THE KING IN EVERY MAN

THE KING IN EVERY MAN

Evolutionary Trends in Onitsha Ibo Society and Culture

by Richard N. Henderson

The King In Every Man
By Richard N. Henderson

ISBN 0-97404-400-8

Originally published in 1972 by Yale University Press

Printed in the United States of America
at Lightning Source, Inc.
LaVergne, Tn

To Byron Maduegbuna, Mike Agbakoba, Obiekwe Aniweta, Ifekandu Umunna, T. C. Ikemefuna, P. Aniweta Achukwu, and the late Ɔkunwa T. B. Akpom. Without them this book could not have been written.

CONTENTS

FIGURES

Introduction to the 2003 Edition

As the author of **The King in Every Man**, I have arranged this eproduction of the book primarily for the Onitsha people of today (and ther Igbo-speakers related to them), most of whom have never had the pportunity of reading it (though many have heard of its existence). The ook is reproduced here in full without any changes except for this brief ıtroduction.

The King in Every Man is in many parts not an easy book to read or non-specialists, especially in those sections that employ rather soteric technical terms and patterns of argument. For those non-pecialists – as most readers of the book today are likely to be, I suggest ıe following pattern of reading.

Begin by skipping (or reading lightly through) Chapter 1, which 'as addressed to issues of social systems theory that were current mong anthropologists in the 1960s and early 1970s – in particular, roblems of "state-formation" – but which are likely to be of less interest) many readers today. (Later chapters of the book do return to address ssues raised in this chapter, but I think readers can follow these later iscussions without reading Chapter 1.)

I recommend that you focus instead on Part I (Chapters 2 and 3), 'hich considers problems and presents inferences concerning the econstruction of Onitsha history. In 1972, these chapters generated onsiderable interest in scholarly circles, and though some 30 years later ıost writers view historical models as much less "authoritative" and ıore relative to authorial perspectives than they seemed when I wrote ıese pages in the late 1960s, I think these interpretations remain seful.

In Part II (Chapters 4, 5, and 6), I think readers may find most ifficult (if not impossible) to follow the subsection entitled "The Major 'ategories of Kinship" in Chapter 5 (pp. 126-138), and in chapter 6 the ubsection entitled "The Conceptual Structure of Marital and Affinal 'elationships" (pp. 207-211). Skim these sections very lightly, and don't llow technicalities to block your reading progress – look for the ummary statements. In retrospect I should have greatly shortened hese analyses when the book was written.

Other parts of the book have difficult sections here and there, but I hink the material remains useful today for anyone interested in the arious contexts and problems of Onitsha history. In particular, I direct our attention to the historical discussions in Part III, Chapter 10, the ection headed "The Significance of Role Differentiation in Onitsha" pages 366-381). I am particularly pleased with this section, which mong other things explored the probable time-depths and dimensions of he historical relationship of Onitsha institutions (Ozo title, etc.) with the ncient Igbo kingdom of Nri (and other peoples of the region), a subject which in the 1960s was being little explored. (On this subject, see also the article co-authored by me and the late Ifekandu Umunna, *"Leadership Symbolism in Onitsha Igbo Crowns and Ijele"* (**African Arts** vol xxi, no. 2, pp. 28-37, 94-97, 1988), which also considers regional historical relationships.

I also think that in Part IV, Chapter 13 in particular provides a contribution to our understanding of the historical and regional, political-ecological contexts of the development of Onitsha Kingdom, anc I recommend your reading it carefully.

Again, addressing Onitsha people who will read the book: do so ii light of what you have learned from your elders about Onitsha (and Onitsha-related) traditions. I want to emphasize that this book undoubtedly contains errors of content, omission, interpretation, emphasis, and conception about Onitsha society and culture. When working with any kinds of tradition (whether oral or written), those who interpret them must juggle alternatives, and I will merely say that I was one such scholar and I did the best I could at the time when I wrote this book. Hopefully, wider reading and research conducted by Onitsha and Onitsha-related people (and others) today will lead to new and at least somewhat different perspectives than those I provided. I myself have some changed perspectives today, and were I to rewrite the book I woulc make some revisions. I will provide here just three examples.

First, concerning emphasis and interpretation, the very title of my book suggests a dispersion – as opposed to centralization – of power in Onitsha society, a dispersion which I emphasized in later chapters wher I discussed the "segmentary" diffusion of social control mechanisms. Tc state this less technically: I tended to stress "democratic" tendencies in Onitsha politics at the expense of the "authoritarian" or "centralized' tendencies, and in retrospect I overstated the case. (In his book, **Studie in Ibo Political Systems: Chieftaincy and Politics in Four Niger States** (published by University of California Press in 1972, the same year as **The King in Every Man**), Ikenna Nzimiro compared Onitsha wit three other Igbo-speaking kingdoms, showing nicely how Onitsha was ir a number of ways more centralized than two of the others. I agree with him on these views, and I should have presented a more balanced argument in my own account of the Onitsha political system. The "King in Every Man" in Onitsha (and, as I might also emphasize today, the Omu or "Queen" in Every Woman) was a metaphorical equation, relevan to motivations and self-identifications of Onitsha individuals within thei kingdom, but not an institutional reality to the degree I tended to imply in some parts of the book.

Second, concerning some specific contents of the book: the sections I presented on the "Distributions and Control of Onitsha farmlands", first on a map on page 185 and then in "Appendix A", pp. 529-533, give an appearance of assured authority which was not arranted by my secure knowledge of facts. Throughout the book, I ›ught to identify meaningful patterns of Onitsha history, sometimes on ıe basis of quite limited evidence. (Indeed, one recent student of Igbo ılture suggested to me that I had "pieced it all together", and I ›ncurred that this was an astute observation given how dynamic nitsha society and culture had become since the coming of European egemony in the late 19th century, and how scattered and fragmentary ere the sources available to me.) Concerning the map of historic land :nure in question, I would emphasize much more strongly that the map as intended only to give readers some general sense of what land oldings may have looked like around 1880, and indeed I might have een wiser not to try to present a map at all, since much of the details as guesswork. I could give other examples of questionable :constructions.

More broadly, I recall the very humble attitude taken by the late nitsha historian Jerry Orakwue, who during the early 1960s often bserved how hard it was for anyone to pose as a real "authority" on nitsha tradition, since every story about the past tends to have differing :rsions which to some degree contradict one another, and with the ›eed of Onitsha social and cultural change the meanings of such ›ntradictions blur through rapidly-receding pasts. As the years have ›ne by since I wrote **The King in Every Man** (and during which I have opefully gained some wisdom while becoming something of an "elder" ıyself), I more fully appreciate the wisdom of Mr. Orakwue's perspective.

ichard Henderson
ucson, Arizona
ugust 12, 2003

PREFACE

This book is primarily a study of the changes occurring in a West African society before its inclusion in a wider British colonial system at the end of the nineteenth century. I reconstruct the history of an Ibo community on the basis of evidence drawn from early written accounts, from oral traditions, and from recent ethnography. In addition, I apply an evolutionary theory of social systems to the interpretation of this history, and therefore the book is in part also a theoretical treatise on change in premodern types of social systems. Finally, I describe and analyze the symbols that delineated and organized the society in question, and in doing so explore some general problems concerning the relation of ideas to human behavior.

The society to be studied was traditional Onitsha, an Ibo-speaking community on the east bank of the river Niger in eastern Nigeria. Precolonial Onitsha was a distinctive variant of Ibo social system; at a strategic site along the river it administered an internationally important marketplace, and while it retained the character of the autonomous, acephalous village-group communities so typical of its Ibo neighbors, it was also developing institutions of royalty, of kingship. This inchoate village-group kingdom had some remarkable characteristics, for it combined diversely organized associations with highly segmented descent groups, and it contained not just one king but a number of them, related to one another in a complex and ambiguous manner. All of this occurred in a compact community within which all members could order their relationships in terms of kinship and which could be readily traversed by foot in a single day.

Premodern societies of this type should be of considerable historical and theoretical interest because they combine characteristics of tribal social systems with certain features of the eastern Mediterranean city-states of classical antiquity, societies that in a crucial developmental sense were ancestral to modern social systems. Thus they represent approximations or analogues to one of the most important transitional forms of society in the history of human social life.

Examples of this kind of combination occur widely scattered in various parts of the world, and their study should encourage systematic comparisons from the broadest theoretical perspective. For several reasons this has seldom been done, though the ingredients for such a perspective have been available for some time.[1] First, such systems are relatively rare in the ethnographic record. Second, documentary historical information has been very limited on those occurring outside the West. Third, ethnographers have generally not utilized theory adequate to the task of bringing both tribal and modern social systems within a single descriptive frame of reference.[2]

This book seeks to transcend some of these limitations. It deals with a highly suggestive illustrative case from sub-Saharan Africa for which a detailed ethnographic account can be provided. Moreover, the situation of Onitsha Ibo society was an important partial exception to the general lack of detailed historical documentation that plagues the students of precolonial African societies. Many of these societies changed very considerably under early European contact and domination, and where detailed documents from the precolonial period are lacking, it is often questionable to what extent social patterns observed or reconstructed in recent times by ethnographers reflect earlier historical realities. Onitsha society also underwent such changes, but it received an early settlement

1. Some of the raw materials were developed in Morgan (1871) and in Weber's (1958) comparative study of the city.

2. Partial exceptions to this in the literature on sub-Saharan Africa include the pioneering comparative study by Dike (1956), and Jones's (1963) comparison of the city-states of the oil rivers.

of Western-educated missionaries well before the time of colonial political domination, and these early observers recorded numerous eyewitness accounts of a people who were very little under their control.[3] For these several reasons there are strong grounds for describing and analyzing Onitsha community in a frame of reference that has general comparative utility.

A theory suited to this purpose is not readily available in social anthropology, for anthropologists have been highly eclectic in their conceptual schemes, and concepts applicable to the study of one kind of social system have not always been useful for the study of others. Often concepts have been employed in ad hoc combinations, without recognition of the wider logical implications of their use. It is therefore necessary to consider theoretical issues in somewhat greater detail than is usually done in case studies of this sort; Chapter 1 is devoted to that task.

The field research on which this volume is based was conducted in Nigeria from September 1960 to July 1962, under the support of a Ford Foundation Foreign Area Training Fellowship. Subsequent supplementary research was financed by the Concilium for International Studies at Yale. Besides those to whom the book is dedicated, many people in Onitsha cooperated extensively in my research, especially the late Obi J. Okosi and Obi J. Onyejekwe; the chiefs of Onitsha, particularly Umera Ozi and the senior chiefs Anatogu Onowu, Mbamali Ajie, Mbanefo Odu, Egbunike Ɔnya, Nwokedi Ɔgene, and Orefo Owele; among many others, D. Molokwu, Ezenwa C. Egbuji, Nnanyelugo J. Enwezor, Akunwafɔ R. Erokwu, Nnanyelugo I. Mbanyugo, F. Nwokedi, Madam N. Obinwe, Mrs. J. Okala, R. R. Olisa, J. Orakwue, Akunne F. Oranye, M. Osaji, and L. Uwechia were exceptionally helpful. The Reverend Fathers of the Roman Catholic Mission and Anglican Archbishop C. J. Patterson also provided valuable assistance. R. E.

3. This is not to imply that the missionaries had no immediate effects on the Onitsha community, for they certainly had. They were a tributary enclave at first, and only gradually began seriously to penetrate the social structure.

Bradbury, J. Gugler, I. Nzimiro, R. A. LeVine, P. C. Lloyd, and S. Ottenberg gave rewarding scholarly advice in the field.

I am indebted to H. W. Basehart, L. A. Fallers, F. G. Lounsbury, S. S. Newman, and D. M. Schneider for intellectual stimulation at crucial stages of my scientific education. E. M. Albert, W. R. Bascom, P. D. Curtin, C. Gibson, H. K. Henderson, R. F. Murphy, H. W. Scheffler, R. F. Thompson, and I. Umunna read various parts of the manuscript and gave helpful suggestions; G. Hershberger assisted in copyediting, A. Greenhill, E. Isaacson, C. McCoy, E. Middleton, and B. Tapper in typing and preparing the manuscript. To my wife Helen and to my parents, thanks for endless supportive services.

R.N.H.

NOTE ON ORTHOGRAPHY

I have tried to render Igbo phonemes and morphemes as accurately as possible in the text; figures are somewhat more conventionalized. Vowel phonemes are represented as: a, e, i, ɩ, o, ɔ, u, and ʋ. For convenience in typing, the following consonant phonemes have been represented in conventional form: γ = gh, č = ch, š = sh. Igbo words are italicized, and their phonemic tones indicated, in first occurrence but generally not afterward. Words are hyphenated to indicate their morphological components; the phonemic tones assigned are those which apply to the morphemes in isolation (morphophonemic effects on tone are ignored). Tone is indicated in a morpheme only initially and where subsequent tonal change occurs. Igbo terms are capitalized only where they begin sentences or are proper names.

1 SOCIETAL PROCESS AND KINSHIP SYSTEMS: AN EVOLUTIONARY PERSPECTIVE

EVOLUTIONARY THEORY IN ANTHROPOLOGY

The application of evolutionary concepts to human societies and cultures has always been controversial, but such concepts clearly form a central current of modern anthropological thought. One set of ideas, developed over the last century, forms a coherent evolutionary scheme that has had particularly strong impact on anthropological theory. It consists of the following two major sets of generalizations. First, social groups are the crucial determinants of human experience and culture, and the forms that social groups take are determined by their economic structures; these structures are, in turn, determined by the technology of material production. Second, the most important directional trend of human social life has been a change away from forms of society whose economies, legal systems, and governments are organized around corporate kinship groups; these have tended to be replaced by societies made up of socially diversified individuals organized by division of labor, impersonal forms of contract, individualized kinship relations, and governments based on territory rather than kinship.[1]

1. The theory has four major sources in the nineteenth century. Maine (1861) first drew a clear outline of world trends in legal systems of societies with his polar contrast between ancient societies, legally based on fixed statuses in corporate kin groups, and modern societies legally based on voluntary contracts between individuals operating within territorial jurisdictions. Morgan (1871, 1877) accepted this formulation and related it to the evolution of kinship terminologies and systems of government, explaining trends toward individualized kinship systems and toward governments based on territory rather than kinship partly by changes in technology and property. Marx (1904) provided a general explanatory underpinning for these schemes, and Durkheim (1964) encompassed the whole with his model of "segmental" or segmentary societies (morally integrated by social likeness among kinsmen) which become transformed into societies composed of diversified units (held together by their interdependence in a division of labor).

This central core of recent social evolutionary theory may be called groupcentric, technoeconomic determinism. Armed with assumptions about the primacy of technological and economic factors, about the overwhelming influence of social groups on the experience of the individuals in them, about the significance of division of labor for molding that experience, and equipped with both a comparative vision of societal differences and the precise structural concepts of comparative jurisprudence, social anthropologists have constructed a substantial edifice of knowledge about determinants of stability and change in societies and cultures throughout the world. There has been good reason for the prominence of technoeconomic and groupcentric assumptions about human behavior in social evolutionary thought, for these assumptions have yielded fruitful empirical results.

In particular, systematic knowledge about the primitive side of the evolutionary spectrum—i.e. the socalled segmentary societies—has progressed greatly in the past decades, with considerable success in isolating determinants of primitive social forms and social change: controlled inferences about the relationship between authority over property and the religious beliefs and rituals of kinship groups; [2] cross-cultural findings about the effects of economically conditioned marital residence patterns on kinship groups and terminologies; [3] insightful models of how segmentary societies maintain structural-functional equilibrium; [4] more broadly comparative classifications and hypotheses about evolutionary types, stages, and transitions; [5] and general evolutionary overviews of human history.[6] Each of these results exemplifies the fruitfulness of some part of the heritage; such successes have encouraged the main proponents of the whole theory to regard technoeconomic de-

2. E.g. Gluckman (1956, 1962), Goody (1962).
3. Murdock (1949).
4. Evans-Pritchard (1940), Fortes (1945, 1949).
5. Fortes and Evans-Pritchard, eds. (1940), Lévi-Strauss (1949), Leach (1954, 1961, 1962), Sahlins (1961), Middleton and Tait, eds. (1958), Steward (1955), Fried (1957, 1960, 1967), Southall (1956, 1965).
6. White (1959).

terminism as a general explanatory law, a view recently reaffirmed by Marvin Harris in his important polemical history of anthropological theory.[7]

However, the broader theory associated with this law has serious limitations; in light of much contemporary knowledge about the nature of man, its major assumptions are misleading half-truths which obscure important aspects of evolutionary process and obstruct further theoretical advance. Most importantly, its major theoretical units are concrete social groups and individuals; in its clearest form the theory takes the group as the basic unit for analysis, leaving individual relationships as a residual category. In extreme forms of groupcentric materialism, the human individual is treated as an ultimate particle whose complex internal states are largely beyond the scope of social scientific knowledge; more typically, the vast range of human subjective experience is handled in terms of simple assumptions that take account only of such general factors as capacity for learning by conditioning or reinforcement and ad hoc motivational elements such as "striving for power." [8]

This kind of theoretical simplification has had considerable utility in the social sciences,[9] for it facilitates systematic concentration upon factors that may be called "external" to individuals: (a) social factors, or the constraints imposed by a few major types of socially structured situations (economic, political, ritual, etc.), and (b) ecological factors (the relationship between technology and environment). By setting all human social behavior within a comparable structural framework, and assuming that each actor acts simply to maximize his own wealth or power and orders his learning processes toward this end, the scholar may readily direct attention to the social and ecological constraints that either pro-

7. White (1949:366), Sahlins and Service, eds. (1960:35), Harris (1968:4). See also Leacock (1963).

8. Radcliffe-Brown (1957), Leach (1954, 1967), Goody (1959), and Needham (1962) exemplify some of the variations on this theme.

9. Classical economic theory is a prominent example closely related to the case at hand.

duce equilibria within and between groups or else tend to change their structures.

Excessive simplification of complex phenomena inevitably impoverishes understanding over the long run, and this effect has become evident in evolutionary anthropology. The crucial weakness of groupcentric assumptions and technoeconomic determinism is that, by focusing attention on social groups as a primary reality and by identifying energy (or energy-producing "material means") as the prime mover of social and cultural change, it leads to dehumanized interpretations of societies or other human social activity, tends to treat human agencies as if they were automata. It has produced some significant results in the study of nonliterate primitive societies, where social forms and cultural patterns are most directly conditioned by technological and ecological constraints, but it has proven less successful when applied to complex modern social systems; even in reference to segmentary systems its weaknesses have become quite obvious.

First, its shortcomings are evident in its unsatisfactory approach to problems of meaning in human society. Although groupcentric technoeconomic determinism ostensibly explains the evolution of human culture and social systems, the terms culture and society are not even clearly distinguished in it. While its practitioners speak confidently about the evolution of cultures, it is often unclear whether they are referring to cultures or to societies. This confusion is not accidental, for no theory can serve to describe or analyze symbol systems (culture) if it fails to take account of the complexity of the human mind, including the human mind's distinctive capacities for organized self-reflection and therefore self-regulation—a phenomenon which the followers of the theory largely exclude from their purview.

Second, it has become clear that no theory which treats individuals and groups as the ultimate units of social systems can handle the sheer empirical complexity of human social life. Another set of concepts has become indispensable to social scientists:

individuals in groups may be analyzed in terms of diverse statuses and roles, which each individual possesses and must organize and segregate according to his definitions of situations. Groupcentric theory fails to provide firm ground for these concepts. Role theory adopts as basic units an organized sector of an actor's orientation —his role expectations—and his meaning as an object of orientation by certain social others—his status definition. This emphasis on variables of orientation implies an emphasis on purposive action, on goals, which in turn implies that the scientific observer must always regard the actor's point of view as both centrally problematical and complex in any action situation. Groupcentric theory tends instead toward a purely objective interpretation of social action, and at best ignores the complexity of subjective factors.[10]

A number of implications follow if one accepts the importance of subjective orientations in social interaction. First, given the wide possible variability of his own actions, an actor must assign meanings to his situation and to his own motivational needs within it; if his situation is a social one, the possible meanings of the situation multiply enormously, because of what Parsons has called the double contingency of alternatives open to multiple actors;[11] unlike classical conditioning experiments, in which the sign is part of an independent, stable situation, in social situations the meanings of signs must to some extent be abstracted and shared by the actors, if the latter are to have any likelihood of reaching mutually anticipated outcomes. Shared cultural schemes of evaluation and normative constraints are essential parts of any stable social system, because they enable that system to persist through self-regulating interaction. Therefore, the cultural patterns (conceptions,

10. An example of the latter is Leach's (1962) attempt to reduce the differences between descent and filiation to a contrast between group-representative orientation and self-interested individualism. Status and role concepts, first introduced in anthropological circles by Linton (1936) and later developed logically by Nadel (1957) and others, have been employed by some groupcentric theorists without full recognition of the radical implications of their use. Examples may be found in Fried's (1960, 1967:29–32) scheme of political evolution and, more fruitfully, in Gluckman's (1962) insightful analysis contrasting "simplex" and "multiplex" social relations.

11. Parsons (1951:10–11).

values, norms) that define the structure of roles and groups in a social system must be regarded as strategically important parts of that system.

For these reasons, role theory entails a generally normative view of social systems rather than a strictly behaviorist view. This does not mean that any given norms or values have causal priority over any given social processes, but it points to an elementary error made by those anthropologists who claim that "action comes first and values come second" in human social life; [12] while the outcomes of social activity do affect the structures of norms and values (as technoeconomic determinists emphasize), it is also true that social action does not occur without an actor's prior reference to some selective standard in terms of which he decides to act.[13] Men may act in terms of selective standards that are part of them (an unconscious process), or may examine such standards critically and with logically alternative criteria in mind (a process of consciousness). Which of these processes occurs first in any given evolutionary sequence must be regarded as problematic; the building of new cultural patterns, as well as the preserving of old ones, may occur partly through acts based on creative consciousness.

This perspective implies, in turn, that the social scientist should describe and analyze the normative structures of an action system before he tries to explain its processes, and second, that causal explanations based solely on technoeconomic factors are likely to be insufficient. Technologies do not develop simply as automatic responses to various environmental conditions; they are socially organized, typically in the interests of pursuing more broadly economic aims. Economic structures and processes tend, in turn, to be regulated and organized by policy-making agencies; and political organizations are themselves given definition and direction by various legal, ideological, and religious agencies that set the

12. Arensberg (1957:105).

13. The distinction between action and behavior follows Weber (1947:88). Cf. Parsons (1961b:323–27).

broad evaluative terms of what is conceivable, desirable, and right for a society as a whole. This self-steering or cybernetic aspect of human social action has consequences for the stability or change of a social system which are as important as those deriving from its continuous demand for energy; a revolution in religious thought in a given society may change the directions and rates of its technological advance.

Most contemporary proponents of Marx and Morgan oriented evolutionary views have come to realize some of these limitations. Thus both Sahlins and Service—among the most prominent of these scholars—have deemphasized strictly economic determinants of cultural evolution, stressing instead the importance of societal political structures; sometimes they even suggest that ideological processes may exert independent effects on other features of social structure.[14] Julian Steward with his multilinear theory has also tried to avoid monocausal explanations. Steward brought taxonomic order to evolutionary theory with his notion of the culture type, an ecologically delimited, adapting unit defined by diagnostic features presumably related to one another by constant functional linkages (primarily but not exclusively economic in nature). He then ordered sets of such types into series of related, emergent levels of socio-cultural integration. By allowing for an indefinite variety of culture types, he took account of the widely divergent nature of historical developments, but he also produced assessable hypotheses about the conditions underlying certain seemingly recurrent evolutionary trends.[15]

If one examines the work of these unusually productive scholars, two salient facts become apparent. First, the most important of their "types of culture" demarcate types of society; the salient cultural elements are those that structure a society as a social system. Steward stated this clearly, without developing a rationale for it.[16] Presumably the society is used as a strategic type unit because

14. Service (1962:178–84; 1968:406–08); Sahlins (1961, 1965a).
15. Steward (1955:3–29, 78–97, 178–209).
16. Steward (1955:187).

societies have been pivotal adaptive units through most of the course of human history. Second, in centering attention on societies as adapting systems, Steward and the others adopted the view that technological elements are not necessarily the prime movers in an evolutionary sequence; other factors, internal or external to societies, must be taken into account. These facts suggest that attention should be concentrated, in any evolutionary scheme, upon the various components of societies as social systems.

If, then, we take the self-regulating character of human social life as a point of departure, while recognizing the continuous importance of energy resources, we can analyze both the organizing, directing mechanisms and the energy gathering mechanisms: the latter provide the necessary conditions and facilities for the former, while the former exercise cybernetic controls over the latter.[17] Viewed in these terms, the explanation of human action must always be multi-factorial; all components of an action situation must be regarded as problematic and subjected to analysis before an explanatory result is fully adequate.

If, moreover, one defines society as that social system which controls a more inclusive range of action than do other social systems, i.e. as the one that attains the highest self-sufficiency as a system in relation to its environments, then obviously societies must be regarded as strategic units in any study of long-term or large-scale social and cultural change.

SOCIETY AS AN EVOLVING SYSTEM

In analyzing the given structure of a society, it is important to distinguish clearly among constitutive symbolism (or cultural charter), values, norms, roles, statuses, and collectivities, for while these structures articulate with one another they may also vary independently. They form the backbone of any description

17. This dual hierarchy of control and conditions, formulated by Parsons (1959), resolves the old dilemma between materialist and idealist theories of society.

and analysis of social structures, and familiarity with them will be presumed in the discussion to follow.[18] Because of our interest in process, two other valuable structural concepts are the notions of personal identity and social identity.[19] These are important because they relate personality to the dynamics of culture and society.[20]

Once the structure of a society has been described and analyzed, and one proceeds to consider its dynamics, assumptions must be made about what societies minimally do as durable action systems; this is the question of "functional requisites." [21] If it is to persist, any social system must first maintain its extant major structural patterns and its actors' commitments to these patterns; it must therefore possess an action sector devoted to linking societal values

18. There are various definitions of these terms in the literature, but it is important to use a conceptual scheme that is logically systematic. For the purposes of this study, a constitutive symbol system is a system of ideas held by members of a social system that defines that system and the bases of its members' commitment to it. Values are standards defining the main directional commitments of actors to social action, without reference to details of situations. Norms are rules which prescribe, permit, or prohibit behavior in given types of situations. A role is the normatively sanctioned behavior of a person in concrete interaction with specific partners; a status is a position occupied by a person in an interactive system, by virtue of certain attributes that he possesses, and which may or may not entail an appropriate role. A collectivity is a bounded system of such role-structured interaction. This formulation is based on Parsons (1951: 25–26, 39, 96–101; 1960:170–80; 1961a:41–44; 1966:33).

19. Identity as defined here does not correspond to the fragmented meaning given it by Goodenough (1965:2–8); it is viewed rather as a synthesis, an overall organization of the meanings of a person as an object, both to himself and to others. Personal identity is an aspect of one's personality that, while formed substantially through identifications with social others, comprises a more or less coherent self-image; social identity is a feature of social structure, comprising the organized pattern of a person's roles, statuses, and general moral standing as assessed by others. Cf. Erikson (1959), Parsons (1968).

20. Cultural components of social identity may come to be internalized in a personality through the process of socialization; conversely, components of personal identity may come to be institutionalized in social norms and moral categories. For example, the impact of a charismatic personality may lead to change in the constitutive symbol system of a society.

21. Numerous attempts have been made by anthropologists and sociologists (e.g. Aberle et al. 1950:100–11; Levy 1952:149–98) to formulate an exhaustive scheme of such dynamic requisites, but the most economic, generally applicable, and the most amenable to general role theory is that developed by Parsons (1961b:311–63; Parsons, Shils, Naegele, and Pitts, eds. 1961:30–79). It will therefore be used as a framework here.

and norms with various systems of belief. This task may be accomplished partly through the building and operation of constitutive symbol systems, partly through systems of socialization. Second, there is a continual problem of regulating adjustments among the organizational units that make up the society: the requirement of integration or maintenance of solidarity. This involves the legal processes and systems of social stratification that order relations among member units. Third, any active society is engaged in goal-directed interchanges with its environment; such goal attainment entails decision-making and implementing agencies. This is the political sector of a society. Finally, with multiple goals in a social system, there is always a problem of producing and allocating the means or facilities for attaining various potential goals. This is the technological-economic sector of a society. These four functional problems or sectors have homologues in every kind of social system; they are all requisite to system persistence and are all likely to be involved in system change.

From this view—that social systems are goal-directed and face these chronic functional problems—and from the recognition that human social action is fundamentally cybernetic or self-regulating in character, it is a short theoretical step to the adoption of an evolutionary frame of reference. The relevant propositions may be stated roughly as follows. First, social systems through their cybernetic character tend to develop (by increasing division of labor) functionally diversified social structures, differing substructures to handle one or another of these functional problems with greater effectiveness for the system as a whole. This process is denoted by the concept of "differentiation." [22] Differentiation may or may not entail organized, conscious culture building efforts, and it may or

22. Differentiation is the process whereby one type of multifunctional social unit divides into two or more units (i.e. collectivities or roles) that differ both in their structures and in their functional significance or "outputs" for the wider system. The point is that such differentiation tends to result in greater output productivity, both within the specialized units and for the system as a whole. This principle, clearly developed by Spencer (see Carneiro 1967:14–16, 82–96), is also a strategic element in Steward's thought. For elaboration on these points, see Eisenstadt (1964b) and Parsons (1966:5–25).

may not occur initially in the technoeconomic sector of the society; it cannot be presumed to be a purely automatic response by a group of organisms, since it involves problem solving and innovation.

Second, such structural and functional differentiation creates new problems of social integration, problems of defining and regulating relationships among the now differing types of units (new and old). The criteria that define these differing units may be mutually contradictory, or the outputs of one unit may be required inputs for another; there may be various sources of potential conflict. Solution of such problems requires development of new legal norms and new patterns of prestige distribution within the wider system. However, such developments do not occur automatically as a consequence of the differentiation itself; rather they require independent innovations, whose occurrence is quite problematic and uncertain, and which are likely to entail conscious planning, culture building, and political manipulation against entrenched vested interests.[23]

There are several possible outcomes to any process of differentiation: isolation or encapsulation of the new structure or structures within the system, without change in old structures; a regression to the previous undifferentiated state, i.e. structural loss through elimination of the new units; or evolutionary advance, through a structural change in the societal system of values and norms resulting in the inclusion and "institutionalization" of the new structures. From the latter emerges a new society simultaneously more generalized and more complex in its constitutive symbolism and its values. The actual outcome appears to depend on several factors, including the presence or absence of adequate mobile resources for sustaining the new units, the presence or absence of certain kinds of elite roles and supporting social strata, and the presence or absence of appropriate ideological structures.[24]

23. This process has been analyzed by Coser (1956) in developing his conflict theory.
24. Eisenstadt (1964a) spells out possibilities and factors in some detail. Parsons (1966:23–24) gives a different range of alternatives.

This theory provides a convenient measure of evolutionary stages: the level of structural differentiation established by a society, as defined by the institutionalized roles and collectivities specialized toward meeting major functional requisites.[25] While structural differentiation may be generated by changes in the allocation of wealth or distribution of power in a society, successful evolutionary advance requires, in addition to such changes, changes in the cultural standards that define social inclusion in the society as a whole, and obligation and prestige allocation within it. Each partial transformation is to some extent independent of the others.

This is not a unilineal evolutionary scheme. It permits various modes of differentiation, and recognizes that structures may disappear as well as emerge; structural loss is a continuous potential in any differentiated system. With its emphasis on culture patterns, the scheme recognizes the tremendous importance of borrowing, including acquiring (from various sources) and manipulating alternative models of social structure. Thus it takes account of the important distinction between a pristine evolutionary advance, its origin independent of pressures emanating from already advanced systems in the external environment, and secondary developments that result from such pressures.[26] However, the borrowing of ideas, or other external pressures, cannot create new systems automatically; structural differentiation must take place in the system, and a new level of integration be attained, before evolutionary advance occurs.

SEGMENTARY SOCIETIES AND EVOLUTIONARY THEORY

The concept of evolutionary advance implies as a base line a primitive stage or stages, and implies sequences between primitive forms and diverse forms of advanced systems.[27] In general, segmentary

25. This notion is, of course, related to Steward's "levels of sociocultural integration."
26. Fried (1960:713).
27. Various formulations of such sequences are available. Steward (1955:43–63) provided an important summary. See Fried (1967), and the broader schemes of Parsons

systems are evolutionarily primitive, using this term in the nonpejorative, purely structural sense—primitive first in that the groups and roles composing them are structurally undifferentiated, are multifunctional social units each much like the other. Such systems are also primitive to the extent that there is no clearly bounded society, no unit symbolically or structurally distinguished from its various environments, therefore no unit even potentially capable of acting as a collectivity.[28] Third, they are primitive insofar as their technoeconomic facilities are limited and fixed in distribution. Finally, they are primitive to the extent that they fail to provide cultural distinctions among the social, cultural, personal, and biological aspects of action in general: they lack formal recognition of the independence or individuality of human personality, awareness of the problematic nature of ideas and other culture patterns, discrimination among the organic or nonorganic environment, social life, and ideas.[29]

The primitiveness of a segmentary system centers on the definition of most if not all of its important collectivities and roles by kinship criteria. The elementary criteria of kinship are beliefs and standards that define *filiation,* the relationship between parent and offspring; these criteria are widely variable, but everywhere they refer to the conditions and responsibilities attendant upon procreation.[30] Because of their grounding in universal situations surround-

(1964, 1966), Parsons, Shils, Naegele, and Pitts, eds. (1961:239–64), Bellah (1964), and Eisenstadt (1964b).

28. Fortes (1949) showed that the Tallensi of northern Ghana fit both criteria. The Tallensi are not among the most primitive societies (cf. Worsely 1956), but their evolutionary development has certainly been retarded and they nicely illustrate these two features.

29. Some of these characteristics, for example magical and sacred attitudes towards the reality of words and belief systems, have been analyzed by Horton (1967) in his essay on personalized world-views in Africa. For a general account of the evolution of symbols of personal identity, see Bellah (1964), especially on Australian aborigines, and for a specific study study that illuminates such development in a rather complex African society, Levine (1965:238–86).

30. I follow Freedman (1964:366) and Gellner (1957, 1960, 1963) in adopting this viewpoint. Some hint of the controversy surrounding it may be found in Leach (1960:9, 1961:16–27), Needham (1960), Barnes (1961), Beattie (1964:102; 1965a:51, 1965b: 51), and Schneider (1964:180).

ing procreation, filiation statuses generally entail distinctive value orientations. Filiation is an ascriptive relationship, given by the conditions of birth; it cannot ordinarily be achieved through one's own efforts, or renounced. It cannot be instituted with any persons who meet universal criteria of membership, as can many other kinds of relationship; it is traced from particular persons to particular persons. The attitudes appropriate to filiation tend to be defined by emotion. Indeed, the affective components of filiation are often symbolically elaborated; they are generally highly relevant when the actors assess the state of the relationship. Social interaction in filiation tends to be judged by consummatory or sacred standards, i.e. by its expression of ultimate values, rather than by the sheer instrumental efficiency of specific acts. And filiation tends to be a collectivity oriented relationship, in which the actors view themselves as a bounded social unit rather than as private parties each interacting primarily to maximize self-interest.[31]

These value patterns extend variably to the derivative relationships of kinship. Relations of shared filiation, or siblings, are most likely to mirror the general pattern; relations of shared descent, which are based on the ancestor-oriented abstraction of certain genealogical continua, are likely to be more specific and instrumental in their definition, but in some systems (especially unilineal ones) descent values may be strongly modeled on those of filiation. Marital and affinal relations are achieved and usually terminable; they tend to be more self-oriented, instrumental, and specifically defined than the other types of kinship. In some primitive systems, however, they are strictly prescribed by prior kin relations. While

31. This viewpoint—that the value orientations of filiation universally tend to be ascriptive, particularistic, diffuse, affective, consummatory, and collectivity oriented—has been widely challenged in anthropology. Considerations of space preclude a detailed development of the position adopted here; it is based on the presumed societal universality of beliefs attributing some intrinsic contribution by each parent to his child's being or identity, of socialization processes facilitating attachments and identifications, and of the associated norms, the incest taboo and exogamy. While such universality at the societal level may not apply in the future, the groupcentric arguments raised against it for the past are entirely unconvincing.

there is wider variability in affinal value patterns than in the others, they tend in general to have a strongly affective tone.[32]

The basic value pattern of kinship is peculiarly appropriate to undifferentiated social structures, and accords with another principal feature of primitive societies, their structural rigidity. Kinship relations, because of their personal and (in general) permanent nature, tend to entail relatively fixed role obligations. Where substantial economic resources or political powers are distributed solely by kinship criteria, such facilities tend to be rigidly fixed in allocation rather than convertible and exchangeable. The classic model of primitive segmentary systems clearly reflects this: each segment unit is an exclusive, multifunctional corporate group defined by a unilineal descent criterion which aligns individuals as permanent members of only one such unit. The group must establish regular relations with other units because its internally unifying rule of descent is associated with a rule of exogamy. In the most primitive systems, marriages are prescriptive alliances that perpetually interlock the units with one another by fixed kinship criteria. These affinal relations complete the role structure of the entire system.[33]

Differentiation breaks through this rigidity. The emergence of new roles, groups, norms, and values within a society frees the distribution of resources to some extent. Diffuseness of kinship roles must be increasingly limited as this occurs, whether the new roles are assigned by kinship or by other criteria. A general evolutionary trend in value configurations was first recognized by Tönnies in his contrast between *gemeinschaft* and *gesellschaft* forms of rela-

32. Scheffler (1966) has neatly analyzed the distinction between filiation and descent; Hsu (1965) has given some indications of the cross-cultural variability in both consanguineal and marital value patterns; Schneider (1968) has analyzed American kinship in terms of its underlying values; Bennett and Despres (1960) have shown how kinship ideology may be used in the constitutive symbolism of nonkin organizations in order to sustain kinlike value patterns.

33. Schneider (1965) has provided the clearest discussion of basic elements in this model.

tionship: a trend of development away from communal role relations of the type just discussed and toward "associational" roles, which tend to be achieved, universalistically and specifically defined, instrumental, affective-neutral, and self-oriented. They form a polar contrast to the basic value patterns of kinship.[34] Given recognition that kinship values have not been eliminated in the course of evolutionary change (though they have been progressively limited in scope and transformed in other ways), this scheme appears to reflect a valid general trend, and it should be a useful guide for considering the evolution of segmentary systems.

Three additional cautions are necessary in applying this evolutionary scheme to the study of segmentary societies. First, this is not a unilineal scheme; there is more than one potential pathway of structural differentiation at any given level of the system being considered. Second, since the conditions that give rise to such differentiation may well differ from those which foster the forming of social strata capable of solving the consequent integrative problems, the outcome of the evolutionary process must depend on many factors rather than on any one alone. Third, cultural models defining a structure in one sector of a social system may be borrowed by actors and applied in whole or in part to another, a process that may considerably increase the complexity of structural change.

Given these strictures on generalization, what kinds of broad trends are evident in the empirical evidence on segmentary systems? Clearly, the most primitive systems are those that lack definite symbolic boundedness, and whose kinship units are locked into interrelationships by a general prescriptive marriage rule. From such primitive base line types, there are several possible directions

34. Tönnies (1957:33–78). Filiation and other kinship relations are forms of *gemeinschaft*. The purposes and activities of an associational relationship (*gesellschaft*) are specifically defined, limited in scope and duration; norms and sanctions apply to specific instrumental acts, and are directed toward encouraging rational efficiency of performances. It must be remembered that each value element in such a configuration may vary independently of the others.

of development.[35] One is the emergence of some kind of non-unilineal descent structure that tends to introduce achievement criteria into kinship-defined roles and groups. Others include the emergence of age-set structures or sex-restricted associations, both of which detach persons from particular family involvements, and integrate society on a more universalistic basis. Such developments may lead to considerable functional differentiation within a segmentary system, differentiation that may have long-run evolutionary implications. Among the many possibilities, three seem most likely to lead to radical transformations of segmentary societies themselves.

The first of these is the emergence of a socially stratified society, one that systematically divides its major kinship units on the basis of relatively high or low prestige. Southall and Mair have shown for various societies in East Africa that this process tends to occur where the ascribing of superior symbolic value or prestige (in the form of religiously defined statuses of royalty, or kingship) to one descent line or group is associated with the concentrating of economic resources and/or political advantages in the hands of that unit, so that the other, relatively disadvantaged units are defined as commoners, and a "pyramidal" or "segmentary state" emerges.[36] Where the problem of integrating these two types of units within one society is solved not through kinship relations but by creating a new form of relationship (the achieved roles of patron and client), there occurs a full separation of kinship roles from roles that perform societal integrative functions. Such a separation of roles may become fully consolidated should the royal kinship

35. Kirchhoff (1959), Lévi-Strauss (1949), and Leach (1951, 1954) first developed precise models for understanding the transformations of such systems.

36. Southall (1956), Mair (1962). The conception here is different from that drawn by Fried (1960), who rigidly binds evolutionary developments of rank and stratification to economic determinants. Clearly, concentration of economic advantages does not in itself automatically produce this development; witness those African segmentary systems where kinship groups that monopolize craft skills such as blacksmithing are structurally isolated as pariahs (Murdock 1959:186, 189, 201). Southall shows brilliantly for the Alur how a stratified society may develop and expand by providing valued cultural services not primarily economic in their initial implications.

group cease to be exogamous and come to prefer endogamy, thus entirely eliminating its kinship links with the commoner units.[37]

Through such processes as these, a fully crystallized two class system may replace a segmentary one. Such a system has differentiated a substructure specialized partly for performing societal integrative functions, partly for providing cultural legitimation of prestige. A distinctively political differentiation in a society appears to develop (in the relatively pristine case) with the further elaboration of bureaucratic administrative staffs within a hierarchical framework of leadership, an officialdom separated from such other specialized units as priesthoods concerned primarily with cultural legitimation. With this separation established, major structural change occurs. The significance of consummatory, sacred values in setting directions of action for the whole society decreases, and the importance of instrumental values in setting directions of collective activity increases. An hierarchical societal system has thus replaced the stratified or pyramidal one, and new modes of collective societal action have been instituted.[38]

In intermediate cases, where the major role differentiations just outlined have been only partially attained, the system is in a condition of internal conflict and strain. Fallers has shown, for example, how in Busoga society the coexistence of corporate descent groups with societal stratification makes for strain and instability, and has illustrated the limitations which the vested interests and values of corporate descent groups place on centralization of power and prestige.[39] However variable such intermediate systems have been, they all indicate that the formation of state systems, through the centralization and stratification associated with the emergence of kings, has been one of the most important and widely recurrent

37. Parsons (1964). Equally, the separation may be in continual danger of disappearing, should kinship ties closely parallel achieved ones—a point clearly seen by Weber (1947:324–86).

38. Parsons (1964). The terms employed here follow Apter (1965: 83–94), who has done much to clarify the significance of the differences between these two types of society. See also Southall (1965:128–29).

39. Fallers (1956).

evolutionary developments in the history of mankind. Some have regarded it as a true evolutionary universal because of its effects of releasing resources from fixed distributions in kinship networks, encouraging more universalistic and achieved requirements or merit as bases of group and role recruitment, and making possible new modes of collective societal action.[40] Thanks to a substantial body of sophisticated accounts of pyramidal and hierarchical systems in Africa, the developmental possibilities in these forms of society are now reasonably well understood.

There are other possible patterns of development from a segmentary system base line than that toward hierarchy. The emergence of other kinds of differentiated structures, in a system also developing tendencies toward stratification and hierarchy, may greatly complicate evolutionary change by generating complex processes of competition for resources and prestige. The importance of such processes was recognized early in evolutionary thought by Morgan. Morgan tried to fit them into a fixed universal sequence by demonstrating that the first evolution of a society from broadly particularistic and ascriptive bases of membership to universalistic and achieved bases—the change that occurred in Greece between the seventh and fifth centuries B.C.—occurred without prior or concurrent elaboration of institutions of kingship.[41] Later research proved this view erroneous, but only partly so, for Morgan had isolated an evolutionary development of great comparative importance. There had emerged in Greece, on the basis of earlier, simple kingdoms, and through the forming of coastal cities in social contexts of intertribal warfare and expanding economic opportunity, a series of nonhierarchical, associational city-states. In a later broadly comparative study of the city, Weber elaborated on the significance of such developments, showing that in various parts of the world, city social systems have evolved recurrent distinctive types of collectivities and roles sometimes destructive of hierarchy. Under cer-

40. Parsons (1964).
41. Morgan (1877).

tain conditions social processes involving these new units have led to great accelerations of cultural, legal, political, and economic change.[42]

Analogues of these processes are evident in some of the nonliterate societies of precolonial Africa. Paula Brown, going beyond Fortes' and Evans-Pritchard's earlier division of African political systems into stateless and centralized types, outlined a more detailed set of types in West Africa on the basis of the additional criterion of associations—nonascriptive corporate groups. She found one type of authority system in which political authority resides only in kinship groups, a second in which it resides in a combination of kinship groups and associations; a third that combines authority in kinship groups, associations, and centralized state organization; and a fourth in which the centralized state system has replaced and downgraded extant kinship groups and associations.[43] That this classification was groupcentric in its predominantly concrete terms of conceptualization limited its heuristic value, but it did point out the strategic importance of nonhierarchical differentiation in both segmentary and centralized societies. At the same time it implied an evolutionary process through which hierarchical structures supersede associational and kinship ones.

A more recent classification of political systems by Eisenstadt has built upon Brown's work, and added to it a fully analytic and functional-requisite perspective that takes as its basic units the society and its component roles. Eisenstadt's criteria for characterizing a political system include not only the nature and articulation of politically important groups, but also the specialization of roles, the relative emphasis on various aspects of political activity (distinguished as technical-administrative, executive, party-political or integrative, and cultural-juridical), and the relation of the political system to the major values and goals of the society in which it

42. Weber (1958). For a recent treatment of the evolutionary significance of ancient Greece, see Parsons (1966:103–08).
43. Brown (1951).

is set. On the basis of roles, groups, and political sector emphasis, he develops the classification summarized here in Figure 1.[44]

This classification makes it possible to relate the structure of political subsystems to the major value systems of the societies in which they operate, and to relate both of these to the conditions in which the society is situated. His distinction of the four major sectors of political function is homologous to the more general functional-requisite scheme discussed above, and it produces valuable hypotheses. For example, Eisenstadt suggests that graded title associations tend to become politically significant in autonomous village settings where instrumental economic goals are the main goals and values of the society, and that they serve the political function of regulating or administering such economic processes where the local units of production are not self-sufficient.[45]

Eisenstadt's scheme is also amenable to interpretation in terms of the evolutionary model previously described. Indeed, if political system types recently distinguished by other scholars [46] are added to those set forth by Eisenstadt, it is not difficult to formulate a coherent multilinear evolutionary scheme that both suggests the likely directions of evolutionary advance from one type to another and specifies some of the conditions under which such advance may occur. Such schemes may facilitate outlining and considering various developmental possibilities and their limitations, but the empirical evidence shows that many societies of precolonial Africa are mixed types in that their assignment to one or another category is largely arbitrary. The virtue of Eisenstadt's approach, as opposed to one that emphasizes only concrete units of comparison, is its analytical nature. The limited number of analytic elements in the model of society makes the model manipulable: various con-

44. Eisenstadt (1959).
45. Ibid., pp. 209–10, 218. Numerous other hypotheses emerge from this study, and it is a pity that it has not received the attention it merits.
46. For example, Middleton and Tait (1958), LeVine (1965), Lloyd (1965), and Southall (1965).

Fig. 1 A classification of "primitive" political systems (after Eisenstadt)

I. SEGMENTARY TRIBES

1. Based on KIN GROUPS, primarily

A. BANDS

loose groupings, each local group has high self-regulation; little personal initiative on societal level; societal goals ecological-adaptive and ritual.

B. CLASSICAL SEGMENTARY TRIBES:

maximal lineages bear political tasks and roles; these units are solidary communities, which in turn are interdependent; interaction between them largely ritual in nature.

C. RITUALLY STRATIFIED TRIBES:

division between noble and commoner kin groups; nobles compete for ritual prestige; self-regulation of units high; a political intermediary, the "client," appears.

2. Based on KIN GROUPS, and OTHER GROUPS and PRINCIPLES:

D. UNIVERSALISTIC (AGE-SET) SEGMENTARY TRIBES:

no corporate lineages; less self-regulation by kin groups; age-sets have war, juridical, party-political functions; societal goals ritual, war.

E. PARTICULARISTIC ASSOCIATIONAL TRIBES:

offices are vested in kin groups, and in associations based on kin and personal links; the various units are self-regulatory; complementary functions of the different units integrate the tribe.

3. NON-KIN based:

F. ACEPHALOUS, AUTONOMOUS (UNIVERSALISTIC) VILLAGE SYSTEMS:

the primary political groups are graded title associations; titles are not hereditary. Interdependence of various associations in the interests of regulating economic activities; specifically administrative roles are present.

II. SPECIALIZED CHIEFDOMS

G. KINSHIP-ORGANIZED: the "FEDERATED" MONARCHY:

kin groups are self-regulating in most matters; offices are controlled by them; feudalistic authority patterns; political competition is between lineages.

H. KIN, plus UNIVERSALISTIC GROUPS: the "CENTRALIZED MONARCHY:

societal membership is by direct allegiance to the king; achievement of offices by commoners; little self-regulation by kin groups; age-regiments often important; strong collective goals of war and expansion.

I. MONARCHIES BASED ON ASSOCIATIONS AND SECRET SOCIETIES:

most positions are kin based, but secret societies do important tasks of administration and social control; king competes with them politically; low self-regulation of kin groups, otherwise like (C).

crete cases may be compared with one another, without continual construction of new types or pigeonholing of new and complex cases into old ones. An analytic model may be used for explanation without proliferating an endless stream of types.

POLITICAL SYSTEMS AND EVOLUTIONARY DEVELOPMENT: THE IBO CASE

The societies of the Ibo-speaking peoples have for some time presented a quandary to students of comparative history. The Ibo live in some of the heaviest population concentrations in all Africa, and they occupy a region long in communication with societies possessing stratified, even hierarchical social systems. Moreover, the Ibo themselves participated extensively and actively in the European slave trade, a powerful external economic and political stimulus that in many other areas along the Guinea coast promoted confederation, centralization, and state formation in diverse indigenous societies. Nevertheless, the Ibo mostly continued to live in small-scale segmentary societies, each structurally differentiated but based strongly on unilineal descent groups. In Eisenstadt's terms, they were acephalous, autonomous village-group communities, but not of an isolated or undifferentiated type—they were open to environmental influences and they possessed rather complex, partially universalistic bases of social order.

There was, of course, considerable diversity of social form in a population of several millions living in such small-scale societies. In the northeast, where they abutted on non-Ibo segmentary societies, some evolved toward age-set segmentary tribes, specialists in undertaking wars of expansion; [47] in the west, in the shadow of the powerful Benin kingdom, some developed small-scale chieftaincies usually tributary to Benin.[48] Throughout most of their territory, however, they remained organized in age-graded village-

47. Jones (1961).
48. Thomas (1914).

group systems that possessed associations of variable importance; as societies they markedly lacked clearcut descent group stratification or hierarchical structures.[49]

Simon Ottenberg has attempted to explain this lack, in his paper on the Ibo oracle cult of Aro-Chukwu, a community located in the extreme southeastern corner of Ibo country near the coastal trading city of Calabar.[50] He shows how, in the absence of political centralization, Ibo religion provided a normative basis for mediating the external expansion of this community's interlocal trade network, which spread to many politically independent village-groups through the medium of a shrine that served as an arbitrating court of final appeal. By using their oracle as a juridical device, members of the Aro-Chukwu community (the "Aro") came to be regarded as holy agents of God, who could travel unprotected and could settle in the various communities of central and northern Ibo country, retaining their commitments to their home base and expanding a trade network that led back to it.

Although the oracle system brought numerous Ibo communities into an expanded communications network, some non-Aro people became assimilated into the Aro system, and in some regions the Aro agents came to control both potent military forces and important market places, Ottenberg shows that there were no evident tendencies toward consolidation of a unified political system and no efforts to establish hierarchical controls; indeed, by the beginning of colonial times, the area was undergoing social disintegration.

Ottenberg explains this lack of political consolidation by several features of Ibo culture. First, he argues, the Ibo in general initially lacked the small kingdoms that elsewhere served as a beginning for political expansion, through the slave trade, into an hierarchical state system. This lack was true of the Aro-Chukwu community

49. Uchendu (1965) has written a valuable general account of these systems that supplements the comparative survey of Forde and Jones (1950).

50. Ottenberg (1958).

itself, for the Aro agents never developed significant hierarchy or centralization even at home; without a hierarchic model from their community of origin, they could hardly develop such a system elsewhere. Second, like other Ibo peoples, the Aro agents appear to have viewed their expansionist activities entirely instrumentally. They were interested primarily in the wealth that came out of the trade, and the methods they employed to insure this were viewed by them as mere techniques; the Aro were therefore not interested in political domination of other groups per se. Finally, Ibo village-groups as a wider communications network of linked but autonomous societies were "segmentary at heart", their interrelations based on complex balances of linkage and alliance that were unstable and underwent continual fission. In this setting, the Aro oracle cult modified and sometimes undercut specific balances, but it did so unsystematically and disruptively.[51]

In a recent, more broadly comparative study of state formation in Africa, Stevenson has carried the problem of Ibo societies in a new direction, by asserting, largely on the basis of Ottenberg's contribution, that the Aro system had actually become a true state, pervading the center of Ibo country. He maintains that the autonomous and acephalous character attributed to the Ibo village-group system by Forde and Jones, Eisenstadt, and others, has been misleading, in view of the range and scope of Aro-Chukwu influence.[52]

Stevenson's argument emphasizes an important aspect of Ibo societies: that they were unusually open social systems in the precolonial period. Spheres of influence and channels of communication could penetrate them despite their local autonomy. What he fails to recognize is that these spheres of influence were multiple

51. Ottenberg (1958:310–14).

52. Stevenson (1968: 188–227). Taken literally, this argument is certainly more misleading than the views it opposes. I suspect that its overstatement derives from pressures set by the general purpose of Stevenson's study, which was to demonstrate a consistently positive correlation between population density and the presence of state systems in tropical Africa as a whole; he appears to have found it desirable in the interests of this thesis to force the Ibo data into a state mold. Still, the interpretation is not without value, for it necessitates some rethinking of Ibo history.

in character and in source, and they overlapped; a variety of them developed, reached well beyond the boundaries of local society, and coexisted with other such channels. Each channel expanded communications and laid a potential basis for wider social integration in its own way, but none—not even the Aro—established exclusive territorial jurisdiction, and none integrated all the requisites for a new level of societal system, much less one of the state type.[53]

The existence of multiple communications networks in Ibo country will have to be considered very carefully in any effort to explain evolutionary trends in the area or any portion of it. Ottenberg's explanation in terms of the basic character of Ibo culture is not general or sufficient, because there were small-scale kingdoms in parts of the area and knowledge of alternative forms of social systems was widespread as a result of these networks. One major network lay well to the west of the Aro-Chukwu sphere of influence, on a north-south axis that followed the river Niger. The present study will concentrate attention on this network, and seek to relate its importance to that of the others.

More specifically, attention will be directed to the "city-state" of Onitsha, a community located at an important crossroads of the region, and one that bears comparison with the city-states of ancient Greece. Like those Greek cities it was located close to important waterway communication routes, like them it grew substantially through an emphasis on trade, and like them it was organized in part for defense against segmentary hinterland tribes. Also like them, it evolved social forms of a type that appears to have developed recurrently in preindustrial communities facing such circumstances. It should therefore prove an illuminating society to analyze.

53. Fried (1960:726–30) has outlined the distinguishing features of state systems.

PART 1

PATTERNS OF COMMUNICATION ON THE LOWER NIGER, CA. 1500-1880

2 PHYSICAL AND INTERSOCIETAL ENVIRONMENTS: PRECOLONIAL LIFE IN THE LOWER NIGER AREA

PROBLEMS OF TECHNIQUE

To develop an adequate reconstruction of Onitsha Ibo society—one both probable historically and intelligible as a model of a system in interaction with its environments—it is necessary to place the community with reference to its geographic, political, and cultural settings during late oral-historic times.[1] Since archeological study of the lower Niger region remains in its infancy and comparative linguistic analyses remain unpublished, the main sources of evidence for such description must be ethnographic, although the historical documents available from the region after 1830 provide invaluable supplementary evidence.

An attempt will be made here to construct an outline of the development of Onitsha community which will suggest major patterns and changes in the structure of the society and in its communications with other important social systems. This requires some statement about the geographical relationships, cultures, political prominence, and trading activities of major centers of regional influence, all prior to the effort of tracing the development of Onitsha itself.

Sufficient ethnographic data are available for an outline discussion of the most important centers of influence on the lower Niger region in oral-historic times, and for one of these centers—the Edo

1. Three major historical periods will be distinguished in this work: the "oral-historic" period preceding the existence of written documents, for which oral traditions are the main evidence; the "exploratory" period when European explorers and missionaries provided documents that supplement oral tradition (between 1830 and 1880); and the "colonial" period of the Niger Company and afterwards, beginning about 1880.

kingdom with its capital at Benin city—there exists an elaborate recorded oral tradition providing reasonably reliable dating of major regional events back to approximately 1500 A.D.[2] The founding of Onitsha community is traced in several oral traditions to this early period, and therefore a base line date can be established for the initial development of Onitsha society as recounted in oral tradition.

From the terminal period of European exploration on the Niger from 1830 to 1880, a wealth of documentary evidence deals directly with Onitsha and relates it to these major regional centers. This material, much of which is still unpublished, illuminates developments in the community and in its external relationships during that time. Since very little of this early historical data has been consulted by the Onitsha people themselves, it constitutes a valuable check on the validity of their oral traditions as historical accounts, and provides independently valuable descriptions of an intact social system.

For these reasons, reconstruction of Onitsha history may depart from a roughly datable base line of around 1500, as substantiated by the Benin material, and end with an exploratory period fairly well documented by historical accounts. There is then an intermediate period of about three hundred years for which Onitsha oral traditions must provide the major data for reconstruction.

To what extent can Onitsha oral traditions gathered in the 1960s be taken as evidence of historical events? The recent situation of Onitsha people must caution the historiographer trying to assess hearsay accounts of the past. When the present research was undertaken in the field before the Biafran war, the native Onitsha community lived nearly encapsulated within an expanding, dynamic, cosmopolitan city that was continually growing by immigration.[3]

2. The primary source for Benin oral tradition is Egharevba (1960). Bradbury (1959) has made a carefully reasoned assessment of Egharevba's dates for the reigns of Bini kings, and has also published the major studies of the political system of Benin (1957, 1964, 1967).

3. From 1967 through 1970, the entire population was scattered because of the Nigeria-Biafra war.

The Onitsha people themselves had long boasted a high literacy rate; many of them had traveled widely and were sophisticated by any standards. Moreover, those residing at home had been active for many years in litigation over their increasingly valuable urban properties, so that not a few local people had developed quite legalistic views of tradition which made likely considerable distortion in their oral testimony. Government officials in the past usually found it impossible, during commissions of inquiry at Onitsha, to distinguish genuine tradition from the welter of imaginative lies promulgated by competing and articulate interest groups.[4]

For a number of reasons it remains possible despite these difficulties to gain valid historical knowledge from Onitsha oral traditions. Traditional Onitsha was, unlike some other Ibo societies,[5] a community strongly concerned with maintaining oral accounts of the past. Onitsha lacked an elaborate mythology as its cultural charter, and instead emphasized a quasi-historical "ideology" based on stories tracing the founding of its villages to prehistoric migrations and political fissions. This concern with the past, moreover, was associated with development of an ideology of kingship and with interest in royal genealogies. These interests had led to the development of publicly acknowledged stories (*ákʊkɔ*) [6] about past events associated with specific lineage and village segments and with the reigns of particular kings. Both factors favored the preservation of accurately transmitted and sequentially ordered tales about the past.[7]

This development of kingship institutions in Onitsha did not lead to the establishment of "official" versions of history, subject to the willful distortions imposed by a ruling group. There tended

4. For example, see O'Connor (1936) and Harding (1963:vi).

5. Forde and Jones (1950) have delineated the major cultural divisions of Iboland.

6. Onitsha people distinguish two kinds of akʊkɔ: the term unmodified may be glossed simply as "stories," but opposed to *akʊkɔ iro*, or "myths and fables," it refers to stories viewed as genuine statements about the past.

7. A valuable analysis of the criteria for assessing the likelihood that an oral tradition may contain historically valid facts has been made by Vansina (1965).

to be as many defended versions of a given recounted event as there were segmental units in the community involved in the event. It was therefore possible to cross-check stories on the principle that where most major divisions agree on a version, while the groups directly involved in the event either distort it euphemistically to minimize their loss of prestige or avoid recounting it at all, the majority version is likely to be accurate.[8] Furthermore, in Onitsha community there were a number of distinct contexts in which stories might be told, and in these contexts various sanctions operated which enable an observer to assess the likelihood of accurate transmission. The first two contexts were public, and the third private or semiprivate.

The first context was that of ceremonial activities in which the unity of Onitsha or one of its segments was publicly affirmed in an orator's recounting of tradition. On these occasions, the "sweet words" which "fill the stomach" by recalling common tribulations and accomplishments of the people were stated in a standardized way and were subjected to affirmation and correction by an audience relishing this appropriate image of their unity. In this context, the criterion of historical truth is secondary, for no divisive, debatable, or status-denigrating stories were acceptable. Since the transmission of the shared tradition was itself subjected to continual public criticism of its accuracy, such accounts may be regarded as accurately transmitted, but they are minimal accounts glossing over details, and the "truths" conveyed in them are often difficult to interpret.

The second context was that of public controversy. Where decision making was at stake in Onitsha public meetings, interested parties sought to fix precedents by citing former abominable acts (*álʊ*) committed by one or another segment of the community, or by citing the historical basis for differences among segments in

8. Vansina (1965:28, 42, 83–84) shows the importance of such comparisons. Where traditional accounts go against the prestige of the group recounting the tale, and do so in a manner complementary to the accounts of most other groups, a tale has an especially high probability of accuracy. This frequently happened in Onitsha oral traditions.

their prestige and their rights over various facilities. In this context, the holders of two social roles would become prominent. The first, the patrilineage priest, was expected to cite genuine tradition about his group in its relations to others. He was subjected to public tests of truth by oath (*íyi*) sworn either on his sacred patrilineage ɔ̀fɔ́ staff of trust or on some more generally feared oath.[9] These oaths provided powerful sanctions for truthful transmission, but when the stakes were high fabrications were likely. In such situations the second role, that of the orator-spokesman (*ɔ́nʊekwulɔ̀ra*),[10] would come into prominence. This person was expected to stand up, as a fearless public spokesman, and state unpleasant truths about past events and about the diversity of origins of various community segments, even when these statements might derogate his own kinsmen and bring about a decision contrary to their interests.

Both priests and orators were highly respected by virtue of their reputations for truthfulness. Their statements were under strong accuracy control, for they were spoken only in the last resort and were subjected by their audience to the strictest tests of truth. Such plain talk, a counterpoint to the sweet words of unity in Onitsha, contained more accurate details of the past.

Finally, knowledge of diverse origins, of abominable or otherwise distinctive past actions, was most assiduously transmitted in the third context: that of the private, ritually sanctioned communication between father and son, and its semiprivate extension to wider levels of patrilineage membership. These tales were usually associated with known ancestors in relation to other ancestral figures in the community. They were linked with rituals directed to sets of concrete mnemonic objects transmitted as inherited property from fathers to sons and valued as treasures and remembrances of past events.[11] Since they were associated with such

9. Chapters 4 and 5 contain detailed discussion of the ɔfɔ and other forms of oath.
10. Ɔnʊ = "mouth," *ekwulu* = "speaks," ɔ*ra* = "public."
11. These symbolic objects are discussed in later chapters.

mnemonic devices and were subject both to personal spiritual sanctions of truth and to more public tests of accuracy, these "private" stories of group differences and activities comprised basic sources of evidence about past events.

It was therefore possible, through careful examination of these forms of Onitsha stories, to develop an overview of major events of the past. However, additional distortions resulted from the manifold social changes which had occurred by the time research was undertaken in the Onitsha of the 1960s.

Such recent changes had by 1960 not only produced considerable discontinuity between generations in the transmission of traditions in Onitsha, but also had considerably secularized the attitudes of people toward the traditions themselves. However, as I have shown elsewhere,[12] the patterning of these changes in their total impact had preserved an overall balance in the traditional social roles of the system, including the maintenance of prestige by the critical transmitters of tradition; it had also preserved the strong general interest in maintaining a continuity of traditional knowledge. In this situation, the mission education received by young Onitsha men even encouraged some serious efforts at recording various oral accounts for their own sake. Numerous genealogies and tales of origin had been recorded, and although the context of transmission had seldom been indicated, some Onitsha students nevertheless showed considerable sophistication in assessing accounts. Although little of this information has been published, many Onitsha families possessed old genealogical lists and other information collected as early as the turn of this century, and such documents provided illuminating comparisons to accounts given by illiterate elders in recent times.

Therefore the effects of a secularizing education on respect for tradition among Onitsha indigenes were in some ways counterbalanced by the advantages of written preservation of traditions. A sufficient diversity remained in the community so that the ac-

12. Henderson (1966:388).

counts of an elderly, illiterate, but reputedly truthful patrilineage priest could sometimes be checked against documents recorded some time ago by literate members of another patrilineage. When the considerable early documentation by explorers and the comparative accounts by ethnographers working the region early in this century are added to this material, enough controlled comparisons can be made to build a reasonably accurate reconstruction, at least for the late oral-historic stages of the community's existence. It must be emphasized, however, that this and the following chapter are intended as initial efforts at such reconstruction; it cannot stand as a definitive account. Conditions of research in 1961 were not conducive to maintaining the standards for the collection of oral traditions that historians now demand.[13]

ECOLOGY: AN OVERVIEW

Onitsha is located on the east bank of the Niger River, approximately one hundred fifty miles north from the delta coast of eastern Nigeria. At this point, the Niger cuts southward through a formation of red sedimentary sands which fold up to the east from Onitsha, forming the Awka-Orlu uplands, and rise again to the west of the river as a series of hills in the Asaba district of midwestern Nigeria.[14] The river meanders through broad, swampy lowlands for many miles to the north of this riverain gap, and south of the gap it flows its entire course through the flat, forested alluvial flood plains which fan out to form the great Niger Delta (see Figures 2, 3, and 5).

Because of its geographical position, the site of Onitsha has long been an important crossroads of this area. The extensive riverain lowlands to the north and south, which receive the annual

13. Unfortunately, in most cases it was not possible to use a tape recorder in my research. However, I did obtain data under conditions that approximated, directly or indirectly, the three different social contexts described above. See Curtin (1968).

14. These are the Bende-Ameki groups of tertiary sediments (Grove 1951:4). Onitsha is situated at latitude 6° 10′ N.

flooding of the Niger, are relatively fertile but difficult to occupy or traverse. They have therefore remained low in human population. The uplands running east and southeast of the river gap, however, contain some of the heaviest population densities in all Africa, and the majority of this population occupies lands that are today in a condition of serious soil deterioration.[15] Onitsha lies between these two major ecological zones; on the fringes of the area of densest population, it abuts directly on the river at a point sufficiently raised above the floodwaters to afford stable docking facilities for riverain people and to provide direct access to the interior uplands. This location has insured its importance as a center of trade since prehistoric times.

Onitsha lies near the northern edge of the rain forest zone, where rainfall averages seventy-five inches per annum, but the dry season is long enough to induce a transitional vegetation.[16] Along the rivers extensive gallery forests remain to this day; on the uplands on both sides of the river, intensive swidden cultivation over the centuries has reduced the forest to an open oil palm bush interspersed with broad patches of derived savanna grasslands. Only the sporadic distribution of sacred groves around villages indicates that the climax vegetation was high forest.

This region has long been occupied by the Ibo-speaking peoples. The riverain or lowland Ibo, who have traded for centuries along the river, call their floodplain environment *ólu.* They contrast this lowland environment with the contiguous uplands, referring to those running east from Onitsha as *ànɩ-ɔ̀chá* ("white lands") and those running west from the river as *énu-ànɩ* ("high lands"), and they often categorize the peoples occupying these regions by these names. The upland Ibo traditionally raised a variety of root crops and livestock, but those occupying the leached white lands of the Awka-Orlu area have long suffered chronic food shortages. The

15. Grove (1951:22).
16. Ibid., p. 8.

soil has in many places undergone such extensive deterioration that it cannot support the dense population, and in these areas textile weaving, oil palm tending and processing of palm produce, blacksmithing, and other specialized economic activities such as slave trading traditionally supplemented farming. In contrast, the lowland-dwelling Ibo have always been able to produce a surplus of yams and to collect enough fish and other river animals for an abundance of protein, but they lack iron, cotton, palm produce, and proper surroundings for livestock raising. Out of such ecological and economic differences developed a trade between these two populations in prehistoric times, and Onitsha has long been a prominent site of exchange in this trade.

CULTURAL AND POLITICAL RELATIONSHIPS DURING THE ORAL-HISTORIC AND EXPLORATORY PERIODS

Although our primary interest concerns Ibo-speaking peoples, the Ibo can be understood historically only in terms of their relations with the peoples surrounding them, who during some periods in the past have actually intruded into their midst and who certainly had strong influences on their culture. Figure 2 indicates the recent distribution of major ethnic groups in the region.

Although this pattern suggests a great historical complexity, some of these distributions have developed through relatively recent and even historically documented migrations, and can therefore be discounted for our initial task of inferring base line cultural influences in the region prior to 1500. The Benue-Congo-speaking Tiv, for example, are known to have expanded northwestward from a more southerly position into the Benue Valley, where they have split up and undoubtedly absorbed formerly Idoma-speaking peoples.[17] The Basa Nge, who have intruded into western Igala country along the lower Niger, did so in the 1840s;

17. Bohannan and Bohannan (1953:10).

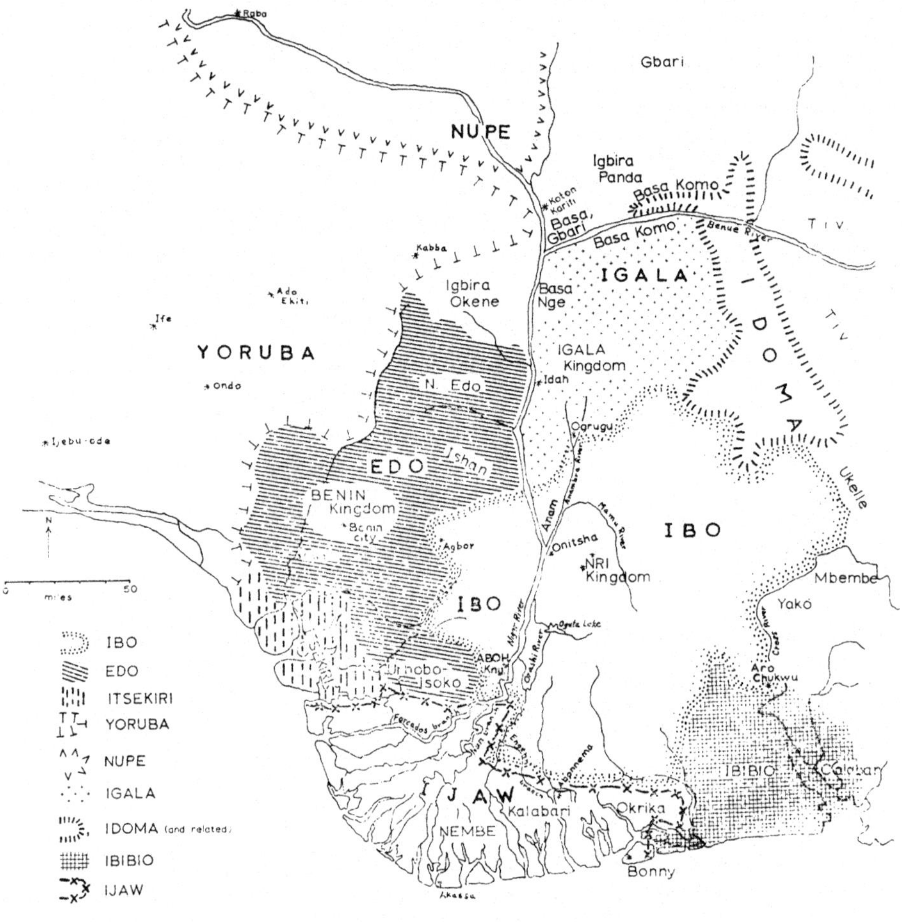

Fig. 2 Language groups and kingdoms of the Lower Niger area

the Basa Komo entered the Niger-Benue confluence region in the 1860s.[18] The Igbira Okene west of the confluence appear from oral traditions to have migrated there from the north during the past few centuries, although this inference is rather less certain.[19]

Since most of the groups under consideration are members of the Kwa-speaking subfamily of the Niger–Congo language family,

18. Clifford (1936:404), Armstrong (1955:77).
19. Brown (1955:57).

the populations can be grouped in accordance with their membership in subdivisions within this family.[20] These linguistic distributions indicate a likely center of origin for the Kwa speaking peoples around the Niger-Benue confluence. That the divisions between the major Kwa groups must be very old may be inferred from exploratory studies in glottochronology; [21] the geographical divisions of the major groups—at least their general contiguous locations—must have been stable for a long time. However, oral traditions and other evidence from language distributions also suggest some subsequent patterns of movement. First, there was evidently an early and long-term spread of speakers of the Yoruba-Igala group west and southward from an origin point somewhere in the northeastern part of their current range. Second, Igala traditions relate their early expansion on the east bank of the Niger, with movement eastward against the Idoma and southward against the Ibo-speaking peoples.[22] Third, the position of the Itsekiri in the southwestern part of the Niger Delta indicates that this Yoruba-group expansion may have occurred prior to the expansion of Edo speakers toward the coast.

An early southward invasion of the Niger Delta by the Ijaw-speaking peoples may also be inferred. This movement appears to have been followed at a later time, first by a southward and east-curving movement of Edo-speaking peoples, second by a generally southward Ibo expansion into the uplands west of the Niger, and third by another Ibo push toward the eastern delta coast, which was still under way during the development of the slave trade. Eastward expansion by the Ibo against Benue-Congo-speaking peoples north of the Cross River has been documented for very

20. Following Greenberg (1955, 1963), the members of this subfamily in the area under consideration are Yoruba-Igala, the Nupe group (including Nupe, Gbari, Igbira, and Gade), Edo, the Idoma group (including Idoma, Agatu, and Iyala), Ibo, and Ijaw.

21. See Armstrong's (1962, 1964) startling suggestion of a 6,000-year depth of separation between Yoruba and Idoma. The time inference must be regarded as purely speculative, but such evidence points to a considerable period of stable divergence of communities in the area.

22. Clifford (1936:400).

recent times.[23] Such late Ibo expansions, associated in part with rising population pressures on the eastern uplands, may have begun only after the start of the slave trade. They may indeed have occurred at the same time as a series of other movements recounted in oral traditions and implied in the intermingling of language groups in the delta. These sources of evidence suggest late expansion of Edo peoples into the central delta, and also of Ijaw peoples dispersing from an early center in the western delta toward the east, where they ultimately came up against the Benue-Congo-speaking Ibibio.[24]

With this background pattern in mind, we may turn to more specific problems concerning the Ibo. To begin by defining them as a traditional unit in their relationships with other populations would lead immediately to difficulties, for it seems clear that in prehistoric times Ibo-speaking peoples had no widely shared conception of themselves as distinct from other populations. They were initially defined piecemeal and from without. During the slave trade the riverain Ibo, and apparently the other river groups who dominated the lower Niger, referred to the dense populations on the Awka-Orlu uplands as *ńdi-ìgbo,* a term which for the former came to mean slaves, and they contrasted themselves as *ńdi-ólu,* "peoples of the riverain lowlands." It has been suggested by one author that this contrast was merely a geographical reference and that the term *ìgbo* referred specifically to hinterland or upland people,[25] but the matter is not so simple.

Some communities in the eastern uplands, like Nnewi, did order their social world by drawing a contrast between *ìgbo-na-ólu,* "igbo and riverain" groups, but the uplands Ibo speakers west of the Niger were not called igbo, and they employed the term themselves to derogate the peoples across the river. Moreover, some Ibo speakers living on the eastern uplands, including those of Nri and

23. Jones (1961).
24. See Bradbury (1957:19–22), Jones (1963:29), and Alagoa (1966).
25. Obi (1963:2).

Onitsha, used the term igbo in referring to populations surrounding them but considered themselves distinct.

The contrasting meanings of the terms igbo and olu appear to have involved a bundle of variable features that were not clearly discriminated by the groups who used the words. Both Nri and Onitsha people employed the succinct proverb "igbo have no king" (*ìgbo énwegh ézè*) to set their neighbors apart from themselves. Their origin traditions stressed the idea that they had intruded into these uplands from other areas. The riverain slave dealers—including Ibo, Igala, and Ijaw speakers—distinguished themselves from ndi-igbo not only by their lowland habitat but also by associating themselves with one or another of the extensive kingdoms on the peripheries of Ibo country, and they claimed possession of kingship institutions for themselves. The contrast of igbo-na-olu therefore involved three independent but often coinciding features: olu meant riverain or riverain-derived, slave-dealing, kingdom-associated peoples; igbo meant upland, slave-providing, kingship-lacking populations. The upland implications of the term further connoted a lack of ready access to water; Onitsha people refer to ndi-igbo as "Those who do not wash," alluding to the traditional custom in the uplands of rubbing the body with palm oil as an aromatic, odor-masking substitute for bathing.

Since it was through kingdom-associated traders that a cultural definition of these populations first developed, consideration of Ibo oral history can best begin with an examination of the major kingdoms impinging upon Iboland. In terms of political and cultural history, the region of Onitsha may be regarded as the crossroads of four major spheres of influence. With the river Niger as a vertical geographical axis, at the northern pole lies the kingdom of Igala centered at Idah, and at the southern pole lies the Ibo kingdom of Aboh. With the uplands as a horizontal axis, the Benin kingdom lies at the western pole and the Nri kingdom at the eastern pole (see Figure 2). The major historical problems concerning these four kingdoms include their relative ages, powers, and interrelations through time, and the relationship of these patterns to the waxing and waning of the slave trade in Iboland. For these problems, oral traditions and historical documents provide our major initial guides.

Of the four kingdoms, Igala, Benin, and Nri appear to be the oldest; Aboh seems to have been derived primarily from Benin. Oral traditions collected from both Igala and Benin suggest that kingship in both these areas was at an early time strongly oriented to the traditional centers of Yoruba divine kingship at Ife and old Oyo. The monumental Benin oral tradition recounted by Egharevba traces the first Benin king or *ɔba* to a period, long before the beginning of the European slave trade, when Oranmiyan, said to be the son of a descendant of the Yoruba culture hero Oduduwa, "brought the first horse" into the Benin region and established his son by a Bini woman as ɔba there.[26] This legend finds echoes in similar Yoruba traditions suggesting an ancient conquest of Ife by the legendary hero Oranyan, who had come from the north (perhaps from the middle Niger area) and established the Yoruba kingdom of Oyo.[27] At Igala, Crowther in the mid-nineteenth century recorded a tradition that long ago a Yoruba king had sent his man the Ata (the title of the Igala king) downriver from Raba on the Niger to seek a new settlement. Landing at Idah, the Ata settled among autochthonous peoples called Akpoto and in time gained precedence over them.[28]

Such origin accounts suggest at the very least an early period of Bini and Igala cultural borrowing from, and perhaps political dependence upon, the Yoruba peoples. Benin traditional history is remarkably rich for a nonliterate society and indicates a long period of changing relationships with Yoruba groups, while at

26. Egharevba (1960:6–8).
27. Biobaku (1958:25–26); Lloyd (1960:223).
28. Crowther (1855:65–66). (All citations of Crowther refer to S. A. Crowther unless otherwise noted.) Akpoto or Akpota apparently may refer to both Igala and Idoma. Tiv use it with reference to Idoma; I have heard Ibo use *Àkpɔta* with reference to Igala.

Igala these relationships are so remote that they are apparently not widely remembered.

Benin

Benin oral history is of particular interest because of its richness, and because it includes a suggestive account of governmental innovations which had an impact over a considerable area. Although it cannot be regarded as directly valid history, its wealth of detail and relative internal consistency have made possible the careful analyses that produce a very considerable yield of historical evidence.[29] At this point it provides a useful guide to historic cultural relations in the area under consideration.

The first king or ɔba, Eweka I, whose regalia came from the Yoruba city of Ife and whose body after death was interred there, is said to have created the first Council of State, composed of the "seven Uzama"; these were the holders of the ancient and highest ranking, strictly hereditary chiefly titles of Benin, who traditionally acted as kingmakers, enacting elaborate ritual roles in installation of a new ɔba. It is said that a later ɔba found these Uzama chiefs appropriating his emblems of authority and conferring new titles, so he removed his palace from their midst, defeated their leaders in battle, and ended their imitating of his royal prerogatives. He also began creating new titles for his domestic servants, thus establishing an inchoate staff of palace retainers.[30]

After this time, warfare apparently spread in the region. It was followed by a period of disorder, culminating in what may have been an invasion and conquest of the city of Benin prior to the Portuguese explorations in the late fifteenth century. The conquering leader, who became the ɔba Ewuare the Great, is said then to have embarked on a series of further conquests to the north into Northern Edo and Yoruba country and also eastward into Iboland, thereby greatly increasing the influence and importance of

29. See Bradbury (1959, 1964), for excellent examples of this work.
30. Egharevba (1960:10–11).

Benin City. He also introduced a number of innovations, including a new title order and council of "town chiefs" (eghaevo n'ore) based on the "four pillars of Benin" (the iyase, esogba, eso, and osuma) whose offices were attainable through achievement, and he organized the achieved titles of his domestic servants into graded associations of "palace chiefs" (eghaevo n'ogbe).[31]

The kings of Benin traditionally sent out their royal sons and junior brothers as chiefs (pl. *enigie,* sing. *onogie*) of dependent communities. This practice, together with the holding of sons of conquered and tributary chiefs as court hostages and trainees, was pursued more intensively as the power of the kingdom increased, with the result that Bini culture as well as political domination was widely diffused into surrounding populations. Ɔba Ozolua, at the threshold of the Portuguese exploration period, is said to have established resident local authorities westward into conquered Ijebu-ode in southern Yoruba country and eastward into Ibo country near the Niger, including the community of Aboh.[32] Most Edo-speaking communities north of Benin state that their political order originated from that city, through either the receiving of a chief sent by an ɔba or the accommodating of refugees who had fled the king's powers.[33]

With the establishment of Portuguese interests at Benin after 1485, European trade goods were first introduced into the kingdom, and in 1515 Portuguese agents may have actually accompanied the king's army eastward on an expedition against Igala armies to determine spheres of power west of the Niger. According to Bini tradition the armies of the king and his Queen-mother Idia, led by the slave commander Gbunmara, routed the Igala and camped on the banks of the Niger before returning to Benin.[34]

31. Ibid., p. 79. See also the very interesting discussion of Ewuare by Ryder (1965: 35–36).

32. Egharevba (1960:24).

33. Bradbury (1957:22, 63, 101).

34. Egharevba (1960:29). Bradbury (1959) has carefully considered the problems of relating these dates to Benin genealogy.

Tributary overlordship was established over many communities west of the river, and thereafter recalcitrant groups there were regularly attacked in slave-raiding wars. According to Asaba tradition, the ɔba periodically sent his agents to fetch water from the Niger,[35] and in some areas this Bini domination continued into the 1850s.

The domination of Benin in the western part of the lower Niger region had two major effects. First, it spread new ideas about chieftaincy and title systems. Bini royal kinsmen placed in charge of subject communities carried with them some of the symbols of royalty, and in many cases they instituted grades of subordinate chiefs modeled on those of Benin. More distant tributary chieftaincies, including Western Ibo communities like Isele-ukwu, were delegated the powers of capital punishment through the conferral by the ɔba of the royal sword (*ádà*). These traditional authorities thereby gained new prerogatives, and their chiefdoms became secondary centers of influence. Second, various Ibo communities were disrupted, and a number of population movements resulted from the large-scale warfare accompanying the extension of Bini power. In Western Ibo country, some groups were forced out of the Asaba-Agbor uplands and into the riverain lowlands near the Niger; others crossed the river to settle in the east.

Among the disrupted and displaced Ibo communities were nine which trace their origins to an ancient Ibo sacred king (*ézè*) named *ishima* or *chîma* (hereafter "Chima"), who ruled a legendary community called *Àdó-nà-Ìdu* ("Ado and Idu") and paid tribute to the ɔba of Benin. Nine towns in the Asaba-Agbor uplands share this Eze Chima legend (see Figure 3), and their oral traditions trace their dispersion from Ado-na-Idu to a dispute between Eze Chima and either Ɔba Esigie or Ɔba Ozolua, one of whom was almost certainly on the throne at the time of first Portuguese con-

35. Spencer (1901). This water was, of course, symbolic of the geographical extent of his control.

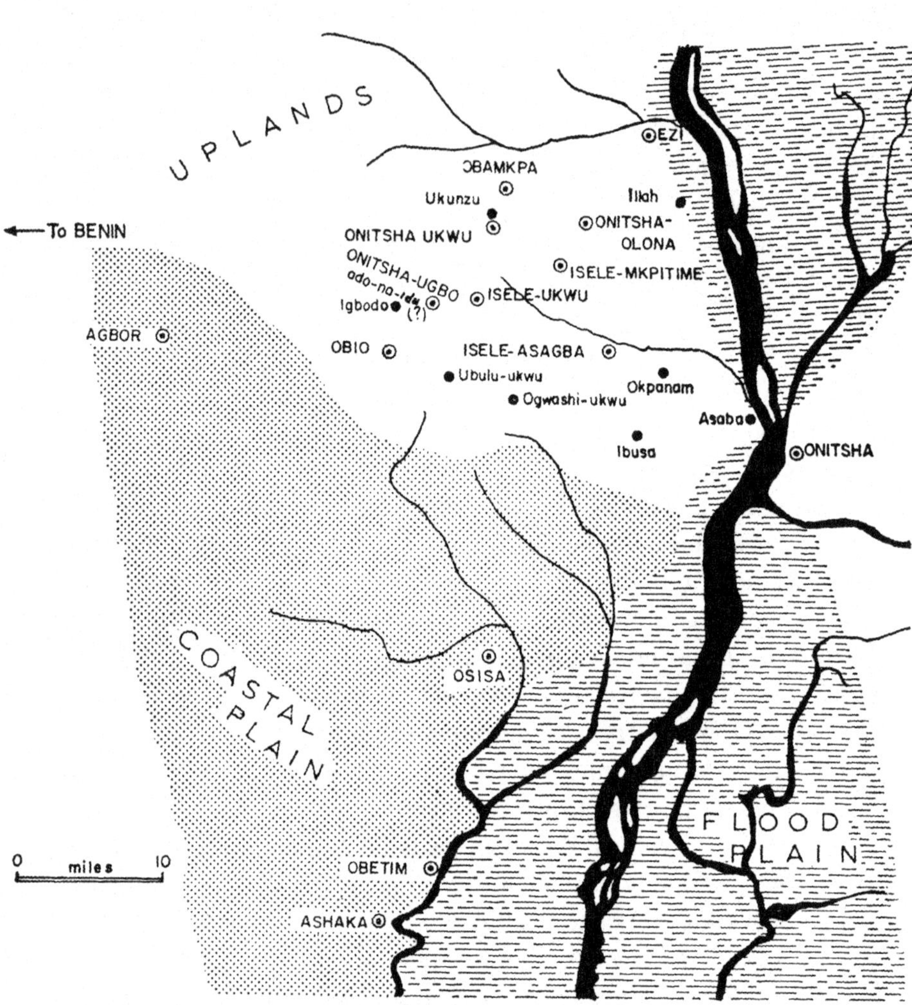

Fig. 3 Western Ibo communities affected by Benin

tact and the Benin expedition against Igala. The ɔba or his queen-mother is said to have sent troops against King Chima, who was forced to flee with his people and in doing so "founded" (or at least linked together) a series of towns along the uplands as well as the community of Onitsha across the river.

Aboh

The riverain Ibo kingdom of Aboh also traces its origin to King Chima and Ɔba Ozolua. According to Aboh legend, their ancestor Chima disputed the right of Ɔba Ozolua to the Benin throne, and when he and his supporters were humiliated and degraded after his failure to win it they left their home near Benin, pursued by Ozolua's army. The group moved southward from the Asaba uplands, founding the related series of communities called Osisa, Obetim, and Ashaka, and, supposedly still pursued by the Bini army, encountered a river running through swamplands which they could not ford. Miraculously, it is said, a group of manatees formed themselves together into a mass and ferried the people of Chima to safety near a site along the Niger. Finding an indigenous Ibo-speaking population called *Ákrì* occupying this desirable spot, the followers of Chima fought them, expelled them, and established for themselves the community of Aboh.

This origin tale links the Aboh community to an initial dependency on Benin, a dependency that Benin oral tradition suggests existed for a considerable period of time after the formation of the riverain town.[36] It also formulates in myth the importance of the ecological shift into a riverain environment. By situating themselves at the apex of the main tributary channels of the Niger Delta, the Aboh people not only put themselves beyond the direct control of Benin but occupied a strategic position for controlling the riverain slave trade, which may have begun not long after the reign of the Benin Ɔba Ozolua.

A glance at any map of the lower Niger (see Figure 2) will confirm the strategic nature of the Aboh location. Near Aboh three major streams of the Niger diverge. The Forcados branch runs through the western delta and connects through a series of creeks

36. Egharevba (1960:41) cites an incident during a reign dated around 1735, when Aboh sent an appeal to the ɔba of Benin, asking him to decide between claimants to the Aboh throne.

with the waterways of the Itsekiri kingdom and the Benin port city of Gwato, the Nun branch flows southward to the sea at Akassa, and the Engenni branch, flowing southeastward through Abonnema and the Kalabari country, is linked through creeks to Bonny on the eastern delta coast. Below Aboh these three major branches of the river are interconnected by labyrinthine systems of creeks which make possible intricate alternative patterns of canoe travel, but above Aboh the river runs through one main channel. Riverain trade northward had therefore to be channeled up the single main stream which passes Aboh. One alternative route bypassed Aboh to the east along the upper Orashi river through Oguta Lake.

The delta regions below Aboh are mostly mangrove swamplands long occupied by Ijaw-speaking peoples organized politically in ancient times in village units divided into extended family "houses" (wari). Their economies were based on fishing and salt production. Not self-sufficient economically, the delta Ijaw exported smoke-dried fish and salt northward into the Edo and Ibo country in exchange for agricultural products, poultry, and domestic livestock. This ancient trade laid the basis for a north–south trade system along the many creeks of the Niger Delta.[37]

With the beginning of the slave trade, European trading vessels entered the lower reaches of the delta creeks and made contact with the Ijaw populations. By the beginning of the sixteenth century, traders from the hinterlands to the north were coming to the coastal Ijaw villages in large canoes, bringing yams, livestock, and slaves which they sold to the villagers in exchange for salt, and which these villagers in turn sold to the Europeans in exchange for copper bracelets.[38] By the end of the seventeenth century, import demand had expanded to include a variety of European manufactured products, and the communities of Kalabari, Andoni, Bonny, Okrika, and Nembe or Brass had become impor-

37. Jones (1963:13–16).
38. Described in Esmeraldo de situ orbis; see Jones (1963:33).

tant trading centers. During the latter part of the eighteenth century, as firearms and cannon became the crucial manufactured imports, intertribal wars proliferated. Ijaw canoe fleets armed with cannons clashed with each other over trading spheres, and local war leaders became "kings" possessing relatively centralized powers of coordination.

The Ijaw kingdoms of Nembe, Kalabari, and Bonny emerged from these wars the dominant trading communities of the eastern delta. Their extended families had been transformed into "canoe houses," trading and fighting corporations built around the management of fifty-man canoes that served both as warships and cargo vessels, and organized on the basis of achieved wealth and power rather than ascriptive kinship criteria.[39] These three kingdoms sought to conduct trade not only within their own immediate creek systems and hinterlands but also more widely throughout the delta, particularly towards the Niger. In their efforts to expand communication, they came into contact with the people of Aboh.

The course of development in the relations between Aboh and these Ijaw states, between the beginning of the slave trade and the start of the nineteenth century, cannot be traced in any detail because no intensive anthropological research has been done in Aboh itself. Nevertheless it is clear from historical accounts of the nineteenth century that prior to this period the Aboh people not only developed an active riverain canoe-based trading economy and adapted their social organization into "canoe house corporations" similar to those of the Ijaw but also succeeded in playing the Nembe, Kalabari, and Bonny states against one another to such an extent that they maintained their political independence and gained political control over access to the Niger upstream.[40] The Landers's 1830 account attests that Aboh

39. Jones (1963:45–47).

40. The clearest evidence of this in the documentary literature is the Landers' being held for ransom by the king of Aboh, referred to as Obi. Obi shrewdly played the Brass and Bonny traders against each other in their efforts to buy the two Europeans. See Lander and Lander (1841:220–22).

> has, for a series of years, been the principal slave-mart for native traders from the coast, between the Bonny and Old Calebar rivers: and for the production of its palm-oil it has gained equal celebrity. Hundreds of men from the rivers mentioned above come up for the purpose of trade, and numbers of them are at present residing in canoes in front of the town. Most of the oil purchased by Englishmen at the Bonny and adjacent rivers, is brought from hence, as are nearly all the slaves which are annually exported from those places by the French, Spaniards, and Portuguese.[41]

The Aboh king at this time, Eze Obi Osai, wore the profusion of "coral" necklace wrappings characteristic of the Bini ɔba, was accorded the most abject prostrations by his people, and extracted regular tribute and obeisance from the king of at least one of the delta states whose leaders were trading at his capital city at the time.[42] His power was based on firearms and cannon, which the people of Aboh had acquired through manipulating a diversified trade network that spread to Benin and to the Itsekiri kingdom as well as to the various eastern delta states.

The Aboh sovereign, modeling himself on the ɔba of Benin, claimed to hold despotic and hereditary powers over his people, but, although some preference in succession was apparently accorded the king's son, as in Benin, the successor to kingship was reportedly chosen in fact by a council of the sixty chiefs in charge of the various villages under the Aboh kingdom. Eight or ten of these titled chiefs (some of whose title names are cognate with Benin titles) resided in Aboh itself, each representing an Aboh local segment and controlling from two to six war canoes operated by twenty to fifty paddlers each. The king himself possessed a total of fifteen war canoes, each mounted with a cannon in the bow, but when he proposed to make war he could call on all his tribu-

41. Ibid., p. 218.

42. Ibid., p. 213; Allen and Thomson (1848:1:171), Laird and Oldfield (1837:1:97, 388).

tary chiefs, those of outlying villages along the river having available from one to four canoes each, depending on village size. In normal times these canoes were employed in trade, and prominent women traders independently managed their own fleets of canoes.[43]

The king, and certainly other Aboh trading chiefs as well, solidified ties with the tributary chiefs by marrying their kinsmen, thus gaining for their sons positions as daughter's children to those chiefs' patrilineages. But these intercommunity ties sharply limited the ability of Aboh to impose decisions upon its tributaries, for such matrilateral kinship bonds divided the Aboh community internally.[44]

Aboh society emphasized status achievement through warfare and trade. Although their canoe-house system was apparently based on an Ibo patrilineage pattern, the extent to which achievement had become the major route to wealth and influence is evident from an early report which estimated the average age of the town's prominent leaders at thirty-five. This figure is all the more striking for a community in which, it was said, "The people live apparently to a good age, for many were observed to be more than seventy years old." [45]

Aboh trade was oriented downriver toward the delta states and upriver toward Ibo communities on both sides of the Niger and, further north, toward Edo-speaking communities on the west bank and Igala speakers on the east up to the Niger-Benue confluence. The direction of their trading expeditions was, however, preponderantly upriver. This upriver trade had an ancient base among the Akri Ibo, the autochthonous, simple descent-organized population that occupied the river area prior to the coming of the Aboh. The Akri are called by other Ibo "Children of the Niger" (*Ụ́mụ̀-ótimili*), and they acted in early times as priests of the river, presenting to it white animals as sacrificial offerings. Ibo traditions

43. Allen and Thomson (1848:1:233–36); Laird and Oldfield (1837:1:99–100).

44. Allen and Thomson (1848:1:240); see also Crowther and Taylor (1859:19) for an example of the divisive effects of such matrilateral ties.

45. Allen and Thomson (1848:1:251).

say that Akri people could not drown in the Niger. They conducted riverain trade with the upland Ibo east and west, with the "Ado" or Edo-speaking peoples further north on the west bank, and with the Igala. In this trade, salt from the delta and fish from the river were exchanged for Ibo yams, palm products, livestock, and camwood, and for ivory and potash from Igala country and beyond. After the beginning of the sixteenth century the upcountry probably began to export slaves as well.

It may be presumed that fairly early in the eighteenth century, Aboh began to acquire cannon and gun powder from the various delta states with which it had established trade relations, for by the end of the eighteenth century its firearm-based power on the river had become legendary. Using their cannon-equipped canoes in massive fleets, Aboh warriors established dominance over the Ibo-speaking riverain communities and encouraged the development of markets trading in slaves. The very right to ply a canoe on the river depended on the paying of tribute to the Aboh king, and a major center of canoe production apparently developed at Aboh itself. The statement in the earliest historical source that the people of Aboh were "famous for making large canoes, and all those of the different rivers, from Benin to Calebar, are constructed by them," while not corroborated by later accounts, indicates the apparent range of their influence at the start of the exploratory period.[46]

The primary source of Aboh slaves was far upriver, and one major supplier of those slaves was the kingdom of Igala. This state long controlled the Niger-Benue confluence region, and comprised the third sphere of political and cultural influence in the lower Niger area.

Igala

Some of the oral traditions collected by explorers and scholars from the Igala capital at Idah suggest ancient connections of Igala

46. Lander and Lander (1841:233).

kingship both with the Yoruba to the west and also with the Jukun kingdom eastward on the middle Benue.[47] These origin traditions are, however, rather obscure; more detailed Igala legends associate their kingship more strongly with Benin, and the late oral-historical Igala kingdoms appear to have been oriented primarily in this direction. British explorers in 1854 were told by an Igala chief that the first kings of Benin, Igala, and Aboh had all sprung from Ado, the country lying westward across the Niger from the capital at Idah. The Ado people had in turn supposedly come from Ife. The first ata of Igala was described as either a hunter or a warrior, who had crossed over the Niger from Ado and subjugated the indigenous Akpoto population.[48]

The royal family in Idah traces its own descent to a brother of a Benin chief who was said to have left that state after a dispute over succession, and who went to Idah carrying royal regalia that awed the Igala into making him their ata. These fabled ritual objects, clearly of Benin origin, are still retained in Igala. Such traditions imply acceptance of an Igala position tributary to Benin, and might be regarded as relating the recent Igala dynasties to a Benin agent imposed after Benin's victory in the Igala-Benin war of the late fifteenth or early sixteenth century. Clearly, both Benin and Igala traditions do recognize a descent relationship between their kings, and both traditions recount the defeat of an Igala army in the Ado country at the hands of Benin.[49]

After this defeat, the Igala kingdom's sphere of control was limited mostly to the east bank of the Niger, although around the confluence it may have extended on both sides of the river. The

47. Crowther (1855:64–65), Seton (1928:255–56), Clifford (1936:395). Boston (1968:9–16) argues that the several Igala traditions which attribute royal origins variously to Benin, Yoruba, and Jukun sources cannot be historically ordered, and must be viewed as mythic structural archetypes.

48. Baikie (1856:286–87). See Figure 2. The term *Ado* was applied by the Ibo to the people living west of Idah, i.e. apparently Northern Edo speakers; the Akpoto or Akpota refer variously to Igala or Idoma, in this case no doubt Igala. See Armstrong (1955:79–83) on these problems; cf. Ryder (1965) concerning the possible historical significance of the Northern Edo area.

49. Boston (1962:380–81).

kingdoms of Nupe and Igbira both trace their royal origins to immigrants who had formerly served the king of Igala; the first Nupe king has been tentatively dated in the early sixteenth century,[50] and the Igbira kings of Funda and Koton Karifi above the confluence apparently remained tributary to the ata until exploratory times.[51]

Igala influence over these kingdoms helped them to develop a domination of trade downriver even though the Edo-speaking peoples on the western bank remained tributary to Benin and hostile to Igala. The Igala acquired slaves, ivory, and other products from the upriver states and from their own eastern and southeastern hinterlands, and these they traded downriver to the Aboh people, in exchange for salt and European manufactured goods. By the beginning of exploratory times the ata of Igala had gained "the reputation of being the most powerful [king] between the sea and Funda," [52] that is from the mouth of the Niger to the confluence.

This kingdom appears to have developed a number of characteristics which influenced the course of its evolution and that of contiguous peoples. The ata of Igala, like the ɔba of Benin, was traditionally a person so sacred that his feet could not touch bare ground; his face should not display human emotions, and his bodily functions were matters of secrecy. A plethora of retainers insured that he was seldom observed by ordinary men, and indeed the early European explorers consistently found the ata to be the most inaccessible monarch along the river. While this royal seclusion was practiced in many west African kingdoms, at Igala it apparently developed to such an extent that the king became effectively imprisoned by several groups of independent retainers.[53]

50. Nadel (1942:406).
51. Allen and Thomson (1848:1:375). See Figure 2.
52. Laird and Oldfield (1837:1:124).
53. Allen and Thomson (1848:1:278–335), Baikie (1856:58–63), Crowther and Taylor (1859:41–48), Clifford (1936:400–17). Boston (1968:191–96) has thrown into doubt the question of the king's divinity, but I do not find his arguments convincing in light of the historical documents. These also suggest, however, that Islam was becoming the state religion in this kingdom by the beginning of the exploratory period.

Igala oral traditions imply sequences in the development of the kingdom. They may or may not be historically valid in detail, but they do suggest some trends in organization which also seemed evident to the explorers of the nineteenth century. First, it is said in one tale that an Ibo wanderer helped an early ruler. In return this man was given the title of *achadu,* and was grouped with the *Gala Mela* or "Nine Igala"—heads of ancient patrilineal clans—to form a king's council. These patriarchs controlled the major divisions of the country (with the *achadu* in charge of that portion of the kingdom nearest to Iboland), acted as kingmakers, and played ritual roles in the installation of new kings. Their titles became hereditary within their clans. They formed the ascriptive base of the kingdom, and as such appear to have played roles roughly comparable to those of the "seven Uzama" of Benin.[54]

Second, the kings expanded their kingdom outward from the core area held by the Nine Igala, colonizing the interior Akpoto regions by sending out sons as titled chiefs to various communities, and also by recognizing heads of certain local clans as nonroyal titled chiefs. In some places, both types of chief were present and competed with one another to the advantage of the king. Other sons of the king were given titles as representatives of the royal clan within Idah itself. All these chiefly titles—both royal and nonroyal—tended to become hereditary within the descent groups of the original holders.[55]

Third, another major category of officials established by the king was that of his palace officials, who supervised domestic life in the palace, insured the observation of royal taboos, and regulated access to the king in the interest of his safety. The most prominent of these were the eunuchs (*amonoji*) ranked in an elaborate hierarchy of titles. The most senior eunuchs became close advisors to the king, might serve as his delegates in judging

54. Seton (1928:269–70); Clifford (1936:395). Boston (1968:16–27) gives a detailed version of the legendary activities of the achadu and the first historical king, which affirms a probable historic significance to this putative establishment of new titles within an hereditary framework.

55. For a detailed description of these offices see Boston (1968:28–127).

cases at the royal court and in putting down rebellions, and played important roles in succession to clan and title offices, collecting a portion of the title fees in some cases.[56]

The other category of palace officials, the *edibo,* were clients selected by the king as his personal servants, bodyguards, and war leaders, and aside from their oath-sworn allegiance to him they were exempted from ordinary law as administered by the chiefs. Most of these clients claimed some kind of uterine kinship link to the royal clan, but they gained their titles through purchase, paying the necessary fees to the ata through his senior eunuchs. Over time they increased in numbers and became scattered through the kingdom as a kind of predatory social stratum, regarding themselves as above the law. Through control of various title fees, the eunuchs continually gained in power, while the edibo themselves came to surround the ata with a kind of blanketing cohort of retainers who had bought their titles and regarded these titles as personal property.[57]

The twelfth ata was reportedly killed at the instigation of the achadu because of his tyranny and, according to one account, the thirteenth (who reigned early in the nineteenth century) retaliated by breaking up the ancient council of Nine Igala which had provided an important conservative counterweight through the power of the achadu. In its stead, the king formed some titled chiefs of the royal clan into a state council, a move that led to continued expansion of royal prerogatives. Whether this particular account is valid or not, by the end of the nineteenth century the king's major councillors were titled royals called "children of the ata," and not the Nine Igala.[58]

These oral traditions may or may not reflect sequential changes

56. Clifford (1936:401–02); Boston (1968:155–75).

57. Clifford (1936:402–03); see also Boston (1968:165).

58. Clifford (1936:400–03, Boston 1968:61–66). Boston (1968:91–92) denies the validity of this historical account, and it does seem doubtful that this process could have occurred during the nineteenth century without considerable evidence of it in the oral tradition.

that actually occurred in Igala society; the most an outside observer can say is that they are not implausible. The accounts of early European explorers do provide evidence that very serious integrative problems had emerged among the various social strata making up this kingdom. Early impressions of a very powerful monarch gave way to the view that the ata was practically imprisoned by his attendants,[59] that prominent chiefs, having established virtually independent fiefs, could dominate him,[60] that law-based social order was rapidly breaking down.[61] Explorers of the mid-nineteenth century clearly felt that Igala was disintegrating through factional disputes and lawlessness.

Two interrelated developments may have contributed to this apparent instability and malintegration. First, after 1810 the Fulani Holy Wars in the Hausa kingdoms north of the Niger-Benue valleys had developed into systematic slave raids and conquests directed into these valley regions. By the time European explorers reached the region of the confluence, the Fulani were widely feared, were laying waste to many communities, and were forcing disrupted populations southwards across the Niger. By 1854 the population of Igala country around the confluence was receiving a heavy influx of refugees from the north. This no doubt created problems of order that the Igala were hard-pressed to solve.[62]

A second development fostering disintegration may have been the king's policy of allowing, under these conditions of population flux, various Igala clans to set up independent outlier stations along the river for the purpose of pursuing the slave trade. The earliest European reports indicate that the holder of the Abokko title had set up an independent trading station along the Niger at Adamugu on the southern frontier of Igala country. This chief

59. Allen and Thomson (1848:1:278–330), Baikie (1856:58–63); Crowther and Taylor (1859:43–48).

60. Crowther (1855:28, 34–35), Baikie (1856:61–63, 268–82).

61. Crowther and Taylor (1859:46).

62. Lander and Lander (1841:70–71, 113, 116–17); Allen and Thomson (1848:1:379–81); Laird and Oldfield (1837:1:241–42, 2:22–23); Baikie (1856:81, 85–86).

and his followers engaged in open warfare with another Igala riverain clan over dominance in this trade, and by the mid-nineteenth century the Abokko's descendants had abandoned their trading activities at the capital of Idah and had instead set up markets near the confluence which entirely bypassed Idah in the downriver trade, reportedly to the ata's disadvantage.[63]

Thus the Igala kingdom shows substantial evidence of instability and strain, due in part to social conditions along the river Niger. It will be shown below that during the oral-historic period, development of Igala downriver trade with Aboh involved a series of defections by Igala subjects who were river traders, a process having some importance to Onitsha. Certain Igala traditions also allude to more ancient defections or migrations from Igala country, specifically recounting early intrusions into Ibo country.

Legends of Onojo Oboni and the Northern Ibo

A complex of Igala and northern Ibo legends describes an Igala warrior named Onojo Oboni,[64] a giant with six fingers on each hand and six toes on each foot. In Igala legend the genealogical position of this warrior appears ambiguous,[65] but he is said to have aspired at one time to the title of ata, and to have built a palace tower near Idah which competed in its height with that built by the ata. He failed in his aspirations, and went to settle in Ogrugu on the upper Anambra River, in southeastern Igala country near the Ibo frontier. There his official seat or stool gained such a reputation through his righteous judicial decisions that the succeeding kings at Idah made gifts of slaves to Ogrugu in order to acquire it.[66]

This legend suggests the presence of a semi-independent, per-

63. Lander and Lander (1841:168–71); Baikie (1856:268, 281–82); Crowther (1855: 171–73). Boston (1968:109–14) gives a detailed account of the conflicts among these Igala riverain clans.

64. In Onitsha and at Nri in Iboland, he is called *Ónojà Òbolí*. To avoid confusion I will use the Igala term throughout.

65. Seton (1928:267–71); Boston (1968:49).

66. Seton (1928:259, 267–68).

haps autonomous state (possibly the remnant of a very old one) on the fringes of Ibo country. Northern Ibo groups from Nsukka to the Anambra River recount traditions that Onojo Oboni raided their areas for slaves and sometimes established his agents there. He is also said to have made it possible in some of these areas for Ibo leaders aspiring to the title of Eze to go to Igala country in order to receive the regalia of "royalty." [67] Onojo Oboni is described by peoples living along the Anambra River toward its confluence with the Niger, as an elephant and slave hunting warrior who terrorized the Ibo populations there, once conquered Asaba, and took a woman of Onitsha as his wife.[68]

The Ogrugu Igala are known to have traded slaves overland between the Nike Ibo country and Idah. These legends of Onojo Oboni indicate that Igala, and Igala-influenced Ibo groups occupying the "Anam" floodplain area between the Niger and Anambra rivers, also operated far down the Anambra river and at one time dominated the key riverside sites leading into the Asaba and Awka uplands. This secondary center of influence on the Niger will be further discussed below.

The "Eze Nri" and His Range of Influence

Another set of Ibo legends traces to the Igala borderlands the origin of several Ibo-speaking communities in the Anambra and Mamu river drainage system, including the historic home of the "Nri king" (*Ézè Ñri*). Nri people say that they are not igbo, for "the igbo have no king," but that they descend from Eri, a man sent from the sky by the great god (*chí-úkwu*). Eri is said to have had two wives, each of whom bore him offspring as shown in Figure 4.[69]

Eri, the first king in this narrative, found himself standing in the morass of the world surrounded by water near what is now the

67. Boston (1960a:56–57).
68. Ibid., p. 55. Onitsha tradition will be further discussed below.
69. Jeffreys (1935:346; n.d.:6:5–7).

hills south of the Anambra River, and complained of his plight to the great god. The great god sent him a blacksmith who blew on fire with his bellows, made the ground dry, and then became the ancestor of the Awka Ibo people who have since that time specialized in blacksmithing.

Later Eri's son Nri became hungry, for the igbo people among whom he had come to live were not farmers but simply wandered about in the bush. The great god ordered him to kill and decapitate his senior son and daughter, and, after cutting their foreheads with marks of sacred ritual purification (*íchi*), to bury their heads

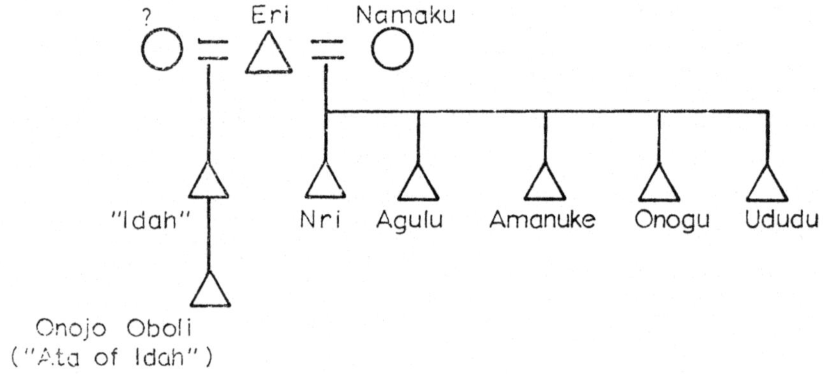

Fig. 4 The children of Eri

as if planting a garden. Nri did this, and after a time out of the head of the son grew yam (*ji̊*, Dioscorea spp.) while out of the head of the daughter grew taro (*àkasi*, Colocasia esculenta).

Since the cultigens upon which the Ibo-speaking peoples came to depend for their food staples were the "son" and "daughter" of Nri, Nri and his descendants gained the right to produce the sacred "yam medicine" (*ɔ́gwờ-jí*) for which surrounding peoples traditionally came to Nri and for which they paid him an annual tribute to insure the edibility of their yams. Since his sacrificed children were the first persons to bear the marks of ritual identity purification, Nri gained the right to confer certain emblems of such ritual purification, and since he was the first to develop a ritual relationship to the land, his people gained the right of spiritually cleansing every community of any sins committed against the land (*ńsɔ-ànι* or alʊ).[70]

It is said that the Nri king traveled southeastward, leaving the original landing spot along the Anambra to be occupied by his brother Agulu, who founded Aguleri. While another brother founded the community of Igbariam, and other siblings settled the communities of Nteje, Amanuke, and Osinagidi, the Nri king himself settled at Agu-ukwu, the great plain on the uplands which became the Nri community. Eventually the Nri community split, one section founding Oreri further south near the contemporary site of Igbo-ukwu where archeological bronzes have been found. Thus two independent centers of Nri kings emerged at some oral-historic period (see Figure 5).

This Nri origin myth forms the great cultural charter of the northern Ibo-speaking peoples of this area, for they all associate their primordial condition with the dominance of Nri. The community of Nri was believed by many surrounding Ibo groups to be the place to which their dead traveled, the Nri "village square" (*Áma-Ǹri*) being a resting place en route to the land of the dead. The Nri king traditionally established the annual calendar schedule and the weekly market cycles of these communities. Nri men who had attained ɔzɔ title purification were, unlike most other Ibo speakers, traditionally free to travel widely through Ibo country, carrying their sacred staffs and medicines which enabled them to cleanse other communities of social abominations. Only they could bestow the final emblems of the identity purification that constitutes the ɔzɔ title system among Ibo, and only they could dispense the sacred yam medicine which ensured edible yams.

This symbolic charter and the rights formulated by it defined a dependence among these Ibo groups upon Nri for their subsis-

70. Thomas (1913:52, 59); Jeffreys (n.d.;6:9–15).

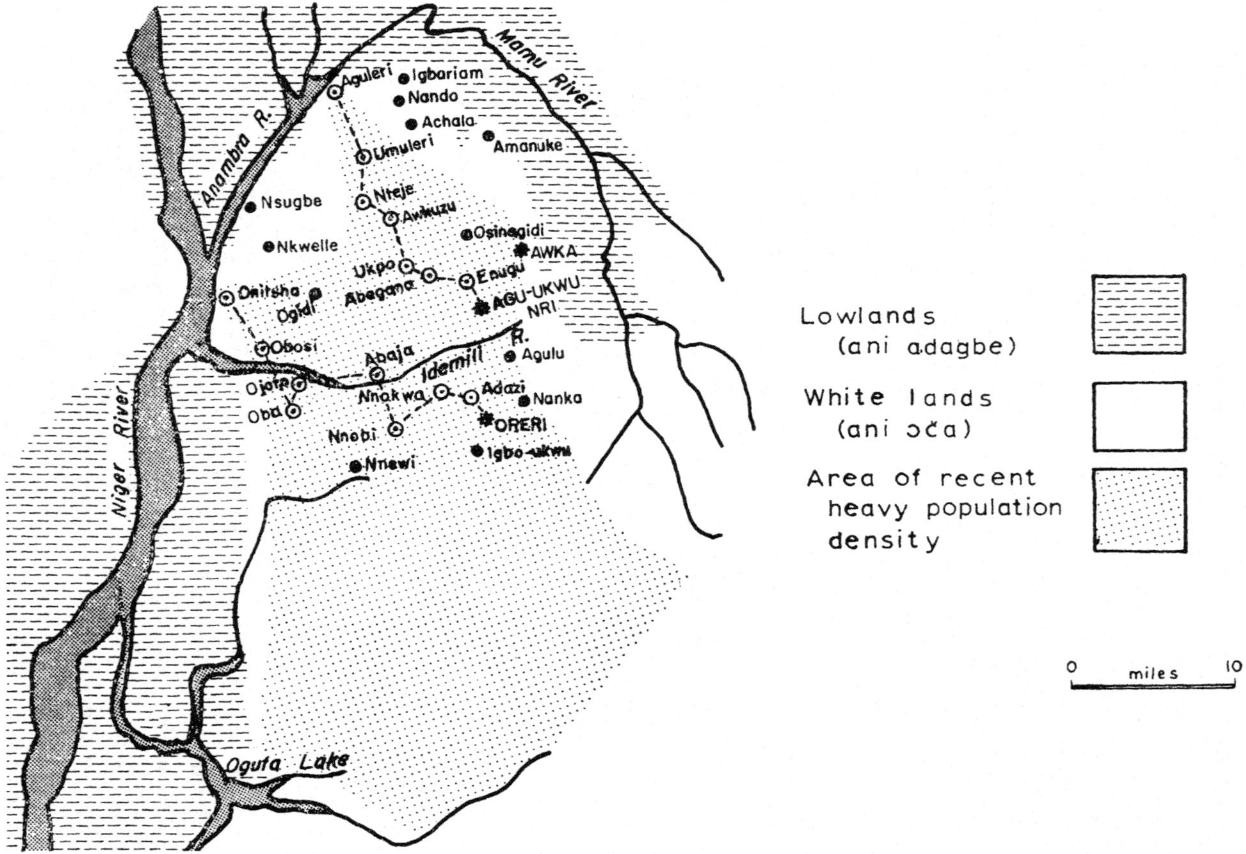

Fig. 5 The centers of Nri ritual influence

tence, law, and attainment of prestige; such dependence appears to have extended in ancient times westward across the Niger. According to some Nri informants it once reached all the way to Benin.[71] East of the river, many towns derive the origin of one or more of their village quarters from Nri, and across the Niger westward such communities as Ibusa, Ogwashi-ukwu, Owa and others do the same.[72]

Such extensive cultural influence suggests the existence of a great and powerful kingdom, and the elaborate bronze castings found by archeologists at Igbo-ukwu near Oreri would seem to support such an inference.[73] The Nri king held regalia, such as the bronze face-mask (ikputu-eze), which would place him in a class with the kings of Benin and Igala, and he was said to be "above the law" as were these monarchs. Since it was traditional for groups within the Nri sphere of influence to send all persons tainted by social abominations to the Nri king, an administered trade in slaves may have been in his hands. However, by the beginning of the exploratory period an almost complete decentralization of power obtained throughout the Nri sphere of influence. The king was selected at Nri not for his capacity to make binding decisions but partly through divination and partly by evidence of prior personal failure and psychological instability.[74] These criteria resemble those used among Ibo in selecting a personal career as a native doctor or diviner (*díbìa*). Once he had been installed, the king lived in seclusion (as did the kings of Igala and Benin), but in a place totally unprotected by walls. Although he had the right to decide cases involving abomination and possessed extensive ritual prerogatives, and although the imitations of warfare in his installation ceremonies seem to indicate a symbolic position of great power, he had very little control over decision making even within his own community, and ɔzɔ men of Nri were free to travel

71. Thomas (1913:52); Jeffreys (n.d.:2:16).
72. Forde and Jones (1950:46–47).
73. Field (1940); Shaw (1960, 1965, 1967).
74. Jeffreys (1935:346; n.d.:7:1–2, 9–18; 12:4–5); cf. Thomas (1913:48–49).

widely and autonomously in performing their ritual activities.[75] In many Ibo towns of the area, the ɔzɔ men of those towns could obtain their own eze or kingly titles.

By the exploratory period the two Nri kingdoms at Agu-ukwu and Oreri centered their activities in the uplands drained by the Anambra, Mamu, and Idemili rivers as indicated in Figure 5. Both had instituted paths of travel which their king candidates would follow in their rituals of accession to the throne. The Agu-ukwu king would pass through Enugu, Abagana, Ukpo, Awkuzu, Nteje, and Umuleri on his way to the primordial origin spot at Aguleri on the Anambra, where he would obtain a lump of clay from the river. The Oreri king passed through Adazi, Nnokwua, Nnobi, Abaja, Ojoto, Oba, Obosi, and Onitsha, culminating the ritual passage with a sacrifice to the Niger.[76] But if these communities and others shown in Figure 5 recognized the spiritual supremacy of the Nri kings, none of them appears to have accepted any direct organizational control by either Nri center.

Complete political decentralization, associated with widespread cultural domination by the Nri communities, poses complex problems which will be further discussed in later chapters. At this point a brief summary of the salient facts of Nri's importance will indicate possible historical trends. First, the evidence suggests that Nri was founded at a period well prior to the expansion of Benin power west of the Niger; at one time Nri priests exercised important influence in the upland areas west of the river, their activities apparently crossing the east–west axis of the uplands. Second, however, at least by colonial times the ritual succession circuit of Nri kings extended only to the east bank of the Niger-Anambra rivers, and they lacked political control even of the communities on these banks. Third, Nri tradition shows a striking lack of the traditions of political development suggested in the legends of Benin and Igala. And finally—to anticipate a further important influence in this region—Nri spheres of activity

75. Jeffreys (n.d.:8:40; 10:10–11, 25).
76. Jeffreys (1935:347–48; n.d.:13:6–16).

appear to have correlated negatively with the expansion of another center of cultural prominence based at the southeastern fringes of Ibo country, the oracle center of Aro-Chukwu. The impact of this center upon the Nri and Onitsha areas will be further discussed in later chapters.

THE DEVELOPMENT OF TRADE ON THE LOWER NIGER: THE IGALA-ABOH AXIS

Given this historical background of the major centers of influence that impinged upon the Onitsha crossroads region, we may now consider the changing patterns of communication in this region. The dominant axis of communication was the vertical one along the Niger, involving expanding trade in slaves between the Igala and Aboh states.

Communication between the riverain Ibo and Igala, based on the ancient exchange of salt and river products for uplands produce, developed into a complex system of trade that distributed a wide variety of goods. The fundamental organizing feature in this system was a boundary market of an almost pure type,[77] located midway between the kingdoms of Igala and Aboh at the confluence of the Niger and Anambra rivers, where the eastern and western uplands meet the river at Onitsha and Asaba. Thus the major marketplace was situated right at the crossroads of the region. Held directly in the middle of the river and therefore dominated by the canoe fleets of Igala and Aboh traders, it was called *ikiri* by the Igala and *onya* by the Aboh, both terms apparently referring to the political boundary character of the site. Onitsha people referred to it as "sandbank" (*úbòm*), because when the river was low it was held on the extensive sand bar which formed an island in the river at this point. When the river was high the market was

77. I.e. the type distinguished by Weber (1958:67–68) as an *umschlageplatz* or intersection point where means of transportation were changed without any attachment of the marketplace to a resident political power.

held in canoes lashed together in midstream.[78] Although the kings of Aboh and Igala apparently controlled the largest number of canoes on the river, this sandbank market was not ordered by any single dominant authority, and it was therefore socially unstable.

The boundary market was not, however, the sole organizing principle of the riverain trade, for during their development both kingdoms set off migratory movements that generated another level of social order along the river. From the south, the Akri people who had been driven from the site of Aboh moved along the river to establish the communities of Akri-uteri, Akri-ugidi and Akri-atani, all of which continued to pay tribute to their former conquerors (see Figure 6). Other riverain communities are said to have been founded by (or at least received increments of) persons who had committed crimes in Aboh or had disputes with Aboh leaders and were forced into exile. According to several accounts, a section of the town of Nsugbe was founded by a man from Aboh who had been exiled for murdering his wife, and the town itself was for a considerable time tributary to the Aboh king.[79] The chief of Oko town at the beginning of the exploratory period was a kinsman of the Aboh king, and the community of Onitsha is said to have sheltered an exiled Aboh "prince" and his followers, who established a major new segment of this town. Such kinship relations remained recognized despite these movements, and developed over time into institutionalized bonds linking Aboh with various related community segments located upriver. The kingdom was able to communicate and trade with these communities without continual direct domination. Aboh women established trading partnerships with women in these riverain towns, and Aboh canoes thereby gained ports of call, backed ultimately by the threat of Aboh power but stabilized by the fundamental values of kinship.[80]

78. See Boston (1960a:53) for an account of the market.

79. For corroboration of this oral tradition, see Baikie (1856:293).

80. Attacks by Aboh against various of her linked communities, for purposes of vengeance, are recounted in a number of historical sources. For example, see Allen and Thomson (1848:1:269).

Fig. 6 Communities involved in the Igala-Aboh trade system

The migrations from Igala areas in the north appear to have been even more extensive than those from Aboh and its vicinity in the south. Some penetration of the lower river by Igala fishermen may have occurred very early, for a few of the riverbank Ibo communities claim that their founders encountered Igala fishermen camping by desired sites, and the Igala themselves say that such lower river towns as Okpaiye, Umuolu, Onya, and Ndoni were originally Igala-speaking.[81] Much later, organized flights took place from Igala country and its peripheries, and one of them is detailed in the oral traditions of the towns of Osomari, Odekpe, and Oko. The legends of these old riverain Ibo towns recount that their founders were originally subjects of the ata who lived in the lower Igala country near the Anam floodplain. Attacked, according to their tradition, by an army of warrior ants sent by the ata to plague them, they fled southward by canoe and founded first the town of Oko on the west bank, then the towns of Odekpe and Osomari on the east bank. Locating themselves in the forested, swampy lowlands protected from direct contact with the Ibo hinterland and also from surprise attacks from the river, these Igala-derived fishermen gained independence from Idah and its Anambra River agents, but came under the influence of Aboh and at some time became tributary to it.

Osomari tradition recounts a subsequent period during which the members of the community were in tributary alliance with Aboh, intermarried with Aboh people and placed their canoe fleet in the service of the Aboh king. Both groups fought against Ibo canoemen of the Anambra flood plain over control of the Niger-Anambra confluence region and its trade. These Anambra River people were called "Anam," and apparently they included a variety of floodplain Ibo and perhaps also the "Ibaji," mixed Ibo and Igala peoples of this area. These appear to have been occa-

81. The Onitsha origin legend, recounted in the following chapter, provides one example of this substratum tradition. See also Boston (1960a:53–54), Forde and Jones (1950:50–51).

sionally tributary to the Igala of both Idah and Ogrugu, and may have mounted canoe forces associated with the legendary Onojo Oboni. Osomari traditions state that after a period of intensive battle against the Anam people, Aboh and Osomari came to dominate the Niger-Anambra confluence region because of the superiority in firearms attained by Aboh.

Osomari is located conveniently near a navigable stream leading out of the Niger and into the Orashi river system which parallels it to the east, draining the Orlu uplands and flowing from Oguta Lake southwards into the Engenni River, which in turn leads to the Kalabari state area centered at Abonnema (see Figures 2 and 6). Osomari traders began concentrating their efforts in this eastern drainage area, developing feeder markets at Okija, Ihiala, and Oguta and thereby becoming the main trading source for the Ibo populations of the Orlu uplands, the peoples whom the riverain Ibo call "Isu-ama." Osomari traders obtained slaves, yams, palm oil and camwood from this area, in exchange for salt and fish from the lower river and ivory and potash which they had brought down the Niger from Igala country. They also began selling their services as mercenaries, using their firearms to help decide intertribal disputes in the Isu-ama area. Moreover, they began developing an Orashi-Engenni trade route to Kalabari and Bonny which bypassed Aboh. Encouraging Bonny traders to utilize this route through Oguta Lake, they began thereby to gain wealth at the expense of Aboh and used their kinship connections with Igala to establish trade relationships far upriver.

A commercial competition thus developed between Osomari and Aboh; it culminated, according to Osomari tradition, in an Aboh armed assault on Osomari town in which the latter successfully defended itself and drove off the Aboh invaders. An oath then sanctioned an agreement between the two groups which gave Aboh trade priority on the Niger but recognized Osomari independence. This treaty was ritualized in the following proverb [82]:

82. I am grateful to Mr. R. R. Olisa of Osomari for this information.

Aboh welu ife;	(Aboh takes a share;
Igri [Osomari] welu ife;	Osomari takes a share;
Aninta gba ubu.	Small countries scramble for whatever remains.)

In this way two separate Ibo trading communities emerged on the lower part of the river, each establishing independent trade linkages to various upriver Igala communities. Some of these Igala communities were, in turn, directly controlled from Idah, but as European exploration of the Niger proceeded, these stations also tended to become more independent of the central authority.

For example, when the Landers made their pioneering journey downriver in 1830, they bypassed Idah out of fear of the king's power and halted instead at a village called Adamugu on the Niger-Anambra floodplain above Anam. Adamugu had been founded by one "Abokka," who, the explorers said, was a half-brother of the ata. He had, the Landers reported, fled Idah after an abortive attempt to usurp the kingship, and had been given land for his followers by a nearby "Ibaji" village.[83] There he was able to act independently of the ata, trading and occasionally waging wars. He ran his canoes from Aboh, where he obtained muskets, soap, cloth, and rum, up to the ikiri market north of Idah where he traded these for ivory, slaves, and livestock. He was credited with founding and controlling such subsidiary riverain trading posts as Okparam Ogbaru and Ute on the left bank north of Asaba, even though both of these communities reportedly spoke the Aboh dialect of Ibo [84] at the time of exploration.

By the 1840s, the family of the Abokko were said to have become dominant personalities at Idah itself. By 1854 they con-

83. Lander and Lander (1841:169–71). This was the holder of the Abokko title (discussed by Boston 1968:109–14), who belonged to a nonroyal clan. The reference to kingship may allude to his alliance with one of the royal lineages.

84. Lander and Lander (1841:169–72; Laird and Oldfield (1837:1:114, 124); Crowther (1855:178); Baikie (1856:290–94). It is difficult to estimate how accurate these reports were, but this clan probably at least had kinship ties with descent groups in these places.

trolled two markets north of Idah and were bypassing Idah completely in the upriver trade. Near Adamugu other Igala chiefs were busy setting up trading posts in competition with them.[85]

This is a rather complicated picture, for most of these riverain trading posts were multilingual, composed of subgroups possessing diverse origins and allegiances, and their external alliances were divergent, overlapping, and shifting. Villages grew through admixtures of Igala, Aboh, upland Ibo, and also Edo peoples, and from these mixtures developed the complex, web-like social order which existed along the river. One very general basis for this order was the ideological conviction held in common by the rulers of both Igala and Aboh that they shared ultimate descent from the Ado/Idu peoples through Benin. The more crucial bases of social relationships had a markedly noncollective bias, perceived by the explorer-missionary Samuel Crowther. In describing the activities of a river trader called Ewonruzo at Onitsha, Crowther said,

> Ewonruzo is an inhabitant of a village between Idda [Idah] and Onitsha, known by the name of Onugba, which signifies in the Ibo language, a mixture, which in all probability may mean a mixture of Ibo and Igara inhabitants. Ewonruzo is half Ibo and half Igara—his mother being an Ibo, and his father an Igara. A person, under his circumstances, has the privileges of both nations. Ibo canoes are not allowed to go beyond Idda market, nor are Igara canoes allowed to go below Abo; but a person under Ewonruzo's circumstances has the privileges of going beyond both points.[86]

Such relationships comprised models for relations between mixed groups as well. Migrations, mixtures, and intermarriage among these riverain populations produced multiple crosscutting alliances that clearly limited the capacity for centralization of

85. Allen and Thomson (1848:1:273–74); Crowther (1855:28, 34–35); Baikie (1856: 268–83).

86. Crowther and Taylor (1859:385). This person apparently played a part in one of Onitsha's kingship succession disputes. See Chapter 13.

power by either Igala or Aboh and transformed the riverain confrontation of the two major political groups into a social interpenetration. Thus there developed along the lower Niger those flexible, sometimes turbulent social patterns which the Lander brothers described during their historic voyage downriver and to whose underlying order they owed their lives.

A typical pattern of trade during the early nineteenth century might be described as follows. At Aboh a chief would receive muskets, gunpowder, cotton cloth, pottery, rum, cowries, looking glasses, salt, and new foodstuffs such as cassava from traders who had come from the coastal town of Brass. He would run these products upriver, stopping at his kin-linked community of Oko and at the sandbank market by the Anambra River confluence, or else continuing via Igbokenyi where he had kinsmen partners and going on to do his major trading at Idah. There he would obtain ivory, slaves, and livestock and would return downstream, stopping at Akri-atani where there was a demand for ivory, exchanging the ivory for yams and other agricultural produce. After a day's rest at Aboh, he would take what remained from trading there on downriver to the onya or terminal Aboh market at the outlet to the Forcados or Benin branch of the Niger.[87] An Osomari trader might begin by receiving similar European products from a Kalabari or Bonny trader at Oguta Lake. He would run these up to the sandbank market or else to Onitsha, where he would find a sizable community of his kinsmen. He would trade there for upland Ibo woven cloth and palm oil, and then continue north to the trading post of Okparam Ogbaru and thence to Idah. On the return trip he would bring potash and ivory for the Isu-ama Ibo peoples east of Oguta Lake, and ivory, slaves, and palm oil for the delta state traders at the lake.

These trading expeditions involved considerable unpredictability at all times, for traders on all sides were armed and the ethical bases of economic relations were fluid. Instability was apparently

87. Allen and Thomson (1848:1:236–37).

greatest at the crossroads leading to the uplands behind Onitsha and Asaba, for neither of these communities ever came under the continuous control of Aboh or Igala, and they therefore remained important independents whose activities further complicated the trading pattern.

The Uplands Trade: Asaba

The instability of social order at the Asaba and Onitsha crossroads was illustrated in the earliest historical account, produced by the Lander brothers on their downriver voyage. When these defenseless explorers were at Adamugu, the Igala chief Abokko apparently contrived to send them (along with an agent of a Bonny chief, who happened to be trading for slaves at Adamugu at the time) through the Osomari route to the Orashi River and thence south to Bonny in order to avoid the middleman's tribute which would have been demanded by the king of Aboh.[88] When the voyagers reached the sandbank market escorted by Adamugu people, they were confronted by a flotilla of about fifty armed Ibo canoes, were summarily looted, and nearly killed; after being rescued by the occupants of a canoe from Kalabari, they followed their assailants to the uplands marketplace on the Asaba riverbank. There a group of traders coming from Bonny, Kalabari, and even from the Igbira Funda kingdom north of the Niger-Benue confluence, supported by some twenty canoe-groups of Adamugu traders, discussed the theft and forcibly restored some of the Landers' property to them. When the Aboh-affiliated canoe pirates attempted to attack and recapture this booty, they were forestalled by the natives of Asaba who sallied forth armed with guns.[89] Other historical accounts indicate that such armed hostile interaction was not infrequent at these crossroads markets.[90]

The scanty oral tradition evidence available suggests that the

88. Lander and Lander (1841:172).
89. Lander and Lander (1841:182–84; 191–94).
90. Laird and Oldfield (1837:1:394–96); Allen and Thomson (1848:1:268–69); Crowther (1855:178).

Asaba community underwent a complex sequence of developments in its relations with outsiders. Igala traditions claim that Asaba was conquered by the legendary Ogrugu chieftain Onojo Oboni during one of his forays down the Anambra River.[91] Asaba tradition derives the origin of the community itself from an Anambra drainage immigrant (from the Nri-linked community of Nteje) who settled among a group of autochthones, began hunting elephants and trading ivory with the people of Aboh, and became so wealthy through this trade that he overshadowed the indigenous people and became their king. He was followed by ten successors who, it is said, were separately crowned by a representative of the king of Nri.[92] These traditions suggest an early dominance of the area by peoples of the Anambra River area, from Nri and possibly from Igala, and an important trade interdependence with Aboh. It is also said that at some time after the death of the immigrant king, his descendants became subject to the ɔba of Idu, the king of Benin, who began sending his agents on annual journeys to fetch water from the Niger there.

By the beginning of the exploratory period, Asaba was clearly independent of both Aboh and Igala, although some contiguous communities said to "belong to" Asaba were also said to have been formerly tributary to the ata.[93] This independence was maintained partly by the encouragement of trade with such diverse people as the Osomari, the Anambra River Ibo, and independent Igala subgroups, and partly by the maintenance of the subordinate relationship to Benin. At the beginning of the exploratory period, Bini traders were coming overland to Asaba market to exchange their upland products for lowland produce from Anam and for Igala ivory and slaves.[94] Although Asaba people spoke an Ibo dialect similar to that of the Aboh, they had reportedly been at war with the latter since the Aboh king had conducted a punitive

91. Boston (1960a:54).
92. Spencer (1901).
93. Crowther (1855:178).
94. Allen and Thomson (1848:1:270–71); Baikie (1856:293).

raid, taking two hundred heads in revenge for the murder of one of his sons at Asaba market.[95] Asaba was able at this time to prevent Aboh people from trading at its market but could not block their activities on the river itself because the Asaba community lacked canoes.[96]

The evidence for Asaba, then, suggests two major periods of cultural and political influence. It underwent an early period of Anambra and Nri dominance, then later it became tributary to Benin and maintained unstable relations with the expanding riverain powers. Such unstable riverain relations also obtained in the uplands community of Onitsha across the river.

95. Laird and Oldfield (1837:2:139).
96. Crowther (1855:178).

3 ONITSHA COMMUNITY: A HISTORICAL OUTLINE

There are two rather different and, to some extent, incompatible perspectives from which the Onitsha people view their community and its history, and the outside observer must take both perspectives into account because they underpin a rather complex form of constitutive symbolism. First, the community is seen as forming a coherent whole by virtue of its derivation from the unifying activities of a glorious founder-king, Chima. When they take this viewpoint, the people minimize the diversity of their origins. However, while the framework of their oral tradition is therefore based on kingly genealogies, Onitsha people also recognize the existence of nine distinct kings at any given time—nine kings representing nine descent groups. When the people take this point of view, they stress the diversity of their origins, and implicitly adopt the perspective of a segmentary system. Oral traditions maintained within the descent group framework indicate that Onitsha was fundamentally heterogeneous in its origins, including elements of riverain Ibo, Igala speakers, Awka-Orlu uplands Ibo, western Ibo, and possibly others. Its cultural heritage contains elements from Benin, Igala, Nri, and the lower river. The synthesis of these elements into a coherent tradition can only be understood, however, by reference to the unifying effects of kingship.

The Onitsha Ibo lack an independent myth of primordial origins. In their cosmogony, they simply relate themselves to the cultural focus of Nri where, it is said, the Onitsha dead go on their way to the underworld. Onitsha origin traditions are clearly more ideological than religious, for they relate to various geographically known communities and migrations rather than to ultimate conditions of being. One of the two primary concepts which Onitsha people employ to refer to the origins of their community is the notion of *Ébo Ìtenáni*. The term ebo refers to an ancient, venerated patrilineal descent group which has long possessed a residentially coherent social organization, and it will be glossed here as "clan" in this special sense.[1] All contemporary Onitsha elders agree that Onitsha has always been a unity of Nine Clans (itenani means nine), but no two persons agree precisely on the names of all nine. To illustrate the range of variation, three lists derived from different informants are shown in Figure 7.

Fig. 7 Informant lists of the Nine Clans

Source A	*Source B*	*Source C*
1. Ɔreze	1. Okebʊnabo	1. Isiokwe
2. Eke-na-Ubene	2. Eke-na-Ubene	2. Umʊ-Dei
3. Ugwu-na-Ɔbamkpa	3. Ɔbamkpa	3. Asele
4. Ɔbiɔ	4. Ɔdɔje	4. Isele
5. Ulutu	5. Umʊ-Arɔlɩ	5. Isuma Ogidi
6. Isele-Awada	6. Umʊ-Ikem	6. Obikporo
7. Ubulu	7. Ɔlɔsɩ	7. Iyawʊ
8. Achala-igwe-ogidi	8. Awada	8. Umʊ-Arɔlɩ
9. Agba-na-Ute	9. Odogwu	9. Ọdogwu

The scholar collecting information of this kind is beset, initially, by considerable confusion, a condition exacerbated in this case by the recent changes in Onitsha society that increased the diversity of informants' access to traditional knowledge. But when the relationship of the narrator to the various social units listed was known, and the context of narration related to the second major concept of Onitsha origins (discussed below), it became clear that some of the terms on one list were subcategories of those on other lists, while other terms referred to more recently established, sometimes composite units that were (by Onitsha categories) villages

1. This usage roughly parallels Murdock's (1949:68) definition of "clan" as a "compromise descent group," but here merely indicates the combination of residential community and descent implicit in the meaning of the term. It does not imply the concepts that Murdock uses.

(*ógbè*) rather than clans (ebo). This distinction will be further discussed in later chapters.

The second major concept of origin is the "Children of King Chima" (*Úmù-Ézè-Chȋma*) legend. According to this tradition, Onitsha people lived originally in a community called "Ado and Idu," Idu referring to Benin City and Ado referring (as far as the writer could determine) to the general country of the Edo-speaking peoples bordering Western Ibo country. Ado and Idu, located, according to one scholar, somewhere near Igbodo on the uplands west of Asaba,[2] was ruled by King Chima but was tributary to the ɔba of Benin. The latter's queen mother, said to be named *Ásȋjie,* once invaded the farmlands of this community to gather firewood and was assaulted by its residents. When she reported this assault to the ɔba, he sent his war leader *Ògbúnwàla*[3] with an army to retaliate. King Chima was defeated by Benin in battle and his people were scattered. Some fled to *Ɔ́bìɔ̀,* while others went to Onitsha-ugbo (see Figure 3). From Onitsha-ugbo, two groups continued the flight, some to the various towns of *Ísèlè* and others northeast to Ukunzu. Enroute to Ukunzu, it is said, a pregnant woman of the group had to stop to give birth, and she and her offspring remained to found the town of Onitsha-ukwu ("Great Onitsha"). From these scattered points, Chima rallied his people, and they moved on eastward. According to some informants, a dispute that had developed in Onitsha-olona brought on this second migration; it began from the northeastern area around Ezi, Onitsha-olona, and Onitsha-ukwu, and drew migrants from Ɔbiɔ, the *Ùbulu* towns, Ogwashi-ukwu, *Ɔ̀bámkpa,* and other towns. They moved eastward to the Niger at Illah, where they made a compact with a group of fishermen who ferried them downstream by canoes to the site of what is now Onitsha.

At this point Onitsha tradition contains some ambiguities.

2. Thomas (1914:8–9); see Figure 3.
3. Recorded as "Gbunmara" by Leonard (1906:35).

Whether King Chima himself ever reached this site, called "Riverain Onitsha" (*Ɔnιcha-mili*) by the Western Ibo, is an issue still debated by Onitsha indigenes. They believe he was buried not in Onitsha but at Ɔbiɔ in the west. The people of Agbor on the western fringes of western Ibo country, on the other hand, claim that their founder was one "Chima," who first migrated from Benin, crossed the Niger to Onitsha, then later returned west to settle Agbor.[4] Onitsha tradition provides another view of the problem, for it is said that before the travelers embarked on the river near Illah, a dispute broke out concerning who would be king in the new community they were about to settle. According to this legend, the names of the disputants were *Ɔ̀rézè* (a son of King Chima), *Úkpali Ézěchi* (or "Agbor Chima"), *Ékeñsu* (also called "Aboh Chima"), *Ɔ́bìɔ̀*, *Ɔ̀bámkpa,* and *Íselè* (and others variably mentioned). Each of these immigrants had brought one of the essential symbols of Onitsha kingship, a pair of the short cylindrical log drums called *ùfie* which the king traditionally used daily to beat out in rhythm the names of ancestral kings as he ritually ushered in the dawn. It was suggested that all contestants destroy their ufie drums. After crossing the river the person who first cut down a tree, then fashioned and beat new ufie drums would be accepted by all as king. Two leaders, Ukpali Ezechi and Ekensu, refused to accept this suggestion and departed, the former returning westward to Agbor and the latter taking most of his followers southward where he eventually founded Aboh. The others agreed to the terms, and all destroyed their drums except Ɔreze Chima, who deceitfully lashed his own ufie beneath the canoe which ferried his group to the site of Onitsha. When they all arrived at the eastern shore and began fashioning new drums, Ɔreze renovated his old drums, beat them, and proclaimed his right to supremacy. The other settlers refused to acknowledge his supremacy and remained with their followers nearby, holding and using their own ufie drums, but by his deceit

4. Forde and Jones (1950:47).

Ɔreze had attained a kind of primacy among them; they agreed to muffle their own drums so the sounds would not carry throughout the community.

No doubt this origin legend is largely a rationalization of relationships established subsequent to any crossings of the Niger that may have been made; indeed, the plot of this tale is strongly reminiscent of certain Ibo animal fables and may well have been drawn from that source. Viewed solely in terms of assumptions underlying the story's moralizing intent, it presumes initial heterogeneity and divisiveness among diverse and relatively autonomous segments occupying a confined area, and points to an existence at the outset of a multiple eze title system in the community.

The site of this original settlement at Onitsha was called *Ȍkpóko,* a low area near the river beside a swampy inlet called *Ǹdé-n̄de* (see Figure 12). The general area was already occupied, according to Onitsha tradition. First, the fishermen who had ferried the travelers downriver had their camps along the riverbank immediately to the north. In legends they are called *Ȕlútu,* and some narrators identify them as Akpɔta or Igala speakers, while others identify them as Ado people from west of the Niger to the north. They eventually became a part of the new community and acted as priests of the land.

Second, it is said that when the migrants landed at Okpoko, smoke could be seen in the hills to the east rising from the fires of the *Ȍze ìgbo* people who lived there. In addition to these groups, the Onitsha immigrants were joined by a group of downriver Ibo people called *Égbemà,* who came from the Ahoada area of the delta near what is now Aboh (see Figure 6). While most of the immigrants remained at Okpoko, the Egbema along with some of the remnant groups mentioned in the river-crossing legend moved further inland toward the hills occupied by the Oze Ibo group. Out of this putative initial heterogeneity a common community was begun.

Interpretation of this origin tradition is difficult. Although Onitsha people speak of the migration as unitary, in some narrative contexts they clearly believe that various "original" units arrived in the community at different times. If one followed the traditional Durkheimean view of oral history as reflecting only contemporary social conditions, one might question whether any massive movements took place at all, and argue instead that the traditions reflect only recently important social relationships obtaining across the river; certainly those groups with traditions of migration from given areas have maintained social ties with people in those areas in recent times.

Such an extreme view is unwarranted, for some extensive population movements did take place. First, the area of legendary origin was clearly subjected to intrusions and disruptions at some prehistoric time; Ukunzu and some other towns in the immediate area were actually islands of Yoruba-speaking peoples within Ibo country, peoples who claimed primordial connections with the travels of the Benin king and with Igala.[5] Second, many towns in what is now the Asaba division of Benin province have variant accounts of this legend; these include nine that have in modern times joined together to form an Ʊmʊ-Eze-Chima Clan Union.[6] These same towns are the ones whose names figure prominently in the Onitsha variant of the legend. Third, the Ibo peoples of both Obosi and Oze towns in the immediate hinterland of Onitsha, as well as the people of Asaba across the river, have traditions recounting a time when the Oze Ibo group occupied the historical site of Onitsha, and tracing the arrival of the people of Chima to a later period.

Finally, there is considerable correspondence between the Ʊmʊ-Eze-Chima origin tale and the Benin legends of their war with Igala. The Onitsha name of the legendary Benin "Queen mother," Asijie, appears to be a rendering of the name of ɔba Esigie, whose reign around the beginning of the sixteenth century was marked by

5. Thomas (1914:2).

6. The nine towns are Ɔbiɔ, Onitsha-Ugbo, Onitsha-ukwu, Onitsha-olona, Ezi, Isele-ukwu, Isele-Asagba, Isele-mkpitime, and Ɔbamkpa, all shown on Figure 3.

a war with Igala that extended into western Ibo country and disrupted many communities there. Moreover, the Onitsha name for the Benin warrior, Ogbunwala, corresponds closely with that of the Benin army's slave commander during the reign of Esigie.[7]

For all these reasons, it is sensible to infer substantial migrations, and even to assign tentative dates to them. The settlement at Onitsha of King Chima or some of his people may be placed well after the beginning of the sixteenth century, perhaps around the beginning of the seventeenth.[8] These traditions also provide a base line from which several stages of oral history may be distinguished. The first stage refers to a riverain substratum of the Ulutu and/or Ado peoples coming from upriver and occupying the river banks, perhaps in a manner similar to that of the Akri population originally located at Aboh. Inland lived the Ibo community of Oze people. This will hereafter be called the substratum stage.

The second stage of oral history may be called the Onitsha-formative stage. This begins with the Umu-Eze-Chima migration that leads to the founding of Onitsha. Onitsha oral traditions recounting the ufie drum legend are followed by a series of tales dealing with problems of defining the scope of the community, of regulating relations with outsiders, and of the development of kingship. A list of "kings" (each associated with a village community of followers) can be elicited for this period from all knowledgeable elders, but their order and the activities associated with them are vague and to some extent inconsistent. Some examples of this variability in narrative are provided below, with putative kings assigned numbers in order.[9]

These three recorded accounts, probably independent of one

7. Egharevba (1960:29–30); R. E. Bradbury, personal communication.

8. A number of cultural similarities between Onitsha and the core area of western Ibo to which the legends refer attests to the closeness of the two peoples, and some of the Onitsha groups named after these western Ibo towns are known to have sent representatives to visit them periodically for ritual purposes.

9. The 1906 account is based on the research of Leonard (1906:36). The 1900 and 1930 accounts are based on old written documents held by recent informants, whose kinsmen were alleged to have compiled them at the times indicated.

another, illustrate nicely the kinds of variations in ordering given by recent informants, and they also show the recurrence in all accounts of some major culture heroes. Except for the ambiguous positions of the ancestral figures Ɔreze, *D́ei,* and *Chîmezíe,* who are considered kings in some accounts but not in others, there is both in old records and in the recent narratives fairly consistent agreement on the names of early kings but not on their ordering. Similarly, there is consensus about major events during the general period covered by all the names listed, but these events are

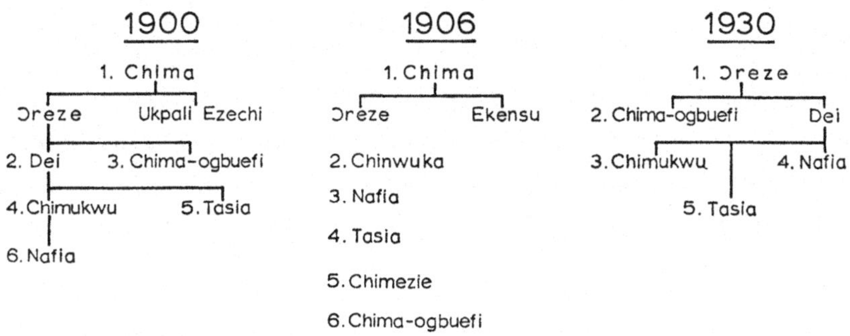

Fig. 8 Conflicting lists of early kings

associated sometimes with one of the kings and sometimes with another.

First, it was generally agreed by recent informants that the most ancient of these kings (eze) were patrilineal "patriarchs" (*d̀iɔk-pala*) selected primarily by ascriptive criteria. Moreover, there was an incessant competition between them suggesting a lack of societal unity. For example, during this period *Ézè Àwuma,* the patriarch of the Isele community living at Okpoko, is said to have proclaimed himself the supreme eze and to have sat upon the royal throne (*ùkpo-ézè*) of King Chima. His opponents hired a magician to place a medicine in the throne, which caused it to heat when Awuma sat there. Overwhelmed by his profuse perspiration while occupying this "hot seat" before his subjects, King Awuma sought relief by sitting on the ground among the commoners. Once he had done this, he was reminded that it was an abomination for the king to sit on bare ground. Therefore he was deposed. In chagrin he gathered his family and went to his home at the lowland area near Nde-nde, where he spoke some ritual imprecations against Onitsha people. Pouring a calabash of water on the heads of himself and his family, he was engulfed, with the core of his supporters, by a flood of water that formed the *Ótumɔyè* Pond which fills this area today.

Another example of disunity is the legend of *Íyàselé Ǹsu* of Ekensu community, who is said to have disregarded the rightful king and to have conspired with peoples of neighboring interior towns (Obosi, Ogidi, Nkpor) to kidnap Onitsha persons and sell them as slaves. Grown wealthy from slave dealing, the iyasele then proclaimed himself king. The Onitsha people organized a secret meeting and prepared a wooden helmet large enough to cover his entire head. They then announced their willingness to accept his leadership and reported their readiness to provide him, in public ceremony, with a wooden headdress appropriate to his dignity. To this public meeting they carried stones concealed in their loincloths. When the great helmet had been pressed down over the pretender's head, they stoned him to death, cast his body into a pit, and poured in boiling water to insure that he would not revive. Much of the land controlled by his community was then divided among some of the Onitsha chiefs.

These and other legends about this period suggest lack of consensus about the definition of "royalty" and even about the boundaries of the community itself. Indeed, legends from contiguous Ibo communities referring to this time describe the Onitsha people as made up of two communities, "Onitsha" and "Egbema," the latter being the group with which Iyasele Nsu was affiliated.[10] However, the stories also imply an internal process whereby defeated aspi-

10. For example, see Iweka-nuno (1924:E79). Stoning was apparently the traditional Onitsha method of deposing a king, however.

rants and their supporters became defined as "nonroyal," for after the defeats of Awuma and Iyasele Nsu in the two incidents cited, their relatives in the Isele and Ekensu clan communities are said to have lost their statuses as full "Children of King Chima." A second series of events recounted for this same era suggests processes of incipient unification. It is said that the people of Aboh began conducting slave raids along the river, and the lowland Onitsha villages found themselves in exposed positions near the river. Therefore, when the Onitsha clan named *Ùte* came into a land dispute with the hill-dwelling Oze Ibo community, some of the Onitsha and Egbema groups joined together and fought the Oze War (*ágha Òze*). They drove the Oze people across the ravine of Nkisi stream, which became the northern boundary of a more united "Onitsha Eze Chima" community centered in the hills above the river.

It is also said that during this early period the role of the king acquired new characteristics. The eze established a new ritual pattern at his meeting-chamber (*òbí*) that involved the distribution of kola nuts by his personal servants; visitors were expected to accept the nuts, thus defining themselves as beneath the eze in status. Salutation patterns were established in which visitors would kneel before the king and place their heads in the dust. The king thereby became *òbí*, possessor of a "court," as well as eze, possessor of ufie drums. Also during this period a group of titled chiefs called *ńdîchie*, their title names modeled to some extent on the eghaevo titles of Benin, came to be selected by the king and emerged as a prominent elite in the community.

Finally, an effort was made to expand the range of Onitsha influence during this early period. After the first Onitsha war with Obosi, referred to as "machete war" (*ágha m̀pama*) because guns were unknown at the time, an agent of Eze Chima was established in Obosi town to collect tribute there. The Obosi people, however, refused to regard themselves as subjects of Onitsha and successfully rebelled. This Onitsha legend is corroborated in the written account of an Obosi historian of the 1920s, who asserted that in ancient times at Obosi a man named "Chima" came from Onitsha and proclaimed himself eze of Obosi, that Obosi people "redeemed" the title of eze from him, and that they fought the "Onitsha and Egbema people" and drove them away in a series of machete wars.[11] This stage of consolidation will hereafter be called the Onitsha-Egbema stage, or the stage of "early kings," both terms referring to the process of developing unification.

After these early and relatively vague phases of Onitsha tradition, a core genealogy develops on which there is substantial contemporary consensus. It is said that during the time of King Chima the Cow-killer (*chȋma-ògbúefi*) the Onitsha people maintained a market at the beach of the Niger, called the "*Nkwɔ*-day Waterside" (*ótu ńkwɔ*, nkwɔ being the fourth day of the Ibo week). For a time the king was forced to transfer the market to more protected ground near the Anambra River when Aboh slave traders began firing their newly acquired cannons at the market traders. Since Onitsha people lacked canoes, they hired expert canoemen from the Anambra drainage to fight the people of Aboh.

After the death of King Chima the Cow-killer, his senior sons are said to have thought themselves "too old" to assume the duties of kingship,[12] so they called upon their most junior brother, *Àrɔ́lɩ*, who "had been sent to Idah" to live with his Igala mother because of his childhood ailments. Arɔlɩ returned in triumph from Igala, and was given a pot with feathers attached, which had been prepared by a magician. He was directed to walk with this pot on his head about the streets of the community so that the ancestral kings might cause a feather to drop where his new palace should be located. This was done, and Arɔlɩ settled in the center of the town amidst the Onitsha hills to found what was to become the largest descent group of Onitsha.

It is said, too, that during the time of Arɔlɩ the great Igala war-

11. Iweka-nuno (1924:E52, E79).

12. According to other accounts, they were eliminated from contention by a diviner. These two sons were *Ébo and Chȋmaʊkwa,* the founders of the social unit named *Ísiòkwe.*

rior Onojo (or Onoja) Oboni came from Ogrugu, raided the river towns for slaves, and took Arɔlɩ's daughter *Ǘssè* in marriage. This Igala influence continued to be important among the descendants and successors of Arɔlɩ, whose genealogical relations are shown in Figure 9.[13]

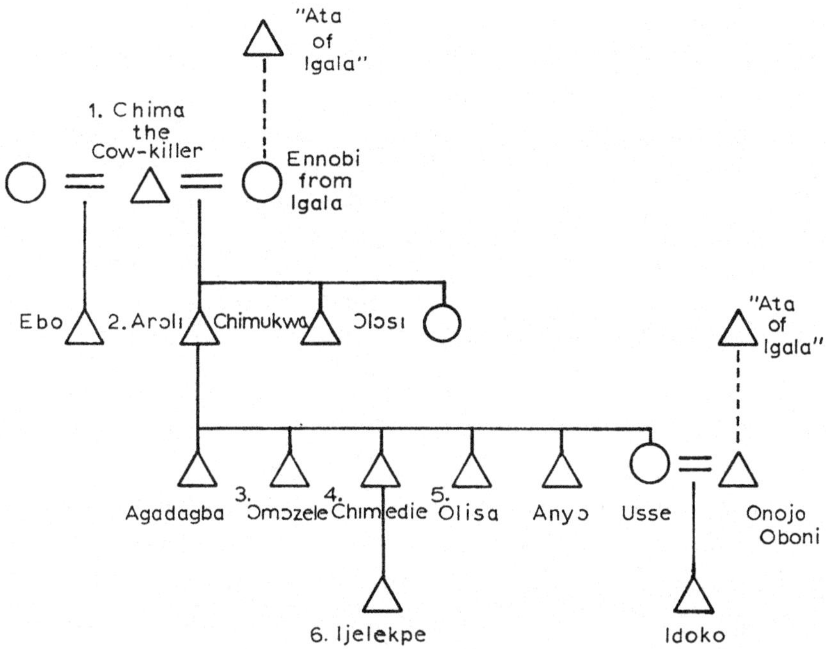

Fig. 9 Igala influence during the reigns of six kings

After the death of Arɔlɩ, his son *Ɔ́mɔzèlé* succeeded him. During his reign, Onojo Oboni and Usse (the daughter of Arɔlɩ) had a son, *Ìdóko,* who first lived with his father in Ogrugu. When Onojo Oboni was near death, he instructed his son to return with Usse to Onitsha, because he feared that his other sons would conspire against their half-brother born by a foreign woman, and that they

13. Chapter 13 gives a much more detailed genealogy and analysis of the oral traditions outlined here.

might sell him into slavery. Idoko therefore returned with his followers to Onitsha.

During King Ɔmɔzele's reign, according to this narrative, Idoko criticized the king's practice of wearing only a loin cloth during his annual ritual emergence from seclusion (*ɔ̀fálà*) and boasted about the fine regalia worn by the Igala king. Ɔmɔzele sent Idoko to Igala to bring some new apparel so that his ɔfala festival would be more splendid. Idoko departed by canoe, but as ɔfala time drew near he had not returned. A diviner recommended that a medicine be made and inserted into the royal ufie drum, so that a message could be conveyed through the drum to call Idoko back from Igala. This was done, and the drum beat out this message:

Ìdóko; Ìdóko; Ìdóko jèlu ólu;	("Idoko has gone to the riverain country")
Ìdóko; Ìdóko; Ìdóko ánatarɔ̀.	("Idoko has not returned.")

Hearing the message at Igala, Idoko returned bringing for Ɔmɔzele a garment made of brown Igala cloth with black spots representing the royal leopard, brass anklets, and, according to some accounts, a brass royal sword (*àbani*). These regalia, worn and carried at Ɔmɔzele's emergence festival, have since been the traditional royal attire for the occasion, when the royal ufie drums repeat the ritual message to Idoko prior to the king's public appearance. Idoko and his people settled on the northern side of Onitsha community some distance from the king's palace.

Idoko and his followers also brought a new religious organization into Onitsha, the *ɔ̀rá-òkwute,* a secret inner council of the incarnate dead, along with their fearful masked incarnation of the elderly dead, the *égwugwu* or "tall ghost." [14] It is said that at first the king made use of these innovations to terrify the Onitsha peo-

14. The meaning of these terms is uncertain. The term okwute in Igala refers to staffs kept by the nine Igala Mela or patriarchs, but in Onitsha these staffs were not part of the organization's paraphernalia so far as I could determine. The "tall ghost" translation of egwugwu is based on one of its Ibo alternate terms, *ḿmʊɔ ógonogo.* This masquerade is also called "riverain ghost" (*ḿmʊɔ ólu*), referring to its derivation.

ple when he announced important decisions, thereby bending them to his will. However, the children of Idoko jealously guarded this organization as part of their Igala heritage, and when they brought it out into the community they would call out, "*Igbo* run away!" (*Ìgbo ḿabò!*) [15] When the influence of the Idoko elder dead began to compete with that of the king, King Ɔmɔzele found it necessary to uproot these immigrants from their separate locations on the north side of the town. He placed them instead in an area amid other Onitsha villages where they could be observed and controlled; the other villages then began to imitate Idoko, developing their own elder dead organizations, and the Igala settlers lost part of their distinctiveness and their independent social sanctions.

These tales associated with the coming of King Arɔlɩ to Onitsha can be correlated with similar stories of nearby communities (cf. Asaba, for example) that refer to the legendary figure Onojo Oboni and suggest an expansion of slave raiding by Igala and Anam peoples down the Anambra River drainage, probably in response to a challenge by Aboh. Onitsha oral tradition suggests that the dominant influence there was established by the Igala-derived groups. Indeed, the story of Arɔlɩ's arrival from Igala implies a direct imposition of an Igala agent as ruler of the Onitsha community, while that of Ɔmɔzele's emergence festival asserts a continuing dependence on Igala for ritual reaffirmation of the king. The claim of incarnate dead superiority by the descendants of Idoko has continued into recent times, and the legend about their elder dead organization's competition with the king indicates that opposition between the two may have had considerable antiquity and may have been an important factor in internal politics.

No external criteria make it possible to fix a time for the dura-

15. Such usages reflect the ambiguous position of the Onitsha people in the igbo-na-olu dichotomy analyzed above. Onitsha people do not class themselves collectively as igbo, but set themeslves apart from the "unwashed" ones as "children of the great god" (ʊmʊ-chukwu). They do not, however, class themselves as riverain (olu) people either; they say they cannot swim, and they accept this usage of the term igbo by the children of Idoko. For historical clues on this problem, see Crowther (1855:179), and Baikie (1856:297–300).

tion or antiquity of this sequence, hereafter called the Igala-Anambra stage. The following stage of tradition, however, emerges into early exploratory times, so that consideration of this next stage will provide a basis for estimating a rough time scale for the genealogy as a whole.

THE EARLY EXPLORATORY PERIOD

After the death of King Ɔmɔzele the genealogy of Onitsha kings as recounted by contemporary informants runs consistently and with little ambiguity into colonial times. Ɔmɔzele was succeeded by his brother *Chímedie,* who took many wives and fathered a large number of male children, thereby founding the largest single segment of the "Children of King Arɔlɩ." During the time of Ɔmɔzele and Chimedie, the increasing prominence of a segment of Onitsha community with strong affiliations to Aboh—the Children of *Dei* village complex—is suggested by tales of the aspirations of its members to kingship, despite their lack of a position as one of the primordial Nine Clans.

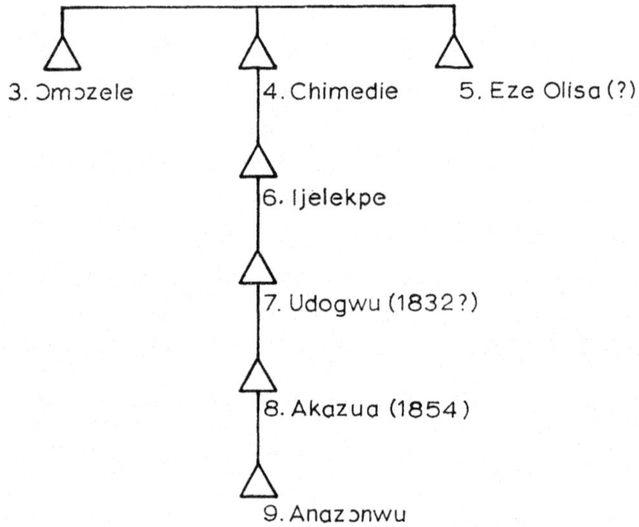

Fig. 10 Kingship succession after King Ɔmɔzele

After the death of Chimedie, his brother *Òlisa* aspired to the throne. Although his name is usually included in the lists of kings, it is universally agreed that he was an unpopular king who did not reign long. Some informants even say that he died while undertaking the rituals of succession.

After Olisa's death, it is said, *Ìjelekpe* the son of Chimedie then aspired to succeed, but his mother objected to his becoming king on the grounds that kings seemed to die prematurely. She and others maintained that the lack of a proper ɔfɔ staff of authority was causing the kings to die untimely deaths. Her brother, a member of Ɔbamkpa community in Onitsha, volunteered to return to the original homeland of Onitsha across the Niger in order to obtain a stronger ɔfɔ. He went to Ɔbamkpa and returned bringing an ɔfɔ staff of iron which had been ritually dedicated by agents of the ɔba of Benin. He then transferred this staff to Ijelekpe, and in return the Ɔbamkpa segment of Onitsha gained the right of reclaiming it during interregnum and conferring it upon succeeding kings.

This ɔfɔ staff may symbolize the occasion on which the Onitsha people first obtained firearms, for it takes the form of a tapering iron cylinder reminiscent of a cannon.[16] Moreover, according to oral tradition, during the time of Ijelekpe, guns were employed in expanding Onitsha's influence among its neighbors. Obosi, Ogidi, and some other communities of the hinterlands to the east became tributary to the king of Onitsha.

The rise of Onitsha dominance over nearby Ibo towns is reflected and corroborated in Obosi oral traditions. The Obosi historian Iweka-nuno relates that

> the people of Onitsha, on their returning for the second time, brought with them guns, which were borrowed for the first time by the men of Obosi, which they used in fighting the people of Umu-oji after which they repeatedly borrowed same for hunting purposes. And according to custom the borrower of a gun was to give a portion of the meat of any animal killed to the owner of

16. I am indebted to R. Thompson, an undergraduate in history at Yale in 1967, for this suggestion. The staff also links the king to blacksmithing.

> the gun. But the Onitshas, as a rule, when a tiger [sic] was killed will not accept the share due to one according to their custom, unless it first be made to pass in the care of their king, which had become the usual practice.[17]

The practice of sending to the recognized head of a domain all leopards killed by hunters of that domain is a widespread mode of symbolizing recognition of superordinate status in the general Kwa-speaking region. In Onitsha the pattern was expanded to include the representation of adjacent communities like Ogidi and Nsugbe at the Onitsha king's annual emergence festival, where dancers and titled men from these nearby towns saluted the king on his second day of ritual emergence into the public arena.

During the reign of Ijelekpe the Obosi people also rebelled, led by their own eze namd *Akwagu,* who refused to continue to maintain the leopard tribute to Onitsha. There followed the second Onitsha-Obosi war, this time a "firearms war" (*ágha égbè*) that continued sporadically for a considerable duration with Onitsha generally dominant. Its dominance ended, however, with a defeat in battle that is recounted by the descendants of both communities. Onitsha people do not detail the battle but say that one of their senior chiefs, a "daughter's child" (*ńwadiàni*) to Obosi, betrayed Onitsha to his mother's community. The Obosi story is more revealing, again as related by Iweka-nuno. The Obosi people offered to resolve their long-standing rebellion against Onitsha dominance, suggesting

> that the men of both towns should meet on the valley between the two towns to settle their disputes and to restore peace, to which the men of Onitsha consented. Obosi then cleared the bush at a certain spot in the valley, and collected as much palm wine as they could, and placed it in readiness at the fixed day. But they also secretly placed their prepared warriors in ambush near the spot, *well armed with many guns, which were newly*

17. Iweka-nuno (1924:E81).

bought from the people of Aro-Chuku, and many also with matchets. The men of Onitsha, quite ignorant of this stratagem, met the men of Obosi in that valley, and, after some discussion and drinking, when the men of Onitsha were found well intoxicated with palm wine, a special sign was given to the ambushers by the men of Obosi, who suddenly came out and attacked the men of Onitsha, killing them in a horrible manner, and when some of them tried to run back to their own town the warriors, in ambush with many guns, attacked their retreat, killing as many as they could; then they advanced into the town of Onitsha, where they committed much havoc to the town and its inhabitants.[18]

This change in the balance of power, repeated in other nearby Ibo towns, involved the tapping of a new source of weapons through the Aro-Chukwu traders who were expanding trading and slave-raiding activities in the interior east and southeast of Onitsha. Onitsha people found their expanding dominance of the hinterland disrupted by the activities of the Ohafia and other slave-raiding warrior mercenaries associated with the Aro-Chukwu trading system, for the hinterland Ibo communities not only obtained new sources of firearms but also hired these mercenaries themselves.[19]

This final stage distinguishable in oral tradition, which will be called the uplands-Aro stage, contains the second fixed reference point for assessing time levels of reconstructed history. Baikie in his exploring voyage of 1854 recorded the contemporary Onitsha king as *Ákazùá,* and was told that the king "Udogu" had been alive at about the time of the Laird and Lander voyage in 1832.[20] These dates fit well with later historical evidence and with the overall genealogy, which may now be correlated with a series of roughly dated stages of prehistory.

18. Ibid. Italics are mine.
19. These developments will be discussed in greater detail in Chapter 13.
20. Baikie (1856:297).

Fig. 11 Inferred stages of Onitsha history

1. *Substratum stage* (pre-1500)
   Igala and Benin kingdoms extant, Benin expanding (Ewuare period).
   Niger riverain area: autochthonous Ibo (Akri peoples) on lower river, infiltrating Igala and Ado fishermen.
   Interior Ibo country: Nri kingdom extant, in communication with Igala through Anambra River drainage.

2. *Onitsha formative stage*
   A. The King Chima war and migration (1500–1600)
   The Igala-Benin wars and their aftermath; movements of groups west of the Niger and along the river. Agbor Chima or Ukpali Ezechi, Aboh Chima or Ekensu, and Ɔreze Chima, together with others of the Nine Clans, found a community on the east bank.
   B. The Onitsha-Egbema phase, or that of the "early kings" (1600–1700)
   Evidence of inter-segment competition for precedence or "royalty"; movement to the hills as the riverain slave trade develops; the beginnings of a unified community with a unitary ideology of kingship. Chimukwu, Nafia, Tasia, Chimezie, Chima the Cow-killer, and Nsu, Awuma, and Egbema.

3. *Igala-Anambra stage* (1700–1780)
   A. Early: dominance by the Anambra-drainage Igala; kingship ritual and regalia derived from there.
   B. Late: expansion of the Dei community with its linkage to Aboh.
   The stage begins with the "return" of Arɔlɩ from Igala, and continues through the reigns of his sons.

4. *Uplands-Aro stage* (1780–1880)
   A. Early: guns facilitate Onitsha independence and expansion of its dominance over the eastern hinterlands; religious linkage to Benin re-emphasized.
   B. Late: Aro-Chukwu hinterland trade brings firearms to contiguous Ibo communities and Aro-associated mercenaries threaten Onitsha; Missionaries and traders encouraged to settle there.
   This stage includes the reigns of Ijelekpe, Udogwu, Akazua, and Anazɔnwʊ, ending with the beginning of Niger Company control in 1880.

THE EVOLUTION OF ONITSHA SETTLEMENT PATTERN

It is possible to trace over time, in broad outlines, changes in Onitsha settlement patterns corresponding to the stages of community development just inferred. The reconstruction can be only tentative, and the prior locations as well as the time of arrival of some old Onitsha villages may forever remain indefinite. When, however, the multiple patterns of Onitsha oral tradition are checked against recent distributions of land holdings and of old shrines and sacred groves, it is possible to formulate general trends. Information from diaries of early missionaries has provided checks against oral tradition for the late periods. One difficult problem for the analyst as well as for the reader is that the names of Onitsha Ibo social units have changed considerably over time. But that such transformations have been recalled over time is both a tribute to the depth of Onitsha tradition and an aid to the student of its history. Most early names of social units are either those of ebo (ancient clan) or of one of the early kings, while later names are those of village (ogbe) or of patrilineage (*ʊ́mʊ̀-ńnà*).

Figure 12 outlines putative settlements and movements during the formative stage; a general pattern may be discerned without further reference to esoteric names at this point. Three sets of settlements may be distinguished for the initial phase. First, there were the autochthonous Ibo people living in the Onitsha hills at the time of migration. These were ordinarily referred to in oral traditions simply as the Oze, but several named subgroups were distinguished within them. Their distribution in a string of hilltop settlements suggests a typical low-density Ibo residence pattern.

The second group of settlements was located around Okpoko and extended up into the area called *Ìwɔ́lɩwɔ*. These were designated by two kinds of names: the names of primordial clans from towns west of the Niger, and the names of early kings or prominent men associated with them.

The third set of settlements was derived from riverain peoples at this early stage of oral history. One of these remained along the river, and the others were located inland near the low hills called Ìsiòkwe, where they were at an early time joined by one of the ancient western Ibo-derived clans. This Egbema group formed a series of clusters contiguous to the indigenous Oze Ibo.

The early formative-stage settlement pattern was thus one of

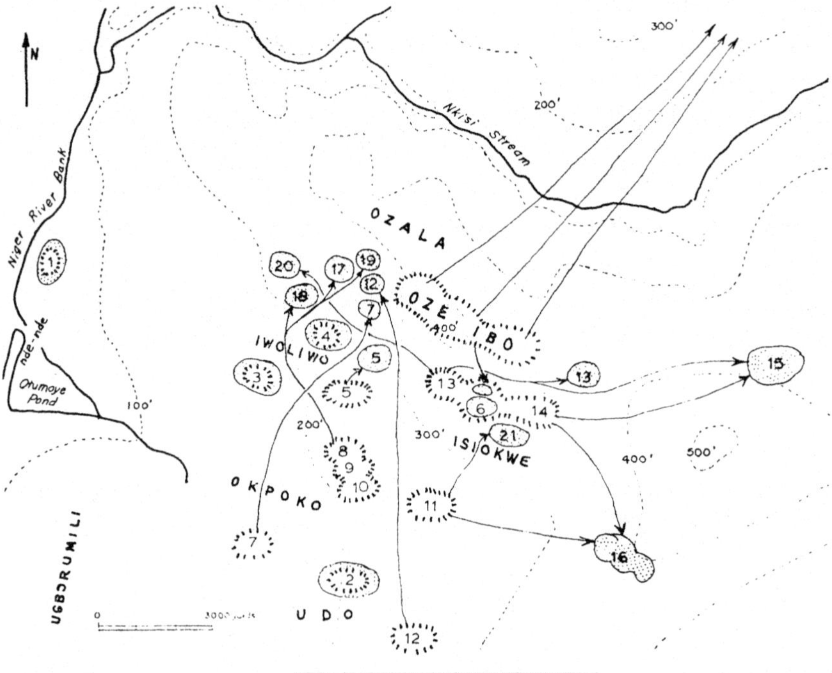

Village position, early Formative stage

Village position, Onitsha-Egbema phase

VILLAGE NUMBER REFERENCE:

riverain substratum:
1. Ulutu-Ado

named after Western Ibo towns
2. Ɔbiɔ
3. Isele-Awada
4. Ubulu
5. Ɔbamkpa
6. Agba-na-Ute

named after early kings & chiefs:
7. Ɔreze
8. Chimukwu
9. Tasia
10. Nafia
11. Chima-ogbuefi
12. Aniemena (Onogbo)

downriver peoples:
13. Ekensu (Aboh link)
14. Egbema

developing in Onitsha-Egbema phase:
15. Ogbe-Olị-Eke
16. Ɔdɔje
17. Ogbe-odogwu
18. Ogbe-mbubu
19. Ogbe-abu
20. Okposi-Eke
21. Isiokwe

Fig. 12 Onitsha settlement patterns: formative stage

three separate village clusters. Most of the primordial clans retained lands and shrines in the Okpoko area into recent years, and the name of Ɔreze, the deceitful victor in the ufie drum contest, is directly linked to Okpoko and to a great tree there said to mark the ancient shrine dedicated to Onitsha land.

During the time of the early kings, when the Okpoko cluster joined with the Egbema group in a war against the Oze Ibo, there were changes in the settlement pattern. The Oze were expelled across the Nkisi stream, where they took refuge with the Nkwele villages northeast of Onitsha (leaving behind some remnants that joined certain villages of the Egbema group). Then a series of movements into the hills resulted in an expansion of the various immigrant groups out over the available uplands. Subgroups of the Egbema cluster, who were renowned as warriors, moved out to the east and southeast and formed (after several movements and splits) two new village clusters. Most of the villages named after early kings moved from Okpoko northwards into the western part of the uplands. Finally, it is said that at this time the early king named Chima the Cow-killer established his residence in the hills of Isiokwe, where he lived near several remnant groups. At the conclusion of the process summarized in Figure 12, only three of the ancient clans remained near the initial residence around Okpoko.

The result of expansion during the latter formative stage was the widest geographical spread that Onitsha was ever to attain as a system of settlements, and this was probably associated with a low level of unity within that system. Traditional tales suggest, for example, that the settlements on the eastern and southeastern frontier tended to join socially with the communities located beyond them in those directions.

Things changed after the coming of King Arɔlɩ from Igala. During the Igala-Anambra stage, new social units were established through immigration, various residential groups underwent differential expansion, and various attached units developed as the slave trade expanded. These changes are outlined in Figure 13.[21] The village unit of the "Children of King Arɔlɩ" expanded greatly, and drew around it such immigrant segments as the Children of Idoko from Igala and those of an Ibo blacksmith said to have worked for Arɔlɩ and impregnated his daughter Ɔlɔsɩ. At the same time, the village called the Children of Dei was established amid the descendants of the early kings, derived some of its most important members from Aboh, and expanded at a much more rapid rate than the older social units with which it was associated. The descendants of Ɔbamkpa also expanded, drawing to the group a number of immigrant attached units. The rest of the primordial clans remained small or even decreased in numbers.

During this period soil exhaustion in the southern farmlands forced an increasing emphasis on exploiting farmlands toward and across the Nkisi stream northward. This more northerly emphasis is also evident in the development of the "international" market along the Niger, the Otu nkwɔ. Beside it a shrine dedicated to Onitsha land (*ànɩ-Ɔ̀nɩcha*) was controlled by the king but given sacrifice by the descendants of the original riverside occupants. To this market came traders from Igala, Aboh, Osomari, and the delta states, who provided the trade goods that gave Onitsha increasing power over the populations to the east.

Finally, during the uplands-Aro period of increasing firearms trade and warfare, a riverside village closely related to the Osomari people of the lower river grew in numbers and became a part of Onitsha community. During the latter part of the period, the entire residential community of Onitsha contracted its spatial dimensions. The villages on the eastern and southern fringes of the community moved from their frontier positions to more central locations, and the riverside units moved beside the Children of Idoko into a consolidated "Riverain village" (*Ógbè-ólu*). Thus

21. A careful reader will note some minor discrepancies between this figure (which mostly indicates residence shifts during the nineteenth century) and Figure 37, which diagrams the area of stable traditionalist residence as of 1961. These differences have no significance for the arguments of the present volume.

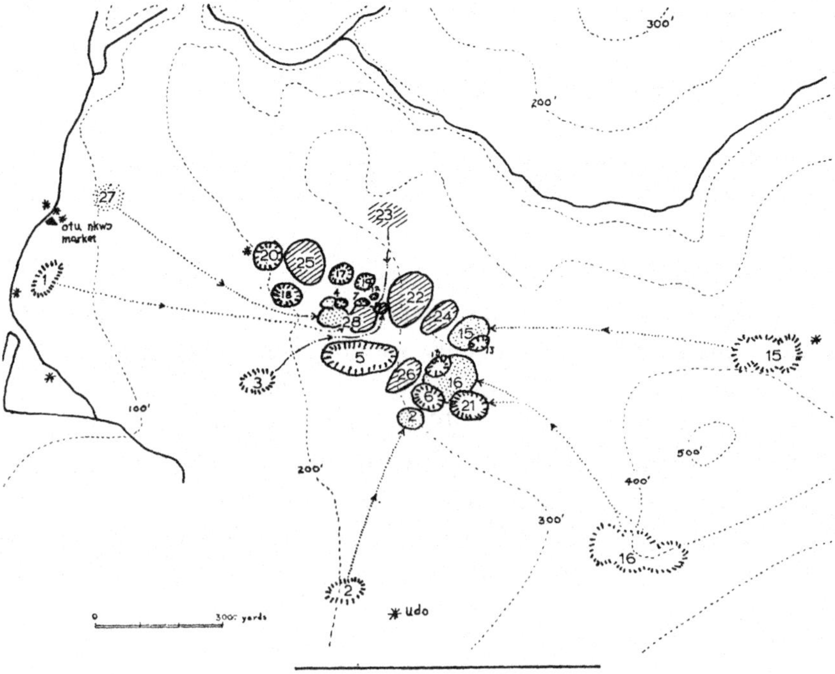

✱ Spirit shrine

VILLAGE POSITIONS:

Position at beginning of Igala-Anambra stage

Established during Igala-Anambra stage

Movement " " " "

Established during Uplands-Aro stage

Movement " " " "

Terminal position

VILLAGE NUMBER REFERENCE:

1. Mgbeleke (Ulutu-Ado)
2. Ɔbiɔ
3. Ogbe-Ɔzɔma (Isele-Awada)
4. Ubulu-na-Ikem (umu-Ikem)
5. Umu-Ase (Ɔbamkpa)
6. Agba-na-Ute (part of 16)
7. Umu-Ɔreze (part of 28)
12. Umu-Onogbo (Aniemena)
13. Ekensu (parts of 15 & 16)
15. Ogbe-Oli-Eke
16. Ɔdɔje
17. Ogbe-odogwu
18. Ogbe-mbubu
19. Ogbe-abu
20. Okposi-Eke
21. Isiokwe
22. Umu-Eze-Arɔlı
23. Umu-Idoko (Obikpɔro)
24. Umu-Ɔlɔsı
25. Umu-Dei
26. Iyawu
27. Ogbe-otu
28. Ogbe-olu

Fig. 13 Onitsha settlement patterns: later stages

by the final stages of the developments under consideration, the Onitsha community came to present a residentially compact village-group formation to the outside world.

Oral traditions of the latest contracting movements are partially corroborated by early written accounts, which also provide brief descriptions of the Onitsha settlement pattern obtaining at mid-nineteenth century. When the Sierra Leonean missionaries and traders first settled at Onitsha, they found its commercial activities centered at the riverside market. There between four hundred and eight hundred people were estimated to congregate on any given market day, and up to two thousand on "great market days."[22] A "very good road" led from the marketplace in a gradual ascent "between extensive cultivations of yams and Indian corn, among which young cotton plants were just growing up," to the entrance of the "town," about a mile and a half from the river and a hundred feet above it.[23] The westernmost residential cluster first encountered was

> about one mile in length, if not more, through which one broad road runs lengthwise, which divides it into two sections. On either side are groups of houses, a little remote from the high road, ruled by heads of families or inferior chiefs. Both sides of the road are either covered with bushes or plantations, till you come to an open road, leading to a group of houses further back, but some of the groups are close, and open to the high road, where also a market is held occasionally.[24]

When the Reverend S. A. Crowther first observed this pattern, with house-clusters dispersed on high ground amid gardens and linked together by pathways and "streets," he counted twenty-six such groups of houses which he estimated "contain at the lowest average 250 persons each, which gives 6,500 souls in the town of

22. Crowther (1855:24); Crowther and Taylor (1859:249, 255, 256, 288).
23. Crowther and Taylor (1859:24).
24. Ibid., pp. 28–29.

Onitsha"; later knowledge of the more distant community segments induced him to double the population estimate to thirteen thousand.[25] The southeasternmost village-cluster (*Ɔ́dɔjè*) was estimated at that time to contain "nearly one-third" of Onitsha's population; later it was described as a "suburb" of the town which "stands apart about one quarter of a mile from the nearest group at that end of the town, built on both sides of a wide road about half a mile in length on the summit of the hill, among a group of lofty trees." In 1868, however, after a series of internal misfortunes and under the pressure of external threats, all its inhabitants were observed to have "deserted the village and removed to Onitsha" where they established themselves in the area around Isiokwe.[26] During the same period it was reported that because of the continual war with the community of Ogidi to the east, "a great many good houses were deserted at the east end of the town, where a constant look-out was kept for the approach of the enemies, and the inhabitants have removed to the west parts, which are safer." [27] This reference may reflect the retreat of the easternmost village indicated on Figure 13, dating the westward contractions to between 1850 and the 1870s when the warfare threat from the east was at its peak.

Early descriptions of the community vary widely in the number of residential clusters distinguished. One observer suggested that the entire town was walled around as a unit:

> A wall covered with vegetation surrounds the town; the entrances to it are artificially constructed by training straight trees, closely planted into a screen work. At each side of the trees . . . a narrow passage introduces you into a dark arbour, and passing through you enter the town. All about these entrances, and in all places of public resort, rude images of their favorite evil spirit appeal to the generous public.[28]

25. Ibid., pp. 32–33, 426.
26. Crowther (1868:81).
27. Crowther and Taylor (1859:32).
28. Witford (1877:171–72).

However, this description may have referred to a single large village unit rather than to the town as a whole. In 1879, the community's population was estimated at ten thousand, and it was said that "the town consists of five villages, with a little interval of bush between each," [29] while a later observer reported that Onitsha was divided into ten "districts or villages," each presided over by a chief;

> These villages are surrounded by a thick hedge, the only entry being a rough gateway of upright poles. Within the gateway stands a juju or fetish house, and scattered amongst the undergrowth and trees are the dwellings of the people invisible one from the other.[30]

In recent times such gateways and fences have been constructed by each village and subvillage seeking to establish its independent identity, and this pattern was probably the one described here. The variation in number of reported villages may reflect the segmentary and "nested" character of these social units, which the observers could not have understood. In general, the accounts suggest a series of residential groupings (with the number reported varying between five and twenty-six) each protected by surrounding hedges and separated from the others by gardens. The general pattern of house-clusters, dispersed on high ground amidst a concentration of towering trees and linked together by pathways into "streets" where markets were held, suggests a typical Ibo community of recent times.

29. Great Britain (1888:9–11).
30. Mockler-Ferryman (1892:21).

PART 2

THE ELEMENTARY STRUCTURES OF ONITSHA SOCIETY

4 MAJOR VALUES AND RELIGIOUS DOCTRINES

The traditional Onitsha community was a society in terms of the criteria adopted for this study. Analysis of the traditions of origin reveal a reasonably coherent system of constitutive symbolism, a system that contains evidence not only of what the community meant to its people but also of the development of that meaning over time. After the beginning of the Igala-Anambra stage, well before the beginning of the exploratory period, this was certainly a bounded social system, although the oral tradition also suggests that this boundedness evolved over time and probably did not obtain early in the formative stage.

There are many other forms of evidence that Onitsha was a self-sufficient social system—that it was so legally, politically, economically, and as a preferentially endogamous community. The question is not so much to what extent Onitsha comprised a society, but rather what kind of society Onitsha was and in what directions it may have been changing. Clearly it was not totally unified, for the ideological view of the system was, as we have seen, twofold, both stratified and segmentary. Moreover, it obviously was not a totally undifferentiated society, a number of its distinctive organizational features having been traced to this or that stage in oral history.

Nevertheless for two reasons it will prove illuminating to begin the analysis of Onitsha society as if it were entirely kinship based. First, kinship values and norms pervade this society, and a procedure that systematically analyzes Onitsha kinship will not fall very far short of encompassing the society as a whole. Second, following this procedure we can better perceive how and where structural differentiation has occurred, and what implications it has for the kinship system of a society undergoing such change.

Any analysis of Onitsha society should begin with an exposition of major religious beliefs and values, because there is a profound interpenetration of the religious beliefs with the kinship ideology, indeed with the definition of all kinds of statuses, roles, and groups. This will set the stage for understanding the far-ranging importance of kinship and also for anticipating some of its limits.

Most of this chapter and of Chapters 5 through 11 are written in the present tense for convenience of exposition. The time level reconstructed is just prior to 1880, but many of the patterns discussed remained in effect at the time of my research. Where I wish to emphasize that a pattern was strictly precolonial, the appropriate tense will be stated clearly.

The major values of social life in Onitsha are rooted firmly in notions of filiation and descent. When Onitsha people assess the career of a person, their primary criterion is the number of children he has raised to support and survive him. Children are extolled in proverbs above any other good, even above the accumulation of wealth (*àkʊ*); "children first, wealth follows" is a proverb affirming the route to success.[1] Onitsha people say that a wealthy person who has no children will reap a bad destiny, for his own relatives may conspire to seize his fortune. He may very likely die a "bad death" (*ájɔ ɔ̀nwʊ*).

Onitsha proverbs make it quite clear that maintaining life is a justifiable end in itself only to the extent that it is productive or nurturant of more life. This overwhelming concern with the production and the continuity of life is basic to the fundamental concept of Onitsha philosophical and religious thought: the idea of

1. Proverbially, Onitsha people liken children to the tie-cloths that support a person's belly, helping him to walk the road of life. It is said that when one dies, his offspring should be as numerous as the grains of sand that bury a yam. The value of children is often affirmed in the personal names given them, for example, "Child surpasses money" (*Nwá-kà-égo*), "Child is shelter" (*Nwá-bʊ̀-ǹdo*).

chí.[2] Chi is "life" (*ńdʊ*), or life conceived as an animate self that guides the course of existence. The most directly important manifestation of this for any person is the "chi in me," which is thought of as a spiritual essence of the living self that guides and determines the course of that person's life from birth to death. It is believed that when an individual chooses "to enter the world" (*ínye-ʊ̀wa*), he makes a pact with a particular essential being (chi), selecting his length of life and his future activities; the choices so made are marked by the chi on his hand as his *ákàla-áka* ("marks of the hand"), or "destiny."

Any person is thought likely to be uncertain about the nature of putative life choices he has made (although some people are suspected, on the contrary, of knowing them and keeping them secret). Should anyone become anxious about this he can communicate with his chi to ascertain what these choices were. He can then affirm and adhere to these choices, or attempt to modify them if he regards them as undesirable. The chi is prominent when people consider making an overall assessment of the career of each individual, for a person is measured by the quality of the chi: for example, it is said that "one who dies without children, though he be rich, has a bad chi (*chí ɔ́jɔ*); a poor man who leaves many children behind him has a good chi (*chí ɔ́ma*); and a man who dies wealthy and is properly buried by his many children has a very good chi indeed."

Since chi refers then to a single life acted out by each person, there are as many chi as there are living individuals. However, not only does chi have a more general and inclusive meaning as the essence of life, it is also projected as a life essence attributed to the entire universe, a universal self called *chí-úkwu* or *chúkwu,* literally "great chi." The term chi-ukwu designates an ultimate self ordering the course and character of the universe as a whole, which in turn is conceived as a multiplicity of "worlds" (*ʊ̀wa*).

2. My analysis of this subject is indebted to the work of Talbot (1926), Horton (1956, 1961, 1967), and Bradbury (1960).

This universal self is addressed in prayer as *chí-úkwu-òkike,* "great chi the creator"; as *chí-nà-élu,* "chi in heaven"; and as *òlisa-èbúlu-ùwa,* "divinity who supports the world." [3] Chi-ukwu is said to have created all physical phenomena and endowed them with force and direction: the sky (*ígwe*), the heavenly bodies as his "messengers" and eyes, the earth (*ànι*) and the great river Niger (*òrumíli*). Chi-ukwu sent trees to grow on the land, animals to roam it, men to occupy it, yams and other foods to feed people, and various objects as "medicines" (*ɔ́gwù*) to help them in the course of their lives. When a person dies, his chi ceases to exist as an independent entity, returning to the great ground of being in the sun or in the sky. Chi-ukwu exists as long as the universe which it personifies.

It is implicit in the logical structure of these terms that chi-ukwu is a subcategory of chi rather than the more general class within which chi may be categorized.[4] We may view the meaning of these concepts as a semantic structure, whose unmarked terms point to the general category within which the marked terms are a subcategory. It is reasonable to translate chi as "god," and chi-ukwu as "great god." However, Onitsha people also say that the great god is the source from which all particular gods of persons originate; it might therefore be equally valid to translate chi-ukwu as "god" and chi_2 as "personal god." We will hereafter use the terms "personal god" for chi_2, "great god" for chi-ukwu, and "god" without qualifier for chi_1; in the latter sense, the term also refers to daylight. (See Fig. 14.)

If the description of the Onitsha belief system thus far makes a concern with life and lifelike forces appear central, individual life itself is conceived not solely in opposition to the notion of

3. The latter term is clearly related to the Benin term for the high god: Osanobua. Olisa is a term often used by riverain Ibo as equivalent to chi-ukwu.

4. This analysis differs somewhat from that of Horton (1956), but does not contradict it. Onitsha people say that a person plagued by misfortune sometimes prays to chi-ukwu to give him a better chi in his next incarnation, and the chi returns to the sky after death. Talbot (1926:2:40–41) clearly perceived the central significance of the notion of chi and its relations to conceptions of self and universe.

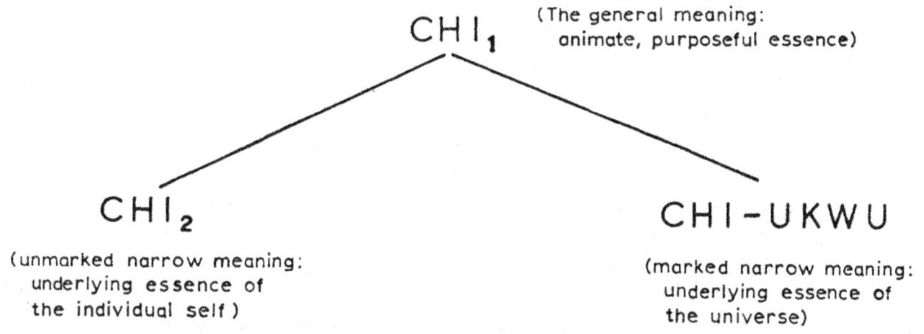

Fig. 14 The semantic structure of chi

death (*ɔ́nwʊ*), but partly as an imperfect approximation of it. Indeed, acts of attaining the heights of prestige by individuals in Onitsha are marked by identity-changing rituals that bring them closer and closer to death. The ultimate goal for every person is to lose his chi and thereby to become a "dead person" (*ḿmadù ɔ́nwʊ*), a "ghost" (*ḿmʊɔ*). The concepts of "god" and "ghost" form the major contrast pair in Onitsha religion, two forces in opposition which, however, interpenetrate through the process of reincarnation.

Onitsha belief postulates a multiplicity of worlds (*ʊwa*) in which existence occurs. The number of these worlds is indefinite (some say there are eight, some say seven, some four worlds) but from the viewpoint of men occupying this one, the other worlds are all "lands of the dead" (*anɩ mmʊɔ*), into which all persons who die should subsequently be incarnated. On the other hand, these lands of the dead are also the sole sources of all new human beings in the empirical world. Men, wherever they are, are believed to be always "looking into" the other worlds, communicating with people there, and considering being incarnated there anew. All the dead are believed to take a continuous interest in this world. Indeed, some never leave it, and wander it in a state of perpetual, incorporeal unrest; these are "bad dead" (*ajɔ mmʊɔ*) who have violated the world order. They belong nowhere and do little but make trouble. The dead viewed hopefully as sources of new human beings are those who lived lives of fulfillment here in the past, who were sent out of this world with glorious funerals which facilitated their subsequent establishment in other worlds, and who consequently look back here with pleasant memories and thoughts of returning. These dead are exhorted by the living to return as infants and, periodically, in other forms.

The worlds of the dead are conceived as located nearby, in the vicinity of the earth in which they were buried, and it is believed that the closer a person was buried to a house, the more likely he or she will choose to reincarnate there as an offspring of its occupants. Hence highly valued persons are buried within their own house to facilitate their return, while those whose life courses have been condemned are cast away into distant bush so that they will not return. Those buried in or near their houses also continue to observe and protect their living children; they may be periodically invoked to return physically to this world in the form of "incarnate dead" (*mḿanwʊ*) to inspect and judge the community—to express their pleasure at the celebrations of their living kinsmen or to demand that laws they have helped to support be upheld. They may also be invoked to enter incorporeally into objects constructed in their name to be fed, venerated, prayed to, and thanked for their spiritual assistance in maintaining long lives for their children and in bringing more children into this world.

The notion of reincarnation (ɔ́ *bìalu n'ʊ̀wa* ɔ́zɔ—"one comes to the world again") thus defines personal identity in terms of its relation to the dead. It is a dead person, or mmʊɔ, who chooses to return to this world in the form of a newborn child. To do so, the ghost walks to a crossroads (*ába-úzɔ*) of the two worlds, where it meets a personal god and makes a destiny-defining pact with that personal god. Through a creative act of the personal god, the ghost enters the body of the infant at birth, becoming the "seeds of heart" (*ńkpʊlʊ-óbì*) which provide the motive force underlying life, and the body emerges into the world as a living infant whose personal god has marked the lines of his destiny enigmatically into his hand.

The production of new lives, at this conceptual level, is believed to require two elements which, together with the empirical beliefs about conception, constitute the three necessary and sufficient agencies of birth. The first is the development of the physical body. In Onitsha theory, this entails the implantation of the male's "child seed" (*ùré nwá*) into the female's womb (*akpa nwa*). Ure is regarded as a category of blood (*ɔ̀bala*) that possesses a seed which grows just as a yam will when planted in good soil. If a man's ure is good and a woman's womb in proper condition, conception is certain to follow repeated sexual intercourse.

But the formation of a human being as distinct from a mass of flesh or a monster depends upon the second and third agencies, the choices of a dead person or ghost, who becomes the motive force driving a life by making its pact with a personal god. Evidence of the character of this ghost is sought by the parents in the infant's physical appearance and in certain observed behaviors, for it is believed that the ghost determines physical characteristics and certain putatively intrinsic tendencies such as "hot temper" (*óbì ɔ́kʊ*). It is hoped that the dead person is a revered ancestor returned, but often malicious beings from unknown worlds may capriciously decide to enter this world. Equally capriciously, they soon will choose to depart. Parents hope the infant is a returned ancestor who was buried nearby, i.e. one (or more) of the deceased fathers, mothers, father's mothers or other ancestor who had observed local community life from the nearby subterranean locality, found it good, and has chosen to return.

Among the Nri-Awka Ibo peoples around Onitsha, each individual tries to determine, at some stage of his life, which ancestor has formed that compact which has resulted in his identity. Once this ancestor has been determined by a diviner, the person makes an objectification of the personal god, in the form of a stick from an *égbò* tree (Newbouldia laevis) which is cut, placed in a bowl, and periodically "fed." This stick is called *ókposi* and symbolizes both a dead ancestor (mmʊɔ) and the individual's personal god (chi). When he dies, his personal god has departed and therefore, after funerary rituals have assisted him to reach the spirit land, this stick is discarded. His sons then fashion a new okposi stick, to represent him as a ghost (mmʊɔ) who still takes interest in his offspring. Thus in the object of the okposi, the notions of god and ghost are conceptually linked.

In Onitsha, however, the practice and belief are more complex, for here a personal god is represented not by one wooden stick but by five sticks called "seeds of god" (*ńkpʊlʊ-chí*), which are kept in a wooden "vessel of god" (*ɔ́kwa-chí*). Hence the essence underlying an individual's life course is represented not as an undifferentiated particle, but rather as a compound of units which, taken together, determine his character and life. Four of these sticks also refer to ancestors; some Onitsha people say that they represent ghostly contributions from the ancestral worlds of the father, the mother, the father's mother, and the mother's mother. The fifth stick, however, represents dead who are not ancestral. It is called *ɔ̀gbɔ́nùke* or *ɔ̀gbɔ́-nà-ùke,* which Onitsha people translate as "age-set and misfortune," and its link to other worlds is not to ancestors but to "one's comrades" (*ńdi-òtu-ýa*), or ghostly contemporaries regardless of their ancestry. Attached to this age-set representation is a wooden image of a man with ram's horns on his head, usually holding a machete in his right hand. This image, called *ìkéngà,* represents the essence of a man's will to success; it is viewed as part of a man's personal god, more specifically part of his ɔgbɔnuke.[5]

In Onitsha, then, the structure of a personal god contains these five components, which are usually worshipped as a unit but, in the case of ɔgbɔnuke, sometimes separately. Although the personal

5. The term ɔgbɔ means "age-set," and the Onitsha people translate uke as "fortune" implying "misfortune." See Jones (1962:192), where uke clearly means an "association."

god is identified with the entire life course of a person, it is not thought to be strictly localized inside the human body with which it is identified (though there is some hint of its relation to the head). The ghostly components supposed to determine basic features and tendencies are thought to be located in the heart, but they are also often externalized in the wooden objects that represent them, and the whole personal god is said to reside in its vessel.

When a man dies, all his chi sticks are discarded, for the personal god has departed forever. But the senior son of the deceased person will then "bring his father into the house" by collecting four large egbo sticks, which are also called okposi and represent the ghosts, plus (sometimes) a fifth object, his father's ikenga. Thus the set of symbols of the dead that a man acquires after his father has departed is homologous to the set of objects that represent his own character and destiny, his personal god. If one were to quantify human character in Onitsha terms, four-fifths of a man's personal identity would appear (at this point) to depend upon the choices of ancestors, one-fifth upon a preincarnate pact made with his spiritual contemporaries. In this set of ideas, the social categories of kinship and age-set gain unitary religious foundation through the linking of a person's god with various kinds of ghosts of the dead.

The major categories of Onitsha religion have not been exhausted in this discussion of personal god, its related but "universalized" concept of great god, and ghosts; for the objects of the physical universe which may represent these components are appropriate symbols because they are believed to be imbued with intrinsic forces and intentional powers that are also relevant to the needs of the living. These forces and powers are subsumed under the terms "spirit" (*álʊsɩ*) and "medicine" (*ɔgwʊ*). With introduction of these two terms, we encounter the full complexity of Onitsha religious belief, for their meanings interpenetrate not only with one another but with the ideas of god and ghost. Medicines, retained over time, can become spirits; spirits, under certain circumstances, can make pacts with personal gods and thereby become attached to individuals; and spirits are regarded as such partly because their power attracts the ghosts of the dead. To make clear their importance in the belief system, some extended discussion of spirits and medicines is necessary, because through them the belief system is charged with a contrast like that between the sacred and the profane.[6]

The Onitsha people believe that when the great god created the universe, he endowed some of its objects with spirit. These spirits are abstract but purposeful forces that reside in natural objects, possess moral commitments, and may help men or harm them. Unlike the personal god, they are limitless in duration. Unlike the great god they are spatially localized forces that act directly and intentionally upon men, and negotiations can be made with them.[7] For example, the sun (*ányanwu*) and the moon (*ɔ́nwa*) are regarded as "messengers" (*ńdi-ózi*) of the great god; they traverse the sky (*igwe*) over the land (*anι*) in intersecting paths which divide the earth into quadrants associated with the four days (*ékè, óyè, àfɔ, ǹkwɔ́*) of the Ibo week and with markets.[8] Thus a conceptual linkage is made between time and space, for each Ibo day is identified with a particular market place held in a particular community and associated with a particular sector of earth. All these phenomena—days of the week (often represented as four women carrying market baskets or as a four-faced person), sun, moon, and land, are thought to be imbued with spirit. The river Niger (orumili) is the "king of spirits" (*eze alυsι*) for it was created at the same time as the (female) land, and the egbo or *ogilisi* tree, the first tree to grow on the land, is regarded as the "age-mate" of the land. It therefore also partakes of spirit. This is why it alone is suitable as an objectification of a personal god and as the tree-shrine of land.

6. Durkheim (1915) :37–41).

7. The nominal form of the term spirit will be used in the special sense indicated here throughout the volume.

8. Cf. Horton (1956).

Although the meaning of alusɩ varies among different Ibo communities, and there are many varieties of such spirit in any single community, in Onitsha the meaning of the term becomes clear when one considers the most revered and most ancient spirits. These are called "oaths" (*íyi*). When a major dispute arises in the community and each party refuses to admit that the other is right, an object may be brought from the shrine of a fearsome and revered spirit and presented to one of the parties to swear upon. If that party's representative swears the oath (iyi) and dies within a specified time thereafter, it is believed that the spirit has killed him for denying a crime of which he was guilty; if he lives, the spirit has exonerated him and his cohorts. In brief, these spirits bring illness and death to whoever has violated their moral standards, and this power to harm is the basis of their veneration. They are critical sanctions of morality in the Ibo community, and one major mode of their operation is through the oath. When they kill, they draw the ghosts of their victims to their spirit abodes, and the presence of these "bad ghosts" further enhances the fearsomeness of these abodes.

The most ubiquitous spiritual moral agent is the land, for its sanction is inescapable. All strongly valued social norms are "things of the land" (*ɔ̀dɩnanɩ*), a term that covers a range of meaning. Within this category two kinds of sacred violation are distinguished: acts that are *ńsɔ*, "forbidden," and acts that are ńsɔ ànɩ, "forbidden by the land." Onitsha people attach different sanctions to these. "Whoever commits nsɔ, must undo the nsɔ" (*ónye ḿe ńsɔ, ɔ́ g̀a èmégha ńsɔ*); this refers to a restitutive sanction: one must perform a ritual act that negates the violation. If a son should push down his father, he must perform a ritual to lift him up again. However, "whoever commits nsɔ of the land, has committed an abomination; he must cover the abomination" (*ónye ḿe ńsɔ ànɩ, ḿe álʊ; ɔ́ g̀a íkpʊ álʊ*). An act such as incest cannot be undone, but can only be covered over, as one heaps earth over feces. If a ritual that "covers the abomination" is not performed, the land will become so hot with anger (literally, a "fiery surface,"*íru ɔ́kʊ*) that it will cease to be inhabitable.

Not all norms are subject to these two kinds of sanctions. Onitsha people broadly distinguish "good" (mma, ezigbo) and "bad" (ɔjɔ) kinds of "action" (*òmumé*), but not all bad acts are violation of land custom (*ɔdɩnanɩ*). There are many kinds of "rules" (*ìwú*), some of which are regarded as having been devised by men and are therefore modifiable. Violation of the latter may be sanctioned by fining (*ídà ńra*) without any need to undo or cover the act, because they lack spiritual value.

Spiritual value is bound up with the notion of nsɔ. This term has several related meanings. A thing or event may be nsɔ: birth, a newborn baby, and the great god are all nsɔ, but not quite in the same sense. Used most generally, nsɔ does not necessarily mean forbidden; for example, the great god is not ordinarily thought of as forbidden, but revered. Asked what property such things have that is different from the forbidden, Onitsha people say that they are "holy" (*asɔ*), holy things that are nsɔ but not necessarily forbidden.

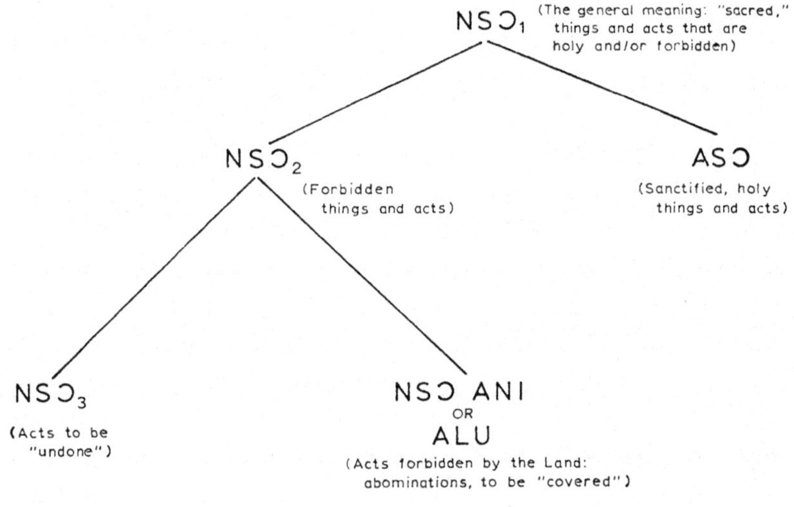

Fig. 15 The semantic structure of nsɔ

We are dealing with a three-level semantic structure in this class of religious norms, as indicated in Figure 15. Broadly, anything identified with gods, ghosts, and spirits is nsɔ. Thus one's identity is fundamentally sacred simply by virtue of its definition through the personal god; in addition, its close association with a particular land brings it under the nsɔ of that land. Other forms of spirit are also associated with personal gods and uphold a variety of sacred moral standards.

Regardless of the kind of morality they support, two distinct kinds of spirit may be distinguished in any Ibo community: those associated with the personal gods of particular human beings, and those with power over a collectivity, in some cases over an entire community, for example the land of a minor descent group or a village-group. The same distinction applies to most other kinds of spirit. There is an important dynamic relationship between these two categories; specifically, there is a general tendency, over time, for personal spirits to become collective ones. Before this process may be understood, we must first consider the problems of knowledge and communication in this personalized universe.

Men know that there are gods, spirits, and ghosts, know something about their putative locations, and know that the agencies may act upon them directly. However, while the courses of human lives and communities are presumed to be set by these wills, they are largely unknown to men. Men therefore continually seek to bring them into personal or public awareness through acts of communication. "Messenger spirits," such as the vulture (*ùdene*), are believed to serve this purpose, but communication through them in turn requires physical media. These physical media are medicines (ɔ*gwʊ*). Medicines are putative intrinsic properties of physical objects—bones, plants, liquids, stones, metals, body parts and effluvia of animals and men—which are believed to produce certain effects automatically by virtue of these properties.

For example, the fish called *ázʊ̀-ísi*, "head fish," has a very large bony head. It is believed that the eating of this fish makes a person's head strong and resistant to attacks by enemies. The young green shoots (ɔ̀mʊ́) of the oil palm (Elaisa Guineensis) are medicines the carrying of which automatically protects persons who must associate themselves with corpses or with the threat of death. Various plants when eaten are believed to produce automatic magical effects on a person's body. There are also "bad" medicines or poisons (*ńsi*), such as excrement (*ǹsí*), the bile (*ònunu*) of various animals, the juices of certain plants, etc., which are thought to produce various harmful effects. Both kinds of medicines may be used in varying combinations for a variety of purposes.

The most important medicines are thought to possess intrinsic association with important spirits and the dead, and thereby they serve as powerful media of communication with these forces. The tunneled clay of a termite hill (*ńkpu*), regarded as a channel of communication with spirits and dead located in the earth, is therefore used in making especially powerful forms of medicine. White "chalk" (*ńzu*) represents the cleanliness of the ghosts and is thought to be a favorite food of spirits. The body of a human being, especially its blood and certain internal parts, is a most powerful medicine because of the association of these parts with various spiritual and ghostly forces. The nut of the kola tree (ɔ́jɪ, Cola acuminata) is believed to have been the first fruit which the great god caused to grow on the land. Its consumption is therefore always an act of commensality with the great god and with land. Similarly, the sticks of the egbo tree (see above) are media of communication with land and other spiritual forces residing on it.

Perhaps the most important medicinal medium is the tree called ɔfɔ (Detarium senegalese). Its twigs are somewhat phallic in shape and fall naturally away from the branches of their parental tree just as, it is said, human sons grow as dependents of their fathers but in time become separate from them. These twigs, picked from the ground by males and appropriated as their personal property, are called ɔ̀fɔ́ ɔ́*kpala* and represent the supposedly intrinsic qualities of individual maleness and paternity, through which a man can control his wives and children. However, the ɔfɔ is not simply a medicine of raw male power: the ɔfɔ tree is also said to grow in the great god's compound, and it is therefore a part of the ultimate truth (*ézi*) that the great god represents. The holder of an ɔfɔ stick can thus communicate directly with a great variety of sacred forces, including his own personal god, various spirits, and the dead.

Although there are many kinds of ɔfɔ staff, the basic form, i.e. the one derived from the ɔfɔ tree itself, is intimately linked with paternity. There is an analogous medicine appropriate to maternity, called *ɔ́ma* or *ńdi-ńne*. The ɔfɔ and ɔma are the most important medicines intrinsically associated with individuals. Control over them may be succeeded to by the offspring of individuals, and they may thereby come to be associated with collectivities.

Important medicinal media such as ɔfɔ and various complex medicinal combinations cannot simply be obtained and utilized by persons on an ad hoc basis, for specialized knowledge is required to make them work. It is believed that the great god at one time sent a series of spirit messengers to teach men about the medicinal properties of physical objects. One came to teach them about herbs and roots, one to show how to mix and heat powders, plants, and animal parts together in water and oils, one to teach the use of iron and other objects in preventive medicine, and one to teach the use of poisons. This knowledge has since been pooled among "doctors" (dibia) who also control medicines giving them relationships to the messenger spirits that enable them to practice divination. A person is "called" to be a doctor-diviner when it is determined that his personal god is intimately associated with a spirit called *ágwʊ̀*. Agwʊ acts as a generalized spirit messenger (represented in the form of a vulture), and tends to compete with and overshadow the spirit ikenga identified with normal men. These doctor-diviners are trained by other doctors. They learn the methods of divining the various intentions, demands, and influences present in this personalized world, and they develop the art of combining medicines into powerful concoctions which may operate independently of spiritual forces. They supervise the construction of objects representing each person's god, of certain shrines dedicated to spirits associated with that personal god, and of objects dedicated to the ghosts of the dead. They also supervise the dedication and rededication of shrines to various localized spirits associated with collectivities, and the consecration of ɔfɔ and other medicines which may be controlled either by individuals or by collectivities.[9]

Once such representations, shrines, and medicine collections have been established, they may be directly utilized by the persons and groups owning them, provided that periodic consultation is made with the doctors to ascertain the state of current relationships with the spiritual or ghostly components associated with them. Modification of such presumed states is then effected by various ritual activities.

An outline of the major sectors of Onitsha religious belief as delineated thus far may assist the reader in comprehending the dynamic relationships among these ideas and their representations. Figure 16 distinguishes the major categories of this personalized universe.

Medicines and spirits are placed in the same sectors on this figure because of the high degree of conceptual overlap between them. This is particularly true for the spirits and medicines intimately connected with the personal god. Onitsha people are usually not willing to draw sharp categorical distinctions when talking about ikenga, ɔma (or ndi-nne), and ɔfɔ. A person's ikenga, for example, is sometimes characterized as spirit and sometimes as ghostly, but it is also consistently linked with the personal god, particularly with that aspect of it which reflects the spiritual influences of age-set relationships (ɔgbɔnuke). The maternity em-

9. See Shelton (1965) for a detailed account of divination procedures among Ibo of the Nsukka area, which are similar in general form to those of Onitsha.

Fig. 16 The categories of Onitsha religion

1. THE GREAT GOD: Personalized universal cause, the underlying determinant of all things and events.

2. THE PERSONAL GOD: The individual's underlying self, whose orientations were set by pre-natal choices and conditioned by various potentialities derived from the dead. It has two sets of components:
   A. *Okposi,* the ancestral components participating in the pre-natal pact; represented by four *egbo* sticks;
   B. *Ɔgbɔ-na-uke,* whose character is determined by the pact of ghostly associates and contemporaries; represented by one *egbo* stick;
   These are kept in *ɔkwa-chi,* the vessel of god. At the time of death, the personal god departs, returning to the great god, and the entire assemblage is discarded.

3. SPIRITS AND MEDICINES ASSOCIATED WITH THE PERSONAL GOD: The following major types:
   A. *Ɔfɔ ɔkpala,* medicinal essence of paternity, profoundly related to god; represented by an *ɔfɔ* tree twig.
   B. *Ɔma,* medicinal essence of maternity, believed to influence the personal god; represented by a conical clay mound.
   C. *Ikenga,* the spirit for normal men, attached to the *ɔgbɔ-na-uke* part of the personal god; represented by a wooden figure of a ram-horned man.
   D. *Agwʊ,* the spirit for doctoring, attached to the *ɔgbɔ-na-uke* part of the personal god of a deviant; represented by a wooden figure of a vulture.
   E. *Anɩ ezi,* the courtyard land spirit of a particular man, marked by an *egbo* tree.
   F. *Ogwugwu, urai,* and assorted other medicines that may be obtained by individuals with the aid of a doctor.
   Control over the objects representing all such spirits and medicines may be jointly acquired by the successors to a parental estate.

4. SPIRITS AND MEDICINES ASSOCIATED WITH LOCALITIES AND COLLECTIVITIES: two main types:
   A. The sun, moon, sky, market days, and other prominent givens of the natural environment, which may or may not be related to particular communities.
   B. Other, more localized objects related to particular sub-groups or communities:
      1) The *ɔfɔ* of groups;
      2) the *ɔma* of groups;
      3) the *ikenga* of one's father (ordinarily kept only by one person if at all);
      4) Spirits jointly served by doctors;
      5) the *anɩ* (land) of groups;
      6) the *ogwugwu, urai,* and other medicines of groups;
      7) rivers, ponds, rocks, and trees located on the land of groups.

5. THE DEAD: two main categories may be distinguished:
   A. Those properly residing in lands of the dead:
      1) dead ancestors (*ndi-mmuɔ* proper), who have been buried in appropriate

earth and who may become associated with a personal god through reincarnation; represented by four *okposi* sticks;

2) dead associates and contemporaries (*ndi-otu, ndi-ibe*), who are connected with *ɔgbɔ-na-uke.*

B. Those not residing in the land of the dead: the "bad dead" (*ajɔ mmuɔ*), who have not received proper burial and who instead become attached to the spirits that have killed them.

blem, ɔma, is equally ambiguous in classification, for it "contains" ghosts and is believed to have a direct effect on the course of life set by a woman's personal god. The ɔfɔ medicine is associated with the ghosts and with spirit as well as with a man's personal god, and when he dies his ghost may become attached to it.

Generally, the difference between a medicine and a spirit is that spirit is holy (asɔ) while medicine is not. A medicine may be forbidden (nsɔ) if it is dangerous; other medicines are profane remedies unless they are associated with other forbidden or holy things. This leads to a final important point: over time, a medicine may become a spirit.

As we have seen, when a person dies the elemental ghostly components of the personal god ordinarily return to the land of the dead, whence they may be born again through a compact with another personal god. If, however, a person has died a "bad death" at the hands of a wrathful spirit, the ghostly components become attached to the shrine of that spirit and are not reincarnated but remain dangerous to the living. In any event, the personal god and its ghostly components are dissipated from their former structuring.

However, the spirits and medicines that were associated with this particular personal god may not be thus dissipated after a person's death. They may instead be retained by his descendants, thereby becoming, over time, objects of collective interests as symbolically perpetuated parts of his socially recognized self. Personal medicines so retained over time may, if they demonstrate their powers through effective results, become the spirits associated with particular groups. They tend to focus collective reverence precisely to the degree that they have killed sinners and drawn the malevolent ghosts of these sinners to their shrines.

It may be instructive to represent the dynamic aspects of Onitsha religion schematically (Figure 17). This suggests a developmental process that relates persons to roles, collectivities, and to the conceived moral order of the universe. The left side of Figure

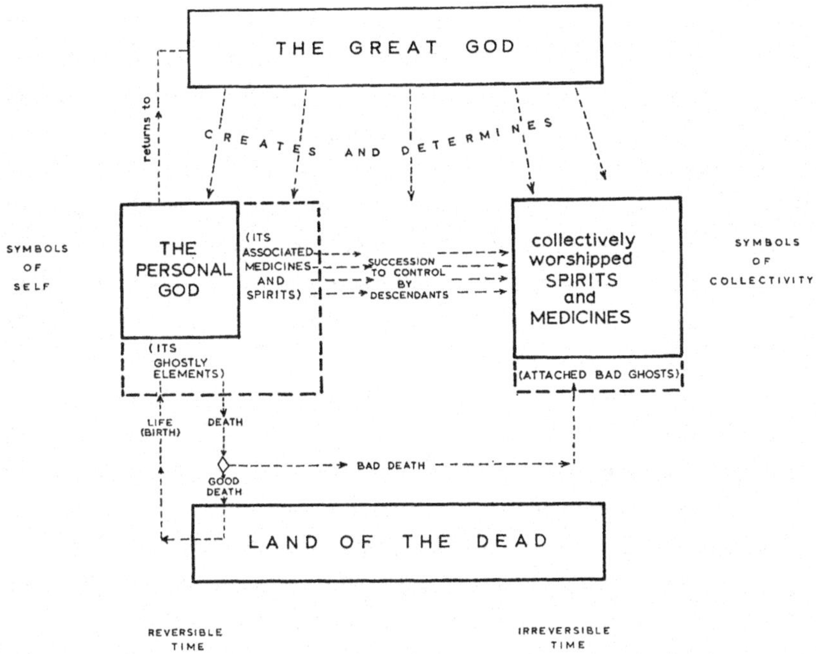

Fig. 17 Religious symbols of self, role, and collectivity

17 summarizes the ideal, static system of cycling reincarnation that human beings undergo in terms of their personal god pact. The Onitsha personal god represents, in a sense, the assumed core of one's personal identity, i.e. self-image as a configuration of attributes that one knows or suspects himself to possess. Closely attached to this core and to some extent viewed as part of it are other elements (ghosts, spirits, medicines) that accrue to the per-

son at salient points of his life history. These elements, thought capable of modifying and molding his life, round out an overall personal identity, giving it (ideally) style and coherence culminating in a "good death."

Various of these elements—ghostly, spirit, medicinal—are of social importance, and some designate socially recognized moral qualities, statuses, and social roles. Some of these elements may thus be said to define a person's social identity. Through these ideas, Onitsha religion links personal identities, social identities, and a series of collectivities, all within the framework of a moral universe. Through the idea of god (chi), man becomes a microcosm of the universe and the universe becomes moral in man's image; through the ideas of spirit, medicine, and ghost, the character of man, collectivity, and locality become refractions of one another.

The use here of such terms as personal identity and social identity must not mislead us into imagining that Onitsha beliefs define persons in analytical terms, for they do not. Instead, multiple concrete concepts are used to explain human complexity, and the human identity defined in such terms is not thought to be localized inside the human body to which it refers. Its various aspects are externalized, thought to reside in various symbolic objects as well as being related to various body parts. For this reason, these objects may continue to be of great social interest after a person's death, for they retain part of his essence, and control over them may be acquired by his descendants.[10]

However, social interest in many of these objects is likely to be

10. These points emphasize a divergence of this analysis from those of Horton (1961, 1967), who has shown how some African religious ideas parallel the Freudian distinctions of conscious vs. unconscious self, and who regards such ideas as basically "explanatory" schemes. The first point that needs to be emphasized concerning African religions is that, although we may isolate ideas that parallel concepts in Western psychology and sociology, this kind of thought system lacks the basic assumption that the self and its will are physically bounded entities, confined within the human body. Second, in belief systems of this kind, reality therefore tends to be profoundly moral in its significance, and it is thus not possible to draw a clear separation between scientific and religious thinking. For this reason, "explanation" itself generally possesses a moral dimension, and is not equivalent to positivist scientific explanation.

maintained over time only to the extent that the social situations of the descendants of that person, and of those who interact with them, are imperfect—characterized by misfortune and "bad deaths." The potency of these collective symbols is measured largely by the evidence of their vengefulness. Thus collective identity of a group may be measured partly by the number and kinds of spirits the group worships as a collectivity; and this in turn partly reflects the imperfect nature of their past history. Onitsha religion is, as we shall see, very much bound up with the problem of evil, and with a sense of pollution accumulating over time.

5 THE ONITSHA PATRILINEAGE SYSTEM

Since the central components of Onitsha religious belief involve both parent-child relationships and modes by which descendants inherit and share spiritual objects, these religious beliefs are intimately bound up with the kinship system. We are now in a position to examine that system in detail. In this chapter, I shall first outline the statuses delineated in Onitsha kinship terminology, and then relate these statuses to religious concepts, to social roles, and to the ecological situation of the community.

THE MAJOR CATEGORIES OF KINSHIP

I showed in an earlier study that groupcentric assumptions about kinship and kinship terms are insufficient to account for the semantic structure of Onitsha kinship terminology, and that assumptions and methods congruent with those set forth in the first chapter of this book are essential.[1] A brief outline of Onitsha kinship semantics, based partly on the findings of the earlier paper, will suffice for our requirements here.

The verbal symbol that identifies Onitsha as a single community is the notion of "Onitsha the Nine Clans" (Ɔnɩcha ebo-itenani). The ideal implied in this conception is an image of nine localized descent groups, each one an exogamous unit that obtains its wives from the others, thus generating a simple, web-like segmentary system. This ideal has been considerably distorted in reality, although not so much as to lose its value as a frame of reference.

1. Henderson (1967). The groundwork for that exposition may be found in Schneider and Homans (1955), Schneider and Roberts (1956), and Lounsbury (1964a, 1964b, 1965).

However, coexisting with it is another ideal of "Onitsha of King Chima" (Ɔnιcha Eze Chima), the community led by its great ancestral king. If in recent times one asked the headmen of the various clans who were the true descendants of King Chima, each headman would include his own clan in that category—adding (in most instances) the modifier "across the river" (*ùfesí-m̄ili*) to indicate that the members of his clan had been duped of their rightful status at the time of the legendary Niger crossing. Through this second notion, nearly all Onitsha people trace their descent to a single royal ancestor (though nobody would agree that everyone else in the community may rightfully do so). Thus the entire Onitsha community is defined in terms of kinship ideology, although in two different senses; in one sense descent entails exogamy while in the other it does not.

Two widely used terms denote consanguineal kinsmen. The prefix "children of" (*úmʊ̀-*) denotes shared filiation or descent, while the term "kinsmen" (*íkwu*) denotes (in its most general sense) any consanguineal relative. When an Onitsha person wishes to identify himself with a specific descent category or group, he uses the first term (together with the name of the ancestor or ancestress of reference); when he wishes to identify himself with a wider social community of relatives, he uses the second. The term *íkwu-n̄a-ànyí*, meaning roughly "our people," is used to imply shared commitments within such a grouping.

Another term roughly equivalent to "our people" is *íkwu-n̄a-íbè*, which may be translated as "kinsmen and associates." This term also specifies a sense of community, and such usage indicates that the sense of community extends beyond kinship, for *ibe* includes not only "in-laws" (ɔ́gɔ̀) but also "others" (*ńdi*-ɔ̀zɔ́) who are regarded as members of the community on grounds other than kinship.

Thus in Onitsha the broad definition of community includes two major kinship categories, ikwu and ɔgɔ (together with a residual category of non-relatives). These categories do not correspond exactly to the Western dichotomy of consanguinity and affinity, for the Onitsha people treat some "affinal" relatives as if they were consanguineal. In this chapter, only kin types that are from the Western observer's viewpoint consanguineal will be considered.

The basic structure of Onitsha consanguineal terms is generated by two pervasive dichotomous variables of degree and agnatic-linkage. The foundation of this terminological system is a set of terms that refer solely to relations of filiation (in their formal, reference usage).[2] This set includes the terms "father" (*ńnà*), "mother" (*ňne*), "child" and "children" (*nwá* and *ʊmʊ*), "man's senior son" (*ɔ̃kpala*), and "man's senior daughter" (*àdá*). All these terms are glossed with the English labels because they refer only to that specific kin type. Linguistically they are all simple unit terms, and they refer to what may be called "first-degree" relations, in contrast to all other relations, which may be called "further degree."

Since in Onitsha terminology, all further-degree consanguineal relations are designated either by combinations of first-degree terms or of a first-degree term with a modifier, they are all structurally complex. If the distributions of these complex terms are examined, it turns out that the kin type references of many of them can be predicted from the literal meanings of the combined terms that compose them. For example, *nne nna,* meaning literally "mother of father," does indeed apply only to FM (father's mother), and hence the literal meaning is also the acceptable gloss. Such terms will be here called "descriptive complex terms," and while there are many such terms in Onitsha, they pose no problems

2. The distinctions between reference and address usage in Onitsha, and between primary and secondary usage, were discussed in Henderson (1967). In the present study, an effort has been made to simplify wherever possible and to eliminate details. There has also been one shift of empirical classification. In the 1967 article, I regarded the term "man's senior son" as applicable to father's senior son as well as to man's senior son. While this is valid as a secondary, informal, general reference, I now think that a more accurate reflection of all my data is to regard the formal, concrete application of this term as limited to the context of primary filiation. The same applies to "man's senior daughter." I am indebted to Ifekandu Umunna for clarifying the context variations in use of these terms. See 1967 article for basic data.

of meaning in themselves although their distribution in the wider system is of interest. However, other complex terms are not predictable as to kin type from the combined terms that compose them, and such complex terms are problematic: they evidently form semantic units in their own right. These will be called "classificatory complex terms"; they include *nwá-ńnà* (literally "child of father"), *dí-ɔkpala* (lit. "master senior son"), *ísi-àdá* (lit. "head daughter"), *ńnà-óchiè* (lit. "old father"), *ńne-óchiè* (lit. "old mother"), *nwá-ḋi-ànι* (lit. "child of the soil"), and *nwá-nńe* (lit. "child of mother").

The nature of the terms discussed thus far indicates the general character of this semantic system. Clearly, those terms designating first-degree relations must be viewed as its basic units, for they are ubiquitous, and in combination they preserve their primary kin type meanings, with the exceptions just listed. Since this is true for the system in general, we may safely assume that the primary meaning of any exception, i.e. any classificatory complex term, is given by its "focal kin type(s)," i.e. by the kin type referents closest to a first-degree relation; and the secondary meanings of the term are "extensions" of this primary meaning. For example, if the classificatory complex term *nna-ochie* includes among its kin type referents MF (mother's father), MFs (mother's father's son), MFFs, and MFss, then the primary significance of the term may be glossed as "mother's father," and the term's general meaning extends that primary meaning to the other kin types (according to specifiable semantic rules that state their equivalence to the focal kin type).[3]

The classificatory complex terms can be translated and then grouped into subsets of reciprocals as follows:

1. *nwanna:* f.t. (focal type) *Fc;* g. (gloss) "father's child;" (pl. *ʊmʊnna:* f.t. *Fc;* g. "children of father")
   appropriate reciprocal: *nwanna;* but also depending on

3. Lounsbury (1964a) gives an account of the logic behind equivalence rules.

seniority(+):
diɔkpala: f.t. *Fs+;* g. "father's senior son";
isiada: f.t. *Fd+;* g. "father's senior daughter."

2. *nnaochie:* f.t. *MF;* g. "mother's father"
   nneochie: f.t. *MM;* g. "mother's mother"
   (pl. *ndiochie,* f.t. *MP;* gloss "mother's parents")
   appropriate reciprocal: *nwadianı:* f.t. *dc;* g. "daughter's child"
3. *nwanne:* f.t. *Mc;* g. "mother's child"
   appropriate reciprocal: *nwanne*

Our findings thus far have been reached by simply following the implications of the fundamental semantic contrast between first-degree and further-degree kinsmen. There is a second basic semantic variable in this system: that of agnatic-linkage, which divides the first-degree terms themselves into two asymmetrical subsets of reciprocal terms:

1. agnatically-linked: father/child
   father/senior son
   father/senior daughter
2. non-agnatically-linked: mother/child

These instances alone suggest that the variable is agnation rather than agnatic-linkage; that it is a more general variable is revealed only when further-degree kinsmen are considered.

Attention may first be concentrated on the terms applied to further-degree lineal kinsmen, i.e. the direct ancestors or descendants of ego. For these kinsmen, wherever the kin types that link ego and the kinsman of reference are only F or s (father or son), that kinsman of reference is designated by a descriptive complex term. It makes no difference whether ego or the kinsman of reference is male or female, so long as all the intermediate links are male. This includes, of course, persons who are agnates, e.g. one's FFF is called "father's father's father" (*nna nna nna*), and reciprocally his ssc is called "child's child's child" (*nwa nwa nwa*). It also includes persons who are not agnates but agnatically-linked in the sense just indicated, e.g. one's FFM is called "father's father's mother" (*nne nna nna*) and reciprocally her ssc is also called "child's child's child." In contrast to this pattern, all those further-degree lineal kinsmen for whom any one of the intervening links is female are classed in the categorical set of "mother's parents"/ "daughter's child." For example, both one's FMP (father's mother's parent) and MFP (mother's father's parent) are classed as "mother's parent," and reciprocally both one's dsc (daughter's son's child) and sdc (son's daughter's child) are classed as "daughter's child."

These examples show why this variable must be viewed as one of agnatic-linkage rather than a more limiting one of agnation per se, and they also point to a pattern of interest. The immediate ancestress of an agnatic line is treated in the same descriptive fashion as her husband, the founding ancestor of that agnatic line. Both are contrasted with all other further-degree ancestors, who are in contrast classified together as "mother's parents."

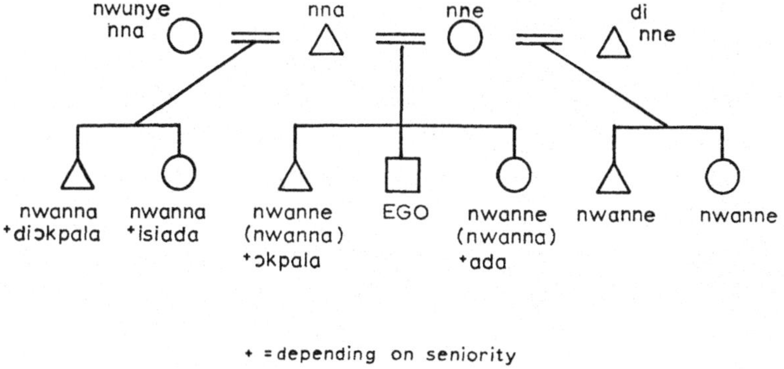

Fig. 18 The terminology of shared filiation

The variable of agnatic-linkage operates much more pervasively to categorize collateral consanguineal kinsmen. The preceding list of classificatory complex terms shows that there is no Onitsha term precisely equivalent to "sibling" in designating shared filiation, but rather two distinct terms, "father's child" (nwanna) and "mother's child" (nwanne). This pair can be understood only in light of agnatic-linkage. In the genealogical context specified in Figure 18, agnatically-linked (patrifilial) half-siblings can only be called "father's child" (nwanna), while non-agnatically-linked (matrifilial) half-siblings can only be called "mother's child" (nwanne). Full siblings are also referred to as "mother's child," unless one wishes to specify patrifiliation; then "father's child" may be used. This suggests that the term nwanne has two levels of meaning. Its general meaning designates a super-class of "siblings," specifying "mother's child" without specifying patrifiliation, i.e. Mc who may or may not also be Fc (or perhaps Mc who is assumed to be also Fc). As such it contrasts with its own marked subclass, nwanna, which is appropriate in those particular contexts where agnatic-linkage is to be stressed. More narrowly, nwanne operates as an unmarked subclass contrasting with nwanna by specifying "mother's child, *not* father's child." The categorical structure of the set is diagrammed in Figure 19. Thus at the general level of meaning, "mother's child" transcends the variable of agnatic-linkage, while at the lower, narrower level it stands in opposition to the agnatic-linked category "father's child." At this narrower level, shared-filiation kin types cannot be regarded as B ("brother"), S ("sister"), or "sibling", but must be distinguished according to parental link.

The term "father's child" is widely extended to collateral kinsmen, but only where linkage is entirely agnatic. One's FB, for example, may be called "father's child" only where he is FFs, i.e. where he is a paternal sibling of father; should he be only FMs, a maternal half-sibling of father, the term cannot be used. In a full range of collateral kinsmen, extension of the term "father's child" is governed by the following rule of agnatic linkage: "let any agnatically-linked collateral kinsman be regarded as equivalent to father's child." This rule may be expressed diagrammatically thus[4]:

$$(1)\ (F^{m}s^{n})c \rightarrow Fc$$

The operation of this rule, which contains its own corollary, is quite general, covering a large number of kin types. All these, or any subset of them, may be referred to collectively as "children of father" (ʊmʊnna). The application of either the singular or plural

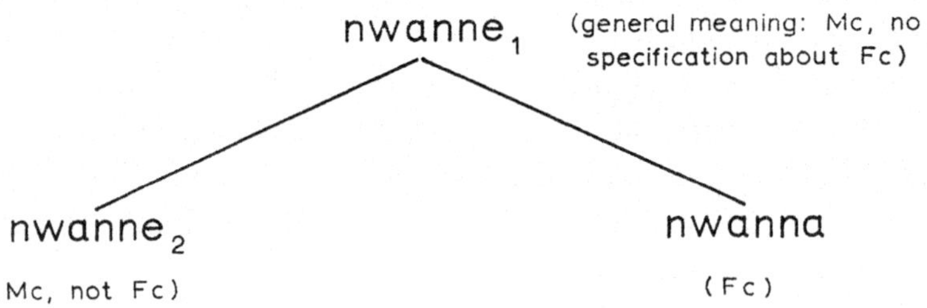

Fig. 19 Semantic structure of the sibling class, nwanne

form of this term clearly involves a reference to the apical ancestor of the collateral chain, for that ancestor is specified by name after the term in order to delimit the range of category. Thus "father's child" and its plural "children of father" specify shared descent statuses, and define these statuses in terms of shared filiation.

Within this general category of "father's child" falls another set of classificatory complex terms having a specialized distribution: the terms diɔkpala and isiada. The term "father's senior son" (diɔkpala) refers not only to that specific kin type, but is widely extended, and the term "man's senior son" (ɔkpala) from which this complex term is derived is applied not only to a man's

4. Here m, which specifies the number of links traced through fathers, may be any positive number, while n, which specifies the number of links traced through sons, may be any positive number or zero. The arrow means "is structurally equivalent to." For example: "father's father's father's son's son's child is structurally equivalent to father's child" ($F^{3}s^{2}c \longrightarrow Fc$).

first son, but to successively senior sons upon the death of the senior one. The same kind of succession obtains for "father's senior son," but this applies to a much wider series of successively senior male kinsmen linked agnatically to ego through an apical ancestor—indeed it applies as widely as the range of "father's child." Thus while "man's senior son" signifies lower generation to ego, "father's senior son" applies in theory only to persons of generation equal to or above that of ego; it is always associated with an ancestral referent. Even ascending generation lineal agnates may be called "father's senior son" if they are the most senior living descendants of a given ancestor. Thus ego may call his FFs "father's senior son" of FFF, if FFFs and FF are dead. Then when FFs dies, FFFss may become "father's senior son" of FFF, and after him, F. Ultimately the referent of the term may reach FFss and male ego. The complete reference for a kinsman holding this position is "father's senior son of the children of father X" (diɔkpala ʊmʊnna X), where X is the name of FFF.

The term "father's senior daughter" (isiada) is extended, similarly, to successive senior living collateral female agnates. For example, ego will call his FFFsd "father's senior daughter" (of FFF), then after her death will call his FFd by that term, and so on. Thus this term too is associated with an ancestral reference.

The "senior daughter" term is not entirely a parallel to its male counterpart, for it is also modified by prefix as nwa-ada (literally, "child-daughter"), a term applicable as a direct equivalent to "father's child" for female agnates. This is pluralized as ʊmʊ-ada when referring to a collective category of female agnates, and in both singular and plural forms it emphasizes the filial character of the female's status in her agnatic category. Of the two distinct prefix-modified terms, one emphasizes seniority among "senior daughters" (ísi-) and the other their overall status as "children" (nwa- or ʊmʊ-).

Among the non-agnatically-linked sets of classificatory complex terms, the reciprocal set "mother's parents"/"daughter's child" is widely extended to both lineal and collateral kinsmen. As might be expected, the extension of "mother's parents" terms consistently involves linkage through a maternal kin type at some point, and reciprocally the extension of "daughter's child" always involves linkage through a daughter kin type. Obviously linkage is non-agnatic. Nevertheless, agnatic-linkage is not irrelevant to the application of this set, as Figure 20 shows.

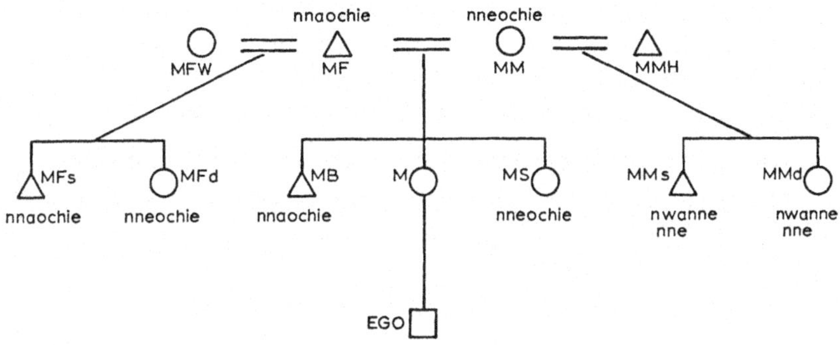

Fig. 20 Terminology for maternally linked kinsmen

Figure 20 indicates that extension of the "mother's parent" terms consistently involves kin types that combine a maternal link with agnatic-linkage. Indeed this is quite general in the Onitsha system: if rule 1 is applied to all the collateral kin types to which "mother's parent" is applied, all are reduced to MFc, MMFc, or FMFc.[5] A rule which converts these reduced categories to MP or some higher generation equivalent is the following: "let mother's father's child be regarded as equivalent to mother's parent." This rule may be diagrammed thus:

$$(2)\ \text{MFc} \rightarrow \text{MP}$$

Rule 2 in a sense modifies rule 1 wherever an Fc link occurs after an M link, and its operation is quite general throughout the Onitsha

5. The latter two may be regarded as equivalent to the first, for all practical purposes. See Henderson (1967:30).

system. It has the following logical corollary: "let father's daughter's child be regarded as equivalent to daughter's child:"

$$\text{Fdc} \rightarrow \text{dc}$$

The corollary reduces all collateral extensions of the "daughter's child" term to their focal type (or some lower generation equivalent).

The set "mother's parents"/"daughter's child" is a "matrifilial-agnatically-linked" category, since agnatic-linkage penetrates these non-agnatically-linked terms. Here again the critical variable is not agnation per se but rather agnatic-linkage, for MM is of course not an agnate of M; however, as in the case of FM and other agnatically-linked ancestresses treated in the same way as their husbands, MM is evidently treated as an ancestress of mother's agnatic line and classed with MF.

The self-reciprocal term "mother's child" is extended to such a wide variety of kinsmen that it is rather difficult to analyze, but it has two related meanings. The general meaning is "mother's child, no specification about father's child" (nwanne_1), and the narrower meaning is "mother's child, *not* father's child" (nwanne_2). Extensions of the term involve both meanings.

The following general rule converts to Mc all the kin types to which this term is applied: "let any ancestor's mother's descendant be regarded as equivalent to mother's child":

$$(3)\ \text{P}^{m}\text{Mc}^{n} \rightarrow \text{Mc}$$

Rule 3 thus may be regarded as a "shared ancestress reduction rule." It operates after rules 1 and 2 have been applied and is consistent with their operation. For example, the kin type MMdsc is called "mother's child." It entails the general meaning of this term, for it makes no difference should MMdsc also be MFdsc, since the operation of rule 2 reduces the latter to MMsc, and rule 3 then applies to this kin type as well. On the other hand, for certain kin types extension of "mother's child" involves the narrow meaning of the term (i.e. "mother's child, not father's child"); for example, MMsc is called "mother's child" only if he is not also MFsc; for should he also be the latter, rule 2 would operate to make him equivalent to "mother's parent." Finally, although "mother's child" must be regarded as a non-agnatically-linked term, it applies to agnatically-linked collateral kinsmen where this agnatic-linkage is assumed. For example, it may refer to FFMssc who is also FFFssc. This kinsman is, by rule 1, "father's child," but he may also be called "mother's child" by rule 3, in the more general sense of that term.

Thus, three basic rules of equivalence underlie the classification of consanguineal kinsmen in Onitsha, and there are two major semantic variables. The results of the analysis are displayed in Figure 21.

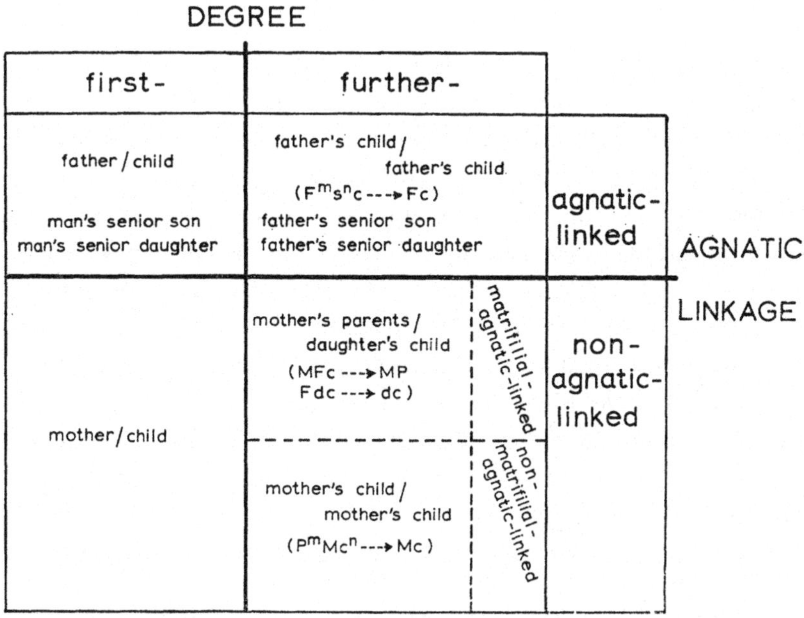

Fig. 21 The major categories of kinsmen

Figure 21 vastly simplifies actual Onitsha terminology,[6] but it outlines the basic structure of the system. Lineal agnatically-linked kinsmen are treated with descriptive complex terms, while lineal non-agnatically-linked kinsmen are classed as "mother's parents"/"daughter's child." Otherwise Figure 21 gives the essential information: 1) the underlying structure is given by the terms of primary filiation, patrifiliation being provided with the most diversified terminology. Further-degree relations are modelled on those of filiation. 2) Agnatic-linkage penetrates throughout the universe of kinsmen, even retaining some relevance for the "mother's child" category. It is now necessary to inquire to what extent these status categories structure social roles, and to consider whether the major equivalence rules just formulated isolate significant collectivities.

KINSHIP CATEGORIES AND SOCIAL ROLES: THE ONITSHA PATRILINEAGE

In Onitsha society, kinship norms are generated through an articulating of religious beliefs and kinship categories which links personal identities and collectivities into a single moral system. Two crucial religious objects which provide this mediation are the medicinal ɔfɔ and ɔma. The ɔma is of secondary importance; much more important to the kinship system is the moral connection between kinship concepts of agnatic-linkage and religious imperatives, which is governed by the medicine called ɔfɔ ɔkpala. This medicinal twig, symbol of paternity, is the primary mediator of the power attributed to a person in his roles as husband and father. The ɔfɔ ɔkpala can be used by its holder to inflict sickness and death. Onitsha people say, "ɔfɔ is might" (*ɔ̀fɔ́ bù íke*), for it conveys its holder's wishes to the spiritual and ghostly sources of power and links these wishes to the ultimate truth represented by

6. In that it omits all descriptive complex terms. Especially significant are the further-degree agnatically-linked lineal terms, but there are others. For more complete coverage, see Henderson (1967).

the great god. A father can use it to bind his children to a course of action, even to curse or ostracize them, and he can employ it to curse anyone (including his wives) who may seek wrongly to harm anyone or anything under the protection of his ɔfɔ. As a device for testing truth, it is used as the prototypical oath (iyi) within its sphere of influence. In all these uses, it is a double-edged sword, for if the father administers it wrongfully and deceitfully its power will be directed against him and may kill him. The meaning of ɔfɔ encompasses the notion of "right," and when one affirms, "I hold ɔfɔ," he is saying, "I hold the power of righteousness."

Since according to Onitsha standards of value the father's major social duty is to maintain the lives of his children, this spiritual authority must be exercised with great restraint. Once a curse or oath is made upon ɔfɔ its effect is believed to reverberate throughout the family group wherever deceit and injustice have been practiced. Onitsha people believe, therefore, that the basic paternal authority is too dangerous for frequent application within the family and that it can more safely be applied in just causes "against the outside." The full name of this paternal object, "ɔfɔ of the senior son" (ɔfɔ ɔkpala), reflects the belief that it bears most powerfully on the social relationship between a man and his senior son. It is thought to bind them so closely to mutual truth that any curse uttered by the father against the son would certainly kill one of the two persons. The inescapable dependence of the senior son upon the will of his father through ɔfɔ is a central tenet of Onitsha belief.

When the father dies, his senior son must ultimately "bring the father into his house." In doing so he takes hold of his father's ɔfɔ ɔkpala, which thereby becomes ɔfɔ diɔkpala, "ɔfɔ of the father's senior son." Holding it in his right hand and resting it on the shrines dedicated to the ancestral dead, he administers the ritual communication with these ancestral ghosts (now including his own father) whom he and his junior agnatic brothers and sisters serve and supplicate. The role of the senior son thus perpetuates the filial relationship shared by the agnatic sibling set. When this senior son dies, his next junior brother will take up the ɔfɔ symbolizing the continuity of this filiation, and will thence be called father's senior son."

The original senior son in this paradigm will also have acquired his own ɔfɔ ɔkpala, which he uses in ritual mediation vis-à-vis his own children and in controlling various objects that he has personally acquired. When he dies, although the ɔfɔ of his father passes to his junior agnatic brother, his personal ɔfɔ passes only to his sons and their children. Consequently a continually segmenting system of spiritually sanctioned control is automatically produced, within which the terms ɔkpala and diɔkpala designate the priests of the ancestor cults shared by various ranges of collective "children of father" (ʊmʊnna).[7] The term diɔkpala may thus be glossed as the "senior lineage priest" among a set of such priests. All priests may be called diɔkpala, but they are further ranked according to the level of paternal ancestry each represents. It is possible for one person to act in the role of senior lineage priest not only to his deceased father, but also to his father's father, his FFF, and so on. The highest level of priest in such a series, who is by definition the most senior in all shared parentage sets in which he is involved, is called the "head priest" (*ísi-ɔ́kpala*).

The "daughters" (ʊmʊada) of the collective "children of father" also fall within that father's righteous power, and they too are ordered in a series of roles coordinate with the hierarchy of lineage priests. Although the paternal ancestors associated with ɔfɔ objects are believed to abhor menstrual blood and the touch of women, the daughters are defined as quasi-male. A senior daughter whose father is deceased may, in her role as "head senior daughter" (isi-ada), hold an ɔfɔ object which has been delegated to her by the senior lineage priest. This object, the ɔfɔ-isi-ada, has power

7. The multiple nested series of collectivities specified by these norms indicates the presence of a segmentary lineage system. The classical case of this type, analyzed by Fortes (1945, 1949), shows many formal similarities to that of Onitsha.

over the entire patrilineage, but it is especially important in directing the collective activities of the daughters in a manner to be further considered below.

When patrilineage daughters die, they cannot transmit this delegated ɔfɔ to their children. Instead, it reverts to the senior patrilineage priest for re-delegation. The spiritual presence of such daughters is preserved in a set of flattened oblate clay shrines called ʊmʊ-ada, which are periodically served by the senior patrilineage priest. The ɔfɔ ɔkpala system thus provides the religious basis for the social organization of the Onitsha patrilineage. The values it symbolizes are enduring and solidary relations based on ascriptive paternity, which involve the entire lives of the people it embraces. Although there are multiple ɔfɔ ɔkpala within any patrilineage system, it is said that the ɔfɔ of a father supersedes that of his son. Thus the entire patrilineage is ideally a single, united collectivity.

There are other implications in the meaning of ɔfɔ ɔkpala. Since father-child and agnatic relations are regulated by the power of ɔfɔ, and since ɔfɔ operates by inflicting death, the incidence of deaths in any given family or lineage serves to indicate the spiritual health of that unit. This especially concerns the order in which deaths occur, for appropriate succession to the control of ɔfɔ ɔkpala requires that members of the group die in the order of their seniority. Onitsha people are emphatic in their assertion that whenever the order of deaths within a social unit repeatedly violates this norm something is radically wrong with the spiritual conditions of life in that unit.

The Basic Forms of Ritual Action

If the ɔfɔ symbol provides a general evaluative model for agnatic relationships in Onitsha, the concrete form of social interaction which best illustrates how this model works to order such relationships is a complementary pair of ritual acts called *ífè ǹrù* and *ígɔ ḿmuɔ*. In Onitsha ritual, two kinds of action recur in a wide variety of contexts. The first is *írù*, "to venerate" (nominal form, nru), which implies a total commitment to the object, a "worship" despite whatever contingencies of life may intervene. The second is ígɔ, "to beg," which is associated with requests for valued things, made to a superior by his dependents.

The duty of a child is to venerate (iru) his parent, and to demonstrate this veneration by continuing acts of service (ife). An Onitsha proverb states that "the child who serves his father will eat well," emphasizing the rewards which follow if one subordinates his own interests to those of his father. This service includes not only instrumental and sometimes onerous tasks, but also the regular performance of a ritual act symbolizing self-sacrifice. This act is ife nru, "serving homage." Any child who has reached the age of basic moral understanding is expected periodically to bring his father a gift. Any man (or woman) who makes a formal visit to his father should perform this homage service with a few cowries and some kola nuts (ɔjι).[8] When he does this, he kneels before his father, hands him the gift on a plate, and says, "Father, pray for me to the ghosts" (*ńnà, ĝɔlúm ḿmuɔ*). Given this request, the complementary paternal act becomes appropriate.

A simple, almost prototypical, situation of this kind involves the acts of presenting, breaking, distributing, and consuming the kola nut in the context of "begging the dead." The father takes one of the kola nuts presented to him by the person serving homage, hands it to his wife to be washed, then holds it in his right hand, and, blowing on it to indicate that both the kola and the words he will utter are clean, he begins his prayer.

> Olisa-who-supports-the-world, receive kola nut. Eat the entirety of the kola, while we eat it in pieces. We, who are dirty, beg you, give us long life. Land, receive kola; we beg you, feed us, give us long life. Ancestral ghosts [named in series] receive kola; give us long life. Kola has come; whoever brings kola, brings

8. The actual objects used in homage service have changed considerably over the past hundred years, but there can be little doubt that the pattern described here was the traditional form of the ritual.

life. We shall all live. Let him who wishes ill to others have that evil fall upon him; a careful man never harms others.

[Addressing the supplicant], may it be good for you and for all of our family. May good thoughts enter your belly, may good things come to you. That is my prayer. When a thing is well started, it is well ended.

After this prayer, the sentences of which are punctuated with utterances of "*ìsé*" ("so be it") by all persons present, the father breaks open the kola nut, picks off the germinal sprout—called "head of kola" (isi-ɔjɩ), the senior portion—and drops it on the floor as an offering to the dead. Breaking the cotyledons up into as many pieces as necessary, he takes the best as his priestly prerogative, calls the person who has performed service to receive a piece of kola directly from his hand, and transfers the remainder in a tray to the most junior person present, who then serves the others in descending order of seniority. All must eat of the kola to affirm the meaning of the prayer.

There are two ways to present kola: by dropping it into the recipient's cupped hands, or by serving it in a tray. The first is a fundamental prerogative of a man when giving it to his children and his wives. The second is more generalized; it expresses the giver's seniority. A person who receives kola from a tray may take it in his left hand, thereby communicating that he is a slave (*órù*); he may simply take it with his right hand, communicating that he is a freeman and the server is a slave; or, appropriately, he may touch the tray with his left hand and take the kola with his right, thereby communicating his generic equivalence to the giver within a framework of collateral seniority relations. This is the usual mode of distributing kola between paternal siblings, for example.

This ritual act is perhaps the most pervasive phenomenon of Onitsha social life; it occurs in the context of most other forms of religious action, and is a prerequisite for proper social visiting where other ritual is not planned. Its basic significance is that the eating of the kola nut by the recipient demonstrates his trust in the giver—for the nut could be secretly poisoned if the giver's intentions are evil—and his acceptance of the sentiments expressed in the giver's prayers. By eating a portion of the nut himself, the giver demonstrates the goodwill he has previously expressed in prayer.

In addition, the acceptance of kola that has been broken and divided in this way signifies acceptance of differential prerogatives among the actors concerned. Onitsha people say that "maltreating an Onitsha man is in the kola" (*ḿmegbu nwá ónye Ɔ̀nicha ʋ̀ ǹa-ɔ́jι*), indicating that this is the only circumstance in which an Onitsha man will accept another man's right to appropriate a much larger share than his own. In distributing kola, a priest presented with three kola nuts may simply take two of them for his own, after he has broken the third and taken the best pieces of that.

The meanings associated with kola become most impelling when the ritual act is validated by the breaking of the kola nut against the ɔfɔ staff, and the use of this staff to convey the prayers to the dead. The ɔfɔ should always be brought forth when more complex ceremonial activities are to be undertaken which include formally "begging the dead." The major forms of such activity include the celebration of "feasting the dead" (*ílɔ-ḿmʋɔ*), the performance of "venerating spirit" (*iru-alʋsι*), and the act of "driving away [evil] with sacrifice" (*íchʋ-àja*).[9] The latter two are usually acts of expiating some divined evil and involve the complete sacrifice of some living thing. "Feasting the dead" is a festival of thanksgiving in which the participants partake of the cooked sacrificial offering; during such occasions "begging the dead" occurs repeatedly.

In the typical case, a person when troubled, sick, or about to embark on some new venture consults a diviner, who tells him that some ancestor or ancestor-affiliated spirit requires a festival and

9. The description given here may be compared with that provided by Basden (1938:56–67). The latter is semantically inaccurate.

desires certain specified foods. The person must then consult with his father or with a senior lineage priest who mediates relations with the spirit or ghost involved, and arrange for the occasion at which the priest will be presented wtih the appropriate materials for sacrifice. Such ceremonial occasions must be scheduled considerably in advance, so that all participants may abstain from sexual intercourse for several days beforehand, since the ghosts are believed to abhor any taint of female sexuality.

If the sacrifice is to be a "festival," the lineage priest brings out the okposi sticks representing the dead and places his ɔfɔ staff upon them; beside these objects he sets the vessel representing his personal god, his personal ikenga statue, and perhaps various treasure boxes and staves.[10] These objects are all placed together upon the "face of the throne" (*íru-ùkpo*). When the congregation has gathered, the priest occupies his throne. He is presented with a bowl of water, washes his hands in order to cool them, washes the kola nuts set before him, and then sprinkles water on the dead to quench the heat in them. The opening prayer and distribution of kola are validated by the priest's spitting chewed kola upon the accumulated shrine objects and his touching these shrines and the ground with his ɔfɔ stick.

The person who has requested the feast then steps forward and, addressing all assembled persons in appropriate order, recounts the conditions under which he has asked for the activity, presents the goods he has brought to the lineage priest, and requests the priest to utilize them in worship for the benefit of everyone present. Several steps of begging the dead follow. The priest first receives a cup of palm wine presented him by the supplicant, and pours a small portion of it upon the objects representing the dead while he prays to them. The remainder he hands back to the supplicant, who kneels to take it, calling the honorific name of the priest then drinking down the cup of ritually blessed liquid. The priest then calls all others under him whom he wishes to honor—his wives,

10. These latter objects are further discussed in Chapter 7.

his children, his junior brothers, etc.—and they too kneel in sign of their homage (nru) and call him by his honorific name. When the priest is satisfied, the other lineage priests present may follow the same pattern, taking cups of wine which they bless through libation and calling upon their subordinates to receive and drink then in recognition of their priestly right to beg the dead. Gin may then be served in the same ritual pattern.

The major phase of begging the dead begins, however, when an animal is sacrified and its blood runs freely upon the shrines. At this time, the priest first takes hair or feathers from the neck of the animal and places it upon the various shrines; then, begging the ancestors to receive and be contented with this blood, and to leave their descendants to live in peace, he cuts the animal's throat and directs a spray of blood over the shrine objects. The sticks representing his personal god must not be touched by the flowing blood, which is food suitable only for the dead. The remainder of the blood is collected in a pan, cooked, and served out to the participants under the priest's direction. Again, patterns of redistribution are followed in accordance with seniority and superordination, each distribution being associated with a defined prayer-homage relationship binding giver and receiver.

In each such ceremonial act, the father or lineage priest performing the ritual receives a special portion of the animal killed (e.g. an "arm" of a goat, while the supplicant receives the skin and head). He is also provided an extra portion of food so that he can feed all the small children who have joined the congregation. At the end of such ceremonies, speeches are made by the senior lineage priest, the supplicant, and others, summarizing and assessing the significance of what has been done. Then "money for the dead" (*égo ḿmuɔ*) is brought forth by the supplicant and presented to the presiding priest. The priest takes an initial portion as representative senior son of the dead, and then every person present, including the priest, receives a personal portion as a gift "for one's own god" (ego chi). The ceremony closes with the priest's prayerful avowal that the action has been properly intended and performed, as he beats his ɔfɔ emblem on the ground to send that message of validation to the land of the group and to the ancestral dead.

The articulated model acts of serving homage, prayer, and sacrifice thus spell out patterns of deference and demeanor associated, in the case of paternity, with the power of moral right, and extended, through the rights of succession to the ɔfɔ, to all members of the patrilineage that "serves" a common patrilineage priest.

The Moral Relationship among Father, Sons, and Agnatic Siblings

The binding moral character of father–child interaction is most strongly emphasized in the model of deference and demeanor between father and senior son. The father is expected to direct his parental indulgence elsewhere, particularly in the form of periodic "free gifts" to the most junior child and to the next senior one "who has brought his junior sibling into the world." His moral training in patrilineage responsibility is concentrated upon the senior son (and to a lesser degree upon the senior daughter). Both senior children are expected in turn to educate their junior siblings. An Onitsha proverb states that "the child [carried] at the back never knows how difficult it can be to learn to walk," referring to this expectation that younger children will be cared for by elder ones who have been controlled more directly by their parents.

The senior son serves as the model of appropriate father–child relationships, and his interaction with his father is constrained by numerous proscriptions of acts that are defined as forbidden (nsɔ). He must never overtly challenge his father, lest he be thought eager to replace him. Of all members of the parental household, he alone is forbidden to enter his father's private "treasure room" (*òlisiliɔ̀kʊ̀*) so long as the father is alive, for it is believed that by doing so he might learn the extent of his father's wealth and wish to succeed him immediately. Since the father and senior son interact in a context defined by the imperative of strictest truth (ɔfɔ), their relationship should concern matters of moral knowledge and responsibility, not possibilities of future economic gain. If the father wishes to confide in any kinsmen about the extent of his hidden wealth, he is expected to turn to his junior sons, to his wives, or to his daughters, but not to his senior son.

If a son should insult his father or push against him physically so that the father falls to the ground, the latter may declare a "forbidden act" that must be undone ritually under the sanction of ɔfɔ. Petty thievery or other selfish acts disturbing members of the household are similarly sanctioned, often with fines levied, but repeated acts of defiance may be handled by a parental vow of ostracism (*ńsʊpʊ̀*), which is tantamount to a declaration of abomination (*nsɔ anι* or *alʊ*). Such an act must be "covered" by the son's ritual confession, atonement, and oath of intentions to conform. The declaration of abomination is so dangerous to the entire patrilineage that a wide latitude of deviance may be permitted before it will be openly made. An act such as sexual intercourse with one of the father's wives must, however, be declared an abomination.

Many behavioral prescriptions bind father and son (especially senior son), and most emphasize that a son should submerge his personal will and interests in the will and interests of his father. They also point to the perpetuity of the relationship; it is, for example, the unrenounceable duty of the senior son to perform his father's first and second funerals, and to "bring him into the house" as an ancestor after these funerals have been completed. While the father is alive the senior son's acts of homage are carefully measured, and the son may be fined or otherwise punished for shoddy performance.

However, certain beliefs limit this submergence of the senior son in collectivity with his father. First, it is said that a father must exercise extraordinary care in directing his senior son; should he chastise the son excessively the son may fall into a "prideful lament" (called *ákwa àlılı* or *ífu àlılı*), and, it is thought, pine away and die. That would jeopardize the spiritual health of the household and deprive the father of his most reliable support for his old age. Second, that father and senior son are so tightly bound in their mutual behavior is thought to make them closely equivalent in status; proverbially, it is said that "father and senior son are of the same age-set." Although the father may call all his wives, daughters, and junior sons to kneel and receive ceremonial drink and food from him as a sign of their utter dependence upon him, he ordinarily should place that of his senior son before him on the ground as a sign of the latter's incipient social equality with him. Third, the Onitsha father must respect the right of his son to accumulate his own personal property, even though the son should voluntarily contribute the wealth obtained from such property primarily to the furthering of his father's glorification. If, for example, a mother buys seed yams to be planted in her son's name when that son is too young to engage in farming work, the father must plant and harvest these yams separately from his own. After the harvest, he must receive the boy's verbal permission to merge any part of this harvest in the common pool.

Thus there is in the Onitsha patrilineage a tension between the son's subjection to a wide number of norms sanctioned by the father's ɔfɔ and the recognition of the child's independent identity and private, personal rights. All sons of a man share this tension, which also exists in the seniority relations among them, especially in norms governing their interaction that are formally similar to those between a father and senior son. If the senior son and his junior brother attend a festival and their father is absent, each must receive an equal share of the food (or money) that is divided. The right of each person to appropriate an individual share must be separately asserted; then, however, the junior brother is expected to take a portion of his share and add it, as a prototypical act of the homage service he will always have to render, to the share of his senior brother, who is viewed as standing in the role of the father in the latter's absence. This separate "share for the father's senior son" is a general phenomenon in the division of valuables within the patrilineage.

The moral character of the relations binding the children of one father is enforced by their father's right, as holder of ɔfɔ, to "repair disputes" (*ídozi ókwu*) among them, to act as their "court" (*íkpe*). The "bringing of complaints" (*íkpelu*) before the throne of their father is done in the ritual context of begging the dead: both parties must bring "kola for talk" (*ɔ́jɩ ókwu*) and, if the case is serious, "wine for words" (*ḿmanya ókwu*). The father breaks the kola, begs the ghosts to hear the case, listens to both sides, and then "pronounces judgment" (*íkpe m̀alu*) against one party. He may simply "advise" (*ídʊ̀ ɔ́dʊ*) both parties to change their behavior, or he may levy a fine (ɩda nra) against the culprit. If the dispute is highly rancorous, he may require the two sons to "bind [their] lives" (*ígbà ńdʊ̀*) by swearing they will not "look for one another's lives" and then drinking blessed wine from a single cup. All such proceedings are regarded as under the sanction of the paternal ɔfɔ, and they therefore devolve upon the senior son after the father's death.

The kinds of complaints which may be brought before the holder of ɔfɔ ɔkpala range from simple bad behavior to forbidden acts to full abominations, all the major Onitsha categories of offenses, all of which he may judge. However, it is said proverbially that "abominations stick [*tá ḍo*] to the body," and that "a madman [*ónye-ála*] is not nearly so ashamed of his condition as are his mother's children [ʊmʊnne]." Therefore, when abominations are committed within a narrow range of kinship grouping, there is intense pressure to keep them secret, and when the ceremonial "covering of abomination" occurs it is done with as few people aware of it as possible. The taint of abomination is difficult to remove, and it spreads to close consanguineal kinsmen. Concern about abominable acts therefore runs high among the "children of a father."

One important form of abominable act is homicide. This may or may not come before a patrilineage court. If a slaying occurs involving two members of one patrilineage or clan, the first questions concern evidence, intent, and segmentary subdivision memberships. If the slaying was publicly witnessed and intentional and both slayer and victim were members of the same immediate ancestral house, the victim's collective mother's parents may directly approach the murderer, give him a rope, and command him to hang himself. The hanging is regarded as a sacrifice that partially neutralizes the act forbidden by the land, but the murderer's immediate agnates must then also perform rituals "covering the abomination." If, however, the two parties come from different major segments of the lineage, judgment may be pronounced by the head priest of the clan; the victim's segment then comes to demand the hanging of the killer and a compensatory transfer of a patrilineage member from the killer's segment to that of the victim.

In both cases, if it is agreed that the killing was inadvertent (*ɔ̀ghɔ́m*), the killer may flee to save his life. If he does so, whatever the circumstances, the wrath of the land remains unassuaged and warriors from the immediate patrilineage of the victim must attack the premises of the killer's immediate ancestral house. They drive off all its occupants to take refuge with their mother's parents, and they burn and destroy its houses, crops, and animals and cut down its shade trees so that the land becomes a barren "fiery surface." In this they act as the agents of the wrathful spiritual land of the clan. The killer and his lineage segment may later return, but they provide a compensatory transfer of one of their members to the victim's segment and must "cover the abomination" and "cool the land." Reconciliation is effected when the two parties "bind their lives." Similar processes may occur in cases of vengeance between different Onitsha patrilineages, and between an Onitsha unit and one outside Onitsha.

Thus the Onitsha patrilineage possesses a wide-ranging judicial autonomy. When the father dies and the senior son has taken control of the parental ɔfɔ, he thereby gains the right both to hold court among his paternal siblings and to vow the ostracism or death of any paternal sibling who deviates from his directives concerning objects under that ɔfɔ. Since it is he who must vow to the death that his words are just, he also bears the brunt of potential spirit and ghostly wrath. The senior son is expected therefore to maintain rigorous spiritual intentions, to avoid misdeeds which may have spiritual impact upon his lineal segment. If an external dispute should arise, he must take an oath upon his life, then go into an ascetic retreat to protect himself and his kinsmen. Junior siblings are not subjected to these spiritual constraints, although they are bound to serve periodic homage to their priest.

Junior brothers do, however, gain some spiritual independence when they establish their own households. If the father is dead and the senior son has "brought his father into the house," his junior brothers may also "bring the ghosts into their houses," setting up altars and mediating relations in their own households through their own personal ɔfɔ staffs. This gives them spiritual control over their personal property and relationships. However, they remain perpetually dependent upon their senior patrilineage priest for the slaughtering of animals and for access to all other joint rights devolving from the father, rights that include all forms of sharing among the siblings and that may be voided by a declaration of ostracism. Moreover, the ɔfɔ diɔkpala that control more senior segment levels of patrilineages tend to include control of mediation with the powerful spirits associated with these patrilineages. Senior patrilineage priests control access to the shrines of some of most fearsome spirits in the locality.

Aside from the serial hierarchy of lineage priests, the Onitsha patrilineage is organized by a twofold division of labor between "elders" (*ńdi-ìkenye*) and "youths" (*ʊ́mʊ̀-ílo,* "children of the square"), a division defined by the criterion of marriage. These two categories operate as subcollectivities which in some circumstances orient to one another as units. The unmarried youths have precise collective duties to perform. They are subject to the authority of their elders in the performance of these duties, but they also have clearly defined rights to be rewarded by shares of ritual wealth, and are capable of going on strike against the elders if they believe their rights are being violated. The married elders join as a unit with their senior priest to arrive at decisions affecting the entire patrilineage, and each elder has the right to an equivalent "share" (*òke*) when parts of the patrilineage estate are divided. When, however, kola is divided, whether real or symbolic (e.g. kola for talk), equivalence does not apply to the senior priest. He may appropriate as large a share as he sees fit, even if by doing so he "maltreats" his fellows.

The Roles of Daughters in the Patrilineage

A daughter (*nwa-ada*) is expected to act toward her father in a manner formally similar to that of a son, with the perpetual duty of serving homage. Display of her potential sexual role before her father is forbidden, for persons interacting under a common ɔfɔ cannot intermarry, and sexual play among persons linked by direct filiation or as siblings is an abomination. So long as a daughter performs her appropriate service and remains a proper subject of his ɔfɔ, the father can never deny her refuge in his house in times of need, and he must act as her protector against the world. The disposition of the daughter is largely in his hands, for he must approve her marriage, set and accept the terms of exchange which send her out of her natal home, and accept her in his charge should she find a marriage unbearable. When the father dies, his daughters must play a major part in defining the meaning of his death and in ensuring that his funeral is properly completed.

The relationship among a man's daughters and sons is similarly ascriptive and irrevocable. According to an Onitsha proverb, "on the day of the sibling [nwanne], one's lover departs"; among other things this reflects the overriding ascriptive right which sisters have to the attentions of their brothers. When a man is single, it is believed that a sister is likely to drive his paramours away in order to retain his affections for herself; the senior sister knows that when a man marries, the obligatory symbolic gift of the kidneys of any animal killed by him must go no longer to her but to his senior wife. Once a man is married, his sister watches carefully that his wife meets all her connubial obligations. No man can deny his sister refuge in times of need, and he is expected to be willing both to help her in her trade and to be one of her regular "exchange partners" (*ónye-áfia*). It is a woman's duty to feed her brothers when they visit her, to see that they are at peace with one another and faring well, and to render periodic homage service to the senior patrifilial brother. If her father has died, that senior brother stands in his place.

An Onitsha proverb states that "the body of the sibling stings," indicating that the affection between brother and sister must always be asexual. This asexual quality gives a man's paternal sister the right to enter her brother's house and ritually purify it, an act which men of the patrilineage and their wives cannot do because they are contaminated by their past or potential passions and sexual intimacies. Among the wider range of agnatic "daughters" (ʊmʊ-ada) of the patrilineage, "father's senior daughters" through their control of the ɔfɔ-isi-ada gain the right not only to "calm the [patrilineage] houses" (*ɩ́jʊ̀ ʊ́nɔ̀*), but also to enforce the making of peace between disputing patrilineage segments, to supervise the wives of their collective "brothers," and to subject these wives to ritual ordeals of confession on a number of occasions. Should a wife give "bad mouth" to her husband or to the daughters, the latter may declare a forbidden act, and seize the offender's cooking utensils until she ritually revokes the act and pays a fine; if they dislike her sufficiently they can have her ejected from the lineage premises.

The daughters control a variety of ritual prerogatives that define acts necessary to the spiritual health of the patrilineage, and all these prerogatives are predicated on the daughters' asexual role in controlling the "head daughter's ɔfɔ." When a new wife enters the patrilineage fold, the senior daughter must subject her to a confession of her prior sexual exploits and must then "cleanse" the husband in his introduction to the strangeness of his wife's sexuality. The senior daughter must perform a similar ceremony for every pubescent child of the lineage; she tests the child's knowledge of basic ancestral customs and cleanses him of his "strangeness" to lineage affairs. If a person has committed any abomination which contaminates his house, the senior priestess of the patrilineage must perform the "oath [quenching] the fire" (*íyi ɔ́kʊ*) which makes his presence dangerous, by beating a fowl around his body so that the bird absorbs the "heat" of his condition. Finally, the daughters play a fundamental role in the funerals of all patrilineage members. Only they can wash the corpse, for their ɔfɔ protects them from sexual or other attack by the newly dead and angry ghost. They must utter the double-edged curse against the supposed killer of the deceased.

The daughters possess a simple but strong formal organization which partially parallels that of the men of the patrilineage. The head daughter's position reflects that of her senior lineage priest and is dependent upon it, for as the status of senior lineage priest rotates, the new priest confers the ɔfɔ-isi-ada upon his own senior agnatic sister or her nearest equivalent. The close administrative relationship between the priest and his priestess makes it convenient for her and her juniors to mediate disputes that may arise between the priest and other members of the patrilineage. The ɔfɔ of the senior daughter gives its holder the right to receive periodic homage from the daughters, and portions of animals, palm wine, and other sacrifices which are then shared with her senior priest as he shares patrilineage tribute with her.

The daughters are further organized in terms of a status dichotomy between unmarried, pubescent girls (*ʊ́mʊ̀-àgbɔ́*) and married daughters (ʊmʊ-ada proper). The pubescent girls form an organization emulating the activities of the married daughters. Both groups learn, practice, and perform funeral dances for the lineage, and each group marches en masse about the village when one of its members dies. The married daughters themselves are roughly divided into two groups according to age as measured by the attainment of menopause, and the ɔfɔ-isi-ada can be held only by a woman who has passed child bearing age. Should a woman who still menstruates occupy the prime genealogical position for holding this object, she must delegate her right to a more elderly woman. All daughters are expected to bring homage tribute when visiting such senior women.

The most striking feature of the norms defining patrilineal roles and collectivities is the extent to which the "children of a father" are inextricably bound together in a set of genealogically designated roles that perpetuate their common filial dependence on paternal "righteous power." Remarkably, both male and female members share control of the spiritual authority that underlies their interdependence, which is irrevocable and all-embracing. The basic role structure is linked to the statuses of "senior sons" and "senior daughters," but not all the internal organization of the patrilineage is spelled out in the kinship terminology. Important divisions are based on marital status, physical age, and other factors.

SETTLEMENT PATTERNS, PROPERTY, AND PATRILINEAGE STRUCTURE

Thus far in Onitsha kinship, the normative structures of agnatic relationships have been grounded solely in the superordinate direction of cultural ideology and religion. The institutions of agnatic kinship must be grounded as well in the ecological relationships of people located in physical space. The ecology of Ibo-speaking groups in the Onitsha area has some distinctive properties and tendencies, and it will be illuminating to consider Onitsha ecology both in terms of its history and in terms of its formal similarity to the various patterns of community settlement in the neighboring Ibo hinterlands.

In Chapter 2 the geographical position of Onitsha was briefly described as a meeting point between eastern uplands and riverain lowlands (see Figures 3, 5, and 6). The uplands which extend from the east to reach the Niger at this point are covered with "acid sands," free-draining, red-to-orange loamy sands derived from an underlying mantle of red or yellow earth which in turn is the product of deep tropical weathering of lower sandstones and clays. These acid sands are low in organic material, high in iron content, and easily leached; near Onitsha outcroppings of ironstone indicate how readily leaching and bacterial action can produce extensive soil laterization and sterility. Although rainfall levels and temperature conditions are sufficiently high to encourage rapid growth of a wide variety of crops as well as natural secondary vegetation, this soil rapidly deteriorates once it is exposed to the eroding effects of the tropical climate. In any event it cannot sustain successive plantings of food crops without extended fallowing to permit soil regeneration. Since approximately ninety percent of the rain falls between early April and late October, and often comes in violent and damaging storms, both runoff control and waterlogging of the soil can be chronic problems to farmers in various areas. On the other hand, although the average humidity is over seventy percent, there is insufficient moisture during the dry season to support planted crops, and therefore during this period little planting or growing of the staple yams can occur, because tubers are likely to decay if they are left in the ground.[11]

These conditions obtain over most of the leached Onitsha hinterlands, which the Ibo call "white lands" (anι ɔcha) after the predominant soil coloration further in the interior. Different ecological conditions hold in the adjacent lowlands floodplain, variously called olu or *ádàgbe*. These lowlands, which include part of the Anambra and Mamu River drainage system, contain lateritic soils annually subjected to flooding and silt refertilization. They tend to be waterlogged, pose great difficulties of habitation, and have

11. Jones (1961) has described the essentials of this pattern.

therefore always been underpopulated, even though in recent years they have increasingly borne the burden of staple food production for the whole region. The recent distribution of population density in the Onitsha vicinity correlates closely with this topographical division, as may be seen in Figure 5. Since the Onitsha people have always farmed mostly on the uplands, the following description concentrates on the uplands pattern.

Lacking sufficient livestock to maintain stable fertilization of their farms, the uplands Ibo devote most of their effort to swidden hoe cultivation of yams. Each year a new plot of ground is cleared of saplings and undergrowth, and the debris is then burned to produce a layer of ash which neutralizes the acid soil and provides important plant food minerals. Holes are dug at intervals, and ash-rich topsoil is scraped into them. A corm-bearing portion of yam tuber is planted in each hole and a mound of soil including twigs and leaves is scraped up over it with an iron hoe, to about eighteen inches in height and two feet in diameter. Long poles are stuck into the mounds to support the climbing stems. Intercropping is begun after the yam has sprouted, with yam-beans (*ókpodùdu,* Sphenostylis stenocarpa) planted on the mound and trained onto the pole, and maize (*ɔ́kà,* Zea mays) and cotton (*òwú,* Gossypium spp.) planted between the mounds. Later, when the yam stalks are growing well on the poles, cassava may be planted in the same fields, to be harvested in the following year.

This intercropping pattern is said traditionally to have produced high initial yields. The mounds insure sufficient drainage to protect the yam tuber from rotting, while the intercrops provide some protection for the mounds. However, the soil is rapidly exhausted by such cultivation, although if cassava or cotton is not interplanted it may be possible to repeat planting in the following year, a practice called *igbu ogbo,* "cultivating the same place." Ordinarily, in the following year, a "new farm" (*úgbo ɔ́fʊ*) must be cleared. Previously cultivated land is then fallowed, if possible until the secondary growth has reached a height of about fifteen feet, at which time the saplings are long enough to be used for yam support poles. Five to seven years is the desired fallow period, which means that each farming unit should have half a dozen available plots, but in few areas of the white lands is this length of fallow possible.

Centuries of swidden horticulture on the uplands around Onitsha have produced what Keay has called "derived savannah" vegetation, an open bush with heavy concentration of oil palms (*ńkwʋ*, Elaeis guineensis), interspersed with areas of high grassland (*ɔ̀zala*) resulting from overconcentration of swiddens, insufficient fallowing, and repeated firing of grasses.[12] The area with thickest oil palm distribution is coextensive with that of heaviest population density and severest soil deterioration. Only the sporadic patches of relict forest around villages and in sacred groves provide evidence that the original climax vegetation was high semideciduous forest.[13]

One cannot understand the horticultural and settlement patterns of this region without recognizing that Ibo draw major, ecologically relevant distinctions between "houseland" (*ànɩ-ʋ́nɔ̀*) and "farmland" (*ànɩ-úgbo*), and between these two and wild bush or forest (*ɔ́fia*). The latter is symbolically cold and fearsome, the former two relatively warm and predictable.

The distinction between houseland and farmland coincides with a contrast between relatively "intensive" (permanently cultivated plots) and "extensive" (recurrently cultivated swidden) horticulture. This contrast is also symbolically important, delineating somewhat different spheres of land tenure regulation and different patterns of forbidden activity. In Onitsha belief, farmland and houseland should ideally be separated in space, for somewhat different spiritual forces control the two areas. Farmland is the home of the yam spirit (*ɩ̀fejíɔkʋ*), who is believed to abhor the presence of women, and it is forbidden for them to sleep where

12. Keay (1949).
13. Grove (1951:15–19).

he resides; banana trees (ɔ*gede,* Musa sapientum), the symbols of the domestic domain of small children, should not be grown on farmland. Residence land, in contrast, is the proper domain for women and small children; banana trees are grown there, and taro, exclusively a woman's plant, is grown in household gardens along with a variety of condiments, spices, and vegetables planted and tended mainly by women. In the household vicinity, domestic refuse is used to fertilize the soil so that perennial cultivation is feasible.

It should not be inferred, however, that this dichotomy is followed rigidly. A man may ritually establish the yam spirit in a corner of his compound, in a small area forbidden to women, and he may grow some of his prize yams there where they can be fertilized by household refuse. Residential land is the domain where most of the economically valuable trees—oil palm, kola, kapok (*ákpʊ,* Ceiba pentandra), breadfruit (*ʊ́kwà,* Treculia africana), iroko (ɔ́*jì,* Clorophora excelsa), native pear (*ùbé,* Pachylobus edulis), star apple (*ʊ́dalà,* Chrysophyllum africanum, C. albidum), calabash (ɔ́*bà,* Lagenaria vulgaris), black plum (*ele-de,* Vitex cienkowski), etc.—are selectively preserved, and most (though by no means all) of these trees are controlled by men who have planted or preserved them. Women, on the other hand, do participate in farmland cultivation and they have partial claims on the cotton harvested there; however, farmland is viewed as a zone transitional to dangerous wild bush (a domain mostly reserved for men), and is therefore more suitable for men to work in than for women. Few economically valuable trees survive the burning of farmland areas, unless they have been left long in fallow, in which cases there may be in an area several transitions between relatively treeless farmland to fallows that have reverted to thick bush. In contrast, in the village, where large trees have been preserved or planted (according to various rules of location), the land has the appearance of a controlled form of forest.

The ideal traditional Ibo settlement pattern is a group of villages on high ground, clustered around a village-group center but sufficiently dispersed among mazes of walled or fenced gardens to make effective surprise attacks difficult. Extending out from each residential nucleus, and away from the community center, lies an expanding segment of farmland controlled exclusively by that village, as schematized in Figure 22.

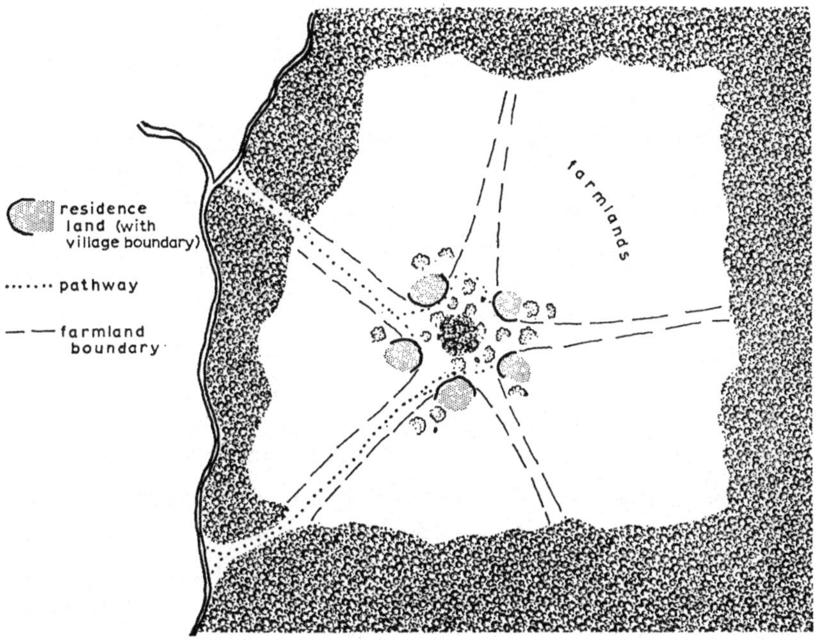

Fig. 22 Ideal Ibo settlement pattern, colonization phase

This pattern of clustered settlements, each abutting on unoccupied land segments radiating outward, is regulated by the fundamental principles of Ibo land tenure so well described by G. I. Jones:

> that the land ultimately belongs to the community and cannot be alienated from it without its consent; that within the community the individual shall have security of tenure for the land

> he requires for his compounds, his gardens, and his farms; and that no members of the community shall be without land.[14]

As Jones has observed, this settlement pattern serves

> to allow a number of villages to live reasonably close together as a single local community and yet be able to expand without too much friction. It achieves this by zoning them around one or more than one central meeting place and at the same time giving each village the right to occupy the land extending in a specific direction away from this centre.[15]

Since each village is, ideally, a patrilineage, the expansion of each lineage unit will be directed away from other such units, rather than colliding or intermingling with them. As a result, "the correlation between the territorial and lineage structure is closer among the Ibo than among many other Nigerian peoples, for, following the layout pattern, all expansion of a maximal lineage has to be contained within the lineage territory." [16]

This settlement pattern has certain ecological limitations imposed by the conditions of farming and population density. Since the major portion of village food is obtained from the farmland and not from the houseland, the major economic decisions concern the swidden cycle. Toward the end of the dry season, the collective decision must be made about which sector of the farmland will be cleared for new farms. Since the clearing of overgrown fallow land requires massive labor, the work is done by all adult males of the patrilineage unit. After the bush has been cleared and fired, the land is divided into family plots and planting begins. Planting and building of yam mounds must be done hurriedly once the rainy season begins, because the torrential rains erode the mounds and engender rapid weed growth. This means that a relatively brief period of planting is quickly superseded by a long

14. Jones (1949:313).
15. Ibid., p. 310.
16. Ibid., p. 311.

period of tending the mounds, collecting and erecting the support poles, and removing the weeds which spring up amid the various crops. As the yams ripen, the major task of harvesting follows, for they must be removed from the soil to prevent rotting, and large open but sheltered barns must be constructed to protect and aerate the tubers. After harvest, a period of enforced idleness follows.

These problems and conditions severely limit the amount of planting, and therefore the size of farm, that a given number of people can handle. Much more labor time must be expended in preparing the fields, collecting and erecting stakes, weeding, and harvesting than can be applied to the planting process.[17] Since the Ibo householder seeks to plant the maximum amount of land he can possibly manage, this is a very important limitation.

The second limiting condition concerns population pressure. As population increases, residence land expands into the contiguous farmland more or less automatically. As farmland becomes scarcer, the lineage units must send their members further into the peripheral bush to clear new farms. This extension in distance cannot continue indefinitely, because the requirements of continual tending of the farms make it uneconomical for farmers to traverse great distances between their homes and their farm plots. Moreover, the community will inevitably encounter the peripheral farm lands of other communities, and boundary definition will become a problem.

Jones has distinguished three evolutionary stages in this ecological relationship between an Ibo community and its land.[18] In the initial, and ideal, "colonizing" stage, the compact residential units of the community lay claim to unoccupied peripheral lands for subsistence exploitation. Under such conditions of low community population and requirements of deforestation for farmland, the nucleated community provides advantages for purposes of defense, while collective control of farmland meets the heavy labor require-

17. Jones (1961:119).
18. Jones (1949:310).

ments of forest clearing. During this stage, as the Ibo state it, community demand is for more people rather than for more land.

As population increases, new problems emerge. Since some villages or village segments may increase in population more rapidly than others, advantages accrue to land-pressured but enterprising individuals or subgroups who go to the peripheries of communally controlled lands and clear their own farms independently of village control. Through this and other processes, farmland control begins to subdivide below the village level. Also, as the community confronts the peripheral lands of other village-groups, boundaries are defined and the territorial limits of the community become established. This may be characterized as the "consolidation" stage of settlement pattern. Later in this stage, when the distance from residence to major farm plots of a subvillage (whether these plots are controlled directly by the subgroup or "leased" from other village groups) becomes too great for effective continual cultivation, subgroups begin to "hive off" from the parental nucleus, establishing new residential nuclei in the midst of their farmland. This process is diagrammed in Figure 23. Such nuclei may retain their membership in the parent village, but if distances are great enough and the subgroup can attract sufficient population, new villages may be established.

Ultimately, if the population continues to increase, the expansion of houseland absorbs farmland until all lands of the community have become filled with residences amid surrounding household gardens. Under these conditions, effective day-to-day land control becomes highly individualized since clearing of forest is no longer a communal labor problem, although ultimate disposal of residence land remains in the hands of the village. Onitsha people would say that "land has now become more valued than people."[19]

19. This tendency to individualize land holdings in houseland correlates with the intensive horticulture practiced there and with the distinctive labor requirements entailed by this kind of cultivation. Cf. Netting (1965).

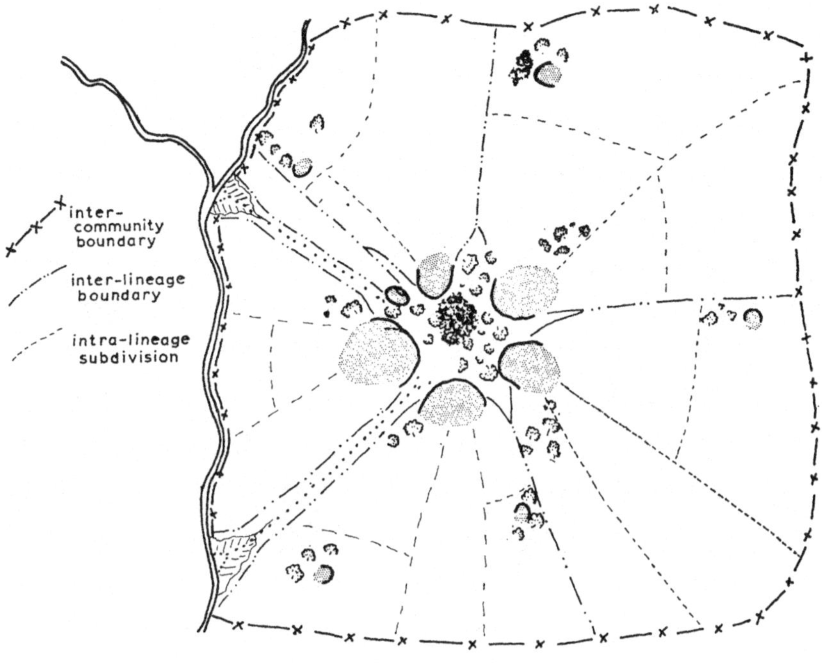

Fig. 23 Ibo settlement pattern, consolidation phase

Soil fertility decreases under such pressure until the community is no longer self-sufficient in subsistence. This has been characterized by Jones as the "disintegration" stage of settlement pattern; it exists in communities like Nnewi in the Onitsha hinterland, where the population has reached densities of over one thousand per square mile. In recent times, communities at this ecological stage have handled their land problems by seasonal farming migration into adjacent lowlands or by urban emigration, but in precolonial times various forms of economic specialization and trade were undertaken. The oil palm, nurtured in increasing quantities in the diffusely settled gardens of such communities, acquired greatly enhanced importance as a trade crop, while various towns specialized in such pursuits as iron-working, weaving, doctoring, and, formerly, slave-trading.

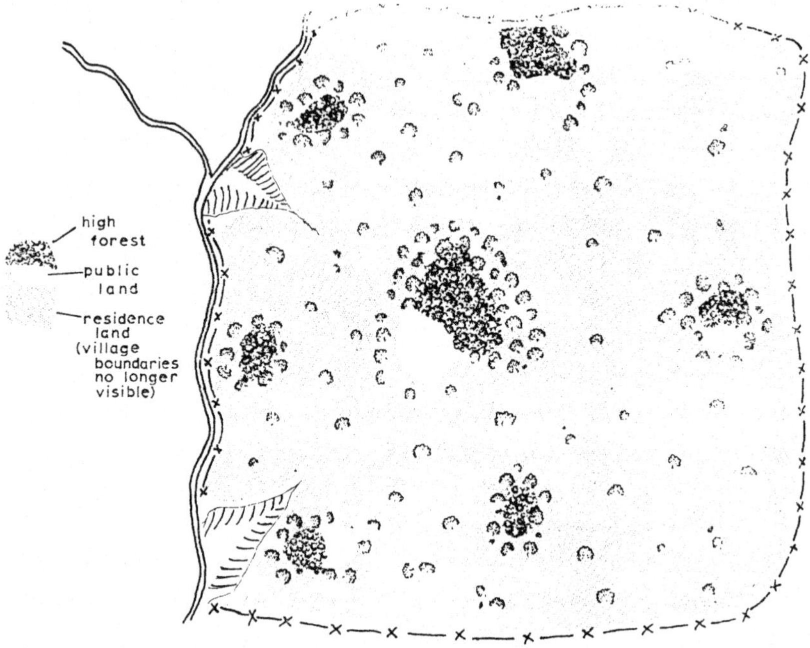

Fig. 24 Ibo settlement pattern, disintegration phase

This discussion of changing settlement patterns has direct relevance for the Onitsha community. Reference to Figures 12 and 13 will confirm that the Onitsha settlement pattern has not been static; there is indication of an early "hiving off" of settlement clusters during the period of the early kings (c. 1600–1700), followed by a contraction of the community into a nucleated pattern during the uplands–Aro period (c. 1780–1880). The following analysis deals with land occupation patterns obtaining at about 1880.

Residence Land and the "Ancestral House"

In its ideological definition, each Onitsha village (ogbe) is regarded as a patrilineage unit (ʊmʊnna). Therefore the social order of the village is ideally regulated under the ɔfɔ of its senior lineage priest. In Onitsha belief the identification of a man's personal rights with his ɔfɔ ɔkpala is part of his identification with his personal locality of land and with an "ancestral house" (*ìba*). All villages are ordered in terms of structured relationships between residence land and ancestral houses.

The Onitsha ancestral house (Figure 25) differs from those of

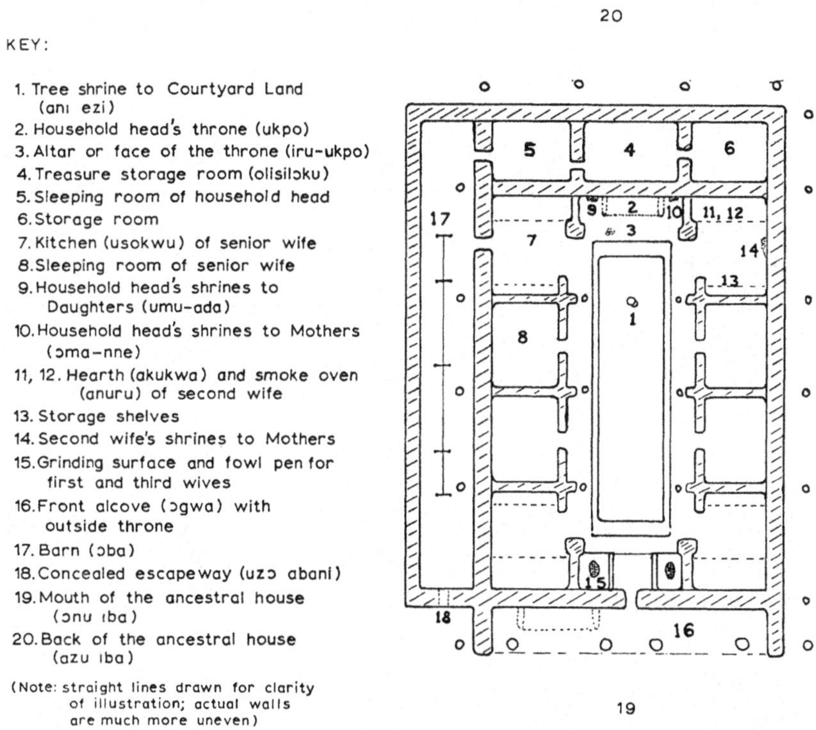

Fig. 25 Structural features of the ancestral house (ıba)

contiguous Ibo peoples, but it resembles houses of the Western Ibo, Benin, and Yoruba.[20] Unlike the simple thatched single-gable mud rectangles built for young men, resident divorced daughters, or slaves, the ancestral house is constructed around an open-air interior courtyard. A long rectangle of coursed-mud wall is laid, with an entry door at one end. Inside, extensive mud living sur-

20. See Mbanefo (1962).

faces are raised along each wall, leaving a depressed central rectangular area which contains a living egbo tree dedicated as a shrine to the spirit of the courtyard land (ànι-èzí). This central courtyard is drained by a small slab-lined tunnel (*úlòlo*) which runs under the front end of the house. Each wall, with its associated raised interior living surface, is protected by a full gabled roof of thatch, supported on the outside and inside both by walls and adjacent wooden support pillars. The interior gables drain into the sunlit central courtyard.

Externally the ancestral house has a fortress-like appearance, for its interior is illuminated solely by light falling into the court from above. It has a single doored entryway, outside which is a sheltered, mud-surfaced alcove (*ɔ́gwa*), containing a mud bench. The alcove faces out over a clean-swept open meeting space, called "the mouth of the ancestral house" (*ɔ́nʊ ìba*).

Inside, the ancestral house is oriented around two major unifying features, the central courtyard about which domestic life revolves and the "throne" (ukpo) of the household head or patrilineage priest. The throne, a symbol of prestige superiority that raises the priest above the surfaces on which his congregation sits, is situated at the opposite end from the entry door and faces toward it. Before the throne is a structured floor surface called "the face of the throne" (iru-ukpo), the altar where the objects representing the ancestral ghosts, personal god, and spirits are placed during ceremonies.

Behind the throne is a specially constructed room, the "storage place for wealth" (*ófili* or olisiliɔkʊ), which is protected with thick mud walls on all sides and a mud-covered bamboo ceiling intended to make it fireproof. Major treasures and shrine objects controlled by the household head are stored in this room. To the right of this room is the household head's sleeping room, and to the left is another storage room for various implements, medicines, drums and other patrilineage and personal properties.

The throne and courtyard provided a unifying center for social life. Each morning, the household head occupies his ritual seat; he is brought water to wash his hands, breaks kola, and, throwing a piece of kola out to the land shrine tree, prays to the great god, to his personal god, and to the courtyard land to preserve the life of himself and his household subjects.[21] At each evening meal, he receives dishes of food from his various wives and calls his children to kneel before him and receive ritually blessed gifts of food. On ceremonial occasions, he sits on the throne to preside over the prayers to the ancestors and spirits, while his congregation sits on the ledges running around the courtyard.

If throne and courtyard unify the ancestral house, the kitchens (*ùsókwu*) of the various wives divide it into domestic segments. Each wife has a separate cooking and sleeping area along the flanks of the courtyard. The kitchen of the senior wife (*ànasi*) is symbolically located to the right of her husband's throne to express seniority, that of the second to its left. Additional wives occupy spaces near the entry door. The kitchen of each wife centers around the hearth (*ákìvukwa*), a tripod of clay-covered stones on which cooking pots are placed; the children of a woman are identified with this hearth, being referred to as akwukwa Nweke (if the mother's personal name is Nweke), since they all eat from a common dish of food cooked at this hearth. Over each hearth is constructed a mud-lined, bamboo floored storage bin (*ánʊrʊ̀*), which serves as a smoke-oven for drying and preserving corn, meat, and other perishable foods. Each wife also has her own storage shelves (*àkpáta*) for storing her water pots. Near these may be personal shrines dedicated to her "mothers" (ɔma-nne or ndi-nne), a series of mud lumps placed along the floor by a wall.

Beside the entry door are facilities shared by the wives, i.e. one or two mud-lined boxes for keeping domestic fowl, on top of which are grinding stones and other shared domestic utensils.

21. The shrine to the spirit of courtyard land is closely associated both with the personal god of its founder and with the great god. Its tree links them to the land itself. Prayer addressed to this shrine consistently refers to the "Olisa who supports the world."

Alongside the main house structure to its right is a mud-walled roofless enclosure which contains a pole-rack "barn" (*ɔ́ba*) for storing yams in the open air, and along one wall there are pens for keeping goats at night. To the rear of the structure extends an open area, the "back of the ancestral house" (*àzʊ́-ɩba*), which is usually fenced with living egbo saplings to form an enclosed garden "compound" (*ògige,* literally "fenced").

Thus the ancestral house represents a self-contained center of polygynous family separateness, and much of Onitsha life is conducted within its boundaries. It may also become a church for a wider patrilineage sphere. When it is used for such purposes, the wives are dismissed, while the congregation of lineage elders assembles to sit along the bench perimeters of the courtyard and the unmarried young men sit as guards along the external alcove. If a very large meeting is to be held, the priest uses the alcove bench as his throne and the congregation sits at the mouth of the ancestral house. In its entirety, the ancestral house is regarded as a holy place; in various ceremonial contexts—the daily ritual washing of its external walls, the seasonal rubbing of live fowl and white snail shell along its walls to relieve it of pollution, even the actual damaging of it during a funeral—it is treated like a human body.

The ancestral house (and its associated gardens) has a natural history in terms of occupation and usage. A young man lives with and works for his father until he can obtain his first wife; but by the time he marries he should have constructed an independent house, preferably on the compound land of his father. Initially, the father allocates land in the back of the ancestral house to each of his wives as "household gardens" (ugbo ʊnɔ), with each garden fenced to keep out goats. When a boy attains the position of young man (*òkólɔbìa*), he departs from his mother's quarters and is authorized by his father to build a "house of [elephant] grass" (*ʊ́nɔ̀ àchala*) in his mother's garden land. There he sleeps and there his mother sends his daily meals. When he is ready to marry, this "stick house" may be replaced with a permanent mud-walled structure. Even if the son chooses to build this structure within his father's household gardens, he must seek out the senior lineage priest of the widest range of patrilineage group from which he will also require assistance in house construction, so that this priest can perform the ritual of "softening the land" (*íkpʋba-ànɩ*).

If the lineage priest agrees, he arranges a meeting of the lineage males at the site of the new house. The supplicant (represented by his father, if he is alive) presents a hen (since the female land requires female animals), palm wine, white cloth, kola nuts, and a small live stick of the egbo tree. The lineage priest plants the tree that marks the site of the courtyard land, raises a small clay mound beside it, "dresses" it with white cloth to exalt its purity, presents it with chalk food, then sacrifices a hen, sprinkling its blood over tree and clay altar. He calls the ancestors and lineage members present to share in the feast venerating this land, and to witness the identification between the land and the new householder. At such ritual occasions, the lineage elders specify the extent of the area that the builder will be expected to maintain, corresponding to the land spirit which sanctions his area of control.

This "softening the land" for a household demonstrates a set of mutual concessions made by the participants. It indicates that the land on which a house stands is part of the general spiritual domain of the senior lineage priest at a certain level of lineage segmentation, thereby marking the householder's obligation to pay homage service (directly or indirectly) to this priest and to observe the obligatory sharing of fire, hospitality, and trade that are articles of faith among the members of the lineage and their wives. Simultaneously, it commits all members of the lineage to recognizing and upholding the householder's inviolable rights to this land: one portion of the residential area is now identified with him and his personal god; he can never be evicted from it unless he sins against the land itself, whose spiritual forces have become in a sense an extension of his own moral right.

Thus there is a close relation between the ɔfɔ ɔkpala of each man and the land of the household that he has established, which gives him "righteous power" over his household area, so long as he observes its morality. Within that sphere, his personal ɔfɔ is dominant "as against the world"; his children and his wives are under its spiritual control. This legal separation of each paternal household from all others may be viewed as a correlative of the important symbolic distinction between first-degree and further-degree kinsmen in Onitsha kinship.

Such a structure may not become an ancestral house, and it will not initially be built in the appropriate form for such a holy place. The usual form for a subsidiary house is a single-gabled rectangle, with the land shrine located outside its entry door. Even if this house falls apart from age, however, the tree remains to mark its site and its founder's sons hold a perpetual right to occupy that residence land. What actually happens to any house depends on patterns of death in the patrilineage.

The ideal order of succession to occupation of an ancestral house follows the model of ɔfɔ ɔkpala. Figure 26 suggests the ideal pattern.

Assume that A occupies a house which he has constructed, and has allotted to each of his two wives garden areas which they have cultivated. His senior son B has established his separate house in the garden of his mother, A's second wife. Later B's junior agnatic brother C establishes a house in the garden of his mother, who is A's first wife. The senior son must always marry first in any agnatic household, regardless of the seniority of wives. B raises a son D, and C raises a son E; each son first lives with his father but later establishes a separate house in a subsection of his father's garden land.

When A dies, he is buried inside his own house, which by virtue

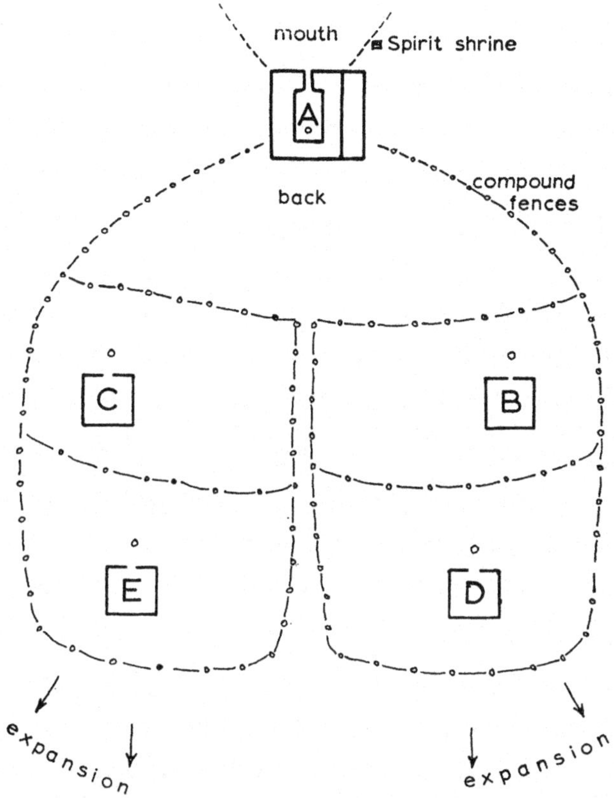

Fig. 26 Ideal succession to the ancestral house

of that fact becomes his ancestral house. After his funerals have been completed, senior son B is entitled to take control of his father's ɔfɔ, and he therefore moves out of his own house and occupies the ancestral house of A. He may take all his wives with him, or he may leave one or more of them in his own house. Since the father's house has become a "house of death" (ʊnɔ ɔnwʊ), all the ancestral shrines which A kept have become "hot" in anger over the death and have therefore been removed to an outside shed. B must go about the process of "bringing his father into the house," thereby "cooling" these ancestral objects and gaining the right to communicate with them. Once they are reinstated into the ancestral house, B has the right to receive periodic tribute from C and D as the senior lineage priest of A.

When B dies, he will also be buried in the ancestral house. When his funerals have been completed, C will then leave his own house and go to occupy the ancestral house, while B's son D will move into B's original house. C will "bring in his father A," and D will "bring in his father B." When C dies, he too will be buried in the ancestral house to be occupied by D and ultimately by E.

Thus in theory, even as the patrilineage grows and the number of personally owned houses increases, one ancestral house remains the focus of an ever-widening range of lineage interests. Since responsibility for the welfare of widows falls primarily upon the succeeding patrilineage priests, and since expansion of lineage affairs converts the original ancestral house into a continually utilized assembly hall, the lineage members will expand the barn structure into a second major chamber (duplicating the structural features of the original house) to provide domestic space for wives, children, and widows. This will be reserved for affairs of the priest's immediate family, while the original ancestral house will be used more and more for meetings of wider segmental scope. In time, this ancestral house may expand into a multi-chambered structure. Such a structure is called "the great ancestral house" (*n̄nukwu ìba*).

Each of the major chambers of this structure serves both as a church and as a court (ikpe) for the patrilineage segment attached to it. In the primary chamber, disputes between members of the maximal patrilineage are heard and judged by the senior patrilineage priest, while the lower-order chambers serve as courts of lower-order segments, presided over by the same person acting as priest of a less distant ancestor. The higher the level at which a dispute is heard, the more public it becomes; commission of an abomination is more likely to be openly proclaimed in a great court than a small one, and the associated shame will be more widely publicized.

As a holy place, the ancestral house becomes an object of special veneration. The ritual "rubbing" and decorating of its surfaces becomes a communal concern, and the area comprising its "mouth" is cleared by the patrilineage youth to become a playground as well as a meeting place for elders. Special clusters of ritually significant trees are planted about its flanks, and communal medicines and spirits are enshrined along its margins.

The expansion of patrilineage residence occurs toward the "back" of the ancestral house. Areas outside the fenced compounds or gardens are classed as "latrine land" (*ànι-òwele*), for it is in such marginal areas that fecal matter is deposited and domestic animals are allowed to wander. Such areas are considered houseland, and the first step of expansion into it is ordinarily the planting or claiming of valuable economic trees there. Eventually E of Figure 26, for example, may require additional garden lands for one of his wives, and he must obtain permission, through a conclave presided over by the senior patrilineage priest, to extend his fencing into the latrine land. Thereafter one of his sons may build a house there.

Thus the residence pattern of the Onitsha patrilineage combines an unambiguous focus of social unity with open possibilities for segmented expansion. As a symbol system, it formulates a model of persons (ancestral houses) facing towards a common center. As a social system, it operates to insure the continuity of social patterns predicated on the ascriptive values represented by paternal ɔfɔ; a man has only to "stand and wait," serving homage to his senior patrilineage priest, until in time he too will occupy and be buried in the ancestral house.

However, for a variety of reasons there may come a time when the great ancestral house is abandoned to fall into decay, and this development represents a crucial change in residential pattern. The continued occupation of any house depends upon a proper spiritual relationship with the land on which it stands, and a major index of this relationship is the incidence of deaths among patrilineage members. If many people occupying the area around an ancestral house die, and worse, if they die out of proper order, the belief must inevitably arise that the vicinity of the house has become a "fiery surface" (iru ɔkʊ) for its occupants, that the land is angry about their immorality and is killing them. When this occurs, the family abandons the house, leaving only the growing egbo tree which represents the land spirit. Bush will be allowed to grow up in the avoided location.

In general, bush (ɔfia) is regarded as dangerous wilderness by Onitsha people, but some kinds of bush are more dangerous than others. Beyond the peripheral limits of residential latrine land, and enroute to the village farms, each Onitsha village maintains, by avoidance, an area of uncultivated woodlands called "bad bush" (ajɔ ɔfia). This is used as a dumping-ground for dangerous things. The shaved hairs of children, nail parings, and other magically dangerous substances are deposited there. More important, corpses of "abominable infants"[22] and persons who have died "bad deaths" (ajɔ ɔnwʊ) because of their imputed sins are cast without burial into this bush, and their "bad ghosts" (ajɔ mmʊɔ) are believed to lurk therein. Such an area of bad bush may in time come to be identified as the residence of a powerful spirit.

The site of an abandoned ancestral house is ipso facto a residence of spirit, for it contains the shrine tree marking the location of the original courtyard land of the founder. As an uninhabited area, it serves as a dumping-ground for persons whose bad deaths have been divined as caused by offenses against that land spirit. When the forest grows up in that area it is regarded as the "[sacred] grove of the land" (*òkwú ànɩ*), a grove inhabited by bad ghosts and other dangerous forces. Powerful protective medicines made by native doctors may be deposited there for safekeeping, thus adding to its awesome nature. Paradoxically, this fearsome and forbidden forest, located near extant villages and full of vile and terrible things, is regarded as the source of a power to

22. See Basden (1938:262–63) for a list of types.

protect as well as to destroy the people associated with it. It is viewed with veneration as the source of local morality and power. It is an object of continual active worship.

Cases have been recorded in Onitsha tradition in which entire village areas have been abandoned as "fiery surface," but more commonly only the ancestral house is abandoned. Thus the land of a village has a natural history depending on the kinds of deaths which have occurred on it. Many modes of death are distinguished by Onitsha people.[23] There are a number of kinds of outright "bad death": a death associated with swelling or prior rotting of certain portions of the body, death from smallpox, death as a consequence of witchcraft conviction, and so on. Any child who dies under the age of six and before its mother has borne another baby is regarded as a capriciously reincarnating infantile ghost (*ɔ̀gbánje*). Such beings were traditionally, in the words of the first Christian missionary in Onitsha,

> put into an earthen pot, squeezed into the narrow shell, and sometimes the limbs are cut off to make the shoulders get in. This being done, they are carried and thrown out into the fields, a prey to the multitude of vultures that are soaring over the country.[24]

More generally, any death which violates seniority order in the patrilineage is regarded as a kind of "abomination," but degrees of violation are distinguished, and various categories of residence land are in a sense defined by the kinds of corpses which may be interred in them. Any child who dies young, but has "encouraged" a junior sibling to be borne after himself, is a "child who brought child" (*nwá sɔ̀lu nwá*). He is buried with a proper two-stage funeral, beside the "mouth" of the ancestral house, where his ghost may observe his living contemporaries playing there and eating the

23. Noon (1944) lists Onitsha categories of death.

24. Aside from this very early account in Crowther and Taylor (1859:308), some other early reports suggest that the corpses of such children might be beheaded and burned to forestall reincarnation. See George (n.d.:018/19).

bananas from their trees growing there. A young man who dies before marriage without any other evidence of bad death may be buried within the area of his father's compound fences. However, any man, married or unmarried, who dies in the presence of his father (*ɔ́nwʊ n̄a íru ńnàya*), thereby commits a muted form of abominable act; he cannot be buried in his father's ancestral house, but may if married be buried in his own residence if he shows no other evidence of bad death.

When a man who has died out of order is buried in his own house, a new ancestral house is created. This is called a "small ancestral house" (*óbele ìba*) to distinguish it from the "great" one, but it is a permanent fixture of the community. Moreover, the sons of this man can no longer expect to succeed to occupation of the great house; they have become perpetually "junior sons" of the patrilineage at that level of lineage segmentation and can never control the ɔfɔ of their grandfather.

Therefore there is a major exception to the basic patrilineage rule of seniority succession among siblings, and this exception also applies if a man dies while his senior patrilineage "brother" occupies the lineage throne. The logic of this rule system entails a rigidly ascribed ordering of deaths. When that order is broken, status relationships in the patrilineage are permanently altered. Thus Onitsha people inevitably show extraordinary concern with, and interest in, the facts of death: the sequence of deaths, the conditions under which death occurs, and the social definition of its character through funerary ritual. These normative concerns are the key to understanding the central importance of funerals in Onitsha society.

Since inevitably the empirical order of deaths will violate the normative order, inevitably the number of ancestral houses in any village will multiply. In the course of a typical village development, the primordial ancestral house is eventually abandoned, so that two or more great houses coexist with several smaller ones. A likely empirical outcome of the ideal model presented in Figure 26 is diagrammed in Figure 27.

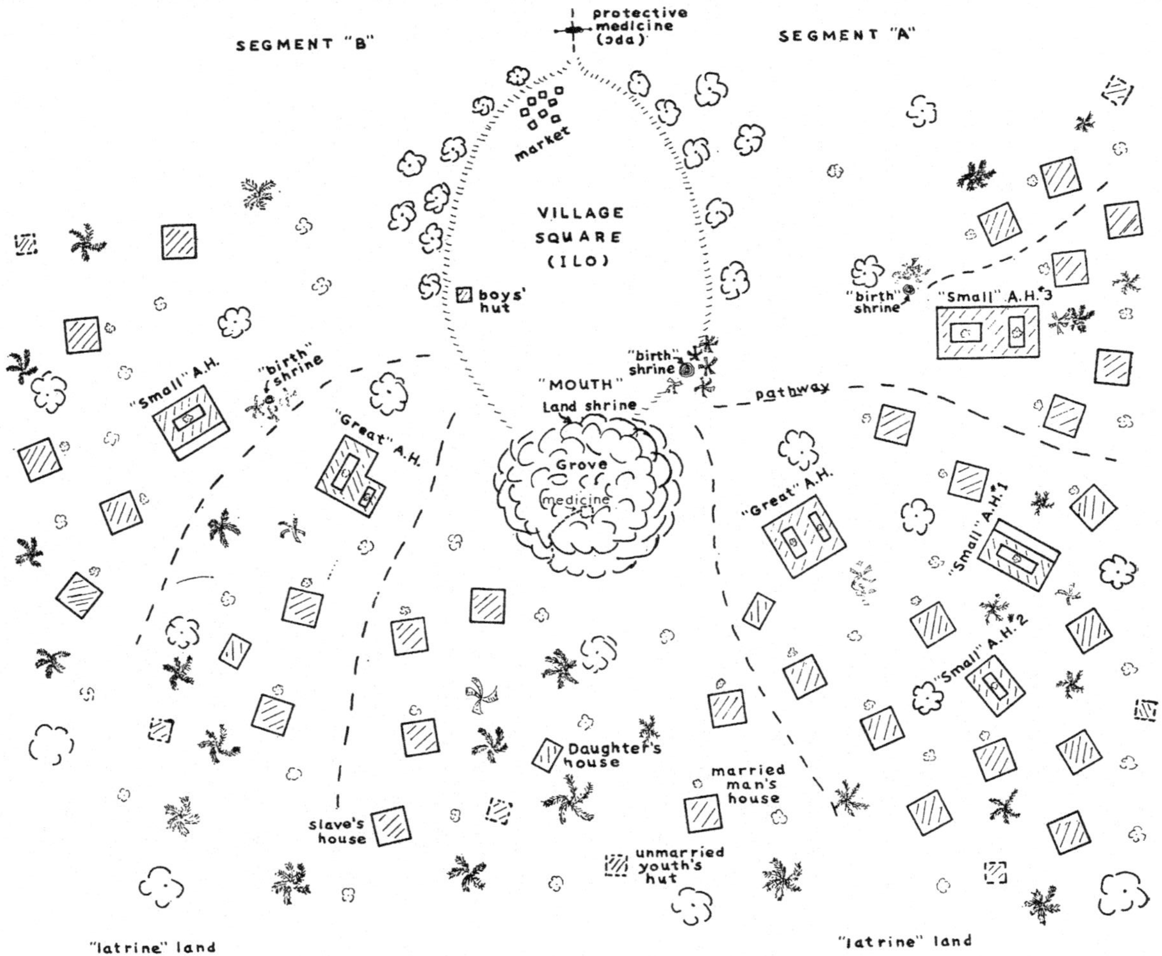

Fig. 27 Typical village residential pattern

In this case, the original ancestral house has been abandoned and allowed to grow up into a sacred grove beside which is the land shrine marking the site.[25] There are now two great ancestral houses, occupation of which is succeeded to by members of segment A and B respectively. However, the senior patrilineage priests of segments A and B are both eligible to act as priest of the entire lineage, so that the ɔfɔ and other objects held by the founding ancestor "travel" from one house to the other when the incumbent priest dies, and a system of role rotation therefore obtains.

The "mouth" of the original house has become the "mouth of the [village] square" (ɔnʊ ilo), a cleared, sandy area which serves as a general meeting place. In its primary and geographical meaning, ilo refers to an open and maintained plot of ground on both sides of which people live, but it also connotes opposition. Groups living on opposite sides of this arena refer to one another as "those across the square" (*ńdi-ùfesílo*), and they represent opposing segmental units. However, the arena is also an area of economic exchange, debate, communal ritual, and play, all activities being sanctioned under the moral order of the land. On its flanks is the "birth medicine" (*ɔ̀mʊmʊ*) devised to increase the population of the entire village; annual communal sacrifice is made to it and beside it are planted the banana trees that are regarded as communal property of the village children. These children are referred to collectively as "children of the square of village X" (ʊmʊ-ilo-ogbe-X), and small boys maintain a play hut there (*ʊ́nɔ̀-ìfufe*, "breeze house"). The wives and daughters of the village operate a weekly market in the square, presided over by the senior daughter, and the warriors of the village who have become "killers" (*ńdi-ògbu*) plant their kapok tree shrines along its flanks.

Thus the village square is the focal center of communal village activities. However, in Figure 27, segment A has three "small"

25. The maze of compound fences and pathways is not shown in this figure. Indeed, it is not possible to be specific about such patterns for Onitsha, because the compound system was no longer intact at the time of research.

houses, suggesting that some of its subsegments have lost the right of succession to the great house and are increasingly oriented to their separate ancestral foci. In segment A small house no. 3 has established its own birth shrine, indicating that it is beginning to compete with the rest of the segment in terms of population; a similar condition has developed in segment B. In this way new subvillages and eventually new villages may arise.

It is likely that a series of villages-within-villages will develop in local groups, generally in accord with genealogical division and with differential population expansion. Figure 28 shows the extent of village differentiation in the major "royal" lineage segment, "Children of King Arɔlɩ" (ʊmʊ-Eze-Arɔlɩ). In this large and highly segmented patrilineage, several levels of village organization have emerged, the major one a threefold division. Two positively defined units, "High Grass Village" (*Ógbè-ɔ̀zala*) and "Low Village" (*Ógbè-ǹdɩda*), have emerged among the descendants of *Chímedie,* while those of the other four sons of Arɔlɩ remain as a collective residual category called "Children of Arɔlɩ." Ogbendɩda, in turn, has emerged from a former position within Ogbeɔzala, for it was in the 1930s still sometimes referred to as "Ogbeɔzala-ndɩda," i.e. the low-lying portion of that village.[26] Lower-order villages (ogbe) have developed within various units, and in fact there is greater differentiation than can be illustrated here.

This pattern can be related to the conception of the patrilineage. The basic patrilineage term, "children of father" (ʊmʊnna), has an indefinite, sliding application, from the children of one man to those of the remotest recognized agnatic ancestor. Figure 28 shows that the term village (ogbe) may have a similarly sliding range of application. In the ideal situation for Onitsha people, the widest range of patrilineage and the village unit should coincide as a unified entity. Chapter 3 introduced the concept of clan (ebo)

26. A report from 1872, during a major fight between these two units that may well have marked the beginning of their permanent separation, referred to this village segment as "lower Ubozra." See Langley (n.d.).

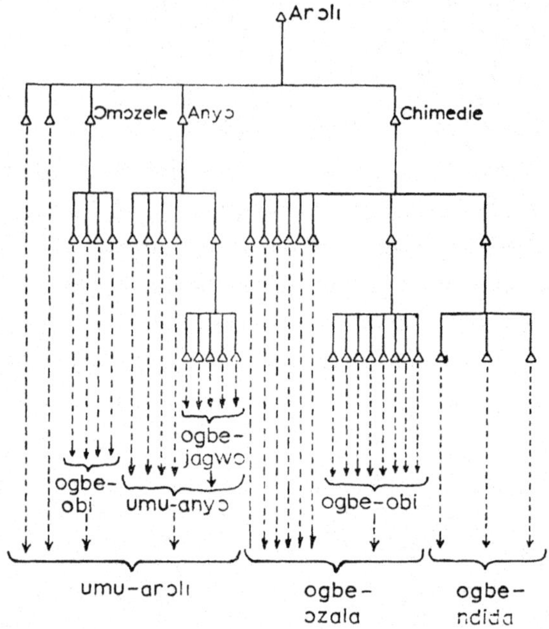

Fig. 28 Village subdivisions among the Children of King Arɔli

as an ancient, venerated descent group which has long had residential unity, and Onitsha people always attempt to describe their society as a unity of "nine clans." That these categories do not coincide is an index of diverse and contradictory pressures within the system.

From this perspective the developmental processes of village formation cannot yet be fully understood, but in every case they involve the orientation to a separate ancestral house or to its putative abandoned site. This reflects the fundamental importance of the ancestral house in Onitsha, for this structure links social roles to the spiritual sanction of the particular land in which ancestors have been buried. When a man sits in his ancestral house and beats his ɔfɔ staff on the floor there, he is certain that the message will be conveyed not only to the land but to the ghosts of ancestors buried there.

The essential definition of the status of a freeman is given by his relationship with a particular land. People who visit a village square from afar may find that "the winds of that land blow ill for them," causing them sickness or misfortune. Domestic slaves (oru) are without rights precisely because they have no ancestors buried nearby to validate their link to the land, and their residential structures hence lack associated land shrines. If, however, a slave is subjected to severe mistreatment, he may force justice upon himself by smashing his master's clay shrine to courtyard land. By defiling this shrine, committing what would be an abomination for legitimate members of the family, he throws himself on the mercy of the land and thus places himself in a forbidden state; no member of the family dares to tamper with his condition. If the land does not subsequently kill him, he obtains a new order of status.

The relations among land, ancestral house, and patrilineage ɔfɔ define major dimensions of property control and inheritance. The major corpus of heritable wealth in Onitsha is "wealth of the ancestral house" (*ɔkʊ ɩba*). This includes most things associated with that structure—shrines, residential and farm land, certain trees, domestic animals and utensils kept there (except for those of women, which will be inherited by their immediate daughters), rights to certain shares of daughters' bridewealth, and most importantly, the ɔfɔ and certain "treasure boxes and staves." These include two kinds of property, "permanent wealth" (*ɔ́kʊ̀ ɔ́kpʊ*) and "transitory wealth" (*ɔ́kʊ̀ m̀gbe,* literally, "wealth-time"). The latter is usually divided into "shares" (oke) in the process of "inheritance" or "sharing" (*ɩ́fe ńkètá*), but the former is conserved in the patrilineage unit. This permanent wealth includes not only the house and its associated land, but shrines, trees, and the ritual objects and "treasures" associated with ɔfɔ. If, as in the case of the major village unit diagrammed in Figure 27, the primordial house no longer exists, these "treasure" objects are classed as "wealth which travels" (*ɔ́kʊ̀ ńfè ǵhalɩ*), passing in rotation between the two great houses of this unit as patrilineage priests die.

The property a man has obtained by his own efforts is "wealth grasped in the hand" (ɔ́kʊ̀ áka ǹkpa), and by definition his to dispose of; it becomes wealth of the ancestral house after his death unless he chooses to divide it among his sons. If a man follows this latter practice with farm land he acquired, it is said that "he shared out the land" (ɔ́ *kèlu ànɩ*). Eventually, however, such wealth becomes attached to an ancestral house.

Thus the ancestral house, with the land shrine and patrilineage ɔfɔ kept in it, serves as the keystone of property control and status definition in the patrilineage. In the case of Figure 27, the great land grove, the shrines, trees, medicines, and structures located about the communal village square, and the "wealth which travels" remain as the property shared by the descendants of the original house, while clusters of separately controlled property adhere to the separate houses which have emerged. For example, the residential land around small ancestral house no. 3 is under the administration of that patrilineage priest rather than his superordinate in the great house of segment A. Should a dispute arise over its occupation he will exercise his "righteous power" in order to retain that control.

Farm Land: Its Control, Utilization, and Redistribution

Figure 29 indicates the range and subdivision of Onitsha farmlands, in relation to the patrilineage and village units that control them.[27] The tenure patterns evident in this figure suggest an early

27. The details of tenure as represented by numbers on this map will be found in Appendix A; only an outline summary is given here. The tentative nature of these findings must be stressed. For some parts of the area, especially to the north and east of the community, there have been few attempts to survey land divisions systematically. Moreover, the Onitsha people were no longer farming their own lands to any substantial degree at the time of research, and it was difficult to arrange to get clear indications of boundaries. I was not able to gain access to the Onitsha high court records that would have facilitated study of land tenure, though the Native Court records were of some help. For these reasons, the divisions indicated in Figure 29 for the areas north of the Nkisi stream, and for the areas numbered 26 and 28 just south of the stream, must be regarded as informed but incomplete estimates; I cannot testify to their accuracy. For example, the Children of Ɔlɔsɩ have some land in this area, but I was not able to determine where. However, I believe that the remainder of the map is quite accurate as historical reconstruction.

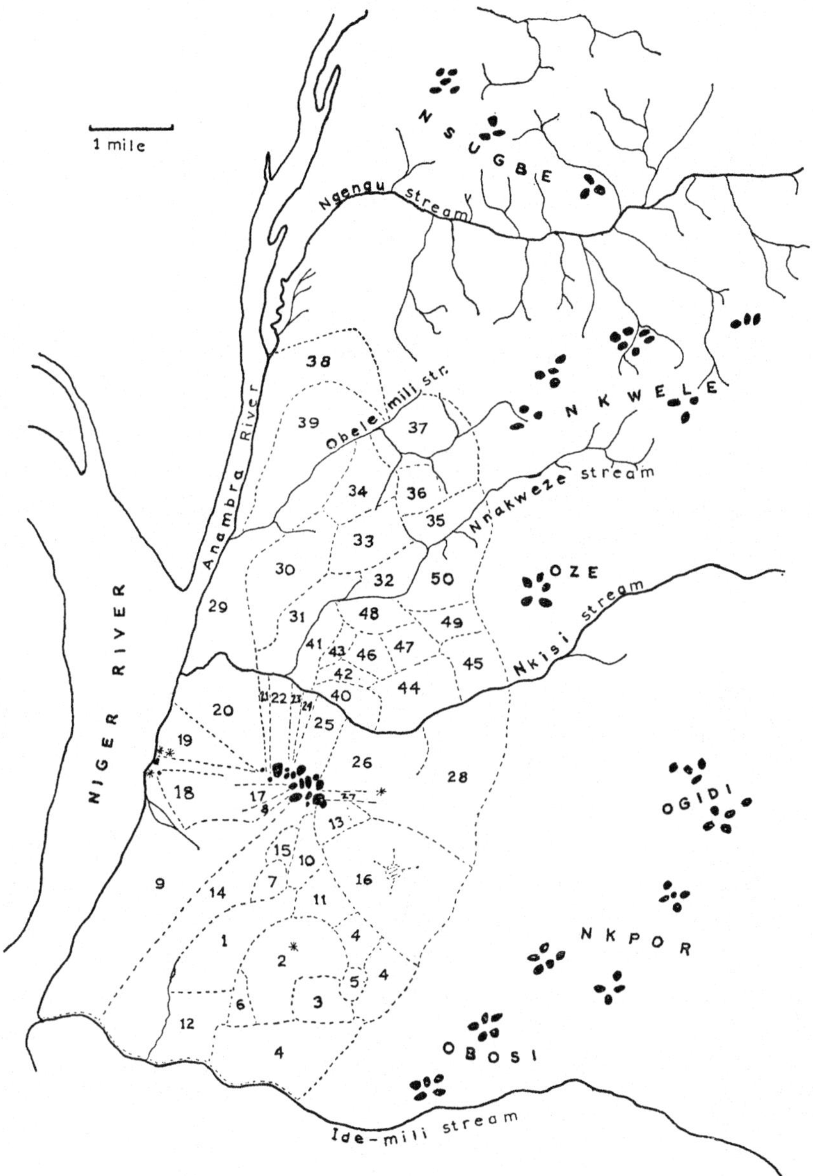

Fig. 29 The distribution of Onitsha farmlands

consolidation stage of settlement, save for the complete absence of residential hiving-off to the peripheries. The historical evidence already presented revealed a late contraction of the residential community, due in part to external pressures that presumably discouraged such hiving-off. Even so, this characterization by stage also conceals some important variations by area, for there are differences in land tenure patterns between lands south of Onitsha and those to the north, especially north of the Nkisi stream; there are also some anomalies east of the community.

South of the community, the uplands are fairly flat. Farmlands in this area are traditionally held outright by the Onitsha people, but the distribution of the holdings manifests a distortion of the radiating segment pattern. Oral tradition suggests that this distortion occurs because this area, centering around Okpoko, was originally a residential center. In recent times, the most venerated and ancient clan units, whose members trace their former home sites to this area, have continued to hold blocks of farmland there, and the sacred grove of the early kings is there. However, oral tradition also suggests that these ancient clans (mostly small in population) have consistently lost substantial portions of their former lands to more recently established, numerically more successful groups (for details, see Appendix A).

It is said that by the end of the precolonial period, Onitsha people tended to rely less heavily on the land to the south, because of its decreased fertility. The Obosi community, pressed by heavier population densities to its southeast, was taking increasing interest in the area and Onitsha patrilineages were leasing out parts of these farmlands to Obosi people. Meanwhile, members of the Onitsha community were making increasing efforts to exploit lands to the north.

North of the Onitsha village-group cluster, two areas may be distinguished, the lands south of Nkisi stream and those to the north. The stream itself is regarded as a spirit guardian of the community, and sacrifices are regularly made to it. The major part of the communal water supply is drawn from it; all Onitsha villages share pathways to it and cooperate in the clearing of these paths. Much of the land south of the stream slopes in fairly steep gradient to the water, and several areas are defined as bad bush, but much of it is farmland and all is controlled by one or another contiguous village unit; throughout this limited area the outward-radiating segment division is present except toward the east where there is a break. Parts of this latter area were, it is said, seized away from the followers of the early king usurper, Iyasele Nsu, after the latter had been killed (see Chapter 3) and were reallocated to some of the leading chiefs of the town. Their descendants have since held strips of land there. These eastern lands have remained reasonably fertile, and they were subject to increasing contention between Onitsha and the communities of Ogidi and Nkpor.

North of the Nkisi stream, the topography contrasts sharply with that to the south of the community, in that the uplands are deeply dissected by streams, and parts of this area border on the adagbe lowland country of relatively low population density. Very different conditions of land tenure occur in this area, in that ultimate control of these lands was traditionally vested in the communities of Oze, Nkwele, and Nsugbe. Over time, portions have been obtained from them by Onitsha people, in various forms of perpetual lease arrangement. It is not certain that all these lands have been so obtained, but there can be little doubt that most have; in general, the more distant lands are controlled by the largest descent group units, whereas some lands nearest the Nkisi stream and Onitsha community are or were at one time controlled by very small units.

A final area of farmlands is a strip running from the western edge of the community residence nucleus down to the Niger banks where the great Onitsha market is held. This area, including the great market, the shrine to Onitsha land, and shrines to other powerful community spirits is traditionally regarded as under the control of the Onitsha king. The exact extent of this strip cannot be precisely determined today; whether it included contiguous farmland, as suggested in Figure 29, or was limited to the main roadway and market area, is uncertain.

Farmlands are said to "adhere" to ancestral houses, but the size of patrilineage unit that controls such lands is by no means invariable. Examination of genealogies suggests that a plot subjected to communal patrilineage exploitation ordinarily involves a lineage having fifteen or more living adult males. Such a plot is ideally divided into seven strips, one of which is cleared each year. In January, at the height of the dry season, a meeting is called in the house of the senior patrilineage priest to decide which new strip will be farmed. A representative of the senior priest then surveys the strip, marking its subdivisions. The essential principle is to allocate roughly equal amounts to each householder, giving the senior patrilineage priest and other lineage priests somewhat larger shares in areas protected from external attack.[28] Men who have large families and many slaves may, however, be given more extensive portions on the remote side of the farm. Once the site has been marked, the men of the lineage go out to the land and the senior lineage priest ritually softens it (ɩkpʊba-anɩ), rebuilding the land shrine there and sacrificing a female goat.

Around the end of January each householder ritually establishes the yam spirit on his plot. The land is cleared and the debris burned at about the end of February, a procedure coordinated by the senior priest. The entire patrilineage unit works to clear the plot held by the senior lineage priest, who is expected to expend little effort on his farm because of his frequent ritual duties. In theory, each householder should devote some part of every fourth day to "work for the senior lineage priest" (ɔlʊ *diɔkpala*), for senior priests are regarded as too heavily burdened with the spiritual welfare of the patrilineage to undertake all their own farming. In addition, the unit cooperates in building the communal yam

28. For example, in land block no. 31 of Figure 29, the senior priest of the patrilineage is given land beside the Nkisi stream, while lesser men receive plots at the more distal end.

barn which is maintained on the farm site. This barn is subdivided into sections, one allocated to each householder; it is guarded by young men and, traditionally, slaves.

The amount of land that a householder can clear and plant is limited by the range of supporters he can muster at the crucial times. For this purpose men call on their unmarried sons and the latters' age-mates, their daughters' suitors or husbands, their collective mothers' parents, and their slaves. Men who can mobilize many supporters are likely to seek greater amounts of land than are available within the patrilineage. As a result of their demands, transfers continually take place.

The first means of obtaining new land is to clear unexploited and unclaimed forest. Only a man with strong social support is likely to undertake such a dangerous venture, called "brushing and taking land." Such land becomes his personal estate, but when he dies it remains part of the property of his ancestral house.

More commonly, the enterprising man goes to the people of his mother, his father's mother, or his wife, if any of these have large holdings, and requests an allocation of land for a given season. This involves simply petitioning the senior patrilineage priest of the unit, with a present of kola and palm wine, and arranging a lineage meeting at which the decision will be made. If his request is granted, he will be expected to donate labor periodically to this unit's patrilineage priest and to bring a harvest "homage" (*íbute ńrù*) in yams. This yam "tribute" is divided by the patrilineage priest: one share for the "great ghost" (*úkwu ḿmʊɔ*), which the priest represents; another share for the priest himself; and one share for each married man of the patrilineage. Such seasonal transfer of land is tantamount to making the lessee a temporary member of the unit, for he participates in the farming activities of that unit.

However, such seasonal transfers may in time come to be regularly arranged between one lineage and a person acting as representative of another lineage or village unit. In this case, whether the arrangement is made between Onitsha units or with a unit from another community, the relationship is routinized through an oath. The senior patrilineage priests of the donor and receiver units come together on the farm and "bind their lives." The donor unit brings a yam which is split lengthwise, then rubbed on one side with salt and on the other with palm oil (two condiments regularly brought together in Onitsha ritual feasts) provided by the lessees. The yam is bound back together, and committed to the earth, as the donor priest swears he will not evict the receiver from the land unless the latter commits an abomination, and the receiver priest swears he will not try to usurp the land, put further tenants on it without the donor's consent, nor fail to pay annual homage tribute to the donor and his people. Both groups swear that they will not "look for the lives" of the other group, and the donor priest performs the "softening" of the donated land at this time and whenever the land comes out of the fallow cycle. Once this ritual has been performed, the recipient unit may place its own seasonal tenants on the land.

One important variant of this procedure is the transfer of a block of land by a father, on the occasion of the marriage of his daughter, to his son-in-law. The land is treated as part of the gifts provided by the father to "lead [his daughter] home" (*ídu ún̄ɔ̀*). Another variant is the act of "pledging" (*ígba íbe*) land to a person in exchange for a large store of yams or other form of liquid wealth. In this case the land may be deeded outright unless the debt is repaid within a specified number of years. This form of transfer is traditionally frowned upon by Onitsha people, but the marriage transfer is an institution of major importance.

Finally, any patrilineage or village may attempt, as a collectivity, to expand its farmland at the expense of other landholding units, within or outside the community. They simply assert control of an area formerly held by another unit, a procedure which may involve the use of arms. Threatened units may send their members to the priests of some widely feared spirit and arrange to "place the spirit on the land." The spirit selected is one regarded as a powerful oath (iyi), which will kill persons who assert a right that they do not legitimately possess. If a large segment of a patrilineage attempts to usurp land held by a smaller segment of that patrilineage, the ɔfɔ and land of the total unit may be invoked as an oath, requiring the usurper to "speak on the land" and swallow kola or palm wine containing sand from that land, a concoction believed to be quite lethal to transgressors against it. If the dispute is between different lineage units within Onitsha, famous oaths may be brought even from outside the community.

The senior patrilineage priest of the usurping group, who acts as the living embodiment of righteous ancestral claim to any land, is the person who must take such fearsome oaths. He becomes a living test of the wrath of the oath. Any man who takes hold of the small oath sticks, touches them to his mouth, and speaks his truth, thereby becomes forbidden. He must retire into the seclusion of his ancestral house, for since his life is under test, it is believed that his opponents will attempt to poison him if possible. He cannot cut his hair as long as he remains in his forbidden state. If he survives for the thirteen months of the Ibo year, he then emerges in triumph and dances in the company of his people through the streets and into the opposing unit's priestly compound; there he shares kola with that priest, thus freeing both groups from their mutual ostracism. He is given chalk by the losing priest, as a symbol of his righteous purity and right to hold the land, and he retires in glory to his ancestral house. Should he die before the thirteen months have elapsed, the other side undertakes the celebratory march and gains control of the land.

In this case, as in that of succession to the ancestral house, the pattern of deaths determines personal and collective moral rights. This mechanism of spirit oath restrains arbitrary usurpation of land within the community, not only because of the fear for life that it imposes upon those who actually swear, but also because its consequences are believed to ramify and to affect descendants as well as the immediate actors involved. It is believed that when the disputants are consanguineally related neither side can win in the long run, and such oaths are employed only as a last resort.

Clearly the patrilineage priest plays a central role in the regulation and control of farmland usage. Through farmland the senior priest's wealth in tribute is expanded. It is to his interest to coordinate land usage in such a way as to maintain the unity of the exploiting group. If a patrilineage unit splits or becomes too small, it is in danger of having its land usurped. It may then be forced to form cross-lineage alliances which amount to partial transfers of land control.

However various the procedures through which land may be transferred, by far the most common ideal model employed by Onitsha people to explain historically known transfers is that of the "gift" transfer leading the daughter to her husband's home. To determine why this is so requires the examination of marriage patterns, and of the roles of the daughter's child (nwadianɩ), the "child of the land." Relationships among "in-laws" (ɔgɔ) gain structural permanence only through the development of mother–child bonds, and it is to these relationship patterns that we must now turn our attention.

6 THE SOCIETAL WEB OF KINSHIP: MATERNAL, MARITAL, AND AFFINAL RELATIONSHIPS

MOTHERHOOD

For every male member of any Onitsha patrilineage there is a close relationship between the number of supporters upon whom he can reliably depend and the amount of land that he can exploit. Since these supporters are expected to be primarily his own children, every man is strongly motivated to sire as many offspring as possible. A major focus of the collective interests of every independent lineage segment is its common "birth shrine" which contains objects representing the wombs of all wives of the group. Each patrilineage and every adult male must constantly search for more wives, and wives in Onitsha are valued primarily for their potential roles as mothers.

The importance of the mother role-set in Onitsha correlates closely with the prominence of reproduction in male values. The primary criterion of fulfillment for a woman is the number of children she has successfully raised to survive her. Intimately associated with the personal god of every woman is the spirit called *ɔ́ma,* objectified in the form of a small rounded conical clay mound set against the wall on the floor of the woman's kitchen. Called "the mothers," this symbol represents maternity as a perpetual force which acts upon all descendants of a woman. When a woman sits before this shrine (built in a series of three mounds representing her M, MM, MMM, MMd, etc., if these persons are dead), she may perform ritual acts of begging the dead similar to those performed by a patrilineage priest. Since the mothers are not communicated with through ɔfɔ, the normative component of righteous power associated with males is absent in such ritual communication; instead, the worship of ɔma evokes associations of maternal indulgence and loving filial dependence.

The mother's fundamental duty to her children is defined as "child care" (*ɔ̀zuzu-nwá*).[1] This refers narrowly to the two-and-a-half-year post-partum period when she is expected to abstain from sexual intercourse and to devote herself to serving the needs of her child. It refers more broadly to the expectation that she will perform lifelong acts of nurturance, so that her children are said to have the perpetual right to "suck breast" (*ánà ámɩlɩala*) from her. She is expected to keep her children physically contented, so that they will wish to remain in this world. It is recognized that when each son reaches the age of six, his discipline is not her responsibility, whereas her daughters must learn from her the technical skills and moral proprieties necessary to good wives and mothers. But it is believed that all children actively seek control over their own activity, and that a mother's primary duty is to encourage such autonomy rather than inhibit it.

In return children are expected to remain morally dependent upon their mothers, regardless of their other positions in life. Proverbs state that a person who has a living mother remains a child, that a man in this condition "has no age-set," for it is unthinkable that a child could ignore his mother's desires or neglect, abandon, or harm her. It is expected that children will seek to glorify their mother since in doing so they glorify themselves. If in anger a child should push his mother to the ground, he has performed a forbidden act and must "lift her up" by a ritual that absorbs the injury and insult to her. Each child owes his mother periodic gifts of ritual homage (ife nru) analogous to those owed the father.

It is believed that through ɔma a mother's spiritual power can make her children sick, barren, or impotent. Should a diviner determine that a person is being harmed by his mother's ɔma, that

1. An Onitsha proverb (also a female personal name) states, "Who gives birth [to a child], cares for [rears] it" (*Ɔmʊlʊzʊa*).

person must provide food for a sacrifice to it which will be attended by all who are "in ɔma" to the mother. The wrath of ɔma indicates a neglect of filial duties.

Children born of one mother are expected to behave maternally towards one another as the children of one father are not. This applies particularly to the surrogate performance of child care by older maternal siblings. As a collectivity, the children of mother (ʊmʊnne) define their relations in terms of this mutual nurturance and mutual dependence upon ɔma.

The condition of being in ɔma to the mother lasts beyond her lifetime and may therefore be considered as part of a descent relationship. When the mother dies, and her funeral ceremonies have been completed, her eldest daughter will "bring the mother in" (*ínyedo-nne*) to her kitchen, where the small clay mound is molded along the floor against a wall. It is then treated as a permanent force acting to benefit or harm her descendants. When this senior daughter dies, her next younger uterine sister will succeed her in performing this ritual, thus acquiring spiritual control over all descendants of the original mother. In time, she will be succeeded by the senior daughter's daughter. The mounds multiply with each dedication, and all descendants of the original mother, male and female, can be affected by their force. All descendants who worship a common ɔma in this way remain "children" of the same "mother" and—most importantly—they cannot marry one another. Exogamy is associated with this ideology of descent.

However, if the ideology of ɔma is "matrilineal" in that it is thought of as a descending line of mothers, the normative criteria fer perpetuation of "in ɔma" relationships are not unilineal, for sons of a woman also transmit the condition of being "in ɔma" on to their children. A person may stand in ɔma not only to his mother's mother, but also to the "mothers" of his father, and of his father's father. A man may also under certain conditions "bring his mother in" to his house and collect the ɔma shrines beside his household throne.

In contrast to patrilineage relationships, the relationships defined under ɔma lack the righteous power associated with the patrifilial ɔfɔ. The maternal representative cannot curse the descendants of a mother for their lack of filial piety, and the mother–child relationship lacks the moral strength of that between father and child. Relationships of ɔma can be ritually severed much more easily than can those involving ɔfɔ. This process of severing may be clarified by considering the requirements of exogamy.

THE REQUIREMENTS OF EXOGAMY AMONG KINSMEN IN ONITSHA

The control over persons and things that is symbolized by ɔfɔ extends to the reproductive powers of the patrilineage daughters, but it would be a sin against the land for patrilineage members themselves to impregnate these women. It is believed that should the "children of a father" try to procreate among themselves, they would all die. Therefore, the exchange of marriageable women is a major interest of every patrilineage unit. It is said, moreover, that "one who partakes of the vagina uninvited does not beget the child" (*ónye éche ɔ́ru ádâmʊ nwá*). This "invitation" to obtain the right to procreate with a woman, the fundamental marriage norm in Onitsha, entails a pact made between patrilineages.

The first criterion of eligibility is that the prospective spouse be a freeborn Onitsha man or woman of established genealogy. This requirement is more strongly enforced in the selection of husbands than wives, but it points to a positive preference for community endogamy and genealogical purity.

However, within the range of this sphere of preference there are a series of proscriptions which, if rigorously followed, would make intracommunity marriage practically impossible. Onitsha people say that *any* genealogical connection between two persons should prevent marriage between them. Since over half the community traces patrilineal descent to the founder-king Chima, agnatic genealogical criteria alone would entail an exogamous moiety situation for all "Children of King Chima." Also, once a bond has been formed through marriage, it cannot be repeated by descendants of the persons concerned; once two patrilineages are linked by marriage, the immediate segments so linked become exogamous.

These general proscriptions are modified by specifying a more limited proscription: those who worship together, who have common shrines to the ghosts and a common patrilineage priest to whom they regularly serve homage, cannot intermarry. The requirements of such worship make sexuality abhorrent within a group. Therefore if a patrilineage expands and segments into a series of major villages, its members may fight one another and subsequently "scatter the ghosts" so that they no longer share religious orientation to a common village square. Afterwards, when they have made peace, they "kill a goat to the ancestor" (*ígbu éwu ḿmʊɔ*), begging their remote common forefather to accept this offering as a final collective gift and thereafter to permit the two groups to intermarry without his retaliation. As an accepted prelude to this ultimate fission of patrilineages, when segments have substantially separated their interests but have not yet come into conflict, casual sexual relationships form between the young people of the two units. These preferred premarital sexual liaisons serve as the wedge for a later "scattering of the ghosts" and the establishing of marital relations.

Similar severings occur between maternally linked kinsmen. Two people in ɔma to a common ancestral mother, or linked through a common shrine dedicated to daughters, cannot intermarry because they pay common reverence to the ghosts associated with these shrines. A modifying rule states, however, that "daughter's children of the third generation" can intermarry if a diviner determines that the ancestral ghost will accept the sacrificing of a goat and permit the marriage to be fruitful.

In Figure 30, the sex of the persons (A,B) linking the potential spouses (C) does not matter. In case 1, the persons of the third generation can go to the ɔma of the apical ancestress and, with the permission of the keepers of that shrine, present them with a goat to be sacrificed to the ghost, so that the marriage may be fruitful. In case 2, they go to the shrine dedicated to the daughters of the indicated apical ancestor and arrange the sacrifice of a goat to these daughters.

However, such severing of genealogical ties is by no means an automatic process; it occurs through collective decisions that are subject to a number of exigencies. As I have shown elsewhere,

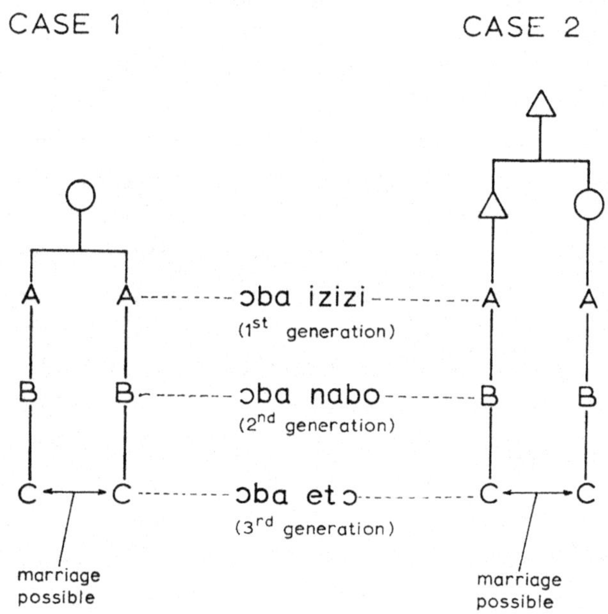

Fig. 30 Limits of prescriptive exogamy between maternally linked kinsmen

maternal linkage can generate perpetual alliances of mutual exogamy between patrilineages, one patrilineage being defined as daughter's children to another. Such alliances are frequent and are of particular importance to numerically small units, which may maintain them to great genealogical depths. Non-agnatic exogamous relationships may also emerge among the collective descendants of an ancestral mother without any mediation of patri-lineages; such groups are ephemeral and structurally unimportant at the society level, but they indicate the structural strength of maternal linkage.[2]

These rather complex patterns of exogamy indicate a structural antipathy between two different sets of values and rules. On the one hand, the mutual dependence upon ancestral shrines and their associated ritual activities is regarded as a basic good. The accumulation of wives is an equally basic value, and the "best wives" are Onitsha women. Hence there is a constant tension between expansion of descent groups oriented to common ancestral shrines, and the need to break up such co-worship in the interests of obtaining marriageable Onitsha women.

One implicit consequence of this situation is that the search for Onitsha wives must be widely diffused through various segments of the community; whenever a lineage begins a search it must scan sectors of the community marriage market that have not been tapped recently. A second consequence is that if genealogically related men desire many wives, the search for women must sometimes lead them outside the community. Onitsha people claim that in precolonial times an Onitsha man who failed to find a suitable home girl for his wife would search across the Niger among the highlands western Ibo before he would accept an Ibo woman from the eastern interior (although genealogies indicate that large numbers of such marriages were contracted). The strategic position of Onitsha with its great riverside market made it advantageous for eastern Ibo to marry their women to Onitsha men, because this link could give them access to the market. Onitsha women were not traditionally given to eastern Ibo men, but they were given to riverain Ibo and to Igala. In this part of Ibo country, women have traditionally moved in the direction of wealth and power. As in other prominent trading towns at the beginning of the colonial period, polygyny was probably the statistical as well as the pre-

2. Henderson (1967:44–49).

ferred pattern in precolonial Onitsha, and the associated influx of non-Onitsha women into the community created important external ties.

THE ESTABLISHMENT OF MARITAL BONDS

Since the ever-ramifying web of genealogical links poses difficult problems for those seeking to establish a marriage contract, many persons must be mobilized for the search. It is a rule among the children of a father that the senior son and senior daughter must marry first, followed by the remaining siblings in order of age seniority, and that all agnatic siblings should devote effort and wealth toward this end. A wealthy woman may establish an infant betrothal for her own son which upsets this pattern, but the senior children must be the first to found their own marital households.

Initially, the search for a suitable spouse is begun by the boy's or girl's mother, who gathers genealogical and other information from the sources most readily available to her: her husband's daughters and village wives, and the daughters and wives of her own village. Aside from genealogical criteria, the major characteristics sought in the family of a potential spouse are positive evidence (in the form of wealth, health, and numerous offspring) of good personal gods and the absence of witchcraft, madness, unresolved oaths, recent abominations, or bad deaths. Personal characteristics sought in a woman are physical perfection, obedience, and avoidance of slothfulness and adultery; in a man, industry, assertiveness, generosity, and "sense" or foresight (*úchè*). If either party should fall seriously short in any respect, a remote genealogical link can always be found (even one previously severed) to bar the wedding.

Betrothal arrangements are always formally initiated by the suitor's patrilineage, although the mothers of the prospective marital pair may effectively arrange the match and have what amounts to veto power over the selection. "Taking a wife" (*ínu nwũ̂nye*) entails a definite series of steps that begin when the suitor's father (or immediately senior patrilineage priest) has obtained the consent of patrilineage elders. The first step is "rubbing the ears" (*ígba ɔ́kɔntì*) of the girl's people; the suitor's father goes alone to the girl's father and presents him with "kola for rubbing the ear." The sharing of this defines an initial interest and good will. After some days, during which the girl's father directs his own intelligence network to determining the social status of his visitor, the latter returns to "peer into the house" (*ínyò ʊ́nɔ̀*), presenting a bottle of gin. At this meeting, blessed by the offering of gin to the girl's patrilineage ancestors, the suitor and the object of his interests are specified. The girl's mother then undertakes detailed research into the character of the young man. If he and his family are found acceptable, the information is transmitted to the girl's senior patrilineage priest, whose consent must be obtained. The priest then designates acceptable times for the next stage of courtship.

This stage, called "carrying palm wine for wife" (*íbu ḿmanya ńwũ̂nye*), consists of ritual presentations of wine by the suitor and his immediate patrilineage elders, as directed by the girl's father. The series begins with an "afternoon palm wine" at which the girl shares a cup of wine with her suitor to signify her acceptance. Her father then lists kinsmen who must be served palm wine in their homes: his senior patrilineage priest and other lineage elders, his daughters, his mother (who in turn will list her own kinsmen to be served, including her senior lineage priest), and the "mediator" (*ónye-ʊ́kɔ̀*), a lineage member who will witness all future matrimonial ritual and mediate disputes between the prospective husband and wife. After these presentations, the girl's father directs the suitor and his father to greet the girl's mother with palm wine. She then directs them to present wine to her patrilineage elders and to her own mother (who in her turn will specify additional kin to be served). In this way, four distinct patrilineages ratify the betrothal.

Until the carrying of palm wine has been completed, all the suitor's presentations are regarded as free gifts. Thereafter all exchanges become refundable and the use of affinal terms between the parties begins.[3] At this point, the girl's father announces the stages to follow: a period of several years during which the husband will provide bridewealth in kola presentations to the girl's kinsmen. The bridegroom is also expected to "do work for the in-law" (*íje ɔ́lʊ ɔ́gɔ̀*) by helping on his farm and performing other labor services, to serve the girl's father yearly homage on the model of that rendered to the patrilineage priest, and to provide the girl with "body gifts" (*ífè árò*) for her adornment.

When the marriage negotiations reach this phase, the girl should have attained the stage in life of "developing breasts" (*íkpʊ̀ ála*); at this time her village age-grade performs ceremonies associated with premarital "betrothal visits" (*íje úrì*). The boy should have attained young manhood and be in a position to establish his own household. Ritualized visits are exchanged between the two while the young bride remains in her father's home. The patrilineage "brothers" of the husband periodically "go outside" (*íje ílo*) to visit the bride's village home and play the role of her potential husbands. These visits include serious attempts at seduction as a test of the bride's upbringing; but since it would be an abomination for lineage brothers to have sexual intercourse with the same woman, anyone who succeeds in seduction is expected to refuse consummation of the act and to report the matter to her prospective husband.

After the great harvest festivals at the end of the rainy season, a ceremonial "cooking" feast (*ósisîte*) marks the beginning of these betrothal visits, when the age-grade of girls who have reached puberty divide into betrothed and unbetrothed segments to perform their group dances in a community square. At this time, each be-

3. As this point, acts of generalized reciprocity have established tentative interpersonal commitments. Affinal roles are now being defined, in terms of strictly balanced reciprocity.

trothed girl "carries back the pot" (*íbu ńata ìte*) in which the palm wine of marriage was brought to her home. Escorted by another girl of her patrilineage, she makes a four-day visit to her prospective husband's community, where she performs domestic duties under the supervision of his mother and is given gifts by the householders of the patrilineage to carry home to her people.

These preliminary visits continue for three years until the bridewealth kola has been paid. In the second year the bridegroom should receive permission from the bride's father to have sexual intercourse with her at the groom's home. This act is viewed as an important test of the girl's character. A white cloth is placed under the couple, upon which blood should fall as proof of her virginity. If this evidence is obtained, the groom publicly rejoices by "leading the wife back home" (*èkené ídʊ ńata ńwũ͡nye ʊ́nɔ̀*) with a full pot of palm wine which he presents to the girl's mother in recognition of her educational efforts. If the evidence is lacking, he presents a contemptuous half-pot of wine and may demand refund of bridewealth. For a girl, prebetrothal sexual intercourse is a forbidden act, and a child born of such a union would in traditional times be abandoned in the bad bush as an abomination.

If sexual consummation is properly completed, the girl returns home for a year during which she is free to establish copulative relationships (*ιyι ɔyι*) with any nonrelated lovers of her choosing. She thus acts as a major focus of competition and a sexual outlet for the community's unmarried males. Her lovers are defined as rivals of the groom, and their relations with him are hostile.

This period of female sexual freedom ends only when the full bridewealth has been paid. As Figure 31 shows, bridewealth "kola" (in traditional times, actually considerable wealth in cowries) is not only distributed through the patrilineage structure of which the girl is a member, but also, through women, it reaches the hands of three other patrilineage units.[4] The distribution thus falls within

4. Following the numbers on the diagram, (9) receives "father's kola," the greatest single payment given by the bridegroom (18); (10) receives "mother's kola" and

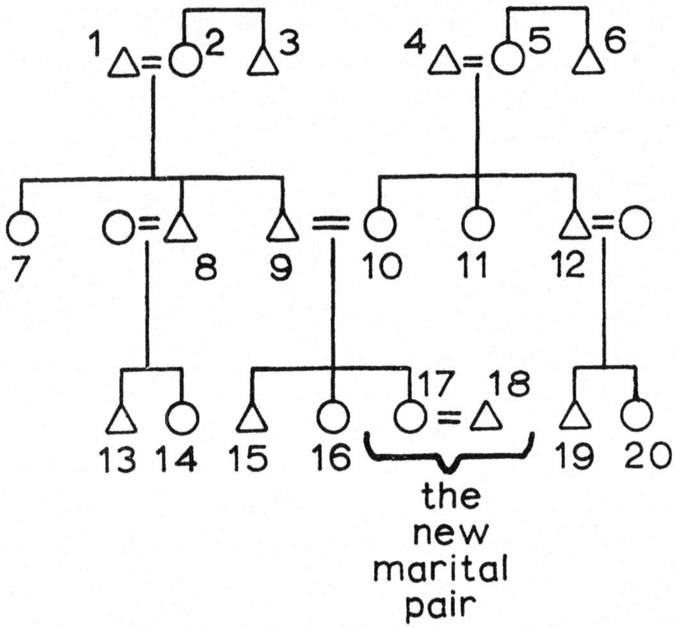

Fig. 31 The distribution of marriage kola

the prerogatives of the lineage priests. At the same time it singles out certain actors (the father, the mother, etc.) for special shares. The scope of interests that various actors and groups hold in the future course of the marriage is thereby precisely defined.

also "kola for childcare [of the daughter]". However, if the girl is her first daughter, she will pass the "mother's kola" on to (5) (her senior sister), retaining it only when her younger daughters marry. If (1) is living, he will receive "kola for the senior lineage priest of the father"; if not, (8) will take it assuming he is senior to (9). If (9) is senior, he will pass it on to the senior lineage priest to whom he pays homage at a higher genealogical level. If living, (4) will receive "kola for the senior lineage priest of the mother"; if not, (12) takes it. "Kola for the daughter" on the father's side will be shared by (7) and, if she is married, (14), and a similar share is divided on the mother's side by (11) and (20). Separate kola shares are given to the father's mother (2) and mother's mother (5) or, if they are dead, apparently to their respective patrilineage priests, (3) and (6). The "kola for the mediator" is given to (8), (13), or whoever of this patrilineage has been selected to play this role. If the father (9) is dead, his brother (8) should receive the "father's kola," but only for the senior daughter, assumed in this case to be (17). When (16) marries, (8) will then be given only "lineage priest's kola," while (15) will receive the "father's kola."

After the full distribution of bridewealth, the groom and representatives of his patrilineage arrange the ritual "notification of receiving the wife." They meet at the house of the bride's father, and his senior patrilineage priest occupies the throne in presiding over prayers to the ghosts of the girl's patrilineage ancestors. The groom and his senior representative present homage service in money and palm wine to the senior priest, who prays to the ancestors to make the marriage fruitful, "feeding" the ghosts kola and palm wine. Then, exhorting the young couple to live well together and to bear many children, he calls them to drink wine from a single cup as they kneel before him. This ritual act defines both bride and groom as parties to a pact sanctioned under the ɔfɔ of her patrilineage. It is followed by a further distribution of blessed wine to the entire congregation. The husband's lineage representative then entreats the priest to release the bride to them immediately, but he is refused; finally, the priest is cajoled to specify a date on which his people will lead [the wife] home (idu ʊnɔ).

For this final "leading home" ritual, the young unmarried boys and girls of the bride's patrilineage escort her festively to her husband's house, where she kneels before his patrilineage priest and accepts a drink of blessed palm wine that defines her as dependent upon the ancestors of her husband's people. As a result of these acts, two separate spheres of ɔfɔ control overlap: that of the husband and that of the wife's father, each within his own patrilineage system.

An important aspect of the final leading home is the transfer of gifts borne by the bride's escort to the husband's new domicile. These gifts, freely provided by the girl's people, are defined primarily as her domestic stock of utensils, yams, and firewood, but to establish a strong relationship between the girl's parents and her offspring, quite valuable property (including rights over economic trees located in the girl's patrilineage home and, in some cases, rights over a section of farmland) may be ostentatiously transferred in this process or at least defined as a part of it.

The final act that brings the new wife into the social order of her marital village involves her ritual "confession" (*ísà ífì*) of her previous sexual relationships before the assembled daughters of the husband's lineage and some female representatives of her own group. In this ordeal, the head daughter of the husband's lineage holds her ɔfɔ and begs the dead to witness the new wife's performance, then tears the beak of a fowl when the wife begins her confession. Confession includes the naming of all partners, and the death of the fowl is evidence that the number of lovers has been exhaustively detailed. The daughters then exhort the wife to be faithful to her new husband, and they all go to the husband to clear his body (especially his mouth and throat) of the potential taint of her sexual offenses. Until these acts are performed, it is believed that the ancestors will kill any children born to the couple and that the husband will be magically sickened by any food he eats from his wife's cooking. The husband, informed of the names of all his wife's lovers, demands ritual sacrifices from each, so that he and they may safely share food and drink at communal meetings in the future.

These confession and cleansing rituals express a central theme of Onitsha thought, the belief in the potentially dangerous effects of female sexuality on males. All the stages of marriage negotiation are closely coordinated with the sexual states of the girl: betrothal occurs when she reaches puberty; the successful completion of the early stages depends on her virginity; she is subsequently permitted a period of sexual wantonness; finally, she must confess and her husband be ritually cleansed of her past sexual behavior. Her entry into her husband's household brings a sexually dangerous stranger into his patrilineage domain, and this danger must be minimized by a ritual that brings her under the control of the ɔfɔ of the patrilineage daughters.

Once all this has been done, the wife is settled in her husband's household. The gifts brought by her people to her new home give her an initial prestige there. They help her to establish a familiar space within the household, one containing her own property. She also brings a representation of her personal god to worship, and may keep a medicine for her personal protection.

THE CONCEPTUAL STRUCTURE OF MARITAL AND AFFINAL RELATIONSHIPS

We have seen that the act of marriage is socially defined as "taking a wife" (inu nwunye), a process in which a man and his agnates negotiate with a woman's parents and her other kinsmen while the woman herself plays a predominantly passive role as an object of value. A woman may refer to her own participation in these activities as "taking a husband" (*ínu dí*), but publicly the process is defined from the husband's point of view. Moreover, marriage establishes an achieved relationship between parties, denoted by the concept ɔgɔ, in which the wife does not actively participate in her role as spouse. This conceptual asymmetry in Onitsha marriage generates some complexity in the categories of affinal relationship.

Formal semantic analysis of marital and affinal categories has lagged considerably behind that of consanguineal kinship (with the exception of prescriptive alliance systems, which bring the two together), but methods employed for one may serve for the other. Some of the difficulty in analyzing marital and affinal systems derives from the increased open-endedness of relationships that often results from tracing linkages through spouses: one must deal not merely with first-degree and further-degree, with lineal and collateral kinsmen, etc.; one deals in addition with spouse's kinsmen, spouse's kinsmen's spouses, and so on. I have undertaken an analysis of Onitsha marital and affinal terminology, and present a brief outline of the results here. The details of the analysis are in Appendix B.

There are three major terms applied to the relationships established through marriage, which may be glossed as follows: "husband" (*dí*), "wife" (*nwu͡nye*), and "in-law" (ɔgɔ), the glosses being based on the focal kin types to which the terms refer. Each of these terms is extended to a considerable range of relatives, and each is combined with modifiers in application to still other relatives. "In-law" is a self-reciprocal term that is applied to two distinctive focal kin types, wife's parent and daughter's husband. Thus its primary meaning must be regarded as either "man's parent-in-law" (wife's parent) or "son-in-law" (child's husband).

Given these primary meanings, the following rules of kin type equivalence account for the extensions of these terms to more distant relatives.

First, let husband's kinsman be regarded as equivalent to husband (corollary: let kinsman's wife be regarded as equivalent to wife). This may be regarded as the fourth rule of Onitsha kinship terminology; it applies to such relatives as husband's grandparent's grandchild, grandparent's child's wife, etc. To one kin type the rule and its corollary apply simultaneously: husband's kinsman's wife is regarded as equivalent to husband's wife, or "co-wife" (nwunye-di).

Second, let wife's kinsman be regarded as equivalent to wife's parent (corollary: let kinsman's husband be regarded as equivalent to child's husband). This may be regarded as the fifth rule of Onitsha kinship terminology; it serves to make wife's collateral kinsmen equivalent to parents-in-law, and to make one's collateral kinsmen's husbands equivalent to son-in-law. One kind of kin type, wife's kinsman's husband, is such that the rule and its corollary apply to it simultaneously. This kin type is reduced to a special category, "co-in-law" (ɔ́gɔ̀ *ńgɔ̀kɔ́*).

Third, let wife's parent's spouse be regarded as equivalent to wife's parent (corollary: let spouse's child's husband be regarded as equivalent to child's husband). This may be regarded as the sixth rule of Onitsha kinship terminology; it may be employed following the application of rule 5.

It will be noted that rules 4 and 5 bear a formal resemblance to consanguineal system rules 1 and 2 respectively, but also that they take a more general form and apply to affinally related "kinsmen" as broadly defined (. . . $P^m c^n$ . . .) rather than to agnatically-linked affinal kinsmen (. . . $F^m s^n c$ . . .) only. Onitsha people clearly indicate that agnatically-linked categories (e.g. HFsc) are the primary relatives to which such "spouse" and "in-law" terms are extended, other kin types being so called by courtesy; rules 4 and 5 may therefore be regarded as affinal-context transformations of rules 1 and 2.

Although I have stated rules 4, 5, and 6 very generally here, there are some definite restrictions in their application that must be specified in the formal statement of the rules. The following categories of affinally related kinsmen are excluded from reduction to spouse or in-law categories through these rules: 1) kin types defined through linkage to a husband's senior generation lineal kinsmen, or to senior generation lineal kinsmen's husbands, or to a combination of these types of relation; 2) kin types defined through linkage to a wife's junior generation lineal kinsmen, or to the wives of such kinsmen. Such kin types are handled by descriptive complex terms, e.g. FMH is called "husband of father's mother" (di nne nna). These are all lineally linked relatives; they include some of those who are, from the analyst's viewpoint, "stepkin." To be precise, they entail the kinds of linkages most likely to be assimilable to consanguineal role relations in the Onitsha social system. I will henceforth refer to such descriptive combinations as a distinct category of "potential kinsmen," i.e. potential consanguineal relatives, under the assumption that they are being so treated by Onitsha people.

Thus there are three major categories of kinsmen related to ego through marriage: "spouses," "potential kinsmen," and "in-laws." The overall structure of these categories may be illuminated by comparing the Onitsha system with two other systems for which similar analyses have been undertaken. Lounsbury has compared two systems, the Trobriand and the Pawnee, which happen to be matrilineal but which indicate general patterns of variation in the relative priorities assigned to sibling solidarity and spouse solidarity. This variation is diagrammed in Figure 32. In the Trobriands, spouses are identified with one another in relation to spouse's parallel siblings, in that ego employs the same term that his or her spouse does in referring to the latter's parallel siblings. Among

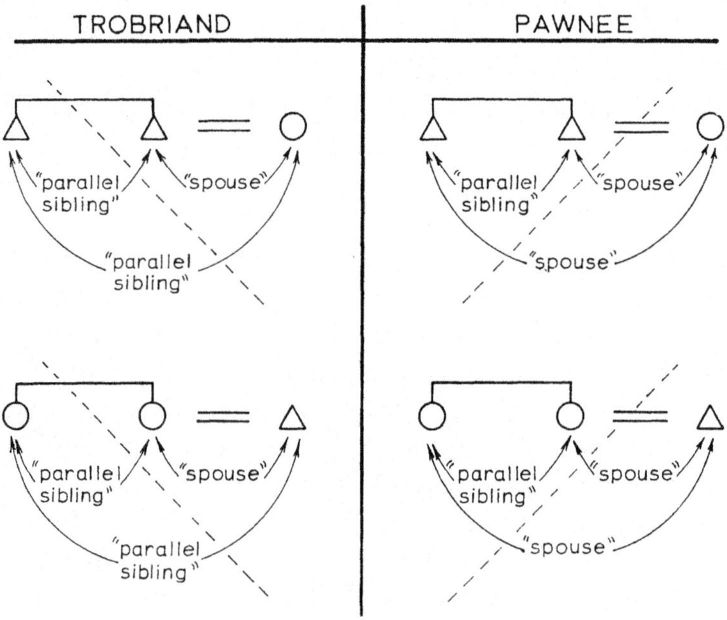

Fig. 32 Spouse solidarity vs. parallel-sibling solidarity in two matrilineal systems

the Pawnee, on the other hand, mutual identification of parallel siblings is primary, in that ego's parallel sibling employs the same term as ego does in referring to the latter's spouse. Lounsbury relates these differences to such variables of social structure as presence (Pawnee) or absence (Trobriands) of extended families based on sibling solidarity.[5] The Onitsha system contrasts with both of these types, as Figure 33 shows. Here the major categories are included in a somewhat more complex diagram.

5. Lounsbury (1965:177–78).

The first obvious difference between Onitsha and the other two cases is that in Onitsha, sibling solidarity takes priority over other relations, regardless of the sex of the sibling. It is with regard to the status of spouse that sex differentiation becomes important. Whereas siblings of both sexes adopt the status of their male sibling in his position as spouse, neither sibling does so for a female sibling in her status as spouse. While she relates to her husband and his kinsmen as "spouse," her own siblings set these relatives apart as "in-laws." Moreover, a wife identifies herself with her husband and his siblings in this regard, for she too distinguishes

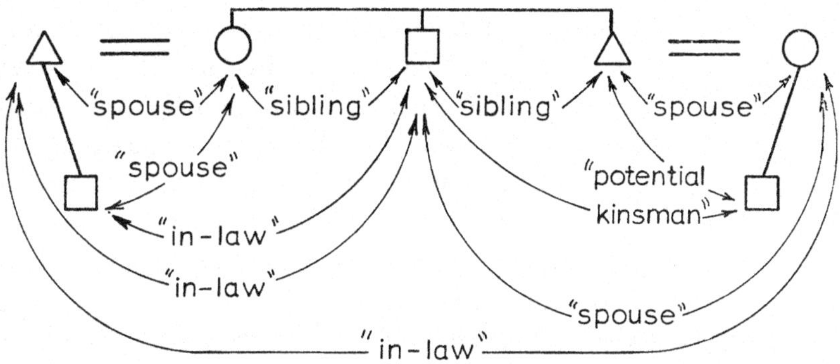

Fig. 33 The structure of Onitsha marital and affinal categories

the spouses of her husband's sisters as "in-laws." Obviously a wife tends to identify herself with her husband and his kinsmen, but a husband does not make such identification with his wife and her kinsmen. In its conceptual perspective, the Onitsha patrilineage is structurally more open to its in-marrying females than to its in-marrying males.

THE SOCIAL STRUCTURE OF AFFINAL RELATIONSHIPS

Marital and affinal relationships center on the roles of husband and wife, defined in the spiritual context of the household head's ɔfɔ with its relation to the courtyard land of that household. By coming to occupy her husband's household, the wife brings herself within the jurisdiction of this spiritual complex and therefore under the authority of her husband. By accepting this position, she commits herself to "serving homage" to him and through him to his patrilineage priests and daughters as well. A wife may bring her personal god, her shrines to mothers, and certain protective medicines into her section of the household, but she may rightly do so only if her husband ritually sanctions their presence. She trusts her personal god and her destiny partly to his priestly care, and his ritual activities become the prominent points of reference in her daily life. The husband largely controls his wife's spiritual condition, for he may declare her guilty of forbidden acts or abominations, and he may fine her for violating the rules of household life. Since she comes from outside his patrilineage, he may insure her social reliability by requiring her to take an oath on one of the lineage spirits—an oath not to steal from her husband, not to send her wealth home to her patrilineage, not to have sexual intercourse with other men, not to bring dangerous medicines into the house, and so on. Such oaths are most likely to be required when the wife comes from outside Onitsha; otherwise they are imposed only if there is reason to suspect her good will, for they are regarded as dangerously contagious in their powers of destruction, affecting the children of a marriage as well as the partners themselves.

Norms Governing the Husband–Wife Relationship

These spiritual sanctions controlling a wife are alluded to in the prescription that a wife should "bow her head" (*ɔ́nà èrúbe ísi*) to her husband, should follow his directions and obey his commands. Beyond this, a wife's rights and duties include regular tasks that are viewed by Onitsha people as closely interrelated: preparation of food, sexual reproduction and child care, and trading.

First, a wife must provide regular daily meals for her husband

and her children. She manages her gardens and extracts oil from the palm fruits allocated for her domestic use, provides and mixes ingredients for soups, and pounds yams or corn into the cohesive mash which constitutes the basis for almost all meals. It is also her duty to collect water and firewood for domestic use, and to do the daily sweeping of the house area and the ritual washing and rubbing of the house walls. Second, the husband normally has inviolable and exclusive rights of sexual access to his wife; should he discover her feeding a man who is not his or her kinsman, he may beat her, accuse her openly of committing an abomination, and demand that she undergo ritual confession. A wife has no grounds for refusing her husband's sexual overtures except when she is menstruating or performing child care. Third, she is responsible to her husband for adequate performance in her role as mother. Finally, every wife has the right to engage in trade with the support of her husband, but she is expected to employ most of the gain she derives from it for the ultimate benefit of her household.

Onitsha women are involved in a system of village, community, and intercommunity markets, and it is possible for a resourceful woman to amass considerable wealth through trade. Such wealth should be expended to glorify her marital household, but a wife has the right to make concrete decisions on expenditures. Trading is considered partly independent of household affairs. Indeed it is believed that the more effort a woman expends in trading the less effort she will make to perform her other wifely duties. Onitsha people say that "when a woman gets wealth, children run away," suggesting that a woman who strongly emphasizes trade is likely to abuse her sexual condition. Sexual infidelity may magically affect the food which a wife prepares, so that such food may sicken and even kill her husband or children; traders are thought to be especially predisposed to such infidelity. Moreover, it is recognized that women who travel constantly to distant markets and return home late must inevitably neglect their domestic tasks. The role of trader (onye-afia, lit. "market person") is an emergent one for Onitsha women, not sharply separated from the role of wife, but its normative incompatibility with major features of both wife and mother roles (the spiritual symbols of which are the hearth, the soup pot, and the womb) is fairly clearly conceptualized. Trading may be regarded as a boundary component of the wifely role, a component associated with the attribute of witchcraft.

The husband's major duty to his wife is to provide the conditions for her to maintain a thriving and expanding household. He must provide the domestic setting in which his wife works, and furnish her with a reliable supply of major staple foods from his farms. He must allot a household garden to each wife and provide palm fruits from his trees for her domestic use and for trade. The husband is also expected to allocate his cotton crop for his wife's trade, and to give periodic trade advances in money to finance her market activities.

A wife has the inviolable right to demand regular sexual performances by her husband, but he may seek other wives or engage lovers while his wife is under the long postpartum sex taboo. Male impotence is a problem to which considerable concern is devoted in Onitsha culture; if a man is sexually ineffectual, either he must provide his wife with a secret lover or else her patrilineage kinsmen will do so. Under such circumstances he cannot rightfully apply his ɔfɔ power over her.

Finally, it is the husband's obligation to his wife to insure the social solidarity which keeps the house calm, by performing his requisite priestly acts and by calling in native doctors when his wife is pregnant or when any member of their household suffers sickness or misfortune. The general spiritual health and welfare of the household is in his charge; his ultimate control over his wife's domestic property is associated with his immediate responsibility for her welfare, her debts, and her misbehavior.

This cluster of relationships defines the required role-behaviors of the statuses of "husband" and "wife." When used in non-genealogical contexts, these terms imply a relationship of domestic master and servant in the general sense that can be inferred from the rights and duties indicated above: a combination of masterful control and responsibility on the one hand, compliance on the other. "Husband," for example, is used as a prefix to characterize persons having a high degree of control over some specific set of nonkinship activities; a man who has acquired exceptional mastery of farming may be called "husband [master] of yams" (di-ji), with the implication that yams respond dependably to his command. Similarly, when a man is characterized as a "wife" of another man (done only in certain nonkin relationships), this implies obedient "domestic" service.

A Wife's Relations with Her Husband's Relatives

A woman has important and regular relationships with her husband's kinsmen, primarily his agnates. Among them, a sharp distinction is made between the husband's ascending generation lineal agnates and all others. The husband's father (or his father's father) is an object of particular deference for a woman; his authority over her actually supersedes that of her husband. Indeed, in a sense she adopts her husband's obligations to him, for she addresses him as "our father" and owes him periodic homage service as a child owes it to his parent. The husband's father may, if displeased with her actions, define them as abominable and order her sent to her natal home. On the other hand, if she pays him proper respect on ritual occasions, it is his duty to beg the dead to bless her.

Other agnates of the husband are treated as husbands in every sense except the sexual one. A wife is expected to serve them and follow their directives as she would her husband's, for in theory they are eligible to succeed to his role. However, this set of obligations also applies to the husband's lineage daughters, all of whom both address and refer to their agnate's wife as "wife." The patrilineage daughters, in pursuit of their duties of insuring that patrilineage houses are "calm," can direct their brothers' wives who are expected to "bow their heads" as they would to their husbands. Aside from having the right to test a wife's sexual propriety in the ritual of adultery confession, daughters may impose fines on a wife for disobedience or rudeness.

Beyond the agnatic relatives of the husband, his mother is the most important to his wife. To an outside observer, the husband's mother's position would seem to resemble that of his wife in that both women are in-married to the same lineage, but this shared relation is ignored and the maternal role emphasized. A woman addresses her husband's mother as "our mother" and is expected to do her bidding as a child should. The husband's mother is regarded as an overseer of her son's affinal rights. She may demand that her son's wife take an oath of fidelity, and it is said that mothers generally demand duties from their son's wives which they would never themselves perform as wives. In addition, a woman is expected to cook and do domestic tasks for her husband's mother when the latter is engaged in marketing and other nondomestic activities. The mother has the right to demand that the wife be sent home to her parents if she fails to render these and other wifely duties faithfully.

Other nonagnatic kinsmen of the husband are of lesser social importance; they are treated by a wife as if they were the husband's agnates, in that she verbalizes a wifely deference in addressing them and behaves to them with respect, but this relationship does not entail any definite obligations. A similar lack of formalized relations applies to her husband's kinsmen's in-laws, whom she also calls in-laws.

The Relations between Cowives

Every Onitsha man is expected to obtain as many wives as possible, and it would be improper for a wife to discourage her husband from doing so. Indeed, a good wife should encourage it, especially when she is bearing a child or is subject to the postpartum sex taboo. Polygyny is of the nonsororal type, and full bridewealth kola must be transferred in all marriages.

"Cowives" (*ínyemè-dí*, "wives of husband") are graded by seniority, and the senior wife is given an honorific title, ànasi. She occupies the place of honor in the household; she has ascribed prerogatives that other wives do not share, regardless of how many children she or the others have borne. For example, she receives the kidneys of any animal killed by her husband in hunting, and she is the first to bring him cooked food at ceremonies and receive ceremonial blessing from him. When he performs rituals that raise his esteem in the community, she shares directly in his public acclaim. Whenever goods are divided among cowives, she must take the first share, and is given an extra portion beyond the shares allotted to the others. Finally, she is expected to mediate disputes between cowives when these erupt into overt anger; at such times she must call the wives of the household to bring out their market stools into the central courtyard and sit, with her presiding, until the differences can be discussed and settled.

Although the role of senior wife provides that ordering mechanism of seniority which appears to be a component of all Ibo social structure, the solidarity of the group is also predicated upon the strict norm of an equal and independent share (oke) for each wife. Each must receive equal allocation from the husband's food store (aside from the symbolic extra portion given the senior wife), equal access to his sexuality, an independent garden area, separate financial advances for trading, and equal opportunities to provide his main meal and receive his approval and acceptance. Cowives are expected to "move together" as a unit, in fetching water or firewood, or in trading, but this unity depends upon individual rights to shares carefully measured by the participants.

This prescribed solidarity among cowives is reinforced by its duplication in a higher-level organization, the "village wives" (*ìkporó-ógbè*, lit. "women of the village"), a group socially ordered by seniority of marriage into the lineage unit. This group comprises the widest range of in-married women under the power of a lineage head daughter's ɔfɔ. It also corresponds to the range of prescribed extension of the term "wife of husband." The village wives share two symbols of unity, a large conical gong (*íboma*) of hammered sheet iron, kept in the home of the senior member (called the "head," isi-ikporogbe), and a "dance box" (*ʊ̀kpá égwu*) kept by the woman selected as "head singer," and used to receive monetary offerings from admirers of the group's public dance performances. The most recently married wife in the group acts as a messenger who distributes shares among the group and conveys decisions about the scheduling of their activities.

The head wife convenes meetings by sounding the gong in front of her house, where the wives assemble to discuss their affairs. The primary interest is group funerary dancing, an activity that provides Onitsha women with their main opportunity for individual aesthetic performance and which is awarded with public acclaim. The wives also discuss conditions in the village market, coordinate their travel to other markets, and schedule cooking duties for major village ceremonies. The group is expected to uphold the general standards of wifely performance, and senior wives may criticize young wives who are thought to be neglecting their duties. The group may fine any member who fails to attend a given meeting and may also fine any wife whom they convict of disrupting the village by quarreling. The village wives can exercise some social control within the wider residential unit, for if a husband should repeatedly maltreat his wife they may boycott all forms of ritual cooperation with him and subject him to public gossip until he agrees to pay them a specified fine. Although the primary goals of the group are emotional-expressive in nature, this organization must be taken into account by husbands in ordering their relations with their wives.

The Changing Position of a Wife as Mother

When a wife bears a child, all her husband's kinsmen refer to and address her by a new form that tends to replace "wife": "mother of [child's name]." This usage is especially stressed when the child is male, for when a woman bears a son her relationship to her husband's kinsmen changes quite substantially.

These changes do not eliminate, but tend to overshadow, her designation as a wife. She becomes eligible, with age, to attain a relationship with these kinsmen that links her with their ancestors: she may be installed as "mother of the incarnate dead" (*n̄ne ḿmanwʊ*) and thereby incorporated into one of their social organizations. Moreover, by raising a son she gains the right to be buried in her son's residential land when she dies. She will thus be brought into the ancestral system of the group. These ascriptive changes reveal the extent to which a mother has a membership in her marital social unit; they may be regarded as sociological correlates of the special position accorded her in the consanguineal kinship terminology (i.e. as an agnatically-linked kinsman).

"In-laws" (ɔgɔ): *A Husband and His Wife's Relatives*

The single term in-law designates relationships between persons treated as of differing generations. There is no distinct term indicating the asymmetry; a man may distinguish the two types of in-law by saying, "he gave me a woman" (referring to father-in-law) or "I gave him a woman" (referring to son-in-law). It is clear, however, that the designated relation is asymmetrical, for the two kinds of affinal relatives that are exceptions to this asymmetry are given distinctive terms. The first are men who are "co-in-law" (ɔgɔ-ngɔkɔ) to the same set of parents-in-law. The second are men who have each married a woman from the other's patrilineage, and who therefore owe one another the same kinds of affinal obligations in different social contexts. They call one another *ógɔ̀ ńgɔ̀líta*, which may be glossed as "reciprocally in-law." To distinguish the primary, cross-generational in-law relations from these more complex relationships, the terms father-in-law, mother-in-law, and son-in-law will be employed.

The most important in-law of a husband is his father-in-law, for these two men have overlapping ɔfɔ jurisdictions over the same woman. The father-in-law is spiritually senior, for when he and the son-in-law meet, he always blesses and divides the ritual kola they share, in analogy to the division between parent and child. Concomitantly, the father-in-law's ɔfɔ power over his daughter overrides that of a husband over his wife; a man may order his daughter to leave her husband, and she must obey or endanger her life.

The son-in-law may therefore expect marital stability only if he faithfully does certain services for his father-in-law or the latter's successor. These include, first, periodic work on the latter's farm, second, annual homage service, and finally—and most important—"covering cloth for the in-law" (*íkpù ákwà* ógɔ̀) and "providing goat for the in-law" (*íkpuga éwu* ógɔ̀), prescribed funerary gifts from a son-in-law for his deceased parent-in-law. So long as these duties are adequately carried out, the father-in-law should act to maintain the marriage. If the first two services are neglected, he may find some excuse to call his daughter home and to exact a fine from her husband; if the third is neglected, the wife may leave her husband by her own will. If the father-in-law receives consistent reports of misbehavior by his daughter's husband, he may also call for her return. A son-in-law may require, however, that his father-in-law swear a formal oath that he will not use his control over his daughter as a means of capriciously extorting fines. Such an oath fixes the relations between overlapping ɔfɔ powers.

The second most important in-law is the mother-in-law. She lacks ɔfɔ control over her daughter but is nevertheless believed to exert strong influence upon her. During the marital negotiations, she must be pleased with the suitor or else the negotiations will be terminated, and of course she acts independently in accepting a portion of the marriage kola. She has an obligation to assist her daughter during the first twenty-eight days after childbirth, and she must be rewarded for this service with a symbolic gift of cloth from her daughter's husband. A son-in-law also owes her funerary duties equivalent to those owed the father-in-law. Finally, a mother-in-law is expected to oversee her daughter's comforts and privileges as a wife. Should the daughter's position become intolerable, her mother may separate the pair, either by inciting the father-in-law to call the daughter home or by encouraging her to flee directly to the home of her mother's natal patrilineage (i.e. the daughter's collective mother's parents). When this latter separation occurs, a husband must approach his wife's mother's kinsmen first through his father-in-law, who will then direct him to consult with (and pay a fine to) the mother-in-law. In such a situation the husband cannot approach the mother-in-law or her people directly.

Other kinsmen of a wife who are classed as the husband's "in-laws" have relationships with him that vary according to their linkage to the primary parent-in-law. Generally, all classificatory parents-in-law are given deference in the ritual sharing of kola, in that they may bless and break the fruit their son-in-law shares with them. Their more specific significance to a son-in-law depends on whether they may be substituted for, and/or control, the focal parents-in-law, and on whether they have been assigned a share in the bridewealth kola. Therefore the most important are members of the wife's patrilineage and of her mother's patrilineage. The roles of a wife's close agnatically-linked kin or of her mother's immediate kin become most important on funeral occasions; when a wife or a direct parent-in-law dies, these persons may act as assessors of the husband's performance of his funerary obligations. Parents-in-law may require their sons-in-law to contribute to the funerals of some of these kinsmen (e.g. the wife's mother's mother), particularly if they are actual or potential protectors of the wife's rights. A wife's other kinsmen who do not occupy such positions may act as parents-in-law only on occasions of dividing kola, except that, if they play the roles of consanguine kinsmen at the funeral of a wife's parent, they are then entitled to receive a token "covering cloth" as parents-in-law. Thus a daughter's child of wife's parent may be called "our parent-in-law." More remote relatives linked through wives, such as co-in-laws lack even this regulatory norm for ordering their behavior, but they are expected to treat one another cordially.

The position of persons who take the role of parent-in-law (primary or substitute) changes considerably when their daughter bears children, for they then gain the right to penetrate into the affairs of their son-in-law's lineage and they may, in some situations, actually mediate his affairs there. They do so, however, primarily in their roles as mother's kinsmen (ikwu-nne) or mother's parents of the son-in-law's children. The parent-in-law role attains its most pronounced and permanent importance when it is associated with this consanguineal role.

Relations between Step-kinsmen

Because step-kin are conceptually divided into three categories ("spouse," "potential kinsman," and "in-law"), and because spouse and in-law relations have already been considered, the discussion of these relatives will be limited to the focal types and children of the ascending-generation focal types.

1. Father's Wife and Husband's Child: In both reference and address these relatives call one another "spouses"; only if father's wife has nurtured her husband's child from infancy as a foster mother will she be likely to be defined as a mother. The husband's senior son is expected to succeed to the role of husband of his father's wife, and to be succeeded in turn by his immediate junior brother. However, only if the senior son actually performs his prescribed autonomous role in the funeral of his father does he gain

the right and duty to control the disposition of his father's wives and their unmarried children; if he is unmarried and not financially independent and the father's junior brother performs the funeral, then the latter gains this control and may succeed as husband.

There are four possibilities in disposing of a widow under these circumstances: she may be sent to her natal home to be maintained by her people there; she may return to her natal home but continue to be maintained by her husband's successors; she may be allowed to "remain for her husband," living in his house and continuing to bear children in his name; or she may be formally taken over in marriage by his successor or the latter's designated equivalent. Any woman who has raised children for her husband has the right to demand that her deceased husband's successor maintain her and her children by providing her with a house, a garden, and food. If the senior son "takes over the wife" (*íkùchi ńwṹnye*), he must bring palm wine to her parents and gain their permission to succeed as the husband. No additional bridewealth is entailed for such succession, but should the wife prefer another man of the patrilineage over the rightful successor, then the former must refund the entire bridewealth to the latter, for by succeeding as husband a man gains rights and duties over the bridewealth of his wife's children.

A woman may, instead of being remarried, be asked to "remain for her husband" only if she has no living male child by him. In this case she still receives support from her husband's sons, and her subsequent children are regarded as legitimate—though they may be referred to as "[those who] happen at the back" (*òmen-azʊ́*). Should a widow who has not remarried decide to return to her natal home, she and any children borne by her there must likewise be maintained by her husband's successors; otherwise the successors will forfeit their rights over her remarriage kola, over her property, and (if childrearing expenses are met instead by her own patrilineage members) over the children born in their mother's natal home. Sending a wife home without support is viewed as an act of divorce by Onitsha people, and it frees the woman and her kinsmen from any future obligations to the husband's people; it is likely to occur only if the woman has no surviving male children.

2. Mother's Husband and Wife's Child: If both members of this relationship are of the same patrilineage, then the mother's husband is ordinarily regarded as father's successor, is expected to stand in loco parentis, and is addressed as "father." If the situation is normative, this person will also be father's senior son, i.e. the senior paternal sibling who has taken charge of his deceased father's ɔfɔ and thereby gains rights and duties as receiver and provider of the bridewealth of his father's wife's children. This is particularly important for unmarried children, who thereby become fully dependent upon their mother's husband for arranging their marriages. Under these circumstances the role of the immediate senior patrilineage priest of father's ancestral house merges with the social role of substitute father. However, if the senior son is unmarried at the time of his father's death, and one of father's collateral junior agnates meets the major expenses of his funerary rituals, this agnate will succeed to the role of mother's husband. He will not succeed to the ɔfɔ of the deceased, but will keep it in custody until the senior son marries and performs the rituals of "bringing in his father." The mother's husband will in these circumstances provide and control the bridewealth of the children, and he is expected to act as a father to them in other ways until the senior son attains adulthood.

If mother's husband and wife's child are not of the same patrilineage, then divorce (and bridewealth refund) has occurred and the two persons will refer to and address one another as "potential kinsmen" (descriptive terms). In reference ego will distinguish between "mother's old [former] husband" (*di-ochie nne*) and "mother's current husband" (*di-ɔfʊ nne*). Former husbands of mother are not socially important to ego, except indirectly through her children by them; and mother's current husband from another patrilineage has little more significance (except in the unlikely instance that a child attaches himself to this person so that the latter plays the role of father). If a child were to be reared and cared for by this person without support from his natal lineage, however, a dispute would probably arise over his paternal filiation. Ordinarily, a man refers to his wife's child from another patrilineage by the child's father's name ("child of X"), or by the name of the child's patrilineage. In this situation the "potential kinsman" terminology appears to emphasize the structural separation between the two parties, for any tendency for a man to regard this child as his own would certainly lead to interpatrilineage disputes.

3. Mother's Husband's Child and Father's Wife's Child: Again, the crucial issue for this pair of step-kin is whether they are both members of the same patrilineage. If they are, that status defines their role relationship, and they ordinarily refer to one another as "father's child" (nwanna) rather than employing the step-kin terminology of "potential kinsmen." They treat each other accordingly as patrilineage mates at a given level of segmentation. If they are not members of the same patrilineage, then distinctions are made as above according to whether the other person is the child of a present or former spouse of one's parent; and the "potential kinsman" terminology applies. Under such circumstances, these step-kinsmen have no clearly defined relations with one another. Their relationship is only "potential," in that, if father's wife's child becomes attached to father's home, he may become incorporated into one's own patrilineage.

Step-kinsmen and the Problem of Legitimacy

This brief analysis of step-kin relations raises the problem of legitimacy, because under certain circumstances a child's filiation may be transferred to his step-parent of another patrilineage.

Within one patrilineage, step-parentage poses no great problems of conceptual definition, for relationships to the religious objects ɔfɔ ɔkpala provide a fixed reference to which children ultimately orient themselves. Where divorce has occurred and a woman has remarried into another patrilineage, problems may arise concerning the paternity of children she bears after leaving her first marital home. Since in traditional terms the possession of children supersedes almost all other values, it is regarded as improbable that a woman might return with her children to her natal home without the children's agnates continuing to claim them. If bridewealth is repaid at or after a wife's separation from her marital residence, controversy may arise over whether children born thereafter belong to her current or former husband. This problem is resolved by requiring the woman to take a public oath, at the time of bridewealth refund, that she is not pregnant. This requirement reflects the basic Onitsha norm of legitimacy, summarized in the proverb, "He who partakes of the vagina uninvited does not beget the child." The transfer of bridewealth publicly legitimizes this "invitation," which proclaims the husband's rights over access to the woman's vagina and the fruits thereof. Any child sired at the time of bridewealth disposition is treated as if the husband were the procreator, regardless of his actual physical interaction with his wife.

Certain features of the marriage process become significant in light of these norms. During the sequence of betrothal visits, for example, a bride returns to her natal home and takes lovers, after the groom (having paid part of the bridewealth kola) has first sexually consummated their marriage. Edmund Leach has interpreted this kind of marriage custom as

> a symbolic gesture which serves to discriminate the fact that while the marriage ceremony has served to transfer to the husband's lineage all offspring of the bride, however begotten, the physical person of the bride herself has not been transferred.

> She remains a free and independent member of her own original patrilineage.[6]

Although this interpretation has some relevance here, the Onitsha custom has a somewhat different meaning. For although the husband cannot stop his bride from pursuing these licentious activities, as soon as the full bridewealth has been transferred he has the right to exact fines from these lovers retroactively, and any children born during this period are treated as if he had sired them. The customary taking of lovers, then, does not emphasize the separation of social rights over offspring from physical rights over the woman herself, but stresses the connection between bridewealth and the husband's control over *all* rights of sexual access to the woman, rights which cannot be violated with legal impunity. It is not that procreation is irrelevant to fatherhood here, but rather that bridewealth determines who will be treated *as if* he is the genitor, regardless of whether he is in fact. Onitsha people do not, so far as I could determine, draw open social distinctions between genitor and father. Instead they follow the path of legal fiction.

These legal fictions are manifold and extensively employed. They range from requiring a woman to "remain for her [deceased] husband," from engaging secret substitutes for impotent husbands, to allowing barren women to "marry" a wife, and even to retaining a daughter at home who acts as the putative (but not actual) "wife" of her father (in the precolonial practice of *ìdigbé*).[7] In all cases, legitimacy depends on treating the payer of bridewealth as "husband" and therefore as if he were the procreator.

6. Leach (1957:52).

7. Details on this custom, probably of considerable importance in traditional Onitsha, were exceedingly difficult to obtain during my research, probably because the practice had been so long discontinued. Onitsha people in retrospect emphasize its acceptability, but its incidence cannot now be assessed. For a more detailed account of the custom as it varies among different western Ibo groups, see Thomas (1914:78–85). According to Thomas, the practice of "woman marriage" has a geographical distribution similar to that of idigbe.

ALTERATIONS IN MARITAL STATUS

The Death of a Spouse

When a man's wife dies at his home, the husband is expected to participate in funeral rites in which his role parallels that of a successor to a deceased patrilineage member. Ideally the wife is buried in the residential land of her husband's home, but this ideal obtains only if the wife has living sons. The wife's patrilineage jointly participates in the funerary rites, and the interlocking claims over women emerge clearly in this ritual. The husband is expected to make a series of ceremonial announcements to representatives of his wife's patrilineage, to provide cooked food and other ceremonial paraphernalia for the daughters of this patrilineage, to provide a cloth for covering the body of the deceased for its travel to the land of the dead, and to "carry the body" to its burial.

If a man performs these acts properly, then after the full funeral is completed he may take charge of the property that his deceased wife brought into the marriage. He does this, however, in trust for his immediate sons and daughters, for he acts in their name. Sons properly take joint control of their mother's land, money, and animals, and daughters take her cooking utensils, clothing, and personal ornaments. If there are no living sons, the husband should nevertheless perform these funerary acts, except that he carries the body to the woman's natal home for burial, and he may thereafter appropriate the movable property which would have gone to her sons. It is possible, if there are no surviving children, for a husband to renege on his funerary responsibilities entirely; should this happen, the woman's natal patrilineage then carries the body home and the husband forfeits all interest in his wife's property. Such neglect would be likely only if the couple were already separated. In cases of separation, if a woman has borne a son for her husband, that son or the husband acting in his name must carry her body to the land of the son's patrilineage for burial.

After the death of a woman, the mourning period for her husband is expected to be brief and relatively burdenless. Since a husband is not closely identified with his wife, after her funeral rites have been completed her relevance to him is minimal except through the connection between his children and her kinsmen. This is another example of the asymmetrical relationship between husband and wife, for a wife's funeral duties are quite different from a husband's.

When a man dies, his immediate wives are expected to perform a series of funerary acts that stress their identification with him. They cook a final bit of food for him, and they feed his patrilineage daughters who act as "husbands." The wives must "tie a cloth on the husband" (*íjebe dí ákwà*); this cloth decorates his deathbed and is placed in his grave at burial. They must, finally, undergo a long seclusion under harsh conditions, that emphasizes their close connection with the deceased. Each widow, for example, must reside outside her marital home in a small hut constructed of the mats in which corpses are wrapped for burial and of which the lamentation coffin (*igbudu*) [8] is made, and she must sleep in a bed of ashes. This period of seclusion may last more than a year, during which time the widow is in constant danger of coming in contact with the ghost of the deceased, and her ordinary domestic life is totally disrupted by this state of contamination. The village wives also participate in the funerals of any of their patrilineage "husbands," but not at all in this identification with them.

After the widow has completed her onerous mourning (which may also involve demands that she undergo adultery confession

8. For a detailed account of Onitsha funerary ritual, see H. K. Henderson (n.d., pp. 326–433). The "lamentation" (*ìkwa ózu*), defining social identity, is the second stage of an Onitsha funeral. The first stage is the "announcement" (*ìkpɔsu ózu*), including "burial" (*ínì ózu*). Lamentation is often translated by Onitsha people today as "second burial," for within the lamentation coffin is blaced a banana tree stem representing the body of the deceased, and this coffin is ordinarily buried at the site of the actual burial.

and other hardships), she is reintroduced to society. Her husband's patrilineage successor then must build a house for her and maintain her. Normally, the deceased husband's senior son holds the right of first request to succeed to the wife (ikuchi nwunye), but the widow may refuse him or anyone else who asks to take her over as spouse. Any patrilineage member who has sexual intercourse with her thereby gains the sole right of succession as far as members of the patrilineage are concerned. The widow may refuse them all and go to another husband, provided the bridewealth is refunded and she takes an oath that she is not pregnant at the time. A widow does not succeed to any of her husband's properties, but only to these rights of maintenance, which she may refuse in favor of other options.

So strong is the ritual dependence of a woman on her husband that even if the couple has been separated a woman must return to his patrilineage after his death, must undergo a posthumous "reconciliation" through his patrilineage daughters, and must mourn him according to custom. If she did not do this, she would be continually endangered by the ghost of her husband, and her children would remain in a state of spiritual contamination, unable to inherit from him. Once the separated wife has been reconciled in this way, she gains the rights of maintenance.

Separation and Divorce

A number of beliefs and social organizations encourage a woman's commitment to her marital community, especially if she has children there. It is also proverbial in Onitsha tradition that a "husband and wife build a house and then furnish it with disputes," and that a very high rate of marital separation occurred.

Onitsha Native Court records from the first half of this century suggest that at least half the serious cases of separation involve co-wife conflict,[9] and Onitsha people confirm this in their normative

9. Court cases from this century cannot of course serve as an infallible guide to practices in 1880; I mention them only as circumstantial support for the informants'

statements about married life. Onitsha people make frequent overt assessments of their spouses' behavior, and much of this assessment concerns cowife relations. Cowives are in no way insulated from the frequent comparisons of prestige made within the household, for their kitchens and sleeping quarters face directly onto the interior courtyard where domestic life centers. Their quarters are arranged around the throne, which symbolizes their husband's control of his household. From it he daily indicates how he assesses his wives: their relative seniority, their trading contributions to the wealth of the household, and their care of their children.

The position of senior wife is prestigious. It is said that traditionally some girls would be taken to diviners to determine whether they should accept only marriages as senior wives. Probably the ritual activities of this role give it a greater stability than junior wives enjoy. Nevertheless, successful child rearing and wealth in trade are more important for a wife's social standing than this ascriptive ranking, and in these matters the senior wife has no particular advantage. When an Onitsha woman worships her personal god, she is likely to beg for children and wealth, in that order.

"When a woman gets wealth, children run away." A good mother should be kept busy in continual periods of child care, and indeed the quality of a woman's mothering is thought to be magically demonstrated if she becomes pregnant again as her latest child approaches the age of three. It is believed that when a woman completes the task of child care, and returns to sexual intercourse with her husband, her first child will spiritually "invite" another infant to join him in this world if he is contented with his life thus far. If the child dies, or does not invite others to follow him in birth, then his relation to the conditions of this world, particularly the performances of his mother, becomes the subject of gossip and debate.

---

statements about the past. In ten of twenty cases sampled from Onitsha Native Court, cowife conflict was overtly mentioned. It was probably relevant in other cases as well.

If a wife cannot conceive, or miscarries, or her children die, or if she bears only a single female, then her marital status is in jeopardy. When a barren woman (*àga,* a forbidden term not employed in address) dies, and is returned to her natal patrilineage for burial, her corpse is stabbed in the groin so that should she reincarnate her womb will be open next time. Such ritual aggression indicates that her life course has been assessed as a pact with a bad personal god.

Whereas a fertile woman should spend most of her time in child rearing and have correspondingly little opportunity to develop trade contacts (since infants cannot ordinarily be taken to market), the sole route to prestige for a woman with few or no children is through trade. Therefore variation in fertility determines a fairly sharp (though normatively disapproved) differentiation of wifely roles, about which Onitsha people have developed clear stereotypes. If a childless woman is to maintain her position in her marital household, she must gain sufficient wealth through trade to provide her husband with the means to take another wife, must directly increase his wealth through gifts, and should ornament herself to glorify him. She should buy ingredients to make him the most delicious soups. Onitsha society provides no clear normative standards for redistributing such wealth or for allocating the tasks of child rearing between wives, and this informal differentiation of roles therefore tends to create irreconcilable jealousies. A trading wife is not expected to share out her wealth among her cowives or their children, and wives are afraid to share feeding or other aspects of childcare with cowives who have had poor success in child rearing: hence imbalances within the household tend to be exaggerated.

A childless wealthy woman inevitably becomes the object of aggression from others in the long run, for without children a woman has no significant committed defenders in her marital home. She is essentially at the mercy of her husband, her cowives, and their children. A cowife with many children is free to taunt a childless woman for her trading proclivities and to cast doubts upon her spiritual cleanliness or her ancestry. If a childless woman speaks angrily about her cowife's good fortune in having children, she has "invoked the dead" (*ígbà ḿmʊɔ*), for in counting a person's children one is said to "look for their lives." The patrilineage daughters then step in, verify the offense, and fine her under threat of ostracism; if any children in the household die thereafter, she will be accused of feeding them poisonous foods or killing them with secret medicines. If she subsequently bears a child and it dies, she will be accused of "eating" her own offspring by witchcraft. Indeed, Onitsha informants tend to depict the traditional household as a kind of cowives' battleground, an image confirmed by the missionary-ethnographer Basden, who painted this rather lurid picture of Ibo marital strife:

> It is impossible to prevent quarreling, and women who have no restraint often develop fiendish proclivities. The outcome is frequently devastating . . . leading to wounding by snatched-up implements, teeth or nails. . . . It not infrequently happens that conditions become so bad, and jealousy so acute, that the only safe procedure is for a mother to send her sons away from the compound; she is afraid of the machinations of her other wives, fearing that her son is in danger of being poisoned.[10]

Although violence within the household is proscribed and its perpetrators liable to fines, there is a variety of means by which wives seek domination in the household. Both wives and husbands are said to employ a "control medicine" (called *èkẃu èkẃe,* "talk-agree") to make spouses responsive to their requests, and women are said to mix poisons (medicine) and essence of witchcraft into foods they serve to others. These indices of deception and distrust suggest high tension in the household, and it is said that wives tend to depart from such households when they feel threatened, returning either to their natal homes or to those of

10. Basden (1938:237).

their maternal grandparents. When such separation occurs, children under the age of six years usually accompany their mothers, and older children who feel insecure may do likewise.

From a wife's point of view, there are many advantages to separation, for a daughter who remains at her natal home has many ascribed prerogatives and her position may be preferable to that in a highly competitive marital household. This is particularly true for a woman who has no children or whose children are in a drastic minority in the polygynous unit. A woman can always be certain that her patrilineage or maternal kinsmen will provide a home for her and welcome her children, behaving like "mothers" to the latter and treating them better than their own patrilineage sons.

Such separations are not formalized; they may occur after a wife has been beaten by her husband, if she or her children become ill and she believes her cowives are implicated, or if she feels oppressed by any member of the household. A husband who wants his wife to return to him must undertake formal visits to both of his parents-in-law or their successors, bearing ritual gifts of drink. The parents-in-law may, if they wish to obstruct reconciliation, require a series of such consultations, but there are dangers in retaining a daughter in the face of demands by her husband's lineage. If one of her small children should die under these circumstances, the husband's patrilineage may demand a replacement from the ranks of the wife's kinsmen.

It is said that brothers or parents of a woman who is a wealthy trader may well be eager to repay her bridewealth and help her to maintain her trade from a base in her natal home. During the early colonial period and into recent years, a frequent practice of prominent trading women was to marry only long enough to gain valid marital status, a practice called "to answer a name" (*ízalu áfà*). It was also called "I do not seek complaint" (*áchɔrɔm íkpe*), alluding to a separation after which the woman takes no interest in reconciliation and instead refunds the bridewealth out of her own trading income. Such women, having satisfied the prescription that females must ordinarily marry, might even go on to play a male role, paying bridewealth for women who would bear children in their names.

A husband may drive his wife away in divorce (*íchʊpʊ̀ ńwũ̂nye*) by the ritual acts of breaking her cooking pots or destroying her hearth. Should he wish to accuse his wife of abominable acts, the husband washes his body in her sleeping quarters, symbolically removing the contamination that her acts have allegedly caused. In all these cases, the husband renounces all claims over the wife and over any future children she may bear.

Certain other traditional practices increase the incidence of divorce. Onitsha villages are said to compete openly for beautiful wives, by seduction or abduction with promises to the woman of material advantages she will gain. If the woman is willing to remain with her seducer or abductor, he merely repays the bridewealth to her parents (who transfer it to her former husband) and the new husband has "taken another's wife" (*íkwulu ńwũ̂nye*). Cannon shots are fired in the village of the abductor to mark this prestigious accomplishment, which is regarded as a legitimate way for a group to avenge a minor wrong.

It is difficult to estimate the incidence of separation and divorce in traditional Onitsha, but Onitsha people believe it was quite high, and tend to think of their women as strongly trade-oriented and independent-minded spouses despite the norms of obedience to which they are subjected. Certainly separation must have been common; villages expect to have a core of daughters in residence and to provide them with houses. Trade in village marketplaces appears to be organized largely by its daughters.

MOTHER'S PARENTS AND DAUGHTER'S CHILD

The status of a parent-in-law gains its greatest significance by association with that of mother's parent, for the latter has structural permanence. This status, extended to persons agnatically-linked to actual mother's parents, draws on the symbolism of motherhood for its role definition. In connection with the cultural construct ɔma, it was shown that mother-child filiation is elaborated into a symbolic perpetuity that gives it a "descent" significance. Mother's parents are not closely associated with ɔma, but they are linked with a number of other symbols of motherhood. In this way, in this most strongly patrilineal society, an ideology of maternal descent is transformed into a mode of defining relations between patrilineages.

"Whoever has a living mother has no age-set"; in other words, children always remain loyal, dependent children when they deal with their mother, and the same is true in dealings with their mother's agnates. Since these kinsmen are regarded as mothers, the relationship does not include the power of ɔfɔ, but is rather one of motherly nurturant indulgence and childlike gratifying dependence. Any person classed as a mother's parent always has the right to break kola for his daughter's child. This is true regardless of their other social roles. The daughter's child "can do no abomination" in the home of his mother's parent, and he has the perpetual right to "suck the breast" there. He may enter the house and demand food, may enter a room and appropriate some object which strikes his fancy. The daughter's child must be unfailingly loyal to his "mothers," which means that they can always rely upon him to help them and to support them in need. The symbolic model for the relationship is clearly expressed on ritual occasions when the mother's father begs the dead for his daughter's child; as he pours palm wine to the ancestors and calls his daughter's child to kneel before him and drink from the cup as a sign of subservience, he says, "come and take the breast."

The strength of this relationship is supported by powerful religious sanctions. It is believed that the major spirits associated with a patrilineage especially "love their daughter's children," and therefore bring these kinsmen benefits or misfortune depending on whether or not they receive proper worship. When a woman fails to conceive after marriage, she may be told that a spirit of her mother's patrilineage is troubling her and demanding veneration. A man seeking greater prosperity will "fête the spirit" (and simultaneously feed his mother's people as well) to give thanks for previous benefits and to request more. The very origin of lineage spirit shrines tends to be traced either to patrilineage daughters who died at their ancestral homes in some unusual way, or to mothers who brought medicines associated with spirits of their paternal homes into their marital homes, medicines subsequently worshipped by their sons and daughters as spirits. Most major communal shrines are identified with women in one way or the other.[11]

This ritual dependency of daughter's children is also activated during the annual ceremonial cycle, for they are expected to render homage service to their mother's parents when either set of kinsmen performs certain ceremonies. When a daughter's child performs his new yam ceremony, for example, he places one wing of the sacrificed fowl on the shrines dedicated to his mother, and then sends it as homage to the senior patrilineage priest of his mother's people. Finally, the daughter's child has the right to mourn at his mother's parent's funeral, dancing proudly in public and carrying the horsetail of mourning, but free from the responsibility of contributing to the funeral expenses.

Together with these symbolic and ritual components there exists a very important set of rights and duties between the parties to this relationship. Mother's parents guarantee and protect the daughter's child's social status, within his own patrilineage. When he seeks to establish important gains in social prestige and responsibility

11. For example, a woman named Ojedi, who had no children, was a great trader and a daughter of the major patrilineage of Children of Dei. The shrine bearing her name is located near the central residential area of this large localized lineage, beside a great grove of trees where a coven of witches is said to gather regularly by night. Ojedi is worshipped by all Children of Dei and by their daughters' children, and it is said that "nobody worships the spirits more fully than one who worships Ojedi." The daughter's children to the Children of Dei regard Ojedi as one of their mothers' parents. There are numerous instances of this phenomenon in Onitsha.

within his patrilineage, his mother's parents must join the gathering as observers who will witness all his transactions so that he cannot later be cheated; indeed, he cannot safely undertake such important activities without their consent and support and must therefore never remain in dispute with them for any length of time. When the daughter's child dies, his mother's parents will enter immediately into the funerary consultations, and if some of his patrilineage survivors claim that he has died a bad death, the mother's parents may demand the mother's right to mourn her child in peace. If, on the other hand, they suspect that there has been foul play within the patrilineage, they may demand to know who within the patrilineage has caused their child's death; if murder has occurred they may demand that the murderer be hanged; if he escapes, they may raze his compound and demand compensation. These are precisely the duties of a natal patrilineage when someone from outside kills one of its members. In these ways, the mother's parents actually breach the sovereignty of patrilineages.

Reciprocally, daughter's children are expected to act as peacemakers in the interests of their mother's parents. Should a fight break out between their own patrilineage and that of their mother, it is their duty to plead the case of their mother's people and to call for a peaceful settlement. They can travel in safety between both sides to mediate cessation of hostilities, for neither side dares harm them. So strong is this duty that Onitsha people demand that all the great political leaders of the town must have Onitsha mothers. This demand is justified by the story of a great man of Onitsha whose mother came from a town against which Onitsha planned a war. He betrayed the town in order to protect his mother's parents.

It is said that every Onitsha person must maintain an active relationship with his mother's kinsmen if his life is to be at all secure. Ideally, a man should have at least three sets of mother's parents, in decreasing order of importance: mother's patrilineage, father's mother's patrilineage, mother's mother's patrilineage. So important are these exogamous relationships that they tend to become permanent and collective on both sides. Numerically small patrilineages uphold their structural independence within Onitsha society by maintaining such collective relations with groups of daughter's children bound to them in mutual exogamy. For the daughter's child, on the other hand, the home of the mother's parents stands as an ultimate refuge. We have seen that in cases of marital separation small children remain with their mother when she returns home. If there is a killing within a patrilineage, and a person is expected to hang for it, that person may flee to the home of his mother's parents and find refuge there. If there are many disputes in a patrilineage, and so many people die there that the land becomes a "fiery surface," all members of the group may scatter to the homes of their mothers' parents.

The concept of daughter's child has a strong connotation of relationship to locality. Not only is the term said to mean "child of the soil," but it may be used in a relativistic way determined by location of utterance. For example, it is not unusual for two men from different patrilineages to be daughter's child to each other, as traced through different links. When this occurs, the usage of the reciprocal terms mother's parent/daughter's child depends on the locality where interaction occurs. If A is in his patrilineage homeland, he calls B "daughter's child"; if the two meet in B's home territory, the terminology is reversed. This connotation of territoriality implies, moreover, that the child of the soil is eligible to commit himself permanently to the land of the maternal patrilineage, and to be buried there. The ancestors, the land, and the other spirits of the patrilineage will not object to his presence, for he is one of their children. A man can, therefore, choose to become a member of his maternal patrilineage.

In general terms, given localized patrilineage groups competing for existence in a tribal setting, two basic problems seem relevant to each group: the need to gain more members as supporters, and the need to seek more land for food production. The existence of localized patrilineages and their differing "natural" expansions over time makes it likely that both problems may arise, although it is said that in traditional Onitsha "people were more valuable than land." For a numerically small unit with abundant lands, there are several ways to increase support. A traditional technique most stressed by Onitsha informants is the transfer of farm land through the "leading [the wife] home" marriage gift from a wife's parents to her husband. This is actually a gift to daughter's children, for unless the marriage is fertile such a gift would not be regarded as permanent; it is viewed as a means of tying the daughter's child more closely to the maternal patrilineage, while meeting the demand for land by members of another group. A second way is to allocate farm land to the daughter's child within the regular plot allocations made during the farming cycle, thus bringing him into the farm-clearing team of the patrilineage. Finally, the patrilineage may encourage their daughter's child to live with them as a permanent patrilineage member.

LAND TRANSFERS AND KINSHIP

There is considerable oral tradition evidence for land transfers during the precolonial period, but it refers to quite remote times and its significance is not easy to assess. The incidence of transfers as reported in these traditions may be taken as a rough measure of the stability of relations of groups to land.[12]

For lands south of Onitsha, the traditions suggest transfer of substantial blocks of land, mostly from small village units to large ones, but also from segments of one unit to segments of another regardless of size, through the leading home marriage dowry. Probably every major, named block of land in the south has undergone either total transfer or dimunition by the transfer of one or more of its subdivisions at some time or another. Most lands north of Onitsha have been transferred from the nearby outside communities, again mostly through putative leading home dowry. Subse-

12. The details of this evidence are given in Appendix A.

quent transfers within these areas have been mostly from small villages to men of larger ones, by the same method. To the east of Onitsha, a new process of transfer is reported, i.e. the redistribution of a block of lands among various chiefs. This was not done extensively, for only one case is known.

Thus oral evidence suggests considerable flexibility, over time, in the relations of groups to the lands they farm. In the vast majority of cases for which any evidence was available, these transfers were remembered as the results of leading home dowry provided by a group when their daughter married the man who sired the recipient group. The transfer, symbolized as the concomitant of a marriage, actually constitutes a transfer not to the husband but rather to the daughter's children.

It is extremely unlikely that all these oral tradition "records" reflect what really happened. Clearly, the institutionalized pattern of the leading-home dowry has here become a symbolic model for rationalizing most forms of land transfer however they may have occurred in historical fact. There is evidence that some Onitsha people have used this model to justify claims over lands which they did not control at all in precolonial times. Nevertheless the model is important, because both donor and receiver groups usually agree on the marriages specified and can name both the men and women involved in them; the deviant cases, of redistribution among chiefs, have not been rationalized in terms of marriage dowry. It is probable that a common pattern of actual transfer was for underpopulated groups with land surplus to grant usufructory rights to collective sets of daughter's children who needed additional land, thereby binding them as allies; the gradual takeover of such lands by the patrilineage descendants of the original daughter's children was then rationalized ex post facto as a "dowry transfer."

KINSHIP AND SOCIETY IN ONITSHA

Fundamentally, what we are dealing with in Onitsha is a system of internally segmented patrilineages, whose internal solidarity is predicated on the normative model of the father–child relationship but whose monolithic separateness is breached by relationships modeled on the mother–child relationship. From the perspective of the society, the central function of marriage is to legitimate and stabilize these two basic modes of social linkage. The pattern is one of a classic system of undifferentiated segmentary lineages engaged in exchange of women, a process producing a web of maternal interlinkages across the seams of patrilineage boundaries.

We have seen how this structure emerges through an articulating of kinship categories, religious beliefs, and ecological exigencies. In their kinship relations, Onitsha people live in a basically moral, collectivity-oriented community located within a generally moral universe. The beliefs and norms that identify persons, physical spaces and structures, and social groups, are systematically interconnected—indeed are refractions of one another. The system as analyzed thus far is "primitive," then, in the sense that these various domains interpenetrate so deeply with one another. It is also primitive in the sense that the boundaries of the societal community are not fully distinct: marriage and maternal relationships, land-holding and other relationships with people outside Onitsha are common, both in genealogical depth and in recent times.

The pervasive importance of kinship and marriage in Onitsha is clearly shown by the way in which all social encounters may be defined under the kola-breaking rules applied to consanguineals and affinals. Within the patrilineage, seniority by birth or generation specifies the breaker of kola at a meeting of any two persons; outside the patrilineage, structural seniority also determines this right: husbands break kola for wives, mother's parents break it for daughter's child, and wife's parents break it for child's husband.

Where there is no specifiable kinship seniority, the determination is made by other criteria such as relative age. This elementary structuring applies generally throughout the community.

It is nonetheless evident that this is not a primitive community in the sense that the individual self is totally submerged in his primordial collectivity; in both world view and normative system considerable structural space is allotted to individual distinctiveness and to the possibility of an individual's playing multiple social roles. Moreover, we have encountered some evidence of an incipient "freeing" of both human and nonhuman resources from the fixity of ascriptive bases. At the societal level, the clear preference for endogamy reflects a definite sense of the community's separateness and distinctiveness from those around it.

Not all functional sectors of the society have been covered in these descriptions and analyses of kinship relations. A major part of the economic base has been examined, fundamental legal and status structures have been considered in light of the educational milieu within which they are largely defined. These topics have not been exhausted, and we have barely considered the macropolitical level of social organization. Kinship and descent remain crucial to the Onitsha political system as to all other sectors of the system, but in order to deal fully with this topic we must go beyond kinship (while taking full cognizance of it). We are now in a position to examine the patterns of structural differentiation apparent within Onitsha society.

PART 3

STRUCTURAL DIFFERENTIATION IN ONITSHA

7 THE ƆZƆ TITLE SYSTEM: A PATHWAY TO SELF-PURIFICATION

It is not an easy matter to analyze Onitsha society in terms of its structural differentiation, for two reasons. First, various social structures are deeply embedded in the kinship organization, i.e. they interpenetrate with kinship structures. Such interpenetration is of course partly due to the pervasive range of kinship relations in Onitsha, but it also appears to be due to a basic tendency of Onitsha people to ground their more specialized norms and concepts within a symbolic framework of simpler ones. Second, once such differentiated structures have been isolated, there remains the task of showing whether or not they are historically more recent than the basic kinship structures. This is necessary if a solid case is to be made for the operation of evolutionary processes.

The interpenetration of kinship and other social structures is evident everywhere in Onitsha, beginning with the basic concepts for localized groups. For example, the notions of "patrilineage" (ʊmʊnna), "village" (ogbe), and "clan" (ebo) are intimately intertwined in the minds of Onitsha people, because ideally they should coincide with one another. The basis for this belief lies in the relation of these concepts to that of the spiritual land. The village is a local unit sharing a "village square," the patrilineage is a set of persons bound by norms of shared descent, and the clan is a venerated descent group which has long had "village" status. Now, the sanctity of the village square is insured by the land shrine located at its "mouth," and the adoration of this shrine must be mediated by a patrilineage priest. The square is tended by village youths who are the young unmarried men of the patrilineage. Ideally, this relation of a patrilineage to its village residential land should be perpetual, a "clan" relationship.

Nevertheless, there are three distinct terms referring to the localized group, and the meanings of these terms differ. The distinctions between them are related to some of the major emergent roles in the society: the notion of "clan" is linked to the idea of "king," while the notion of "village" is related implicitly to the identity of "chief" and of incarnate dead. Other roles and collectivities also have relevance to these distinctions, and all are embedded to some extent within the matrix of kinship.

Each of the differentiated structures possesses an ideological framework, a set of ideas that specify distinctive identities and relationships and entail or imply certain role qualities. Each, moreover, constitutes an organizational system that is adjusted to the kinship matrix, and is to some extent based ideologically on kinship concepts. It would be feasible to start by describing those structures which are ideologically most remote from kinship relations, in order to draw the sharpest possible contrast with them, but it seems preferable to trace the structural patterns of Onitsha society through a chain of diminishing embeddedness in kinship.

In Onitsha religion the assessment of an individual's personal god depends primarily on the number of his living children and only secondarily on other circumstances, such as wealth. It is also believed that success in other spheres of endeavor may contribute to successful raising of children. Another, directly visible representation symbolizes the publicly accepted quality of one's personal god: ideally, a man should keep the sticks that represent components of his personal god stored in a divine vessel (ɔkwachi) carved from the wood of the star apple tree, and by gaining the right to do this one signifies that his particular personal god is "bathed in wealth and purity" in a way that an ordinary person's god is not.

Also, the pivotal status of patrilineage priest has been described as one attained by the purely ascriptive criteria of birth order and death order. The Onitsha proverb which expresses this says, "patrilineage priesthood is reached in turns" (*ɔ̄kpala bʊ̀ èlumelú*). After the death of a father, his ɔfɔ ɔkpala must pass to his senior son and only to his senior son. Playing the *role* of patrilineage priest cannot, however, in the nature of role-playing, be purely an ascriptive matter. One must act, and in Onitsha this right to act as priest entails first "bringing in the father" to his ancestral house. In addition, there are usually certain other objects present which are regarded as part of a father's heritage; these remain forever associated with his ɔfɔ and are believed to be so "pure" that an elaborate chain of ceremonial acts of self-purification is necessary before the new patrilineage priest can gain operative control over them.

The shrines called "ghosts" (ndi-mmʊɔ) that a man brings into his house under ɔfɔ include the four okposi sticks; these represent the collective ancestors, named and unnamed, remembered and forgotten. Any man who has "brought in his father" can "beg" these ghosts and render them service. However, the objects representing the ghosts will very likely also include one or more "sacred treasure boxes" (*ókpùlúkpu*) and "staves" (*ɔ́sìsɩ*), and such ghosts cannot be in the physical presence of a person who has not "washed his hands" (*íkwɔ áka*), i.e. undergone self-purification.

The sacred treasure box is made of two identical blocks of kola wood about a foot and a half long, each carved in the shape of a low rectangular truncated pyramid and each dug out in the base, so that when the two blocks are fitted together, one atop the inverted other, a sizable chamber is formed inside. The box is decorated with linear carved designs to give it individuality, and in it a man stores his personal treasures, his own and his senior daughter's ɔfɔ sticks, his kola nuts, and other valued personal relics.[1] Associated with this box is a ceremonial staff, a star apple stick about four feet long, carved at both ends and ringed with three iron bands that jingle when the staff is stamped on the ground. Both box and

1. The treasure box is illustrated in Mbanefo (1962:18). In recent times, personal names of the owner have often been carved into the boxes in English script, but there are also more traditional forms of marking.

staff can be possessed only by men who have "washed their hands" and who therefore will not contaminate them.

Both sacred treasure boxes and staves follow the model of succession to the ɔfɔ ɔkpala. They have a prominent position on the altar before the throne of the patrilineage priest, and, unlike the okposi sticks which represent all the ancestors, they are specifically named for their original owners and hence represent those specific ancestors who have washed their hands. Each treasure box serves as the repository of that particular ancestor's ɔfɔ, and the ancestor himself can be ritually evoked to "enter" its chamber; as such, it symbolizes his ancestral house in microcosm. The staff is regarded as equivalent to the ɔfɔ. It is said that when a man holds his staff in his right hand and thumps it on the ground so that its iron rings jingle, the ancestors in the land of the dead hear it as clearly as they hear the message of ɔfɔ. Moreover, the staff can be used to sanction the sacrifice of a goat to be shared by "purified" men, while the ɔfɔ alone cannot.

Thus whenever the ghosts are assembled at the Onitsha patrilineage altar, the staves and treasure boxes are placed beside the okposi sticks and all are given sacrifice together. Only the ancestors who are evoked to enter the treasure boxes must be mentioned in prayer by name, and they can be given sacrifice only by a man who has "washed his hands." The patrilineage priest who has not done so cannot retain these objects within his house.

Indeed, the character of these staves and treasure boxes underlies the general requirement that every man must build his own house when he marries, for these objects are so pure that they cannot reside in a house where unpurified persons have sexual intercourse. Therefore they serve as a residentially centrifugal force, driving young men out of their fathers' houses at marriage. On the other hand, at maximal levels of patrilineage organization, they may serve as a binding, shared estate substituting for an ancestral house that has disappeared. As "property which travels," they pass in succession from segment to segment together with the position of senior patrilineage priest, and they constitute some of the most valued emblems of the ancestral estate.

In Onitsha the color white is the essence of purity.[2] If it is said of a person that "his clothes are white" (ɔ̀*chá*), they are clean (as opposed to *l̀ulu ínyi*, "permeated with dirt"). Although "white" may be used this way whatever the actual color of the cloth, white cloth is a prime symbol of purification. Purity or "whiteness" also entails both the absence of the "heat" of anger and hostility and the absence of contamination by female sexuality. "Whiteness" and abhorrence of sexual contact with women are the most consistently emphasized elements in the notion of purity or "washing the hands" (the application of water to the hands is viewed as a cooling and decontaminating act).

Such personal purity cannot be inherited but must be obtained through a long process of ceremonial acts. In these acts the individual communes with his ancestors, becomes himself increasingly ancestral in personal and social identity, and eventually takes on the essential features and attitudes of his patrilineal ancestors: the physical color of whiteness and the abhorrence and avoidance of the contaminating qualities of women. At the end of this process he will don white cloth as do the ancestors; he will be brought before the sacred relics of the clan and his body will be covered with white clay, thus assuming the white appearance of the ancestors themselves. Without undergoing such purification, the patrilineage priest cannot "beg" or "fête" the purified ghosts, nor kill a goat to be eaten by purified men of his patrilineage, for both purified ghosts and purified living men abhor his contamination. Only a person who has spiritually "died" and been reborn in such purity can act as their priest.

2. See Turner's (1966) masterful study of color symbolism, which suggests how widespread in Africa are certain basic notions about white, red, black, and other colors.

THE PROCESS OF PURIFICATION: BECOMING A "SERVANT OF NZE"

The primary process of purification is called "attaining ɔzɔ [title]" (*íchi* ɔ́zɔ).[3] It is not a single step but rather a long series of arduous tasks that must be undertaken, the whole conceived as a unity divided into two major stages. Onitsha people view the purification of the personal god and the conduct of a successful life as a continuous process of ever closer approximation to death, and the process of "attaining ɔzɔ" entails continual tests and transformations of a man's relations with his ancestors and with the spirits of his patrilineage. It is part of a continuum from the funerary acts of rubbing the father's grave and bringing the father into the house, to the goal of bathing one's personal god in wealth and purity. At the end of the task, a man covers his new, boat-like vessel of god with white chalk, making the sticks which represent that god as white as the revered ancestral ghosts.

The critical ceremonial acts of course involve not only the ancestors but also the living members of the clan, and entail "carrying money for the ghosts" (*íbu égo ḿmʊɔ*). It is of great importance that the ideology of purification is conceived and the carrying of money conducted within a patrilineage context, for this complex gives the Onitsha patrilineage an additional valued estate.

After a man has brought in the ghost of his father (and of his mother if she is dead), he may begin the task of becoming an ɔzɔ man. In doing so he must follow a set sequence of performances. His first step is "to notify the kitchen" (*ńkàtá ùsókwu*), drawing his siblings by the same mother to a meeting at which he presents them with palm wine and calls upon them to support him in his coming effort. He then calls a meeting "to notify the ancestral

3. This account is indebted to the descriptions of Onitsha title-taking published by Orakwue (1953) and Ifeka (1962). Orakwue's work gave valuable leads for field research, and Ifeka's study provided some useful additional perspectives.

house" (*ńkàtá ìba*), including all his patrilateral siblings from whom he hopes to gain support. His next step is "to notify the patrilineage" (*ńkàtá ómʊ̀ńnà*) by requesting the senior patrilineage priest to convene a meeting in the great ancestral house. This meeting will involve the widest group from which the man hopes to gain assistance in preparing for the ceremonial steps of purification; it is generally the group that he joins in farm clearing as well as his basic funerary unit—that is, the group to which he has made the formal ceremonial announcement of his father's death. Here he speaks out, requesting their backing, calling for the blessing of the senior priest and receiving it. Finally, he must approach the senior priest of the entire clan, the "maximal lineage" representative who controls a sacred object called *n̄ze* (the medium of purification), to receive his blessing for beginning the long task ahead.

All these acts are defined as "rubbing the ears" (ɩgba ɔkɔ ntɩ) of his kinsmen. At such meetings, any grievances against the candidate will be voiced and proper settlement demanded. These first steps cannot rightly be undertaken by a junior brother before his senior brother has completed them; should this be attempted, the candidate must be turned away with the demand that he first support his senior brother in seeking purification. In this process, the particular patrilineage priests approached and the specific sources of patrilineage support drawn upon affirm and set patterns of permanent reciprocal commitments.

After these initial steps of notification, the candidate arranges a series of prayer meetings for begging the blessings of the ancestors, including those of his own patrilineage, his mother's patrilineage, his father's mother's patrilineage, and, preferably, other maternally related patrilineages. On these occasions, the ɔzɔ-purified men of each patrilineage group meet to perform the prayer; the senior patrilineage priest presides, serving palm wine and other liquor provided by the candidate and calling upon the ancestors to accept the candidate's previous conduct and to guide him in good health through his arduous task of purification. The candidate's senior wife, his senior son, and his senior daughter are also called to the altar by the priest. They receive drinks dedicated to the ancestors, thereby partaking to some extent of the candidate's spiritual condition and being set apart from his other wives and offspring.

With the initial goodwill of the ancestors established, the candidate begins living a new life with spiritual propriety. His words must now become those of a man continuously responsible to his ancestors, for the ghosts will listen to him and "his words rebound against him." He cannot speak casually in anger or profanity. He must observe ritual periods of chastity and avoid casual contacts with women. Most importantly, he must begin carrying money for the ghosts. He must be very careful to avoid giving social offense during this activity, for he is especially liable to incur "public fines" or to be required to "undo forbidden acts" in his precarious spiritual condition.

Carrying money for the ghosts is a closely accounted redistributing of the wealth that the candidate has managed to mobilize. The money is first blessed and then shared among those descendants of the clan's ancestors who have themselves taken the ɔzɔ purification and who therefore deserve equal shares as representatives of the purified ancestors and as "servants of nze" (*ágbàla-nze*). Although members of the candidate's maternally related kin groups do not ordinarily share in this distribution of wealth, they must be present at each transaction to act as witnesses.

At each harvest season, the candidate goes to his farm with his clan ɔzɔ men (and some mother's parents as witnesses), and they haggle over the value of that portion of his yam harvest which he has set aside for ɔzɔ redistribution. He also calls upon his siblings to augment his fund with portions of their harvest, and as daughter's child he goes to close agnates of his mother to "suck their breasts" and receive financial assistance from them. He exhorts his sons to work hard in the interests of a bumper crop next year, calls on his sons-in-law to "work for the in-law," seeks extra aid from his age-mates and requests that his wives contribute their trading income to him so that he can meet the demands of carrying money for the ghosts.

This effort traditionally stretches over a period of years, during which the candidate pursues his goal with single-minded will, while the title-purified members of his clan continually haggle for larger and larger shares from him, in order to insure that his purification is complete. The candidate's ability to haggle the fees down to an attainable level is largely dependent upon the demands made by his maternal kinsmen for reasonableness, since no formal limits are set on the amount of ghostly money which may be requested.

The number of ɔzɔ men who share this wealth distribution varies widely, depending on the number of purified men in the clan.[4] However, the total amount transferred within any clan must remain roughly comparable with that of all other Onitsha clans; should it not be, the quality of the clan's standard of purification would become denigrated. This requirement of interclan comparability indicates basic segmental equality in Onitsha. In patrilineages of large membership, the money is divided into two equal portions. Half of it, called "money for the house" (ego ʊnɔ), is shared equally among the ɔzɔ men of the candidate's major patrilineage, i.e. his farm-cooperative unit or a higher-level segment if the clan is sufficiently large. The other half, called "money for all" (*égo ìra*), is shared equally by the ɔzɔ men of the entire maximal patrilineage—ideally, the clan.

Each stage of money transfer is followed by one in which the titled men of the group concerned assess the candidate's ceremonial efforts; these efforts are invariably found to be wanting, and additional fees are levied. The levies made on the candidate are so repetitious that observers in the nineteenth century reasonably interpreted title-taking as a kind of purchase:

4. Or splinter-group of the clan. In oral tradition and in known history, fights over ɔzɔ fees have sometimes been followed by fission of groups sharing ɔzɔ money.

> Among these people the love of riches is very great; it is a result of offices and dignities being sold. Everybody hoards up in order to be able to buy them some day, or to reach a higher grade; for on passing from one rank to another they must every time pay a fresh tribute.[5]

Completion of the carrying is followed by the ceremony of "assessing wine" (*ígbàkɔ ḿmanya*), in which the candidate must distribute more than one hundred pots of palm wine to the ɔzɔ men. This marks the end of the first qualifying preliminaries.

The first named title in Onitsha purification is *ǹkpălo,*[6] a position attained after a ceremony that follows the wine assessment, and which is referred to as "consorting with the ghosts" (*íkpa ḿmuɔ*). The candidate meets the head patrilineage priest and all ɔzɔ men of his patrilineage and presents them with additional money "for the ghosts." The head priest of the clan then sacrifices a goat upon the collected okposi sticks representing the ghosts ancestral to the candidate. This act indicates to them that the candidate now asserts the right to "beg" them with wine and blood sacrifices, and it constitutes a prayer that they will accept such offerings. After this, the candidate kneels before the altar to receive from the senior priest a cup of sacred fermented corn drink. The senior priest then sacrifices a he-goat (*mkpi*) upon the ghosts, an act which sacrificially cuts off the candidate from his past impurities and forbidden acts. Finally, the candidate is led forth and seated upon a goat skin, where he is handed a cupful of the corn wine and for the first time "serves wine" (*ítʊ ḿmanya*) in a ritual libation to his "fathers."

This ceremonial sequence brings the man to the position at which he may now actively adopt the role of patrilineage priest, for he has attained sufficient purity to serve palm wine to the ancestors, to beg them for blessing, and to call his children to drink

5. Burdo (1880:132).
6. The meaning of this term could not be analyzed.

this blessed wine from his hand as a sign of their subservience. He must sit on a goatskin, for he has now become too pure to sit directly upon the ground. He may now call his children to drink wine blessed by him, may expect periodic homage service from them, may pray to the spirits and ancestors of the group in communal ritual. He may also join in the company of chiefs when the latter participate in major funerals, and he is entitled to share the loin of funerary sacrificial goats with other nkpalo. Most importantly, he may wield his father's ɔfɔ with full authority. However, he remains too impure to perform sacrifices for those more purified men who have "died" and then returned reborn as ɔzɔ men; he may not kill a goat for such men to eat.

The attainment of nkpalo by the senior son marks the end of the junior paternal siblings' obligation to submerge their private interests in the collective support of their senior brother. Once he has reached this title, they may begin seeking their own ends.

The candidate who wishes to go beyond the level of nkpalo to gain full purification must again carry money for the ghosts. Some of this second installment of ghostly money is distributed to the "hands of the house" (aka ʊnɔ), some to "hands outside" (aka ilo). This redistribution of wealth is done in a context of "feasts for the ghosts" that tend increasingly to focus upon direct wealth exchange. Various ceremonies called "planting the Iroko tree" and "nurturing the Iroko tree" are quite attenuated acts of exchange, entailing a minimum of ritual but considerable expense.[7]

The final major steps of purification emphasize increasingly elaborate rituals. There are preparatory ceremonial "notifications" of paternally and maternally linked kinsmen similar to those undertaken at the initial stages of candidacy. The candidate then isolates himself from his wives and from the female sex generally. He arranges to acquire the major symbols of his career effort:

7. These rituals are paralleled in more elaborate form in other Ibo areas, suggesting that Onitsha ɔzɔ rituals have become attenuated from an older and more widespread Ibo pattern. The Iroko tree is also symbolically associated with kingship.

the wooden divine vessel, the staves, the sacred treasure box, and an elephant ivory horn.

The five egbo sticks representing components of his personal god are placed in the wooden ark carved with representations of elephant-tusk horns symbolizing the fusion of wealth, strength and purity. The entire divine vessel and its contents are to be covered with white chalk and placed alongside the ɔzɔ man's altar at every sacrifice he performs. As a representation of the essence of his self, it cannot be touched by the sacrificial blood offered to the dead, but it is fed yam food as are the ghosts that lie beside it. It can be carried about only by a virginal, prepubertal girl, for it is an emblem of the man's socially purified identity. It will receive blood sacrifice only once, at that final phase of his funeral when his personal god is said to have departed to the sky and his life force (mmʊɔ) has returned as ghost to the land of the dead. It will then be discarded, for such purity cannot be inherited.

Second, the candidate obtains his personal sacred treasure box, carved to his order with decorations. This will serve as a permanent mnemonic record of his achievement, ultimately to become part of his patrilineal descendants' estate and a symbolic dwelling place into which his ghost can be invoked by calling his name. Finally, he collects two staves. One of these represents the mortal nature of identity purification, for it is not banded by iron rings and will be cut to pieces by the ɔzɔ men immediately after his death in order to cut him off from his title shares. The other, banded with three iron rings, becomes an equivalent to his ɔfɔ; when it is carried as a walking stick en route to a ceremony, the sound of its jingling thump on the ground with each step he takes is heard by the ancestors below. Where ɔzɔ men meet together in a ceremony, it must be beaten on the ground to validate the decisions taken there. Onitsha ɔzɔ-titled men sometimes even speak of the staff as a replacement for the personal ɔfɔ; they consider it more important in their regular ceremonial activity, and they tend to forego the handling of ɔfɔ. Men who have not obtained ɔzɔ purification, however, claim that the ɔfɔ as an instrument of medicine is more powerful and dangerous than the staff.[8]

The climax of purification is the ceremonial dedication of the candidate to the sacred mystery of the clan, the symbol called nze. Secluded from his wives in a major ancestral house of the patrilineage, he is ritually shaved (except for a small tuft of hair); this act, otherwise performed only at his death or when he is mourning, is done by the head daughter of the clan. He is then led by night to the sacred "grove of nze" (okwu nze), where the mysterious nze objects are stored in a small gabled hut and no female being, human or animal, may enter. Significantly, the ceremonies are undertaken at night, which is ordinarily regarded as dangerous. At night deaths are announced, ritual initiating journeys to the land of the dead are undertaken, and dangerous, mysterious, reincarnate ghosts emerge from the bad bush to roam at large through the community.

The nze itself is known by ɔzɔ men to comprise the great ɔfɔ of the clan's founding ancestor with his sacred treasure box, which contains venerated, holy, mysterious relics including in some cases objects made of bronze. The awe and reverence associated with this set of objects are based upon veneration of the founding ancestor, who is viewed as the most purified ancestral being; it constitutes the most general basis of the commitment to patrilineage and to clan. Employed as an oath device for the confession of incest within the widest patrilineal descent group, nze is the most revered and mysterious relic of the clan estate. Its "abhorrence" of sexual contamination suggests its character as a patrilineal symbol.

With the priest seated within the hut of the nze, the candidate kneels before the sacred objects. He repeats oaths that he will henceforth speak with responsibility and avoid the pitfalls of or-

8. This exhaltation of the ɔzɔ ɔsɩsɩ staff at the expense of the ɔfɔ is, it should be noted, unusual in Ibo country. For example, elders from the powerful riverain community of Osomari expressed sharp disagreement with this radical viewpoint.

dinary men, that he will uphold the purified status honor of the ancestors. He is then taken, in darkness, into a hidden part of the chamber, where the priest anoints him with white chalk taken from the nze, thus cleansing his body of his past sins, making him like the ancestors themselves. A feather taken from the vulturine fish eagle (*ùgo*), said to have the remarkable medicinal quality of shedding all filth that touches it, is placed in the small tuft of hair remaining on his shaven head, and he is dressed in white cloth. A he-goat is sacrificed to the nze, and the candidate's new staves are smeared with its blood. Grasping the ɔfɔ of nze, the senior priest of nze validates the achievement of ɔzɔ purification, addressing the initiate by his chosen title (usually a name which reminds the addressor of the vast wealth which its holder has distributed, e.g. *ɔ́kʋ̀-nwá*, "Wealth of the child"). The candidate has now become a "servant of nze" (agbala-nze).

Hearing the new title name, the ɔzɔ men of the clan cheer the initiate, and escort him in a procession through the village, chanting "has money, has money" (*ńwe égo, ńwe égo*); as he walks, he is followed by the virgin girl dressed in white, who serves as his handmaiden by carrying his vessel of god. He is led to the great ancestral house, where the ɔzɔ men of his clan hold a festive nocturnal vigil (*ína òbibi*) during which the initiate, now saluted as "King of ɔzɔ" (*ézè* ɔ́zɔ), distributes still more wealth and kills two goats. He cannot yet return to his own house, for he is too pure to enter it or to have contact with members of his family.

After this vigil, the initiate retires within the ancestral house, and on the following morning his colleagues go to prepare his wives for renewed contact with him. Each wife must hand these visitors ceremonial gifts of food and drink, and each then takes a title name glorifying herself. In the afternoon during the public "Dance of ɔzɔ" (*égwu* ɔ́zɔ), the initiate and his wives are reunited. The initiate arranges for two cows to be killed and provides fish for a general banquet. Dressed in white cloth the ɔzɔ men assemble and emerge in procession to the village square where they dance, circling round the initiate and his handmaiden. They sing out praises to him and his family, addressing him by his title name, and blowing elephant ivory horns in his honor, while he dances, chanting "I have emerged!" The dominant theme of the dance itself is one of profound contempt for those who have not taken the title, as can be seen in some of the words of the song which accompanies it:

A minor speaks out,	ádι nànta kẃue ǹ'ókwu-o
a nobody responds to him;	ádι nìmó áwolʊ̀ya
replying thus, he gets back anger;	ówolùya ówolɔ̀numa
carrying anger to go forth in the world.	éweluɔ̀numa éje ǹ'ʊwa

During this song, any ɔzɔ dancer may ostentatiously thump his staves on the ground before an untitled acquaintance as a gesture of arrogance, and it is said that elderly untitled men avoid attending the dance because of their frequent humiliation. At the climax of the dance before the initiate's own house, he and his senior wife approach, dance, and ultimately embrace publicly[9] beneath an arch of egbo limbs. She presents him with a goat, fish, and other presents which validate her new identity as "wife of his god." Husband and wife then return together to his house.

The "recounting of ɔzɔ fees" (*ígbà ʊ́gwɔ* ɔ́zɔ̀) follows this crucial public ritual. The ɔzɔ men of the clan try to extract more wealth from the candidate by fining him for any ceremonial errors he may have committed, and he must satisfy these demands before gaining the right to an equal share in all the future title fees of the candidates of his clan who follow him. As at all other exchanges, his collective mother's parents bear witness to his final validating payment.

Thereafter, the initiate performs ceremonies which express the magnitude of his accomplishment. As a new ɔzɔ man (*ónye*-ɔ́zɔ), he holds a mock market (*ízʊ̀ áfia* ɔ́zɔ) in the village square, during

9. Such public behavior, ordinarily subjected to disapproval, proclaims their renewed sexual compatibility.

which he makes gifts of food to members and wives of his local group. He then goes with the men of his patrilineage out to their farmland, where he presents himself to the guardian spirit of yams and performs a ceremonial feast there to thank this spirit for securing him the fine yam harvests which made possible his title. Finally, he performs a feast for the land of his village, thanking it for recognizing his worthiness to take the title by preserving his life during the difficult undertaking.

With his ceremonial distributions completed, the title-holder has become fully purified, and he now begins publicly to assert his prerogatives. For twenty-eight days, he does little other than perform the cermonial feat of "washing hands of ɔzɔ" (ιkwɔ aka ɔzɔ) in various houses of the community, to which he has been invited to spread the blessings of his new holiness. When he enters a house, he is handed a calabash of water by a virgin girl of the household. Seated on a goatskin, he immerses his hands in the water and prays for the good health of all members of the family there. After any other ɔzɔ men present have also dipped their hands in the water, the calabash is returned to him and, again placing his hands in the water, he picks up the money which his hosts have placed in the bottom of the vessel and retains it as a sign of the prerogatives associated with his new state of grace. The young girl then takes the calabash outside the house and pours its water through the main entryway into the room, so that these blessings of purification will flow in to benefit all it members.

THE SIGNIFICANCE OF ƆZƆ PURIFICATION

In Onitsha social life, ɔzɔ men dress in white cloth and wear the fish eagle feather on ceremonial occasions as visible symbols of their spiritual proximity to the divine. These objects embody the attributes of purification. It is said, for example, that "the eagle feather does not tarnish" (*ùgo áda ágbachu*). This notion includes elements of both luster, or polish, and cleanliness. "It has tarnished" (ɔ́ *chúrugo*) may be said of a metal object which has rusted, and also of cloth irreparably stained. It may also be applied to a person who has become disesteemed. Thus the essential components of the purification idea include images of permanent luster and cleanliness.

In their social activities, ɔzɔ men are expected to evince this purification. When they speak at patrilineage or public meetings, their words should bear evidence of their diplomacy and honorable character. They should refrain from careless speech, casual committing of forbidden acts, and abominations, for the ancestors and the patrilineage spirits are believed to heed carefully what the ɔzɔ man says, and to act accordingly.

Ɔzɔ men carry round leather fans (*àzuzu*) which "cool" situations and enforce peace among disputing nontitled men. Ɔzɔ men may therefore preside at village meetings where controversial decisions must be made. In ritual celebrations, they carry the great elephant-tusk trumpets (ɔ́*dʊ*) whose sounds proclaim that ɔzɔ men, mighty as elephants, are present to dignify the occasion.[10]

The bodies of ɔzɔ men are holy. They cannot sit directly upon the ground and they cannot be asked to dig a grave or to carry a corpse, because in their proximity to the purified ancestors such contact might cause their own deaths. They cannot be expected to demean themselves by communal labor. If a nontitled person strikes an ɔzɔ man, or insults him directly, he has committed a forbidden act and must ceremonially undo it just as a son must if he strikes his father. The ɔzɔ man's body is particularly endangered by the defiling properties of women, and therefore no menstruating woman may be allowed in his presence.

Only an ɔzɔ man should undertake construction of a house in the form of the ancestral house, with its interior courtyard. Al-

10. The elephant-ivory horns simultaneously represent purity (in their whiteness), wealth (because of their rarity), greatness (the size of the elephant), and the new voice attained by the initiate (the trumpeting sounds). No untitled man may carry or blow such a horn in public. The importance of this emblem is such that another way of referring to the achievement of ɔzɔ title is the "taking of the horn."

though an untitled patrilineage priest may occupy his deceased father's ancestral house, only an ɔzɔ man may build one for his own use. (Since such ancestral houses become great meeting halls and foci of patrilineage unity, this structure influences lineage division and separation.)

Only a patrilineage priest who has "washed his hands" may kill a goat and serve blood to the purified ancestors in public communions at which ɔzɔ men are present, and ɔzɔ men may eat only of goats killed by a purified priest. In any ceremonies that they attend, ɔzɔ men are served prior to, and receive larger individual shares than, the untitled.

The ɔzɔ man's purity reflects on his senior wife, so that she may act as "wife of his god," ritually "washing" his vessel of god in white chalk prior to important ceremonial occasions; she may also prepare food for the purified ancestral ghosts and for the spirits of his patrilineage. No other wife may do such things, for in general ɔzɔ purification entails the strictest circumspection in all relations with females. The head daughters of each clan unit must also undertake a kind of self-purification analogous to that of ɔzɔ, which gives them sufficient prestige to "quiet the houses" of ɔzɔ men. This entails carrying money to the senior priests and to other head daughters, the ceremonial wearing of white cloth, and the like.

STRUCTURAL IMPLICATIONS OF THE ƆZƆ IDENTITY

It is of great importance in Onitsha social life that these socially significant characteristics of ɔzɔ purification are shared by all descent groups, that the style of life of an ɔzɔ man is recognized and acclaimed as honorable by all members of the community, and that, at the same time, this identity transformation occurs within a social context overwhelmingly defined in descent group terms. Ɔzɔ statuses are achieved, and the roles played by an ɔzɔ man strongly emphasize his achieving, but the attainment of the identity itself occurs inside the highly ascriptive social context of the patrilineal descent group.

A problem inevitably arises in the relationships between senior patrilineage priests at various levels of lineage segmentation and ɔzɔ men who are junior members of such units. According to Onitsha dogma, in the ideal, ancient state of affairs, only a senior patrilineage priest would find it necessary to become a "servant of nze." Ideally all his junior agnates rallied around him to help attain that purification. Perhaps others might then follow him in order of seniority. However, Onitsha people also recognize that for generations, a practice known as "uprooting the trunk" has been in operation. In this procedure the senior paternal brother is assisted in reaching the partial purification of nkpalo, so that he can do basic libations to the ancestors and receive agnatic homage. Then his junior brothers race competitively to be the first to acquire full ɔzɔ title. Such internal competition, universally deplored, indicates a deep normative conflict within the patrilineage system.

A similar ambivalence has emerged at a more abstract symbolic level as well. The importance of "clan" in the ideological definition of Onitsha community depends primarily upon the clan's holding the institution of ɔzɔ as part of its joint estate. This in turn is based upon control of the symbolic objects called nze. The nze is an essential part of the patrilineate in Onitsha, for its symbolic properties serve to legitimate exclusive patrilineal rights. Its ultimate abhorrence of female sexual contamination, expressed for example in its use as an oath in intrapatrilineage incest confession ritual and in the ban on any pre-menopausal woman's entering the nze grove for any purpose, is one side of this pattern. The positive ancestor orientation in ɔzɔ purification itself is the other side of the pattern, emphasizing linkage to agnatic ancestors and identification with them. Thus it would seem that the nze must be held by a patrilineage priest of the highest order of seniority.

However, the idea of self-purification, while related to the image of ancestors, is a more general notion than that, for the personal god has a wider meaning than mere association with ancestors. The purification of self transforms one's general identity to bring a man close to the divine order of things. Moreover, the founding ancestor whom the nze symbolizes could not himself have been an ordinary man, for the nze includes not only his exceptionally sacred ɔfɔ but also his treasure box of purification, which contains mysterious holy relics. All these features suggest that only a priest who has himself attained an extremely high order of purity can hold effective control over the nze; achievement is implied at the highest clan level also. The processual implications of these pattern conflicts are central to the social system as a whole, finding only a partial resolution in the institution of kingship.

8 KINGSHIP: THE FUSION OF ONITSHA VALUES

Kingship in Onitsha is based on a complex of intersecting, only partially separable symbolic components; together they outline a coherent social identity, analyzed separately they relate to a variety of different structures, even different traditions. The three major terms referring to the king are *ézè*, concerned fundamentally with his relationship to the sacred nze complex; *òbí*, which alludes to his providing a secure forum for public meetings and court proceedings; and *ígwe*, "the sky." The various role aspects of kingly identity are suggested by these and other titles.

EZE AS "FATHER," AND HIS POSITION IN THE CLAN

The king is referred to as "our father" (*ńnà-ányi*), and his identity is closely bound up with patrilineage and clan symbols. In the Onitsha hinterlands, contiguous peoples use the term obi to refer to the public meeting house of the senior patrilineage priest. Onitsha elders say that at the time of the early kings, the kings were indeed senior priests. Remarkably, Onitsha kingship recognizes not just one eze, but nine, one from each of the legendary nine clans said to have founded the community. In eight of these clans, the kings, called "hidden kings" (*ézè ídi*), should also be the head patrilineage priests of their clans; each hidden king holds the clan nze and uses it to confer purification on his clansmen. In each of these eight groups, the nze objects consist of a single massive ɔfɔ placed atop a sacred treasure box.

The ninth clan is the "Children of King Chima," whose king cannot be the most senior patrilineage priest of the clan but nevertheless holds the clan's sacred nze. This nze, unlike that of the nonroyal groups, consists of nine ɔfɔ sticks bound together with a loop of iron wire at each end. One stick, larger than the others and representing the royal clan, is bound with three rings of iron; the smaller sticks are bound with a single ring of iron. Together, the sticks represent the nine primordial clans. When men of the community bow before the eze of Onitsha they are saluting this nze object. With this instrument the Onitsha king confers ɔzɔ purification upon members of the royal clan, thus playing a role similar to that of the head priest of a nonroyal clan, but the multiple structure of the instrument implies a recognized higher prestige for his own ɔfɔ nze than for that of any other group. It is proverbial that, as holder of this nze, the Onitsha king must always wear white cloth while in seclusion.

The king of Onitsha holds a tapering rod of iron, called "anvil ɔfɔ" (*ɔ̀fɔ́ ótùtu*) or *ɔ̀fɔ́ òbí*, "king's ɔfɔ."[1] The tradition of the bringing of this object from the town of Ɔbamkpa across the river Niger justifies the right of the Children of Ase in Onitsha to appropriate this staff after the death of each king and confer it upon his successor. This gesture is said to symbolize the acceptance by the nonroyal clans of the king's authority, for it is largely by virtue of the nze and the anvil ɔfɔ that the king's premises became a court (*únɔ̀ íkpe,* literally, "house of complaint") in which disputes heard and judgments pronounced become binding upon the entire community. For this reason the king is regarded as obi by all Onitsha people, and he holds the sacred bell (*ḿgbilimgba*) rung to command silence in such public assemblies.

In the anvil ɔfɔ the meaning of ɔfɔ shifts beyond the descent group per se. First, the anvil ɔfɔ is made of iron rather than wood from the ɔfɔ tree, and its form is more like a cannon than a phallus. It is also doctored with medicines to enhance its potency, e.g. the potion called "when the strength of the aged one is finished,

1. There is some evidence that this anvil ɔfɔ was traditionally regarded as part of the nze complex itself. In recent times the two were treated as separate objects.

he takes a walking stick," which is intended to invigorate old objects.[2] The feathers of a variety of birds are attached to it, including a parrot's red tail feather called *áwʋ̀ḿme*, otherwise worn only by men who have killed a leopard. Finally, some representation of the chameleon (*ówʋ̀magana*) should be placed on the royal ɔfɔ, for the chameleon is a major symbol of the king's powers. Onitsha people avoid this animal, saying that no one can know the chameleon; "if it sees black, it blackens, if it sees white, it whitens" (*ɔ́fʋ óji ójighalia; ɔ́fʋ ɔ̀chá ɔ̀chághalia*). These attitudes suggest an ambiguity and unpredictability in the king's use of his staff of authority that does not apply to the basic ɔfɔ.[3]

Thus the king holds two ɔfɔ-like objects, the prototypes of which are held by patrilineage priests, but both represent modifications from that base. His nze represents ancestral purification and gives him the right to bestow such purification only on members of his clan; however, its sanctity is greatly respected by all clans, and its holder is not and cannot be senior patrilineage priest of his own royal clan. His royal anvil ɔfɔ is conferred upon him by the nonroyal clans, and it has symbolic components representing a normative freedom from strict "ancestral truth" (alluded to particularly by the chameleon element) which the patrilineage ɔfɔ does not possess.[4]

2. *Ikwegwu ágadi òwelú ɔ́kpɔ̀si.* Another medicine applied to the anvil ɔfɔ is called *ɔbala ɔra,* the tonal pattern and meaning of which was by oversight not determined during research in the field. It might mean "blood of the public" (*ɔ̀bala ɔ́rà*), but that is speculation. Both medicines are said to have been brought from Ɔbamkpa town.

3. The chameleon, a widespread symbol of kingship in west Africa, is regarded in Ibo country as both cognitively unclassifiable and behaviorally anomalous. Some amazing feats are attributed to it in Ibo animal fables. One salient feature is its apparent imperturbability in the presence of fire and other mortal dangers, when it is said to proceed with continued slow and measured movements. The Onitsha symbol appears to include attached elements representing "control" of these forces, for a royal ɔfɔ probably manufactured in 1962 showed a chameleon "caged" within four iron wedges.

4. The Onitsha king holds still another emblem of apparently ancestral authority called *ǹgʋ ágʋ̀lʋ́ga,* a brass spear with six short longitudinal rods bellying out at its mid-portion. Onitsha people in recent times could say little about its significance, but it is clearly similar to staves held by ɔzɔ men in various Nri-dominated communities. The significance of this will become apparent later.

Another of his titles is ghost (mmʊɔ), for when he is installed his accession rites bring him fully to the social condition of the dead. Not only is he, like the ɔzɔ men, identified as quasi-ancestral, but his final installation ceremony (ɔfala) serves as an enactment of his final funeral. During it he enters then emerges from a death-like seclusion, reincarnate and renewed. This ceremony is repeated annually to test the spiritual health of king and community.

Possessing the social status of a ghost, the king is expected to act in certain ways that are inversions of normal procedures. He carries the horse-tail switch (*ótîn̄ri*),[5] which normal men may hold only as mourners during funerals of their kinsmen, and he holds it in the left or death hand; but he does this on ordinary occasions, never when one of his kinsmen has actually died. Being himself an ambiguous kind of ghost—one who remains in the land of the living—he cannot undertake the kind of ritual communication with ghosts that ordinary men have. He cannot, for example, see or have the ordinary man's relationship with those ghosts who take the visible form of the collective incarnate dead (mmanwʊ). However, since he has become fully deceased, he may no longer retain the identity of the quasi-ancestral ɔzɔ man, and must therefore transfer this ɔzɔ title to his senior son. He does of course possess the ancestral holiness of body, and in enhanced form: not only may he not sit directly upon the ground, he must have specially constructed seats, pillows, and arm-rests to support his body at rest. In this sense, his body is regarded as the ultimate in corporeal holiness; he is defined as having no bodily functions, and his latrine is a palace location forbidden to all but his most trusted servants. He must display no evidence of emotions in public, and it is proverbial that no one should see his mouth open or observe him eating or drinking.[6]

5. This term means "it hits people," the imagery implying that one who holds the switch swipes away pestering people like a horse swipes away flies with its tail.

6. Orakwue (1953:52) lists the objects used for supporting the royal body. There is a proverb concerning the king's impassivity: "if the king smiles, the chiefs crack up their heads [laughing]" ("*Ézè ḿʊa ámʊ, ǹdîchie étiwasia ísifa*).

For these and other reasons, although the king is referred to as "our father," he cannot participate in the roles of the head patrilineage priest for the royal clan. Although he has appropriated one of the central objects of priesthood (the nze), he has also become something different from a patrilineage priest.

THE KING AS SERVANT TO SPIRITS, AND AS HIMSELF SPIRIT

The Onitsha king has such close relations with powerful spirits that he tends to be identified with them. His title salutations include a number of such identifications, e.g. he is called "Great river which can dissolve endless salt," and "Rock which stems the flow of the great river." [7]

The king must propitiate several very powerful spirits whose influence is believed to affect the entire community. Most of these are located near the great nkwɔ day waterside market at the bank of the Niger. Immediately east of this market is located a shrine to the land of Onitsha (anι Ɔnιcha), marked by a large sacred grove near which a "great ebenebe" (*n̄núkwu ébènébe*) tree was long ago planted by Onitsha women. A spirit called "She Lives in the Water" (*òbinam̄ili*) is said to reside in the river where it runs past the market, and a great whirlpool, *ìte ófe* ("soup pot"), north of the market where the Niger and Anambra rivers converge, is said to protect the town from evils coming from the north. On a promontory of rocks along the edge of the river south of the market is the spirit called "it eats Nri [man]" (*óli-n̄ri*); this is believed to protect Onitsha not only from incursions from the south but also from improper behavior by men from the cultural center at Nri. Since the Onitsha king is responsible for mediating relations with these spirits, his representatives, together with mem-

7. Such salutations have multiple meanings. Here he is identified with the river Niger (regarded as a mighty spirit), while the reference to salt dissolving alludes to his putatively insatiable proclivities to consume valued goods which others must present to him. The image of a great rock also implies spirit, and in this salutation implies a force immobile, stolid in the presence of continuous flux.

bers of the Ulutu-Ado clan who were the ancient inhabitants of the waterside area, must be present when any sacrifice is made to them.

To understand fully the relation of the Onitsha king to spirits, it is important to recognize that in the Ibo communities of the hinterlands certain statuses and roles that Onitsha people attribute to their king are attributed either to spirits or to those who serve such spirits as "cult slaves" (*òsú*). A central meaning of spirit is the property of oath (iyi); in Onitsha, oaths may be vowed on the king himself. He maintains a collection of secret objects which he administers as oaths to those who become chiefs, but it is also possible for an ordinary person dissatisfied with other oaths to take his vow on "the life of the leopard" (*ńdʊ̀ ágʊ*). This is an "oath on the king" (*íyi òbí*), an act requiring only the eating of kola received from the king's hand.

Spirits are also said to draw to themselves objects of propitiation, atonement, and retribution, including the ghosts of those whom they have killed for transgressions. All objects that remain in prolonged close contact with spirits tend to become both fearsome and contaminated; the groves of spirits, for example, are both holy (asɔ) and bad bush (ajɔ ɔfia). In Ibo country near Onitsha, the most powerful spirit shrines of each community attract cult slaves. Cult slaves are dedicated to a spirit; they become the property not of a human being but of that spirit. They care for its physical shrine and watch over its sacred grove; they oversee its propitiation and uphold the observance of its laws among freemen.

Since a spirit may "inherit" the property of persons it has killed in an oath, the cult slaves may as its servants share this property among themselves. Since their bodies become physically associated with the spirit, no freeman dares to shed their blood, and they may commit offenses that no freeman dares attempt. Because of their close association with the dangerous spirit, and with the "malevolent ghosts" believed to hover near spirit shrines, their bodies are also regarded with fear and loathing. No freeman will eat with a cult slave, much less marry one, for any person contaminated by such contact with a cult slave must himself become one.

By the logic of this relation, moreover, any person who has become a criminal in the eyes of the community may escape human retribution by fleeing into a spirit grove; he obtains permanent sanctuary there, but he becomes forever a cult slave to that spirit. All children born of cult slaves remain cult slaves and as such are "sacred," in the general Onitsha sense of being both "holy" and "forbidden."

Early observers of Ibo peoples found it difficult to accept the notion that such mediators between men and their gods could be so despised, so ostracized from the world of freemen, but the seeds of these attitudes run deep in Ibo beliefs about spirit. An analogue to the sanctuary rights of cult slaves exists in the Onitsha treatment of domestic slaves (oru), who may claim the shrine of courtyard land as a moral sanctuary. As the early ethnographer Leonard reported, merely by touching or breaking the land altar in a household

> belonging to some big patriarch or chief . . . a slave or dependent belonging to some other person is able to obtain, or in fact to compel, justice. For in this way he places his person under the protection of the god [i.e. spirit] himself, and no man who has the smallest regard for his own well-being as well as that of his house would dare to incur the displeasure and most probably the wrath of his god.[8]

In Onitsha itself only one kind of person approximates the condition of a cult slave, and that is a king.[9] He approximates this

8. Leonard (1906:420).

9. This statement is accurate for recent times, but may not have been true in the precolonial era. Female slaves apparently acted as servants and priestesses at the shrine of the protective spirit called "old woman" (*ágadι ńwânyι*) at the eastern frontier of Onitsha community (John n.d.), but it is not clear whether such women were classed by Onitsha people as cult slaves or ordinary slaves (c.f. Horton 1954). In recent times, informants stressed their lack of the osu custom except in the case of the king, who was viewed as at least metaphorically a cult slave, though he was not publicly referred to as such.

condition in his relation to the great spirit *Údo,* whose worship is controlled by the numerically tiny but highly revered Ɔbiɔ clan. In the central ritual of kingship succession, the successor is dedicated by the hidden king of Ɔbiɔ to this great spirit, whose shrine is said to represent the burial place of the ancient kings. Like the cult slaves of the Onitsha hinterlands, the new king is thereafter regarded as a living sacrifice of atonement and is the object of attitudes of mingled awe and revulsion. Unlike the cult slaves of the hinterlands, he does not automatically transmit this condition to his children. The dedication is ritually revoked after his death by the Udo priest. Because he is thus simultaneously revered and abhorred, he must be secluded from contact with ordinary men. There is danger on both sides in such contact; because he is so pure, he is exceptionally susceptible to pollution. On the other hand, those who come into sexual contact with him, i.e. his wives, are thereby contaminated by his powers and must join him in seclusion. Escaped criminals or slaves may run to him for sanctuary, and by doing so they become forever his slaves. The same is true for any persons so bold as to touch him or to sit upon his throne: they cannot continue to exist except through identification with him. Therefore they become his slaves.

Through his cult relationship to the Udo spirit, the king is freed of ordinary behavioral proscriptions, not only with regard to ordinary freemen but particularly with regard to his own immediate agnates. It is said that "the king does not experience judgment or guilt"; because he is identified with spirit and cannot be accused of abominations or required to take ordinary oaths, he is free to attempt things which others cannot essay. He can pronounce judgments of death, and he directs the major annual sacrifices of expiation to the community spirits, most importantly to the land of Onitsha and to the river Niger. The responsibility for such duties is believed to be more than ordinary men can bear.

THE KING AS GOD

The third element in Onitsha belief is an emergent notion of the king as god (chi) of the Onitsha people.[10] The most common indicator of this is the salutation "sky" (igwe), the term most frequently used to address him. As the sky the Onitsha king holds the royal drums (ufie), a pair of short cylindrical slit drums, the beating of which is believed to usher in the dawn. The king rises from slumber when the royal drums are beaten, and the sound also defines the beginning of daylight and morality for the entire community: if a person leaves his home before "royal drums" and happens to be killed, there may be no public inquiry about his death, for it is assumed he went out for an immoral purpose; if a cock crows before "royal drums," it has committed an abomination by presuming to herald the dawn and it must be killed.

After the king rises in the morning he bathes and, as the royal drums call out the names of previous kings, he grasps his nze and offers each deceased king a prayer and kola. Then he takes the anvil ɔfɔ and offers kola to ancestors of the nonroyal clans. Afterwards, he makes a circuit of the mouth of the open square within his palace grounds, offering food and salutation to trees along its flanks that represent various aspects of his spiritual self. One of these, the "mouth egbo" (*ɔ́nʊ égbò*), is associated with his personal god and on important occasions receives human sacrifice. Another, an Iroko tree, enshrines the spirit of his greatness.

In additional and related senses the king approximates god. First, he not only ushers in the day, he also sets the calendar by proclamation, prophesies forthcoming seasonal events, and participates in ceremonies during this cycle without which, it is be-

10. I use the term "emergent" because most Onitsha people did not make this identification; only a few from the royal clan did. Others told about it found it plausible, because the king is clearly associated with the spirits closest to the great god, i. e. the sun, moon, and sky. I did not hear of his association with thunder or lightning, though it may well have formerly been believed.

lieved, the seasons would fail to run their expected course. Second, in this ceremonial participation, the king in traditional times performed human sacrifices; for he is also saluted as "He kills a person on the day that one most values life," i.e. he may intervene in the life course set by one's personal god, for his own holy purposes. In taking human life for pursuit of a higher aim, he therefore approximates god and spirits. Human sacrifice was in the traditional system the consummate act of kingship. The king is called "The great snake whose prey comes to him," and is represented in art by a coiled python and also by a coiled black cobra, sometimes depicted holding an egg in its mouth.[11] Since the egg symbolizes life in Onitsha thought, this image shows the king holding this ultimate value in the balance. For human sacrifice, he keeps a curved sacrificial sword (*ádà*), an instrument said to derive from Benin. It is also said that in ancient times only the king could kill cows for sacrifice; therefore only he could be called "Cow Killer" (*ògbu-éfi*).

These intimate relations of the king to the day, to seasons, and to the control of life appear to underly the use of the emblems of sun and moon to represent him in art. On the cow-leather fans held both by chiefs and by ɔzɔ men, the servants of nze, these emblems are prominent. They link their holders to a source of authority who is at once human and divine.[12]

THE KING AS WARRIOR

His capacity to kill points to a final major aspect of the king, namely his position as the greatest of all "killers" (ndi-ogbu), or "warriors" (ńdi-ìkẽnga). The Onitsha king is identified with the leopard (*ágʊ*), regarded as the animal most dangerous to man

11. The salutation is *ágbu ànι ǹa-ánɔ̀ ànι íɟe ógèlí à ɓialu-ỳa*. The phrase *ágbu ànι*, literally "ground rope," refers to a type of python. The black cobra, *ágwɔ ɔ̀la*, is said to have a ridge running behind its head; another variety, *ágwɔ ɔ̀lιla*, is said to be brownish and spotted, also with a ridge behind its head.

12. The divinity of the king in this sense is beyond doubt, but I did not elicit any other clear associations between him and the sun or moon.

and called king (eze) of the forest. Only a king can sit on leopard skin, and most of the artistic emblems in his palace are covered with leopard spots.

This identification is so thorough that whenever a hunter kills a leopard, the body of the animal must be brought before the king to determine by inquest that it is not the king himself. Seated on his throne, the king throws a spear at the animal to "kill" it; then it is dissected and its gall bladder (*ónùnu*), considered a deadly poison, is removed and given to the king as evidence and insurance of his own safety. As killer of the leopard, the king also retains the animal's skin and head but gives the hunter part of the carcass, replenishes his gunpowder, and adorns his head with a fish-eagle feather as a reward for his courage. The hunter is thereafter regarded as one of the community's killers. The king has the right to receive this leopard tribute (which includes in fact all large animals, all fish eagles, and any "stray men," *òse,* caught wandering) from any community which accepts his superior identity as warrior.

This aspect of the king's character implies a three-way identification of king, hunter/warrior, and leopard as killers. When any Onitsha man kills a person in war, that man must also be brought before the king to receive a fish eagle feather, representing an enhanced self-purification and luster. The king, like the leopard, is a purposeful hunter and killer of men; the hunter who kills a leopard or a warrior who kills a man thus dangerously identifies himself with the king, and for this reason the latter must legitimize the act. The fish eagle feather that the king bestows proclaims that the killing is positively valued, and permanently enhances the killer's prestige. (Only a king may keep fish eagles penned in captivity for such purposes.)

More directly symbolizing the king's prowess in battle are his titles "Cannon containing powder" (*ógbondù-na-éjì-ńtʊ*), "Hand which smote the Ibo" (*áka-ḿelu-ìgbo*), and "Arm of the elephant more mighty than its thigh" (*áka-ényi-ká-ólu-ʊkwʊ-ýa*). The latter two salutations allude to the personal spirit ikenga, which represents the glories of aggression implemented through the power of a person's right arm. Some central items of the king's regalia also stress his powers. He controls a set of war drums (*égwu-ɔ́ta,* lit. "shield drums"), including the double iron gong (*ózì*) that calls chiefs to perform the dance of war. One iron gong of the set, called *ɔ̀génè,* is beaten by his messengers around the town to announce decisions such as those for intertribal warfare. This gong is regarded as the king's mouth and voice. The king also holds the double-edged "ceremonial sword" (*ḿmà àbani*) of brass; this weapon for leading soldiers to war is touched to the ozi gong to direct the sounding of the war drums.

At the annual "killer's feast" (*ɔ̀gbalido*), celebrated only by accomplished warriors and warrior chiefs, the king receives the highest tribute from all participants in recognition of his position as the greatest of warriors. When he emerges later from seclusion, he carries his ceremonial sword and wears his great headdress tableau of intersecting wooden arches, all stuck with feathers taken from a variety of birds that symbolize his bravery, purity, wealth, and power; this capping array has the appearance of a great tree in which many birds are perching. His more usual "royal crown" (*òkpú ézè*) is of cow leather, stuck with multiple fish eagle feathers tipped with brass.

Beliefs about the king's fearsomeness through his links to spirit, and his dangerousness as warrior, intermingle in his identity as the holder of dangerous medicines. The king is the keeper of the poisonous sasswood medicine (*ɔ̀ráchi,* erythrophloeum Guineense), which he employs (for a fee) to test Onitsha women accused of witchcraft (and to test both Onitsha and non-Onitsha people accused of other kinds of crimes). On those rare ceremonial occasions when he emerges into public view, he carries his horsetail fan, the handle of which is said to be laden with medicines for protection against, and application of, "sorcery" (*íkʊ-ńsi,* literally, "hitting with poison"), and he wears on his left arm a brass band (*ɔ́dʊ ɔ́nà*) heavily doctored with prepared protective medicines (*ɔ́gwʊ̀ ágwɔ̀lagwɔ́*). Anyone in his presence is greatly endangered when the king moves into public gatherings, for Onitsha people have sorcery in mind when they say, "if two pots collide, the smaller one must break."

THE IDENTITY OF THE "HIDDEN KING"

Onitsha people are emphatic in stating that the "hidden kings" are kings in the full sense of the term; they differ primarily in the range of loyalties that they can command, and indeed some of them are considered in some ways more sacred than, and senior to, the king of all Onitsha.

The hidden kings, like the king of Onitsha, hold the nze objects of their clans, and like him they bestow ultimate ɔzɔ purification by chalking the candidates of the clan. They too are saluted by Onitsha people as "the sky," and like him they hold the royal drums (ufie) whose beating ushers in the day. They are defined as "dead" and celebrate their own joyous funerary "emergence" annually; at least some of them hold the royal ceremonial sword (mma abani) and are related symbolically to the leopard. They are, finally, dedicated to the major spirits of their respective clans and to the great community spirit of Udo, thereby approximating the condition of cult slaves.

The clan with a hidden king can have cows killed by him for the group, and when one of its members kills a leopard or captures a fish eagle or a "stray man" in its territory, these trophies are brought before the nze holder of that clan. The clan with a hidden king, moreover, may hold its own court and therefore salute its head as obi. Its king can pass judgments on its own members, including, apparently, the judgment of death.[13]

13. It is not possible to be certain about this because the title of hidden king, disregarded by the British, therefore lost its autonomy and raison d'être early in the colonial period. In recent times its holders have continued to fulfill some of its role requirements but not the more crucial ones. The evidence on traditional murder cases

The hidden king is therefore truly a king and not a quirk of terminology. The most revered of these personages is the eze idi Ɔbiɔ, the senior patrilineage priest of the smallest clan in the community, who can serve here as a type-case. The hidden king of Ɔbiɔ holds his own ceremonial sword, made of brass just like that of the king of Onitsha, and he holds two royal drums regarded as senior to those of the Onitsha king. When he approaches the king of Onitsha, the latter must rise from his throne and pace about; the Ɔbiɔ king enters, addresses him with arrogance, ultimately orders him to take a seat, exchanges salutations with him as an equal,[14] then actually sits beside him on his throne in ultimate mutual identification. Moreover, the Onitsha king must serve homage annually to this more senior king.

The other hidden kings do not have so exalted a position, but they have similar qualities which place them on a level with the king of Onitsha. All of them also differ from him in important ways. First, the range of recognition for some of their qualities differs. The hidden king is obi (and therefore, court) only to his clansmen, and only his clansmen will bring leopards and other stray beings before him. Only his clansmen (and other obliged kinsmen) will attend his annual ceremonial emergence. Second, some of their qualities are attenuated in comparison to those of the Onitsha king. Although the hidden kings hold royal drums, these drums are "muffled," they may not be heard throughout the community. And although they have associations with certain spirits of their clans, the spirits associated with each are fewer in number and variety. Finally, there are important qualitative differences in the two types of king. Although a leopard, for example, is brought before the hidden king of its killer, the animal must then be taken to the king of Onitsha for its ultimate disposi-

---

suggests that they held the right of death judgment, and their visits to the Udo shrine suggest human sacrifice. Probably, however, this right was in some way limited and subject to the participation of a representative of the king of Onitsha.

14. The Onitsha king addresses him as "sky" (igwe), and the Ɔbiɔ king responds by saying, "leopard, your life" (*ágʊ, ńdʊ̀yí*).

tion. Although the nze of the hidden kings is employed as an oath in cases of incest confession, the nze of the king of Onitsha has lost this function. The king of Onitsha no longer oversees incest confession for the royal clan, because the royal clan is no longer an exogamous unit—sexual intercourse and even marriage are possible within some of its major segments. Although both kings are considered "deceased," the Onitsha king is more drastically cut off from the position as senior patrilineage priest of his clan; the other kings are expected to hold this position, although they delegate most of its role requirements to others when they assume their identities as hidden kings.[15]

This complex system of meanings in kingship identity appears to be a fusion of diverse major religious ideas and values rather than a fully rationalized synthesis. That this fusion is an historically complex phenomenon is suggested by the existence of nine kings possessing different clusters of qualities. The hidden kings have close ties with patrilineage, with godhead, with spirit, and, to a lesser degree, with "warrior" qualities. One king, the king of Onitsha, differs sharply from the others in relating less to the patrilineage priesthood and more to the warrior.

NORMATIVE STRUCTURES: THE SECLUDED ONITSHA KING AND HIS RELATIVES

The most striking feature of the Onitsha king's life is his seclusion. Simultaneously too pure and too abhorrent for contact with ordinary men, he must live obscured from public view. The "king's palace" (*íme òbí*) is located in thick forest, the sacred "grove of the king" (*òkwú ézè*), and it takes the form of a multi-chambered

15. It would seem that as kings they could not have taken the kinds of oaths in their clans' names that senior patrilineage priests are expected to do. The character and prerogatives of the hidden kings appear to have been quite variable. For example, according to one early account, if a man shed the blood of another Onitsha man, he had to pay a fine and deliver up the weapon—not to the Onitsha king, but to the hidden king of *Eke* clan (Williams n.d.). Since Williams's account appears quite accurate on other details, the practice was probably a traditional one.

ancestral house. One enters this grove only through the medicine-impregnated archway (*ɔ́dà*) marking the sacred limits beyond which the king should never travel and through which the incarnate dead should never enter. Inside the archway opens the wide, sandy "mouth of the king's square" (*ɔ́nʊ ìló ézè*), flanked on both sides with trees marking his spirit shrines, with the palace complex at the far end.

A detached structure in front of the palace, facing the square, consists of a thatch-roofed, low-walled mud dais with a throne set against the back wall. This is the "house of breezes" (*ʊ́nɔ̀ ìfufe*), a sacred place for the king's communion with the sky and with the cosmos in general. It may be screened in with mats to conceal his presence or left open so that he may receive refreshing breezes. He regularly occupies this room during the heat of day, and he sits on this throne to receive the salutations of his people during his annual emergence. He also retreats into this room to enter the spiritual dreaming trance when it is time for him to divine the omens of the yearly cycle.

The main palace structure was described in an early account as "a vast shed carefully closed on all sides." [16] The major door into this structure leads into the great public chamber, called *ʊ́nɔ̀-ɩba, ɩba-áfa*, or *òbí-ézè*. Beside the entry door,

> heaps of spears, guns, bows, arrows are deposited resting against the wall, for the visitors are compelled to enter the palace without their deadly weapons. . . . The reception place is 120 feet long and 50 feet wide; it is open in the centre, and the sides, about six feet wide, elevated above the centre are sheltered by palm-leaf thatch.[17]

At the far end, opposite the entry door, stands the king's leopard-skin-covered throne (in the same position as the throne in any ancestral house). On the wall behind it is a representation of the

16. Burdo (1880:29).
17. Witford (1877:172–73).

king as a coiled snake. Before the throne is a raised altar with two altar pillars at each side, before which slaves stand to screen off the king's throne with cloth.

In this chamber great plenary intracommunity meetings are held. It is not used for any private purpose by the king's family. Left of the entryway a door leads to the second major chamber, the "consultation room" (*ʊ́nɔ̀ ùme* or *ʊ́nɔ̀ ɩgba ìzu*). This room also possesses a throne for the king with a representation of the king as leopard on the wall behind it. This is the room in which the king and his six senior chiefs privately confer and arrive at decisions.

Behind the consultation room lies the third major chamber, called "servants of the king" (*ágbala-ézè*). This area possesses the courtyard land shrine of the king and is reserved for his family and servants. It is used only for meetings of his patrilineage, and no other persons except his personal slaves and kinsmen may enter it. Finally, at the rear of this chamber lies the king's sanctified private kitchen (*ùkóni*), where his food is cooked and served by prepubertal boys. Here he eats in total privacy, and beside this room is his private latrine. Between these major chambers is the king's private resting sanctuary, in which he sleeps on the floor.

Although the king sleeps inside the palace, his wives must not remain in this structure during the night. They occupy a chain of separate rooms behind, and to the left of, the main structure. The king inevitably takes many wives, for it is said that he may simply seize any woman who strikes his fancy. If his slaves bring a woman to him by force, he may mollify her family by sending them gifts. Since the king is above customary procedures, in theory he need not do this. It is said that a husband may deal with an incorrigible wife by handing her over to the king.

The king's wives are treated like cult slaves in that their bodies are forbidden.[18] They cannot leave the palace area and cannot associate with other men or women except their kinsmen. Since their

18. Note that they are not fully categorized as such by Onitsha people. If they were true cult slaves, their children would inherit this condition.

adultery would be a deadly contamination for the king, they are secluded and guarded by the king's "naked slaves" (*m̀gbálɔtɔ ézè*). These slaves may at one time have been eunuchs (*ónozi*), but in historical times they have been prepubertal boys. The naked slaves escort the king's wives when they go to fetch water or on any other trip outside the entryway to the king's grove, and all persons encountered must make way before them. Most important, the wives may not go to the market or trade like ordinary women, but must remain dependent upon a special market periodically conducted for them outside the palace gates by the women's trade organization. The sexual propriety enforced in the palace area is such that no man and woman may touch one another there; should this happen, traditionally a human sacrifice would be required to "calm the house." In the most recent remembered case of a royal wife's infidelity, she was dragged around the community as a sacrifice to "cover the abomination" that she had committed.

After the king's death his wives must lament him for a year totally isolated from other people in the bush. They may never remarry but must remain widows. It is said that in precolonial times they were likely to flee the town immediately upon learning of his death, a tradition that suggests some of them may even have been sacrificed at his funeral.

The naked slaves form the king's corps of household servants and perform many of the domestic duties normally done by a man's wives and children. They also bear his royal swords and fan him while he sits on the throne. Other "royal servants" (*òdibo ézè*) represent him in public, conveying orders in his name. All the king's slaves are marked by the shaving of one side of the head. Oral traditions suggest no high degree of organization among these palace slaves. It is clear, however, that large numbers of them were killed at the king's death; their ranks had to be refilled periodically.

The king's children and his immediate paternal siblings form his most important body of assistants, confidants, and court intermediaries. His children do not share the disability of their mothers, are not contaminated by their contact with him, and may both enter the palace and participate in other community activities. Both sons and daughters marry in the normal way. It appears that their patrilineal heritage shared with the king overrides the more dangerous features of kingship, which the king does not directly inherit but acquires through his actions.

There is no evidence that the children of the king are raised very differently from others in the community, beyond the effects of their mothers' lessened freedom to move about. They participate in wider patrilineage affairs, and both they and the king serve homage to their senior patrilineage priests. The main difference between the king's sons and other persons of the royal clan lies in their numbers and therefore in the influence they necessarily wield as a disproportionately large patrilineage segment.

It is also proverbial that "one does not judge the son of a king," for the king is of course in an excellent position to protect him from judgment. The king's senior son shares a unique consanguineal identification with him. The first European contact with the Onitsha king in 1857 was arranged at the "house of Odiri, the king's son," who lived near his father and took a prominent part in court discussions.[19] A somewhat later European observer who was received at the king's court remarked that "The King's favourite son, a tall handsome youth of the same bright colour as himself, sits at the foot of the throne, armed with a daggar." [20] This social prominence is based on the king's transferring his ɔzɔ title to his senior son

19. Crowther and Taylor (1859:23–26).

20. Witford (1877:174). This pattern differs from conditions reported by Basden (1938:277) among the communities living west of the Niger towards Benin:

> On the western side of the Niger . . . it is the custom for the heir to live elsewhere so long as his father is alive. Usually, he resides with another king who undertakes to train the young man in the duties and responsibilities required of him when he, in his turn, becomes king.

Onitsha informants agree that this is true for some western Ibo groups, but they deny that any such separation of father and son ever occurred in Onitsha. The only

upon taking the throne, making him eligible to play a new set of roles. This custom, "ɔzɔ of the child" (ɔ́zɔ *nwá*), bestows the right to speak with purity and responsibility upon a man whose father is alive (although the king is socially "dead"); its critical importance lies in the considerable competitive advantages thereby conferred upon the son of a king.

Beyond his immediate filial relationships, the king's relations to his patrilineage retain much of the basic form: e.g. homage service is paid in the regular way but through the king's representatives. However, the king's control of nze removes one valued element from control of the royal clan patrilineage priesthood. Concomitantly, the royal clan is no longer an undivided exogamous unit; intermarriage may occur within its major segments, and the royal nze no longer defines the boundaries of incest. The sacred nze still means purity, but it is no longer identified with the patrilineage priest and with incest proscriptions. This does not imply that the royal clan is tending to become an endogamous unit; one of its major segments is the largest exogamous unit in the entire societal community. Nevertheless, it does indicate that there are important structural modifications under way in this clan.

Other modifications evident in the relations between the king and his kinsmen are in his relations with his mother and his mother's parents. The rule is that the king should not have a living mother, obviously a device to minimize the powerfully binding effect of maternally linked relationships. This separation of the king from his mother is extended to his mother's parents, in that they cannot make overt claims on him as daughter's child. Another rule, however, suggests the tenacity of this link, for it is also stated that only a man with an Onitsha woman as his mother should be king. This rule is of recent (though precolonial) vintage.

Similar attenuation obtains in the relations between the king and his wife's parents. Although the king is expected to extend

tradition suggesting this concerns King Arɔlɩ, but that is very dubious evidence of the practice in question.

courtesies to such in-laws, they lack the usual leverage over a son-in-law, for his wives are bound to him for life. On the other hand, the king as parent-in-law has full rights over men who marry his daughters.

KING AND COMMUNITY: INTERNAL RELATIONS

The king of Onitsha is called "He who owns the town" (*ónye ńwe òbodo*). His right to receive leopards and stray men symbolizes his position both as an object of homage service and as holder of reversionary rights within the community as a whole. Refusal to render him this service would constitute secession from the societal community. His reversionary rights include the right to hold in trust (with his chiefs) land that has become the object of unresolvable disputes between townsmen.

The king's palace serves as the court of the entire community; complaint to him is the ultimate recourse when disputes have not been "repaired" by the procedures available within and between villages. Judgment in this court is said to be final, for the king is also called "He speaks, it is final" (*ókwue ɔ̀bé*). "Meetings" (*ńzùkɔ̄*) of all kinds are held at the palace whenever decisions are required that will affect the entire community.

In 1877, a European trader named Witford sought to open a trading warehouse or "factory" at Onitsha waterside near the great market. When permission was initially requested, the king sent word through an intermediary that certain gifts should be brought to the king at night, rather than being "given along with inferior gifts to the head people, lest their envy be prejudicial to his happiness."[21] The standard requirement was that "one does not approach the king with empty hands."

Witford then found that he had to provide "kola for words," similar to that for the patrilineage priest holding court, but involving a considerably expanded range of persons:

21. Witford (1877:172).

> The time for audience was fixed two days before it took place, as the king had to consult his magicians on the subject. Silk-velvet robes, bright cotton prints, turkey red chintz, razors, powder in kegs, bars of iron, guns, swords, knives, looking glasses, and demi-johns of the darling rum, were divided; so much for 7 chiefs, the same for the old women who constituted the Board of Trade, and about a similar quantity, but less rum, for the young dandies about the court, who were too full of natural vigour to require any stimulant.[22]

On the appointed day, these gifts were brought in procession to the primary chamber of the palace. When the people had assembled, with Witford seated facing toward the throne, the king came through a door on the left, members of his family shielding him from view; he stepped behind some men seated in the far left corner and emerged, dressed with a red cloth cap, a few brass rings on his arms, a coral necklace, and a yellow silken robe. He sat on a throne

> concealed by bright patterned mats and soft leopard skins. A hard leathern, elbow-accommodating seat, like a double Mexican saddle placed sideways, affords grateful rest for the royal arms. In one hand, the King wields a long black horse's tail fixed into a handle, with which he smites at insects. Convenient to his other hand is a bell about the size used by British bellmen in remote villages. He has frequently to use this bell and ring it violently to obtain silence in the court.
>
> On the right of the king are assembled chiefs. . . . Below them are a few sensible old women representing trade. Beneath the shed on the left are the commons, and in front, like the crowded tiers in the gallery of a theatre, are a lot of boys, and just as other boys do, they make fun of what is going on; but they get terribly wolloped for doing so. It takes several lords-in-waiting to keep order. The sheds are crammed with spectators, two or three rows standing against the wall, and those in front

22. Ibid., pp. 172–73.

> squatting. Through an opening on the right, the women of the royal household peep, but they are driven away by the king's brother, who roars like a bull at them. They go away, but stealthily return, when the interest in the debate causes them to be partially unnoticed. But as they converse in loud whispers, like ladies caged in the house of Commons, they are again and again driven away and still return. . . .[23]

This vivid description of assembly proceedings roughly outlines the major groups participating in them as evident in more recent times.

The seating arrangements in this major chamber are ordered from the perspective of the king. On his throne, he is flanked by two naked slaves and one or more sons or brothers. To his immediate right in the corner sit the senior patrilineage priests of all Onitsha clans, or the hidden kings; they sit to the right because in a sense they are senior to him, his "fathers." To his immediate left sit his "junior chiefs," referred to as his servants (odibo) or "wives." Down the length of the courtyard, to the king's right beyond the senior priests, are members of his immediate family and his slaves, who guard the entry doorway leading into his domestic chambers. Beyond them sit the "senior chiefs," in descending order of rank; they "oppose" the king on his right. Beyond them on the right are the "ranking chiefs," subordinate to, but also equivalent to, the senior ones. At the far end of the hall opposite the king sit the senior representatives of the women's trade association or "queen's councillors" (*òtu ɔ̀géne*), also called the "women of Onitsha" (*ìkpóro Ɔnıcha*). Along the length of the courtyard to the king's left, ɔzɔ titled men sit beyond the lesser chiefs; behind them near the entry door are the untitled men.[24]

Onitsha people formulate the major divisions among these ranks in the following way. First are the king and the hidden kings, sec-

23. Ibid., pp. 173–74.

24. Several early reports indicate that children might sit in the center courtyard, regardless of the seriousness of the subject to be discussed. See, for example, Johnson's (n.d.) reference to their "ridiculous antics" during the signing of a treaty with the British Consul of 1877.

ond the chiefs (ndichie), and third the rest of the populace classed together as "Those who support and dignify" (*àgbála-nà-ìrégwù*). This latter term includes all ɔzɔ titled men who are not also chiefs. Witford's interpretation of them as "commons" is appropriate, but distinctions are also recognized among them, including head priests, ɔzɔ men, holders of the nkpalo title, elders, and young men.

All persons present save the king must be bareheaded and must sit on bare earth (except for the hidden king). A meeting begins with salutations to the king. The senior chiefs salute him with clenched fists, offering him the strength of their arms, then kneel to simulate paddling as his canoemen, and finally bow their heads low while standing before him. Lesser chiefs must touch their foreheads upon the surface in front of the throne after saluting him, in recognition that their lives depend upon his will. Ordinary men simply prostrate themselves.

The king then opens the proceedings by breaking kola nuts, which the crowd will eat to signify their confidence that he does not intend to poison them. After offering a prayer, the king breaks open a nut and calls the supplicant who has asked for the meeting, dropping a piece directly into his hand. Thus he defines himself as father (or husband) to the supplicant. Then the king distributes kola nuts to his senior chiefs, elaborating on the kinship model of kola distribution: for each senior chief, he drops a kola nut into the cupped hands of his servant, and the servant then walks to the chief and drops the nut into the chief's cupped hands. In this way, the king simultaneously communicates an identity as father (or husband) and affirms his physical distance from other men, for people are "in awe of him" (*n̄a-àsɔ ya*) and must avoid his touch. All other persons in the assembly, in order of seniority, then receive with their cupped hands pieces of kola nut distributed by the king's servants.

This distribution marks the king's full appropriation of fundamental symbols of husband–fatherhood, an innovation attributed to the time of the early kings. Although the senior patrilineage priests are superseded in this way, they retain important prerogatives. They must be represented in attendance if decisions reached at a plenary meeting are to be legitimized, and when wine is served they have the right of senior priests to break open the seal.

Once the kola has been eaten, the talk may open. The supplicant begins discussion. If the topic is a complaint, he is followed by the person complained against. Questions and statements of opinions may then be made, but they must begin with the most senior chiefs who wish to speak and must follow descending order of seniority. When general discussion (*íkwu ókwu*) has been exhausted, the assembly breaks down into "private meetings" (*ígba ìzuzu*). The most central is the meeting between the senior chiefs and the king in the consultation room, but all interest groups among "Those who support and dignify"also have consultations and may have their views conveyed to the king.

When the king and senior chiefs return to the primary chamber, the king calls for presentation of the "kola for talk." It is said that he has the right to appropriate fully half the total share, but he must then immediately depart from the scene. If present he would have to supervise the subsequent divisions and would therefore expose himself to physical attack, since these divisions of shares are not precisely defined but are worked out through controversy. It is said today that of the remaining half-share, the senior chiefs may appropriate three-fifths, and more junior chiefs may then claim three-quarters of the remainder. The rest is divided among "Those who support and dignify," with the ɔzɔ titled men obtaining perhaps eight-tenths of that. If the women's trading organization is represented, the pattern of shares is considerably modified.[25] It appears that in Witford's time, just as today, this public controversy over shares could reach high intensity. Witford

25. Witford reported that a rather large share went to these women, no doubt because of their direct concern with the European's trading activities. I was not able to determine the full range of situations in which these women got shares.

reported that when his presents were distributed, "great confusion" followed, and "hatred and malice came out strong." [26]

Only when the division is completed does the king return to his throne. The most senior chief, who acts as spokesman, then stands forth and announces the decision in the king's name. Regarded as a "regulation" (iwu), it is promulgated as such by the king's messenger slave, who beats the ɔgene gong throughout the town, proclaiming that the king "beats" (*tìlu*) the order (iwu) that the decided policy will be followed.

The matters that the king's court may handle differ from those handled by an ordinary patrilineage priest less in kind than in the range of persons implicated. The king hears complaints about major abominations, but he also deals with lesser forbidden acts and other kinds of "bad behavior" as well. What distinguishes the court of the Onitsha king is that it concerns matters in which lower-level decisions have been unacceptable or unobtainable, or matters implicating two major village or clan units. However, complaints that reach his court do tend to receive more serious definition than they would were they settled within the villages.

For example, when one person is believed to have been killed by another, an abomination is mooted. The action taken depends partly upon the circumstances of the killing and partly upon the relative strengths of the two parties involved. It will not necessarily come before the king's court for a decision. The Onitsha king is notified about proceedings, but his role may be limited to announcing their nature through his messenger and perhaps mediating the process of reconciliation. For example if giving poison (*ínye ńsi*) is suspected within the clan but the suspect denies it, the matter should be handled within the clan by subjecting the suspect to an oath on the clan land. If the circumstances or even the fact of slaying are cloudy, or if the killer's patrilineage segment is much larger and stronger than that of his victim, the king's role may become more important. If the victim's people are convinced that though a slaying has occurred the suspect's kinsmen

26. Witford (1877:175).

will protect him from all retribution, they may bring the matter before the king.

If the suspect denies in the king's assembly that he attacked the deceased, and the evidence about the death is sufficiently equivocal, e.g. if the agency is believed to be witchcraft, giving poison, or sorcery, the king, in consultation with the assembly, may direct the suspect to take sasswood poison. Only the king holds this poison, and the accusers must pay him a considerable monetary fee for its use. If the accused dies after drinking the dose at the palace assembly, his corpse is cast into the bad bush and his kinsmen must pay compensation for the murder; if he survives, the accusers must pay him compensation.[27] If the evidence given at court is reasonably clear, the king may simply pronounce in assembly that the suspect must hang or take flight.

The king's participation is most likely when a killing involves two different villages. Again if the victim's village is strong enough they may simply see the killer hanged, or raze his entire village while its members flee. However, if the village of the accused refuses to give up their member to be hanged, civil war will break out between them unless the king's court is used for mediation. The king can enforce attendance in an assembly to decide such matters by sending his messengers to the ancestral house of the accused and placing the palm leaf (*ɔ̀mú*) that symbolizes the dead on its roof; as a ghost himself, the king can command with ghostly sanctions.

The king's right to call persons to such assemblies covers a range

27. To judge by historical records from the 1860s, during that time the Onitsha king was employing sasswood largely in cases of witchcraft accusation. A woman accused by members of her own patrilineage could take an oath on the patrilineage land, but if others (e.g. her husband's patrilineage) accused her, her sons might arrange to send her to the king. If he and the chiefs decided that the rite of "eating sasswood" (*íla ɔ̀ráchi*) was necessary, the sons paid the king a fee of 3120 cowries (plus a discretionary additional fee if they hoped to have the dose weakened). After the woman had made a final sacrifice to her personal god, she was dressed in white cloth, given a ritual farewell breakfast, and was then led to the palace where the sasswood dose was mixed in her presence and administered to her. If she survived, she and her sons organized a public dance of triumph during which her accusers were openly ridiculed, and the king summoned them to pay money "to wash the body of the accused." See Meek (1937:228) for additional details.

of problems far wider than homicide, but most assemblies concern abominations that touch the community as a whole, including major imputed transgressions in funerary ritual, in patterns of performing the ceremonial cycle, and in accession to titles, as well as matters of physical violence or treachery.[28]

Whenever people act on an intervillage level, the likelihood that abominations will be publicly proclaimed increases. In all these matters a considerable variety of experts and authoritative officials play important roles. A pivotal right of the king is his right to select the Onitsha chiefs (ndichie) and the "queen" (*ɔ̀mʊ́*), for these officials have important voices in the making of decisions both within and between villages, and they play prominent roles in prestigious ceremonies during the seasonal cycle. Although his selective rights are central, the acceptance of his selection by other chiefs is necessary for an installation to be completed. Once installed, neither chiefs nor queen can be deposed; the appointments are for a lifetime. The chiefs should pay the king annual homage service, on the model of children to their fathers. Upon accession they commit themselves by oath to be loyal to him and to comply with any decision agreed to in his consultation chamber.

The king's control of crucial community shrines near the great waterside market is associated with an important right shared by him, his chiefs, and all the senior trading women of Onitsha: the right to annual tribute from those who enter that market to trade. This tribute, called "covering the canoe" (*íkpù úgbɔ*), involves periodic appropriation of trade goods by the king's slaves, particularly from outsiders. Aside from this tribute neither the king nor his wives can participate in trade directly.

The king maintains ties with the women's trading association. The traders consult with him to report problems or violations in the market, and they play prominent roles in arranging major sacrifices by the king to expiate community evil. They deal with him not directly but through one of the chiefs.

28. It is evident from historical accounts that he could not take this step if the leaders of the village of the accused did not concur.

Despite his multiple relationships to his chiefs and people, it is proverbial that the king tends to be isolated from active community affairs because of his continual seclusion. To overcome this isolation, he selects a set of secret "eyes in the village," unknown but presumably important persons from each village who meet with him separately or jointly as the "king's secret council" (*ùlóko òbí*). These are men titled or untitled, whom the king trusts to inform him about current civic affairs.

Finally, a continuous communication between king and people occurs in the ceremonial cycle, for even in seclusion the king reaches out through his messengers into the community. He announces the scheduling of ceremonial activities; in some ceremonies he participates as an ordinary member of his patrilineage, in others he becomes an object of tribute and veneration. In still others he ritually expiates the abomination of the entire community. The funerals of important men of the royal clan cannot be concluded without his representative's participation. In a variety of ways, his agents coordinate those activities which, more than any others, define and maintain the structure of the solidary community.

THE KING AS AGENT OF EXTERNAL RELATIONS

As promulgator of decisions made in consultation with his chiefs, the Onitsha king regulates boundary relations with other communities. By sending his bell-ringer through the town, he can forbid trade with external communities whose actions have been deemed offensive. Similarly, the king may prohibit the people of any offending community from attending the great waterside market, the most important boundary structure relating Onitsha to the outside world. Any town whose people want to trade there must make arrangements through an assembly at the palace, at which they may be allotted an area of the market for their stalls, and their participation may be ended through a confiscatory raid by the king's slaves.

The king guarantees and symbolizes the territorial integrity of the societal community. When there has been warfare between Onitsha and another town and peace is to be made, he must send his agents to the boundary to witness an oath "binding the lives" of the two communities. He himself can never step outside the town; he can never cross a stream, nor set eyes on the Niger, for it is feared that he might see a canoe similar to the plank coffin in which he is to be buried, and consequently die an untimely death.

Nevertheless, in an ultimate symbolic sense he is the great warrior of the community, for it is said that should he take up his ceremonial sword and go forth to fight, all warriors would know that survival of the community was at stake and they would then fight to the death. When the assembly decides that the entire community should wage war, the king announces the decision through the town, and directs the beating of the royal war drums.

Aside from his capacity as symbolic warrior of the town, the Onitsha king's reputation as a court of appeal reaches well beyond the community itself. His control over sasswood poison is recognized, for example, across the Niger in Western Ibo country. Describing a custom at Ibuzo, Thomas reported:

> The Olinzele chiefs were summoned in the cases of suspected murder, and asked the culprit to drink inyi [sasswood]. He was taken to Onitsha by his accuser and the umunna of both parties accompanied them. If the man died he was buried in the bush at Onitsha. If not, he came home and rejoiced, and the accuser paid 5s. compensation to him.[29]

In general, the Onitsha king is known to expect tribute from the adjacent hinterland communities. In Obosi it is agreed that at one time the Obosi people paid "leopard tribute" to the Onitsha king; it was customary for the towns of Nsugbe, Nkwelle, Oze, and Ogidi to send representatives to salute the king during his annual emergence, so it is likely that these towns too paid leopard tribute

29. Thomas (1914:91).

at some time. The development of this tribute system appears, however, to have been quite unstable, and it did not last into the 1880s.

All the communities contiguous to precolonial Onitsha were strongly linked in ritual dependence to the kings at Nri. Nri representatives had to officiate at the ɔzɔ title ceremonies in these towns and enter them as priests to supervise the "covering of abominations"; in some cases the Nri king himself entered the community during his accession to make sacrifice at major communal shrines. Throughout Iboland, it appears that kings expanded their sovereignty first by establishing the right to give sacrifices to the shrines of new communities, thereby gaining rights to receive homage service. Expansion of such rights by Onitsha east of the Niger was almost certainly inhibited by the prior existence of such powers in the hands of the Nri kings.

Indeed, the Nri king based at Oreri included Onitsha as part of his sacrificial round during his succession to the throne and therefore considered it part of his domain.[30] He was expected to make sacrifices at major Onitsha shrines, including Onitsha land and the river Niger. As Jeffreys describes it, when the Nri king wished to perform his final great ceremony of sacrifice to the river, he would find that "Eze Onitsha locked one of my followers up in a room and said I would have to ransom him." According to Jeffreys, "This procedure is customary, each Eze Ndri Oreri must rescue or ransom his man from the Eze Onitsha." [31]

These patterns suggest a structured ambiguity in the relations between the Onitsha and Nri kings. By early exploratory times a kind of joking relationship had developed between the two, in which the king of Onitsha permitted the king of Nri to sacrifice at the major shrines to land and river in recognition of his spiritual superiority, but seized the latter's followers for ransom as a sign of his superior strength. Nri spiritual superiority extended

30. Jeffreys (n.d.:12:14).
31. Ibid.

to the requirement that Nri men enter Onitsha to supervise any "covering of abomination" that involved the use of scapegoats or humans in sacrifice, but it did not include the right to confer ɔzɔ title, for the kings in Onitsha severally held their own nze. The Onitsha king also controlled a spirit shrine along the Niger called "It eats Nri [people]," alluding to its capacity to consume Nri men who misbehaved while in the community.

THE SUCCESSION AND DEPOSITION OF KINGS

Kingship succession in Onitsha brings into play the full segmentary system of descent groups, for succession is viewed as a process by which patrilineage ritual relations are progressively widened, culminating in the establishment of ceremonial relations between the king and the major spirits of every one of the nine clans. It also follows the model of the king's funeral, which proceeds through a series of announcements to widening segments of the royal clan and then to all the nonroyal clans. The actual public funeral of the king simply repeats the form of his annual ceremony of joyful emergence, except that it is the king's senior son who emerges into public view, wearing the king's attire, carrying his ceremonial sword, and dancing to the war drums along with the senior chiefs.

Thus, formally, the funeral of a king seems to express the right of his senior son to succeed to the throne. However, all Onitsha funerals are characterized by this assumption of the father's formal attire by his senior son, and junior sons also participate, parading in their father's dress. Onitsha funerals strike a normative balance between the senior son and junior paternal brother of the deceased; both are his successors, and the balance of rights distributed between them depends on their actual performances in the funeral. If, for example, the senior son is unmarried and only beginning to establish his economic independence, the deceased's junior brother assumes the predominant financial responsibility for the funerary arrangements, and when they have been completed he will hold the bulk of the deceased's property in trust, receive the bridewealth due for the deceased's daughters, and also be responsible for getting the senior son a wife. If the senior son is wealthy and the deceased's junior brother elderly and poor, the latter acts as central symbolic "mourner" while the senior son bears financial responsibility, takes over the bulk of his father's personal property and gains control of his sisters' bridewealth.

The Onitsha funeral is not, in fact, a clear model for succession by primogeniture. Only after the funerary emergence does the actual process of succession begin. It is clear that Onitsha people do not share any precise delimitation of kingship succession right and very likely have never done so. Historical accounts suggest that by killing sixty slaves at the funeral of his father, the senior son of the king established a prestige making him heir-presumptive. In recent times, however, the interpretation of succession right has varied according to the segment of the royal clan consulted, and there is good evidence that this variance obtained well before the turn of the twentieth century.

One generally accepted standard has been formulated in a proverb: "Patrilineage priesthood is reached in turns; kingship is given by the public" (*ɔ́kpala bʋ̀ èlumelú; ézè bʋ̀ ìra ṅyelu*). This contrast suggests a lack of fixed, institutionalized delimitation of eligibility.

A candidate for the Onitsha throne should be a male agnatic descendant of King Chima. His mother and father must be dead. It has been emphatically stressed during this century that his mother must be an Onitsha woman. The candidate must be married, must have sired living, healthy sons, and should possess no visible physical deformities, for sexual potency and physical luster are very important symbolic qualities of the king. Otherwise, it is stressed, he need possess no special qualification, might even be a "wastrel" (*ónye-éfùléfù*), except that he must hold ɔzɔ purification.

As the funeral of the king cannot begin until twenty-eight days after his death, so the candidacy of his successor cannot be activated until twenty-eight days after the funeral ceremony. During this time, the candidate begins "rubbing the ears" of the various senior patrilineage priests of the royal clan, the senior priests or hidden kings of the nonroyal clans, and also the various chiefs, particularly the most senior one, who will hereafter be called the "prime minister." To each of these he must present wine and beg for support. Thus proceedings begin in a manner similar to the ɔzɔ title purification; but in this case holders of nze other than that of the candidate's own clan as well as chiefs from various clans must be approached.

Chiefs must be approached because of their abilities to mobilize their villages to support a candidate. Among these chiefs, the "prime minister" becomes an especially pivotal figure because he directs the scheduling of the king's funeral and that of the succession procedures as well. He "stands in place of the king" during interregnum.

In the absence of the king, the senior patrilineage priests of the royal clan also gain strategic positions, for a candidate must progress from his immediate priest through the segmentary hierarchy to the most senior or head priest of the royal clan, and each must beg the dead to support the candidate. Ultimately, the candidate should be given the ritual of bodychalking purification *íma-ńzu*) by the head priest of all the Children of King Chima. In becoming king, then, the candidate treats the royal clan as if it had not been modified by kingship but remained a single unit of worship. The range of a candidate's support and commitments is defined directly by the level of priestly seniority to which he has served homage.

While he is making arrangements within the royal clan, the candidate must seek out the hidden kings of nonroyal clans, to arrange rituals that "cut off" the relationship between their spirits and the deceased king and dispose them favorably to him as a successor. He must also obtain the ritual blessing of his mother's and father's mother's patrilineages. Normally the candidate avoids competitive confrontations as long as possible, while progressively widening his ritual support, but the pivotal senior patrilineage priests and the hidden kings inevitably become objects of competition, for each can legitimately give ceremonial support to only one candidate. Various chiefs can influence villages to support one candidate or another, and village opinion can sway the priests' intentions. As the mobilization of support for the ceremonial steps to kingship proceeds, the various candidates must take ceremonial short-cuts, and thereby open themselves to accusations of abomination.

For example, a central requirement for a successful candidate is to gain the ritual support of the hidden king of the Ɔbiɔ clan. In the strictest sense, the numerically insignificant Ɔbiɔ clan controls the avenue to kingship because of its spiritual seniority. First, the candidate must go to the hidden king of Ɔbiɔ and arrange for him to make sacrifice to his shrine dedicated to the spirit ɔgbɔ-na-uke, representing the ghostly peer group of the king. By killing for this spirit a black goat (provided by the candidate), the Ɔbiɔ hidden king cuts off the candidate from harm by the ghosts of the late king and his contemporaries.[32] Then the candidate must provide a ram to be sacrificed to the nze shrine of Ɔbiɔ. Associated with nze of Ɔbiɔ are two small royal drums, representing the ultimate right of the Ɔbiɔ clan to confer kingship. This blood sacrifice to the drums notifies the nze of the desires of the candidate. Finally, the candidate must provide materials for animal sacrifices to be made both to the land of Ɔbiɔ and to yet another major spirit of that clan.

The candidate must also arrange with the hidden king of Children of Ase village (Ɔbamkpa clan), who controls the disposition of the anvil ɔfɔ symbolic of nonroyal recognition, for a similar series of sacrifices to the nze and to major spirits of this clan, and

32. This is the only instance I know of a collectively controlled shrine dedicated to this spiritual force in Onitsha. Some of the shrines mentioned in this paragraph were almost certainly given human sacrifice in precolonial times, for such sacrifices were proclamations by the candidate of his kingship. See Appendix D.

for preliminary blessings of the anvil ɔfɔ. He must arrange with the hidden kings of the nonroyal clans Isele-Awada and Eke-na-ubene for sacrifices to their major spirits, and with the Children of Ósùmá, from the Village of Oli-Eke, for sacrifice to their shrine dedicated to the "malevolent ghosts" (*ékwensu*). Finally, the candidate must approach the "Children of Ɔlɔsɩ." Although they are regarded as members of the royal clan, it is said that Ɔlɔsɩ was a daughter of a king; therefore her descendants must act collectively as daughters in every Onitsha king's funeral. They oversee the care of his corpse and supervise the disposition of his property; they also take charge of burying him, but instead of merely shaving his head as do the daughters of an ordinary deceased person, they remove his head and carry it off to their village. The candidate for succession must deal with them to establish ritual relations with the heads of former kings.[33]

In these preliminary sacrifices, the candidate establishes initial commitments with the various royal and nonroyal units that must legitimize his succession. When the preliminary arrangements have been made, the candidate is presented to the senior patrilineage priest of the entire royal clan, who is a representative of the royal unit called Children of Ɔreze. In a ceremony at the candidate's ancestral house, the Children of Ɔlɔsɩ, acting as daughters of the royal clan, enter, "calm the house," chalk the candidate's body, and bring him before the senior priest, who leads him out to his throne. The priest then "[forcefully] places him on the throne" (*ídɔkìwasɩ n̄a-ùkpo*), and ceremonially transfers the royal clan's nze into his hands.[34]

33. I was unable to determine with assurance what happened to the head of the king in former times. Some informants claimed that the head was buried in the village of Ɔlɔsɩ; others maintained it was handed over to the new king to be buried in the floor in front of his throne. Possibly the head was buried for a time, and then the skull was handed over to the successor. In any event, in recent times it was said that the head of the king was merely shaved, the cuttings being taken by the Children of Ɔlɔsɩ. Only they could attend the actual burial.

34. It is said that at some point in this ceremony, the Children of Ɔlɔsɩ perform "adorning with brass feather" (*ítube èle ɔ́nà*), providing a brass feather-holder to be stuck in the king's leather crown, and also "tying thread on the leg" (*ígèdo òwúlu*

After this ceremony, the candidate retires into seclusion for twenty-eight days, "guiding course" (*íche ńdu*), assuming the title "Sky," and ceasing to touch other persons because of his new purity. He will henceforth wear white cloth at all times and establish a life style of exceptional purity and atonement. During this period of guiding his course, the candidate sends his kinsmen to present the animals and other materials for sacrifice to the various major spirits of the nonroyal clans. They act as his agents in these sacrifices. Finally, the hidden king of Children of Ase, as representative of the nonroyal clans, comes to the home of the candidate, who fêtes him. In the presence of all major patrilineage priests, the hidden king prays for the candidate's life, presents him with the anvil ɔfɔ, and salutes him as obi, or court of the people.

After receiving this emblem of the nonroyal will, the candidate is escorted by the Onitsha people to the compound of the most senior chief or prime minister (the *Ónôwú*), where he is subjected to the ritual humiliation of "performing work for Onowu" (*íje ɔ̄lʊ Ónôwú*). He is publicly addressed by the prime minister in ceremonially insulting language,[35] and is commanded by chiefs to perform domestic services with implements that he must first purchase from them. A chief shows him how to chop wood with an adze; then he does it before the people. He carries a pot of water on his head, scrapes the bark off a yam, pounds a piece of yam in a mortar, and climbs a ladder to repair thatch in the prime minister's compound. These are the last insults he will receive from the general populace, and the last work he will ever perform for them. Only after he has completed this public domestic service for the senior chief does the king-elect gain the right to take up the ceremonial sword that marks him as the greatest of warriors.

ǹa-ókwʊ). According to some accounts, a plenary civic meeting is to be convened by the prime minister at this time, during which the chiefs and other persons may speak out their opinions of the candidate, and the candidate displays his powers of oratory.

35. Although I witnessed two examples of the ceremony in 1962, I was unable to obtain a text of this language; the details of the custom were not known by those in charge of the ceremonies. I suspect, however, that the king was traditionally slapped in the face and addressed as a wife.

The candidate must then "go to Udo" (*íje Údo*), escorted by the young warriors of all Onitsha, and remain there for twenty-eight days.[36] At Udo, the "sacred grove of the early kings" at the southernmost fringe of the community, the candidate for kingship must submit to the authority of the hidden king of Ɔbiɔ clan, who escorts him inside an enclosure made of burial mats at the mouth of the sacred grove. While the young men of the community stand in waiting outside, the hidden king performs a number of rituals within this coffin-like seclusion. In precolonial times, after human sacrifices had been made during the night to the major spirits of Udo, and white animals had been presented to them as living sacrifices, a human sacrifice was made to the candidate's royal drums, sanctioning the transfer of powers of the Ɔbiɔ king's ufie drums to those of the king-elect. After these ceremonies, the king sleeps the remainder of each night beside the "king's termite hill" (*ńkpu-ézè*), to commune with the ghosts of former kings who are said to look out at him through the apertures.

Before the last dawn of the twenty-eight-day period the hidden king of Ɔbiɔ escorts the candidate before the Udo shrine, publicly insults him, slaps him on both cheeks as a gesture of superiority, and commands him to chop wood and to perform other domestic tasks for him. Then he demands that the candidate remove his old loin-cloth and presents him with a new, white one (which the candidate himself has in fact provided but must "redeem" from the hidden king with money). The hidden king of Ɔbiɔ then pushes the candidate down upon a goatskin-covered stool, places a white cap with a fish eagle feather on his head, and rubs chalk over his legs and forearms to complete the first stage of his new purification.

The head daughter of Ɔbiɔ is then called to Udo, and she shaves the head of the king-elect, leaving only a small tuft on the right

36. The sequence of this reconstructed version of the ceremonies of succession does not accord with recent practice or with recent accounts of the succession. My version is based partly on unpublished documents from a committee of the Onitsha people who worked on the 1931–1935 interregnum contest. Today, Onitsha people themselves express considerable confusion over the sequence (for an account of this confusion, see Harding 1963).

side. Some of the shaved hairs are thrown into the sacred grove, to mark his dedication to the Udo spirit, and the hidden king completes the purification by rubbing chalk on the initiate's head, upper arms, and finally his chest, as the assembled warriors cheer his glory.

The king-elect is then escorted in the early morning to the king's termite hill, where his old loin-cloth and the remainder of his shaven hairs are deposited. In the old days, a slave was sacrificed over them so that the blood would run into the apertures.

With these acts, the king-elect has been fully dedicated to the Udo spirit. He is handed the sticks for beating the royal drums that announce the dawn, and they are beaten for the first time. From this time on, the king, as cult-slave of Udo, is defined as free from charges of abomination. He is regarded as "dead" and therefore free from requirements of funerary performance. He must renounce his ɔzɔ title, bestowing it on a son and sacrificing a sheep to validate the transfer.

After a cow has been killed at the termite hill, and is divided among the young warriors escorting the new king, they carry him shoulder-high back into the town, where in a morning procession he is carried past the major spirit shrines of all the clans of Onitsha. Along the way, he throws powdered white chalk to all persons who come out to greet him (each rubbing the chalk on his own face, arms, and chest to share the king's purification), and casts chalk into each of the major shrines that he has propitiated: the Otumɔye Lake, shrine of the unsuccessful early king Eze Awuma of Isele-Awada clan; the Ukwu-Ake shrine of Isele-Awada; the shrine of the early king Chima the Cow-killer at Isiokwe bush; the ògwugwu medicine of the early royal pretender Iyasele Nsu of Ekensu clan; the malevolent ghost shrine of the Children of Osuma in Village of Oli-Eke; and finally, to the "Iroko tree killing men" (*ɔ́jì ògbúgbu m̀adu*) held by Village of Oli-Ɔlɔsɩ.

From this point, the new king is carried in procession to his new palace grounds, which have been cleared of all vegetation. At the entryway, where the two egbo trees support the protective medicinal arch beyond which the king may never travel again, he formerly sacrificed two human beings to these trees, emblems of his spiritual self. He is then carried before his house of breezes, where he must be met by two major civic representatives, the head priest of the royal clan and the prime minister. While the head priest sits on the floor to the right of the throne, the prime minister takes the king-elect by the hand, escorts him to his throne, and forcibly pushes him down upon its leopard skin. The king takes up the royal crown of cowhide stuck with brass-tipped fish eagle feathers, and he receives ritual salutations first from his chiefs and then from the rest of the community.

The final ceremonies of accession take the same form as the king's annual emergence, when he dances in his royal square to display his prowess before his people. It is said that traditionally, at the conclusion of his accession, the king performed "ruling Onitsha" (*íchılı Ɔ̀nıcha*), presenting sixty slaves to be divided among all nine clans of Onitsha; their clans' acceptance of these slaves signified their final acceptance of him as king of all Onitsha.

These ceremonies of accession to Onitsha kingship entail much feasting (with resources provided by the new king) and numerous transfers of valued objects that he has accumulated. These include the presentation of slaves as well as many other valuables to some of the hidden kings. A partial account of objects probably demanded for accession during the 1870s is recorded in Appendix D. Although the requirements have changed radically in recent times, it is clear that wealth redistribution has always been an integral part of the installation process; in many ways the process of becoming a king parallels that of obtaining ɔzɔ title purification. The differences lie in the varieties of spirits with whom relations are established, and the kinds of valued goods (including human beings) exchanged or sacrificed.[37]

37. There is some doubt about all the details in the process, for the entire pattern was broken in 1900, and when later resumed was of course radically modified. In recent years, cows were divided among the clans. Bishop Crowther (n.d.) reported

In this elaborate sequence of ceremonial activities, the candidate begins as an ordinary ɔzɔ man and establishes new relations that transform his identity. The personality which emerges is an ambiguous one, for he appears at one point a person to be humiliated or degraded, at another an object of atonement or sacrifice, at still another a person of exalted purification. As in the case of the ɔzɔ title, the candidate becomes more unified with the ghosts, more ancestral, as the sequence progresses, but at the same time he is becoming associated with appalling events like human sacrifices, and his identification with fearsome spirits grows. Thus, while he becomes increasingly ghostly, he has some of the attributes of a "bad ghost."

During this process, the leaders of the community publicly demonstrate that their decisions create the identity of kingship; they force the candidate to occupy his thrones, after first expressing their contempt for him and their power to control him. In this visible way, their actions punctuate the transformations of his identity; they state that these are the last times he will be overtly insulted or asked to do service, but they also affirm that the new powers he will wield are granted by representatives of the people in recognition of his role as their servant.

This affirmation is part of the significance of the proverb stating that "kingship is given by the public." As holder of nze, the king directly symbolizes an ultimately desirable and exalted state. As an agent of killing, he may also evoke great fear and revulsion.[38] The installation ceremonies bridge the dualism implicit in his identity by demonstrating that both kinds of qualities are the outcome of the collective will, and that both are joined in him.

Once installed, the Onitsha king reigns for life from the confines of his own sacred grove. Since he cannot go outside it, his

---

that 60 human sacrifices were made during accession, but there is no indication of how or where this was done. It was necessary for the king to take ceremonial steps to "enter the house," but I got no details of the requisite procedure.

38. However, if analogy is made to emotional tones evident during cattle sacrifices, this was not the only kind of reaction aroused when human sacrifices were performed.

farmlands must be worked regularly for him by members of his clan, as nonroyal clansmen work for their senior patrilineage priests; at the same time he must pay annual homage service not only to his own senior patrilineage priest, but also to his senior, the hidden king of Ɔbiɔ. It is said that he is above accusations of violating land custom, for "the sky is higher than the land," but "while the king cannot be judged guilty, if he is advised to be more careful he will know that he has been judged guilty."

Since the king is a ghost who remains in this world contrary to the normal order of events, and since the collective incarnate dead are ghosts incarnate who have followed this normal order, he must never encounter these masked beings. Should the most feared of the incarnate dead, the tall ghost, ever pass beneath the archway guarding the entrance to the palace, and thence enter the king's square, the king would have to step down from his throne, and he would be deposed. For although the king is above ordinary laws, he is not greater than the dead and in fact must answer to them. Like him, the tall ghosts are identified with the hooded cobra (agwɔ ɔla), one of the deadliest snakes of the forest; they can be the agents of his demise.

The accession rituals of the hidden kings cannot be described in any detail,[39] but they appear to parallel the ɔzɔ title sequence more closely than does the accession ritual of the Onitsha king. The purification process is confined more strictly within the clan, and candidacy is not supposed to be open to competition, for the right to senior priesthood is "reached in turns."

However, the would-be hidden king, in order fully to activate his potential role, must also go before the Udo shrine escorted by the hidden king of Ɔbiɔ, and must be dedicated to it. He must mobilize sufficient wealth to present one slave to the king of Onit-

39. No hidden kings have undergone the full installation procedure since early in this century, and no such installation has been described in the literature. After the establishment of colonial rule in Onitsha, the hidden kings lost many of their prerogatives, and the identity has never again been fully assumed. Nevertheless, it retains considerable importance.

sha, and must provide him money in cowries any time the king sends his servants to visit. All except the hidden king of Ɔbiɔ must undertake to serve the Onitsha king an annual homage of ten yams.

The new hidden king must also present the senior chiefs five bags of cowries, and the lesser chiefs three bags. After such ceremonial transfers, the new hidden king undertakes his own annual ceremony of emergence, inviting representatives of the Onitsha king to sanction and witness his assumption of the right to kill cows for the people of his clan. Once this has been done, the hidden king has full ritual rights within his own jurisdiction.[40]

The hidden kings reign for life within the confines of their sacred groves, and their farm fields are worked for them by their people. Like the Onitsha king, they are regarded as "above the law," but primarily in their own clan areas. Like him they may be deposed by the tall ghosts as agents of the collective incarnate dead.

THE ONITSHA "QUEEN" AND HER COUNCILLORS

The organization of Onitsha women reflects that of the men, but is more completely embedded in the kinship structures of Onitsha society, and thus points to important features underlying the wider system. This women's organization cannot be analyzed in detail, for since the turn of the century many of its features have become defunct.

The major Onitsha women's organization is known as the *òtu ɔ̀gené*. *Ɔ̀gené* is a title of one of the senior chiefs, but in Onitsha this chief has no special relationship to this group, which will be referred to for convenience as the "queen's council" or the "women's trade organization," depending on its representative func-

40. The evidence on this matter does not make clear whether hidden kings could attain the right to make human sacrifice. I suspect that they could, because they could definitely obtain the right to kill cows within their clan jurisdiction, if they established the arrangement with the king of Onitsha. The early historical accounts link the right to kill cows and the right to make human sacrifice, but imply that only the king of Onitsha held these rights.

tion in a given context. It in turn is a part of the larger organization called "women of Onitsha" (ikporo Ɔnιcha), to which all women who are or have been married belong. The woman who presides over these organizations is called ɔmʊ. Since her role closely parallels that of the Onitsha king, she will be called "Queen." She is not the king's wife, but a person who is genealogically distant from him. Her "councillors" (ndi-otu-ɔgene) are women with title names in some cases identical to those of Onitsha chiefs.

Onitsha women play prominent roles in two arenas outside their households and natal homes. The first are the village and community squares where they hold their markets. The most important of these is the great waterside nkwɔ day market along the Niger, a recognized domain of the women; the second is the large "lowland square" (*ìló m̀gbedémgbè*) which is the accepted location for plenary meetings of the women of Onitsha. Both squares are associated with powerful medicines said to have been buried by the ancient mothers of Onitsha, and with spirits peculiarly linked to the community women. The second arena in which women are most active is at the boundaries of Onitsha residence lands, which are marked by medicinal arches beneath which the women of Onitsha perform important ceremonies.

Onitsha women, particularly those who become the queen and her councillors, are regarded as the "prophets" (*ńdi-ámʊma*) of the community, for they often dream of spirits who come to them warning of imminent dangers and demanding sacrifices. These women take charge of "sacrifices driving [evil] from the town" (*íchʊ àja òbodo*); seasonally, for example, they take burning firebrands from their hearths, wave them about their households and compounds, and carry the fiery heat of accumulated abominations outwards through the medicinal arches protecting the town. On the side toward the eastern hinterlands, they cast the firebrands out on the "Ibo road" (*úzɔ ìgbo*), and on the side toward the river they carry them down past the great market and throw them into the river, which "quenches the fires" of abomination. Such acts are directed by the queen in consultation with the king.

The medicinal archway over the path leading toward the riverside market is called *Ɔ́da Átàgbusi,* in honor of a legendary metamorphosing woman who, it is said, still appears in the great market on market days and entices people into it with her magic fan. This woman, Atagbusi, is said to have been a daughter of the tiny clan called *Ókposi-éke,* a descent group renowned for its native doctors and responsible for magical protection of the northwestern bush outskirts of the town. She was believed capable, as are other persons of Okposi-eke, of transforming herself into various large and dangerous animals, and it is believed that she concocted the medicine that protects the community on its western front. Onitsha women often make collective sacrifices at her medicinal archway. A second archway is located near the protective spirit shrine called "old woman" (*ágadi-ńwa͡ñyι*), on the eastern outskirts along the Ibo road. This shrine is served by a woman.

The images of prominent women as prophets and as agents driving evil from the community are combined with their image as "witches" (*ńdi-ámʋosu*). The major meeting places of women, at their marketplaces near the sacred groves of village squares, are believed to hold conclaves of witches by night. It is said that by day the queen and her councillors sit on their market stools near the sacred grove and supervise trade, but by night they adopt the forms of birds and gather in the trees of the sacred groves to discuss nefarious plans. Men of Onitsha avoid the marketplaces and the lowland square where the women meet in plenary sessions, because they fear both the medicinal powers buried at these places and the women who as witches may seek them as victims. The connection of men with market trade comes mainly through their individual sponsorship of their wives or daughters as traders. Symbolically, the marketplace is defined as outside the sphere of assertion by males, whether human or animal; any cock that crows there during trading hours must become the property of the queen.

The women's organization is basically an organization of patrilineage and clan daughters. The queen should be head daughter of her segment of the royal clan, and her titled councillors should be head daughters of their clan or village units. Thus they are tied to the ascriptive base of descent group membership. The queen is handed her ɔfɔ ɔmʊ by the king of Onitsha, and the titled councillors receive their own head daughter's ɔfɔ from their own senior priests and hidden kings. However, in order to participate actively in this council, women must first "put on ivories" (*ígbʊ ɔ́dʊ*), by obtaining and arranging to wear ivory bracelets and anklets as visible signs of their purification. This means that they must mobilize wealth to redistribute among previously purified persons.

The bodies of the queen and her councillors become holy as do those of purified men, in that anyone who abuses one of them physically must pay a fine and perform ceremonies to undo the forbidden act. The queen must always wear white cloth; she holds a ceremonial sword (mma abani) like that of the king, carries the leather fan (azuzu) for making peace, and maintains her own special set of women's war drums (*ìzabu*). She has her own palace (constructed ordinarily at her marital home), performs her own annual ceremony of emergence (ɔfala) some days after that of the king, and emulates his activities in a number of other ways. She also possesses a market throne (ukpo), a decorated market stool carried for her by her own slaves. Her councillors also wear white cloth and have slaves to carry their market stools to the great market.

The queen and her councillors directly control the activities in the great market. Trade cannot begin before they have arrived and occupied their stalls. In public women's meetings at the lowland square they regulate what products may be sold in the market, by whom, and at what price. They oversee orderly trading and may handle market violations in their court. They may judge disputes, require suspected offenders to take an oath on the women's medicine, levy fines, and report to the king any violations or problems that they cannot handle themselves. They receive regular tribute in kind from all trading women in the market.

Most of the unscheduled expiatory sacrifices made to the spirits near the great market are undertaken at the demand of the queen and her councillors, who observe the spiritual health of the market with great sensitivity. When, for example, bees rage out from certain trees near the Onitsha land shrine, beneath which the ancestral Onitsha mothers long ago buried their women's medicine, the councillors infer that the spirits are angry and they consult with the king to arrange for sacrifices. The market is closed whenever Onitsha women find it necessary to "venerate spirits" or "drive away [evils] from the town," and the goods of anyone violating such closure are confiscated by the king's naked slaves.

The Onitsha king has formal channels of communication with the women of Onitsha. One of his junior chiefs ordinarily acts as their representative to the king and his council, but they represent themselves in any matter requiring a decision that will affect them directly. The queen and her councillors each pay the king annual tribute, but they are not under his command in market affairs. Indeed, the queen is regarded as the king's equal in some ways; her palace can serve as a sanctuary to anyone who has incurred his wrath, and she may actually compete with him in splendor. She is regarded as greater than his chiefs, and through her prominence in trade she can mobilize the power of Onitsha women. Her decision-making capacity in community affairs is quite substantial.

Although women control the major marketplaces, much of the trade in slaves was traditionally conducted not in the open market squares but in the ancestral houses of chiefs and prominent titled men, and in the compounds of outstanding women traders such as the queen. Neither the king nor the queen dominated this trade.

Every member of the queen's council undergoes an installation procedure which begins with the candidate's making ritual notification to her descent group, then to the women of Onitsha, and finally to the king and his chiefs. All these groups receive wealth distributed by the candidate, but the largest share goes to the women of Onitsha, and of that a disproportionately large amount is shared among the queen and her councillors.

The procedure of accession to the position of queen is in general form similar to that for kingship, although the expenses are lower. However, the queen does not go to the nze of her clan, but must receive her investment from a representative of the Nri king. It is said that the king of Nri sends a female dwarf who confers queenship upon the successor and thereafter witnesses her annual ceremony of emergence.[41] Therefore, although the Onitsha queen bows down to the Onitsha king, she is also ritually subservient in a quite different direction: toward Nri. This is remarkable, for the institution of queenship occurs in Ibo country mainly west of the Niger and northward toward Igala. Onitsha people themselves say that the queenship was a recent phenomenon in Onitsha, and they link its establishment to Igala and to Asaba across the river. Nevertheless, it is Nri that serves as the fountainhead of the queen's identity, and this relationship also occurs in disguised but not quite obliterated form for the Onitsha king himself.

Thus the women's organization is grounded in descent memberships, parallels the patterns of kingship in its institution of queen, possesses titles in some cases terminologically identical with those of Onitsha chiefs, and has an international relationship in the form of ritual ties with Nri. Oral tradition traces only two or three queens prior to the 1880s, but the generally accepted practice of addressing each clan's daughters by a distinctive chiefly title indicates that the overall form of the association has considerable antiquity.[42]

41. Dwarves are defined as holy agents of the Nri king, and any dwarf born within his spiritual domain must be sent to live with him. In recent years, the accession of any king (eze) in the Ibo communities of the Onitsha hinterlands was witnessed by an Nri dwarf, as was the annual emergence of that king.

42. For detailed analysis of the roles and collectivities of women in Onitsha society, see H. K. Henderson (n.d.).

9 THE INSTITUTION OF CHIEFTAINCY

The Onitsha term that may be translated "chiefs" or "chieftaincy" (pl. *ńdîchie,* sing. *ónyîchie*) is not readily analyzed by Onitsha people. Many argue that it is a distortion of the term *ńdi-óchìe,* "old persons" or "maternal grandparents," and that it thereby identifies the chiefs with the ancestors. Certainly the term can refer to the revered deceased as ancestors, a usage that occurs also among contiguous Ibo communities. Others in Onitsha maintain that its stem is *íchi,* "to achieve, attain." (In referring to an ɔzɔ man, one says, "he has completed ɔzɔ," *óchiligo ɔ́zɔ.*) Either interpretation might be etymologically incorrect, but that would not make them irrelevant. Another term referring to chiefs is *òlíñze or òlíñele,* which may be glossed "he has consumed nze," implying complete dedication to the clan's nze shrine. (It is said that in ancient times chieftaincy was attained, like ɔzɔ purification, by sacrificing a goat to nze.) The essential feature of chieftaincy then is achievement, but the chiefs are also symbolically related to ancestral qualities.

Three ranks of chiefs are distinguished in Onitsha: *ńdîchie ùme, ńdîchie ɔ́kwa,* and *ńdîchie ɔ́kwaraezè.* Onitsha people give variable meanings to these category terms, including etymological suggestions which analyze the latter term into ɔkwa-ra-eze, "rank below the king," or ɔkwa-ra-nze, "rank below nze," etc. These clearly unstablized rationalizations suggest that the terms derive from external sources, i.e. western Ibo or Benin.[1] There is also little agree-

1. Meek (1937:189) suggested that *araze* may refer to the *arase* titles of Benin, apparently titles of the Ibiwe house in Benin, the most junior of the three Benin palace associations (see also Talbot 1926:3:585, and Bradbury 1957:37). Only care-

ment among informants concerning the meaning of the term ndichie ume, though some said that the phrase means "dynamic chiefs." (*Ǜme*(*le*) does mean "active," or activity, but not everyone would subscribe to this translation of the title.) The category of ndichie ume will be glossed here as "senior chiefs." These are six in number, and their symbolic characteristics epitomize chieftaincy. The ndichie ɔkwa may be referred to as "[second] ranking chiefs," since ɔkwa means "rank" and the translation is reasonably appropriate for their roles. These traditionally number about thirty. Some (but not all) can substitute for the senior chiefs in their absence. Finally, the ndichie ɔkwaraeze will be called "junior chiefs" because they are more fully in the king's service than the others, who have more independent rank. They also number about thirty.[2] Both the ranking chiefs and junior chiefs will be distinguished from the senior chiefs as "lesser chiefs."

An initial understanding of the meaning of chieftaincy can be derived from the names given the six senior chiefs. They appear here in descending order of seniority.

1. The *ónôwú,* also called *íyàséle.* Onowu is formally an Ibo term, but its analyzable meaning, "he swallows cotton (thread)," is not apparently relevant to the title. This term is also used in Aboh and other riverain Ibo. Iyasele is related to a senior title name found in Benin and among the western Ibo. Among most western Ibo, the iyasele acts as the spokesman for the town and as its representative in formalizing settlements of intercommunity wars.[3] In Onitsha, his other title names are "Mouth of the stream" (*ɔ́nʊ-íyi*) and "Branch of the great river" (*ǹgadaba òrumili*), alluding to his role as spokesman for the king, his importance as a branch of

ful comparative linguistic analysis of these terms among Benin, western Ibo, and Onitsha peoples could pin down derivations. In Obosi, a title higher than ɔzɔ is *ɔkwaranze,* implying a relationship to the nze shrine, but this is probably a secondary elaboration of a term borrowed from Onitsha.

2. In recent times, the lists of both ranking and junior chiefs have never included more than twenty, and I was unable to fill in a list of thirty titles for either of these categories.

3. Thomas (1914:33–34, 42–45). For Benin, see Bradbury (1957:36).

the king's great force, and also his own turbulent forcefulness. According to some informants, he was once the war leader charged with defending the side of the town facing the Niger, and historical accounts suggest that he did have some jurisdiction over settlement near the river.[4]

2. The *àjíè*, also called *ísàgbá*. Ajie is also a prominent title at Aboh and among other riverain Ibo, while the term Isagba (or Asagba) is widely distributed among the western Ibo and probably derives from Benin.[5] This chief's other title names are "Discussion is worthy of respect" (*úkà-d̃́i-ùgwu*) and "Center-post supporting the palm-frond [signifying justice]" (*ìdé-j̃́i-ógù*), both referring to his powers of arbitrating and solving disputes.[6]

3. The *ódù*, also called *ósòdi*. Odu, possibly an exception to the general western and riverain associations of these terms, formally means "he leads." The term Osodi is obviously related to the Bini title Oshodi. In Benin this title-holder has jurisdiction over the king's wives,[7] but this is not part of his role in Onitsha. His third title, "Great basket that contains water" (*ǹ̃kata úkwu ńeche ḿili*), alludes to his abilities to perform improbable feats.

4. The *ɔ̀nyá*, also called *ɔ̀zɔ́ma*. These are both western Ibo titles, and the latter at least is probably related to a Bini title.[8] He is also called "Worm that penetrates Iroko" (*úka ńagba ɔ́jì*), a reference to a parasite that can bore into very hard wood which alludes to his capacity to pierce to the core of any difficulty. A final appellation, *asakalakpobi*, apparently untranslatable, may be a compressed Ibo phrase which at one time had meaning.

5. The *ɔ̀gené*, also called *ònírà*. Both terms are found as titles

4. This is implied in the early mission accounts, concerning both settlement by the missionaries themselves and by Aboh and other traders. See Crowther and Taylor (1859:290–92); also George (n.d.:018/22–23).

5. See, for example, Thomas (1914:42).

6. The palm frond (ogu) represents power of righteousness in a sense analogous to that of ɔfɔ.

7. Egharevba (1960:79), Bradbury (1957:38–39).

8. The term ɔnya is widely distributed between Asaba and the various Onitsha towns west of the Niger. The term ɔzɔma may be related to the Bini ezama (see Egharevba 1960:79).

among the western Ibo. Ɔgene literally means "he supervises," and may derive from a Bini title.[9] He is also called "Oil bean tree" (*ʋ̀kpáka*), an allusion to the explosive seedpods of this hardwood tree.

6. The *Ɔ̀wélè,* also called *Osowa.* Owele is limited as a title name to areas east of the Niger; to western Ibo ears it bears a connotation of "latrine," or "lowly." [10] Osowa is a title among western Ibo probably derived from Benin.[11] He is also called *ji odibo anya,* a phrase not evidently translatable that appears to imply the role of servant. In Onitsha society the most junior member of any social grade becomes the "divisor" of shares. This is the task of the owele among the senior chiefs.

In general, the first title of each senior chief is his usual appellation for common people; the second and other titles are used by other chiefs in various contexts of address. The first title is related to local, riverain, or western Ibo terms, the second is Benin-related, and the others are local Ibo terms of description. The meanings include forcefulness, decisiveness, firm leadership.

Among the lesser chiefs, the most common metaphors in title names allude to power; one title literally means "might" (*íke*), while others identify specific chiefs as "one who curses" (*òjíàbʋ́*), "one who devours" (*ónoli*), and the like. Other terms suggest roles in discussion and mediation, but the notion of power predominates in the terminology of the chieftaincy. Many titles for lesser chiefs are clearly related to western Ibo and Benin titles (e.g. the ranking chief ɔ́mɔd̀i is saluted as *d̀aíke,* a term clearly related to the Benin title edaiken taken by the senior son of the Benin ɔba), but many others are probably purely local in origin. There appears to be no pattern of terminological derivation according to chiefly grade;

9. The term onirhe occurs in various western Ibo areas, and is probably related to the Bini eholonire or ehanire (Egharevba 1960:79–80).

10. Cf. "latrine land" (*ànι òwele*) in Onitsha, i.e. land bordering residence land, into which people go to defecate.

11. See Egharevba (1960:79), the title osuan.

indeed the distribution of titles seems almost a random mixture of local and western derivation.[12]

THE IDENTITY OF THE CHIEF

The senior chiefs epitomize the fundamental qualities of the chief; all of them are defined as killers (ndi-ogbu). According to the idealized ancient practice of selecting chiefs, the king would merely send his war drums to be beaten in the compound of an outstanding warrior, place a fish eagle feather in his hair, and this act would confer upon that warrior the right to begin trying to become a chief. During his installation rites, the senior chief must plant a kapok tree, the spiritual emblem worshipped by man-killers and linked with their personal ikenga spirits; he must henceforth give this tree an annual sacrifice of a dog (the animal that symbolizes killing).[13]

All chiefs carry a brass sceptre (*ɔ̀gbanchí*), which has a forked top and a spear-point base. The spear-point is thrust forcefully into the earth when the chief speaks his will; like the ɔfɔ ɔkpala it validates his statements, though with a different connotation. Each of the six senior chiefs holds a set of war drums like those of the king (including the ɔgene iron gong beaten to announce decisions), and like him each also carries the double-edged ceremonial sword with which he dances threateningly to the sound of the war drums, exciting in his followers the sentiments of battle-lust. At festivals each wears a woven grass tableau hat like the king's, adorned with bird feathers which represent his courage and luster.

The chief is surrounded with an aura of malevolence and of ghostly contamination deriving from his practice of killing. He is

12. Appendix C lists as many titles as I could elicit in 1961.
13. Playing of the war drums must always be accompanied by a dog sacrifice.

believed to hire native doctors who gird him with medicines, both for protection and for use against his fellow chiefs; these doctors train him to become an expert practitioner of the art of sorcery. The chief carries the large, stout-handled circular leather fan (azuzu) waved to enjoin peace between disputants, but the handle of his fan is likely to be wrapped with magical preparations that cause the wind stirred by its movement to carry death to those nearby. He may, during a festival dance, point his ceremonial sword and drive invisible barbs into the hearts of his enemies. During his installation, the would-be chief is believed to practice his sorcery by killing ordinary people in preparation for confronting his future colleagues among the chiefs; afterwards, it is thought, he is likely to "suck the lives" of his kinsmen in order to increase his strength for conducting his battles.

A chief is therefore dangerous to all in his presence. The malevolent ghosts (ekwensu) of those he is believed to have killed tend to cluster around him, increasing the danger. For these reasons, whenever a senior chief travels outside his compound, he is preceded by escorts, one of whom carries a warning bell (mgbilimgba, or *ídùluma*) like that used by the king to enforce quiet at assemblies. This bellringer warns the populace of an approaching dangerous presence, and it is said that the ringing also drives off the malevolent ghosts that threaten the chief himself. Meetings of chiefs are regarded as highly inflammable occasions, for "when two great pots collide, the smaller one must break."

The chief is not, however, simply an agent of amoral force, as he holds a "chiefs' ɔfɔ" (ɔfɔ ndichie). This ɔfɔ differs from that of the patrilineage priest and is a derivative form, for it is not made of wood from the ɔfɔ tree but rather from that of the egbo, the kola, or the star apple tree. Instead of being left in its intrinsic or "natural" form, it is carved into a slender wooden cylinder with an expanded conical head, giving the object a strikingly dart-like (one might say phallic) appearance, and it is banded behind the head and at the base with an iron ring. Unlike the ɔfɔ of the patrilineage priest, it is multiple, consisting of a set of nine such sticks linked by an iron wire loop run through the head of each.

The chief's ɔfɔ cannot be used for patrilineage ritual, and it is regarded as spiritually inferior to that of the senior priest within the descent group, but its form suggests its meaning: it is based on an ideology of intrusive force, and it may be used wherever multiple descent units are interacting. Its ritual use links its holder not to his ancestors but to deceased chiefs, and the oaths associated with it are usually oaths to kill enemies. The meaning of chief's ɔfɔ has undergone a subtle transformation from "power of truth and righteousness" toward "the righteousness of force."

The chief carries this ɔfɔ with other medicines in the goat-leather pouch of chieftaincy (*ákpòsi*), which has a leather loop at the top for its servant carrier to use as a head strap; to this pouch is attached the warning bell of the chief. When chiefs go to a meeting, they are preceded by their carriers; when they arrive, they cannot sit alongside other men, for the dangerous forces around them require their separation. Reverend Crowther was the first observer to draw clear attention to the distinctiveness of Onitsha senior chiefs:

> There are two classes of great men among the Ibos. . . . One is a class of men who, upon paying about 15 goats, 200 fowls, about 100,000 cowries, and a large quantity of yams, accompanied with a large supply of palm wine, are admitted into the class of gentlemen called Ndi Nze . . . ; now, as a mark of rank, each is allowed to carry a horn-like shaped ivory, with a hole made into it to blow into, which makes a shrill discordant sound. . . . The other, and higher class, who are considered above carrying a horn, carry bells, which are attached to their bags, and borne before them by a little boy; thus a continued jingling noise is made wherever they go. . . . There are only about six of them in Onitsha. . . . called ndidzi-boriba [ndichie-mgbilimgba]. . . . Upon their entering a room, every

> one must stoop, and address each of them by the title he bears; thus if Onowu, he is addressed, Onowu, Onowu, Onowu, ever so many times. . . . It is a great insult to salute these gentlemen with the common salutation, except by the title they bear. Each one must occupy a separate seat: a bench may be twelve feet long but as soon as Onowu, or Adze [ajie], has made towards it, it must be quitted by all its previous occupiers, in honour of him; on this account, each one carries his sheep-skin or goat-skin about with him, and sometimes his stool.[14]

Thus at meetings outside the palace, when a senior chief enters the gathering he must either occupy the throne or else be accorded a separate seat. The need for separation of such a chief from ordinary men is so great that even if he is ascriptively eligible to become a senior patrilineage priest, he cannot perform this role but must delegate his ascriptive rights to others of his patrilineage who are not senior chiefs. He must cut himself off from praying to his patrilineage ghosts, and he may not handle the ancient ɔfɔ or staves of his ancestors. He concentrates his ritual concerns more strongly upon his ikenga, the personal spirit representing the value of aggressive power, than upon his ancestral ghosts.

Another aspect of chieftaincy emphasizes this separation from ordinary men, for chiefs also possess qualities of purity and delicacy. The senior chief must wear white cloth when he ventures out in public, and like the king he does not touch ordinary people. He must live in a multichambered ancestral house with a "sacred kitchen" (ukoni) like that of the king, where he sits in seclusion to eat food prepared by persons who have not known female sexual contamination. His personal attendants must be prepubertal boys.

A senior chief emulates the king's quasi-ancestral identity. Like the king, a senior chief cannot mourn the deaths of his children, for he cannot view a corpse lest it cause his own death; he is "beyond sorrow" (as indicated by his absence of facial expressions)

14. Crowther and Taylor (1859:433–34).

and must appoint others to do mourning for him. Like the king, the senior chief may not travel beyond the boundaries of the town, cross bodies of water, or eat food cooked outside his own sacred kitchen. Like him, he may not take oaths on behalf of the groups he represents. That in a variety of ways the senior chiefs approximate the king both in purity and in symbols of power is of central importance for their relations to him.

In turn, the top ranks of the lesser chiefs approximate the characteristics of the senior chiefs, while the lower junior chiefs approach positions as servants to the king and are referred to as his "wives." Both ranks lack war drums and ceremonial swords,[15] and it is said that traditionally they lacked the warning bell and the sacred kitchen.[16] The five senior ranking chiefs are called "throne chiefs" (*ńdîchie ùkpo*), because they are considered pure enough to sit upon the thrones of the senior chiefs in their absence, and, like the lesser senior chiefs, they have three title names. The remainder of the chiefs have two, or in some cases only one, salutation. The junior chiefs all possess the other symbols of chieftaincy, including the chiefs' ɔfɔ (the number of dart-like sticks varying according to rank). Like the senior chiefs, they have the right to dance whenever the war drums are played, but they must stop dancing when a senior chief begins his dance. Their bodies, like those of the senior chiefs, are regarded as purer than those of other men.

Since all chiefs share this characteristic of exceptional purity, and since their state of grace encompasses that of ɔzɔ title, anyone who wishes to become a chief must first undergo ɔzɔ purification. While the ɔzɔ man wears a single fish eagle feather in his cap, the chief may wear multiple feathers, and while the ɔzɔ man must not sit upon the ground but on a goat-skin, the chief must do so as

15. With the exception that the osuma, the senior ranking chief, carries a small ceremonial sword, in recognition, it is said, of his seniority. Some say it also indicates his position as a demoted senior chief.

16. At least in recent times, junior chiefs have emulated these items of the senior chiefs' regalia. The statement by Crowther just quoted suggests that in the 1850s possession of the warning bell, at least, was limited to senior chiefs, but he may have been in error.

well, but he may also use specially constructed leather seats and armrests like those kept by the king to support his body and keep it holy. In their manifestations of holiness, the chiefs stand between ɔzɔ men and the king, with the most senior chiefs approximating the king very closely.

THE CHIEF AND THE COMMUNITY: INTERNAL RELATIONS

Fundamentally, the status of every chief is grounded in a given residential area, i.e. in a village (ogbe). A chief's jurisdiction covers the territory over which he can have a gong beaten to announce decisions in his name. Within that residential area, a chief is in many ways socially inferior to its reigning senior patrilineage priest, but in representing the unit "against the world," he becomes a central actor for the group. For example, when a complaint is raised within a village, the patrilineage priest may judge the case without bringing the chief into the affair, but if the complaint is a matter of divorce and therefore involves two village units, only chiefs may preside over the settlement and refund of bridewealth. For this reason, although the priest presides over marriage negotiations, chiefs are always brought as witnesses when bridewealth is formally exchanged. The patrilineage priest, on the other hand, must not attend meetings where bonds for which he prayed to the ancestors are being broken; therefore he must not witness bridewealth refunds.

Village units compete to fill vacant chieftaincy titles, but no village may reserve any particular title for its members. Since Onitsha villages display a segmentary, "nested" structure coordinate with patrilineage segmentation, one encounters villages within villages, units that might be called "subvillages" and "supervillages" (such terminological distinctions are not made by Onitsha people). The senior chiefs generally represent major villages, while lesser chiefs tend to represent subvillages, although this is not a normatively stabilized pattern. There is, however, one important norm that tends to structure this situation. Major villages are the central funerary units in Onitsha; whenever an important person dies in a village, all the men of the major village unit join to do the "dance of rage" (*ígba óziza,* literally "running in rage"), a restrained, symbolic version of a village's aggressive, destructive response to the murder of one of its members. This performance of collective, simulated warfare at a funeral is associated with a second requirement of funerary ritual: during the "lamentation" rites for any titled person, the lesser chiefs must perform a war dance that recounts the great battles in the life of the deceased and marks separation of the living warriors from him; in doing so they dance to the war drums.[17] These war drums should be provided by the senior chief of that village, and unless the dance is performed the senior son of the deceased cannot begin the post-funerary ritual of "bringing the father into the house."

Villagers therefore depend upon the services of a senior chief; if they lack one from their own village, they must become dependent upon one from another unit for providing them with war drums. In accepting these drums, they symbolically become the fighting men of that chief, giving the senior chief strong control over their loyalties. If, for example, one of the villagers insults him, thus offending the holiness of his body, he can insist that the offender "undo the forbidden act." Should the culprit refuse to comply, the chief can block the completion of any funerals in which the person participates, and he may raise his accusation to the level of an abomination. However, he must gain the acquiescence of the senior patrilineage priest for such intervention in ritual affairs to be effective.

The control of war drums by a senior chief gives his village crucial autonomy as a fighting unit, and this autonomy includes the right to fight other Onitsha villages. Reverend Taylor, the first missionary to reside in Onitsha, observed intracommunity battles shortly after his arrival in 1857. Living near the major village

17. For a detailed analysis of Onitsha funerary ritual, see H. K. Henderson (n.d.).

of Children of Dei (Ʊmʊ-Dei), led at the time by the prime minister, he observed the following sequence of events:

> *November 23*— . . . The sound of the war-drum was heard in the village of Umude, on account of the audacity of Wabuvo [*Nwabʊfo,* the ɔgene], the chief of Odojari [*Ɔdɔje* or *Ɔdɔjele*], who had incurred the high displeasure of the people of Umude, and yet headed his troops and encouraged them to persevere in the combat. They were defeated, and were obliged to retreat: on either side there was no loss sustained.
>
> *November 25*—The konko [the ɔgene war drum] was again sounded, for the counsellors of Umude to assemble themselves and discuss the conduct of Wabuvo. Last night he sent some men to take away the large drum of Umude. They came to this conclusion: that they would not first kill any man belonging to them [i.e. *Ɔdɔje*], but that if he dared to retain the drum, and persisted to occupy that portion of land, they would certainly carry on war with him, and were determined to do so. They arose, and one of them took a wooden bowl filled with pebbles and a stone, going round them three times; then they all unanimously burst out, 'According to this oath, so would we have it.' Towards the evening when the young men had retired from their field labours, the counsellors collected them, and told them to be ready at all times, for they had determined to wage war with those of [Ɔdɔje]. I saw a black stone placed on a green leaf, and the young men, all of them, stood up, and one of the counsellors took up the stone with the leaf, going round them. He said, 'Young men, be on your guard, and fight for your right: none must be a coward, but be bold and manly. Remember this iyi (oath-stone): it has been done so in bygone days by our forefathers. . . .'[18]

In this description two senior chiefs represent their major villages in a land dispute. The prime minister, from Children of Dei village,

18. Crowther and Taylor (1859:312–14). Ʊmʊ-Dei and Ɔdɔje, major villages at the time, were spatially separated by other major villages.

sounds his war drum through his village, calling his "counsellors"—probably lesser chiefs and senior patrilineage priests—to a meeting at his ancestral house. At this kind of meeting, the senior chief occupies the throne, but the decision to wage war is made in discussion by all chiefs and senior lineage priests. Once such a dangerous course is chosen, it is validated by an oath, and an oath for warfare courage is given to the young men of the village who will fight.

This description also substantiates what oral tradition asserts, that chiefs of the same rank cannot rightfully command one another even though they are graded by seniority. Even the king was unable to stop the fighting in this case, for the holding of war drums confers the right to make war.[19]

Within a village, senior chiefs can command junior chiefs, but this command is not without redress. The formal "warfare organization" of Onitsha (outlined in Appendix C) does not coincide with the distribution of chiefs in villages, but rather crosscuts it; this pattern gives junior chiefs alternative directions of appeal should they find the senior chief of their own major village attempting to dominate them. This organization is mainly a ritual relationship, involving certain annual ceremonies; it does not actually operate in warfare. It represents none the less an important structural shift away from primarily village-based relationships.

In general, chiefs are expected to "make talk about the town" (*n̄'èkwú ókwu òbodo*), and they may meet for this purpose in conclaves of any numbers. In considering a major village's policy toward some general matter, the senior chief of that village may meet with lesser chiefs representing various minor village segments, in the presence of the most senior patrilineage priest. For decisions implicating the town as a whole, chiefs all congregate at the ancestral house of the prime minister, unless the king himself summons them. For example, when in 1858 Taylor visited the prime minister's house, he found convened there "the old men

19. It will be observed, however, that this case involved "war" conducted with restraint, with an effort to avoid killing. It might appropriately be called feud.

called Ndi-itshe, i.e. 'old counsellors' " seeking to decide about an unpleasant event that had occurred two days before:

> A young man had a wife who was born in this country and whose parents are still living; and as he had a dislike to [sic] her, he went and sold her in private. Another had taken his own child and sold it to Asaba, because it was so weak in body. The chiefs said that it was an omen of evil on their country, and they resolved to make a strong law against the practice, and to do everything to prevent slavery in their land.[20]

The last phrase may have been an addition suggested by Taylor, and the decision made was clearly not a new law, rather a proclamation about the enforcement of an old one. Such administrative operations are major activities of the chiefs. They also serve continuously in judicial roles for village and town as described in the section on kingship.

The senior chiefs may "stand in the place of the king," in the sense that the most senior may convene plenary meetings and preside over them in the absence of a king. Therefore the prime minister (or, if there is none, the next senior chief, and so on) directs the town during interregnum and oversees the installation of a new king. Although senior chiefs are not regarded as rightfully eligible to become king, their emulation of many of his qualifications validates their substituting for him in plenary meetings. Such plenary meetings must be held at their own ancestral houses; they cannot sit upon his throne under any circumstances.

Below the senior chiefs, the five senior ranking chiefs are called "throne chiefs"; they may sit upon the thrones of the senior chiefs to chair meetings in their absence, and may also occupy the senior chiefs' thrones whenever animal sacrifices are to be made for the ghosts served by the latter. In this sense, they stand between highest chieftaincy and the positions of other men, for they may substitute

20. Crowther and Taylor (1859:360).

for senior chiefs and yet may also perform the roles of senior patrilineage priests. No one other than throne chiefs and most senior patrilineage priests (including hidden kings) may sit on a senior chief's throne.

At plenary meetings, the senior chiefs may speak first, after the king, in descending order of seniority, and no decision can bind any of them who refuses to give his consent. Other chiefs also speak in descending order of rank. Since chiefs do not speak the last words at such plenary meetings, they cannot simply impose their decisions. Moreover, they cannot provide plenary meetings with the ritual validation necessary for their decisions to become binding; senior patrilineage priests or hidden kings must be present to break ritual kola when there is no king, and even senior chiefs are spiritually beneath these major priests. This spiritual validation is even more important in those intravillage meetings where matters of traditional rights are discussed; senior chiefs may not chair such meetings or sit on the throne of the senior priest, and they lack a deciding voice in such situations.

In plenary meetings with the king present, the six senior chiefs clearly stand in structural opposition to him, and the prime minister in particular is nearly equal to him. Ordinarily, persons who wish a consultation with the king must first approach him through both the prime minister (or the next senior chief if he is absent) and a close patrilineage kinsman of the king. In all major meetings the prime minister acts as the king's spokesman, uttering the decisions in his name. Since the six senior chiefs go into private consultation with the king before these decisions are announced, their views greatly influence decision making. It is not possible to be specific about this today, but it appears that the situation in such summit consultations closely approximates majority decision, with the king having decisive power only when the senior chiefs are evenly divided.

The lesser chiefs also consult at plenary meetings, and they report their views to the king before his decisions are reached. Since they are subordinate to the senior chiefs both within their own villages and within the war organizations, lesser chiefs are expected to escort them on ceremonial outings and pay them periodic homage service, to serve as messengers for their seniors, and to support their decisions. The most junior chiefs, regarded as "wives of the king," also act as his attendants and messengers. In the king's palace, some junior chiefs hold weekly consultations with diviners and consult with the queen's councillors and the king about important civic sacrifices; others direct the decoration of the palace for the annual festival.[21]

In their relationship with king, senior chiefs, and members of their own grade, the junior chiefs exercise roles of variable influence and compliance. Throne chiefs who preside over large villages may have considerable independence, and aged chiefs renowned for their sorcery may gain respect far beyond their formal rank. Since all lesser chiefs may retain their positions as senior patrilineage priests, they can combine seniority in internal village affairs with prominence in intervillage matters. The senior chiefs depend on them for performance of chiefly ceremonies that address ancestral ghosts of chiefs.

In addition to the three ranks of chiefs, there is a specialized mediary role between the chiefs and the king called *Òkwûgbá*. This term appears to mean "speaks plainly," and it refers to a man appointed by the king for exceptional merit who acts as both "senior wife of the king" (anasi eze) and "servant of the chiefs" (odibo ndichie). Not truly a chief, the Okwugba nevertheless wears chief's regalia and has the right to initiate dancing when the royal drums are played at the palace. Moreover, although he need not hold ɔzɔ title, he may openly question the decisions of both king and chiefs. His closest relationship is nonetheless to the king, whose household

21. See Orakwue (1953:44–5). The details of this organization were difficult to determine, but it does not appear to have been complex even in precolonial times. It certainly had not evolved into a true system of "palace chiefs."

he supervises and for whom he acts as "lookout [spy]" (*ḿgbamà ézè*).[22]

A final—and crucial—set of relationships maintained by all chiefs within and between villages consists of their ties with the age-sets and the collective incarnate dead. In Onitsha, the ultimate means of administration for enforcing decisions is the combined action of these two groups, which are organized at both village and town levels.

The relations between the chiefs and these groups are ambiguous. On the one hand, chiefs may mobilize them. For example, certain age-sets make it their duty to "smell out" witches. They report their findings to the chiefs, who may then direct them to escort the masked incarnate dead to drive the accused witches out into public view. Similarly, any lawbreaker may find himself confronted by the unanswerable power of the massed collective age-sets and the wrathful incarnate dead; when this occurs on a plenary level, it is ordinarily the prime minister who must summon the meeting that decides to employ this sanction. In their village units, chiefs may summon the leaders of age-sets and incarnate dead, who meet and may ultimately decide to mobilize their organizations into concerted action. Therefore chiefs have at hand the most powerful enforcement agencies in the community.

On the other hand, the relation between chiefs and these enforcement organizations is limited, for the chiefs cannot directly participate either in the meetings and performances of their own age-sets or in the meetings and ceremonial invocations of their group of collective incarnate dead. They cannot demean their fearsome and holy identities by interacting with peers in the egalitarian situation of the age-set; and because of their relations with malevolent ghosts, they cannot have close contact with the incarnate dead.

22. Unfortunately, it was not possible to ascertain how long this role operated in Onitsha. Remembered holders of it lived late in the nineteenth century and early in this one.

Therefore they must not take direct control of the meetings held by these two groups, and both units can make their own decisions, not only within villages but also in the community as a whole.

In a variety of ways chiefs serve as agents of community mobilization and regulate that type of decision making that involves multiple descent groups. Beyond this, they, together with the king, represent the community as a whole. The king and his chiefs may as a group hold community land in trust, if there is an intractable land dispute between descent groups and representatives from one group approach the king and his counsellors asking them to restrain both sides from appropriating the land. The disputants place the land in their trust until the litigation is properly resolved; such land may remain fallow indefinitely, and before it may be used again, it must be redeemed from the king and chiefs.

CHIEFS AND COMMUNITY: EXTERNAL RELATIONS

In 1859, Reverend Crowther observed that the law of a life for a life is a central feature of Ibo society; moreover it tends to insist upon the exchange of equals for equals: "if the person killed be a great person, and the manslaughterer be an inferior person, that person will not be accepted for the payment of the superior; but some person of equal worth in the family must be delivered in his stead." Should such an exchange not occur, Crowther said, years might pass and then, when the matter appears forgotten,

> one of the injured family aims a deadly shot at a person of worth, equal with his slaughtered relative. It was on this account the inhabitants of Onitsha, *especially the chiefs,* were afraid to venture out of their town, not knowing but someone might waylay them to avenge the death of some one killed by the people, either accidently, maliciously, or in war.[23]

23. Crowther and Taylor (1859:430). Italics are mine.

Crowther apparently saw that Onitsha chiefs had become symbols of the aggressive and homicidal components in intergroup relationships, and connected this with their inability to go beyond the boundaries of the town. This is probably an accurate inference; historical reports show that, even within Onitsha, the chief who goes outside his village is likely to become an object of attack whenever his people have incurred the wrath of some other chief. Clearly, if a prestigious person in one village has been killed, the chief and members of his immediate family in the village of the killer become the prime objects of demands for retribution.

The chief is a physical symbol of his village's jurisdictional boundaries, and his movement outside those boundaries must therefore be a ceremonial and well-escorted action. Chiefs also symbolize the boundaries of the societal community; as such they must not under any circumstances step beyond them.

Each chief whose village or subvillage controls land at the peripheries of the town's farmland guarantees that boundary. Until this century, several small markets were located at land boundaries between Onitsha and adjacent communities. For example, at a palm wine market at the extreme southern end of Onitsha farmland, Onitsha women bought wine from Obosi tappers; the market was called *Mkpukpa Agbakoba*, after the junior chief Agbakoba, the representative of the descent group in Children of Ase village that controls that land. Another market located on the northern periphery was called *Anam Odu,* after the senior chief odu, who represented the descent group in Children of Dei village controlling that land; this market served Onitsha women who intercepted traders coming from across the Anambra River floodplains to the north. Such markets are ad hoc forms whose social order is guaranteed in each case by the chief concerned.

Although these markets are ephemeral, their names suggest that chiefs in Onitsha tend to be identified as a source of order equivalent to the spirit shrines. Similarly, a market held within a village controlled by a given chief tends to be identified by his title name. Although the ultimate order of such a market is sanctioned by its associated land spirit, any market disputes that the women cannot solve are likely to be referred to that chief. Specifically, the chief guarantees outsiders' safety; he can therefore demand periodic homage service from the market participants.

The wives of chiefs, unlike the king's wives, may readily gain prominence in trading because they have a strong guarantee of safe conduct, and the same is true of close lineage daughters of chiefs. It is said that chiefs traditionally participated directly in the intercommunity slave trade of Onitsha, a trade whose extent may have caused the road eastward from Onitsha to be called by some peoples the "road of slaves" (ʊzɔ igbo).[24] This trade was organized noncollectively; it was not monopolized or closely regulated by anybody in the community (at least throughout the European exploratory period). It could be undertaken by any man or woman, and was based on personal trading and/or kinship relations with members of hinterland Ibo communities, the riverain and western Ibo, or the Igala. However, Onitsha people say that the passage of unfree people between communities was always a dangerous matter, and that chiefs, who were able to ensure safe passage, were therefore ideal trade "customers."

The chief's house should include a private chamber, with a secret entry and escape door, where slaves (ndi-oru) might be held while negotiations were made with downriver customers.[25] They might be openly bargained for in the waterside market, but they could be held more securely in the chief's ancestral house. Traditionally, chiefs accumulated slaves; they were expected to maintain substantial numbers of them as servants. Such personal slaves were ritually dedicated to their master's ikenga spirit, the personification

24. See Thomas (1914:118). It is not at all clear how widely this phrase may have been employed among riverain and western Ibo. It was used by Onitsha people themselves, but for them the connotation of igbo was not "slave" in any simple sense.

25. The word ukoni, which signifies the sacred kitchen of a chief or king, also means (at least in recent times) "prison."

of his personal aggressive powers. In the ceremony of dedication, the master's patrilineage daughter shaved off the slave's hair and placed it on the master's ikenga shrine. Since those chiefs defined as the bravest of warriors are themselves referred to as "ikenga persons," it is evident that the symbolic association among this spirit, chieftaincy, and the keeping of slaves is close. The dedicating of a person's slave to his ikenga rather than to his ɔfɔ grounds the relationship in aggressive dominance rather than righteous power.

Chiefs, finally, are the recognized agents of intercommunity warfare. In theory, it is the king whose war drums should be beaten throughout the community to announce declaration of war, and the king who orders his ikenga chiefs to guide the town's warriors in battle. But the senior chief of a village directly threatened on its boundaries by a contiguous town may mobilize his own warriors to battle, and historical evidence suggests that much Onitsha intercommunity warfare was fought in this way rather than by troops drawn from the town as a whole. However, when peace is to be made, both the king and the prime minister must mediate the settlement.

This latter practice was clearly described by Reverend Taylor in 1857, when he reported that the king had sent an escort to accompany the prime minister (and some of his village supporters) to their boundary with the town of Nkwele, where they were to meet with people sent by the king of Nkwele, "that they might settle their matters and take a solemn oath." [26] This refers to the covenant "binding the lives" of members of the two communities. The prime minister and a representative of the king must witness such a settlement, which includes the setting of homicide compensation standards between the two communities, and they must also witness any actual compensation transfers.

26. Crowther and Taylor (1859:297).

INSTALLATION AND SUCCESSION: CHIEFS AS AN ELITE COLLECTIVITY

A vacancy in a chieftaincy title ordinarily arises only when the previous occupant has been formally "cut off" from his position.[27] Usually this is after his death, when his lamentation rites have been completed; for this reason, when a person as prominent as a senior chief dies, Onitsha people say that "the road has been blocked" (*ógwè ȁachili* úzɔ̀), meaning that no other lamentation rites may be undertaken until twenty-eight days after completion of those for the deceased senior chief. This requirement recognizes the importance of having active senior chiefs, and places great pressure upon the family of a deceased chief to complete his lamentation as quickly as possible.

A vacancy may also occur through promotion. Any person who is not a throne chief or senior chief may apply to the king for succession to a newly vacant title. If the king accepts a lesser chief as candidate, that chief's old title-occupancy must be annulled before the new one is conferred. Throne chiefs and senior chiefs may also aspire to titles as hidden kings, but not to the title of Onitsha king.

Candidates begin succession to any title by "striving for chieftaincy" (*ńgbakwu ńdîchie*), approaching close agnates of the king who can help them to gain an audience with him. Many such audiences may be granted, each with the proverbial understanding that "One does not go to the place of the king with empty hands" (*ádagba áka èjé bè ézè*). Ideally, the candidate goes with the supporting presence of one of the senior chiefs, preferably the prime minister; in any case the king directs the petitioner to consult the senior chiefs in descending rank order so that they may assess him. A prerequisite to obtaining such an audience is possession of ɔzɔ

27. Ifeka (1962) and, to a lesser extent, Orakwue (1953) were valuable sources of supplementary information on succession procedures.

title, for no chief would assess a man without basic purification as suitable. The actual assessment is done partly by sorcery, each senior chief testing the applicant's ability to tolerate the dangers of chieftaincy.

Final choice among candidates is made by the king, though he may summon a meeting of the senior chiefs if their support appears to be deeply divided. The king announces his decision by sending a message through the prime minister, directing one of the petitioners to begin the second stage of succession, called "killing a goat given at the palace" (*ígbunye éwu n̄a íme òbí*). The following account describes the installation of a senior chief.

The candidate comes to the palace with his kinsmen, bringing a goat, palm wine, and liquor, and the prime minister receives them in the public chamber. The royal war drums are played, to represent the presence of warriors; when the king has occupied his throne the prime minister leads the candidate before it, directs him to kneel in front of the royal altar, salutes the king, and says that the candidate has been found worthy of chieftaincy.

The king takes a kola nut presented by the petitioner, and prays with it to the deceased chiefs and kings, calling on them to insure the successful completion of the task. Palm wine and gin are presented in libation, with half the remaining liquor retained by the king and the other half distributed by the prime minister. Then the candidate presents the goat to the king, who directs its sacrifice at his altar, praying again to the deceased kings and chiefs for their support. The king retires to his chambers while the meat of the animal is cut up and distributed. One foreleg and one hindleg go to the candidate, the portion covering the vertebrae and ribs to the prime minister and other senior chiefs, one hind leg to other chiefs and titled men, and the head, liver, heart, foreleg and hide to the king.

The king then returns to his throne, and the candidate steps before him. Three times the candidate addresses the king by one of his standard salutations, and the king responds each time by calling the petitioner's ɔzɔ title name; after the fourth salutation the king addresses the candidate by his new chiefly title. Escorted by the king's kinsmen and his own agnates, the rejoicing candidate returns to his home, where he sacrifices a goat to his ancestral ghosts in the presence of his own village chiefs.

This ceremony is repeated as "killing a goat given at the house of the prime minister." In both cases a substantial sum of money is transferred to the ceremonial host, that received by the king being three times that given to the prime minister. These two ceremonies emphasize the joint social primacy of king and prime minister and formalize their good will and support for the candidate. After they have been completed, the candidate goes to the houses of the other senior chiefs, presenting them with liquor and palm wine. They formally salute him as a chief for the first time.

The third stage of installation, "begging the dead," parallels the basic ritual of patrilineage priesthood. For a senior chieftaincy candidate, it is performed first at the king's palace, then at the house of each senior chief in descending order of rank. At the palace, the king first receives the candidate in his private chambers, and is given a substantial sum of money. In the public chamber he prays to the ghosts with kola, wine, and liquor for the long life of the candidate, affirming a commitment to the aspirant and openly proclaiming a share of spiritual responsibility for his fortunes. Thereafter each senior chief receives the candidate at his house, the war drums are played, and both participants perform the dance of war while testing one another with sorcery. Later the candidate gives the chief one third as much money as he gave the king, then presents a goat for sacrifice to the ghosts of the host chief, who prays for the long life of the petitioner. The meat is cooked and consumed by all witnesses to the ceremony.

This sequence of praying to the ghosts establishes a bond between the candidate on the one hand and his king and future colleagues on the other, formally similar to that between the senior patrilineage priest and his "father's child." When his hosts pray for the aspirant's life, they affirm commitment to him, and this commitment is the candidate's first guarantee of his autonomous identity as a chief. When this sequence has been completed, the king then calls all the senior chiefs, with the candidate, to his palace where they share wine provided by the candidate and affirm their acceptance of him into the chiefs' rank.

The fourth stage of installation is called "bringing money" (ibu ego), a process analogous to that for ɔzɔ title achievement. The phrase "for the ghosts" is omitted, although ceremonial libations are also made on these occasions. The prospective senior chief must present money first to the king, then to each senior chief, and finally to the assembled lesser chiefs as a group. These distributions entail a sum considerably greater than that which has been provided before, with the king receiving three times as much as any senior chief and about as much as all the lesser chiefs together. The money for the lesser chiefs is withheld until a later stage of the installation.

After the money has been distributed to king and senior chiefs, the king directs the candidate to arrange the fifth stage of installation, called "cooking food in the sacred kitchen" (*ísi ńni úkoni*) and held at the ancestral house of the prime minister. For this ceremony, the candidate must assemble massive amounts of food—two hundred twenty yams; baskets of fish; calabashes full of pounded castor oil bean, pepper, salt, palm fruits; and much wine and liquor.[28] After the senior chiefs have inspected and accepted this food, they instruct the candidate in the practices a senior chief must follow when he dines. Then the ranking chief, called akpe, who is regarded as the "senior wife" of the senior chiefs, takes some of the yams and condiments and prepares a meal in the prime minister's sacred kitchen. This meal is consumed by the assembled group, and then the foodstuffs are divided equally among the senior chiefs.

28. See Ifeka (1962:June 9) for a list of the traditional foodstuffs demanded. As far as could be determined, this list is accurate for the custom early in this century.

The sixth step in the installation of a chief is called "redeeming the cap" (*íwèta òkpú*). At an appointed time, the candidate comes with his people to the palace, bringing his chief's attire—his cap, leather fan, ceremonial sword, spear staff, and leather bag. Led by the prime minister into the king's private chambers, he takes a secret oath of loyalty to the king. When the king has taken his seat on the throne in his public chamber, the candidate kneels before him while the king instructs him on the conduct appropriate to his rank. He is exhorted to remain loyal to the king, to keep peace in his village, to avoid all public display of disruptive emotions, and to guard land customs by his own exemplary conduct. He is told that since he will now become a man of the king, he should emulate the king's behavior.

After the required style of life has been communicated to the candidate, his regalia are brought before the king, who calls out the name of each item. The candidate "redeems" the item by paying the king a fixed sum of money. The appropriate attire is then presented by the king to the aspirant, and the transfer culminates as the king places the cap on the candidate's head and salutes him by his new title.

The new senior chief is then led home by his kinsmen, who chant the praises of senior chiefs and their activities in war. Members of the royal clan take the king's own war drum to the initiate's ancestral house. A dog, the usual offering of warriors, is sacrificed there and its blood is poured on the war drum. The new chief dances to the distinctive tune that is always beaten on the drum when his own particular title is proclaimed. Later in the evening, he kills a goat for his ancestral ghosts in gratitude for their support.

On the following day, the seventh step of installation proclaims the initiate's new identity both among the chiefs and within his own ancestral house. This is called "cleansing" (*ḿmacha*), in reference to the purification of the initiate that is necessary before chiefs can consort with him. The initiate wears his finest white robes and receives all the chiefs, who come to his house escorted by processions of villagers playing the major village drums. When the senior chiefs have seated themselves in a row along the ledge that is his throne, the initiate presents title fees to the lesser chiefs as a group, a lesser amount to the remainder of the townspeople as "Those who support and dignify," and a small incremental fee to each of the senior chiefs. Having distributed this "money to wash the hands of the chiefs" (*ego ιkwɔ aka ndichie*), he is led by the prime minister to the throne. Joining the initiate's right hand with his, the prime minister pushes him down onto the throne in his proper seat amid the other senior chiefs, as the assembled crowd calls out his praises.

The eighth stage of installation also takes place in the initiate's house and is called "gathering together ɔfɔ" (*ίkpʊkɔ ɔ̀fɔ́*). After all the chiefs have assembled, the prime minister takes his seat upon the throne, followed by the other senior chiefs. The initiate is called forth, holding his goatskin bag. He takes from it his new set of ɔfɔ sticks, places them on the altar, and then occupies his new position on the throne. Once the other senior chiefs have placed their ɔfɔ ndichie upon the altar, the prime minister leads the congregation in prayer. Prayers are offered in this ceremony on behalf of the entire community, but they focus primarily upon the relations between deceased and living senior chiefs. The standards of chiefs' conduct that the king has previously specified to the initiate are repeated here, as the senior chiefs pour libations over their ɔfɔ and the prime minister dedicates that of the initiate. A fowl and a goat are sacrificed at the altar and their blood sprinkled over the assembled ɔfɔ. By these acts, the ɔfɔ ndichie of the initiate is accepted among those of the senior chiefs, and simultaneously the entire group of senior chiefs reaffirm their vows in the presence of the other grades and the ghosts of deceased chiefs. These vows include their renunciation of the right to perform the role of patrilineage priesthood and to carry the ɔzɔ staves. As senior chiefs, they are expected to mediate relations with deceased chiefs of the community, rather than with their own ancestral dead.

After the sacrifices to the collected ɔfɔ ndichie, the assembled chiefs subject the initiate to "assessing accounts" (*ígbà ύgwɔ*). Any debts or complaints against him are raised at this time and must be settled before he may hold his title in good standing. Having settled these matters, the chiefs inspect the food that the initiate has accumulated for a final distribution to the chiefs. Once they have approved and divided the foodstuffs (the same as those required for "cooking food in the sacred kitchen"), the senior chiefs remove their ɔfɔ ndichie from the altar and leave the throne. Every chief present then addresses the initiate by his new chiefly title. The crucial transformations of identity have been completed.

The ninth stage of installation, called "running outside" (*ígba ílo*), formally proclaims the initiate's new status. First, he goes around the community to the square of each major village and is welcomed to the place of the senior chief residing there; the war drums of the host are played for the two colleagues to dance to them in turn. The initiate then enters his host's house, where he receives gifts symbolizing his new prestige and purification. After going to each of the senior chiefs in this way, the initiate visits various kinsmen and receives gifts at each residence he enters.

The tenth and final ceremony of installation is called "stepping into the water" (*ízɔ̀nye ύkwυ n̄a ḿili*). Escorted by his villagers and their drummers, the new chief travels out through the arch guarding the town entrance and traverses the path leading down to the great waterside market. The procession halts beside the sacred grove of the Onitsha land shrine, to which the candidate presents himself in dedication, then proceeds through the great market down to the banks of the Niger River, where the initiate steps into the water, cleansing his feet to proclaim the conclusion of his installation journey and to indicate that he will never again cross any waterways. Rejoicing, his people dance with him back to his compound, and his installation is complete.

The installation procedures for lesser chiefs follow the general pattern set for the senior chiefs, but differ in emphasis and expense. They do not include "cooking food in the sacred kitchen," for the lesser chiefs traditionally lacked this facility. After the three initial phases of installation, the ceremonies of "bringing money," "cleansing," and "gathering together ɔfɔ" are all performed on the same day on the residential grounds of the candidate, with each grade of chief housed in a separate chamber. Money is brought for every rank, but in amounts smaller than those for a senior chief; and distribution favors the candidate's own future colleagues in rank. After the other grades have received and divided their fees, they depart, while the members of the aspirant's own grade remain in his ancestral house. The most senior member of the grade, occupying the throne, first "begs the ghosts" on behalf of the candidate and his closest relatives. He pours a libation and calls first the aspirant, then the aspirant's senior wife, senior son, and senior daughter to drink blessed wine from his cup. In this way the lesser chiefs are less sharply separated from their kinship relations during the installation process than are the senior chiefs. Their ceremonial advancement more closely resembles that of ɔzɔ title. After the candidate has presented "money to wash the hands" of the chiefs, and the members of the grade seated on the throne have set out their ɔfɔ sticks together upon the altar, a fowl is killed and the initiate's ɔfɔ sticks sacrificially merged with those of his colleagues; but the oaths taken on this occasion do not include vows to renounce patrilineage priesthood.

The elaborate procedure by which an ɔzɔ man transforms himself into a chief insures him of an identity largely autonomous of the will of both the king and his other ranking superiors. Having validated his position among warriors of the community, living and dead, he has attained irrevocable rights. He cannot be deposed as chief, and all members of his rank would join him in opposing an attempted deposition. He may be convicted, by the king in council or by members of his rank, of an abomination, and he may be ostracized (nsʊpʊ) from chiefs' meetings, but in theory he can never be deprived of his privileges, including his earlier rights to share in ɔzɔ title fees of his clan and the title fees due members of his grade.[29] The title of chieftaincy, like the ɔzɔ title, is held for life; its purification is attained through communication with the dead and with spirits, and it cannot be revoked by mortal men.

29. This was consistently reported as an ideal, but it could hardly have amounted to effective power to receive chief title fees while cut off from the king or from members of one's rank. It probably means the retention of the right to receive fees retroactively, if the ostracized chief should later remove the cause of his ostracism.

10 OTHER DIFFERENTIATED STRUCTURES: THE AGE-SETS AND THE COLLECTIVE INCARNATE DEAD

Like the descent system, both the age-sets (*ɔ̀gbɔ́*) and the collective incarnate dead (*ḿmanwʊ*) are symbolically grounded in notions of reincarnation. Their alliance produces the most forceful internal mobilization of manpower in Onitsha society.

THE CONSTITUTIVE SYMBOLISM OF AGE-SETS

The personal god of every human being is symbolized by five objects representing five relations or commitments that fix the individual's life course. Four of these represent prenatal choices by various kinds of ancestral ghosts. The fifth is called ɔgbɔ-na-uke. The term *ɔ̀gbɔ́* may be translated as "age-set"; *n̄a* as "and"; *ùke* in Onitsha connotes spiritual misfortune, troubles. Some say there is a troublesome spirit called uke. Roughly, then, Onitsha people translate ɔgbɔ-na-uke as "age-set and (mis) fortune."

Onitsha people say that when a ghost from another world decides to reincarnate and makes a prenatal life-determining pact with his personal god, he simultaneously makes this in part a communal pact with "his associates" (ndi-otu-ya). They are said to vow an "oath on the world" (*íyi-ʊ̀wa*), agreeing to remain a certain length of time in the world, to accomplish certain tasks in their life course, and then to depart from the world. In this way a mystical identity of destiny is specified for every person and his "associates" (ndi-otu). In empirical life, such "associates" are not defined by kinship but by voluntary camaraderie among persons of roughly similar ages.

The notion of "association" (otu), rooted in the premise of identical, shared destinies, implies a rejection of prestige differences among associates. Associates are expected to interact as equals, with the sole exception that they observe age seniority in the division of "shares" and in other formal situations where precedence must be ordered. The age-set (ɔgbɔ) is regarded as a type of association (i.e. as otu ɔgbɔ, "age-set association"). Its men's destinies are so bound together that the ɔgbɔ-na-uke receives separate sacrifice on occasions when it is believed that a man's dead comrades are calling him to return to the other world, to fulfill the pact they shared. Whenever divination identifies this as a cause of illness, the supplicant's comrades join him in rituals of "begging the dead."

Onitsha people distinguish two kinds of spirits viewed as constituting, intimately related to, or perhaps emanating from this complex of "age-set and (mis)fortune." These are called agwʊ and ikenga.

The term agwʊ refers to a spirit symbolically associated with the vulture (udene); whenever a child has unstable and unrewarding relations with his peers, a condition usually associated with other symptoms of personal disturbance and instability, agwʊ is likely to be identified as the cause. A person recurrently troubled by agwʊ may be directed to set up wooden images of this spirit and to seek training as a native doctor and diviner, for agwʊ is the messenger-spirit for diviners. Since it symbolizes the negative pole of age-set ideals, a person tends to emphasize it when he is incompatible with his age-mates.

The second manifestation of "age-set and (mis)fortune" is ikenga, the personal spirit intimately linked to this fifth aspect of the personal god. Among some Ibo groups, ikenga is clearly defined as a spirit.[1] In Onitsha it is said to be "under the personal god," specifically under that aspect of it called "age-set and misfortune." Since it receives blood sacrifice during the lifetime of

1. See Jeffreys (1954) for some indication of the variable views about ikenga.

its owner while the personal god does not, it cannot be regarded as an integral element of the personal god.

Every man establishes his ikenga in the presence of his age-mates, and when he singles it out for special sacrifice he does so in a congregation composed primarily of age-mates. This spirit epitomizes age-set goals and values by exalting the fruits of warlike self-assertiveness and aggression. Its shrine is the wooden figure of a man, out of whose head sprout the horns of a ram (*èbunu*). These elements are essential to the form of the ikenga, although the head may be very abstractly rendered and the body little more than a cylinder of wood. In its most realistic form, the carved figure is shown seated on a wooden title stool and clothed in the grass skirt of the warrior. It is often carved so that the penis is visible beneath the skirt; it may hold a warrior's machete in the right hand and a severed human trophy head in the left. This attire represents that worn by killers in Onitsha when they perform their annual warrior's dance, holding their machetes and the jaw bones of their victims.

This figure thus associates the stubbornly assertive, butting head of the ram and the power of the right arm with achievement and success (the trophy head). Some ikenga statues show not a trophy head but rather an ivory horn held in the left hand, associating aggressive assertiveness with the attainment of wealth and ɔzɔ title purification. The ikenga is the personal spirit that personifies achievement of prestige through aggressive, warlike performance. It is usually identified with the force of one's "strong right arm," and some Onitsha persons analyze the term ikenga as meaning "[let my] strength progress." It objectifies a major masculine role-orientation.

A man compares his own accomplishments with those of his associates. If he feels that he is failing in comparison with them, he calls his age-set, especially the most prestigious men among them, to attend a sacrifice to his ikenga. The attendance of the successful men at such a ritual is believed to assist the less successful supplicant, and such differences cannot be viewed invidiously among age-mates. When a man's wife becomes pregnant, she will call on him to salute his ikenga in gratitude for his potency, and when traditionally a man acquired a slave, he dedicated the slave as a servant to the power of the master's ikenga. Age-mates attend such ceremonies to share in the good fortune of the celebrant.

Thus the age-set context is defined as outside the realm of competition for purification and its prerogatives; but it is also the arena in which the virtue of striving itself is inculcated and emphasized. In age-set meetings, an untitled man has freedom to insult and make jokes at the expense of his titled colleagues, acts that in ordinary situations would earn him a penalty for committing a forbidden act against the purified. For these reasons, the king and the senior chiefs cannot participate in the meetings and decisions of their age-mate colleagues, for their prestige would have to be shared in this social situation. Although certain warrior chiefs are identified as themselves ikenga, they may not directly dominate members of their age-set.

THE CONSTITUTIVE SYMBOLISM OF THE COLLECTIVE INCARNATE DEAD

It is believed that the ancestral ghosts of Onitsha community can be invoked to enter this world in incarnate forms. These forms are called mmanwʊ, a term also used among themselves by those living men who have been confronted by the incarnate ancestors and accepted as their genuine descendants. Such men may enter the secret "room of the dead" (*òkwúlè ḿmʊɔ*) maintained in every village. They may communicate with the dead, calling them to emerge through insect holes in that room to walk forth in this world. The most senior of these men are referred to as ɔra-okwute.[2]

2. A term that cannot be meaningfully analyzed and that appears to be Igala-derived. Cf. Seton (1928:264, 269).

All the men who embody, invoke, and escort such beings are referred to here as the "collective incarnate dead," and the senior grade of these as the "elder dead."

The incarnate dead appear masked as ancestors temporarily revisiting this world, and they are addressed individually as "father" or "mother of the dead" (and also by other terms). Some of the most important are specific, named ancestors. Their costumes are differentiated in form according to age of the ghost represented, and the physical and behavioral characteristics displayed correlate closely with characteristics attributed to persons of these ages.[3]

The most elderly and most venerated forms of incarnate dead are the "tall ghosts" (mmʊɔ ogonogo), also called egwugwu, whose forms are said to have come originally from Igala. These are tall figures, wrapped in a highly valued, designed Igala cloth which drapes from the head to form an elongated cone, somewhat rounded toward the top. Above it, the "head" is a snake-like, cloth-wrapped protuberance which may, when the figure bends over, strike out capriciously at bystanders with blows said to be deadly. These figures are individually named incarnations of great men, almost always deceased chiefs, and they are deeply feared. Generically called "hooded cobra" (agwɔ-ɔla), they may be seen in public capriciously attacking and cowing even the most esteemed elders of the community. Between such attacks, they rest their deadly snouts on the backs of escorts, for since they are of advanced age it is said that they tire easily.

The next eldest forms of incarnate dead are those called *ìjelè*. These represent male elders (ndi-ikenye), but unlike the tall ghosts they are not elders weak with age. The ijele are stately figures wearing magnificent headdresses covered with fish eagle feathers and brightly colored cloth. These headdresses, made of intersecting stick arches built up over a flat circular wooden base, duplicate

3. See Boston's (1960b) excellent description of Nri-Awka area masquerades, which are very similar in form to those of Onitsha.

the festival headdresses worn by the Onitsha king and his chiefs, except that in the middle of the arched tableau there is a close-set pair of large ellipses of white-embroidered, yellow-rimmed black cloth, which give an illusion of two multi-faceted eyes peering out through the tableau. From the circular rim of the base hang broad strips of black cloth embroidered with sunbursts and reaching nearly to the ground, and shorter multicolored cloth tassels. Partially hidden by these cloth strips is the cloth-covered human figure itself, its face visible as an intricately embroidered mask with high-arched brows and a small, circular mouth, its chest marked with four embroidered sunbursts separated by two intersecting cross-hatched lines, its waist and thighs covered with a kilt of multicolored horizontal cloth strips. The ijele is regarded as "beautiful" (*ùgólò-ɔ̀chá-ḿma,* literally "fine white seeds"). It moves with the stately grandeur of a person who has attained an honored position in life. It is generally escorted by men in their forties to sixties.

The next senior group of incarnate dead takes a variety of names (most prominently, *ágaba* and *ɔ̀ǵan̄achí*) and diverse forms, but they always appear as massive, lumbering, aggressive figures. The "head" of this type is a great wooden mask from the top of which sprouts an array of curved wooden horns; to these are attached a few fish eagle feathers. A ring of small spikes may run around the head at the base of the horns. The face is characterized by massive brows, usually bulging eyeballs, and a broad, open, often leering mouth filled with spike-like wooden teeth. Often the whole face juts forward like the snout of a dog. The body of this figure is covered with a rattling mass of hard seed covers or metal bangles sewn in overlapping layers on heavy cloth, and the figure strides with a powerful, clattering, unhesitating gait which often changes direction abruptly and gives the impression of uncontrolled, irresistible force. This figure is escorted by adult men who are actively raising families and striving to establish or improve their positions in the community. Figures of this type are not regarded as beautiful, and some forms such as the ɔganachi are renowned for their repulsive appearance, which is the object of considerable awed delight.

Of the variety of forms of youthful incarnate dead the most prominent is the *ùlaga*. This figure has a tiny head of a bird with a long beak (in some cases a small crocodile head) tied on top of the impersonator's head so that rapid, athletic movements will not be restricted. Immediately beneath this small head, the figure's body takes the form of a great billowing, seemingly feathery mass of raffia reaching to the thighs, while the legs are covered with cloth tights, simulating the legs of a bird. These athletic beings run gracefully about, especially at the funerals of young men, carrying light, stinging raffia whips, and they especially enjoy chasing nubile girls. They are usually escorted only by boys who are "children of the square," i.e. unmarried but post-pubertal.

Finally, a series of forms is associated with prepubertal boys and publicly defined as masquerades, i.e. forms worn by children and escorted by their peers in simulating the behavior of "real" incarnate dead. These also have raffia bodies and small face masks with smooth, delicate, and symmetrical features like those carved on the wooden dolls given as toys to Onitsha children.

Female forms of the incarnate dead are also distinguishable in form according to age. There are "maiden ghosts" (*àgbɔ́gɔ-ḿmuɔ*), small-breasted figures covered with cloth masks and tights, whose elaborately embroidered designs are similar in general effect to the ijele and similarly regarded as beautiful; and there are "mothers of the incarnate dead" (*ǹne-ḿmanwu*), with horns and broad, toothy, grimacing mouths reminiscent of the middle-aged male agaba. Living females are in general forbidden to participate in the embodying and escorting of the incarnate dead, because of the abhorrence the ancestors are believed to have for female menstrual blood, but mothers who have raised successful sons may, after they have passed menopause, be inducted into the collective incarnate dead as mothers of the incarnate dead. They serve as the living counterparts of these ancestral forms. The forms themselves are however embodied and escorted only by males.

Thus the forms assumed by the incarnate dead correspond generally to patterns of life associated with major age-grade categories in Onitsha. Formal escorts for these figures are also persons in age levels appropriate to the figures. Such correspondences also hold for the night ghosts, groups of incarnate dead called *àyáka* and *ònyékùlúm*, who emerge seasonally from the bad bush and grasslands adjoining the community, and wander through the town by night, chanting mysterious songs and visiting assorted households. There are also transitional forms; for example, men who have reached the adult, warrior stage may continue to invoke the ulaga athletic incarnation of youth (defined in Onitsha by the mask set atop the wearer's head which permits greatest freedom of movement), but the mask itself then takes the form of a dog-faced humanoid with horns (the dog symbolizing warfare), more like the agaba and other adult figures.

The significance of the incarnate dead to the Onitsha community rests on the belief that when these beings emerge into this world from their contiguous land of the dead, they come as ancestors to inspect their community and to enforce the land customs which they as good ghosts have always upheld. A command uttered by one of the incarnate dead permits no appeal or defiance. To resist would be to "defy the dead," and the dead themselves would rise to carry away the culprit forever. This standard applies to all persons in the community, including the Onitsha king himself.

THE STRUCTURAL ARTICULATION OF AGE-SETS AND THE COLLECTIVE INCARNATE DEAD: THE EDUCATION OF MALES

Although socialization in Onitsha is bound up with primary kinship relations, it is also characterized by an implicit "tyranny of the peer group" from the beginning of a child's life. Infants are holy and forbidden, quite possibly not human beings at all. They may be maliciously reincarnating beings (*ígbanje*). Even normal infants are presumed to be in continual communication with ghostly associates who may query them about conditions in this world and try to entice them back to other worlds. This communication is not limited to deceased age-mates but may include the ghosts who are potential junior siblings of the child.

In Onitsha the two-and-a-half year postpartum sex taboo for a mother insures a separation of at least three years between maternal siblings; the period of this taboo coincides closely with the span of Onitsha age-sets. Therefore maternal siblings are not likely to be grouped in the same set, and sibling seniority is not leveled by the egalitarianism of age-sets. Early in life, however, age-grades, the fixed age categories through which age-sets move, are most significant socially. The most important general age-grade category for Onitsha boys is called "youths of the square" (*ʊ́mʊ̀-ílo,* literally "children of the outside"), a basic reference group within which education of youngsters is conducted.

Each patrilineage divides its male membership into elders and youths of the square; this is true of any segment wide or narrow. The socially most important groupings share a named square. A residential unit with such a square is usually labelled a "village." It is the collective duty of the village youths to clean this square, to clear its pathways, and to cooperate in preparing for the collective rituals held in it. A residential unit with this organization will also have a common "ghost room" where its own tall ghost is invoked, and concomitantly maintains an autonomous organization of the collective incarnate dead. It also is likely to have a distinct, unified group of village wives and a separate group of patrilineage daughters, divided by age into maidens (ʊmʊ-agbɔ) and daughters proper, organized under a common head daughter's ɔfɔ. The existence of a square is associated with the crystallizing of several unifying features of social organization.

The crucial age-grade reference group for Onitsha boys is at once an age-grade and a unit in the patrilineage, in the village, and in the collective incarnate dead. A meeting-ground in which these various frames of reference are commonly embedded, it fuses them organizationally, although in other contexts they may become separate from one another. For full membership in this age-grade grouping, a boy must first be accepted by a representative from the incarnate dead and learn their mysteries; to do this, he must courageously journey to the land of the dead.

Children who have passed the period of child care and have begun to join their peers in intravillage play are referred to as "children of the year" (*ʊ́mʊ̀-árò*), a term which applies from the age of approximately three to nine. At first such play occurs mostly within the parental compound and the sexes remain undivided; at about six years of age, boys segregate themselves from girls by joining the "mbekwe club" (*òtu m̀bekwé*), an association of village boys organized around the dancing and following of a child's doll-faced masquerade called mbekwe. Membership is attained when a child's mother provides a feast for the members of the club. After this the boy begins to follow the masquerade, coming under the direction of older boys who wear the mask, carry whips to discipline the neophytes, and teach them discipline and cultural lore. Parents deflect their own child-discipline problems by warning their small children about the wrath of the incarnate dead against filial disobedience; from the age of six boys are made to live under the shadow of this threat.

Young boys also establish more informal teams called "age-set for hunting lizards" (*ɔ̀gbɔ́-n̄achɔ-n̄gwele*), small gangs led by older uninitiated boys of the village. These become training grounds for wrestling, hunting, and fighting more independent of normative constraint or demands for unquestioning discipline than is the mbekwe club. Within the hunting group, boys learn to stand up for their rights and to strive for excellence; they learn to wrestle while their elders criticize and praise them; they learn to divide meat according to ritual standards. When they encounter equivalent groups from other villages, they learn how to fight together as a unit.

The mbekwe club is the primary agent for inculcating the cultural tradition of the incarnate dead. The most senior uninitiated boy becomes its "headman" (onye-isi) and does most of the whipping. Under his direction, the boys build their own hut on the edge of the village square. They call it the "king's house" and inside they hide their ceremonial paraphernalia. Although the group is rooted in the descent system, their songs emphasize independence from filiation (one chant runs, "On the day that you die, your mother won't know, your father won't know") and stress unquestioning dependence upon the incarnate dead (another song chants, "Let mbekwe devour me"). The children are governed by the fear that if they do not learn their tradition well and follow traditional rules in solidarity with their mates, the incarnate dead will in fact devour them. Children who follow the mbekwe masquerade may be referred to as children of the village square in a general sense, but they do not meet one of the critical criteria for full membership in this category. Only a person who has been initiated into the collective incarnate dead can bury corpses, the primary ritual responsibility of the village youths.

At the age of nine to ten years, a boy is expected to begin his incorporation into the collective incarnate dead. His father makes the necessary arrangement with the secret elder dead. Since money expenses are involved, at this first stage (as at every other) the initiation process does not strictly follow age criteria, because the initiation of a poor man's child may have to be postponed. In this first stage of incorporation, a group of boys "goes to the land of the dead" (ibe-anɩ-mmuɔ). Certain members of the collective incarnate dead (but not their fathers) escort the boys at night to an enclosure hidden in the bad bush, and make them lie down naked. After a time, a figure of the incarnate dead appears and, in the shrill and squeaking voice of the dead, accosts each boy as an unwelcome "intruder," threatening to tear off his genitals and eat them. The initiated men present try to dissuade this apparition by defending the past activities of the boy being assaulted, or by promising that he will attempt to improve his ways and behave like a real village member, and they present a bribe provided by the boy's father. When eventually the incarnate ghost departs, the boys are directed to begin a sleep during which, it is said, they will travel to the land of the dead. Next morning the boys awake to find their bodies covered with earth-stains marking their difficult passage into the other world. Each boy is then met by his obviously relieved father to be escorted home by youthful incarnate dead who extort gifts of food from his mother before permitting her to see her child again.

After this inititation a boy is referred to solely as a village youth; he remains a junior and subservient member of the group. He is not allowed to know the mysteries of the incarnate dead, but may follow its escort team. He must participate in the junior drumming group of the village youths in funeral processions, but he may not yet engage in burial activities. He takes full part in cleaning the village square and subjects himself to the discipline of the senior village youths who have attained full manhood through acceptance by the incarnate dead. He may be fined for failing to do his part in the collective tasks, and should he prove recalcitrant or obstinate in refusing his duties, the senior village youths may invoke one of the incarnate dead to enter his compound and seize property belonging to him or his parents.

Neophytes generally endure approximately six years of apprentice membership in the village youths before undertaking their final initiation into the collective incarnate dead at about the age of fifteen. Each youth must undertake and finance his own transition, paying fees to the initiate group and providing various ritual items. He is taken this time to the ghost room, where he hears the ghost being invoked. Again it accosts him as an "intruder." He may be severely tortured at this time if his behavior has been very deviant. Then the ghost is revealed as a masquerade, and the initiate learns the technical and symbolic secrets of the paraphernalia. He takes the secret oath of the collective incarnate dead, learning that immediate death is the price of "defying the ghosts" or revealing their secrets.

This initiation marks a major transition in the life of a boy, for by completing it he becomes a young man (okolɔbia) who may now move freely through the whole town instead of being largely restricted to his own village square. Although he remains a village youth, he can now attend the actual invocation of the incarnate dead and escort them when they travel through the entire community. He may escort the youthful *ɔtúiche* ghost figures that circulate from one village square to another in a game of chasing the congregated youths. He participates in the wrestling contests between young men of the various Onitsha villages which are held in various village squares; and within his own patrilineage, he becomes a member of an interest group that collectively asserts its rights in patrilineage affairs.

Through extra-village activities established by the collective incarnate dead, and through various "select associations" (*írɔ̀ òtu*) established by informal choice among men of similar ages from different villages, persons fifteen to eighteen years old gain knowledge about men of their age throughout the community. It is at this time that community-wide age-sets are established among the young men.

Among the associations established at this time, the age-set association is by far the most important to the community as a whole. As young men begin to obtain their personal ikenga shrines, each calls his age-mates to witness and share in the ceremony and feast of dedication. This ceremony constitutes a kind of fee for joining an incipient age-set. As the group expands, it takes a name and makes a concerted effort to establish full membership throughout the town among young men of the three-year age-span below the most recently formed named set. Although more than one set may for a time compete to represent this age-span, the age-set which succeeds becomes structurally separated from the village youths system, and it begins to operate on the community level.

Although the age-set thus established breaks away from the village square complex, its members retain interest in masquerading. They acquire their own incarnate dead figure, which is initially some variation on the agaba pattern, or perhaps a transitional ulaga with the face of a dog. As they come to be regarded as the warriors of the town, they are sometimes called upon to act as the armed escorts of the "nine incarnate dead" when these nine ghosts —representing the collective will of the nine clans of Onitsha—go forth into the community to announce and enforce some important decision.

AGE-SET ORGANIZATION

The Onitsha age-set system cannot today be reconstructed as a rigidly ordered, neatly sequential ascriptive system, such as appears to have existed in some other northern Ibo communities. Apparently it has always been flexible in that groups adjacent in age-range may at certain times merge their organization, and competitive in that each named group competes for civic prominence with age-sets adjacent to it.

Talbot reported that Onitsha age-sets were actually associations (otu).[4] Although his data are not entirely accurate, they reflect an important fact of the system: membership criteria are flexible throughout. It is possible for a person to join a "high age-set" (ɔ̀gbɔ́-*énu*), i.e. one above his actual age-level, or a "low set" (ɔ̀gbɔ́-*ànι*). This flexibility also extends to fission within a set, for splinter groups may emerge and compete with one another. Sets may also fuse, for especially at the upper age levels adjacent groups tend to merge through co-optation into a single named unit.

As is typical in age-graded systems, the collective activities of sets vary as they pass through different age-grades. Initially, the young men who have just taken a common name are regarded primarily as village youths. They escort the youthful incarnate

4. Talbot (1926:3:550–51).

dead at festivals and funerals, they compete to seduce girls who have started "taking lovers," and they occasionally perform as work teams in special farming tasks for a member's father. Their organization is based on simple age seniority, with the oldest youth chairing their meetings, and the youngest acting as the messenger (onye-ozi) who serves at ceremonies and divides shares. In addition the youths seek out a patron, a wealthy and prominent older man who becomes "father of the age-set" (*ńnà-ɔ̀gbɔ́*) or "father of the dance" (*ńnà-égwu*). This man provides them with a house for meetings and gives them a feast when they bring out their own incarnate dead for a celebration; in return, he can count upon their occasional assistance in his farm work and their attendance at funerals that he performs.

As youthful age-sets gain organizational experience, they are expected to take more active interest in intercommunity competition and warfare. The most aggressive youthful age-set becomes identified as warriors, on the basis of its reputation for fearless adventurers willing to go out to the peripheries of community territory to collect thatching grass, or to go on expeditions into territory that is actually hostile. Age-sets are not actually regimental warfare units, for fighting is organized primarily at the village level, but they compete for warfare reputations, and a set with several members reputed to possess strong ikenga may be given a new collective name, such as "Club [that] seeks palaver" (*òtu ńachɔ ókwu*). Such an age-set comes to be identified with the fighting spirit of the community as a whole, and it will generally be chosen for such dangerous tasks as escorting the nine ghosts when they go through the community to "smell out" witches or to enforce some law being violated by powerful men. Age-sets which gain prominence in such activities range in age level from the early twenties into the late thirties. Most members of these groups undertake their first marriages in their early twenties.

As the members of such sets grow older, they become less active in warfare and more concerned with internal community politics.

The art of physical fighting becomes less important as a basis of leadership than the arts of oratory and argument. As an age-set becomes a group of "elders," its reputation is founded on its fearless public efforts to support community welfare and solidarity and to advocate strong measures against external enemies. A new social role emerges in this context, the leadership role of the "orator spokesman " (*ónye-ńekwu-ɔ́nʊ-ɔ̀ra,* literally "person who speaks the mouth of all;" or *ɔ́nʊ-ékwulu-ɔ̀ra,* literally "mouth that speaks for all").

One arena in which age-set competition becomes important is the palace community meeting, where binding public decisions are made. Once the chiefs and titled men have exercised their rights to speak out first on an issue, any man fearless enough to do so may stand forth and assert his views. The orator-spokesman is a person who does stand up and speak, forcefully and clearly, from the point of view of the public weal and in the name of land custom. A man is not regarded as an orator-spokesman simply because he is articulate and clarion-voiced; he is so regarded because he dares to challenge the views of chiefs. It is said that he may publicly denounce another man's effort to defraud even if that man is his own maternal brother. A tactic expected of him, but not of other men, is to reveal in public some embarrassing facts about his own forebears, and then to assert that certain men greater than he possess equally embarrassing histories. Such speech is appropriate only when important public decisions are at issue, but it appeals greatly to age-set egalitarian values and can therefore have a powerful impact on decisions at these meetings.

The orator-spokesman is so much a part of Onitsha's social fabric that he should speak at every major community decision even if no factions are evident; he clearly represents the political consensus of "Those who support and dignify." However, the nature of the role works against self-seeking or the amassing of a personal following. Indeed, the orator may well be an unpurified, untitled man. He does not gain wealth from such efforts, and may in fact have so many enemies (including close kinsmen whom he may have exposed in the interests of truth) that he is unable to achieve a title. Today, such men are referred to as "awesome" (ɔ́ *dì égwù*, "he is awesome"), but this does not imply diffuse esteem. Esteem for truth is, however, involved, for at critical times the orator-spokesman is heeded, and he mobilizes mass support by appealing to universalistic age-set values.

An age-set in which a number of spokesmen emerge over the years, gaining for it a reputation as a courageous group active in civic affairs, is likely to be selected by the community as the "age-set controlling the land" (*ɔ̀gbɔ́-ńachi-ànι*) when its members become relatively senior elders (escorting their own ijele incarnate dead). This group is selected by a competitive process in which older sets may be passed over and a more dynamic younger unit installed. This "controlling age-set" then co-opts outstanding men from immediately older and younger age-sets, thereby becoming an association rather than strictly an age-set, although it retains its former name.

The controlling age-set, in some nearby Ibo communities called "land is good" (*ànι-dìńma*), is expected to protect community welfare and stability in all matters concerning land custom. Its members may consult the women's trading organization concerning sacrifices necessary for the spiritual health of the community, and they have the right to direct the junior age-sets in public projects. They also meet when issues arise about customary practices and they may formulate new regulations to present to the king and chiefs for discussion. If the latter accept the new rules, the king's bell rings the decision throughout the town.

The controlling age-set is regarded with high esteem throughout the community, so long as its rulings promote solidarity rather than divisiveness. When, inevitably, a time arrives for a new organization to be selected, this process involves the relationship between the controlling age-set and the collective incarnate dead.

THE ORGANIZATION OF THE COLLECTIVE INCARNATE DEAD

After the governmental activities of the collective incarnate dead were suppressed by the early colonial administration in Onitsha, this structure underwent not only change but decay. Enough remains and enough is remembered, however, to present a general outline of its organization.

The collective incarnate dead is said to be divided into nine distinctive clan units that coincide with Onitsha the Nine Clans, but this ideal does not accord with the facts. Any village unit with its own tall ghost possesses an independent organization, and these number far more than nine. Each is an internally autonomous unit with a series of stages by which members move into the inner circle of elder dead (ɔra-okwute), but the exact number of these stages is not known. Initiations that move men through these stages do not revolve around wealth distribution (although expenses are incurred). Instead they entail oaths to keep secrecy and to uphold traditionalism. The criteria for moving into the inner circle of the elder dead emphasize personal history of honoring land custom and previous decisiveness in supporting the public welfare and law enforcement. In short, the values of the elder dead are very similar to those of an orator-spokesman and those of the leaders of the controlling age-set.

When the controlling age-set promulgates or demands enforcement of an important civic regulation, the elder dead, acting as their hidden counterparts, may proclaim their backing of this act by sending a man through each village of the town by night, playing the "arrow flute" (*ɔ́ta úfèle*) that represents the incarnate dead. The incarnate dead themselves are invoked in a number of contexts, and in each instance the consent of the elder dead is required. Because of their control over this invocation, the elder dead are sometimes referred to as "those who control the land" (*ńdi-náchi-ànɩ*).

In the villages, the elder dead bring out their apparitions for funerals, because unless the deceased have a ghostly escort to the land of the dead the funerary sequence cannot be completed. The elder dead also invoke the night incarnate dead, who come out seasonally from the bad bush in massed, chanting groups, to enter their darkened village, threatening and extorting gifts from households where the women have been misbehaving or where there has been much quarreling. Some night groups merely ridicule persons of the village who consistently do forbidden acts; others may actually destroy property and threaten to kill offenders. When the collective incarnate dead of a village propose to enforce village law with violence, however, they are expected to consult the most senior chiefs of that village.

The elder dead are also organized at the community level. Any invocation of the incarnate dead throughout the community must involve nine figures and follow a meeting at which elder dead from all villages are represented. This meeting is traditionally held by night in the village square of Obikporo village, the group whose ancestors are said to have come with Idoko from Igala bringing with them the first tall ghosts and the institution of the elder dead. In such meetings the Obikporo elder dead have strong influence in decision making because of their seniority, but only as a primus inter pares. The prime minister of Onitsha should convene these assemblies.

The nine incarnate dead may be invoked for the banishing of witches, or to ridicule a village whose elders are failing to perform some ritual civic duty. They may impose the extreme penalty when someone has defied, revealed, or inadvertently learned the mystery of the incarnate dead. The elder dead and the prime minister make the decisions jointly in such cases.

Since the decisions of the incarnate dead are irrevocable, the early missionaries at Onitsha found their activities most difficult to counteract. Reverend Strong, describing them as imposters with wooden heads, who dressed in rags and carried machetes or jangling iron rods in their right hands, reported their significance in the following way.

> The [mmanwʊ] are . . . the highest and supreme authority to legislate, execute, enact and repeal all laws binding the people as a nation . . . in this one regard [the king] is inferior to the [mmanwʊ] and is himself bound to abide by the decision and judgement of them in any political matter. In fact, the [mmanwʊ] can control him, repeal his laws and dethrone him and appoint a successor of their choice if needs be. The king under such a circumstance is not above law but the [mmanwʊ] has no superior and is under no human law.
>
> Each village or town has its own [mmanwʊ]—supreme authorities and great self-defense . . . The [mmanwʊ] of one village is not in any way inferior to those of other villages. . . . Equal power, reverence and honor are due to every one.
>
> The [mmanwʊ] of all the different villages meet together . . . form a general parliament and at such a meeting all laws to be made or to be revoked are fully deliberated. But laws respecting a particular village are to be made by the [mmanwʊ] of that village. From the Court of the [mmanwʊ] there is no appeal, no, not even to the Kings of the country or to other [mmanwʊ].[5]

The primary decision makers within the collective incarnate dead, the elder dead, do not necessarily include the village chiefs or the senior patrilineage priests. It is true that chiefs participate in some of the decisions arrived at by these elder dead, and that senior patrilineage priests may be among the elders; nevertheless the organization is clearly regarded as independent of these two roles. The elder dead are said to act as advisors to the senior

5. Strong (n.d.: June 18, 1886). This unpublished quotation from the 1880s fully corroborates my own ethnographic findings on these matters. Strong uses the term "Mor" or "Mors," mixing an English plural with what is apparently a rendition of ghost (mmʊɔ). The difference between this and incarnate dead (mmanwʊ) is difficult for non-Igbo speakers to detect, especially since the meanings of the two words greatly overlap.

priests of their village, and the senior chiefs cannot participate actively in invoking the incarnate dead or dictate decisions to the elder dead. Instead, the independent powers of the collective incarnate dead can be brought to bear to work against the chiefs, and can bring against them a massive force backed by the age-set system.

THE RELATIONSHIP BETWEEN AGE-SETS AND THE COLLECTIVE INCARNATE DEAD

Onitsha men agree that it is appropriate for the age-set controlling the land and the elder dead, or those who control the land, to be the same people. The age-set holding this status will be deposed whenever so many of its members have died that only a few of them remain in strategic positions in the various village organizations of incarnate dead. (When this happens the age-set has lost control of its most important basis of legitimacy.) The group charged with everyday enforcement of the sacred laws of the community and that group possessing the charisma for enforcement may tend to disagree; this possibility is minimized when they are largely the same people.

The relationship between the age-sets and the collective incarnate dead gives the political structure a spiritual validation. Age-sets may escort figures which are their own property, but such figures are invoked primarily for entertainment; when the age-sets escort incarnate dead for law enforcement, the figures are owned by villages and patrilineages. Thus the political mobilization of age-sets cannot become capricious or subject to the will of a powerful man, because it is tied to the ideals of descent.

Both the collective incarnate dead and the age-set controlling the land are, for some purposes, politically subject to the chiefs. Chiefs seek to become patrons of age-sets, to widen their social support and gain additional sources of occasional labor. The chiefs also attempt to maneuver both the controlling age-set and the village-based elder dead into enforcing directives that the chiefs have made. However, since chiefs can neither invoke the incarnate dead nor participate in the meetings of their respective age-sets, it is possible for these organizations, stimulated by the exhortations of orator-spokesmen, to act in concert against the chiefs, as they can against the king himself.

The collective incarnate dead symbolize recognition of the limited control that men have over their world, and emphasize that under these circumstances the only sure guide to action is ancestral tradition. They are predictable only in this sense: they will emerge and act when land custom has been violated. They show that even a man who has visibly demonstrated the *probable* worth of his personal god may come to grief, if he violates the will of the ancestors. Thus it becomes understandable how an unpurified man who has placed himself close to the incarnate dead may thereby gain considerable influence by becoming an orator-spokesman, and why such a person is ideally suited to act as the political voice of "Those who support and dignify."

THE SIGNIFICANCE OF ROLE DIFFERENTIATION IN ONITSHA

As Talcott Parsons has pointed out, if social systems are structured around their most general cultural patterns of value-orientation, then such social systems "evolve" only if these general cultural patterns evolve.[6] Examination of the overall character of Onitsha social structure in relation to the historical development of the various structural components should reveal the evidence for evolution in this sense.

Figure 34 summarizes major Onitsha roles and collectivities, in terms of the general value standards upon which status membership criteria are based. The major alternatives indicated are particularism versus universalism and ascription versus achievement.[7]

6. Parsons, Shils, Naegele, and Pitts, eds. (1961:985).
7. The relations of various roles to the collectivities in which they are embedded

A continuum, beginning in the embracing matrix of descent groups, from the fixed statuses of patrilineage priests, to titled men and kings, culminates in the primarily achieved roles of chiefs. Objects of interest to descent groups, chiefs represent the local units of which they are members, but they are also structurally outside

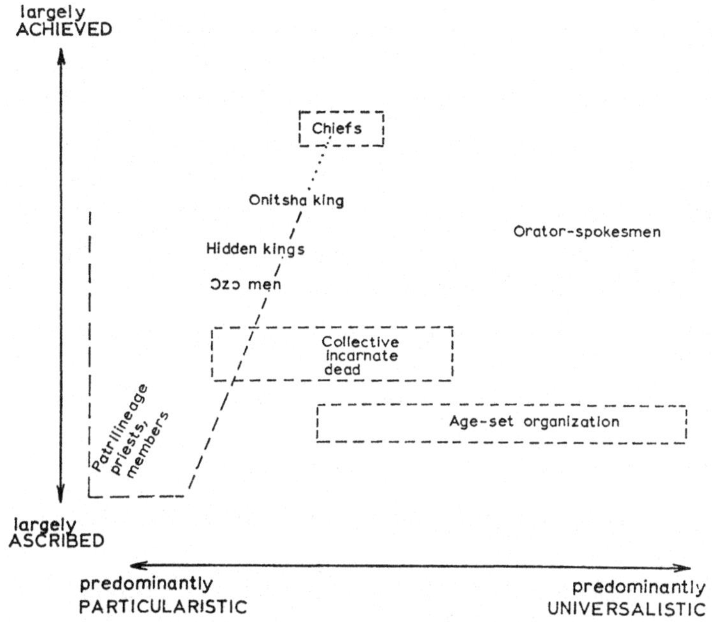

Fig. 34 Onitsha role differentiation: criteria of membership

these units. Chiefs form a distinct collectivity, while the other roles remain rooted in the descent group matrix. All the roles just mentioned are particularistically defined, in that they represent specific descent groups and villages. With increasing achievement emphasis associated with increasing importance of general criteria of ex-

are indicated in Figure 34 by dotted lines suggesting collectivity "boundaries." The basic collectivities in Onitsha, the patrilineal descent groups, are indicated by an open-ended set of dotted lines. The multiplicity of these groups is not illustrated in any way here; what is suggested is the manner in which they are structurally opened by roles whose external orientation increases along with their increasing definition by achievement.

cellence, there is less dependence upon particular positions within descent groups. Thus this series of roles shows a trend toward universalism. If this analytic continuum is also an historical one, a strong case could be made that evolution has occurred at least in this sector of the Onitsha social system.

There can be little doubt that the Onitsha patrilineal descent system, and the kinship categories so concordant with it, are old patterns. The ɔfɔ symbol, the basic legitimizing device throughout Ibo country, is based on paternity, while its derivative forms legitimize authority in other relationships. Variants of the Onitsha form of kinship terminology appear to be widespread in Iboland, although the varieties have never been systematically compared. Patrilineal ideology and patrilineal norms provide the basis of a diffuse model for human relations in which ultimate truth (in terms of ɔfɔ) is related both to the great god and to the ancestors buried in the land. This basic structural component of society binds man to his past, to a particular land, and to his ancestors, since truth (and morality) is identified with tradition and locality. The statuses of patrilineage priest (and priestess) are thus the most fixed, and most particularistic, reference points in Onitsha society. They may also be the oldest.[8]

The ɔzɔ title complex adds a second basis for legitimacy in Onitsha society; to fulfill his life a man must act positively, must seek public spiritual purification. Men must "bring money for the ghosts," becoming cleansed at the font of nze, the sacred symbol that joins the notions of ancestral truth and the acquisition of treasured, mysterious objects. A unit sharing nze has a king (eze), the holiest living representative of exalted ancestral essence. Since the relation between nze and eze is close, the nze complex in turn brings the ɔzɔ titled man and the king into a near equivalence, evident in

8. The Onitsha symbols of "mothers" might be viewed as residual elements of an older matrilineal pattern, by the methods of kinship system reconstruction established by Murdock (1949:184–259). This possibility cannot be pursued here, but the notion of ɔma is not universal in Ibo country. Other forms of motherhood images are widespread, but their historical significance cannot be assessed at this time.

the direct and detailed correspondences between their processes of initiation. In a sense, the king bestows upon the ɔzɔ man some of those qualities that make him king, so that the ɔzɔ man shares in his divinity, becomes in a sense a king unto himself. Indeed, Onitsha people frequently characterize the titled man as eze ɔzɔ, "king of ɔzɔ."

Onitsha kingship and ɔzɔ title are clearly related historically to the Nri kingship complex. Interestingly enough, some practices associated with ɔzɔ title in Nri or other nearby Ibo areas are associated only with kingship in Onitsha. For example, early phases of title taking in some nearby Ibo areas include taking each candidate to the Udo spirit shrine, where the "king of Udo" presides over an initiation ritual; in Onitsha, only the culminating phase of kingship installation establishes a relationship to the Udo spirit. At Nri and other areas, all ɔzɔ men hold iron spear staves called ngʊ agɩlɩga; at Onitsha only the king holds such a staff. Onitsha ɔzɔ men instead hold ɔsɩsɩ staves formally analogous to the uxhure staves of Benin. Thus the combinations of symbolic elements making up different complexes vary, complicating the task of interpreting the development of titles in Ibo country.

This difficulty arises in part from the historical disruptions described earlier, which appear to have led to the formation of Onitsha itself. Moreover, the distributions of the various title systems found in Ibo country have never been satisfactorily delineated or compared. Across the Niger in Western Ibo country, for example, ethnographic accounts suggest the presence of two distinct variants of ɔzɔ-like title pattern: an eastern group near the Niger possessing full ɔzɔ and eze institutions including dependence on Nri and application of ichi facial incisions, and a more westerly group employing different title terms and using uxhure-like staves similar to Benin's, but also including features similar to the first.[9] These may or may not represent two distinctive systems; the Onitsha system includes some but not all elements of both types as described.

9. Thomas (1914:54–57).

The variation in pattern is not endless, however, for the elements of nze, eze, and ɔzɔ appear to be interconnected everywhere in the northern Ibo area and in at least part of the western Ibo country as well. This constant relationship derives its symbolic rationale solely from the mythology of Nri.

At Nri, the ɔzɔ title and kingship are closely interrelated. It is said that Nri himself was the first man to take this title, becoming the eze Nri; thereafter other men who took title became eze ɔzɔ. Accession to both kingship and ɔzɔ requires the establishment of a relation to nze, and in both cases the candidate "dies" and becomes ghost-like. At Nri and also in other Nri-related towns, there are kinds of kings other than the eze Nri. Although available information is scanty a relation between kingship and nze appears quite general. The Nri king differs from ɔzɔ men, and from other forms of eze, in one critical way: he is identified as a mythological participant in the creation of the world, and each new king must reenact this role during his accession to office.[10]

According to Jeffreys, after completing his initiatory "death," "burial," "mourning," and "resurrection," the prospective eze Nri must travel to the town of Aguleri beside the Anambra River, "where all things began," to reenact the great god's initial gift of dry land to the founder of the Nri people, Eri. At Aguleri, the king-elect points his ɔfɔ staff first at the water then at the sun, praying that the river will begin to dry up. Thus he reenacts the predicament of Eri, who, standing in a morass, begged the great god to bring him dry land. When the river does recede, the new king must obtain from its bed a lump of the white clay called odudu, and bring it (carried in a vessel by a virginal boy) back to Nri town, completing the first stage of creation. The possession of this clay lump gives the new king the right to sit on his throne.

Second, the new eze Nri bestows upon his first son and daughter the ichi face marks of ɔzɔ title, reenacting the first Nri king's an-

10. For background to this discussion and what follows, refer to chapter 2, and to Jeffreys (n.d., 1935, 1936, 1956), Thomas (1913:137–38), and Talbot (1926:3:592–98).

cient sacrifice of his firstborn son and daughter which induced the great god to preserve certain social prerogatives for Nri.

These prerogatives and rights, which Nri people claim once extended beyond Ibo country to the west, include the following. The Nri king, it is said, has the right to send the appropriate ɔfɔ to any man wishing to take the eze title. His representative must be present to tie the ankle-cord for any man taking ɔzɔ title. The king himself has the right to prepare the yam medicine for everyone to use each farming season, and to initiate the various phases of the agricultural cycle by appropriate symbolic action. At the end of his installation, he ceremonially establishes the four days of the market week (reenacting the sending by the great god of the four market-strangers to Nri himself). Because of his role in creating the land, only his representatives may cleanse the land after abominations have been committed, and only the king himself has the right to redefine the acts held to be abominations in different areas. Finally, when crops, animals, and persons are dying on a given area of land that seems to have become a "fiery surface," the eze Nri must be consulted for medicines to render the land cool again. All towns in the area of Nri ritual influence continued to accept at least some of these traditional rights throughout the precolonial period.

This complex of ideas relates the Nri king to the cosmic order with a logical consistency not approached in the ideology that legitimizes, for example the king of Onitsha. The Onitsha king accepts the right of Nri representatives to enter Onitsha to cover all abominations, and traditionally granted the right of the king from Oreri (the Nri-derived community near the Igbo-ukwu archeological site) to enter Onitsha to make sacrifices to the river Niger and to Onitsha land; but Onitsha people today deny that Nri have the right to change standards of abomination in Onitsha, though no one in Onitsha itself is traditionally granted that right. The Onitsha queen must have an Nri agent attending her accession, but the Onitsha king does not. Onitsha people do not require Nri agents for their ɔzɔ title ceremonies, for which such agents are elsewhere required (nor, it may be noted, do they perform the ichi scarification with which Nri is traditionally associated.)[11] The Onitsha king annually acquires his own yam medicine from an Onitsha village whose founder immigrated from Nando, a community associated with the "children of Nri." The Onitsha king controls the calendar for his community, but so far as could be determined no mythical rationale for this control has been elaborated in Onitsha. The spiritual transition land for Onitsha dead is at Nri, and those persons who have committed abominations too vile to be covered must be sent there.

These inconsistencies in Onitsha kingship and religion all point to a symbolic dependence upon Nri and suggest that royal independence from Nri is recent. Onitsha kingship appears closely modeled upon the older pattern of Nri.

In Onitsha, both kingship and ɔzɔ title share an abstract quality that summarizes the object of achievement: purification, a spiritual condition of luster and cleanliness visibly symbolized by white chalk, white cloth, and the white fish eagle feather. This symbolic complex, too, finds its probable prototype in the Nri kingship, for a crucial part of the Nri king's installation includes both his emergence from burial with his body covered with shining white chalk, and his wearing white cloth and fish eagle feathers in his crown.

Evidence at both Onitsha and Nri suggests that ɔzɔ title is a kind of partial kingship, a metaphor of kingship attainable by everyman. The ɔzɔ man dies and reemerges as a whitened ancestor; the king's installation takes this process further, with his funeral ceremonies actually performed during his lifetime.[12] The taboos that the ɔzɔ man must observe are clearly cognate with those of kingship, but the king has added taboos. From another point of view, then, Onitsha kingship might be regarded as ɔzɔ title, with some-

11. For example, apparently the ɔzɔ ritual of "tying cord on the leg" (*ígèdo òwúlu ná-ʋkwʋ*), done elsewhere by an Nri agent, was in Onitsha performed by the nze holder of the clan, but this is not certain since the practice was defunct in recent times.

12. Cf. Nri royal installation ceremonies in which the king-elect is actually entombed for a brief period within a plank-covered vault.

thing added. The above description of Onitsha kingship has clarified the nature of some of these added elements, which appear to have been prefigured in the symbolic representations in bronze and other remarkable products found in the archeological sites near Oreri dated tentatively to around 1000 A.D.[13] These ancient objects suggest that symbolic components of kingship important in nineteenth-century Onitsha were also important at Nri long ago. Onitsha kingship does not, therefore, derive from either Benin or Igala in any simple way; its major historical roots reach much deeper in time, at Nri. The residual symbolic prerogatives recently held by the Nri king over this entire region seem to point to an ancient kingdom of much greater power, which existed before the eze title came to be widely emulated at the local level in Ibo country. This emulation, in turn, probably developed on the basis of earlier widespread diffusion of the ɔzɔ title, originally controlled from Nri.

The Onitsha ɔzɔ title and kingship, then, including most of the multiple cultural components which define kingship, are old institutions. Indeed their age may be comparable with that of the patrilineal descent system in which they are embedded, although they logically presume the existence of that descent system; for they do not simply articulate with this system, they penetrate to its matrix, so that achievement norms directly affect the operation of the patrilineage priesthood itself.[14]

Some aspects of Onitsha kingship do not derive from Nri. These

13. Shaw (1965, 1967). For example, in a pit at the Igbo-ukwu site, among a number of objects suggesting kingship, there was a remarkable pottery vessel decorated around its shoulder with four objects in relief: a ram's head with curving horns, a coiled snake, a chameleon, and a rectangular object suggesting a woven cloth. Taking Onitsha as an analogue, the first three features suggest the king as warrior (i.e. as ikenga), as "Snake who waits for his prey," and as the inscrutable one (chameleon). I suspect that the raised concentric circles on this pot symbolized the king's relation to the spirit land; quite likely the pot itself represented the land, and the cloth a "body covering" for it. My reference to the date is based on Fagan (1966:496).

14. Figure 34 does not satisfactorily illustrate the continuity between these roles. In a sense, the hidden king is closer to the patrilineage priest in ascriptive character than is the ɔzɔ titled man, since the criteria of eligibility to the status of hidden king are in theory much more fixed than are those for eligibility to ɔzɔ title. Attainment of hidden kingship, however, entails a greater series of achievements than does attainment of ɔzɔ. Figure 34 does not fully distinguish the criteria of status eligibility from those of validated attainment, and understates the universalistic esteem for titles.

aspects link it with the institution of chieftaincy and point to later historical derivations from Benin, Igala, and Aboh. In Benin oral tradition the major developments of chieftaincy ranks are associated with reigns of specific kings and with relatively systematic diffusion of these institutions eastward into Ibo country. Onitsha people also affirm the Bini derivation of their chieftaincy, and the detailed correspondences between title salutations make this relationship almost self-evident. Three of the top seven Onitsha titles are cognate with three of the "four pillars" of Benin. Moreover, the ceremonial sword carried by the Onitsha senior chiefs as their basic symbol of identification is indubitably Benin-derived, although this borrowing may have occurred through Igala.

The critical innovations evident in Onitsha chieftaincy are symbolized by elements the chiefs share with the Onitsha king: the ceremonial sword and the war drums. Since control of war drums gives each senior chief a measure of control over the fighting men of a village, he leads an independent fighting unit. The separation of these senior chiefs from roles as patrilineage priests, and their positions at the top of chiefs' ritual organizations clearly separated from village units, differentiate these roles most sharply from the kinship system of any of the roles discussed thus far. The king's partial control over the selection of particular candidates, of course, enhances the possibilities of such separation.

Oral traditions suggest that this separation has developed over time. In nearby Ibo communities, titles classed under the term used in Onitsha for chiefs (ndichie) tend to be held as the corporate right of particular village units. Onitsha people say that in the early days a chieftaincy title was taken by killing a goat as sacrifice to the nze, a practice suggesting an organic linkage not only with ɔzɔ title but also to particular Onitsha descent groups. Toward the beginning of Igala–Anambra dominance, the king appears to have gained control over the allocation. In recent times, village units constantly tried to reassert such ascriptive claims on various particular titles, and it is clear that the trend toward differentiation of chieftaincy roles from descent and other structures has not been continuous.

The chiefs' use of their ɔfɔ in begging the dead relates them symbolically to ancestor-oriented components of social structure. On the other hand, their symbolic identification as killers relates them also to age-set values through ikenga, a cultural pattern exalting warfare achievement that is of considerable antiquity in northern Ibo country. The requirement that chiefs first be ɔzɔ titled men and become increasingly purified as they increase in rank appears to be related to the view of righteous killing (by a warrior) as itself a means of progress toward a state of grace, for righteous killing is defined as such when the king bestows upon the killer the basic emblems of purification: the eagle feather and white chalk. This allies the warrior to the meaning of the ɔzɔ complex, but it does not enable him to bypass it.

The symbolic relationships of chiefs to ikenga, to ɔfɔ, and to purification, then, simultaneously legitimize the chiefs' access to various means of power, and limit their differentiation from other social roles. The symbols defining chieftaincy, like those of kingship, form a complex bundle of messages concerning role definition, different elements of which are shared with various other roles. A striking example of this overlapping appears in the sharing of rights to possess basic warrior symbols between senior chiefs and Onitsha king. This sharing is in effect the major device that distinguishes the Onitsha king, as a leader of warriors, from his hidden king counterparts, but it also sanctions a general (though not unlimited) emulation of his qualities by the senior chiefs, and limits his differentiation from them.

The cultural grounds of such emulation appear to lie in the Onitsha practice of defining increasingly prestigious roles through the accumulation of symbols, predominantly symbols of purification related to the ɔzɔ-nze complex. Even among the women, the roles of Onitsha queen and her councillors have come to mirror those of the king and his chiefs in their meanings, partly because the women have developed a simulated purification symbolized by the wearing of white cloth and white ivory anklets, and there has clearly been a tendency for prominent women to accumulate male symbols of prestige.[15] Indeed, the queen has at times so extensively emulated the king that she has threatened his position. More generally, the king's distinctiveness has been constantly threatened by the similarities of the chiefs and the hidden kings to him. The limits of their powers to emulate him must be a major consideration of the following chapters, since the evidence concerning Nri suggests that such emulation led to structural loss of what was probably a substantial kingdom centered there.

The status of the warrior-chief has symbolic roots in the age-set system, but the role is differentiated from it. Age-set systems like that of Onitsha, predicated on universalistic but ascriptive criteria, are general throughout Iboland, and they are probably old institutions. It is not known at present how widespread is their cult relationship to the ikenga spirit and its associated aggressive ideology, but it does appear that men worship their ikenga while attended by their age-set peers in at least some other parts of the Nri-Awka area. It is likely, then, that age-sets in this area were formerly more directly concerned with warfare organization than they appear to have been in recent times.[16]

It might appear paradoxical that a cult such as ikenga, dedicated to the success of the aggressive individual, would find its context of worship in the age-set organization, which stresses an identity of members and minimizes invidious comparisons of individual achievement. This occurs in Onitsha through the relationship of ikenga to ɔgbɔ-na-uke, the personal spiritual force of "age-set and (mis)fortune." An individual's achievement depends on the spiritual goodwill of his age-mates, and conversely worship at the shrine of a successful man's ikenga will spread benefits to all

15. In recent times, for example, prominent women have indubitably kept small ikenga shrines, although the male elders of the town claim they do not do so.

16. Jones (1962) scarcely mentions warfare. Talbot (1926:3:837), on the other hand, describes traditional Onitsha warfare as based on age-sets.

age-mates who attend. In this sense, the age-set as a unit inculcates self-assertiveness, but excludes from its midst the resulting competition. The ikenga receives separate sacrifice in the presence of age-mates, but it may also be worshipped in various ritual contexts in which age-mates may not directly participate.

Age-sets are compatible with the ethic of individual achievement, so long as they avoid invidious prestige comparisons. Senior chiefs, who are strongly oriented to their individual ikenga, must nonetheless be isolated from active age-set participation. Junior chiefs and ɔzɔ titled men may participate in and gain social support from their age-sets, but age-set gatherings institutionalize joking hostility toward them.

Age-sets are even more compatible with the profoundly ancestor-oriented, and most secret, organization of the collective incarnate dead. This social unit, with membership thoroughly embedded in descent groups, nevertheless has a leadership that does not coincide with the formal hierarchy of patrilineage priests. It links men for certain purposes into wider groupings than can be mobilized by descent groups. It is independent of the requirements for public purification, and entails instead an esoteric commitment to continual concern for expressing the will of the ancestors. Such organizations, holding an estate of mask costumes employed to embody the hallowed dead, are also widespread in Ibo country and are probably of very considerable antiquity. The Onitsha form has some distinctive features which appear to have undergone change over time.

Onitsha people claim to have derived the form of their collective incarnate dead organization from Igala, and they can relate its coming to the time of a specific king. This legend refers specifically to the elder dead, the inner leadership of these units, and to the possession of the tall ghost form of incarnation, which represents the most aged and chiefly dead. It suggests that the introduction of this new organizational form, through incorporation by the king of an Igala-derived descent group into the community, was followed by competition between the incarnate dead and the king, and by a separation of the organization from any direct relationship to him.

The general importance of this organization lies in its inaccessibility to public discussion (though all male adults except kings and slaves are members of it), in its direct access to ancestral legitimacy without public proclamations of purification, and, of course, in its structural independence from kings with its close link to the age-sets. More than any other structural feature in Onitsha, the collective incarnate dead grounds the organizational coherence of villages, and this fact brings them also into direct relationship with the chiefs who represent such villages. Indeed, chiefs and collective incarnate dead together provide the constitutive symbolism that generates a village out of one or more descent groups: any descent group with a chief and a collective incarnate dead organization is regarded as a village. Within a village, the secret organization provides a counterpoise, primarily ascriptively oriented, to the achievement oriented chief.

The same counterpoise operates at the civic level, where both chiefs and collective incarnate dead form town-wide organizations. Here another role emerges, the least formalized of those we have considered and the freest from both particular social structures and fixed qualifications. The orator-spokesman may be any freeman, regardless of his descent group background, and he holds his position only so long as he continues to validate it by performances approved by a critical public. An effective role of this type presupposes the structural autonomy of age-sets and collective incarnate dead, for these are the pillars of his support. The orator-spokesman is the public expression of the covert alliance between these two organizations.

It is difficult to assess the antiquity of this role, about which oral tradition is largely silent. Analogues to it, widely distributed throughout Ibo country, suggest that something like it is found wherever there are both structurally autonomous masquerade systems and age-sets. At Onitsha, there are, however, indications of development in this role. Possibly the quasi-chief position of the okwugba reflects an attempt to formalize this role and bring it under the control of the king and his chiefs. This would provide some rationale for the ambiguous character of the okwugba—his simultaneous roles as wife of the king, servant of the chiefs, and legitimate challenger of their decisions despite his lack of purification. The king's secret council (uloko obi) may reflect a similar effort by the kings to bring such orator-spokesmen under royal control.

Finally, we may examine the general character of this complex role structure by considering the communicative distribution of kola. This crucial medium for defining the differential seniority of statuses can be considered in two contexts: the basic interactive situation and the settlement of disputes. In the first, kola exchange gains its primary meanings within the kinship nexus, and is then secondarily applied to other kinds of social contexts. Generation seniority and birth order define the right to break kola in a gathering. Onitsha people say that these criteria apply rigidly in all situations, so that for example a mother's father who is a commoner has the right to break kola for his daughter's child who is a chief.

It is also accepted that differences in age and/or title modify the pattern. If a chief meets his commoner mother's father, the latter will first be handed the plate of kola for the breaking; he will then waive his right, touching the kola with his right hand and saying to the chief, "I have given you the power" (*ényigom-ǵhi íke*). If the meeting is a large and heterogeneous one, the chief may be handed the plate first, but he must ask if his mother's father wishes him to break the kola. After such permission, "the fire placed in the child's hand does not burn him," i.e. because the chief has been accorded a privilege he does not violate the land custom. Thus kola exchange remains symbolically and normatively rooted in kinship relations but is elaborated to express the prestige of title or age.

Such modifications are important, for the fee rights associated with dispute settlement or other policy decisions are also defined in the idiom of kola ("kola for talk"), though the fees may actually be paid in money. Since "maltreating an Onitsha man is in the kola," the chief or king who chairs a dispute settlement may appropriate a share limited only by his own discretion. Chiefs and the king can enrich themselves by appropriating half-shares (and even more) of such public fees.

This mode of allocating kola fees appears to be a symbolic form that defines the breaker of kola as a "corporation sole," in that in this role he represents a collectivity, claiming a share equal to that of its entire membership. The king and chiefs are not differentiated from the senior patrilineage priest in holding this right; their right is indeed modeled upon his, and what distinguishes them is rather the achieved basis of their claim to it. The Onitsha king merely goes a step further, for symbolic purposes, and claims for public occasions the kola-breaking rights of the husband/father as well as those of the lineage priest.

To what extent, then, does the historical evidence on this diversity of roles and collectivities suggest the operation of an evolutionary process of differentiation through time? Clearly, there is evidence that several achievement structures have been increasingly freed from the fixity of descent group ascription, undergoing elaboration and differentiation through time. This is apparent in the roles of both chiefs and Onitsha king. However, it is also clear that achievement through spiritual purification is a very old pattern, far predating any base line that we have been able to establish in this study. The relatively ascriptive collective incarnate dead have also undergone developments which sustained and perhaps increased their importance. Differentiation has occurred, but the pattern is not a simple, unidirectional one, for there have also been some trends toward formal convergence of roles (e.g. those of senior chiefs and king).

A second question is to what extent the historical evidence points toward evolution operating in the social system as a whole. Can it be shown that Onitsha history illustrates the evolution of a society from a segmentary, primitive system in the direction of a hierarchical one? Strong evidence has shown that the symbolism constituting the societal community itself had developed toward a stronger ideology of unity. Moreover, the Onitsha people classify the statuses of this society into three broad categories, king (obi), chiefs (ndichie), and Those who support and dignify (agbala-na-iregwu). Such categorization clearly suggests a coherent stratified system, but there are nine kings, distributed in different descent groups; while there is some stratification of such descent groups, there is also a strong sense in which the various descent groups are equivalent. Nevertheless, there is a distinction between royal and nonroyal clans. The picture here is a complex one also. The questions raised here must be left open at this point.

PART 4

EQUILIBRIUM AND SOCIAL CHANGE IN PRECOLONIAL ONITSHA

11 THE ONITSHA CEREMONIAL CYCLE

In Onitsha ceremonial life myriad complex processes articulate the diverse social units of the community with one another and integrate its roles within a single system of prestige and solidarity, while symbolically relating this social life to a wider reality. The year (*árò*), the pivotal unit of repetitive social processes in the community, is ecologically divided into two major seasons. The wet season is viewed by Onitsha people as a time of hunger, arduous work, and ultimately harvest reward; the dry season is a time of idleness, play, lavish funerary rituals, warfare, and disease. The basic sacred divisions of the year are set by the phases of the moon; the Onitsha king proclaims each of the twenty-eight-day lunar months (ɔ́nwa) and defines the ceremonial sequence in terms of the seven four-day weeks (*ógè ìsa,* literally "seven times") that comprise each month.

The Onitsha year begins approximately in late January,[1] toward the end of the dry season and after a series of expiatory rituals designed to remove the accumulated pollution of the preceding year. The king then announces the time for the first major ritual of the new season, "giving homage to the yam spirit" (ifejiɔkʊ).[2] The presence of this guardian spirit of yams must be ritually established each year in that strip of farmland to be cleared and cultivated by each patrilineage.

1. Unfortunately, the calendrical principles upon which the durational division of ceremonies was based could not be precisely determined, and the account that follows relates events to the Gregorian calendar rather than to the thirteen lunar months of traditional times.

2. This is not a precise gloss of this term, the form and meaning of which appear to vary in different parts of Ibo country. The elements *ji-ɔkʊ* mean literally "roasted yam," but roasting plays no part in the ritual and Onitsha people do not find this additional semantic component meaningful.

The worship of the yam spirit is primarily the concern of each patrilineage that holds farmland and maintains a common barn (ɔba) on that farmland. After the patrilineage elders have decided upon the farmland to be cleared, each household worships the yam spirit independently. Each of a man's wives prepares taro (the major food grown by women), which is used to feed the male yam spirit. Each householder goes with his sons to the farm, carrying farming tools and a live cock. The toe of the cock is cut and its blood is dripped over their seed yams, over the farming tools, and over the egbo sticks that are to be planted to represent the yam spirit, while the household head prays for a greater harvest than before and exhorts the farming tools not to slip in use and injure their users. The men then return home, carrying some of the yams for use in the "feast for the dead" to be performed over the ancestral shrines.

The householder brings out his symbols of the dead and places them before his throne, beside his ikenga and his vessel of god. As he sits on his throne, he receives a bowl of water and washes his hands; he sprinkles water over the assembled symbolic objects—the ghosts, staves, treasure boxes, vessel of god, and over the yams and farm tools, so that they may all "wash their hands" and become cool. His senior wife washes and hands him a kola nut. Holding his ɔfɔ (or his staff if he is a titled man), he begins a long prayer calling the represented ancestors, the yam spirit, and his own personal spirits and god to assemble and receive food. He vows his purity of intention, calls on the yam spirit to support him and his people in the growing of yams, and exhorts the spirit to attack anyone who intends to harm others. He then breaks the kola, divides it, drops the germinal sprout on the altar, and takes a piece for himself, handing the rest in a plate to his servant to be distributed to all persons present. He continues his incantation, chewing kola and spitting it on the assembled objects so that they may both witness his words and taste the kola, and he beats his staff on the ground to validate what he has said.

Palm wine is served in the same way and poured upon the objects.[3] The senior wife's cooked taro is then presented to them; pieces of it are dropped upon them, then distributed to all persons present. The smoked "head fish," whose bony head symbolizes resistance to external aggression, is broken into pieces, mixed with palm oil and salt, and served to the congregation. Finally, the cock whose toe was cut earlier at the farm is held with the staff and offered to ancestors, to the yam spirit, and to the householder's personal spirits. Its feathers are plucked from its neck and placed upon the shrines and upon the yam; its throat is cut and the blood sprayed over the objects and the yam, but not over the personal god. The dead cock is placed on top of the treasure boxes and left there while the feasting concludes.

Although the yam spirit ritual is regarded primarily as a personal sacrifice, it is followed on the same day by extended distribution of food between households. Each wife sends out many plates of taro to those whom she wishes to recognize and from whom she wishes to receive a prayer to the ancestors. She may send a plate to members of her husband's patrilineage, to her own senior patrilineage priest, to her own daughter's children and those of her husband. In return, the recipient must "cover the plate" with yams when returning it to the woman, in balanced reciprocity.

In the afternoon of the feast day the youthful incarnate dead emerge from the "room of the dead" to chase the children and young women about. The following morning, the youths of the square from the patrilineage march around to each household and collect a portion of each bird killed as annual compensation for their farming assistance, grave digging, and cleaning of the village square.

One wing of each bird is taken to the head patrilineage priest as an annual homage service. The priest uses this tribute for a census: counting the total number of wings sent him, he determines whether

3. Except the vessel of god, which can never receive any alcoholic beverage lest the god become disoriented and lead its ward astray.

the number of householders under his ɔfɔ has increased or decreased since the last farming cycle began. If he is dissatisfied, he calls the patrilineage together to consider whether a feast for the dead should be given for their childbirth medicine.

The childbirth medicine shrine is found only in a patrilineage segment that has become collectively concerned with its size as compared with other segments. When such concern first develops, the priest consults a diviner, who manufactures the medicine bundle. A roof-protected clay mound is constructed (usually on the edge of the square), the bundle is set in place beside it, and each wife of the patrilineage presses into the mound the curved base of a pot, symbolizing her own womb and her role as nurturing mother. Banana trees are planted near the mound to encourage ghostly children to seek rebirth there, and these trees become the communal property of the small children of the patrilineage. A ritual, including all men of the patrilineage and their wives and excluding all others, is held at this shrine after the yam spirit festival; all husband-wife disputes must be settled at this time so that the couples may have sexual intercourse immediately after the ceremony.

The king announces the ritual but otherwise plays no distinctive part in the ceremonial sequence at this time. He and his people perform the rites within their patrilineage and give the usual patrilineage tribute to their immediate senior priest; the same is true of all other titled persons.

After the yam spirit worship, the serious tasks of farming begin. The grasslands are fired, animals flushed out are hunted, and from late January through March the tasks of clearing the farmland bush are performed. It is believed that the firing of the grass arouses the ancestral ghosts who reside beneath termite hills, and that these irritated ghosts, called ayaka, converge upon the town at night. Men of the junior levels of the incarnate dead take most active parts in these incarnations, which are arranged by the elder dead. The ghosts besiege households, demand settlement of intrafamily disputes, and extort gifts from disputants or from prominent men whom they then honor and praise. They also rage about villages at night to honor the funerals of great men.

Funerary activities continue during this period into March, when the first real "month of work" (*ɔnwa ɔlʊ*) begins. The undergrowth of the farms is cleared and piled to dry for burning; then there may be a period of restful waiting for the rains while funerals are completed.

From the south come the first thunderstorms in late March, signalling the beginning of intensive preparation of the farms and gardens for planting. During this period, each man should in theory donate one day of every four to working for his senior patrilineage priest. Once the rains come, constant tending and guarding of plots is necessary.

From March onward the months of work are also the "time of hunger" (ugani), for although Onitsha traditional subsistence economy produces a substantial normal surplus beyond minimal needs, the social requirements for conspicuous consumption, redistribution, and waste all mean that the period of most intense work is generally a time of shortage. As the season progresses, the celebrations of lamentation that have marked the funerary season after harvest cease to be performed, and simultaneously the incarnate dead disappear from community view.

At the time of peak rains and hardest farming effort, the king announces the ceremony of "beseeching god" (*àja-chí*), in which every adult makes independent sacrifice and feasting for his own god, begging it to guide him in his labors, to witness his humility, and to help his crops prosper. Although beseeching god marks the first farming festival, it is performed privately, in a spirit of humility for weakness and shortcomings. Women perform their own ceremonies in their kitchens, setting their sticks representing god alongside their shrines to mothers. The household head brings out all his shrine symbols, and his senior wife washes his vessel of god in chalk. He sacrifices a cock to his various ghosts, beginning his prayer by affirming that his destiny lies in the hands of his god, and giving thanks for the successful completion of planting. He begs for a bountiful harvest, and also calls on the great god and on the great spirits of the town to guide and benefit him and his kinsmen.

In traditional times, during the afternoon of beseeching god, the king, having performed personal sacrifices in his palace, sent out his slave representatives dragging a living human being by a rope. This human victim was dragged to all the major village squares of the town, where the head priests came forward and confessed openly the sins of their "children" and symbolically cast these misdeeds onto the victim. The victim was then dragged to the riverside and thrown to one of the great spirits of the river.[4] This sacrifice may have been witnessed by the missionaries in 1864:

> The head slave, who was the director of this cruel action, made a short address, with flowing gesticulations, to the river, in the following manner: "River Niger, the King of Onitsha sends his compliments to you, and thanks you for the same. He is not a wizard nor a profane person. As my subjects have committed many grievous sins and wickednesses, I appease your anger by this sacrifice.[5]

Thus the king expresses the generality of many separate and independent acts of atonement and prayer. This pervasive sense of personal and public expiation brings this ceremony, although technically a feast, under the category of beseeching.[6]

In July the first harvest of maize ends the hunger time and begins a series of harvest festivals. First is the *ùmatɔ* festival, in which great men redistribute their new consumable wealth to end the hunger of their dependents and subordinates. This redistribu-

4. This was the spirit that eats Nri people (oli-nri).
5. Taylor (1865:149).
6. "Beseeching" is not an exact gloss of aja, usually used in the phrase ɩchu aja, "driving away [evil] by sacrifice," but it best conveys the significance of this ceremony, which is certainly also a sacrifice.

tion publicly proclaims the ranking of spiritual prestige among various statuses in the community.

The king begins the umatɔ festival by killing a goat, which the senior chiefs divide and share, thus accepting the king's sequence of ceremonies. On the appointed day the senior chiefs come to the palace in their ceremonial finery, escorted by the junior chiefs and ɔzɔ men of their major villages, and bearing tribute in harvested corn and "old yams" to the king. The royal war drums are beaten, and the chiefs perform their warlike dances. After ceremonial greetings in the palace, the king ritually feeds the senior chiefs by placing garnished pounded corn food directly into their hands. This redistribution emphasizes his responsibility for insuring that his people are fed and underlines the dependence of even the greatest chiefs upon him. Great heaps of food are then brought for division by the lesser chiefs and commoners. The following day the king gives the chiefs palm wine as a reward for their dancing.

After a waiting period, the hidden kings of the nonroyal clans perform a similar ritual for their subjects, and the next day the senior priests of the major segments of the royal clan follow with their rituals. The chiefs of each village attend their patrilineage feasts as other lineage subjects do; but an attending chief is given his own food to be sent to his home, and he retires to another chamber while his senior priest performs the ritual acts, for a chief should not be seen kneeling before anyone save the king.

After an additional interval, all senior chiefs perform umatɔ; they are attended by the junior chiefs of their respective villages, who undertake the actual sacrifices to their ancestral shrines. The day after the chiefs' redistribution of food, the ɔzɔ men of each village who wish to assert their individual affluence by redistributing corn food are permitted to do so within their own spheres of control.

The women of each household end the umatɔ by a ceremonial sweeping out of the hunger time from their kitchens. During all such ritual festivals, no woman may attend market; all markets are therefore closed. After the conclusion of umatɔ, the king announces the climactic ceremonial sequences of the Onitsha year, the central event of which is the "new yam festival" (*ɔ̀wʊ́waji*).[7] These ceremonies express two major mythological ideas interwoven in the ritual activities.

It is said that when yams were first brought into Onitsha, all the people were afraid to eat them for fear that the strange tubers might be poisonous. The king called upon his special doctor/diviners, members of the *Ʊ̀bulu-nà-Ìkém* clan, to provide a medicine that could be smeared over the yams to make them safe for eating. The king directed the doctors to supervise the initial eating of the yams, which was to be done by certain specified social units and statuses before others would follow. The reasons given for this sequence vary, depending on whether the informant partakes at the beginning of the sequence or toward the end: members of the royal clan say that the doctored yams are served first to the least significant members of the community, so that if they die the loss to the community as a whole will not be great; members of the clans eating yams first say that they do so as the most daring and courageous members of the community, and the less courageous then follow. After a considerable series of ritual tests, the most valued (or most discreet) members of the community feel safe to eat yams, including ultimately the king himself.

Second, the new yam festival is also the time when the Onitsha king must retire to "dream" (*ńlɔ*), to enter into a trancelike state during which he communes with figures from the mythical past, assumes all the community's burdens for the year, and seeks through this communion to divine the future. It is hoped that he will emerge from this trance filled with power, to dance triumphantly before his people as living testimony of the town's strength

7. A strict gloss for this term appears to be "splitting yam," but the translation given here is the popular one in Onitsha. See Nzekwu (1959) for a good account of this ceremony.

and spiritual grace. In this dreaming activity, he is guided and assisted by the clan of Ubulu-na-Ikem.

The ceremonies begin [8] with the "new yam festival of young men of Isele-Awada" (*ɔwʊwaji ikolɔbia Isele-Awada*), numerically perhaps the smallest clan in Onitsha.[9] The youngest (and bravest) men of this clan are the first persons to test the adequacy of the medicine. On the following day comes "new yam festival of head patrilineage priests of Isele-Awada" (ɔwʊwaji ikpala-isi Isele-Awada), in which the senior priests (including titled men and chiefs) of the clan first eat new yams. The same sequences of named rituals are then performed in two other nonroyal clans, Eke-na-Ubene and Ubulu-na-Ikem.[10]

Each of these one-day festivals follows a similar procedure. Every householder conducting the feast brings out his shrine objects on the morning of the festival day. When all household members have gone outdoors, the head daughter moves through the village repeatedly performing the ceremony of "calming the house" (ɩjʊ-ʊnɔ). Standing by the threshold of each house where the ceremony is to be performed, she exacts tribute in yams from each wife of the household and in return provides each with salt, fish, and oil for the day's ceremonial cooking. This is a symbolic statement of the ideal trade relations between lineage daughters and wives. Then, holding a live fowl in her left hand, she enters the house and drags the fowl's body over the floor and walls in order to draw into it the heat of evils that have accumulated there. Holding a white snail shell (*éjùna-ńzu*) on the end of a stick, she

8. The details of sequence in this festival series appear to have varied somewhat over recent times, and it was not possible to reconstruct the precolonial pattern with certainty. Documentary evidence suggests that recently observed rituals reflect the earlier ones at least in general outline.

9. This makes up the small village *Ógbè-ɔ̀zɔ́ma*. One of its ancestors was the dethroned early king Awuma.

10. The festival of Eke-na-Ubene is performed both by members of the Village of Oli-Eke and by members of the village of Ɔdɔje; within Ɔdɔje, however, the royal clan subvillage Isiokwe does not undertake the festival at this time. The festival of Ubulu-na-Ikem is performed only in that subdivision of Riverain Village (Ogbe-olu) called Children of Ikem (*ʊ́mʊ̀-Ikém*).

touches it to the same surfaces, to cool the house. As she performs these acts she chants repeatedly:

> Let all forbidden things clear out of the house;
> let money come;
> children will come;
> strong health will come;
> let evil clear out, and sickness depart from the house.

After this is done in each house throughout the patrilineage community, in descending order of patrilineage seniority, each household priest begins his ceremony, calling upon his dependents to receive food and drink from him, and sacrificing a cock (and if possible, a mammal). He then sends annual homage service (ife nru aro) to his immediately senior patrilineage priest, in the form of ten yams and the wing of the cock sacrificed. A daughter's child to the clan performing the festival may also celebrate the occasion by killing a fowl on his shrines to "the mothers" and sending a wing of the fowl to his mother's senior patrilineage priest.

No senior priest may eat the new roasted yam until he is fed a portion of it, placed on the end of a stick, by an agent of the Ubulu-na-Ikem clan. These agents go to the clan performing the ritual on a given day, receive a tribute in yams, and in exchange doctor and administer the roasted yams. After the first participant clans in the sequence (as outlined above) have been fed, the senior priests of the doctoring Ubulu-na-Ikem clan begin the second major phase of the ritual, when they "enter into dreaming" (*ínye-ʊkwʊ-ńa-ńlɔ*). They retire into a ritual chamber in their village, where they do divination prior to preparing the king for his own spiritual retreat. When the omens indicate that they are ready, they emerge, rejoicing, and proceed to the king's palace. They meet him in his private familial chamber (agbala-eze), where he presents them with white chalk, and they perform a ceremonial chalking of his body to purify him in preparation for communion with the dead.

After this is done, the king enters into dreaming; clothed as a mourner (wearing only a loin cloth) and covered with white chalk, he retires into his house of breezes. There, on each side of his throne, fires are kept burning; for the only time during the entire year, the king behaves like a senior patrilineage priest, sitting beside a fire to fast and mourn for all his people who have died during the year. He also communes with the great god, with Onitsha land, with other great spirits, and with the ghosts of former kings. During this time he takes no food, only liquids.

While the king is in retreat, the festival continues to proceed toward a climax, with the new yam festival of ekwensu (ɔwʊwaji ekwensu), performed by the young men of Children of Ase village. The men of this village are metaphorically called malevolent ghosts (ekwensu) because of their traditional reputation as fierce warriors who, as agents of "bad deaths," are therefore endangered by the malevolent ghosts of their victims. On the day after the new yam festival of ekwensu, the head priests of Children of Ase village eat their first new yams. From this time on, the youthful incarnate dead begin to appear in the community for the first time since the hunger season began.

After the new yam festival of the head priests of ekwensu, the "killers' feasts" (ɔ̀*gbalido*) are performed by the chiefs and warriors of the community. Each killer goes to the kapok tree planted in honor of his warrior feat, carrying the lower jaw of his victim in his left hand and the "killing knife" (*ḿmà-ògbu*) in his right (thus emulating the ikenga figure). Singing praises to the potency of his ikenga spirit, he dances before the tree and then sacrifices a dog, the animal associated with malevolent ghosts. He also sacrifices a cock to his ikenga in gratitude for his good fortune. On the day all the chiefs perform this sacrifice, the senior chiefs bring forth their war drums and call the chiefs officially under them in war to come and dance. The senior chiefs kill rams to their ikenga, honoring their powers.

While these killers' feasts are performed, the king remains in retreat. However, as the greatest of all killers, he sends his slaves to visit all the chiefs' houses, where they collect one foreleg of each dog sacrificed. Thus he participates vicariously in the ritual, and gains some of the strength of the warriors.

After four days of communion, "the king emerges from dreaming" (*ínyepu-ʊkwʊ-ńa-ńlɔ-ézè*), having assessed his relationships with god, ghosts, and spirits, and returns to the palace, where his body is washed to signify the end of his mourning. The junior chiefs are called to the palace to prepare his dress and to direct the adornment of his throne, while the doctors of Ubulu-na-Ikem continue to fortify him with medicines.

The climax of the sequence occurs on the following day with the king's annual emergence (ɔfala) [11] from seclusion. He demonstrates that he has survived another year as a living atonement for the sins and misdeeds of the Onitsha people, that he has mourned the community's dead and been shown guiltless of their deaths, that he and the community have been filled with strength, fullness and richness of life, and that he has foreseen the events of the year and found them to be good.

Festive cloths are tied around the throne in the house of breezes, where the king has fasted. Messages are sent to all of the towns around Onitsha that recognize the greatness of the Onitsha king, calling them to send dancers and chiefs further to glorify the festival. The royal war drums are set up beside the throne, and traditionally a slave was tied near the trees at the entryway to the palace square where a medicine bundle protects the palace from dangerous forces.

At this great festival everyone wears his finest clothing. The king is dressed in a brown costume covered with black spots, in memory of attire once sent him from Igala, and he dons his great tableau headress which the chiefs imitate on the lesser scale. The queen and her councillors dress in white cloth and wear great ivory leg

11. This term has no clear literal meaning, but the translation suggests the primary meaning of the ceremony.

rings, while the ɔzɔ men wear white cloth, carrying their ivory-tusk horns, and wear their feathered caps. The daughters of the king ring their necks with pipestone necklaces and dance around the palace square singing his praises. Only the king's wives must remain in seclusion during this great celebration.

The senior chiefs arrive, announced by cannon shots and accompanied by the junior chiefs and ɔzɔ men of their villages. Each procession enters through the archway, passing, formerly, the slave tied there and calling out messages for him to deliver to the dead. The most junior of the senior chiefs approaches the house of breezes first and dances to the royal drums, pretending to threaten the crowd with gestures of his war sword. When he tires of dancing he stops the drums with a touch of his sword, and he and his chiefs take their seats beside the palace entry.

All the senior chiefs dance in this way, culminating with the prime minister, who then leads them into the main palace chamber where they privately salute the king. Surrounded by his entourage of chiefs and flanked by slaves bearing his sacrificial and war swords, the king emerges from the palace wearing his great headdress, living evidence of the well-being of the community. According to one early visitor to Onitsha, the king was expected at this time to carry a weight of earth on his back in order to demonstrate his ability to bear the burdens of power:

> . . . ce jour-là, il est tenu de danser devant son peuple, rassemblé sur la place de son palais, avec un énorme poids sur le dos (généralement un sac rempli de terre), afin de démontrer à tous qu'il est encore capable de supporter le poids du pouvoir. S'il ne pouvait pas remplir cette obligation, il serait immédiatement déchu et peut-être même lapidé.[12]

12. Mattei (1890:68). Whether or not this did occur is hard to say, for other accounts do not mention it and it was not done in recent times so far as I am aware. If the practice were followed, it would have had profound symbolic implications. The king is called "sky," and "the sky is greater than the land." Thus, for the king to carry the earth would identify him with the universe and with the great god (olisa-ebulu-ɔwa, "god who carries the world"). Meek (1937:187) thought that the term

Greeted by the cheers of his subjects, the king dances outwards to the entry arch; there, formerly, he touched his sacrificial sword (ada) to the bound slave, who was then killed by a slave executioner. The king then returns to the palace and retires while dancing groups perform. He emerges a second and a third time, going around the square to salute the trees that have ceremonial associations with his personal god. He then retires to the breeze house.

In a recorded instance in the past, the king's performance was followed directly by the entry into the square of the queen, followed by her women councillors:

> the Queen made her appearance with some chief women of rank singing and dancing towards the King showing their loyalty and hearty respect . . . in token of royal acceptance . . . the King stretched out his sceptre to the Queen who touched it and rose up from her knees fully satisfied.[13]

After this salute was completed, the entire congregation sank to their knees, as the king rose to his feet before them:

> his chief minister standing next to him gave out a public royal proclamation to the hearing of all and for the public general good. The sacrifices to be offered during the ensuing year, the victims when so offered and all other religious and superstitious ceremonies to be done were all specified by him. His hearty good wishes were then conveyed to all and his kingly goodbye said to all.[14]

A proclamation of this kind concludes the main emergence ceremony, and the dramatic tension of the day suddenly subsides. This tension reaches its peak when the king emerges to dance in the

---

ɔfala meant ɔ*f*ɔ-*ala*, i.e. ɔfɔ + land, *ala* being an interior Ibo term for land equivalent to Onitsha anị. If this were true, the king then would be testing his ɔfɔ powers by his moral relation to the land of Onitsha. It is doubtful that ɔfala has that specific meaning, but moral relations to the land are clearly involved in the ceremony. This meaning would certainly fit what the king is said to do in Mattei's report.

13. Strong (n.d.: September 25, 1885).

14. Ibid.

escort of his senior chiefs, for when they join together not only do they publicly demonstrate their solidarity, they also test one another by sorcery. Spectators at the scene experience its glory, but they also watch carefully for evidence of magical confrontations. The suspense continues as long as king and chiefs are close together.

On the following day, "the back of emergence" (*azʊ ɔfala*) is held. At this time all of the king's subjects may come forth to salute him, and representatives of other communities come forward as well. The Onitsha queen and the hidden kings also perform their own emergence ceremonies, but these are limited to a fasting retreat and a subsequent celebration involving primarily members of their own clans.[15]

After the emergence is completed, the new yam festival for the head priests of the Children of King Chima, the royal clan, is performed. However, the king cannot yet partake of the yam, for there still remains a more exceptional form of mourning to be done for the dead. A ceremony called *ito ukpukpa,* in which the dead themselves are believed to undertake mourning, follows the king's own period of mourning. The various objects representing the dead are removed from the altar of each household, and three pieces of firewood are marked with chalk so that they can represent mourning fires kept by the dead. These are placed upon the altar, and two okposi sticks, representing all of the ghosts, are set atop the firewood to symbolize the senior patrilineage priest's traditional mourning beside a fire. After four days, the head daughter of each patrilineage must come and calm the house, to remove this taint of mourning. Thus the dead parallel the ceremonial acts of the king.

Immediately thereafter, the king performs *íkelebeji,* his own ceremonial eating of new yams prepared by boiling and pounding, while his subjects limit themselves to roasted yam as a sign

15. In recent times, the Onitsha king has totally occupied the center of the ceremony, for since the colonial period only one king has been recognized. Occasions when the hidden kings performed their own emergence are however remembered from late in the last century.

of respect to him. The hidden kings and the queen also eat their first yam at this time.

The ceremony of "cooking in a pot" (*ósisi-ìte*) ends the harvest cycle and marks the time when betrothed girls begin their ritualized visits to their future marital homes. It celebrates the beginning of mundane daily cooking by the wives and the completion of harvest work. With the cooking in a pot festival begins the "wasted months" (*ógè-ìsa éfùléfù*) of leisure. Interests turn to performances of the night incarnate dead, to intervillage wrestling contests, to warfare, to title taking and to lamentation, the second phase of Onitsha funerary ritual.[16]

The death of any important person in a household causes the objects representing the revered ghosts to become "hot" so that they must be removed; they cannot be returned to the house to reestablish its spiritual stability until both stages of the funeral—burial and lamentation—have been completed.

For the lamentation of a titled man, the "head mourner" (*ónye-ísi-ózu*) must first arrange for the support of members of his patrilineage. Then he must approach the Onitsha king or his own hidden king to arrange for the killing of a cow to announce this second stage of the funeral. Following this announcement, in which the prime minister and any other chiefs and persons from the deceased's village participate and divide the meat of the cow, the senior chief of the village sends his war drums to the compound of the deceased; the lesser chiefs go and dance there to separate the living warriors from their deceased comrade.

Kinsmen notified to send groups to participate later in lamentation include not only the deceased's own patrilineage, but also his mother's, father's mother's, and mother's mother's patrilineages,

16. "Lamentation," though an accurate gloss of the phrase ịkwa ozu (lit. "lamenting the dead"), scarcely conveys the atmosphere of rejoicing evident during these rituals. It would carry us too far afield to describe the lamentation rites here, but they are of such great social importance that some indication must be given of the range of social relations that they mobilize. The following description relies partly on H. K. Henderson (n.d.).

all of which must send their groups of male drummers and their daughters. All of the deceased's sons-in-law are notified and expected to bring drummers. Daughter's children attend as individuals and the deceased's age-set comes as a group. Age-sets of the deceased's sons are also expected to attend.

On the second day of lamentation, goats are killed to send the deceased well fed into the land of the dead. All the chiefs of the community have the right to come to the funeral site and share in the meat. On the same day, the various descent group teams of male drummers dance at the funeral; since they come dressed as warriors, they lend an explosive, competitive atmosphere to the event.

Throughout this ritual sequence, the children of the deceased (one of whom is ordinarily designated as a head mourner) wear his clothing, including his clothing of title, to signify that his existence continues in them and that they aspire to follow in his footsteps. The climax of lamentation occurs in two striking ritual events. First, the head mourner supervises the first (and last) blood sacrifice to the personal god of the deceased; the blood of a goat flows over the vessel of god and the five sticks it contains, indicating that the departed life has been replaced by the different social existence of the dead.

Second, as evening approaches, the collective incarnate dead bring out tall ghosts representing the founders of the patrilineage of the deceased and that of his mother. If the deceased was a very prominent man, and especially if he was a chief, these tall ghosts escort into public view the visible reincarnation of the deceased himself, in the form of an elderly, tall ghost covered with earth-stains indicating his recent arduous journey into the land of the dead.

Lamentation for a prominent man thus mobilizes nearly every major role-dimension of Onitsha society in an interactive process that has as its focus changes in the status of both a particular deceased person and his immediate mourners. The completion of all lamentations for which a survivor is responsible is a prerequisite for anyone who wants to begin the task of taking a title; partly for this reason, these funerary rituals are pivotal social events, to which great public attention is given.

Another aspect of life gains prominence as the dry season begins. In October the flow of the Niger peaks sharply at Onitsha, and the people at the great waterside market must retreat to higher banks as the waters rise. This is a time of greatly intensified trading, with traders coming to this market from distant places; it is also thought to be a time when diseases enter the community. The major spirits of the town, especially those clustered about the riverside market, are believed to begin demanding food and sending disease or disaster because various customs have been violated. The subsequent falling of the river toward December signals the general decline of the year and the time to begin driving accumulated sins from the town, a ritual cleansing in which the force of the river is used to carry away the taints of abomination and disease.

The first public sacrifice of expiation following the harvest season is to venerate the land (iru anɩ). All men are expected to provide an "annual goat" (*éwu árò*) for their senior priest to sacrifice, the chiefs bring a tribute to the king as homage to the Onitsha land, and the king himself traditionally arranged a human sacrifice to the land. According to Basden, among the western Ibo this sacrifice was traditionally performed at the climax of the ɔfala festival.[17] At Onitsha it was done somewhat afterwards, as apparently when, in 1870, "a little girl, about eight years of age, was offered as an annual sin-offering, to atone for the sin of the nation." She was dragged the two miles "from the King's house down to the waterside . . . during which progress . . . everyone, through whose streets the victim was dragged, might pray that his sin might be carried away by this sacrifice, supposing

17. Basden (1938:69).

thereby they are free from punishment for all their offenses." [18] The king's slaves led the procession, beating drums; they were followed by a great procession of young men carrying whips who forced all travelers off the paths, laid waste to the market area, and confiscated the goods of anyone who dared attend market on this day.

During December or January, in preparing for the end of the old year and the beginning of the new one, the Onitsha women consult with diviners and with the king about the sacrifices necessary to cleanse the town of all sins. Each village group of wives first arranges to perform "sacrifices driving away [the evil] of the year" (ιchʊ aja aro) from the village. Early on the designated morning, each wife takes from her kitchen a firebrand smoldering at both ends and brandishes it about the compound crying, "it [evil] is not in our place" (*ɔ́burɔ̀ be ányi*). The women meet at the village square and then drive the evil to the bad bush at the village peripheries. After each village has completed this cleansing, the king announces "driving away [evil] from the town" (*ιchʊ aja obodo*). The women assemble before the palace with their firebrands and carry them down to throw in the river, while the king's slaves carry chalk and other foods to the riverside to feed the spirits.[19]

The extent of sacrifices performed when the year comes to an end depends upon the findings of diviners, upon the dreams of women, and upon the general incidence of social malaise. A prominent woman may dream that the spirit called "She lives in water" (O-bi-na-mili), located near the waterside market, has been blinded by the firebrands thrown into the river during driving evil of the year, and that she is demanding compensation. In February

18. Crowther (1871:128). On this occasion, the sacrifice appears to have been made about three weeks after the king's emergence.

19. I was not able to determine whether fires were ritually rekindled after this rite, or whether the Onitsha king had any role in a rekindling of fire. Ordinarily, fire was shared within the clan.

of 1858, the missionaries witnessed an elaborate sacrifice of atonement; they saw a young woman

> with her hands tied behind her back, and her legs fastened together with a rope, decorated with young palm-leaves.
>
> In this position she was drawn, with her face to the earth, from the king's house to the river, a distance of two miles.
>
> The motley groups who attended her premature funeral cried, as they drew along the unfortunate creature, victimized for the sins of their land, Aro ye! Aro! Aro! i.e. Wickedness! Wickedness! ["Aro!" = "Abomination!" (alʊ)]
>
> The pretended sacrifice was to take away the iniquities of the land. The body was dragged along in a merciless manner, as if the weight of all their wickedness were thus carried away . . .
>
> I heard also, that there was a man killed, too, as a sacrifice for the sins of the king.
>
> Thus two human beings were offered as sacrifices, to propitiate their heathen deities, thinking that they would thus atone for the individual sins of those who had broken God's law during the past year.
>
> Those who had fallen into gross sins during the past year—such as incendiaries, thefts, fornications, adulteries, witchcrafts, incests, wars, slanders, etc., were expected to pay in 28 ngugus, or 2£ 0s 7½d as a fine; and this money was taken into the interior to purchase two sickly persons, to be offered as a sacrifice for all these abominable crimes—one for the land, and one for the river. A man from one of the neighboring towns was engaged to execute this atrocious deed; and twenty ngugus, or 1£ 12s 6d was paid him for the duty. One of them was seen, with his paddle on his shoulders, going down to the river, where he was to paddle out the canoe, and drown the body.[20]

20. Crowther and Taylor (1859:344–45). The last two sentences in the quotation may refer to a requirement for Nri men to participate in this major public ritual to cover the abominations of king and community.

In this major public ritual, performed at the close of an old year and the beginning of a new one, the Onitsha people appear to assess their yearly activities as requiring profound acts of expiation. Acts of atonement are prescribed not only for "those who had fallen into gross sins," but also for the king himself, as father and symbol of the community and even the universe. This sense of community contamination appears related to a sense of failure to maintain an ideal of social harmony.

Several thematic elements make up the complex fabric of the ceremonial year in Onitsha. The year itself seems to undergo changes in sacred tone; the social units that predominate ceremonially change with the cycle, as do the aims of their actions; the focus of sacred events shifts between symbols associated with particular social personalities and roles and those associated with the community and the universe. Sometimes all these elements intermingle in a complex unity.

The year begins in a spiritual atmosphere of purity, abstention from sin, and dedication; there is also a sense of emptiness, a concern over current efforts aimed toward fulfillments yet to come, and a fatalistic dependence on imponderable forces of nature. The early ceremonies associated with the yam spirit and with childbirth commit every person and household to economic production; they relate each person to his economically cooperative patrilineage unit, and orient each patrilineage to its common, separatist reproductive goals. Secondarily, these rituals delineate connections between patrilineages, through acts of ritual reciprocity (a pattern that recurs throughout the year). When the times of heaviest labor and greatest emptiness coincide, all joyous ritual celebrations cease, including lamentation.

The ceremony of beseeching god carries this sense of personal humility, human weakness, and dedication further. Its rituals are also largely private and personal, while the public sacrifice by the king awakens the community to awareness that all its members are affected by these human weaknesses and shortcomings, which they may collectively expiate through communal rituals such as scapegoating. All these early activities may be viewed as sacred means or instrumentalities undertaken in the hope of later rewards.

At the middle of the year, a time of impending and actual harvests, the sacred tone shifts correspondingly to social interdependence, increasing community power, and impending reward. The maize harvest rituals are viewed rather as signals of greater rewards to come than as rewards in themselves, but their ritual message is clear: faithful homage service by status inferiors is rewarded by redistributive gifts of sustenance from social superiors, and the inferiors depend on such rewards for their well-being. The sequence of these rituals publicly proclaims spiritual ranking among the most prominent social identities in the community:

1. The king feeds corn food and serves palm wine to his chiefs, in exchange for their tribute and dancing (ultimately, he feeds all members of the community);
2. the hidden kings do the same for their subjects (including chiefs);
3. the senior chiefs follow in their village domains, assisted by their junior colleagues;
4. the ɔzɔ men conclude the festival in their more limited patrilineage domains.

The status of senior patrilineage priest is notably absent from this "consummatory" stratification of statuses, except insofar as the status is prerequisite to or linked with others.

The new yam festival develops more complex meanings, for it proclaims a climax of sacred rewards that the community has accumulated as the year has progressed. Its sequence of symbolic trials and gratifications certifies each clan's spiritual health and also grades the primordial Onitsha clans in relative community prestige and consummatory value. It matters little that the clans who eat yams first maintain they do so because of their bravery, for in accepting the task they admit what the other clans claim: that they test a dangerous food, thus serving as means toward the survival of other clans. The initial eating by the descendants of the legendary defeated early king Awuma (Isele-Awada clan) and by those of the early would-be usurper Iyasele Nsu (Eke-na-ubene clan), and the penultimate consumption by the royal clan, point to a prestige ranking sanctioned by events at the earliest stages of Onitsha genealogies.

Other ideas are given increasing prominence of expression as this sequence progresses. The second theme is the development of the spiritual condition of the Onitsha king from emptiness and mourning to fulfillment, power, and celebration. In this task the roles played in building his strength by members of the specialist doctoring clan are emphasized; probably the linking of the eating of yams by the warrior clan of malevolent ghosts with the killers' feast is also part of the wider ritual effort to fortify the king's spiritual condition.

Without question, the king's emergence is the high point of the ceremonial year. It builds to a climax in which the major villages support the leading actors in the drama. The sixth minister appears in the royal square first, escorted by his village supporters. By the time the prime minister has arrived and begun his dance, all the villages have assembled to await the combined confrontation of their leaders with the king. This ritual simultaneously symbolizes the king's emergence from the enforced isolation of communal mourning and atonement, expresses his (and the community's) renewed richness and strength, signifies a state of general harmony among the mythical past, the present, and events to come; and—in the king's dancing escorted by the senior chiefs—it expresses both the intrinsic tensions and the tension-transcending solidarity among these pillars of the community.

Although the central drama of the ceremonial year is clearly the Onitsha king's dreaming and his subsequent confrontation and dancing with his senior chiefs, it is of considerable interest that the hidden kings and the queen replicate this emergence ceremony in their own domains. Persons holding these identities transcend the rights of the royal clan, for like the Onitsha king they eat new yams only at the very end of the sequence. Thus the ritual sequence clearly sets these identities apart as the most valued in the community, regardless of clan.

After the new yams of harvest time have been sampled by everyone in the community, the ceremonial year begins to return its emphasis toward the concerns of separate patrilineages, focusing at first briefly on marriage alliances and then on title taking. With the coming of the wasted months after harvest, the sacred tone gradually shifts to an increasing sense of the accumulating pollution and moral decay in the community, while individual interests shift to personal advancement. This sense of pollution is not part of the formal definition of the lamentation rites performed at this time, for lamentations are supposed to be joyous, but rather is to some extent a result of some of the social outcomes of these rites.

In lamentation, persons in mourning are striving to validate their new access to various statuses and roles; they therefore require the support of their descent groups. Chiefs and kings also play indispensable roles in the ritual, as do the collective incarnate dead; age-sets and various external kinship links are also important. Thus lamentation mobilizes nearly all components of community social structure to define the meaning of a given death. This activity is never a purely formalized, stable process; every ceremony in some way redefines the survivors' social commitments, and these rituals tend to become battlegrounds for prestige. In no other Onitsha ritual does such a general synthesis of role activity center around the individual person, and the process excites widespread interest. Unlike the harvest festivals which mobilize status groups in a serial synthesis that expresses the unity of society, lamentation is likely to have unintended disintegrative effects.

Similar effects appear to apply to the title taking rituals also conducted at this time. The intensification of international trade during the post-harvest season has parallel implications, for Onitsha people view trading activity as unclean, especially trading done with foreigners.[21] Ceremonial efforts to expiate and cleanse the community of sins and disease concentrate on the riverside, on the king, and on those known to have committed abominations during the year, and culminate in expiatory rituals using the cleansing power of the river to clear the land of its collected pollution.

Thus Onitsha people make an expiatory final assessment of their year, trying to drive its accumulated evil beyond the physical confines of the town. Some of this evil is thought to have been brought from without, but much of it has taken the form of abominations committed by members of the community. As abominations are expressions of a lack of social harmony, it would seem that, since the earlier phases of calendrical ritual activities both idealize and enact a coherent and harmonious system of prestige and responsibility, Onitsha people in their final annual rituals express a chronic sense of failure to attain these aims of harmony.

There is a proverb that Onitsha people wryly share among themselves which expresses precisely this pervasive sense of moral failure: "Onitsha is like a mother who is pregnant and nursing at the same time." For any Onitsha person, such a condition is an abomination.[22] This proverb alludes to an intrinsic conflict in the community, a conflict between the high evaluation of persons possessing certain statuses and roles, and the abhorrence of some of the means used to attain them and of some of the typical actions by their holders.

21. Interestingly, the warfare activities conducted during this season appear not to contribute significantly to its spiritual tone, but I did not inquire deeply into this question.

22. It indicates violation of the stringent postpartum sex taboo.

12 THE DYNAMICS OF ONITSHA STRATIFICATION: CLAN, PATRILINEAGE, AND VILLAGE

THE EVIDENCE OF PROCESSES

Onitsha distinctions among clan (ebo), patrilineage (ʊmʊnna), and village (ogbe) have dynamic implications: clan implies the primordial legitimacy of an ancient residential unit that holds the nze shrine for bestowing ɔzɔ title purification; patrilineage implies a descent group led by a senior priest; village implies a residential unit possessing several organizational structures. Ideally, the three coincide, for then the past would completely embrace the present. In fact they often do not.

The major categorical distinction drawn in Onitsha community is that between the Children of King Chima and all others. This term has a shifting application, but the shift can be related predictably to social context: when the people talk in terms of the constitutive symbol Onitsha of King Chima, various people in the community who are not popularly viewed as Children of King Chima emphatically claim that they are so regarded across the river (ufesimili), i.e. in their homeland across the Niger.[1] In the social context of Onitsha the Nine Clans, the Children of King Chima are only one of the nine, and that is the sense in which the phrase is being used here: as a clan reference. This is the royal clan.

In recent times, the residual category that contrasts with the royal clan has also been given a single positive designation, "High [people] and [those from] Ɔbamkpa" (*Úgwu-nà-Ɔ̀bámkpa*), a

1. I allude to this usage by showing a general tracing of descent to King Chima in the beginning of the kingship genealogies.

phrase that alludes to the higher elevations occupied by the nonroyal villages except for that of the Ɔbamkpa clan. Historical documents suggest that the use of this term as an amalgamating conception was probably a postcolonial development, and that it earlier referred to the several clans to be found in the nonroyal villages of "Children of Ase," Iyawʊ, and probably a portion of what is now Ɔdɔje village. Another major clan reference term has also traditionally stood in opposition to the royal clan: the group called Eke and Ubene (Eke-na-Ubene), a term referring to two clans with members in the major villages of Ɔdɔje and "Village of Oli Eke" (*Ógbè-Òlí-Éke*). The major village names associated with these nonroyal clans are all frequently encountered in the early missionary records, and they, with the small separate clan units of Ɔ̀biɔ and Isele-Awada (the latter occupying the Village of Ɔzɔma), comprise the major opposition to the royal clan.

Additional distinctions are made with the royal clan itself. In recent times a large subgroup called "Division is Two" (*Òkè-bʊ̀-nàbɔ*) was distinguished from all other royal units.[2] Division is Two includes the descendants of all the early kings from the royal clan except one. Within Division is Two, a further dichotomy is drawn between a group called Children of Dei and all others, including all the descendants of early kings in the division.

The descendants of the one exceptional early king are called "Children of Chima the Cow-killer." [3] These people in turn are divided between descendants of his son Arɔlι and descendants of his other children; the latter comprise the village units of Isiokwe and the "Children of Ɔlɔsι." The descendants of Arɔlι are again divided, between descendants of his sons and of his daughter. The latter form part of a complex major village that also contains, as its core, a small group of descendants of the ancient royal founder

2. This term too may have been a recent conception, for early missionaries appear to have used "Children of Dei" to refer to this major division; but it reflects an old reality and will be employed in the discussion that follows.

3. This major category phrase may also be of recent coinage, but that cannot be determined from available evidence.

Ɔreze, the hero said to have gained primacy for the royal clan by concealing his drum beneath a canoe while crossing the river. With this tiny group are associated the descendants of Idoko (the son of the daughter of Arɔlɩ named Usse), who live in a village called "House of Women" (Obikporo); the descendants of certain riverain migrants related to the Igala-linked river towns of Adamugu and Osomari, who live in "Waterside Village" (*Ógbè-ótu*); the members of the king's doctoring clan of Ubulu-na-Ikem, who occupy a village called "Children of Ikem," and members of the Igala-derived clan of fishermen called Ulutu-Ado clan, who in recent times have been called *M̀gbelekéké̀*. All these villages are loosely grouped into a major village unit called "Riverain village" (Ogbe-olu).

The final residual category in the royal clan includes the descendants of all the Onitsha kings from the time of Arɔlɩ until the end of the precolonial period. In recent times, this major grouping has been called "The Children of King Arɔlɩ" (Ʊmʊ-Eze-Arɔlɩ), a unit that includes three major villages: the "Children of Arɔlɩ" (Ʊmʊ-Arɔlɩ), the High Grass Village (Ogbe-ɔzala), and the Low High Grass Village (Ogbe-ɔzala-ndida). These are terms used in recent times, but oral tradition and historical evidence suggest that two of them have changed over time. According to recent oral tradition, the covering term Children of King Arɔlɩ, which inserts the word "King" to distinguish the category from one of its three major village subcategories, was coined early in this century for collective litigation against members of Division is Two. I employ it here for convenient reference, but this ethnographic information suggests that the unity of this wider grouping has not been constant, but has increased in recent times in response to external threats. Second, in recent years, the "Low High Grass Village" has largely dropped part of its former name and become simply "Low Village" (Ogbe-ndɩda). This suggests that at some point during precolonial times this unit was an integral part of the "High Grass Village," and that there has been a tendency towards fission.

Figure 35 summarizes the categorical divisions among the major Onitsha village units. This structure is implicit in informant accounts, but no informant could have formulated it completely as shown here; it is the resultant of a number of divergent, dynamic, political alliance-oriented points of view.[4]

The relative sizes of these villages is a crucial question, for in Onitsha society all patrilineages or villages competed with one another for reproductive resources and members. The major long-term goal of every significant residential unit was numerical increase in its membership; this was true in recent times, and such concern was surely greater in the precolonial past when social conditions made numerical strength politically crucial.[5]

There are few useful estimates of relative village size in Onitsha from any period, but there are clues in the historical literature, in some oral traditions suggesting past numerical strengths, and in rough census data from recent research indicating recent size differences. One crude map, drawn in the late 1850s by Reverend Taylor, is available, and it includes population estimates; this evidence is shown on Figure 36.[6]

Comparison with historical data suggests that the absolute numbers indicated here are almost certainly much inflated; Taylor was

4. Figure 35 does not indicate all the nonroyal clans, but focuses rather on the villages. The village of Ɔdɔje cannot be clan-categorized (and hence cuts across divisions in the figure) because it contains members from several clans, including some remnant primordial ones; it is an extremely heterogeneous social unit. Moreover, one of the nonroyal clan nze shrines belongs to the Ubulu-na-Ikem clan, whose members live in the Riverain Village, defined as part of the royal clan itself! There are, in addition, higher-level village units than those indicated here; the "Village of Oli" (mentioned frequently in early mission accounts as "Ogboli") is an amalgam of the royal Children of Ɔlɔsɩ and the nonroyal Village of Oli-Eke; Isiokwe, a royal unit, is part of the nonroyal village of Ɔdɔje.

5. During recent years the education of lawyers has been almost as significant politically as numerical strength.

6. Taylor (n.d.). Figure 36 roughly replicates the essentials of the original diagram, which is also quite crude. The dotted lines isolating sets of named numbered units have been drawn in by me, and I have also changed spellings of village names. Clearly, Taylor conceived of Onitsha as laid out on a grid plan. The five units attributed to Umu-Dei correspond to various units of Division is Two; the subdivisions of Obikporo correspond to parts of Riverain Village; the six units associated with Ogbe-ɔzala (which Taylor marked as "the king's village") correspond roughly to divisions of the Children of King Arɔlɩ, and the six units of Ogboli include both the Children of Ɔlɔsɩ and the Village of Oli-Eke. Some small units are not shown.

not one of the most astute missionary observers at Onitsha in those days. The *relative* numerical strengths remain interesting because they must have been based on informant opinion; they bear comparison with data from recent census research. It was not feasible to obtain reliable estimates of total population for each Onitsha

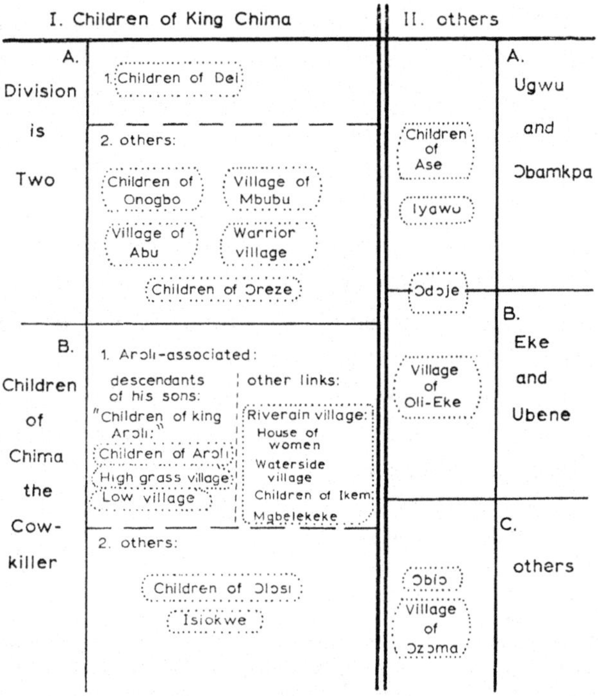

Fig. 35 Village divisions and major clan categories

village in recent times.[7] However, numbers of taxable males for each village were obtained, and these give indications of relative size. This information, with a schematized diagram of recent village residential areas and a list of numbers of ɔzɔ men from each village as of 1962, appears in Figure 37.

7. In view of recent radical changes in residence, occupation, and temporary emigration, such figures would be of limited value in any case. See R. N. Henderson (1966).

When this information is compared with that of Figure 36, it becomes reasonable to assume that the relative sizes and the positions of the major social units have not shifted significantly during the past hundred years. I will therefore assume that recent relative numbers of the major units indicate the balance of social forces in late precolonial times, and will also assume that the trends of

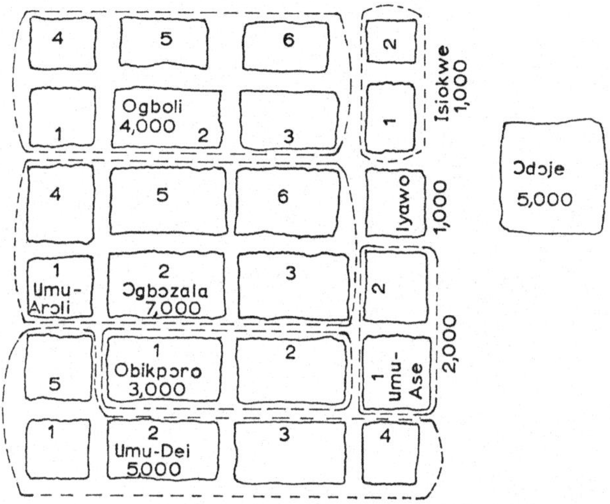

Fig. 36 Village population estimates (c. 1860)

change in relative population size were in general continuous since the beginning of the baseline period and consistent with oral tradition statements. Figure 37 also shows a high correlation between the recent estimates of village numerical size and the recent numbers of ɔzɔ titled men in the village. This points to a close relationship between numerical strength and the distribution of wealth in the community, a relationship that must have been even closer in precolonial times.

These suggestions may be pursued further if the materials just presented are related to the genealogies of the town's major units. If we make the arbitrary assumption that total population has remained largely constant over time, and that the followers of the various clans of Onitsha were at the outset roughly comparable in numbers, then changes in relative numbers of various segments may be plotted as outlined in Figure 38.[8] There can be little doubt

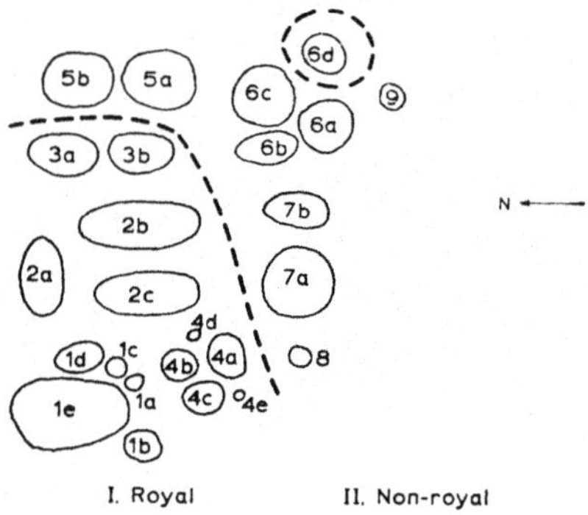

I. THE ROYAL CLAN:	Males	Ɔzɔ
1. Division is Two	350	68
a. Children of Onogbo		
b. Village of Mbubu		
c. Warrior Village		
d. Village of Abu		
e. Children of Dei		
2. Children of King Arɔlı	240	58
a. Children of Arɔlı		
b. High grass Village		
c. Low Village		
3. Village of Oli-Ɔlɔsı	80	21
a. Village of Oli-Agbor		
b. Children of Ɔlɔsı		
4. Riverain Village	100	23
a. Obikpɔro		
b. Obulu-na-Ikem		
c. Waterside Village		
d. Children of Ɔreze		
e. Mgbelekeke		
6d. Isiokwe	50	12

II. NON-ROYAL UNITS:	Males	Ɔzɔ
5. Village of Oli-Eke	80	21
6. Ɔdɔje (minus Isiokwe)	200	59
a. Ɔdimegwugbuagu		
b. Ubene (Eke)		
c. Village of Ndugbe		
7. Children of Ase-Iyawo	125	30
a. Children of Ase		
b. Iyawo		
8. Village of Ɔzɔma, 9. Ɔbiɔ, and others	20	5

Fig. 37 Village size, residential area, and ɔzɔ men

that the size of the royal clan has increased markedly over the years relative to the total community, for oral traditions suggest that in the early times a number of units of nearly equal size engaged in indecisive competition. This condition of relative expansion and contraction is not a general difference between the major

8. The genealogies are presented here in highly schematized form in order to illuminate the general trends. The numerical code for this and the subsequent figure is that of Figure 37.

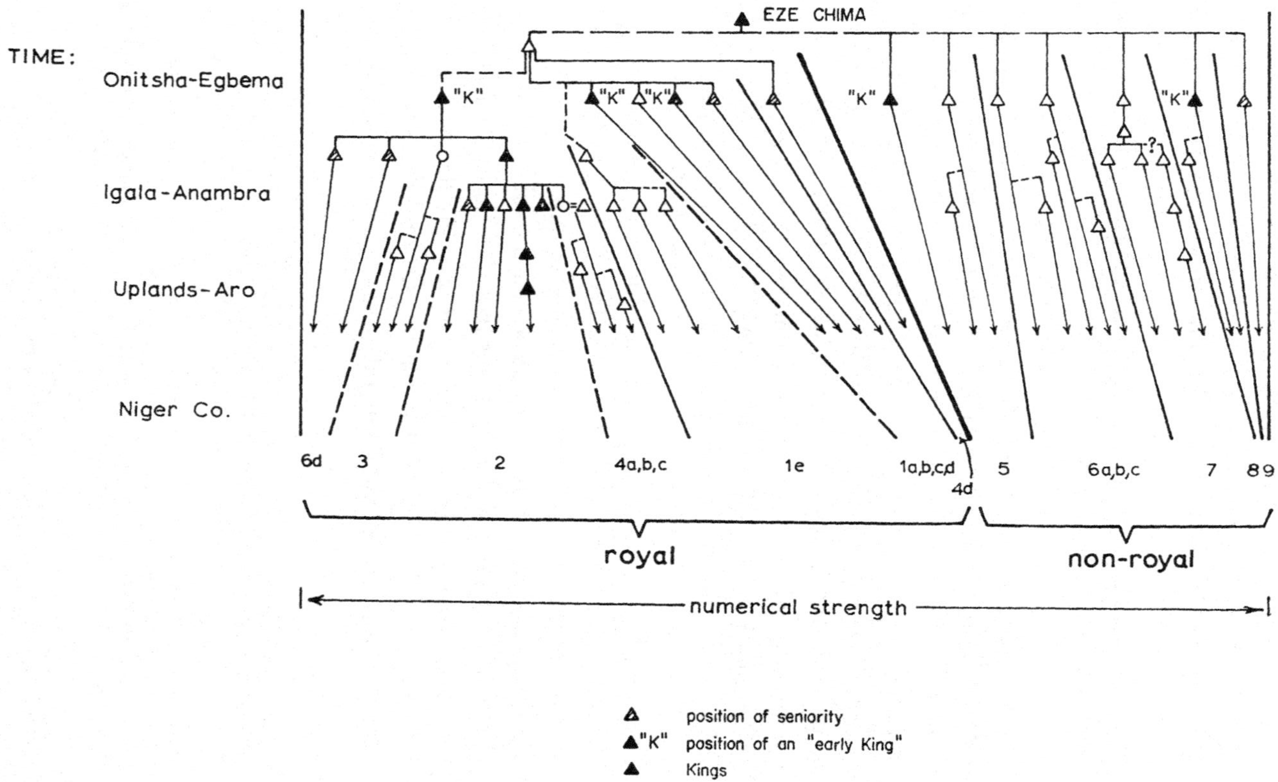

Fig. 38 Villages, time, and numerical strength

categories, but shows marked unevenness within each of them.[9] A distinct unevenness of social process is also evident in the genealogies and segments of the royal clan, and numerous reasons are given for such differential expansion. To illustrate the variations in greater detail, an expanded schematic diagram of the royal unit is presented in Figure 39.

Figure 39 elucidates some curious features of the variable expansion of social units in Onitsha. First, the descendants of the Children of Ɔreze (4d) are very few (recently, nearly extinct), and it is said that they are the only social unit eligible for the senior patrilineage priesthood of the entire royal clan. Second, within Division is Two, all major segments serve homage to the senior patrilineage priest of their total segment, and the sole eligible holders of this role come from the "Children of *Ànι-émèna*," a small subunit of the tiny village "Children of *Ónogbo*" (1a). Among the other segments of "Division is Two," the descendants of the early kings are also numerically few, although they are regarded as senior and venerated for their royal ancestral legitimacy. In contrast, the Children of Dei (1e), the "youngest son" of the group, have been highly successful numerically.[10]

A similarly remarkable pattern applies on the other major side of the royal clan. This segment, too, regards the Children of Ɔreze (4d) as their most senior patrilineage priests. At the next lower level, among the Children of Chima the Cow-killer, all groups agree that the members of Isiokwe (6d) are the sole eligible senior

9. In the nonroyal category, for example, it is said that the Village of Ɔzɔma (8) was formerly substantial in numbers but became greatly reduced, while the clan of Ɔbiɔ (9) has always been very small. The villages of Ɔdɔje (6) and Children of Ase (7) have expanded somewhat over time, while a part of Village of Oli-Eke (5) radically lost numbers after the earliest stages. A variety of reasons is given in oral traditions for these differences. In several cases loss of numbers is related to a defeat or abomination attributed to an early clan leader, but there is no general explanation in the tradition for such disparities.

10. For example, in 1962 the Children of [king] Chimezie, who occupy the Village of *M̀bubu* (1b), had no ɔzɔ men; the Children of [king] *Tásìa*, who make up the Warrior Village (1c), had only seven ɔzɔ men; various other descendants, living in the Village of *Àbʊ* (1d) had fifteen. In contrast, the Children of Dei had a total of forty-six ɔzɔ men, more than double all the others combined.

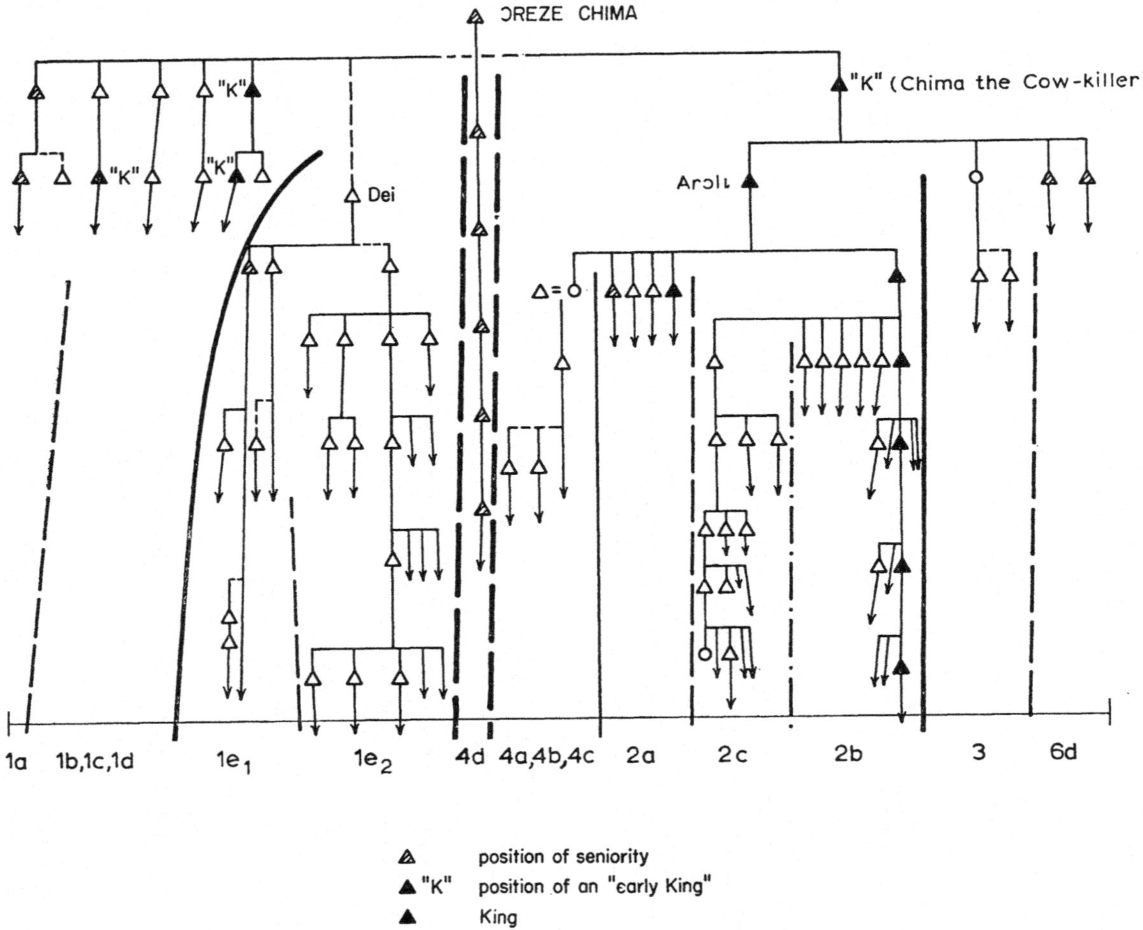

Fig. 39 Genealogies and numerical strength in the royal clan

patrilineage priests of the segment, and they are also the smallest unit in that segment. At the next lower level, among the immediate children of Arɔlɩ, the descendants of only one of his sons are legitimate successors to the senior patrilineage priesthood—and they are extremely few in number.

There is a surprisingly general correlation between ascriptive patrilineal seniority and numerical weakness. This correlation obtains at all levels of social units, and in nonroyal clans as well as the royal one. It is one indicator of a major process of differentiation and of structural change. Onitsha people have some awareness of this phenomenon, but it is not part of their general view of the society. Members of junior but large segments tend to minimize references to their juniority, though they recognize it; members of senior but small segments tend to claim that their priestly dedication to all of their patrilineage dependents has taken priority over their personal pursuit of wealth. Subtly but profoundly, the process has come to pervade the entire system, and it is intimately related to that sense of lack of social harmony which Onitsha people express in their ceremonial year.

STATUS DIFFERENTIATION AND COMPETITION WITHIN THE PATRILINEAGE: A MODEL

From the previous description of the patrilineage, at any given level of the structure the patrilineage priest would appear to enjoy ascribed advantages over those junior to him. He controls the major facilities for making a living. He receives homage service from his juniors, and he can expect them to work in unity toward his uplifting and enrichment, to congregate in unity before his throne in the great ancestral house, each awaiting his turn to become priest and thus to be served by his juniors. However, improper order of death breaks this unity by establishing permanent status differences between siblings and hence between segments of patrilineages, for those who die in their father's lifetime (including those who die during the priesthood of their senior brothers) are defined permanently as junior brothers. They are buried in their own houses, which become thereby small ancestral houses, and their sons can succeed only to these junior levels of patrilineage control. Their descendants are no longer eligible for the priesthood of any higher-level segments. These sons participate most actively in the affairs of their small ancestral house, while they remain junior, tributary, subordinate members of the great ancestral house to which their father failed to succeed.

In this case, the patrilineage faces an incipient split. This can also occur if a great man, such as a senior chief, regardless of his ancestral position, decides to establish a large meeting house for entertaining those who seek him out. A chief is likely to construct his own meeting house for public hearings, leaving the extant great ancestral house for the ritual activities of the senior patrilineage priest. The chief's sons may then direct their attention more toward sharing their father's personal estate than toward higher-level patrilineage segments—especially if their father has acquired other valuable estates.

Both developments generate competition within a patrilineage. When the current rightful priest (from an eligible, senior segment) is untitled, a permanently junior segment may seek ɔzɔ purification for one of its own members instead of assisting that priest to become an ɔzɔ man. It is regarded as a disgrace to a patrilineage if its purified ancestors cannot receive public festival sacrifices, and so long as no titled men are present in the patrilineage, such worship cannot be undertaken. Until a purified man is present, the ancestral shrine objects must be kept in an outdoor shed. They cannot be given their rightful shelter inside the ancestral house. When an ɔzɔ man is established in the patrilineage, the wooden symbols receive shelter in his purified house. Therefore, when a man takes ɔzɔ title within a patrilineage whose rightful senior priest is untitled, the priest must delegate possession of the shrine objects to that ɔzɔ man, even if he comes from a segment ineligible for the priesthood.

The ɔzɔ man then may sit on the throne and perform the communal sacrifices of the patrilineage. This gives him right to participate fully in the decisions and even to override the views of the rightful senior priest—for he holds the staves to which the ancestors are believed to respond just as they do to ɔfɔ. Thus the ɔzɔ man's disenfranchised segment regains effective rights both to share in tribute at this segmentary level and to share decision making in higher-level patrilineage affairs. Junior segments must have ɔzɔ men, for while the ascriptively defined priest always receives deference, other men without ɔzɔ title "have no voice." When the junior segment has obtained full voice by producing an ɔzɔ man and has gained effective control over the ghosts for a time, its members may be reluctant to part with the wooden symbols of the ghosts when men from the rightfully eligible segments do take ɔzɔ title. They may refuse to relinquish this part of the patrilineage estate, and they may swear an oath to their right. Thus, attempted seizure of the shared estate is another form of intrapatrilineage competition, to which the only solution is the making of oaths and curses.

Such usurpation contradicts the ideal of patrilineage unity, for Onitsha people say that "only the senior priest need take ɔzɔ title." A man with important ascriptive patrilineage rights knows that his subordinates depend upon him for proper sacrifices; he therefore believes that his juniors should pool their resources to facilitate his public purification. The holder of nze, the head of the clan, should see that proper seniority relations are followed in ɔzɔ title taking, and that junior brothers have not bypassed seniors, thus upsetting patrilineage ideals. But since the ɔzɔ men of any title-sharing unit are always eager to recoup their own heavy purification expenditures by receiving shares from subsequent candidates, it is quite unlikely, at high levels of lineage segmentation, for a candidate to meet the refusal of any priest to beg the ancestors to affirm his blessing, or the refusal of the holder of nze to bestow final purification.

By the precedent of "uprooting the trunk," the junior segment may assist in financing the rightful priest until he has attained the partial right to sacrifice to the ancestors: the stage of "consorting with the dead" or nkpalo. This man may then preside in communal sacrifice (but not kill goats to the purified ancestors) so long as no fully titled men are present, and his ascribed right has thus been properly upheld. The junior segment is then free, with some disapproval, to establish a fully purified ɔzɔ man as their "voice."

The motivation for such competitive intralineage action is implanted within the primary polygynous family of Onitsha, where mothers regularly exhort their children to fight (and to dislike) their half-brothers.[11] Frequently, it is said, a wealthy group of junior full siblings have been willing to maintain the unity of the patrilineage by contributing to their senior half-brother's full purification, only to be obstructed by the rigidly insistent objections of their mother.[12] At this low level of the patrilineage structure, even though there is great pressure to uphold the requirements of patrilineage seniority, uprooting the trunk has regularly occurred as long as informants can remember. That "improper deaths" inevitably occur in many sibling groups insures that any patrilineage will experience competition between subsegments headed by rightful priests and those headed by junior ɔzɔ men, although ideally it should be a spiritual unity joined in common dependence upon the representative of the ancestral father.

11. Henderson and Henderson (1966:15–16).

12. Such attitudes are compatible with a patrilineage system characterized by a "house-property complex" (cf. Middleton and Winter 1963). Onitsha kinship terminology certainly points to its consistency with such a complex, specifically in the way that wives who have borne children are categorized. Onitsha women do tend to be strongly committed to furthering the achievement of their children, for their own opportunities for social advancement and their own security depend considerably on the success of their sons.

This intralineage competition gains in significance in light of the profound heterogeneity of Onitsha social units, a result of the traditional practice of treating people as scarce resources. In the struggle for wealth and prestige, the number of supporters upon whom a man can rely is the measure of his success. Although any man with farmland can count on his age-set and his nonpatrilineal relatives for occasional help on his land, Onitsha traditional farming is based primarily not on occasional massing of labor but rather on continual assistance. Because permanent dependents are the most important kind of labor assistance, a man tries to acquire as many wives and as many children as possible, and slaves as well. It is said that every man welcomes his daughters' children and hopes to keep them by his side. Within each Onitsha clan, each village, and each patrilineage resides a population of heterogeneous origins. Indeed, as the fieldworker studies almost any segment in any patrilineage in this community, and presses questions about group rights and group divisions, claims emerge that various subsegments derive from daughters' children or from "attached" persons, "those who have come to dwell" (*m̀biambía*) with the original, true descent group members.[13]

There are two major forms of attachment; both follow the same course. First, there is the daughter's child who comes from another Onitsha patrilineage. Such a person holds important ascriptive rights in his maternal patrilineage, and by paying appropriate homage service within it he may obtain farmland and the right to build a house on its land. If he lives in his mother's village as a child he may join the collective incarnate dead there and establish ties that tend to keep him there. Alternatively, he may have fled his own patrilineage to escape quarrels, or the consequences of bad deaths, or the consequences of some offense committed within the patrilineage.

In all such cases, however, he remains under the ultimate juris-

13. In recent years, the term "assimilados" has become a popular equivalent for this phrase among the younger generation of Onitsha men.

diction of his own patrilineage, and he is classed as a daughter's child within his maternal patrilineage, unless he demonstrates an irrevocable commitment to it by attaining ɔzɔ purification within its fold. For—and this is a crucial point—the purification process by which a man dedicates himself to nze can eliminate the taint of female transmission that limits the rights of a daughter's child to participate in his mother's patrilineage; the maternal linkage in descent is impure, but that impurity can be rectified through dedication to nze. Only by becoming an ɔzɔ man does a man obtain full rights within his maternal patrilineage. Then he may no longer be publicly referred to as daughter's child.

It is of course difficult to assess how frequently such transfer of membership has occurred. Cases are privately attested for every patrilineage; but to judge from recent evidence, the frequency is not high. Such transfer is, however, most important as a model for the second form of attachment, which has occurred frequently.

This second form of attachment occurs when a person from outside Onitsha attaches himself to a prominent person and becomes his dependent. Since Onitsha was, even in precolonial times, a center through which scarce goods from riverain and western sources radiated into the areas of dense population to the east, it long held a position of considerable advantage in trading relationships with contiguous Ibo populations. One consequence of this advantage was the influx of women into Onitsha. Some were given as wives, but many were given as maidservants in pledge for debts; such women held statuses intermediate between wives and domestic servants (odibo) to their masters. Non-Onitsha women who had become wives to Onitsha men might also encourage their wealth-seeking kinsmen to come and live with them. Moreover, numerous outright slaves (oru), continually brought into Onitsha for sale, might also be retained as domestic servants.

All these attached dependents could eventually gain incorporation into the Onitsha patrilineage, for their immediate descendants if not for themselves. After a period of faithful service to his master, the domestic servant might take an oath on the shrine to the master's household land, committing himself to follow the justice of that spirit. He was then assigned his own plot of farmland, which he could work when not serving his master; and he rendered homage service to him from the yield obtained there. Later in life he might take an oath before the king, swearing that he will join Onitsha in a war even against his old home community. This oath makes him eligible to join the collective incarnate dead of his master's village. Once he has done this, he is classed as a "child of the town" (*nwá-òbodo*) and may participate in age-set activities.

The attached person (now also called "has returned to dwell," *ńatambili*) must next attempt to obtain an Onitsha woman as his wife. A householder might allot to such a man a badly deformed daughter (e.g. one whose face is grossly disfigured by yaws, such disfiguration being strongly objectionable in Onitsha), or a divorced daughter whose reputation is bad, as a reward for his services. The offspring of such a match become daughter's children to the master's patrilineage.

Every such person, whether offspring of the master by a female servant or of an Onitsha daughter by an attached male, is legally at the mercy of other patrilineage members until he obtains ɔzɔ title purification. Once he has done this, however, his status is radically transformed, for his body becomes holy. He must no longer be addressed as daughter's child or reminded of his ancestry, for such words become classed as a bad mouth offense against him, and he may demand a redress in fines.

Every attached man has an extremely powerful incentive to gain ɔzɔ title, for only in this way can he gain irrevocable legitimacy in the patrilineage. Such a man then becomes not a daughter's child but a junior son, a son "whose father died in the presence of his father." He is therefore not eligible to control the ɔfɔ of the patrilineage segment to which his ancestor was attached.

An illuminating comparison can be made between incentives for a daughter's son and those for a rightful senior patrilineage priest, especially one who is senior at a number of segmentary levels. Unlike the senior priest, the daughter's child may not succeed to control over valuable facilities, and he cannot expect to receive any regular homage service. He must therefore seek the means of taking title through all other possible sources. He must work with sustained effort on his farm. He must willingly perform services for all kinsmen who may later aid him, overfulfilling his cooperative duties if possible in order to build commitments of future support. He must avoid making enemies and try rather to become a peacemaker within the patrilineage, thus improving his prospects through diplomacy.

In contrast, the senior priest controls a body of divine ascriptive rights. He not only has ascriptive control over the paternal estate but also can expect the cooperative support of his juniors. If they do not strive for his glorification the disgrace is their own. However, the senior priest is also expected to devote much of his time selflessly to propitiatory ritual concerned with the welfare of his people, fasting and mourning for lost members of the patrilineage, and the like. For this reason he has little time to work on his farm and his juniors must do this work for him. The priest concerns himself with the strict observation of the basic norms of patrilineage social life, is expected to serve as a repository for truth, and is not known as a peacemaker but rather as a source of demands for conformity.

Onitsha people formulate this structural difference clearly, and the different images that emerge are in striking contrast. The image of the senior patrilineage priest is that of an impoverished person, devoted to atoning for the sins of his people, with little time to seek his own goals, concerned instead with his congregation's adherence to traditional morality and truth. The image of the junior son is quite different. Onitsha people claim that a man whose ancestor was attached can always be singled out by his far-sighted, diplomatic, but always single-minded quest for wealth. It is said that if an Onitsha man's son is becoming unruly, he will never send him to a junior brother for training, but will send him to his most senior brother, the senior patrilineage priest. The priest can be relied upon to train the son according to standards of traditional morality and conduct; the junior brother is likely to manipulate the son for his own personal advancement.

The junior son is not likely to be satisfied with ɔzɔ title. He will be strongly motivated to attain chieftaincy, because this can provide him with the means of building his possessions into an important ancestral estate, of founding a dynasty. The chief gains the right to reincarnate as a tall ghost, giving his children authoritative, potentially autonomous roles in the collective incarnate dead. Moreover, the chief can expand his social influence by granting political protection both to traders from other towns and to persons banished from such towns. Thus he can increase his dependents. The chief controls so many dependable supporters, and has such effective means of maintaining external relationships, that he can risk seeking out new lands for farming at the peripheries of Onitsha territory, claiming such lands for himself. In brief, the chief can found a patrilineage segment possessing sufficient independent resources to become an emergent autonomous village.

The analysis up to this point suggests that attached persons tend to seek ɔzɔ purification and chieftaincy and to found expanding village units, while rightful senior patrilineage priests tend to become relatively poverty-stricken and only partially purified. It suggests, moreover, that this difference may be based in part on the different ascriptive positions held by these two categories of persons, and in the implications of this difference for the orientation of effort. There is good evidence for this structural contrast. In order to establish the case, however, and to elucidate other critical factors that reinforce the tendency, some concrete illustrative cases will now be considered.[14]

14. These cases derive in part from this century and to some extent are based on court records, but the processes described here operated in earlier times.

ATTACHMENT AND SOCIAL MOBILITY: CASES FROM ROYAL AND NONROYAL CLANS

Onitsha people say that in the precolonial days each patrilineage sought people to help them farm the land, whereas in recent times land has been valued over people for the rents it can bring. Although there is certainly substance in this assertion, intracommunity fights over land were occurring at the time of earliest exploratory contacts. For this reason, more recent land disputes can serve to illuminate patrilineage process.[15]

Figure 40 depicts the genealogy of a minor village within a larger patrilineage and village unit of the royal clan. Its members are called not by a village name but rather simply Children of A. They possess a small common village square, on the edge of which stand the shrine to the land of A (marking the location of the founder's ancestral house) and the childbirth shrine which they worship together. They have common paraphernalia and organization of the incarnate dead; they act as a patrilineage unit for funerary activity, and formerly cooperated in farm labor. They are organized under a common senior patrilineage priest who receives regular homage service, and they have a unified group of daughters, the head daughter of which purifies the village on important ritual occasions.

In Figure 40, the genealogy is carried only to a point that indicates relative numerical strengths; living men are two or three generations below. There are five major segments in Children of A, but only three—B, C, and D—are eligible for the senior priesthood of A. The founders of the two numerically largest segments, E and F, are said to have "died in the presence of A," and are therefore ineligible for the position. In segment E many years ago a wife of

15. Since aspects of these cases have remained unresolved issues of recent litigation, names of the groups concerned have been abstracted out of the material presented.

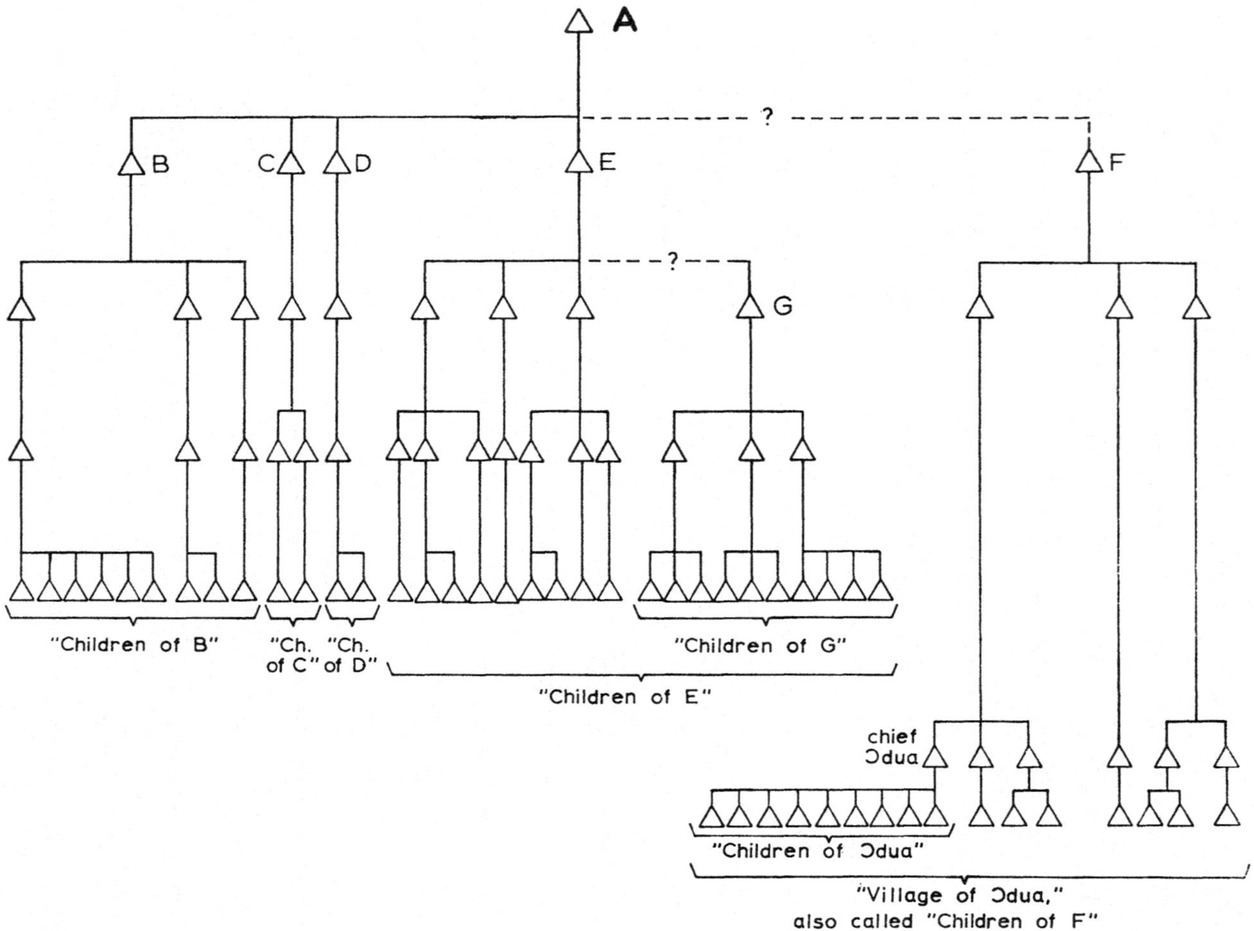

Fig. 40 The genealogy of the Children of A

the village brought childbirth medicine from her home in the highlands across the Niger, and since that time the Children of E have performed annual ceremonies to a shrine that contains this medicine. Segment F maintains a separate land shrine which represents the ancestral house of its founder. Some elders today claim that C also died in the presence of A, but others say that one of the descendants of C recently forfeited his ancestral right of succession by refusing to pay the prescribed homage service to the contemporary priest; the priestly right of C is therefore in question and may become an issue when the current priest dies and the Children of C claim their right.

Children of A is associated with a number of named tracts of land on the north side of Onitsha beyond the Nkisi stream. Block 1 is a relatively small section, located near the village itself and bounded by land of other coordinate segments of the larger patrilineage of which the Children of A are a subunit. Block 1 is held communally by the Children of A; the priest of A controls it and shares out its proceeds to the members. Significantly, the Children of F do not share in these proceeds.[16] Block 2 is a larger segment of land to the east of Block 1 toward the Oze community. It is subdivided into five roughly equal sections, each owned by one of five major subsegments of A and controlled by its priest. Block 3 is closer to the Oze community. It also is divided among the five subsegments, but it is more fragmented in character and is given a variety of subnames.

It is said that the mother of F was an Oze woman. When she came to Onitsha to marry A she was given a large portion of Block 3—owned by the Oze people—as a leading home gift from her parents. This portion became the estate of F in Block 3. The other four major segments claim to have received their portions through permanent leasing from the Oze people, under eternal oaths binding their lives. The mother of F, it is further related, brought with

16. This is strong evidence for the attached origin of F, for if this segment were not a later addition it should have its share in this "patrilineage priest's land."

her from Oze the man named G (or, according to some stories, the three sons of G), and G became attached to E. G or his sons received another portion of Block 3 from his Oze grandfather, and this became a part of the common separate estate of the Children of G.

The Children of F prospered and produced a junior chief, the ɔdua, who, it is said, received yet another plot of land as the share due him as chief when he decided an indemnity case. Since chief ɔdua had many children, the children of F as a whole expanded. Ɔdua dominated the entire Village of A, and after his death and funeral his children began asserting their voices in village affairs. Ultimately, during the funeral of a villager, the daughters' organization of F asserted that the ɔfɔ of the head daughter of F should be placed alongside that of the senior daughter of A, as equal in power to it. The remainder of the daughters of A refused, and the daughters of F boycotted the ceremony. The elders and the village youths of F segment followed the initiative of the daughters, so that the group became autonomous in all activities involving head daughters. They continued to engage in some common masquerading acts but no longer cooperated in funerary activity (except in attending funerals of daughters' children, when they all joined under a still higher village segment).

In recent years the senior priest of A has been one of three brothers who are the sole survivors in segment D. His father, it is said, pledged away these brothers' portion of Block 3 land to a prominent chief from another village, to obtain the wealth to take ɔzɔ title; nevertheless he failed to complete his purification. The senior priest himself is poor, and has waited passively for his people to make him an ɔzɔ man. It is said that in a communal meeting they agreed to sell some of their residential land to provide him with the necessary funds, but after the land was sold, they enabled him to perform only consorting with the ghosts, and they then divided the remainder of the money among the various segments. In bitterness he brought a claim in court that Block 1 belonged not to the Children of A as a group but to his own subsegment D. In court, he received devious witness support from the Children of F, who, in recent years known as the Village of Chief Ɔdua, have sought to sow division among the rest of A internally. In court the complainant publicly exposed the attached origin of the Children of G, and he was forthwith ostracized for having committed an abomination. A rich titled man of segment B, known as a peace-maker, then received the delegated rights of performing the important communal sacrifices, even though it is common knowledge that his father was an attached person.

The Children of G, who have been particularly successful economically, have produced a group of ɔzɔ-titled men. Originally given residential land by E, they have come to desire more land for house-building and have sought a greater voice in the allocation of the residential land controlled by E. They have attempted to assert their rights to a turn as the priest of E, but the incumbent priest, backed by his people, has insisted that they merge their extensive separate portion of land in Block 3 as the price of agreeing to this request. The Children of G refuse to do this, and their wealthy men have continued to construct houses in very limited space.

The Village of Ɔdua (Children of F) has maintained its independence, with a recent population of roughly twenty-seven households, in opposition to the remainder of the Children of A, who number about forty-one households. It produced another chief to represent the Children of A as a whole, and thus dominated wider patrilineage affairs, including leading a land dispute against an opposing royal segment genealogically coordinate with all the Children of A. Recently F too has split internally, since the Children of Ɔdua, i.e. the descendants of actual children of chief Ɔdua, have asserted that the land obtained by their ancestor as a chief belongs to them alone, while the other descendants of F have claimed that it belongs to all members of the wider Village of Ɔdua.

This case manifests an intensity of competition for land probably not characteristic of precolonial times, but the case is typical, not exceptional, and it re-enacts patterns of competition that did occur in the nineteenth century. It illustrates a number of typical features: the nesting of village units within patrilineages, these in turn within wider village units, etc.; the differentiation of senior and junior segments, and the association of junior status with evidence of prior attachment, subsequent population expansion and holding of chieftaincy; the impoverished and isolated position of the senior patrilineage priest; the internal schisms that grow out of these status contasts; the ostracism that follows public exposure of prior attachments; the crystallization of new village units under the leadership of a chief; the divisions that subsequently emerge within the new village between the "proper descendants" of the chief and the other units in it.

The royal segment used in this illustration is generally regarded by outsiders as a genealogical unity, yet considerable evidence of social heterogeneity is present. In some nonroyal units, the heterogeneity is even greater. A case in point is the village of *ɔdakpʊ* (a pseudonym). It is an exceptional case, for unlike most other village units it contains more than one ancient clan, including several remnant clans now in effect extinct. It underwent a resettlement and reorganization approximately a hundred years ago. After its disruption, the units which now compose it established a common major village square, recognized the war drums of a common representative senior chief, joined to perform the massed running in rage at the death announcement of a member, and shared tall ghosts sent forth by their collective incarnate dead to witness funeral performances. They also observed mutual exogamy, though they never established a single structure of patrilineage priesthood.

One of the subvillages of this amalgamation, a unit that will be called the Children of A, is a major segment of the ancient clan Agwɔ (a pseudonym); the other segment of this clan is located in another part of Onitsha. Long ago, it is said, the ancestor of A and the ancestor of the other segment separated after a dispute but continued to share their nze and the ɔzɔ-title fees associated with it; A himself apparently held the nze at one time. A schematic genealogy of his descendants is provided in Figure 41.

After A's death, B, C, and D succeeded one another in the priesthood of A, and each apparently held the sacred nze when his turn came. Meanwhile, it is said, X, a man supposedly derived from a community to the south of Onitsha, became attached to a descen-

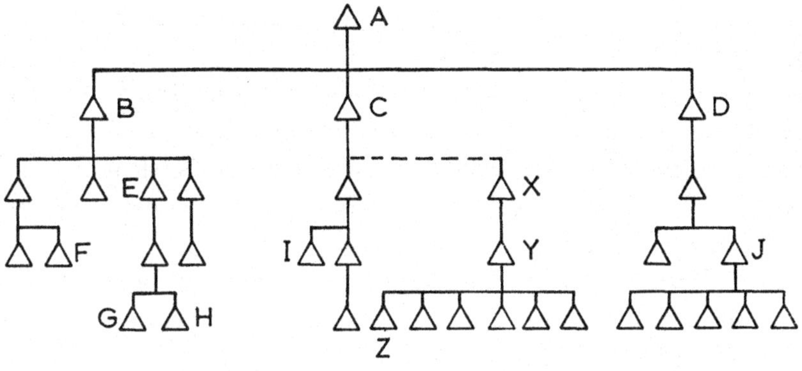

Fig. 41 A nonroyal patrilineage genealogy

dant of C. As a faithful servant, he was eventually given as his marriage partner an attached servant girl who had reputedly come from a town immediately adjacent to Onitsha. A son Y was born of this union, became a wealthy man, and eventually sought to take ɔzɔ title.

E, the titled senior priest holding nze at the time, refused to perform purification on the grounds that Y was not a descendant of the hallowed ancestor. After the death of E, Y went to F and G, the other two titled men of the patrilineage, and asked them to arrange for the title taking, but they also refused. Eventually, Y managed to establish or fabricate a circuitous descent link through his mother to an ancestor in the other segment of Agwɔ, went to the senior priest holding nze there, and arranged to take his title as a daughter's child. Once the act had been performed, he was accepted as an ɔzɔ man in the community as a whole and became a legitimate junior son of the clan.

The fiction perpetrated here is far from unique. What is revealing is that the remotely linked descent group of the Agwɔ clan had no moral concern over the internal status conflicts of the children of A, but were quite willing to accept the title share due them for giving Y his purification.

Later, the titled men F and G died, leaving only Y with ɔzɔ title among the children of A. The rightful person to succeed as the priest of A was I, but he was untitled and not financially able to begin establishing the ancestral symbols in his house. H, who had conducted the funeral of G, was a young man living in the village of his mother; he therefore delegated control of the shrines to the ghosts to Y, who had established himself as a cooperative and generous man.

Y had many wives and sons, and when the right to control the nze was delegated to him, he mobilized support and usurped the title of hidden king of Ɔdakpʊ. He enabled his senior son, Z, to take full ɔzɔ title while he was still alive (precedent for this act having previously been established by a chief who emulated this traditional kingly prerogative). When Y died, his titled son Z then performed the funeral, took over the shrines to A, retained the nze by claiming it as an exclusive right of the children of C, and went on to become a senior chief. His war drum gave him the right to receive funerary tribute from the lower chiefs in Ɔdakpʊ.

Eventually, however, J from segment D also obtained many children, became a successful man, and took his ɔzɔ title. When I, the rightful senior priest of A, died, and J therefore became the rightful succeeding priest of A, he went to Z (who as a senior chief had delegated priestly duties to one of his brothers) and requested him to hand over the ancestral symbols, including the nze. Z and his brothers refused to comply. Eventually J and his sons went to a diviner and learned that the ancestors were offended and were commanding them to set up a separate nze, and to carve new treasure boxes and staves. J immediately complied.

In this example,[17] a successful usurpation of ascriptive rights, followed by an overreaching of attainments, generated a split in the units concerned. In a somewhat similar case, which occurred in yet another, genealogically unrelated, segment of this heterogeneous major village, such a conflict had a different outcome. In this unit, the son of an attached person also rose rapidly to become a senior chief, and he had many children who threatened to dominate the decision making of the unit. The senior patrilineage priest was, however a titled man, and it is said that he foresaw the threat clearly while the senior chief was alive. When the chief died, the senior priest and the elders of the collective incarnate dead discovered that his death had been caused by swelling, which signified a bad death due to abominations that the chief had committed. His body was cast into the bad bush without a funeral, and the intralineage status aspirations of his children were forestalled for a considerable time thereafter.[18]

These examples further indicate processual trends within patrilineage and village units. A contrast in wealth emerges between rightful senior priest and an attached or junior son, and this contrast generates internal conflict. It may be resolved by convicting the vulnerable party of an abomination (a solution that reflects disgrace upon the entire unit); it may be resolved by the splitting of the unit (perhaps with one unit moving to another location); or it may be resolved by the junior man's successful usurpation of the symbols of legitimacy. In the Agwɔ case the usurper gained not only the ɔzɔ title but also the highest social identity available to any

17. The details unfortunately remain somewhat clouded. A combination of old court records, recent oral accounts, and observation of recent social interaction in the village served as the basis of this reconstruction. Unfortunately, research in the field had to be terminated before some of the gaps in this case could be filled.

18. After such an abomination has been covered, the sons may complete the lamentation of the deceased. However, the abomination is said to "stick" to the bodies of the descendants, and this taint can be used effectively against them for some time because other members of the group view it as a disgrace that affects the whole patrilineage.

member of the clan (that of hidden king), and this usurpation was accepted. ("What could our fathers do about it?" say the informants recounting this case. "They had no voice because none of them had taken ɔzɔ title.")

Here the criteria for eligibility to hidden kingship have implicitly become separated from the criteria of succession to senior patrilineage priesthood. Onitsha people say that the hidden king should be the most senior priest of the clan, but they also recognize that the usurper in Agwɔ clan did not meet that criterion; yet all the common people in the town bowed to him in his role. Moreover, informants have cited other cases in which ineligible men who were chiefs also went on to become hidden kings of their clans. It appears, then, that before the colonial period began there was a trend underway toward seizure of these positions by ascriptively ineligible persons, generally chiefs. If this is so, an important implication follows: the criteria for eligibility to hidden kingship were becoming more like those for the Onitsha king and less like those for clan priesthood.

The evidence presented in the preceding section also makes clear that the endemic character of the conflict between poor senior priests and their wealthy junior agnates cannot be accounted for fully by differences in their structurally determined social orientations, for Onitsha people themselves are aware that this conflict tends to develop, and in specific cases they are known to have tried to do something about it. Senior priests can act to alter the course of events; since they control the major fixed resources of their units, there can be no intrinsic inevitability to the process of differential expansion and accumulation just described. Other factors reinforce this tendency, most importantly the politics of kingship.

13 DYNAMICS OF POWER, WEALTH, SOLIDARITY, AND PRESTIGE IN ONITSHA SOCIETY

In the data presented thus far, several societal tendencies seem evident, including a trend toward the establishment of systemic social stratification, possibly even incipient hierarchy. These tendencies prompt questions: in precisely what direction or directions was this system evolving? To what extent have the evolutionary processes operating within it been products of conscious planning by actors in the system, and to what extent have these processes been the unplanned byproducts of actions directed toward other goals? What major resources and obstacles with which the actors have had to deal have channelled their actions, and in what ways?

Explanatory answers to these questions can best be arrived at by first constructing a logically consistent, ideal-type model of rational strategy and tactics from a given point of view inside the system. It will be most useful to assume that the evolutionary aim of certain actors is to produce a stratified and hierarchical society; the model will be based partly on evolutionary theory, partly on the previous ethnographic account of the normative system of the society, and partly on hints in the historical outline presented earlier. Detailed evidence of the genealogical succession of Onitsha kings and chiefs may then be projected against this model, and their rational efficiency in performances assessed. From the errors detected in the actual process observed, it should prove possible to carry the empirical explanation further.[1]

1. I am aware that this model is not fully independent of the data against which it is to be projected; to be so, it would have had to be formulated by someone other than myself, and on the basis solely of theory and of the evidence in the preceding chapters. It still has value in elucidating process and "errors" in strategy, as I intend to show.

A MODEL OF EVOLUTIONARY TRENDS TOWARD STRATIFICATION AND HIERARCHY

To formulate such a model from the perspective of an Onitsha king, assume that he is committed to a social ideology that defines his own descent group as superior to all others, and that his major conscious goal is to increase and secure wealth, power, and prestige for himself and his children. His prime strategy is therefore to limit the total size of his own prestigious descent group, because the larger this group becomes the more widely he must share prestige with his remote clansmen. His second major strategy is to control the flow of wealth in the community, to channel it toward bolstering his prestige and increasing his power. How might the Onitsha king rationally implement these aims?

Four major initial considerations must be taken as givens in the situation. First, each person's base of operation in this system is located at a particular point within a segmentary system of localized, exogamous patrilineage descent groups. The basic resources of land and women are in the hands of these units, and loyalty to father, to patrilineage priest, to father's children, and to clan are part of each person's very identity. This is a basic condition upon which a man begins to build his plans; it is inconceivable for an Onitsha man to launch an attack upon this structure directly, at the outset. Changes in it are therefore likely to occur at first mainly as unconscious byproducts of actions directed to other ends.

Second, a quick route to control of wealth in the community would be through direct control of the trade in the waterside international marketplace. However, the Onitsha king is normatively cut off from this, for women monopolize the role of active traders in Onitsha, a role linked to the roles of wife and daughter. The king's wives (the only women under his undivided control) are identified with him and share the awesome aspects of his nature;

they must be secluded and therefore cannot participate in active trading. Consequently, the king's most feasible routes toward control of wealth are through control of the production of valued goods, and control over men who may undertake administrative regulation of production, trading, and other social activities.

Third, there are various structural sources of manpower in the community that the king might tap for such social control: the chiefs, the ɔzɔ men, the age-sets, the collective incarnate dead. He receives wealth from ɔzɔ candidates under his own nze, and, more importantly, he enjoys some control over selection of chiefs. The latter are his most valuable men, especially the prime minister, who occupies a pivotal position in place of the king during interregnum, directing the process of kingly succession. Since the candidate for succession must seek the blessings of senior priests and hidden kings from all clans, since these clans are associated with villages, and since there are possibilities for competitive confrontation among rivals at every stage of this process, the chiefs of all villages must also be approached and their support sought. Therefore the loyal support of his chiefs is crucial, both for insuring a succession to his liking and for increasing the scope of his administrative control.

Finally, a technique of great potential value for helping the king increase his wealth, power, and prestige is to utilize his relations with those outside the system, incorporating socially useful outsiders into the system in innovative ways. The intersocietal setting of Onitsha seems to have been unusually rich in social resources, because of the presence of the international marketplace.

Given this general structuring of limitations and opportunities, consider first the problem of the size and prestige differentiation of the royal clan. One obvious way of sharply and permanently differentiating such a unit from other clan units would be to make it endogamous; given the basic structure of the system, however, this does not seem even conceivable. Therefore the royal clan must be differentiated from others by its distinctive cultural services and by its wealth and power in numbers. If the king is to realize his prime strategy of limiting the effective size of the prestigious royal group, he must also produce differentiation within the royal clan itself.

The initial major means for attaining these aims are his abilities to manipulate paternally linked and maternally linked relations, and his partial control over the distribution of major chieftaincy titles. The most direct route toward producing a limited royal group under such circumstances is through father–son succession to kingship. This poses problems in two major areas—within the king's own clan, and between his clan and various nonroyal units.

The king must build a base first within his own patrilineage, for no man can act as an autonomous agent in this society without such support. The general principle to be followed is: the closer the agnate, the more reliable he is. However, because of ɔzɔ title competition, at every patrilineage level there is potential conflict, which means that selection of even one's closest supporters must be judicious. The most reliable patrilineage supporters are likely to be a man's own sons, who are bound to him in eternal support, and next to them his full brothers.

The king could be expected to attempt to build the prestige of his favored sons as much as possible, bestowing all feasible advantages on them. Second, all other things being equal, the king would confer senior chieftaincy, even the position of prime minister, upon his full or at least closest brother.

At greater genealogical distance within the royal clan, the king's interests will in general be best served if he weakens the power and prestige of his agnates, insofar as it is both commensurate with and equivalent to his own. To the extent that their numbers are great, their village has power commensurate with his own; to the extent that they are regarded as "kingly," they are potentially equivalent to him. Therefore he will avoid conferring high chieftaincy in distant royal segments if at all possible.

However, he does not wish to alienate these distant royal segments so that they reject all relationship with him, for, given the presence of hidden kings in nonroyal clans, he needs the continued loyalty of remote royal groups if he is to maintain social differentiation from these hidden kings. He must be circumspect in his manner of weakening distant royal segments. Where a large distant royal village can make powerful effective demands, he may be forced to give them a high title; the deleterious effects of this can be limited by selecting candidates from a segment within that village which lacks full ascriptive rights to royalty, for such an act is likely to lead to further dilution of the royal quality of the larger unit.

Even within his own major village of the royal clan, the king must exercise great caution in conferring titles. Specifically, he will avoid bestowing any chieftaincy title higher than that he has given his brother, because if members of another segment of the village had a higher ranking chief, the king's brother would come under the authority of that chief. It would be to the king's advantage to create lowly new titles for candidates in other segments of the royal clan.

As these royal units become increasingly distant from the king's own, he can dilute the strength of distant opposing royal segments without alienating them completely by bestowing on them specialized rights and duties that bear a relation to their royal heritage but that preclude their eligibility to contest for the throne. Another solution involves diminishing the amount of traditional patrilineage affairs undertaken together with the distant segments, using this to justify cessation of exogamy, but continuing to recognize them ideologically as clansmen. Ultimately they become nonroyal but retain specialized abilities and special duties toward the king.

The king's second major problem concerns his relations with the extant nonroyal clans. Initially, intermarriage may align them with him, the most reliable source of strong loyalties being those established with his mother's parents; but he must go further than this if major nonroyal villages are not to secede behind their own hidden kings. He must bestow positions of chieftaincy, including some senior positions, on those persons from nonroyal villages on whose loyalty he can depend. Any king would hope to confer senior chieftaincy on one of his mother's parents, because of their protective orientations to him and the binding integration prescribed for this relationship.

Otherwise, a king may bestow chieftaincy sparingly among the nonroyal villages. Wisdom would dictate that he give it to those units with enough members to make a strong effective demand, and to create new lesser titles wherever possible. Senior chieftaincy should, however, be denied to any nonroyal unit with especially high ascriptive veneration.[2] In contrast, the king would be astute to confer even senior chieftaincy on newcomers who have entered the community possessing craft specialties or trade links to the outside, for through social compacts with such nonroyal units, a king could greatly increase his wealth and his influence without immediately strengthening his competitors. In general, then, he will encourage nonroyals to develop specialized relations with him, relations that facilitate their increasing difference from him as well as their increasing interdependence with him.

This set of rules formulates a guide that an Onitsha king might rationally follow and by doing so, move the system in the direction of his aims. Some of these principles conflict with each other: e.g. satisfying a desire to have a close patrilineal kinsman as a senior chief may frustrate the members of a major nonroyal village who demand such chieftaincy. The king must balance these maxims in the actual processes of choice.

By following these principles thoughtfully and consistently, a king would develop in time a system of chiefs representing villages

2. It would, for example, be folly to select a man from Ɔbiɔ clan as a senior chief. Ɔbiɔ is a very small unit, and its selection would frustrate demands for representation by much larger groups. Even if that were not true, the numerical expansion of Ɔbiɔ clan as a result of obtaining senior chieftaincy might enable it later to compete for community kingship, because its hidden king has even greater ascriptive prestige than that of the Onitsha king.

and sub-villages that are also descent groups; but it would also be a system in which the contrast between royals and nonroyals would increase over time and the size of the effectively royal group decrease while its internal structure would be transformed and its structured relations with other groups modified away from segmentary system forms. The outcome is a society with a centralized stratification, possessing a king who can then go further: he can rationally manipulate the collectivities of chiefs, slaves, and others, in the interests of building hierarchic administrative systems. As these structures become established and strengthened, the king may then manipulate the structures of descent groups more directly, and move to shift the distribution of trading wealth more directly and fully into his hands.

KINGSHIP SUCCESSION, CHIEFTAINCY, AND STRUCTURAL CHANGE: THE EVIDENCE

Changes in patterns of succession to pivotal offices often signal further evolutionary changes in a society. While Onitsha kingship succession engages the full range of segmentary social divisions within the community, the ability of senior chiefs to influence events makes it reasonable to examine the history of this succession with the distribution of senior chieftaincy always in mind. For a variety of reasons, it was not possible during my research to obtain any approximation to a full distribution of chiefly titles by genealogy,[3] but enough information was obtained to make possible a substantial number of inferences about the probable nature of political processes.

Oral traditions concerning the stage of the early kings contain evidence of competition for kingship among representatives of

3. The size and dispersion of the Onitsha population in recent times made an attempt at obtaining any approximation to a complete genealogical record out of the question. In addition, most of the field research was undertaken during a politically volatile interregnum period, which made it very difficult to obtain detailed genealogical information from some quarters.

later nonroyal clans, including Eze Awuma of Isele-Awada clan and chief Nsu of Ekensu clan. These two clans have been regarded in recent times as the least prestigious in Onitsha community, judging by the sequence in which the new yam festival is performed. Since Nsu himself was the Iyasele Onowu, i.e. the prime minister (assuming this title had similar status at that time), the prime minister was competing for the royal throne during the time of the early kings. It is said that Nsu was active during the reign of other early kings who founded various villages in the Division is Two segment of the royal clan. According to one old account, these early kings also competed with one another, as Figure 42 indicates.

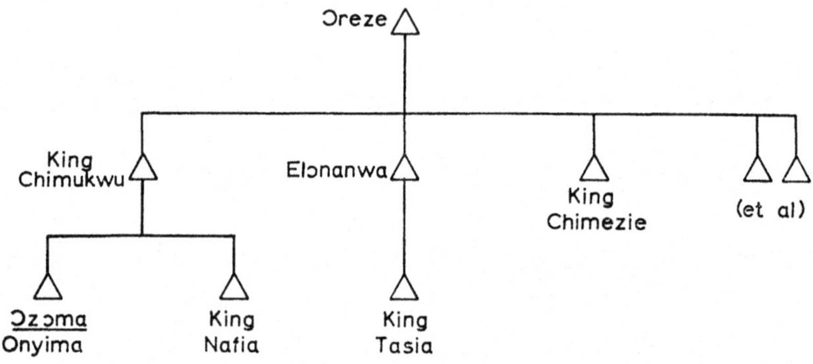

Fig. 42 The genealogy of competing early kings

It is said that *Chímukwu,* a son of the founder Ɔreze, reigned in Onitsha, and when he died his son *Nafia* succeeded him as king. Nafia then quarreled for some reason with his brother, *Ɔzɔma Onyima.*[4] Ɔzɔma Onyima made a curse that his brother would become a leper, then Nafia did contract leprosy (*àrú ɔ̀chá,* "white body," an abomination), whereupon he was apparently deposed. Onyima expected to become king; instead his patrilineal kinsman *Tásìa* was installed. Nafia made a curse for his brother Onyima to die without offspring, and, according to the account,

4. The title Ɔzɔma is the second salutation for what has since become the fourth-ranking senior chief, the Ɔ*nya.*

the curse was fulfilled. Tasia himself died while completing the succession rituals, and the kingship passed to Chimezie.

It was not possible to check the details of this tradition with the descendants of Nafia, but it points to considerable conflict between kings and titled chiefs during the early period. Some independent accounts imply that the reign of Nafia may also have been the time during which control over selection of chiefs first passed into the hands of the king.[5] These legends seem to indicate controversy over both the definition of royalty and the relations between king and chiefs.

The descendants of the persons just discussed are still considered fully royal, but they are also members of very small village units. This is explained by Onitsha people as a consequence of their ancestors' abominations, after which their descendants died while inhabiting a fiery surface at the Village of Mbubu. Some of the survivors then fled to join the Village of *Àbʊ*.

The ancestor who may be regarded as the culminating figure of this early period is King Chima the Cow-killer. He occupies an ambiguous position in the genealogies of various sections of the royal clan. Some accounts from Division is Two emphasize his position as a founder of a tiny village segment in that major group, while others stress his position as father of the Igala-derived king Arɔlɩ and his brothers. One Onitsha writer identified him as founder both of one section of the Village of Mbubu, and of the entire royal clan.[6] From numerous genealogies it is clear that he must be regarded as the father of Arɔlɩ, and that his importance in genealogies from Division is Two probably indicates that he was both an early king among the set of kings later identified with that division, and the ancestor of persons who established a new era of more powerful kings. His own reign is said to have been marked by turbulence, including raids and bombardments of the waterside market by the people of Aboh.

In the oral tradition, the new dynastic sequence developed out of

5. Cf. Ifeka (1962).
6. Okolo (1947).

the relations between Igala-derived Arɔlɩ, his brothers Ebo and Chima-ʊkwa (*Chímʊkwa*), and his sister Ɔlɔsɩ. Some accounts mention a fourth brother *Anwula,* who is said to have become established as an agent of King Chima in Obosi community to the south. There are disputes today about whether Chima-ʊkwa and Ɔlɔsɩ were descended from the same Igala mother as Arɔlɩ, but it is agreed that Ebo, the senior son of Chima the Cow-killer, was born of a different mother from the others, an Onitsha woman.

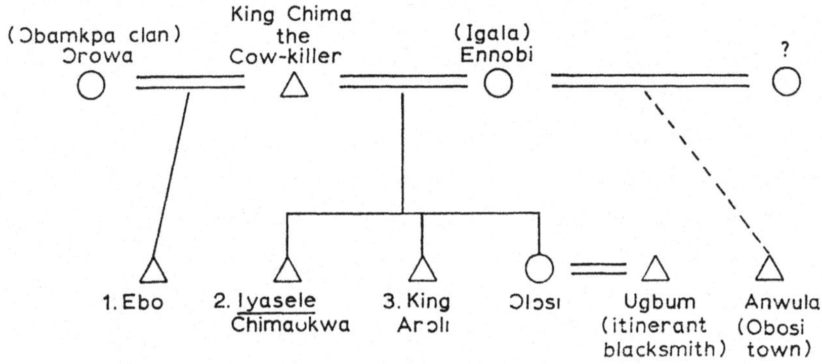

Fig. 43 Arɔlɩ *and his siblings (in order of seniority)*

Several striking features emerge in the traditions recounting the kingship succession following the death of Chima the Cow-killer. First, his death begins what was earlier designated the Igala-Anambra stage of Onitsha history, during which riverain influences become prominent in the oral record. At this point, succession to kingship decisively breaks away from succession to patrilineage priesthood, for the successor Arɔlɩ not only came into Onitsha from life in Igala, but was also the "youngest son" of Chima the Cow-killer. He established his own palace and village area in the center of the community some distance from the ancestral house of Chima the Cow-killer, the putative site of which remains today at Isiokwe village and is worshipped there by descendants of the senior brothers Ebo and Chima-ʊkwa. Eligibility to the position as senior priest of Chima the Cow-killer became limited to the descendants of Ebo and Chima-ʊkwa in Isiokwe.

It is widely held that this village of Isiokwe was formerly large but later lost numbers, and the reason is given in a proverb: "Isiokwe argued in meetings, entered death" (*Ísiòkwe lʊ́lʊ ʊ́kà, bà ḿmʊɔ*). A legend recounts that this once numerous people tried to construct a ladder (*ìgulubé*) that would enable them to climb high above everyone around them. When the ladder was completed everyone in the village tried to climb it simultaneously. As a result it collapsed and most of them perished. It is said that, even today, "they can never agree." [7]

At this time too an itinerant Ibo blacksmith named *Ʊ̀gbʊ́m* is said to have settled with King Arɔlɩ and impregnated the latter's sister Ɔlɔsɩ. Their offspring became accepted as members of the royal clan, but in a special relation to the king; they became collective daughters of the royal clan, taking roles analogous to those of daughters in controlling the burial of deceased kings and handling the disposal of their heads. Thus a village unit grew up to become known as the "Face of the town" (*Íru òbodo*), a term alluding to its position at the northeastern flank of the king's village.

Third, King Arɔlɩ's brother Chima-ʊkwa, a uterine sibling by most accounts, was the prime minister. Many informants say that this is how one would expect a king to allocate high titles, but that it was a bad practice not allowed to continue. Nevertheless, this was neither the first nor the last instance in which the king appears to have had a sibling who was a senior chief.[8]

In recent times, both the descendants of Ɔlɔsɩ and the descendants of Ebo and Chima-ʊkwa living in Isiokwe village have intermarried with the Children of Arɔlɩ. According to oral tradition, this intermarriage began after the people of Ɔlɔsɩ and Isiokwe

7. As an honorary member of this patrilineage, I was present at one of their meetings where (it was later alleged) disagreement medicine had been secretly planted.

8. The last instance occurred after 1900; it generated an almost total split of the community and led to a radical diminution of the influence of the kingship.

fought against the Children of King Arɔlɩ during an ɔzɔ title taking, clubbing each other's heads with their ɔzɔ staves. After this time, the two groups separated, no longer sharing ɔzɔ title money and also ceasing their mutual exogamy. In this third way collateral royal lines have become differentiated from that of the king; the unity of shared descent has been diluted, and the meaning of nze (still shared among them) has become generalized, for it no longer refers to the norms of incest taboo and exogamy. The royal clan does not share the full set of norms associated with nze elsewhere. The fact that Isiokwe and Ɔlɔsɩ came to be socially linked with nonroyal villages also serves to differentiate them from the king's line.

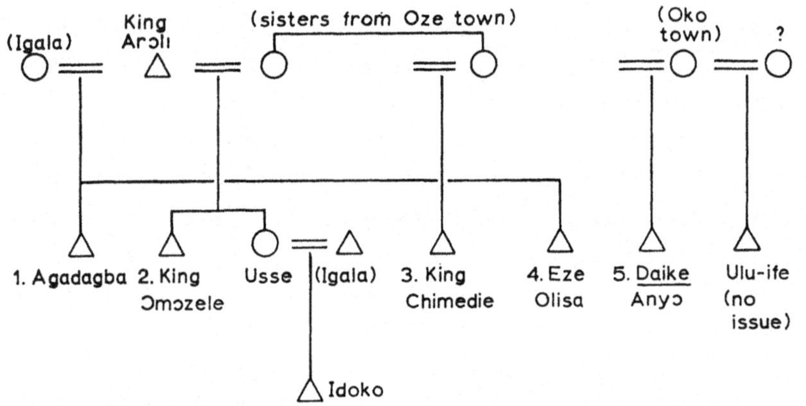

Fig. 44 The offspring of Arɔlɩ

After the death of Arɔlɩ, his sons began succeeding to his kingly title, and other remarkable developments are recounted. First, another specialist community became partially absorbed into the royal clan through the founding of the Children of Idoko (later Obikporo village), the unit derived from a marriage between King Arɔlɩ's daughter Usse and a person said to be a son of the great Ogrugu-based Igala warrior, Onojo Oboni. This village established further relationships with the Anambra people and Igala, and introduced new and fearsome forms of collective incarnate dead into Onitsha. This group was initially associated with King Ɔmɔzele, the uterine brother of their ancestress Usse, who is said to have succeeded his father. According to the legend, at first the Children of Idoko lived apart, supporting the king by cowing the rest of the community with their special form of incarnate dead (the tall ghosts); later they became so feared that they began to compete with King Ɔmɔzele and were sent to reside in the midst of other Onitsha villages. Integrated with other units, they lost much of their distinctiveness but this change also deprived the king of direct access to their special powers.

Second, the statuses of senior patrilineage priest and king are again sharply separated in this generation. An elaborate rationale is provided for this separation in the oral tradition, but the rationale contains fundamental logical contradictions. Informants from the *Àgadágbà* segment say simply that Agadagba was the senior son of Arɔlɩ, but his junior brothers, dying before him, lost their right to succeed to the ɔfɔ of Arɔlɩ. It is, however, also generally accepted community lore that Arɔlɩ reigned for so long that his successor, Ɔmɔzele, was so elderly at the time of his installation that he was at first mocked with the phrase, "What can the aged one accomplish?" (*ágadɩ gà ìmé gínɩ?*). Yet, it is said, Ɔmɔzele astonished his public by reigning wisely for many years. It seems highly improbable that Agadagba, as senior to Ɔmɔzele, could have outlived this venerated sage.

Informants outside Agadagba segment say that Agadagba was originally the most junior son of Arɔlɩ, but the other sons died in the presence of their father, so that only Agadagba lived to bury Arɔlɩ. When I confronted my most reliable and philosophical informants with the logical contradiction inherent in this statement—that if the others had died while Arɔlɩ was alive, they would never have become kings—their perplexity contrasted sharply with the usual readiness of wit that I had come to expect from Onitsha men. A few of these informants responded that the others had died after

Arɔlɩ but before Agadagba, and therefore became kings. If this was true and Agadagba was initially junior, then they all died in the proper order. When this was pointed out, perplexity increased.

The clearly post hoc rationalization involved in this tradition is concerned with legitimizing an ascriptive patrilineage seniority to Agadagba segment. Still other tales recount that *Dăike Ányɔ*, a ranking chief (the Ɔmɔdi), had sexual relations with a wife of King Chimedie—an abomination—and that his descendants therefore lost their right to occupy the ancestral house of Arɔlɩ; similar tales of misbehavior are given concerning Eze Olisa. It was not feasible to check the validity of these tales; the point is, however, that developments occurred which led the community to rationalize the fact that the senior patrilineage priesthood of Arɔlɩ devolves solely upon the Agadagba segment, a social unit which in recent times had no more than half a dozen households located in the village of Children of Arɔlɩ. Thus eligibility to senior patrilineage priesthood is another form of specialization emergent in this side of the royal clan. It is not a fully formulated development, for not only do all these units remain mutually exogamous but at plenary meetings of the Children of King Arɔlɩ, representatives of Agadagba, Ɔmɔzele, and Chimedie must jointly occupy the throne of Arɔlɩ. However, homage service should be paid by all to Agadagba. Socially, this sharing of the patrilineage throne expresses the contradiction between ascription and achievement that is present at this level of the genealogical structure.

A third remarkable fact evident in the genealogy of Onitsha kings at this stage is that all the mothers of the offspring of Arɔlɩ came from outside Onitsha. This contradicts the recent normative criteria for kingship succession, which have emphasized that the mothers of Onitsha kings must be Onitsha women. Onitsha men of recent times have had no explanation for this anomaly, and though some people have found it a relevant issue in recent kingship disputes, most emphasize that as daughter's child a man is expected always to seek the interests of his mother's people, and that a man with a non-Onitsha mother would therefore likely be traitorous.

Among the sons of Arɔlɩ, Chimedie gives the first definite evidence of increasing the wealth, prestige, and power of kingship. Contradictory legends concerning his brother Eze Olisa suggest that the latter may have died trying to succeed to the throne.[9] Eze Olisa is said to have had only one surviving son. Chimedie, in contrast, took many wives and raised eight sons, whose progeny continued to increase.

The sequence of kings from the time of Chimedie down to the reign of *Ȁnazɔ́nwʊ* in the 1870s, as illustrated in Figure 45, indicates major trends that begin after the reign of Chimedie. It has just been said that the descendants of Chimedie did not become the senior patrilineage priests of the Children of Arɔlɩ, because Chimedie "died out of order." This separation of kingship and patrilineage priesthood continues for yet another generation. According to a number of convergent accounts, *Ɔ̀réz̀è Ȍbí*, the senior son of King Chimedie, had received the latter's ɔzɔ title, and seems even to have attained a junior chieftaincy title (obi) under his father, but he died an untimely death while Chimedie was still living. Chimedie was so dismayed at his senior son's death that he proceeded to bestow ɔzɔ title purification upon the three sons of Ɔreze Obi. The second son of Chimedie, *Ɔ̀rɔ́wa,* supervised the funeral of his brother and thereby became the senior son.

After the death of Chimedie the more junior son named Ijelekpe became king, while Ɔrɔwa, the senior surviving son, continued as patrilineage priest of Chimedie. Ɔrɔwa was succeeded in the priesthood by the junior chief Ɔlɔdi Owowo and then by the fourth son, *Nwazago.* It is said that King Ijelekpe died before Nwazago, and that his offspring therefore became ineligible to succeed to the

9. One account alludes to his difficulties, relating that the royal village of Isiokwe discovered a rainstone that ended a serious drought during his rule (and consequently they became rainmakers for kings).

patrilineage throne of Chimedie. Ultimately, only the Ɔrɔwa and Nwazago segments of the Children of Chimedie held the right to this priesthood, for the line of chief Owowo became extinct. Therefore, for fully three generations beginning with Arɔlɩ, the kingship is sharply separated from the senior patrilineage priesthood.

However, this sharp separation of kingship from priesthood does not continue beyond Ijelekpe. *Udogwu*, his second son, succeeded as king, while the senior son *Émeagwalɩ* was given the senior chieftaincy title, Odu (Osodi). Emeagwalɩ, as a senior chief, delegated his patrilineage priesthood to the third son Ezumezu, and when Emeagwalɩ died King Udogwu succeeded to the priesthood and

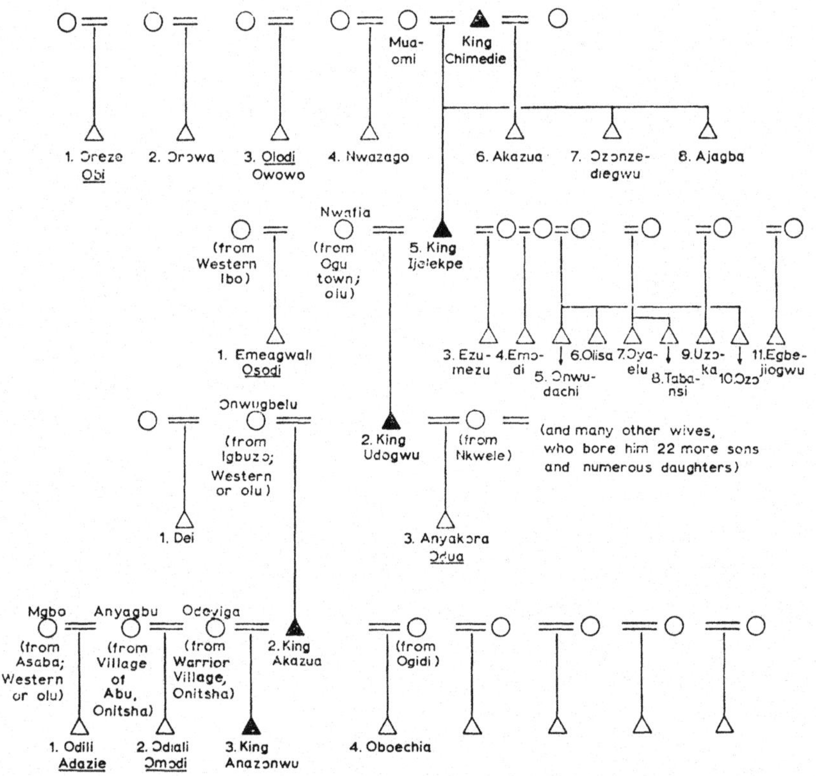

Fig. 45 The Children of King Chimedie

simply continued this delegation. Thus, it is said, the children of King Udogwu retained access to the ancestral house of his father Ijelekpe.

The successor to King Udogwu was Akazua, according to most accounts the former's senior son. An apparently more senior son, Dei, seems to have died without issue, probably while Udogwu was alive. Therefore, the king's surviving senior son succeeded him as king, and the same pattern was followed in the next generation, for Akazua's original senior son *Ódìlí* died in his father's presence, and *Ɔ̀dɩáli* the surviving senior son died while undertaking the ceremonies of royal succession.

There is therefore evident, in the generations below King Chimedie, a progressive drift toward succession to kingship by the senior son of the king, a succession that upholds the right of ascriptive seniority. In recent times, the children of both Ɔdɩali and Anazɔnwʊ retained eligibility to serve as senior priests of the higher patrilineage segments Children of Udogwu and Children of Ijelekpe. This reverse drift suggests a conscious design developed within the families of the kings: initially, to establish a sharp separation between the roles of senior patrilineage priest and king, a process greatly facilitated by assigning them to people in different statuses (status differences passed on to subsequent generations); then, having established this double differentiation (of roles and of descent segments), rearticulating the statuses (but not the roles), in the interest of establishing systematic senior son succession to kingship.

It has previously been observed that the early missionaries supposed that Onitsha kingship succession was determined by the norm of male primogeniture. The missionaries in 1857 found Odili, the senior son of Akazua, prominent in all major civic affairs, and the king's private councillors included not only the prime minister but also Odili (apparently installed as the chief, adazie) and the king's junior brother Anyakora (the throne chief ɔdua). Chief Odili appears also to have acted as the king's public spokesman, together with the prime minister.[10] When Odili became seriously ill in 1865, King Akazua called the Reverend Taylor to attend him, and Taylor reported as follows:

> I had observed during his illness there were eleven goats and fifty chickens offered in sacrifice to propitiate the spirits of his ancestors not to take him away in the bloom of youth, with his 8 wives and children, until he shall have supplied the room in the government after the decease of his father.[11]

Despite all these efforts, Odili died in the presence of his father.

The same orientation towards the king's senior son is evident in the mission accounts after the death of King Akazua. His surviving senior son Ɔdɩali (installed, while his father was alive, as the chief ɔmɔdi) died of smallpox while completing the succession rituals. The next senior son of Akazua then

> came forward to claim the right but proved to be a drunkard, so the elders were indifferent in supporting his claim; others who might come forward, could not with safety step over the rightful heir without opposition and trouble. The younger brother of the late King Obi Akazua, feeling himself to be too feeble from old age to undertake the rein of government, contented himself by acting as a mere president till a king should be elected and crowned.[12]

Since the king eventually installed was Akazua's senior surviving son Anazɔnwʊ, it seems likely that, within the immediate royal unit concerned, succession by the king's senior son had come to be the accepted prescriptive norm.

However, neither historical accounts nor oral tradition suggest that the acceptance of senior son succession to kingship was substantial elsewhere in the community. It is said that Oboechia, another son of Akazua, also contested the throne, but he was disquali-

10. Crowther and Taylor (1859:24–27).
11. Church Missionary Record (1866, p. 206).
12. Crowther (1875:121–22).

fied because his mother came from Ogidi town east of Onitsha. Moreover, the earlier efforts by Ɔdɩali to succeed his father Akazua were in fact contested much more strongly by members of another segment of the Children of Chimedie. Bishop Crowther gave the following report in 1873:

> After the King's death a pretender arose to oppose the rightful prince who was to succeed his father as soon as the funeral customs were over. The pretender was a descendant of a former king, whose line had long since ceased to reign at Onitsha. The pretender had a female relative who was married to a man of the King's family at Idda, in Igara country; she had a son who was grown wealthy by trading. This female relative encouraged the pretender to assert his claim to the throne of Onitsha and that her son from Idda would support him to obtain it. Not long after the son came from Idda, with a strong force to strengthen the pretender at Onitsha. Both united, they commenced threats against the rightful prince and disputed his right to the throne of Onitsha; that it was then their turn to reign. They commenced firing shots at, and set fire to, the houses of the party of the rightful prince. In the meantime he had also collected his party. On the 3rd day they sallied down to the river's bank, with many killed and wounded; the dead being cut to pieces by the limbs, to be feasted upon by the Obotshis [Obosi], notorious cannibals, who had come to help the rightful Prince of Onitsha. The pretender and his Onitsha party had to flee to the neighboring towns and villages for refuge. The son of the female relative from Idda was mortally wounded and died a few days after. Thus Onitsha was delivered from the influence of the Igara people.[13]

While one segment of the royal clan was striving to institute a father-to-senior-son succession, and had managed to establish a de facto senior son succession after the reign of King Udogwu, their effort was being contested.

In examining the question of the political and economic bases

13. Crowther (1873).

of this de facto senior son succession that was replacing the collateral succession of the Igala-Anambra stage, we may best begin with King Ijelekpe, a figure associated with the beginning of the "Uplands-Aro" stage of Onitsha history. The pivotal person is the mother of King Ijelekpe, a woman named *Mua-omi*.

It has been observed that the mothers of preceding kings, beginning with Arɔlɩ, had come from outside Onitsha; the position of Mua-omi is ambiguous in this regard. The people of Children of Ase village claim Mua-omi as one of their daughters, but some outside informants say she came from Ɔbamkpa town west of the Niger, a town regarded as one of the settlements of the original Children of King Chima and linked traditionally with the Children of Ase. A genealogy of that major segment of Children of Ase to which Mua-omi is linked is reproduced in Figure 46.

Mua-omi is said to have been reluctant to permit her son Ijelekpe to become king because the kings had been dying for lack of a proper ɔfɔ. According to the Children of Ase version, the uterine brother of Mua-omi, *Ɔ́dɩ̀égwù* (which means "he is awesome"), traveled with their mother Iba back to her home in Ɔbamkpa, and there received from her people the royal anvil ɔfɔ with its secret Benin-derived medicines. Returning to Onitsha, *Ɔdɩegwu* presented this new ɔfɔ to Ijelekpe, who subsequently enjoyed a long and successful reign.

The possibility that this legend refers to the time when guns were first obtained by Onitsha people has already been discussed. Of direct concern at this point is what rewards King Ijelekpe gave to Ɔdɩegwu for his efforts. First, the Children of Ɔdɩegwu (and later the Children of Ase as a whole) gained the right to reclaim the anvil ɔfɔ after the death of each king and to bestow it on his successor. Second, some informants from Children of Ase maintain that Ɔdɩegwu himself was then made the prime minister of Onitsha. This claim is not generally accepted elsewhere in the town, but it is universally agreed that the senior son of Ɔdɩegwu, *Ókwugbèlé*, did become prime minister. Of the five sons of Ɔdɩegwu, four became prominent chiefs, a development that led to great numerical expansion of the Children of Ɔdɩegwu. *Ʊgboma,* the senior son of prime minister Okwugbele, is said to have succeeded his father as prime minister; the senior son of Ʊgboma in turn began the taking of the Iyasele title, but died during the process. After this failure, the Children of Ase claim, the title of prime minister was wrongfully taken away from their village.

Five generations separate Iyasele Okwugbele (the senior son of Ɔdɩegwu) from his living patrilineal descendants born around 1900. Since there are also five generations between King Ijelekpe and his eldest living patrilineal descendants, it is likely that the bestowal of the title of prime minister on one of Ijelekpe's mother's

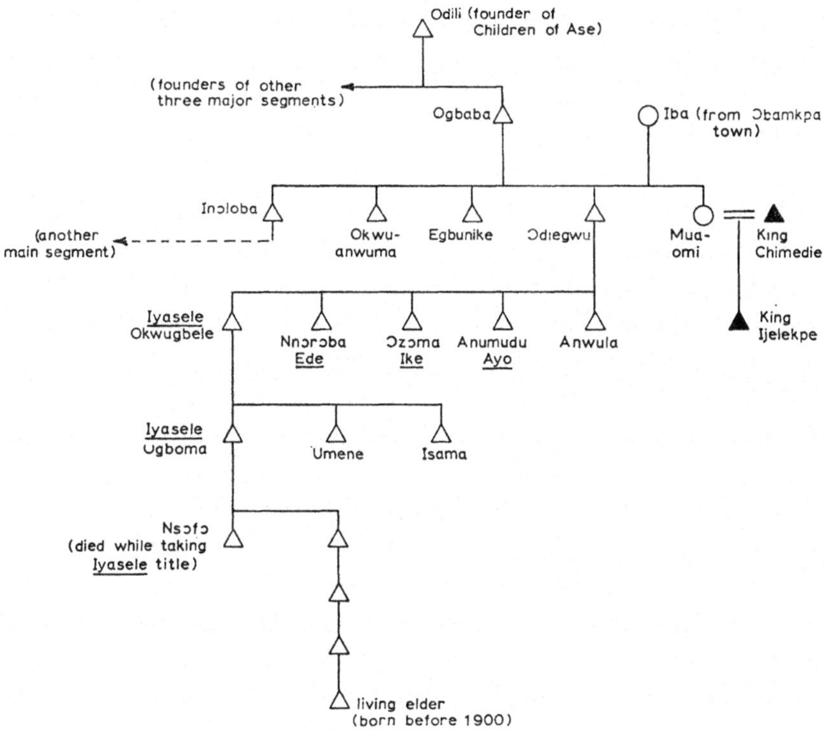

Fig. 46 The mother's parents of King Ijelekpe

parents was indeed done by him. In this way, a basis was probably laid for establishing a father–son succession after Ijelekpe, by insuring the support of the prime minister and the bestowal of the powerful anvil ɔfɔ.

After chief Ugboma, the title of prime minister was taken away from the Children of Ɔdɩegwu and transferred to that branch of the royal clan called the Children of Dei. Figure 47 provides a genealogy that places this segment within the wider framework of the royal clan. Members of the senior generation in Figure 47 are regarded as the founding fathers of Division is Two. It was pointed out earlier that the descendants of Aniemena are the sole eligible senior priests for this major division, and that it is generally agreed (outside Division is Two itself) that only the descendants of the early kings (descendants of Chimukwu, Elonanwa, and Chimezie in Figure 47) have legitimate traditional claims to the kingship of Onitsha. The most junior son of this group is called Dei, a term that informants outside that segment itself say is not in this case a real name but an allusion to a prince said to have fled from the riverain kingdom of Aboh and taken shelter among his royal kinsmen in Onitsha. The Children of Dei themselves do not accept this tradition, saying merely that Dei died in the presence of his father; but they all also claim to inherit his native prowess at canoeing, swimming, and fishing, skills that Onitsha people in general do not share. This unit, possessing by far the largest population in Division is Two, does not share exogamy with any of the other segments.

The most commonly mentioned ancestor of the Children of Dei is Olisa-ololi; his children form the next junior level of the genealogy in Figure 47, a group whose genealogical relations are as difficult to order as those of the preceding level. They might well represent a considerable time span rather than a valid generational unit. Seniority relations cannot be specified for these ancestors, although it is agreed that the descendants of Ɔreze-abo are the sole group eligible for the senior patrilineage priesthood of Olisa-ololi.

What is remarkable about the offspring of Olisa-ololi is that the eight persons listed include four senior chiefs (second minister Ajie Isagba, third minister Odu Osodi, fourth minister Ɔnya Ɔzɔma) and two who attained the position of ranking chiefs (Osuma). The only female of the group, *Òjĕdi*, is said to have

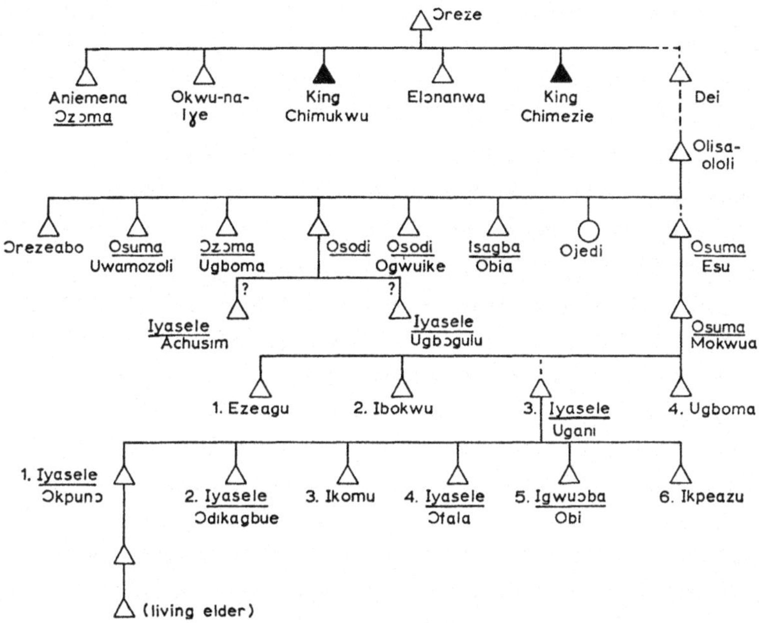

Fig. 47 Senior chieftaincy and the Children of Dei

been a woman of great trading wealth who rivaled her brothers in prominence and was greatly feared for her magical powers. The chief Osodi Idu (hereafter, simply "Osodi"), who according to tradition acquired large blocks of farm land north of Onitsha and whose children form the largest single subvillage of all the Children of Dei, is said to have lived during the time of King Ɔmɔzele and to have competed with him for the kingship.[14]

14. On Figure 47, I have placed question marks beside the putative descendants of Osodi. Unfortunately, I did not obtain an adequate account of his genealogy, and this report of his contemporaneity with King Ɔmɔzele comes from only one informant.

This aggregation of chiefly titles, unrivaled in any other Onitsha lineage, suggests that from the time of Arɔlι the kings began bestowing senior chieftaincy upon the less established and not fully royal segments of the opposing side of the royal clan, at the expense of the more venerated and legitimate segments.[15]

Somewhat later, the title of prime minister was bestowed among the descendants of Osodi. The most probable historical sequence of prime minister succession which I could construct runs as follows, beginning with the time of King Arɔlι:

1. Chimaʊkwa (Isiokwe)
2. Okwugbele (Children of Ase)
3. Ugboma (Children of Ase)
4. Achusιm (Children of Osodi, Children of Dei)
5. Ugbɔgʊlʊ (Children of Osodi, Children of Dei)
6. Uganι (Children of Osuma, Children of Dei)
7. Ɔkpunɔ (Children of Osuma, Children of Dei)
8. Ɔdιkagbue (Children of Osuma, Children of Dei)
9. Osili (Children of Nseli, Children of Dei)
10. Ɔfala (Children of Osuma, Children of Dei)

It appears that the Children of Osodi may have gained the title of prime minister directly after the failure of Nsɔfɔ in Children of Ase (Figure 46); this upgrading over their father Osodi may have been associated with the shifting of the senior chief title of Osodi to the senior brother of King Udogwu (Figure 45).

After Iyasele *Úgbɔ̀gʊlʊ* of the Children of Osodi, the title of prime minister shifted to an even more junior segment of the Children of Dei. Many Onitsha people have claimed during recent times that the Children of *Ósùmá Ésu* (Figure 47) are attached members of the Children of Dei, whose ancestors came from the Anambra River floodplain. The Children of Osuma themselves tell

15. A similar pattern is evident in the genealogy of the Children of Idoko (Igala—born son of King Arɔlι's daughter), who brought the special incarnate dead unit. One of his sons became fourth minister, and two others held the junior title of alamuzɔ.

another story intended to explain this denigration of their ancestor. After the death of Osuma Esu, they say, his son Mokwua took the ranking chief title Osuma. He died soon thereafter, leaving among his widows a woman named Agere, who came from Nzam in the Anambra floodplains and who was the mother of *Ùganι*. It is said that Agere had cause to fear for the life of her son because Osodi, still living but very elderly at the time, was believed to be prolonging his life by magically sucking the lives of his junior kinsmen. Therefore Ugani was taken to Nzam during his youth, and remained there until Osodi had died. After he returned, many people mistakenly believed him to be a native of Nzam.

In any event, Uganι was selected by either King Udogwu or King Akazua, and became the next prime minister of Onitsha. After his death, Uganι's sons succeeded him in order of seniority, and one of them, Ɔdιkagbue, was reported to be completing his title under King Akazua during the first year of the mission establishment at Onitsha.[16]

Thus the title of prime minister, whose holder played a strategic role in the politics of kingship succession, came to be allocated within an apparently Aboh-derived, not fully established section of the royal clan, and it was shifted within that segment to the hands of an even more junior, even less established member when the father-son kingship succession was developing. It appears that this alliance of the later kings with the junior segments of Division is Two generated internal conflict in that unit (the "poor senior priest" vs. "wealthy junior son" dichotomy) and strengthened the position of the reigning king's immediate lineage segment against the other descendants of Arɔlι.

There is good evidence that the king also tried on occasion to confer advantages on ascriptively junior sons within the descendants of Arɔlι as well as outside. After the original senior son of King Chimedie, Ɔreze Obi, died while his father was alive and

16. Crowther and Taylor (1859:283–84).

therefore became permanently downgraded to the position of a lesser son among the Children of Chimedie (i.e. within High Grass Village), the Onitsha kings that succeeded Chimedie are said to have favored the children of Ɔreze Obi over their own brothers as deputies for certain ceremonial purposes.[17] Moreover, either King Udogwu or King Akazua conferred the title of second minister (ajie isagba) upon a descendant of Ɔreze Obi. However, by

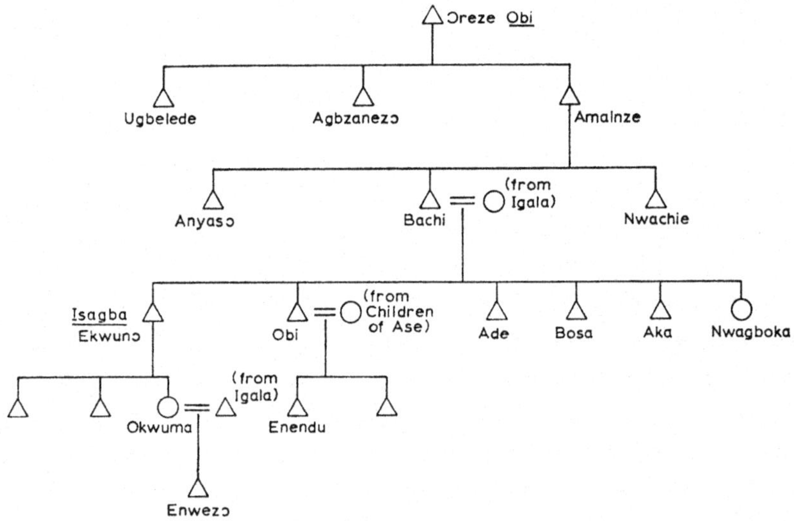

Fig. 48 The Children of Ɔreze Obi

doing so he nearly jeopardized the development of father-son kingship succession, for the relatives of this chief prospered greatly.

It is said that *Băchi,* a grandson of Ɔreze Obi, married a woman from Igala, and his children subsequently grew rich from her trade and her trade contacts. Indeed, her daughter *Nwâgbɔka* eventually became queen of Onitsha (in 1884) because of her great success as an international trader. The senior son of Bachi, *Ékwunɔ̀,* was installed as the second minister of Onitsha; he in turn arranged for

17. Onitsha Native Court (1948).

his senior daughter *Ókwumà* to marry a son of "the Igala king" at Idah, and supervised lucrative trade relations with these riverain people.

Okwuma, encountered by the missionaries, was the first female sufficiently prominent in community affairs to be recorded by name in their accounts.[18] She had developed a substantial external trading network operated through her slaves and her son.[19] She and her close agnate *Énendʋ̀* plotted to use Igala support to bring kingship back to the descendants of the original senior son of Chimedie, and when King Akazua died the drama of interregnum unfolded as described earlier. Onitsha people say that when Enendʋ was defeated he took sanctuary with his mother's people, the Children of (Iyasele) Okwugbele at Children of Ase village. Shortly thereafter, when an epidemic of smallpox raged in Onitsha, the missionaries reported the consequences:

> When King Idiari [Ɔdɩali] died of this malady, his opponent, [Enendʋ] the pretender to the throne, rejoiced at it, when it was at once concluded that it was he who had brought the smallpox to the country to kill the King. The pretender was summoned to a meeting of chiefs, where he was dispatched out of the way.[20]

The people of Onitsha say that the chiefs convicted Enendʋ of an abomination, in helping his patrilineage daughter Okwuma to utilize a variety of medicines that had evil effects. It is said that she secretly cooked the medicinal *ágba* leaf during meetings of various chiefs, so that a number of chiefs were magically seduced to follow Enendʋ, and also that she brought from Igala an evil medicine which kills by producing smallpox. Enendʋ was given a rope and directed to hang himself, thus committing an ultimate form of abomination. After enforcing this act upon him, the chiefs

18. Crowther and Taylor (1859:258–9).

19. Her son *Ènwézɔ̀* is almost certainly the "Ewonruzo" referred to in the Crowther quotation cited in Chapter 2, n. 86.

20. Crowther (1874:154).

manufactured an object representing an oath affirming that henceforth no king or senior chief would ever be chosen from the descendants of Ɔreze Obi (who formed the "Low" part of High Grass Village). The Onitsha people collectively swore upon this oath, and the chiefs then threw it into the river Niger.

Onitsha people cite the outcome of this interregnum as an example of the evil influences brought into Onitsha from other communities during the nineteenth century. The case is revealing. Among other things it shows that both sides were forced to seek military support outside the town, since they were unable to rely upon internally mobilized resources for an effective decision. The outcome itself exemplifies a downgrading of an entire major village of the royal clan, and this was clearly the intention of the chiefs at the time. However, the Low [High Grass] Village remained exogamous with the rest of the Children of King Arɔlι, and a decade later the woman Nwagbɔka, a daughter of this village, was installed by the king as queen of Onitsha, so it is evident that the loss of royal status had not been effectively established.

In recounting this interregnum battle, Onitsha informants of recent times did not mention the role of Obosi warriors, but they emphasized that the bringing of Igala mercenaries into Onitsha was the inevitable evil result of contracting marriage ties outside the community. Such historical incursions are cited as one reason for the requirement that the king of Onitsha have an Onitsha mother. Another tradition recounted as a rationale for this requirement is the story of Osodi *Ɔ̃nwʊadιnsà*, a senior chief from the Ubulu-na-Ikem clan. It is said that early in the reign of King Akazua, chief Ɔnwʊadιnsa, whose mother was from the town of Obosi, betrayed the people of Onitsha to Obosi people and caused Onitsha men to be killed in ambush. This tale may allude to the incident of the late Uplands-Aro stage described in Chapter 3 in which Obosi warriors obtained guns from the people of Aro-Chukwu and then duped Onitsha in an ambush. From the Onitsha perspective, however, it is recounted primarily as an object lesson on the dangers that can be expected when an Onitsha man has a non-Onitsha mother. The genealogy of Figure 45 shows that kings Ijelekpe, Udogwu, and Akazua all had mothers of riverain or western Ibo origin; apparently the interregnum following Akazua marked a shift to the rule that Onitsha kings have Onitsha mothers, a normative change associated with increased emphasis on community endogamy and separatism. The processes of kingship succession recounted here, which were clearly associated with strong receptivity within the system to relationships and resources from outside, led eventually to a sense in the community of the divisiveness resulting from reliance on such external relations, and to intensified demands for closure and unity.

Systematic comparison of the ideal model of kingly procedures with the above sequence of events leads to the conclusion that careful and foresightful planning toward the building of kingly power began during the time of King Arɔlɩ and his sons. The inspiration no doubt came from Igala with Arɔlɩ himself, but the source of the model employed was not Igala kingship.

King Chimedie clearly tried to bolster the prestige of his sons; possibly the practice of bestowing "ɔzɔ for the child" (and even chieftaincy for the child) began with him, though a precedent had long existed in the traditions of Nri. His son Ijelekpe consolidated father–son succession by manipulating the relationship with his nonroyal mother's parents, giving them prime senior chieftaincy and a special right in succession ritual, no doubt in return for their loyalty and support of his own son as successor. His son, King Udogwu, had a brother who was a senior chief, a pattern also evident at the time of Arɔlɩ. From King Chimedie through King Udogwu and beyond, there is evidence of continual effort to build an alliance with senior chiefs from junior segments of the major opposing division of the royal clan, thus strengthening these juniors against the senior segments and fomenting conflict within that unit. While all this was occurring, the king's own major division of the royal clan also underwent progressive transformation at the higher levels, certain segments becoming specialized holders of the statuses and roles of senior priesthood (and, effectively, being denied other substantial avenues of advancement), others being assigned special privileges that distracted them from kingship pretension.

Thus the conclusion seems warranted that systematic rational effort was being undertaken to limit the size of effective royalty, to generate a father–son (and, seemingly, senior son) kingship succession, and to forge specialized, noncompetitive, solidary links with other units. A further pattern is evident in the alliances based on allocation of chieftaincy: no senior title was allowed to become the ascriptive prerogative of any village or clan, although villages pressed claims for such rights. To have permitted this would have been to lose the ability to manipulate chieftaincy, and the kings managed to avoid it. They did permit shortrun father–son and sibling successions to chieftaincy, almost certainly in the interest of insuring their own royal father–son scheme. They would later switch the locus of a particular title, preserving the previous alliance by bestowing other titles.

Some deviations from the model did occur. Although King Arɔlɩ and King Udogwu had brothers who were senior chiefs, this was not a usual practice. From the evidence of the early kings, one may judge that it was a dangerous policy, generating fraternal conflict and perhaps direct competition for kingly prerogatives. King Ijelekpe's uterine brothers might have held chieftaincy titles, but oral tradition states that each of these brothers committed some kind of abomination which forced him to flee from the king's court. These deviations suggest not irrationality of the actors, but imprecision of the model in accounting for the complexity of relations among a king and his close siblings.

A second deviation points to probable changes of certain major tactics over time. There is no evidence that strict father–son succession was sought in the early part of the Igala-Anambra stage beginning with King Arɔlɩ. This is not surprising, since he came from Igala. The first definite evidence appears at the beginning of the Uplands-Aro stage with King Ijelekpe, whose maternal support involved ties to people living in the western uplands toward Benin. This suggests an inference that succession on a Benin model was clearly formulated at this time.

A third apparent error points to failures by the putative planners themselves. The very way in which de facto senior son succession to kingship was attained and established as a rule within the king's immediate family generated structural contradictions in the wider system, contradictions that came to block the establishing of an unambiguously narrow royal line. The role of king was, as shown above, first separated from the status and role of senior patrilineage priest, a consequence of this no doubt being that the two roles became increasingly differentiated in type. From this trend, perhaps, emerged the proverb, "Senior priesthood is reached in turn; kingship is given by the public." Nevertheless, from the time of King Udogwu onward, the kings as senior sons were also eligible to become the patrilineage priests of their fathers. Therefore, although such de facto senior son succession differed from that of the priesthood (where seniority is combined with sibling equivalence), eligibility for senior priesthood could not of itself disqualify a royal segment for eligibility to kingship. The various high-level senior segments of the royal clan continued to view themselves as prospective kings; the acceptance of a strict father–son succession was never established beyond the narrow confines of the High Grass Village (and very likely only within a narrower subsegment of this group).

There was, therefore, an inherent logical and structural contradiction in the device of differentiating these parts of the royal clan as senior priests and kings. Either the early differentiation was largely unintended, and the result of ad hoc struggles for kingship, or else the planners failed to perceive the consequences of their actions for the society as a whole, simply aiming at a Benin-like senior son succession in the most direct way they thought feasible, once the role differentiation between head priests and king had been reasonably well established. I suspect that both possibilities were partially true. The probably unintended consequence resulted from favoring junior segments for chieftaincy: the emergence of an intense, society-wide and unresolved internal conflict between senior and junior sons.

A fourth apparent deviation from the model was the king's evident failure to make effective use of new manpower resources in the form of the fearsome elder dead from Igala, associated with the Children of Idoko (later part of Riverain Village). We have seen how King Ɔmɔzele's efforts to use this group to enhance his royal power led to disorder and conflict, apparently causing a sharp physical separation between king and the elder dead. This may be explained in value terms. The basic status values of the collective incarnate dead, as of the age-sets linked to it, are antithetical to kingship. Apparently the identities of men who became kings had not become sufficiently differentiated from these units to make a direct relationship with the elder dead feasible: if the king tried to control them directly, he had to become one of them. This seems the most likely explanation of this otherwise apparently irrational choice: the kingship could not interact directly with the other group while retaining its independence from it.

There was yet another deviation from the requirements of the model; in terms of the maxims, it was an irrational act for the king to confer the position of second minister upon one of the descendants of Ɔreze Obi, the original senior son of King Chimedie, who had died out of turn; for this second minister built a network of supporters that enabled one of his agnates to compete for kingship against the senior son of Akazua, and in fact very nearly to succeed in radically altering the direction of evolutionary change in Onitsha. The aftermath of that competition did follow the dictates of the model—the losers being formally condemned to an ascriptively second-rate royalty—but the subsequent conferral of queenship upon a member of the unit did not accord with the model very well.[21]

If the previous acts erred, according to the model, then the consistent conferral of disproportionately high benefits upon the Children of Dei, the so-called "junior" segment of Division is Two, was also an error in the long run. This segment had major ties to Aboh, a source of great prestige everywhere along the lower Niger River. The strength and prestige of this segment, however ambiguous its Onitsha royalty, were developing rapidly toward a capacity to claim kingship. To avoid such an error would require an analytical foresight no doubt lacking in the kings who initiated the process; once the Children of Dei had gained such massive members as were evident by the 1850s, it was hardly feasible to deny them high chieftaincy.

These latter deviations suggest the relevance of the flow of wealth and power that was mentioned in the model but not illuminated by the traditions of kingship succession. Moreover, increasing stratification and centralization were not the only trends evident in this system. I have merely argued that the Onitsha king and some of his associates were sources of systematic pressures toward such a trend; other actors performed in different ways and with different consequences.

THE DISTRIBUTION OF WEALTH, POWER, AND SOLIDARITY IN ONITSHA

Early missionaries to Onitsha had few illusions about the degree of hierarchy in its social system. The Reverend Crowther reported in 1857 that

> Onitsha being ruled merely by a nominal king, the inhabitants are very independent, I may say in a great measure lawless, troublesome, and quarrelsome neighbours . . . . The king hav-

21. It is likely that King Anazɔnwʊ bestowed queenship on a member of Low [High Grass] Village because of the strength of its members' effective demand and in place of a more powerful role. Even this led to strong opposition to him by that group.

ing very little or no power, the people fall into all kinds of mischief, to their own inconvenience, being thereby shut up from communication with their neighbours.[22]

Comments like this—that the chiefs were fighting among themselves, that the king was unable to keep order, and so on—are scattered throughout the historical accounts; the Reverend Taylor seemed even to envisage Hobbes's war of all against all when he wrote, "Every man in Onitsha is left to act as he pleases: there is nothing but disorder and confusion reigning in full force."[23] Crowther believed such internal lawlessness was the reason why Onitsha resembled an armed camp when the missionaries first arrived:

> They have a quarrel of one kind or another with the surrounding towns, and hence they are shut up by themselves; and although people from the interior come to them, they do not feel themselves safe to pass through the neighboring towns, with which they are at variance, to visit the interior. They are at quarrel with Ogidi, who lately planted a cocoa-nut, and swore, that till the nut grew, bore fruit, and was eaten, their quarrel with Onitsha should not be settled. Onitsha has been at enmity with Abo from the time of Obi Ossai, who swore that, as long as there was a son of his living, he should be at variance with Onitsha. They have lately managed to pick up a quarrel with Nkure [Nkwele], Obunike, and Nsube [Nsugbe]. . . . Nor are Onitsha and Asaba on friendly terms; so there is no free communication between the two places. Till the factory and our Mission establishment were formed here, Onitsha dared not visit the water-side, except in a large armed body. . . .[24]

These descriptions suggest a beleaguered and disorganized community, at odds with all others but lacking the minimal internal

22. Crowther and Taylor (1859:428–29).
23. Taylor (1865:133).
24. Crowther and Taylor (1859:428–29).

solidarity to cope with the situation. How much this statement reflects conditions prior to the establishment of the mission, and to what extent the mission's very arrival intensified external problems, are matters difficult to assess, but the report indicates tendencies worth examining more closely.

Internal Relations

Historical accounts show that the king could and did proclaim decisions binding upon all the people. For example, the early missionary Taylor provided this quaint translation of one proclamation made by the king's town crier as he travelled through the community:

> "Onitsha! Whereas it has been reported to me by certain parties, that the people of Ogidi have a confederacy with Oboshi [Obosi], I therefore caution all whom it may concern, that from this date, none shall go to Oboshi for trade, until the space of some weeks hence, till information shall have been obtained more satisfactorily from the king of Oboshi, whether he has broken alliance with me." [25]

Taylor reported subsequently that several Obosi men came to Onitsha and were made to swear oaths that they had made no alliance against Onitsha, and several days later "the law which the king had made as to Oboshi was repealed." [26]

Such accounts indicate that the king did act decisively, but he did so only after multiple consultations. After the proclamation cited above, it was said that an assembly of the "Council" was to be convened "to discuss what steps should be adopted." [27] Reports about these decision-making assemblies suggest that decisions were worked out publicly. As the trader Witford observed in the case of his request to establish a trading "factory," "The King con-

25. Ibid.:329–30.
26. Ibid.:330–31.
27. Ibid., p. 330.

sulted his chiefs on the one hand and the commons on the other. Committees of each left for private consultation in another part of the palace."[28] When public discussion resumed, a heated argument began concerning whether another European should be allowed to trade in Onitsha, since previous traders had caused trouble in the community. One of the old women knelt before the king and stated her view; then, according to Witford,

> At length, in a few brief sentences, a very ugly little old man, wearing a sensible head on his shoulders, spoke out, and he was cheered loudly, by a sudden burst of acclamation at each period. So it was settled to allow trade with the white man.[29]

Major decisions rested at least to some degree upon direct public expression of sentiment, though the regulation established was then promulgated as the king's will. The process appears analogous to the people's assemblies in the city-states of ancient Greece, except of course that in Onitsha the mass of the citizenry ("Those who support and dignify") were not otherwise politically passive.

If, for example, a senior chief chose to defy one of the king's regulations, the historical records suggest that the king's course of action depended very much upon the specific character of the situation. Ordinarily a powerful chief could defy the king's will with impunity. Records and oral tradition indicate that there were few meetings of the king's court that were not boycotted by at least one senior chief. A successful "boycott"[30] required the steadfast support of most subordinate chiefs of one's village and (if the village was nonroyal) an alliance with the hidden king reigning there; given such support a chief might defy the king indefinitely. Onitsha people like to recall the prowess of the senior chief of the Children of Ɔlɔsɩ, Ɔgene *Ézè Ɔ́ba,* who not only boycotted King

28. Witford (1877:175).
29. Ibid.
30. The term used is *ńsʊpʊ̀*, or "ostracism," primarily referring to a reaction made by any senior person when a junior refuses to serve homage by attending a meeting to which the senior has called him, but it may be used reciprocally.

Anazɔnwʊ but overshadowed him. As the senior chief in the major Village of Oli, he went beyond passive defiance and even performed his own emergence festival in direct competition with that of the king—a major violation of custom about which the king apparently could do nothing.

Such events sharply contradict the norms of kingship, for the king is said to have had, by virtue of his relation to the Udo shrine, the right to kill his own people and to do other things abominable for ordinary men. However, it appears that hidden kings shared these potentials within their own domains and therefore a senior chief (himself defined as a great killer) in alliance with one of them could gain a legitimacy directly rivaling that of the king.

An important additional development occurred whenever a senior chief took the title of hidden king. This was done, to cite one instance, by the senior chief of Ɔdɔje village, *Nwábʊ̀fó Ɔgene,* referred to in the early mission accounts both as Chief Ɔgene and as "Igwe" (the kingly salutation meaning "sky").[31] The missionaries first encountered King Nwabʊfo when he and the new prime minister, Ɔdɩkagbue, were engaged in a military conflict that the king of Onitsha had been unable to prevent. During this time, when several of the other senior chiefs were requesting the Reverend Taylor to reconcile them because "for seven years they had been inveterate enemies to each other," [32] Nwabʊfo proceeded to take the title of hidden king; his chief's title of Ɔgene was then conferred upon Chief *Ȯbíjiɔ̀ma* of the Children of Ɔlɔsɩ, who later became the royal prerogative usurper Eze Ɔba.[33] Thereafter, King Nwabʊfo emphasized the autonomy of Ɔdɔje village, although it remained a part of Onitsha community; in 1862 he was reported to have assembled "all of his under-chiefs" to hear his plan to establish a mission settlement at Ɔdɔje, despite the Onitsha king's strong disapproval.[34]

31. Crowther and Taylor (1859:261 ff.).
32. Ibid., p. 290.
33. Taylor (1864:140).
34. Crowther and Taylor (1864:21).

The Onitsha king appears to have been unable to prevent any independent actions undertaken by such persons within their own major villages.[35] He endured this weakness because all senior chiefs were extremely jealous of their major village autonomy, no matter how antagonistic they became toward one another, and were unwilling to support any confrontations by the king that might undermine this autonomy. Each village with a hidden king possessed, in fact, the organizational facilities for a complete societal autonomy, with the sole exception of the village's (ordinarily) exogamous nature.

However, this same segmentary system underpinning ultimately limited the independence of chiefs, for the web of ties maintained between villages created powerful pressures for reconciliation. Funerary and other ceremonial requirements, because they mobilized the entire social structure into a coherent process of exchange, made it difficult for a minority of chiefs to continue a complete boycott for a long time, if they wanted to remain members of the moral community at all.

The ultimate test of such community membership appears to have been acceptance of the moral proscription against killing a person from another village. This proscription seems generally to have been followed even by those chiefs from different villages who were fighting each other. The elaborate preparations for civil war between Ɔdɩkagbue of Children of Dei and King Nwabʊfo of Ɔdɔje, described earlier, apparently did not result in any deaths in either village.[36] A case that seems to violate this generalization was reported in the early 1870s:

> Sometime ago a son of a chief, who will be distinguished by no. 1, spitefully wounded a brother of chief no. 2 with an arrow shot from a bow at the time of public amusement at a funeral custom, which proved fatal. According to the law of the coun-

35. For example, a similar situation in the prime minister's village, Children of Dei, was reported by Crowther and Taylor (1859:282).

36. Crowther and Taylor (1859:312).

> try, the murderer must be put to death to pay his life as a satisfaction; but the chief no. 1—the father of the murderer—thought it was hard to deliver his son, the heir, to death; but there was no way of escaping—satisfaction must be given according to law—the murderer must be put to death. . . . chief no. 2 seized the murderer and perceived his death as satisfaction for the life of his murdered brother. Chief no. 1, fired with indignation that his son and heir should thus be put to death, waylaid chief no. 2 and fired gunshots at him as he was returning from the factory at riverside, which wounded him in two places on the right arm, but fortunately not mortally.[37]

"Chief no. 1" in this case was the fifth minister (Ɔgene), Eze Ɔba of Children of Ɔlɔsɩ, the later challenger of King Anazɔnwʊ; "chief no. 2" was the third minister (Odu), *Mòdozíe* of Children of Dei. Onitsha informants recount this conflict as beginning at a funeral, when drumming groups from the two villages spontaneously competed with each other and warlike passions were aroused. It is said that the son of chief no. 1 did not actually fire the arrow, but the opposing village insisted upon obtaining an exchange victim of as high prestige as possible rather than accepting the actual killer, and they therefore demanded the chief's son. Chief no. 1 had naturally been reluctant to comply.

This particular civil war went on for some time, and brought further deaths, but it might not have accelerated in this way had there been an Onitsha king on the throne to arbitrate the dispute. For the historical accounts also tell us that the war occurred during an interregnum, when "No regular king has been appointed. The country, in consequence, is in a state of anarchy," and "in this unsettled state" some of the chiefs began coming into conflict.[38] According to Onitsha oral tradition, when these feuding chiefs were suddenly confronted, sometime in the 1870s, by an

37. Crowther (1875:121–22).
38. Ibid., pp. 88–89, 121–22.

imminent invasion of Abam mercenaries under the direction of the Aro traders, the two chiefs dropped their conflict momentarily and joined to drive off the Abam. Later they resumed their feud.[39]

These accounts indicate that membership in the societal community had reached a level of commitment at which any powerful external threat would probably override internal differences, and that the Onitsha king, who played an important role in mediating these differences, had an integrative effect. Although Onitsha people today claim that most fighting against external communities was done by the village directly offended, some historical accounts suggest that at least in some instances, the king could coordinate effective military action against outsiders.

During the Onitsha–Ogidi war of 1857–58, for example, Reverend Taylor reported "the king's village and other parts busily engaged in making preparations for the ensuing war with Ogidi," noting that "throughout the whole town nothing but preparation for war was heard," and that "the king himself took an active part, and advised his subjects to have courage." [40] He took this active part although originally only the Village of Oli was offended. The war ended with a thoroughly segmentary compensation in which the Ogidi people delivered one of their members to the Village of Oli, the latter killed him in retribution for the earlier offense, and his body was then returned to Ogidi.

Thus it appears that the Onitsha king could perform an integrative role that generated community solidarity whenever a threat to the community was publicly apprehended. Under such circumstances the king should have opportunities to establish new regulations that might gain the force of moral laws. However, the only clear case encountered of the establishment of such a law under conditions of community duress was that which occurred after the kingship succession dispute between Enendʊ and Ɔdɩali (de-

39. I have found no clear evidence that such an attack actually took place, although such possibilities sustained recurrent rumors in the town during the latter half of the 1870s.

40. Crowther and Taylor (1859:432–33).

scribed previously). On this occasion, a new forbidden act appears to have been established by the chiefs in a general assembly, by means of a communal oath-medicine that was manufactured and cast into the Niger. It is said that some features of the king's court procedure were also established in ancient times by an oath, but it is clear that any binding oath which would amount to a change in land custom for Onitsha people had to be established through plenary public assembly. There is no evidence that Onitsha kings were aware of the possibilities for making innovations by means of oaths formulated by them alone; overall, their task was to integrate. Certainly, in the Onitsha–Ogidi war just cited, the king's role was clearly integrative and not mobilizative or powerful; he did not even gain the right to dispose of the man given as compensation.

Prominent chiefs seem to have been more strongly inclined and better able to innovate than was the king himself; they seem to have done so less by promulgating new laws than by violating old ones, within contexts in which community security was not directly threatened. This orientation toward innovation appears related to a strong economic activism evident in the chiefs but absent in the king.

The missionary Bishop Crowther saw great significance in the Onitsha king's seclusion, when in 1870 he reported that

> The King never goes beyond a certain limit assigned him since he was crowned, till his death, otherwise a human sacrifice must be made to propitiate the spirits of the ancestors for transgressing this royal rule. The area of land on which stands the king's palace, very rude, rickety mud walls, without any order, and the houses of his wives, including the open space surrounded with thick jungle to conceal the whole from public view, cannot exceed in all 49500 square yards of ground, in which he is confined for life during his reign. . . .
>
> Hence the King's ignorance of the state of public affairs, and

> the changes in his country, whether for improvement or for ruin. . . . This is the character of the King with whom we have to do in this place, he being ignorant of the real state of affairs, unless he has a faithful servant or representative to look around for him. The people take advantage of his seclusion to make him the dupe of their mischievous designs on whom they wish to injure, and he easily believes anything which anyone may choose to say to him.[41]

This description suggests both the king's relative material poverty and his lack of active daily control over community affairs. Seclusion in Onitsha was based upon the notion that the king was a kind of cult slave to a dangerous spirit; he was therefore, as Onitsha people say, both "above abomination" and "full of abomination." In Onitsha the forest surrounding the king's palace was equivalent to a great spirit grove, and served as a dumping-ground for loathsome things. One of the early mission stations, located on the edge of this forest, was found unsuitable because of the numerous bodies, some of them human sacrifices, that were "thrown out to rot" there.[42]

The mingled awe and loathing in which contiguous Ibo peoples held their cult slaves was similar to that with which the Onitsha people regarded this aspect of the king's identity. Perhaps the direct model for this loathsome aspect is Nri, for Onitsha people think of Nri agents as "full of abomination" because of their practice of travelling about to cover sins against the land. In both cases the kings were viewed as objects of atonement, expiation.

An important consequence of this basis of seclusion was the requirement that the king's wives must be secluded, for in Onitsha a major source of liquid disposable wealth came from the trading activities of its women. The king's wives were a drain on his domestic resources because they could not trade. His daughters might

41. Crowther (1871:125–26).
42. Church Missionary Record (1871–72:131).

become prominent traders, but their wealth was not primarily channelled to him.

Seclusion alone cannot account for royal weakness, for the kings of Benin (and their wives) were secluded, yet those kings wielded great power and wealth. The Onitsha king had to deal with several entrenched sets of statuses, the holders of which formed solidary groups dedicated to conserving their status honor. The most prominent of these were chiefs and ɔzɔ men, for both were "wealthy persons" (*ńdi-ɔ̀galanya*); to dominate persons in these statuses, the king had to mobilize greater wealth than they.

As a communications crossroads, Onitsha based its wealth very considerably on trade. The organization of craft production and trade should be studied from the perspective of the king's ability to control these economic activities, but oral traditions concerning this topic are surprisingly sparse. Whatever crafts were practiced are recalled by their village locations, but no village seems to have held any monopoly or to have developed a remarkably thriving craft. There were blacksmiths in Village of Oli, but also in Warrior Village and among the Children of Dei. Woodcarvers, potters, and weavers were similarly scattered in a number of villages. No village obtained its reputation by virtue of its craft production, and no general form of craft production seems to have been controlled by the king. Local crafts are seldom mentioned in the historical accounts. Crafts must have been unimportant here: men, including chiefs, traditionally prided themselves economically on their abilities as farmers and as title takers, women on their activities as traders.

Traditional reputations of villages do differ, and these differences have social and economic significance. Villages are distinguished from one another proverbially by certain putatively inherent social proclivities of their members. The smaller an autonomous village or clan unit, the more likely that it did some ritual service for the person of the king. Thus the clan of Isele-Awada provided him with certain protective medicines, and that of Ɔbiɔ dedicated him to its Udo shrine. The village of Isiokwe discovered a stone that prevents drought, and have since been his rainmakers. The people of Okposi-Eke (who control the nze in Village of Oli-Eke) protected the northwestern flank of his domain by transforming themselves into dangerous animals inhabiting the bush there, and their head daughter magically drew people into the great waterside market. The Mgbelekeke or Ulutu-Ado people administered the shrine to Onitsha land which he worshipped.

Larger villages are more renowned for their alleged tendencies to do certain things of more directly economic and political significance. The village of Ɔdɔje is famous for its sorcery medicines, said to be used largely by its own members in competing for social prominence (though it also manufactured war medicines), and it is noted for its palm wine traded from Obosi town. The Village of Oli-Eke is known as "those who fly over walls," i.e. for their thievery, and also for warfare. The Children of Ase are viewed as exceptionally fierce and unpredictable people (malevolent ghosts) who would constantly steal, fight, and stir up trouble. On the other hand, in the royal segment Division is Two, the Warrior Village is said to have provided traditional war leaders (ndi-ikenga) for the king. The Children of Dei plied the river and brought fish to trade in the community. In the Riverain Village, the river trading activities of its larger subunits are emphasized.

If this rather curious list of social proclivities is examined carefully, omitting those of the very small units, a remarkable correlation emerges. The inland, nonroyal villages are known for dangerous, disruptive activities, or for certain pursuits linking them to the hinterland Ibo people. These two types of activity are conceptually linked together. The alleged thievery of the Village of Oli-Eke is related to their traditional intermarriage and trade with Ogidi town, whose warriors they sometimes hired to waylay an Onitsha enemy.[43] The people of Ɔdɔje are sometimes referred to condescendingly as "Ɔdɔje of the Igbo Palm Trees," an allusion

43. Buck (n.d.:61) gives an apparent example of this from 1873–74.

to belief that they have excessive ties with Obosi town and are themselves contaminated by Igbo ancestry. The Children of Ase were thought dangerous partly because some of their ancestors are said to have come from the Obosi area. It is also claimed that descendants of the Oze Ibo people who originally occupied Onitsha land may be found in these three villages.

In contrast, the villages located toward the river are almost all defined as royal and most are known primarily for their traditional riverain ties dating from the Igala-Anambra stage or later. Waterside Village emphasized kinship relations to both Adamugu on the Igala side and to Osomari downriver, having been associated with the Osomari migration from Igala; Obikporo village (of whom it is said, "they hold nothing forbidden," because of their strange Igala customs) persisted in calling the rest of Onitsha people "Igbo," and retained social links upriver; the Children of Dei welcomed and protected their Aboh relatives who came to Onitsha marketplace; the Low [High Grass] Village is famous for its trading queens and their Igala ties.

One village, centrally located in the community, is not proverbially characterized by fighting, doctoring, or trading: the High Grass Village, from which most of the Onitsha kings have come. The proverb that defines their behavior is: "High Grass Village are those who lie and deceive" (*Ɔ́gbè-ɔ̀zala, ń̄di ǹtú nà ághʊ̀ghɔ*), a reputation to which recent informants from that village would allude with a certain wry pride.

If the distribution of these specialized activities is considered with reference to the village layout (Figure 37), the degree to which the traditional community was divided by the diverse external ties of its constituent villages becomes apparent. The mostly nonroyal, inland-lying villages were oriented largely toward various hinterland Ibo communities with whom they had long-standing relations, while the royal groups located toward the river maintained a variety of ties with riverain peoples. In their broadly economic interests, then, the major subunits of the community were strongly centrifugally oriented. Since chiefs were the leaders of these villages, they were in positions to control these diverse external relationships directly. Located in the geographical center of this outward-oriented community was the core royal village, famous mainly for its adeptness at social deception, and in the center of this village resided a secluded king who hoped to tap as much of the trade wealth as possible.

The Onitsha king was unable to control this diversity of trade directly, for he confronted a highly organized women's trading association that represented all the women of Onitsha and directed market activities. He had to deal with a series of chiefs who traded through women related to them and carried out many trade negotiations in their own compounds and behind the king's back. The king relied mostly upon his ascriptive rights to receive periodic homage service from the wealthy chiefs and women traders, and his slaves invaded the market from time to time to "lift the covers of the canoes" as a form of taxation. In keeping with his general immobility and his small staff of personal retainers, his trade income came largely from these established rights of prestation—the missionaries, for example, found him an endless source of demands for gifts. He could, of course, close the major market by proclamation, but not for any length of time without the mass support of the community.

The king's other main source of regular fees came from his performance of juridical services. His regular court and its requisite kola for talk have already been described as part of a community-wide pattern of recompense for juridical services. Most important among his sources of wealth from arbitrating disputes, however, appears to have been his control of the sasswood ordeal.

Sasswood was employed by the king for a variety of purposes, from testing a woman suspected of witchraft (when it was drunk by the suspect herself) to testing accused thieves, or chiefs suspected of conspiracy (when it was administered to a fowl). The extent of the king's reliance upon such sources of income is hinted at in the mission accounts, which reported that he received three thousand one hundred twenty cowries for a sasswood draft administered to one witchcraft suspect; when the missionaries admonished him against the practice, they had to report his reply that "he lives by it [administering the drink], as he does not move about to earn his living." [44]

His lack of mobility and his prestation oriented approach to trading distinguishes the king from his senior chiefs. The chiefs expected periodic gifts from traders in recognition of their status, but they did not rely on such tokens or upon their court fees for their major income. Chiefs moved about the town considerably, directed trading activities, and initiated various efforts to augment their wealth and that of their villages. Most major land transfers recounted in tradition appear to have involved the aggrandizement of chiefs; some of the senior chiefs' wives held prominent positions as queen's councillors,[45] and as such held important advantages in trade.

Although the chiefs' emulation of the king fell short of assuming his full condition as cult slave, they shared some of his freedom from traditional norms. They could therefore innovate in a variety of ways. For example, the senior chiefs were free from the requirement of taking oaths as representatives of their patrilineages, and since this meant that they did not have to testify directly by oath to the righteousness of traditional relations, they tended more willingly than others to risk violating these traditions. Oral traditions indicate that chiefs were responsible for most of the attempts to usurp land of weaker patrilineages. It was the senior patrilineage priests who had to take oaths on such matters in court —oaths that might, it was believed, cost them their lives. Since it was a general Onitsha belief that the spirits would kill people who transgressed land custom, a chief who violated a tradition

44. Taylor (1865:147–48). This amount constitutes "money four *ngugu*" (ngugu = 780). At the time, a slave was worth about four times this amount.

45. For example, see Dobinson (n.d.).

and continued to thrive had apparently acted legitimately after all. The usurpation of hidden kingship cited earlier is an example of such an accomplishment.

The chiefs were therefore the source of much important dynamic process in the society. A major example of this was the successful seizure of the king's traditionally unique right to bestow ɔzɔ for the child upon his favored sons. This royal custom had existed at least from the time of King Chimedie, but then (apparently during the reign of King Udogwu or early in that of Akazua), it was emulated by a prominent leader of the Children of Ɔlɔsι, *Nwágbòlu* the Cow-killer.[46] Whenever this emulation was accomplished, its perpetrator did it without relinquishing his previous titles as the Onitsha king had traditionally done; because of this modification, the procedure soon became popular and spread to become common practice. The structural consequences of this change therefore included not only a partial loss of the king's role differentiation from others, but also a general intensification of achievement competition within the society as a whole.

This innovation, one of the more potent devised by persons other than kings in Onitsha, threatened to transform the covert internal patrilineage competition into a more revolutionary situation in which ascriptively senior men might be dominated by their wealthier brothers' sons. This disruptive potential was lessened by setting limits on the son's ɔzɔ rights during his father's lifetime; nonetheless it sharply upgraded achievement values in the community.

It was this capacity of prominent men to emulate some of the king's most important prerogatives (while avoiding some of the limiting requirements attached to him) that continually limited the differentiation of the royal line's style of life. The king, moreover, was unable to block such emulation unless it could be clearly

46. The name suggests that he may have seized still another royal prerogative, but I failed to inquire into the significance of it. This emulation may have occurred when Ɔlɔsι and Isiokwe villages split away from title sharing with the descendants of Arɔlι; such a split could have justified the act.

shown to the public that the security of the entire community was threatened by the change. This fact meant that a thorough emulation of the social identity of kingship itself was a distinct possibility.

Historical records and oral tradition from Onitsha suggest that by the time the British colonial government was preparing to take over continuous social control of the community, toward the turn of this century, the chief Ɔgene Eze Ɔba—who was, incidentally, the son of Nwagbolu the Cow-killer—did in fact present himself as a second king fully on a par with the king of Onitsha. His assumed title, Eze Ɔba, combines the Ibo royal title with that of the king of Benin, and Onitsha people say that for a time he was more powerful than King Anazɔnwʋ. His downfall came not through a direct confrontation with the king but through a covert appeal to the Niger Company that provided evidence of his extensive slave dealings.

An even more convincing case of emulation has come to light in the mission documents from Onitsha.[47] Mission records of the efforts by Enendʋ and his people from Low [High Grass] Village to seize the kingship after the death of King Akazua provide details which clearly indicate that the aims of both candidates shifted during the progress of the competition. *At one stage of the competition, two separate kings were being established in the community.*

After chief Ɔdɩali, the surviving son of King Akazua, began to undertake the ceremonies of succession,

> another man by name Anendo (having one of his eyes injured) said that he too wished to be a king and performed his own ceremonies likewise. The greater part of the town sided with the young Prince, with three of the chiefs at their head. Those

47. I state the point in this way because I encountered this information after this book had been completed in essentially its present form. On the basis of the other information available, I had concluded that a reversion to multiple kingship was imminent in the community, and made this hypothesis part of my conclusions.

who wished that the system of many kings should be introduced, and those who were eyeing the annual presents made to the king joined with the latter.[48]

The missionaries greeted this development with dismay as they anticipated paying what they already regarded as onerous annual tribute to two kings instead of one. They called a meeting to discuss the interregnum, including among their major topics "the evils of the present action of assuming too many kings." Written minutes were taken of this meeting, which included both resident Sierra Leonean traders and churchmen; during it several of them voiced opinions.

The Reverend I. T. George, whose own journals reflect astute observation of local affairs, argued that for both missionaries and merchants, "it is impossible to serve many masters of contrary opinions. It is impossible to give adequate presents to all." But he counselled caution "that we should let our opinions be neutral as regards the nominating one or more persons to be king or kings." J. P. Romaine, a veteran resident trader, agreed with this, and his view was recorded that "it was a past custom of theirs to have more than one king, and that he had met Nzeku's father as a living testimony of his statement. And for ought we know the people would like to recommence the custom."[49] After the meeting, the group tried to arrange a meeting with the townspeople in order to caution them, but were ignored.

The woman Okwuma then returned from Igala, with her son Enwezɔ together with "troops, ammunitions, slaves to be sacrificed and provisions." Each candidate "went on making feasts and killing persons, regardless of the other."[50]

In effect, after these acts two kings existed in Onitsha, for both

48. Buck (n.d.:43). Grammatical errors in these and other quotations in this series are in the original. The reference to one damaged eye suggests a disqualifying physical defect; the reference to three chiefs supporting the prince implies that the other three senior chiefs supported the pretender.

49. Buck (n.d.:44–46). The reference is to the hidden king *Ńzekwu* of Ubene clan.

50. Langley (n.d.).

men were conducting human sacrifices with autonomy and without confrontation. Then, according to the mission account, Enendʊ raised the stakes, sending a message directing King Ɔdιali "to come down from his throne because the town was too small to contain two kings and he Anendo was the king. Obi Ediari told him to be going on with what he was doing and let him and his affairs alone." [51] Enendʊ provoked a confrontation, laying claim to the king's traditional fishing place along the river Niger; Ɔdιali could not countenance this,

> and when Ediari was sending his people to go and maintain his right he told them not to take guns but simply sticks. They were not to kill anybody because all were his people. But the Igara people with Enweruzo at their head and the three chiefs of Onitsha were regardless of life and property and so without any ceremony opened fire at once on their opponents, burnt down their houses and committed fearful ravages many were wounded and one was killed.[52]

After that, King Ɔdιali "sent to a town in the Ibo country for some Ibo warriors," and collected a "grand army" from among them and his own men at home; then he retaliated as, "very early in the morning the Igara people were driven away and a great many of them killed. . . . Nearly the whole of the houses of lower Ubozra were destroyed by fire. Anendo and his party fled." [53]

Thus not only was emulation a possibility, it actually occurred (with the backing of three Onitsha chiefs), and the only reason for its failure appears to have been the hubris of Enendʊ. This emulation would very likely have led to a more general loss of royal differentiation. Such structural loss appears to have occurred somewhat earlier in the Ibo community of Asaba across the Niger from Onitsha. According to an Asaba tradition recorded at the

51. Ibid.
52. Ibid.
53. Ibid. "Lower Ubozra" refers to "lower *Ogbeɔzala*," i.e. "lower high grass village."

beginning of this century, at some earlier time there had reigned in Asaba a King Inalu, remembered as an avaricious and extortionist ruler. After his death, the Asaba people learned that his successor was to be a person equally grasping and oppressive. While the would-be successor travelled to Benin to have his rule legitimized, seven Asaba chiefs took the eze title. When the new king returned, he found himself occupying a position as primus inter pares in a council of eight kings. At about the time that the first Christian missionaries arrived, the process had been extended after an internecine war, so that ten men were reigning as "kings." [54] By the 1870s, one missionary report on Asaba commented about "the alarming increase of kings in the country—we counted no less than four hundred and five." [55] By 1900 there were some two hundred holders of the eze title in Asaba—roughly the same as the number of ɔzɔ men in Onitsha.[56]

The previous evidence suggests that an analogous loss of differentiation was incipient in Onitsha. The threat of structural loss did not end with the death of Enendʊ, for there were other sources of increasingly high conflict within the royal clan. The Onitsha kings' tactic of conferring the position of prime minister on one of the Children of Dei in the Division is Two royal segment was on the verge of producing unanticipated consequences. This unit had become numerically and socially so powerful that its prime minister might, at any interregnum, have seized the opportunity to shift his support to one of the small but royally eligible units of Division is Two. The Children of Dei had actually outstripped the king's village numerically, and such an interregnum would almost certainly have resulted in stalemate.

Such a situation did develop at the beginning of full colonial control of Onitsha, when the king died at the turn of the twentieth century and the prime minister supported the candidacy of a mem-

54. Spencer (1901).
55. D. C. Crowther (1879).
56. Spencer (1901).

ber of Village of Abʊ, a descendant of the early king Tasia. After this pretender had won the throne (through the influence of the Roman Catholic Mission and the British government agents), a senior chief from among the Children of King Arɔlɩ refused to bow, and instead assumed powers equivalent to kingship by appointing his own assemblage of chiefs. This could have been expected had a stalemate developed even in the absence of a colonial power; as hidden kings from the nonroyal segments followed suit in appointing their own chiefs, chieftaincy would have become a village-based title system.

Unless he could generate a public sense of threat to the security of the community as a whole, there was little an Onitsha king could do directly about these threats to his identity. Several sources of structural inertia favored his position: the pressures of ceremonial obligation, the special ritual privileges held by some social units, the chiefs' war organization that cut across village units, the king's commitments to confer chiefs' titles to the chiefs' sons; but all these structures were probably objects of intense political manipulation, especially during interregnum (if recent social processes are any guide to the past). Chiefs were not effectively discouraged by these pressures.

Indeed, chiefs had sources of power not available to the king, for they could participate in decisions to mobilize the collective incarnate dead. For the prime minister, this meant access to power more formidable than any held by the king, for when the incarnate dead of Onitsha the Nine Clans emerged into the community to proclaim or enforce some public decision, the king was helpless to forestall them; the authority of the incarnate dead superseded his own. This power gave the chiefs a potential influence over community events much greater than that wielded by the king through his messengers, because the age-sets—the greatest source of massed manpower available in the town—would mobilize to support the incarnate dead.

However, reliance upon the collective incarnate dead and the age-sets for ultimate enforcement of public order meant, in turn, that the society remained basically segmentary and nonstratified in its distribution of power, because the leadership of these two organizations enjoyed, through their interrelations, an independence from chiefs as well as from kings and patrilineage priests. Their autonomous efforts could operate against the chiefs; the early missionary Reverend Strong saw this happen:

> Onitsha young men about 2–300 came down from the town armed with cutlasses and wooden weapons and occupied our church yard bringing along with them their "egugus" otherwise called "Mors." Nine in numbers—persons dressed in straw, ragged clothes, wooden and rudely carved heads and some other materials all intended to strike any beholder irresistibly with terror and fright.
>
> They intended to occupy the church yard and the ground just below the limit of it where the only 2 roads from the town to the waterside meet in order to prevent any chief or chiefs going to trade in the waterside with the merchants acting directly against the law of the young men and women.[57]

This report indicates that nine incarnate dead represented Onitsha Nine Clans, thus that plenary community action was being undertaken, that the incarnate dead were supported by armed youthful age-sets, and that the mobilization against the chiefs was aimed at enforcing a ruling established by young men and the women of the community, probably the women's trading council. They must have arrived at this ruling through consultation with the elder dead, with the age-set ruling the land, and possibly with the king or with some of the chiefs; but the decision appears to have been substantially their own.

Mission accounts suggest that the orator-spokesman's role operated in every great community decision. It could decisively alter the outcome of an argument because of the public force such a man could mobilize. For example, in 1868 when Christian con-

57. Strong (n.d.), from the section titled "Disturbance 7 April 1885."

verts were beginning to confront and disrupt some traditional social processes, the king, under great pressure from the community, passed a regulation against attendance at church. The missionaries obtained an audience with the king in full public assembly, where they protested their innocence of various charges brought against them. When their arguments had brought the assembly to consider repealing this new regulation, there was an interruption and the

> town orator immediately stood out; and after a long harangue, showing that their ancestors were praying people ere we came into the country . . . he closed with these words—that from this day henceforth no man, woman, or child should be allowed to go to church for public worship, nor be allowed to go to any house for social prayers. The whole assembly with the king gave one unanimous and hearty consent in the affirmative and the orator met with applause from every side.[58]

The mission was then ordered to close. This outcome of the meeting was not merely a device staged by the king or his chiefs, though there can be no doubt that some of them were strongly opposed to the mission. In fact, after the missionaries had made some concessions, the king strove to convince his people to permit reopening of the church, and the chiefs appear to have concurred in this effort.

The orator-spokesmen enjoyed this autonomy as representatives of the age-sets and the collective incarnate dead; they were effective at the community level only when total community welfare was generally thought to be at stake and land custom threatened. Therefore any chief who wished to emulate the king or to create other precedents could do so only if he could be certain of the support of the collective incarnate dead and the age-sets within his major village, for under such circumstances these organizations could not be mobilized as units at the civic level, and the power of the orator-spokesman would consequently be neutralized.

58. George (n.d.:018/25).

The weight of evidence on internal relations in the society, then, supports the view that the sources of societal political power in Onitsha were predominantly segmentary in their distribution and were largely controlled segmentally. In Eisenstadt's terms, the political role of the king was overwhelmingly integrative or party-political; [59] he had little executive capacity and moderate administrative rights. Senior chiefs competed strongly with the king in such party-political activities, and they had seized much of the initiative in executive and administrative matters. As a result, executive and administrative activities were highly segmented in this society: the senior chiefs were multiple and competing, and the strongest agents of enforcement were the autonomous, strongly tradition-oriented age-sets and collective incarnate dead.

The king's isolation from sources of power made him politically merely a primus inter pares among a competitive, deeply divided "patrician" elite social stratum made up of hidden kings and chiefs. The society was socially stratified, but executive political control lay ultimately in the hands of the lower social stratum of "Those who support and dignify," a stratum internally divided among ɔzɔ men, senior priests, Nkpalo, young men, etc., but whose organizing structures were the age-sets and collective incarnate dead, led by a dynamic orator-spokesman.

External Relations

Evidence from Benin and Igala suggests that the Onitsha hidden kings were comparable to the "Seven Uzama" of Benin, and that the identity of the Benin ɔba evolved out of its structural base in this group. The oral tradition suggests that the ɔba institutionalized his differentiation by fighting the uzama when they tried to emulate his rights. This tactic was apparently based on the ɔba's bestowal of distinctive titles on his personal palace retainers, but also on his expansion of the territorial range of his control by sending royal sons out as chiefs of newly dependent communities.

Again, the Onitsha hidden kings appear to have been equivalent

59. See Chapter 1, p. 20.

to the nine patriarchs (gala mela) of Igala. The Igala kings seem to have overshadowed the patriarchs both by sending their sons as chiefs to colonize interior regions, and by establishing personal staffs to eunuchs and of palace servants (edibo). In Igala the palace servants apparently arranged to buy their titles through the eunuchs, thus gaining some structural autonomy even while they remained the king's immediate protectors and while the patrilineal royal family established partially autonomous fiefs.

In both Benin and Igala, the rise of the king's prestige was associated with colonizing expansion, but in Igala increasingly fluid and unstable population conditions in the colonized areas may have contributed to a loss of kingly control. Information from the kingdom of Aboh is insufficient for an assessment of its developmental trends, but the king's use of marriage with tributary riverain trading communities as a means of expanding his control, and the political divisiveness of these external ties within Aboh itself, are relevant to understanding conditions in Onitsha.

Two avenues of colonial expansion by Onitsha were available: to extend the system along and across the river, or to expand into the eastern interior. In either case, there were two broad alternative possibilities of manipulation: to extend cultural-juridical services that would bring increasing prestige and wealth into the community, or to expand the domain by conquest.

Since the riverain peoples provided most of the material advantages that Onitsha held over the hinterland tribes, crucial external relations were river-directed. Indeed, although the traditional view of Onitsha royalty points to ancestry from King Chima, possession of strong riverain ties with Igala- or Aboh-related peoples also seems effectively to have conferred membership in the royal clan on a village unit.

The riverain trade, however, lacked clearly defined structure. Sporadically punctuated with punitive canoe raids by one or another of the river powers, it was otherwise segmented and noncollective in overall operation, in Onitsha as elsewhere. Onitsha trade relations were segmented in that each Onitsha village had its own distinctive favored external ties; they were noncollective in that within each village persons had diversifying external ties to different sets of maternally linked kinsmen. Onitsha people encouraged such relations by giving their daughters in marriage to riverain people while denying them to hinterland Ibo. They were also aware that they tended to separate their roles as daughters' children or mothers' parents from their roles as Onitsha citizens, and that the trade interests of the former might conflict with the political requirements of the latter.

These manifold, diversified, and shifting relationships among the riverain towns, which inhibited the development of stable control over the river trade by any riverain community, generated divisive tendencies within the towns themselves, and intensified conflict within Onitsha, also inhibited unified collective action by Onitsha against riverain groups. The historical accounts suggest the operation of typical Onitsha social processes in trade disputes against riverain outsiders. For example, in 1864 Obijiɔma, senior chief of the heterogeneous Village of Oli, had a dispute with a prominent Aboh trader residing along the riverside under the protection of the prime minister (himself a member of the Aboh-linked Children of Dei). Chief Obijiɔma abducted this Aboh trader's son to his village. The prime minister retaliated by sending his men from Children of Dei to fight the Village of Oli, where they set fire to the chief's house. As civil war appeared imminent, the king had to call upon the missionaries to help mediate the dispute.[60] Evidence of Onitsha unity against a riverain outsider is very rare from any source.

60. George (n.d.:CA3/018/22). In this instance, as in numerous others in the record, a missionary played a mediatory role whose significance is difficult to assess, but the parties did agree to come before the king and Rev. George witnessed the decision. The prime minister paid three bags of cowries and a he-goat to Chief Obijiɔma for the losses due to fire; "the little boy was then delivered, and the national oath being brought, each party swore obedience to the king, and peace and goodwill towards each other henceforth. The assembly then dispersed." The role of mediator between chiefs seems to have been an important but limited intrusion that the missionaries were able to make into the system, an intrusion that sometimes worked but often failed.

Internal divisiveness was related to another factor influencing Onitsha's conduct of its riverain relations: its lack of autonomous military and trading canoe forces. Onitsha people themselves have rationalized this as a straightforward technological limitation by claiming they are inherently unable to swim, but several Onitsha villages had members who built and plied canoes. The failure to emulate seems to have been largely organizational, for Onitsha people developed nothing like canoe teams organized for river fighting and allowed the craftsmanship available to wane without encouragement. Prior elaboration of riverain technology and warfare methods by the Aboh, Osomari, and Anambra river peoples, and the substantially uplands derivation of the early dominant population of Onitsha, probably discouraged systematic elaboration of riverine skills at Onitsha. Because of this lack, Onitsha remained dependent on congenial relations with some of the riverain peoples for a flourishing trade, and this organizational passivity further encouraged a noncollective orientation among those conducting its riverain trade.

Such passivity, in turn, appears to have precluded Onitsha's development as a cultural-juridical center mediating river affairs, despite its position beside a major boundary market of the river system. Its king had some renown for his ability to conduct trials by sasswood ordeal, but this notoriety was apparently more important across the river than along its length. Without some basis for prestige in specifically riverine activities, the people of Onitsha did not conceive of any more general cultural devices that might have given them greater prominence in this area.

Oral tradition suggests that Onitsha did make some efforts toward colonial expansion into its eastern hinterlands: the king once had an agent in Obosi town; several hinterland peoples regularly sent representatives to salute him during his emergence; some of the contiguous peoples paid him leopard tribute in exchange for the loan of Onitsha firearms. As a people, Onitsha community is proverbially regarded by its Ibo neighbors as socially different from themselves. It is said that "the word of Onitsha is not as it is spoken," indicating that they are deceitful and manipulative in their relations with outsiders. Onitsha people concur in this proverbial assessment, saying that the hinterland people are much less artful and diplomatic in social relations than they are.[61] This cultural stereotyping suggests that outsiders attribute to the Onitsha community a colonizing or manipulative perspective similar to that attributed by nonroyal Onitsha villages to the king's village. Finally, Onitsha people were expanding their territory to the north, gradually absorbing farmlands of their Nsugbe and Nkwele neighbors (people classed as *Ìgbo ádàgbe,* closer to riverain people—olu—than to Igbo proper) by peacefully leasing their lands. This leasing was being done mostly by members of villages from the Onitsha royal clan.

All the evidence suggests efforts to expand the Onitsha domain by cultural services linked with economic advantage, and not by conquest (except perhaps the early attempt against Obosi). The outcome overall seems to have been unsuccessful. In cultural legitimacy, the Onitsha king was clearly inferior to the Nri king, whose ritual prerogatives remained a major focus of orientation for the hinterland peoples.[62] Probably the ritual superiority of Nri made it difficult for Onitsha kings to persuade towns to shift commitments to them without applying force or at least controlling a strong, consistent trade advantage.

The leasing of fertile lands to the north by Onitsha royal groups was balanced by an increasing tendency for nonroyal Onitsha people to lease their less fertile lands to the south to Obosi people. The leasing process was in part a response to increasing popula-

61. For example, they ridicule the people of Nsugbe for their alleged crude directness in coming to the heart of a matter, by referring to such behavior as "breaking a coconut Nsugbe style." (This is done by splitting the nut in two with one mighty blow of a machete.)

62. Indeed, there is evidence that the Onitsha king enjoyed greater prestige west of the Niger than in the hinterlands east of it, for of the towns reported to have consulted his sasswood ordeal, several are on the west bank but only one is on the east.

tion pressures from the south; its economic imbalance within Onitsha probably contributed to the difference between royals and nonroyals, but the pattern does not reveal a major economic expansion overall.

No evidence suggests an effort in Onitsha to build a military force capable of assailing the hinterland tribes. Instead, there was ritual lending of firearms and, indeed, the hiring of hinterland mercenaries by Onitsha people to fight some of their own battles. Any goal of conquest was inhibited by the hinterland kinship attachments held by the nonroyal villages, and this may have discouraged attempts to build a genuinely unified military organization.

Other forces at work in the eastern hinterlands themselves had a bearing on the relations between Onitsha and the tribes there. In the earliest explorer accounts, several eastern uplands towns were reported to attend the Onitsha waterside market, and they no doubt depended upon orderly, tributary relations with Onitsha people for access to that market. However, the first missionaries to land at Onitsha thereafter found it an armed camp, apparently besieged by "their Ibo neighbors," and these observers inferred that "in this state of things our establishments at Onitsha were most welcome to them."[63]

By 1865 it was evident that disturbances were occurring in the interior. Reverend Taylor reported:

> There is a war now carried on between Obunike and part of Nkwere, which lies north of Onitsha. . . . Obunike, being valiant, defeated Nkwere, and burnt down their houses and drove them. They took shelter at Nsube. A desperate fight is now carried on between Oboshi and Nkpo, lying eastward of Onitsha. . . . And there is fighting between Ogidi and Umuoji, which lies north-east of Onitsha.[64]

63. Crowther and Taylor (1859:32–33).
64. Taylor (1866:205).

If this account is accurate, all the tribal communities adjacent to Onitsha were suffering the impact of what Taylor described as "fearful massacres." Oral tradition from some of these interior communities suggests that such multiple intertribal wars were taking place throughout the second half of the nineteenth century and had probably occurred earlier. A distinctive feature of this warfare was a general trend toward the specialization, in each town, of warrior associations that not only fought wars for their own communities but also made themselves available for hire to other towns. This practice appears to have had important consequences for the social systems of the area; it had a bearing on the military effectiveness of Onitsha.

The best evidence currently available for consideration of this problem comes from Nnewi, a town some twenty miles southeast of Onitsha which traded with the riverain peoples of Oguta and Osomari and came under the traditional ritual jurisdiction of the Nri-associated Oreri kings.[65] Nnewi was divided into four major social units, each represented by a senior eze, who was succeeded ordinarily by his senior son. Genealogies were obtained for the lines of kings from these four units, *Òtólo, Úruagʊ, Nnéwîchi,* and *Úmʊ̀dim;* events associated with the kings suggest that a series of wars were fought among the units, and between each unit and other groups outside Nnewi, during the latter part of the nineteenth century.

At various times the Uruagu "kings" hired riverain (olu) mercenaries to assist them in subduing other groups, including not only contiguous towns such as Nnobi and Orifite but also the people of Nnewichi in Nnewi itself. On other occasions, they sought the help of Abariba and Ada mercenaries allied with the Aro-Chukwu oracle agents, attacking both other divisions of Nnewi

65. I conducted research in Nnewi for several weeks during my stay at Onitsha. The information obtained during that time was greatly enriched when I subsequently gained access to the excellent study published by the Nnewi historian J. C. Alutu. The account that follows draws on both sources, using my own data partly as a check on the accuracy of Alutu's (Alutu 1963).

and the riverain towns as well. The kings of Otolo, in turn, not only joined with the other two Nnewi groups to fight Uruagʋ, but also, in alliance with communities outside Nnewi, lent their men out as mercenaries to raid the riverain settlements. The kings of Nnewichi fought still other wars with outside communities, obtaining their own mercenary assistance. The people of Nnewi in general characterize as "The Great War" (*ágha úkwu*) one period which, judging from the genealogies, ran from the 1860s to the 1890s.

The evidence suggests that during this period of seemingly continual, constantly shifting warfare, none of the four major units was able to attain any stable domination over the others. A defeated group might temporarily lose part of their land or their control over a valuable market site, but they could simply bide their time, arrange for the military assistance of one or another mercenary group from some other community, and eventually recoup their losses.

As Ottenberg has shown, such patterns of diversified and shifting external relationships also existed in the oracle systems operating in other Ibo areas east and southeast of Onitsha.[66] In conditions as unstable as these, with access to mercenary support a decisive but thoroughly inconstant factor in the intertribal relations of most Ibo communities, it becomes obvious how difficult systematic state-formation would have been. For example, it becomes clear why Nri, even as the cultural center of Ibo country, was totally unable to parlay primordial cultural prestige into an expanding and powerful kingdom during the era of the slave trade. Located in an overpopulated area with relatively poor soils, Nri also had no advantages in access to the most powerful sources of mercenary support: the riverain Ibo and the various warrior groups linked to the Aro-Chukwu. These two sources were becoming increasingly competitive with one another in their services as mercenaries.

66. See Chapter 1, pp. 24–25.

Onitsha had opportunities rather different from those of Nri, but as time went on it faced similar limitations. Although from the beginning of the Uplands-Aro stage it was more favorably located for access to firearms than were its hinterland neighbors, by the latter part of that stage each of these neighbors could also obtain some guns from riverain or Aro sources, and each could establish relations with other groups that might supply mercenaries for specific limited wars. These external conditions made it quite unfeasible for Onitsha to undertake any political colonization of its hinterlands.

Indeed, under the intersocietal conditions in which they lived during the latter part of the Uplands-Aro stage (i.e. by the 1850s), Onitsha community appears to have been "drawing in its horns"; the late contraction of the community nucleus and the growing preference for community endogamy indicated more a rising sense of external insecurity than of increasing unity against outsiders. That Onitsha had little sense of the possibility of mastering the external situation through military action is suggested in two of the mission accounts. One reported a public address by the king that referred to the dangers coming from the river: "for years past we have been under the claws of Aboh. They kill and take us captives from our own market place." [67] According to a later report, a rumor reached the community in 1876 that "the Abams or Abribams were coming in numbers incalculable, and that they fully determined to drive all before them . . . into the sea." The response of Onitsha people as recounted by the missionary was to repair their protective spirit shrine "Old Woman" on the eastern flanks of the town, and when on several occasions the spirit was believed to have given the sign of impending attack, "the whole town was deserted." [68]

67. George (n.d.:018/20).
68. John (n.d.:022/2).

14 EVOLUTIONARY TRENDS IN ONITSHA SOCIETY AND CULTURE

ONITSHA AS SEGMENTARY LINEAGE SYSTEM: A MODEL

In examining Onitsha Ibo society from an evolutionary perspective, one may approach it with different evolutionary models in mind. An illuminating model is that of segmentary systems; if one considers kinship and religious symbols and structures, setting aside all elements that do not fit a classical groupcentric model of segmentary unilineal descent systems, the image of Onitsha society that emerges is almost a caricature of groupcentric segmentary system theory.

The Onitsha world-view (if we abstract out, for the moment, all components that were not kinship-related) defined a man strictly as a microcosm of his community: both individuals and their patrilineal descent groups as collectivities possessed shrines to their land spirits; both had ancestors buried nearby, with whom they were identified; both possessed ɔfɔ staves that provided righteous power in mediating relations between the unit and these spirits and ancestors; both perceived their continuity through time as depending upon patrilineal succession and right. A series of senior patrilineage priests represented both the ancestors and a series of congregations of the living, each associated with ɔfɔ staves of varying power. Since the ɔfɔ of a father superseded that of his son, the identity of the individual was submerged in that of his community: as patrilineage priest or member, he would inevitably act as an agent of his descent group, because that was how he would conceive himself (given the stock of symbols available) and that was what others like him would expect. Viewed over time, the link forged by the symbol system between individuals and collectivities was most intimate.

Juridically, each patrilineage unit was substantially autonomous, regulating its interaction through its own system of courts. It acted as a unit in cases of external conflict, was a unit of blood responsibility and vengeance. It was an autonomous fiscal unit.

When ecological and economic factors are regarded from the segmentary system point of view, it is difficult to imagine a more isomorphic match than that between the units of production and the wider social system and culture in which these structures operated. Onitsha settlement pattern took the form of a set of nucleated, patrilocally and patrilineally ordered village units, each of which faced an outward-expanding segment of farmland held in trust by its senior patrilineage priests and worked jointly by its members and their wives. An authority system based on the paternal ɔfɔ was ideally suited to this situation.

The society as a whole was integrated through its marriage patterns as structured by wide-ranging norms of exogamy. Through marriage, individuals established diverse relations outside their descent groups. If fruitful these relations might be perpetuated (through the mystical symbols of mothers and daughters) as collective, mutually exogamous alliances between sizable segments of different descent groups. Thus a web of kinship wove the diverse patrilineal descent groups of Onitsha into an integrated whole. This societal integration was symbolized in the notion of Onitsha the Nine Clans, conceived as an ancient and sacred collectivity. The boundaries of this societal unit were not, however, very clearly defined; diverse marriage relations and alliances were made with groups outside Onitsha as well as within it.

This outline of Onitsha as segmentary descent group system closely approximates one ideal type of such systems. From the rest of the study we know that this model is seriously distorted and truncated in that it ignores extensive sectors of Onitsha social life; however, no study of Onitsha which failed to take full account of these profoundly segmentary descent group features could be in any sense satisfactory. Such distortion usefully emphasizes and clarifies the nature and scope of these conservative structures; that the Onitsha patrilineage system has such strong potential for normative self-sufficiency is crucial for the structure of the society as a whole. Controlled distortion is also of value in that it directs attention to the significant points of distortion and omission themselves.

DISTORTIONS IN THE MODEL: RELIGIOUS SYMBOLS, SOCIAL IDENTITIES, AND DESCENT GROUPS

Man and Divinity

The Onitsha religious system related a person not only to his ancestors but also directly to divinity. The personal god possessed some aspects that were ancestrally conditioned; other parts of it were nonancestral. It was also a unity greater than the sum of its parts—the being as a whole was part of the cosmic order of the sky, and its "vessel" became purified as a unit through the taking of ɔzɔ title. The broadest implication of the personal god in Ibo religion was that any man might approximate a divine condition, first by taking ɔzɔ title. Moreover, the personal spirit most highly regarded as a means to such attainment was not related to ancestors but rather to age-sets; the ikenga, associated with the strength of a man's right arm and his aggressive will to butt his way forward against obstacles, was viewed as part of his mystical relationship to his ghostly contemporaries, not to his ancestors. Thus the ultimate symbolic references of both ɔzɔ title and ikenga were strikingly universalistic in character, in that they related every man on the one hand to the cosmic order, on the other to persons of the same age as himself regardless of their descent.

Patrilineage Ideals and Ɔzɔ Purification

If these universalistic symbols of achievement are then related to the fact that each ɔzɔ title system as a social structure was deeply embedded in the extremely ascriptive and particularistic context of the Onitsha patrilineage, a profound contradiction is apparent. It becomes partly intelligible in terms of the competition operative in patrilineages, but becomes fully so only in terms of historical inferences. Ɔzɔ title formed part of a very old kingship complex based at Nri town, which at some time in the distant past was widely emulated, its major symbols (nze, ɔzɔ, the eze title) ultimately captured by manifold patrilineal descent groups in various communities of the region. This would explain its direct link to divinity, its being an achievement structure fully embedded in an ascriptive social matrix, and the importance attached to comparing fees between clan units so that a general community standard would be upheld—its universalistic character.[1]

Structuring these religious symbols of personal identity into social roles led to intense competition and conflict within patrilineages. However old this conflict may have been, it is remarkable that patrilineage symbols and norms had not simply given way to and been dissolved by the ɔzɔ system; the two systems coexisted, and the points at which they articulated and interacted may be specified with some precision.

The general significance of the ɔfɔ ɔkpala derived from its mystical righteous power, which bound persons in father–child relationships that were ideally enduring, diffuse, particularistic, affective, consummatory, and collectivity-oriented; it bound them all, theoretically forever, into a solidary system. Associated with this symbol was a social ideal of longterm, generalized reciprocity:[2]

1. Thus the emergence of a universalistic value structure resulted from successful emulation of particularistic kingship.

2. See Sahlins (1965) for analysis of types of reciprocity.

a father first fed his sons and prayed to the dead for them, while they served him homage; later they fed him as a ghost and prayed to the dead for the sake of others who might be reincarnations of him.

From the more detailed norms of patrilineage relationships a different picture emerges. First, the specific acts prescribed of homage service, prayer, and feeding were carefully and continuously measured as performances. Any failure to perform them properly was likely to lead to immediate controversy, fining, even ostracism. Especially at high levels of lineage structure, there was continual testing of specific exchange balances. For juridical and other services, kola payments were continually demanded within the unit. Second, the ɔfɔ system in Onitsha was associated with a strikingly rigid set of norms concerned with seniority and order of death. When any death occurred out of order, ideal patterns of reciprocity and succession were disrupted. Third, although the ɔfɔ of a father superseded that of his son, implying that a son's rights were submerged in those of his father, the detailed norms of property rights spelled out a strong basis of autonomy for every son, including crucial rights to maintain his own gardens and possess his own house. This provided his personal ɔfɔ ɔkpala with a physically separate sphere of operation, and thus secured a substantially self-oriented structure at the heart of an ideally collectivity-oriented system.

These three sets of norms did not correspond to the ideal of generalized reciprocity in patrilineage relations; all involved careful calculation of exchange balances and self-orientations inappropriate to it. All these apparent anomalies represent structural adaptations by the patrilineage system to its internal "contamination" by the presence of the ɔzɔ system. The first and second of these detailed norms appear to be rigid structural responses to the competition engendered by ɔzɔ; such rigid specification of norms is a typical reaction by a strongly ascriptive organization to such internally subversive elements as the uneven redistribution of wealth and influence within the patrilineage that ɔzɔ purification entails.

The third set of norms, however, were predicated directly on the ɔzɔ ideal, for the requirement that every man build his own house gained absolute moral justification from the certainty of sexual pollution facing an ɔzɔ man whose unpurified son married and brought a wife to live in his father's house. Thus the ɔzɔ system sustained a strong norm that upheld personal autonomy and self-orientation within the patrilineage system; a patrilineage member was intrinsically more than that alone, he was also a potentially divine self who had to work out his own destiny on the economic base of his own household and gardens. This norm, another manifestation of the strategic significance of ɔzɔ title, had become a fundamental part of the patrilineage system. By separating a son's household from that of his father, it made his capacity for autonomous economic accumulation secure; by separating him from the achieved purity of his father, it made his autonomous achievement necessary, and prevented the ɔzɔ title itself from becoming ascriptive and hereditary. At this point in its structure, the Onitsha patrilineage had reached an accommodation that enabled it to elude some of the rigidifying tendencies in kinship systems of this type.

Two other sets of norms articulated the patrilineage with the ɔzɔ system. Norms of priesthood delegation modified the relation between patrilineage statuses and roles where other roles were also present. The delegation by an unpurified senior man of some priesthood activities to a more junior ɔzɔ man is one example; the similar delegation by a senior chief or king who was ascriptively eligible for priesthood is another. Such delegation retained certain important rights in the hands of the ascriptively senior man and conferred substantial ones on the ɔzɔ delegate. Finally, the taking of ɔzɔ title by daughter's children provided a pivotal legal fiction through which outsiders could gain legitimate incorporation into patrilineage units. These latter norms adjusted the patrilineage structure to the prominence and importance of achieved roles and to changing population demands and pressures.

The normative adjustment of the Onitsha patrilineage system to the ɔzɔ title system was complex. Some of its structural responses proliferated rigid norms of performance; these rigid responses preserved the basically ascriptive and particularistic character of the system, maintaining the ascriptive role structure and some of its prerogatives at the cost of heightening internal conflict. Other structural responses, however, bent patrilineage norms to the requirements of valued achievement standards and roles; these adjustments gave flexibility and resiliency to the structure. The structure as a whole became a combination of features that might engender high solidarity under some circumstances and intense internal conflict under others; in general it preserved an institutionalized, irreducible sphere of personal autonomy for each of its members. This autonomy was conceived in terms of a religious microcosm attached to the person: his personal god, his personal ɔfɔ ɔkpala, his personal house and land, his personal ikenga, and his personal capacities for self-purification.

Patrilineage and Kingship

Onitsha kingship stood at the apex of the ɔzɔ system and at the apex of the patrilineage or clan; it also partly transcended both. The king's identity had symbolic roots in the patrilineage system, but these symbols were modified and elaborated, and other, different symbols were attached to it as well. Although the Onitsha king's nze shrine was based on the notion of ɔfɔ linked with the treasure-box of ɔzɔ purification, the nature of his ɔfɔ was modified away from the patrilineage form. The role properties designated by this modified ɔfɔ stressed not only purity and righteous power but also vast physical strength, destructive power, and changeability, unpredictability. Associated with the King's ɔfɔ and with the nze complex were the royal ufie drums, which related him—

as an active agent—to the sky, to the diurnal and seasonal changes of the world, and to god. Like senior patrilineage priests, he had relations to spirits, but his relations extended to many more of them; he was actually dedicated as a kind of cult slave to one of the most powerful. He was symbolically defined as warrior, hunter, and leopard, regarded as one of the community's killers. Finally, he was viewed as a ghost, having already completed his first funeral.

All these symbolic increments separated the identity of the king from that of senior patrilineage priest per se, and sets of these symbols designated various distinctively kingly roles not played by senior patrilineage priests but that organized his behavior in the wider community. Nine kings coexisting in this society possessed these symbolic ties with patrilineage, spirits, godhead, warrior attributes, and the dead. Of these nine, eight were expected to occupy the statuses of senior priests of their clans; the ninth was ineligible for this status. In the Onitsha royal clan, the role of king had become decisively differentiated from the role of clan priest, and his status had also been physically separated from that of clan priest. The king remained a member of his clan in status, but his role no longer fit into its patrilineage priest authority framework, and the delimiting of succession to his status had become problematic; the royal clan had not worked out an established structural response to the presence of this new type of social identity.

Concomitantly, the nze of the royal clan had fallen into the king's hands, and its meaning had been changed. Not used for incest confession, it retained only more generalized meanings of purity, and its extended significance implied a general superiority of members of the royal clan. The king's identity was linked with the constitutive symbolism of the society, defined as Onitsha the Nine Clans and also as Onitsha of King Chima, the latter emphasizing the continuity of the royal genealogy and exalting the royal clan. However, this symbolic superiority of the royal clan did not include superiority of its ɔzɔ title system over that of the other clans; by maintaining their title fees at levels comparable to that of the royal clan, all the nonroyal units insured that all ɔzɔ men of the community remained equivalent in prestige.

Thus far, religious symbols and norms associated with segmentary kinship aspects of Onitsha society have been compared, contrasted, and related synchronically to those associated with achieved and socially stratified aspects. However, in the later chapters of the book we traced changes in these normative patterns over time and related them to dynamic social processes. Limitations of space preclude recapitulating the extensive findings of Chapter 13, but the broader implications of those findings may now be considered.

For the formative stage of Onitsha society, the oral tradition suggests the existence of an early segmentary system of multiple clans. Each possessed the eze-nze-ɔzɔ title complex with its "king," and each possessed ufie royal drums. These cultural components of kingship are very old and widespread in Ibo country (the ufie centering west of the Niger, the eze-nze-ɔzɔ at Nri), and on the basis of the archeological evidence at Nri it may be inferred that a complex of royal symbols was available not only in the hands of each Onitsha king but throughout the area, having been widely emulated from the model of ancient Nri and incorporated into each patrilineal unit.

From the base of this formative pattern, there then occurred a progressive differentiation of one clan from all others, as its king became increasingly different in identity from the other hidden kings. These changes resulted from the manipulation of advantageous external relationships by one clan, and the manipulation by the Onitsha king of his control over Benin-related chieftaincy roles. Groups from wealthy and powerful riverain communities either intruded, or were encouraged to settle, into Onitsha community, and these settlers used their riverain contacts for building trade advantages. They also expanded their land holdings into adjacent relatively fertile areas by extending relationships with the

Nsugbe and Nkwele peoples north of Onitsha, peoples defined as "floodplain" (adagbe) rather than uplands Ibo. These riverain-derived Onitsha groups, strengthened in wealth and prestige, were locked into the genealogical framework of the royal clan.

Analysis of the complex changes associated with these external relationships demonstrates the importance of making consistent analytic distinctions between culture and social system for explanatory purposes. Clearly, a culture of kingship was very old in the area; however, changes in the social norms attached to one of the kings began in Onitsha only when external relations were established by one clan with Igala and Anambra contacts. Although new symbols were introduced from these sources (perhaps including ceremonial swords, arm rests, etc.), and a new organization was brought in (the elder dead and their tall ghosts), the subsequent directions of change in Onitsha appear to have been determined not by Igala cultural models or social structures but rather mostly by processes internal to the social system itself. A Benin-derived model of senior son kingship succession was introduced, which affected social development, but its proponents apparently applied it without anticipating the broad effects of its insertion into the society, and the consequences in terms of structural change were surely different than they had expected. It would not have been possible to analyze the complex interrelations between historical developments such as these without employing the fundamental distinction between culture and social system, drawing consistent distinctions among beliefs, values, norms, roles, statuses, and groups, and examining these features in terms of an ongoing, problem-solving social system.

These concepts will assist the attempt to assess the outcome of the evolutionary processes under discussion. We saw that there was considerable cultural differentiation among Onitsha social units; the major categories coming to be distinguishable as types of clans, lineages, or villages were roughly as follows:

I. Royal
   A. Kingly (senior son succession)
   B. Specialized:
      1. Ascriptively senior (priests)
      2. Other ritual prerogatives
      3. Senior chief allies
II. Nonroyal
   A. Ascriptively senior (e.g. ɔbiɔ clan)
   B. Other ritual prerogatives
   C. Senior chief allies

All these categories are emergent in the ethnographic record, and it is clear that a desirable outcome of the evolutionary process for the members of the immediate kingly line would have been the institutionalizing of this cultural differentiation as a general system of social stratification—that is, the correspondence of this cultural differentiation to a clearcut hierarchy of social prestige, matched by differential distribution of wealth and power.

In the previous chapter it was shown that social tendencies did indeed operate in this direction. Moreover, within the royal clan, exogamy had broken down between the village that was controlling royal succession and most of the other, increasingly specialized, royal units; this change could well prefigure a transfer of these specialized units to the nonroyal category. However, in a fundamental sense this cultural and social differentiation between kingly and other royal units remained incomplete and unaccepted, partly because of structural contradictions resulting from the kingly line's succession tactics, but much more broadly because *the ɔzɔ men of all clans, royal and nonroyal, were equal in their prestige.* For this reason, no man of the royal clan could claim that by virtue of his birth he was superior to a nonroyal man, and have that claim accepted. He might claim that he was different in a variety of symbolic ways (in supposedly intrinsic behavioral tendencies, in things eaten or not eaten, in objects manufactured or worshipped, etc.), and perhaps in his effective access to wealth and power, but not that he was by birth superior in prestige or more fit to dominate others than a nonroyal person. The ɔzɔ title made a man equally holy regardless of his clan. By the same reasoning there was an irreducible sense in which the kings of all these units were equal, i.e. in the spiritual holiness of their nze shrines. Thus, *Onitsha as a society was not systematically stratified in terms of royal versus commoner descent groups.* There was differential prestige among the Onitsha clans, but this ranking was secondary to the cross-clan equivalence of ɔzɔ title—the primary career aim of every Onitsha man—which made them all socially equivalent.

It became clear in the previous chapter that the major axis of societal social stratification was the division between kings, chiefs, and Those who support and dignify. These categories cut across descent groups, and the composition of the lower social stratum (ɔzɔ men, nkpalo, elders, young men, the women's trade organization, and—in a secondary sense—the age-sets and collective incarnate dead), shows that *Onitsha societal stratification was substantially universalistic in its basic character.* Relations among the three strata also show that this stratification system was strongly achievement based, for the strata constituted a promotional series through which persons aspired to rise. Within each stratum some gradations of rank were ascriptively defined, but they were distinctly secondary to the crucial tripartite division.

That a multifunctional, segmentary, unilineal descent system also pervades Onitsha social affairs poses substantial comparative problems because of the general notion that such segmentary systems are incompatible with societal communities which emphasize universalism and achievement. Understanding their compatibility depends on recognizing that this system of social stratification was predicated, not on a classification of kinship groups (as in an ideal segmentary system or in a stratified lineage system), nor of social roles (as in a fully achievement-defined system), but rather on a classification of diffuse *career identities.*

CHIEFS, POLITY, AND SOCIAL STRATIFICATION

Four major kinds of symbols defined the identity of the senior chief. His most prominent characteristics—his sorcery, his multiple dart-like ɔfɔ, his war swords and war drums, his stress on his ikenga in ritual—designated him as one of the official killers of the community. This aspect of his character closely resembled the warrior aspect of the king, but was intensified because he lacked some of the king's other characteristics. Second, his killing, symbolically linked to holiness, was therefore endowed with positive value; this, too, resembled the king, and it related the chief to the ultimate base of purified identity, the ɔzɔ title. The chief was intermediate in his holiness between ɔzɔ man and king (wearing multiple eagle feathers while the ɔzɔ man wore only one, eating in a sacred kitchen like the king but not holding nze, etc.). Third, the chief possessed some symbolic attachment to spirit forces and therefore to morality, but his relations with spirits were much less prominent than those of a king. He saluted the Onitsha land during his succession, and he vowed loyalties to the king; otherwise he was largely free of burdensome attachment to the moral forces of community spirits. Indeed the chief sought his closest relationship with a distinctively personal spirit—his own ikenga. Finally, a senior chief was related to the ghosts of former chiefs, but he was not defined as a ghost himself; this freed him from some constraints that bound the king.

These symbols delineated several roles similar to those of the king, and senior chiefs were, during their installation, exhorted to emulate him. However, their role emphases were distinctly different. The senior chief was primarily a warrior and killer, a source of potential intrusive violence. Chiefs were central agents in the dynamics of village formation (the general directions of these dynamics being, however, strongly controlled by the king), and they served as representative agents for furthering the self-aggrandizing, aggressive aims of their villages. Such role behavior was based on the senior chief's separation from the role of senior patrilineage priest, his close identification with his ikenga spirit, and his considerable freedom from various moral constraints. Chiefs mediated relations between descent groups and between villages, but they did so primarily as representatives of their own village interests.

At the same time they were holy men, for they possessed ɔzɔ identity and had undergone additional purifications by distributing their wealth widely throughout the community (including a portion to Those who support and dignify); therefore, throughout the community, their voices demanded respect. Chiefs regulated the markets of their villages, took active part in slave trading, and guided other trading activities undertaken by their wives and daughters; they mobilized the warriors of their villages in battle; and, at least after mid-nineteenth century, they were the most active and innovative leaders in the community. The role of senior chief was clearly developing toward specialization in distinctively political functions, with an emphasis on executive and administrative-regulative activities. These activities were undertaken from a base in the chief's village; but the reason for chiefs' prominence at the community level was the universal respect in which they were held.

Thus the substantial, increasingly political autonomy developed by the senior chiefs had two sources: their relation to the ɔzɔ title, and their rights to possess war drums. Since the chiefs occupied a fully institutionalized position in a clearly defined and coherent continuum of social stratification between ɔzɔ men and kings, they gained the stability and diffuseness of social definition held by each of these strata. The installation of chiefs was clearly modeled on the much older ɔzɔ title system, was socially articulated with it, and by virtue of this fact chieftaincy title became not simply an office but an achieved personal and social identity. Their shared possession of this identity and the style of life that went with it bound the chiefs into an elite that would stand in solidary opposition to any threat to that identity. Also, each senior chief possessed war drums that assured him the military service of members of a major village. He could interact with age-sets and collective incarnate dead, to some extent employing them as means of enforcing his will.

The dynamic historical consequences of these structural facts were traced in the previous chapter. Successful emulation of the kingly prerogative of ɔzɔ for the child led to a general upgrading of universalistic and achievement values in the community. In the nonroyal clans, senior chiefs also aspired to—and in some cases usurped—hidden kingship; and a hidden king who also possessed war drums and other chiefs' regalia was very nearly identical to the Onitsha king himself. In the royal clan, senior chiefs set themselves up as kings competing with the Onitsha king, aided their kinsmen to do so, or conspired to seize the kingship itself. These chiefs' efforts to create new orders of kings had not become institutionalized, neither had they been effectively discredited. Quite clearly, the freedoms available to the senior chiefs, combined with their structural similarities to the king, enabled them under propitious circumstances to challenge the king's distinctiveness, and structural loss of royal differentiation was a real probability by the end of the precolonial period.

We may now go further in attempting to assess and explain the significance of this threatened structural loss. The dynamics of the evolutionary process in Onitsha cannot be fully comprehended without rigorous analytic distinctions between the societal community as a *system of social stratification,* and the *political system* of the society. Chapter 13 analyzed a society whose political system was undergoing disintegration during the exploratory period, but this did not mean that the societal community was disintegrating, for *the major structure of social stratification still remained intact.*

There was disruption of subsidiary patterns of stratification—of the meaning of certain distinctions within and between royal and non-royal clans—but not of the central structure. *It was the incipient differentiation of the political system that was under serious challenge.* This point may be further pursued by comparing the roles of the Onitsha king and his senior chiefs, in terms of their respectively societal and political functions.

For the societal community as a whole, the Onitsha king performed profoundly *integrative* services; his ceremonial activities symbolically determined the spiritual health of the community, took its burdens upon his shoulders and expiated them, and rewarded all its members according to their supposedly just deserts. Through his juridical activities, he sought to maintain a basic solidarity among the diverse segments and role structures that made up Onitsha the Nine Clans. Some of his symbols identified the oneness of the community itself. Since these were his most prominent duties, this integrative function must be regarded as the crucial contribution of his roles. The hidden kings had similar functions within their own clans, but they were also highly valued throughout the community, and through their special ceremonial relations with the Onitsha king they too performed indispensable integrative services.

Among these kings only the Onitsha king also possessed specialized and institutionalized political roles at the societal level. His most important political capacity was his right to select chiefs, and this was above all a party-political function within the emergent political system. He distributed chiefly titles as a means of maximizing societal solidarity for furthering general political aims. To a markedly lesser degree, he claimed assembly decisions as his own, exhorted the mobilizing of warriors, and used his slaves to enforce his commands. The Onitsha kings clearly sought to increase the scope of these executive and administrative capacities, but in this regard they had little success. Indeed, the overall success of their political efforts was very low, over the long run.

Concerning the importance of senior chiefs for societal solidarity, chiefs functioned integratively in exemplifying the attainment of the most widely shared goals of the society: the rewards, followers, and social autonomy that come with the acquisition of social prestige. Among chiefs, relative prestige was closely matched with general and diverse social rewards, so that the chief's career epitomized the most positive goals of the society. This may be one reason why it was so difficult for the king to raise community support against a chief who defied the king's will or emulated one of his prerogatives. In their primarily *political* roles, the chiefs performed predominantly executive and administrative services; partly because of their autonomy and competition with the king in these spheres, they also behaved in politically disintegrative ways. The specialization of the age-sets and the collective incarnate dead in executive, administrative, and juridical activities at the societal level served as a balancing mechanism limiting and dampening some of these disintegrative tendencies in the absence of the king's effective capacity to do so.

To summarize: at the end of the precolonial period, Onitsha society was *socially stratified* primarily by universalistic and achievement criteria. This characterization must then be modified: 1) there was a distinctly secondary and unevenly accepted value-ranking by clans and descent groups, and 2) the major units of social evaluation were not roles per se, but rather career identities carved out basically within the social context of these descent units; once attained, they became a permanent and integral part of a person's self. This is quite different from a much more universalistic system that uses "occupations" as the units of stratification.

Second, Onitsha society's political system possessed unrealized tendencies toward a hierarchical distribution of power between various politically specialized roles. Political power was distributed among three distinct sources: the Onitsha king, the chiefs (and some of the hidden kings), and the alliance of the age-sets and the collective incarnate dead. Among these three sources of power, there were no structurally coherent hierarchical relations; in the absence of such relations, major villages or descent groups operated as major stable interest groups and gave a decidedly segmentary structure to the political system—a system which was, however, predominantly nonascriptive in the character of its political activities.

Third, the *economic system* of the society was organized on a twofold basis. The system of production was organized within patrilineages, and important patterns of produce redistribution occurred through ceremonies and title taking within lineages and clans. However, distribution of trade products was controlled substantially by the ɔzɔ and chief strata and by the women traders, and all of these sought substantially their private interests; strategic limitations had been established on the king's capacity to control trade, although he did play significant roles in trade regulation and redistribution at the societal level.

It is evident that there were two different evolutionary trends operative within Onitsha. The first was a tendency toward increasing universalism and achievement in the system of *social stratification;* some structural changes indicating this tendency had become institutionalized, and the social system upgraded in that sense, by the late precolonial period. The second tendency was one toward increasing centralization of *political* control, both within a royal descent group and in the role of the king. This tendency had not been sustained, because the mode of its incipient attainment within the extant structure had generated profound problems of integration within the fledgling political system itself; during the late precolonial period, the emergent political system was undergoing crises that might have led to structural regression.

A final and crucial problem, then, concerns the likelihood that the various efforts at usurpation might actually have led to a loss of Onitsha political differentiation via successful emulation, by a senior chief or a hidden king, of the Onitsha king's right to select chiefs. The internal weaknesses of the political system are by now evident enough. Would the system of social stratification have supported or inhibited such a change? Although it seems clear that the system of social stratification, rooted as it was in the ancient ɔzɔ system, severely restricted tendencies toward the emergence of political hierarchy in this society, it might not have inhibited changes in other directions. In the abstract, the formulated major pattern of stratification suggests that emulation of kingship might become quickly institutionalized because of the universalistic and achievement emphases of the structure. However, such an inference would reify this formulation; the importance of the subsidiary pattern of stratification must also be taken into account, and analysis carried further. Thus far, Onitsha society has been characterized in terms of its social stratification, political system, and economy. The characterization remains incomplete without consideration of the predominant cultural value patterns of the society.

The culture patterns which most distinguished the Onitsha Ibo as a people were those religious beliefs and values that exalted "individuality"—the set of ideas that placed high positive value on the human individual per se, ideas stressing one's autonomous capacity to realize whatever his personal potentialities might be.

One might leap from this statement to the inference that, since the most esteemed form of self-realization was achievement, Onitsha people might therefore have exalted and accepted the kinds of social egoism displayed by usurping Onitsha chiefs. This inference would seriously distort the pattern being suggested. Individuality" in the sense employed here refers not to psychological egoism or to social independence—rather different matters—but to the elaboration of symbols that delineate, differentiate, and assign value to diverse personal identities.[3] Earlier in this chapter it was pointed out that this exaltation of individuality in Onitsha was rooted in the complex religious microcosm of personal god,

3. I am indebted to Levine (1965:239–41) for his insightful distinctions among cultural, social, and personality dimensions of individualism.

personal ɔfɔ ɔkpala, personal house and land, personal ikenga, and modes of self-purification. These elements as a complex were associated with a close articulation between ɔzɔ title and patrilineage priesthood.

Several avenues of self-realization were open to an Onitsha man. Every man looked forward to ɔzɔ title, which was conceived as a pathway to divinity and in that sense more than an analogical metaphor of kingship. Through ɔzɔ title, moreover, every man could look beyond, to the possibility that he might ultimately become a chief and/or a divine king. Alternative routes could be emphasized in working toward that title and beyond. One might emphasize his age-set roles and try to build reliance on the solidarity of his age-mates; one might emphasize his relations to the divining spirit agwʊ and become a native doctor; one might specialize as an expert in the collective incarnate dead and insure the strong loyalties of his fellow villagers; one might manipulate his relations to his mother's parents; one might rely on the trading prowess of his wives; or one might await his turns at the various statuses of senior patrilineage priesthood available to him and utilize the assistance claims accruing to persons in such statuses.

Most persons would attempt a combination of methods, but the most reliable sources of facilities were distributed at various levels within the patrilineage. While few men would rely on this alone, far fewer would dispense with the ascriptive security obtainable within their natal patrilineages. In the long run, this security would provide the significant power that resided in a man who knew the "truth"—truth conceived as the ultimate order of things in their relation to the past—and wielded an ɔfɔ magically connected with that knowledge and with various valued objects to which the knowledge referred. Even if such a man never attained ɔzɔ title, he was valued as a repository of this knowledge and respected for his ɔfɔ power. Thus the patrilineage priest played a crucial role in conserving the cultural traditions of his people.

Moreover, since ɔzɔ title was fully compatible with serving in the roles of patrilineage priest (indeed was essential for full service), ɔzɔ men were bound to share strong vested interests in maintaining the prerogatives of the priestly role, if not in conserving all of its particular fund of cultural knowledge.

It is therefore clear, that, despite their conflicts in particular patrilineage groups, patrilineage priests and ɔzɔ men shared the ultimate values of maintaining both the patrilineage system and the ɔzɔ system. It was unlikely that they would have supported changes as radical as those attempted by the chiefs, which might have undermined the patrilineage system. Their vested interests in the traditional patrilineage structure were also shared by most of the chiefs themselves, for even those who usurped hidden kingship tried afterwards to claim their descent legitimacy. Senior chiefs displayed their strongest egoism and social independence as representatives of village efforts at self-aggrandizement, and although Onitsha people obviously admired such behavior, it was not likely that other villages would follow capricious changes in structure attempted in any one village.

I therefore infer that the attempted usurpations would not likely have succeeded under existing circumstances. Probably chronic problems of political integration would have continued, but a general political regression would not actually have become institutionalized (as did happen at Asaba across the river).

ECONOMICS AND POSSIBLE ALTERNATIVE EVOLUTIONARY TRENDS

To say that fairly radical change of this kind was probably not imminent in Onitsha society under the existing conditions does not mean that it could not have occurred under somewhat different ones. Consider two possible economic changes that might have affected evolutionary directions.

First, since the king's major trading income came from "lifting the cover of the canoes" in the international marketplace, his wealth would have increased in direct proportion to the incidence of collectivity-oriented trade on the river, trade that he could administer. Given the structure of the system and its situation, the Onitsha king could have accomplished this only by establishing himself in a tributary alliance with the Aboh (or perhaps Osomari) kingdom; had this been done, the king's wealth from taxation would have been greatly enhanced. On the basis of slender evidence, one may, indeed, hypothesize that such an alliance actually existed at some time during the reign of King Udogwu, apparently by far the most wealthy of Onitsha kings.[4] However, while such an arrangement might have increased his wealth relative to that of his senior chiefs, the king would still have had to resolve the emerging structural contradictions between the status of senior priest and eligibility to the role of king, and to solve the problems of controlling his chiefs. Economic factors alone would not have dictated the manner or success of such solutions, which would have necessitated independent innovations on his part. In any event, the instability of riverain trade relations continually undermined the bases for such developments.

A second important ecological and economic change might have resulted from increasing population pressure and increasing immigration from the eastern hinterlands. Near Onitsha where settlement patterns have emerged at the disintegration stage of ecology, as at Nnewi, structural changes have occurred in the patrilineage system; certain patrilineage roles have come to be defined exclusively by primogeniture. Under intensive immigration, emergence of truly cognatic descent criteria for land tenure might in time have occurred. If, as a result of such factors, the Onitsha system of descent groups had broken down into a cognatic pattern in which the role of patrilineage priest had become a

4. Somewhat later, by the middle of the nineteenth century, Aboh leaders strongly affirmed the economic importance of their trade with Onitsha, claiming that it was their "chief oil market" (Crowther and Taylor 1859:17).

residual ritual role of little importance,[5] what would have happened in the rest of the system?

In Onitsha, normative precedents already existed for the transfer of land, for its being held in trust by king and chiefs, even for its seizure and division among chiefs as compensation for social transgressions. What is remarkable is not that such precedents existed, but that their potential uses as means of radical land tenure change had apparently not even been considered. Had the patrilineage role structure ceased to operate, a much higher incidence of land transfers could easily have developed.

The ɔzɔ title system could certainly have been compatible with a cognatic system; it was, in fact, partly a legal-fiction device that fostered covert cognatic tendencies within the patrilineages. In the absence of a patrilineage role structure it could have become a freely accessible title system within a village framework. The village structure as it existed was preadapted to a ward system of residential organization, for both age-sets and collective incarnate dead were structurally independent of the patrilineage role system.

One set of structures would have been directly affected by such changes: those that supported the autonomy of women. More than did men, women required the structural support of corporate patrilineages for their economic independence and broader social autonomy. On the basis of such ascriptive support, Onitsha women had erected a system of councillors and queen that mirrored the men's system and wielded significant power; it is said that at one time the queen led a boycott by all the women of the community against cooking for their husbands, which brought the men to accept their demands. With descent group support undermined, however, the trading roles of women would have been seriously affected. Exactly what changes might have occurred cannot be predicted on the basis of the economic changes alone; they would

5. I do not imply here that I would actually expect economic and residence changes alone to have this effect, as might be assumed from the perspective of Murdock (1949). This assumption is made merely for the convenience of manipulating the model.

have depended on the structure of the political system at the time.

In a system like that existing in the late precolonial period, but with patrilineages destroyed, the senior chiefs, in charge of essentially ward-based village units, could have completed their usurpation of rights to hidden kingship, without bothering to justify such usurpation within a descent group framework; what had been usurpation would become a new kind of norm. These chief-kings, now substantially identical to the Onitsha king, would have been in a position to complete their emulation of him by selecting their own subchiefs from within their heterogeneous village units, and by using their control of ɔzɔ title as a political device within these units. The resistance of ascriptive vested interests would have been fragmented and ineffective.

Under such circumstances for the society as a whole to regain political integration, the age-sets and collective incarnate dead would have had to assert increasing power within the villages, and expand the scope of their activities in the community at large, perhaps embracing the title system within their alliance framework. The outcome of such a speculative series of transformations would have been a society much closer in character to some of the trading states of the "oil rivers" in the delta and at Calabar than to most forms of Ibo society.[6] It would have been a society politically much more centralized within each of its residential units, its system of social stratification more subject to the political control of its chief-kings. If politically integrated by the collective incarnate dead and age-sets, it would have been more strongly collectivity-oriented in its decision making at the societal level. In general, the personal autonomy of each villager would have been substantially lowered. Concomitant with all these changes, *there would have been a significant loss of role differentiation within the society.*

6. Incarnate dead and other types of secret association may be repositories of old kingship culture in a number of acephalous associational societies in this part of west Africa.

My purpose in these speculations is not to suggest that such a change was empirically likely in Onitsha, for it was not, nor that this was the only possible sequence of transformations, given a change in descent groups.[7] It is a plausible sequence, and its plausibility points to the importance of certain of the social structures we have just been considering. *It was on the basis of a stable structural differentiation between patrilineage priest and ɔzɔ title, plus the existence of a common value alliance between them, that the Onitsha cultural tradition emphasizing individuality was conserved and elaborated, and a substantial degree of social autonomy maintained in the social system.* The thought experiment just conducted suggests that destruction of the security provided by the role system of the patrilineage priest would have led to a further loss of role differentiation in the system, and concomitantly to a loss of the very cultural tradition that exalted individuality.

It may be inferred, then, that in the absence of a writing system a cultural elaboration of individuality can be sustained only in a social system that preserves a relatively stable differentiation of non-hierarchically-related roles. This finding has broader relevance than Onitsha alone, for like the city-states of ancient Greece, Onitsha was part of a cultural tradition that transcended any particular political community of Ibo-speaking people. There were multiple channels of communication through the region, people had some awareness of diverse ideas about the world, and they shared a world-view that had some strongly universalistic implications. Through the workings of their own social order, the Onitsha Ibo had formulated some notions about the fundamental equivalence of men regardless of their birth. But where in Greece the

7. Other possibilities are implied in Bradbury's insightful comparison of Benin and Yoruba kingdoms. The Edo and Ibo peoples share an emphasis on partially universalistic title associations at the village and village-group level which is lacking among the Yoruba. The presence of these associations, in the absence of strong descent groups at Benin, may account for the distinctively centralized developments in Benin's political evolution as compared with the Yoruba (Bradbury 1964:158–59).

breakdown of descent groups may have been associated with further radical innovations and developments of social order and of culture, in the absence of a writing system and other means of culture-building the Onitsha Ibo could not go further; to preserve their budding conceptions of personal identity and autonomy, they had to reply on an ancient, stable alliance between a role-type that exemplified universalistic achievement and one that epitomized particularism and ascription. This alliance helped sustain a dynamic equilibrium in a politically unstable society operating in a highly unstable environment. Thus we return to the significance of the segmentary patrilineal descent aspects of Onitsha Ibo society outlined at the beginning of this chapter. It was of great importance for the meaning of Onitsha social life that every man had the potentiality to become a king, but it was also crucial that he retained the potentiality to be a patrilineage priest. Without the latter he might have lost his conception of what it was to be fully a man.

APPENDIX A: DISTRIBUTION AND CONTROL OF ONITSHA FARMLANDS

The following numbers correspond to those on Figure 29.

A. LANDS SOUTH OF THE RESIDENTIAL COMMUNITY

These lands center around the primordial homes of Onitsha people, including the lands called Okpoko (where a great egbo tree is said to mark the ancient shrine to Onitsha land) and Udo (containing the shrine of the ancient kings). In recent times it has been said that all lands called Udo once belonged to the Ɔbiɔ clan.

1. *Okpóko* land, controlled by the Children of Ɔreze. A part of this land was transferred to Children of Osodi (Children of Dei).
2. *Údo* land, controlled by Ɔbiɔ clan. The shrine to the spirit Udo is marked with a star in Figure 29.
3. *Udo* land controlled by the Children of Onogbo (senior patrilineage of Division is Two).
4. *Àpali* land, controlled by the Children of Ase (who trace descent within Ɔbamkpa clan). Also classed as Udo land.
5. *Ákpu* land, controlled by Iyawʊ lineage. Also classed as Udo land.
6. *Udo* land controlled by Iyawʊ lineage, who claim to have received it as leading-home dowry.
7. *Íyi-úkwu* land, controlled by Warrior Village (Division is Two).
8. *Òwele* land of the Village of Ɔzɔma (Isele-Awada clan). A remnant of its former holdings.
9. *Úgbo-Òrumili* land, controlled in ancient times by the Village of Ɔzɔma (Isele-Awada clan), later said to have been given over to Ogbo segment of the Children of Ase via leading-home dowry.
10. *Áwadà* land, controlled by the Children of Ɔlɔsɩ, taken over (according to some informants) from Isele-Awada clan.
11. Awada land, controlled by Isiokwe village, taken over (according to some informants) from Isele-Awada clan.

12. *Úgbo-Úlo* land, controlled by Isiokwe village.
13. *Ísiòkwe* land, controlled by Isiokwe village. Putative palace site of King Chima the Cow-killer is marked with a star on Figure 29. A western portion of this land was transferred to one segment of the Children of Ase through leading-home dowry; a portion on the southern fringe was given to a group of collective daughter's children from the Village of Oli, who were said to have fled their village when their land became a fiery surface due to a murder that occurred there. Some of the bad bush of Isiokwe was putatively given out to a native doctor for a dwelling place; his descendants are said to form Iyiawʊ lineage.
14. *Nkitaku-Akprikpu* land, taken over (according to some informants) from the Children of Ɔreze by Iyasele Okwugbele of the Children of Ase, later shared in part with Onira Village, Children of Dei, via leading-home dowry.
15. *Iyi-ukwu* land, once controlled by the Children of Ase, later taken over by the Children of King Udogwu (High Grass Village). Circumstances of takeover unclear, said to have been some kind of compensation.
16. *Ísi-àfɔ* land, controlled by Ɔdɔje village, the primordial village site of which is marked in the center.
17. *Íwɔliwɔ* land, controlled by Obikporo village (Riverain Village). Part of this area was also held by the Children of Ikem (also of Riverain Village).
18. *Ɔ̀dɔ̃-ákpʊ* land, controlled by Ulutu-Ado clan. A portion at the fringes of this farming area was given, as leading-home dowry, to a segment of Isiokwe village.

B. LANDS NORTH OF THE RESIDENTIAL COMMUNITY, SOUTH OF NKISI STREAM

Mostly these include latrine lands, bad bush, and ritually significant pathways leading to Nkisi stream, held by various contiguous villages. Most of this area closely approximates a radiating segment pattern of land tenure.

19. The king's land, including the pathway to the great riverside market, the market itself, and the shrines around it. The precolonial extent of this land could not be precisely determined, but it included a fishing site along the river bank well north of the market.

20. *Ɔ̀zala* land, controlled by Okposi-Eke lineage (senior patrilineage in the Village of Oli-Eke).
21. *Ɔzala* land, controlled by the Village of Mbubu (Division is Two). Formerly of greater expanse, this land was gradually reduced to include the Nkisi stream pathway only.
22. *Ɔzala* land, controlled by the Children of Dei.
23. *Ɔzala* land, controlled by Warrior Village (Division is Two).
24. *Ɔzala* land, controlled by Village of Abʊ (Division is Two).
25. *Ɔzala* land, controlled by the Children of King Arɔlɩ and by the Children of Ɔlɔsi.
26. *Úgbo-ɔ̀kwe* land, controlled by the Village of Oli-Eke.
27. *Owele* land of Iyi-awʊ lineage, said to have been given by Isiokwe village (cf. 13 above).
28. *Òkwúsi-ńtà* lands (and also *Ɔ̀káfìa* and *Ànɩ-nwókwe* lands), once controlled by Iyasele Nsu of Ekensu clan. This land was divided among the Children of Alibo (Village of Oli-Ɔlɔsɩ), the Children of Alabo (Children of Arɔlɩ), Ɔrezeabo segment of the Children of Dei, Onira lineage (Village of Abʊ), and possibly some others, supposedly after the defeat of Nsu.

C. LANDS NORTH OF THE RESIDENTIAL COMMUNITY, NORTH OF NKISI STREAM (FROM THE ANAMBRA RIVER NORTHEASTWARD BETWEEN OBELE MILI AND NNAKWEZE STREAMS)

This area has two traditional general names: *Àkpákà* and *Ɔ̀tákpo*. All the lands classed as Ɔtakpo are said to have been leased by Onitsha people from the people of Nkwele town.

29. *Akpaka* lands, controlled by Okposi-Eke lineage (Village of Oli-Eke).
30. *Ɔtakpo* lands, controlled by the Children of Ɔrezeabo and the Children of Osodi (both Children of Dei).
31. *Ɔ̀dɔ́-áchɩ* lands, controlled by Children of Osodi (Children of Dei). Also classed as Ɔtakpo land.
32. *Udelili* lands, controlled by Mmenkiti lineage (children of Okoligbo, Children of Dei). Also classed as Ɔtakpo land.
33. *Ákwukwo-óbodobo* lands, controlled by Children of Osodi (Children of Dei). Also classed as Ɔtakpo land.
34. *Ɔ̀yɔlú* lands, controlled by Mmenkiti lineage (Children of Okoligbo, Children of Dei). Also classed as Ɔtakpo land.

35. *Énu-òfufe* lands, controlled by Children of Osodi (Children of Dei). Also classed as Ɔtakpo land.
36. *Ékwulò* lands, controlled by Children of Osodi (Children of Dei). Also classed as Ɔtakpo land.

D. LANDS NORTH OF THE RESIDENTIAL COMMUNITY, NORTH OF OBELE MILI STREAM

The lands north of Obele-Mili stream traditionally belonged to the town of Nsugbe, from whose various villages Onitsha people leased them. I did not determine whether no. 37 belonged in this category or to Nkwele people, nor indeed whether it was a precolonial lease.

37. *Abigwugwu* lands, controlled by Ekwusogu lineage (Village of Abʊ).
38. *Úgbo-Éke* lands, controlled by Okposi-Eke lineage (Village of Oli-Eke).
39. *Ugbo-Eke* lands, controlled partly by the Children of Chimukwu (Village of Abʊ, Division is Two) and partly by Ɔrezeabo lineage (Children of Dei).

E. LANDS NORTH OF THE RESIDENTIAL COMMUNITY, NORTH OF NKISI STREAM, SOUTH OF NNAKWEZE STREAM

There is no common name given to these lands. Some of those nearest to the community are said by some informants to have been cleared from virgin forest, but most were either leased or taken over through leading-home dowry from the people of Oze town.

40. *Ɔ̀dɔ̃-úgili* lands, controlled by the Children of Onogbo (Isele-Awada clan).
41. *Ámaladà* lands, controlled by the Children of Ɔmɔzele (Children of Arɔlɩ), by the Children of Alana (High Grass Village), and by Low [High Grass] Village.
42. *Ákpako* land, controlled by the Children of King Udogwu (High Grass Village).
43. *Àkwʊ́-àchá* land, controlled by Anyo lineage (Children of Arɔlɩ), said to have been cleared from forest by chief Anyo.
44. *Ògwúgwu-ágbu* land, controlled by the Children of Anyo (Children of Arɔlɩ), via leading-home dowry from Oze town.
45. *Ńgidimà* land, controlled by the Children of Anyo (Children of

Arɔlɩ), via leading-home dowry from Oze town. Portions of this land were later leased to men of Children of Ase, Village of Oli-Eke, and High Grass Village.

46. *Ìduma* land, controlled by High Grass Village and Low [High Grass] Village, through leading-home dowry from Oze town.
47. *Ɔ̀zala-úbìli* land, once controlled by Village of Ɔzɔma (Isele-Awada clan), but taken over by Eze Olisa lineage (Children of Aroli), via leading-home dowry.
48. *Ákpʊ-ùgo* land, controlled by the Children of Osuma (Village of Oli-Eke).
49. *Ɔ̀nyilʊ́gʊ̀lʊ* land, controlled by Low [High Grass] Village.
50. *Ɔ̀malíma* lands, controlled by High Grass Village and Low [High Grass] Village.

APPENDIX B: FORMAL ANALYSIS OF ONITSHA AFFINAL TERMINOLOGY

My data on Onitsha affinal terms of reference are not as complete as they should be. This is unfortunate; since there are many alternate terms in Onitsha kinship usage, and since Onitsha people appear to draw less clear-cut boundaries in their affinal categories than they do in their consanguineal ones, many difficulties of analysis consequently arise that cannot be fully resolved. It still seems worthwhile to attempt a formal analysis of what is available, because formal analyses of affinal terminologies have rarely been made and the results may prove useful for limited comparative purposes.

THE DATA: PRELIMINARY ANALYSIS

The following is a list of Onitsha affinal terms, with a range of the kin types associated with each.[1] (The asterisk denotes a courtesy application.)

1. di (and di-anyi): *H*, Hc, Hsc, HFc, HFsc, HMsc, HMc, HMdc, *Hdc, *HFdc, *HMMc, etc.
2. nwunye (and nwunye-anyi): *W*, FW, FFW, FsW, FFsW, FMsW, MsW, MMsW, sW, ssW, dsW, *FdsW, *MFW, *MFsW, *MdsW, etc.
3. ɔgɔ (and ɔgɔ-anyi): *WF*, WFF, WFM, WFc, WFFc, WFsc, WFdc, WFMF, WFMFs, WFW, WFFW, WFsW, WFdsW, WFMH, WMH, WMMH, etc.,
   WM, WMF, WMM, WMc WMMc, WMFc, WMsc, WMFW, WMFsW, WMdc, WMsW, WMFW, FWMdc, FWMsc, etc.,
   dH, sdH, ddH, FdH, FFdH, FsdH, FddH,

1. In all cases, it is presumed that the person listed as one of these kin types is not also related to ego by consanguinity. If the person is, the consanguineal type usually takes categorical priority. For example, if FW is also M, she is referred to as mother and not as "nwunye-anyi." The list is not exhaustive; additional terms will be introduced where relevant.

FdddH, FMdH, MdH, MFdH, MMdH, MFddH, HdH, HddH, HFdH, HFddh, HMdH, HFFdH, HFdHc, HFsdH, WdH, WddH, WddHc, MFdHc, MMdHc, FFdHc, FMdHc, etc.

4. nwunye di: *HW*, HFW, HFFW, HFsW, HFFsW, HsW, HssW, *HMsW, *HMMsw, *HdsW, *HFdsW, *HMFW, *HMFsW, etc.

5. ɔgɔ ngɔkɔ: *WFdH*, WFFdH, WFsdH, WMFdH, WMFsdH, etc.

6. nna di: HF, HFF

7. nne di: HM

8. nne nna di: HFM

9. nnaochie di: HMF, etc.

10. nneochie di: HMM, etc.

11. di nne: MH

12. di nneochie: MMH

13. di nne nna: FMH

14. nwa nwunye: Wc

15. nwa nwa nwunye: Wsc

16. nwadiani nwunye: Wdc

17. nwa nwunye nna: FWc

18. nwa di nne: MHc

Three simple terms distinguish the major relationships established through marriage: *dí*, *nwũ̂nye*, and ɔ́gɔ̀. Each is applied to a considerable range of relatives, and each also occurs combined with modifiers. Each may be combined with the pronominal modifier "our" (*-ányi*); this alternate form is used optionally when the term is extended beyond the focal kin type.

A primary meaning may be specified for each of these three basic terms simply by reference to their focal kin types. The terms di (focal type H) and nwunye (focal type W) form a reciprocal pair, and may be defined as follows.

1. di: ♀\$ (woman's spouse, or "husband");

2. nwunye: ♂\$ (man's spouse, or "wife").

The term ɔgɔ has three equidistant focal types: WF, WM, and dH, which form the reciprocal pair WP/dH:

3. ɔgɔ: ♂\$P / c♀\$ (wife's parent / child's husband).

For convenience, this reciprocal pair will be glossed as "in-law" in the discussion to follow, and the symbols W and H will be employed except where a more general meaning of "spouse" ($) is clearly entailed.

THE EXTENSION OF HUSBAND AND WIFE TERMS

Examination of the kin types to which the term di may be applied indicates that a variety of one's husband's consanguineal kinsmen are treated as equivalent to husband. By prescription, the term is extended only to husband's agnates; therefore, a rule might be formulated as follows: Let husband's agnate be regarded as equivalent to husband:

$$HF^{m}s^{n}c \longrightarrow H$$

This rule could be viewed as a special case of rule 1, the fundamental genealogical rule of the Onitsha consanguineal system.[2] Any of these prescriptive extensions may take the collective form "our husband" (di-anyi).

However, the term di is also extended in this way to those kinsmen of one's husband who are, in terms of the previous analysis of consanguineal kinsmen, his mother's child (nwanne) and his daughter's child (nwadiani). These cases comprise a secondary class membership, especially the daughter's child kin types (overtly stated to be courtesy references); since they are included in the general category and since the available data do not provide sharp formal separation points, these extensions will be included in formulating the reduction rule. A rule that will cover all of these kin types may take the following general form: Let husband's kinsman be regarded as equivalent to husband (corollary, Let kinsman's wife be regarded as equivalent to wife):

4. $HP^{m}c^{n} \longrightarrow H$ (corollary: $P^{m}c^{n}W \longrightarrow W$)

where Pc refers to kinsman ("parent's child") and m or n may equal zero under certain conditions.

In this preliminary form, the rule would reduce all the kin types listed to the focal type H. However, so phrased the rule is too general, for senior generation lineal kinsmen of husband are invariant to it, and are instead assigned descriptive complex terms:

HF — nna di
HM — nne di

2. In its modified form, the values of (m) and (n) would have to be specified differently, so that they may equal zero under certain conditions; husband's lower generation lineal agnates are included in this reduction to husband, and such reduction does not occur in the normal application of rule 1.

HFF — nna nna di
HFM — nne nna di
HMF — nnaochie di
HMM — nneochie di.

While other of husband's kinsmen, both male and female, are called "husband," the kin types listed here are distinguished by sex, and their mode of linkage to the husband is specified. The significance of this invariance becomes clearer when the kin types to which the corollary of this rule applies are considered.

The kin type referents for the term "wife" include only wives of kinsmen, and therefore the reduction corollary $P^m c^n W \longrightarrow W$ is appropriate. This corollary reduction applies more generally than that for husband's kinsmen, for the kin types reciprocal to those ascending generation lineal kinsmen of husband just listed are reduced to "wife" (or "our wife"). Wives of daughter's child and of mother's parent are also included in reduction, although these cases too are clearly regarded as secondary applications. Informants agree that the "wives" of male or female ego include primarily and most importantly those of his agnates, including both ascending and descending generation lineal agnates.

This greater generality of reduction for the corollary of the rule just formulated supports the formulation given (though there is an explicit primacy of agnatic reduction). To the rule "Let husband's kinsman be regarded as equivalent to husband," a restriction must be appended, for husband's senior generation lineal kinsmen are exceptions to it:

$$HP^{\geq 1} c^0 \not\longrightarrow H$$

This form of reduction does occur in some contexts where the husband is not the initial link in the kin type chain; a linking relative's husband's senior general lineal kinsman is treated as equivalent to linking relative's husband:

$$\ldots HP^m c^0 \longrightarrow \ldots H$$

This strongly suggests that one's husband's senior lineal kinsmen are, indeed, treated as members of the "husband" class. Their formal reduction to "husband" is suppressed in the interest of demarcating them as a special subclass.

Rule 4 reduces not only the kin type referent of husband and wife, but also the more complex kin types of the type husband's kinsman's wife ($HP^m c^n W$). These are referred to as wife of husband or cowife (nwunye di) as indicated above. Here the appropriate side of rule 4 is $P^mc^nW \longrightarrow W$, which reduces all kin types, including wives of husband's ascending generation lineal kinsmen, to the focal type HW. In this case also class membership is divided between prescribed extensions and courtesy extensions; here informants draw rather sharp distinctions between husband's agnates and their wives and his other kinsmen and their wives. The tracing of nonagnates as linking relatives for this HW reduction is regarded as marginal; since it can be done and is done, it has been included in this analysis.

EXTENSION OF IN-LAW TERMS

Reduction rules appropriate to this class will have to reduce some kin types to WP (wife's parent) and others to cH (child's husband), since these are the reciprocal focal types. A scan of the evidence listed above indicates that all the extended cases contain the kin type . . . WP . . . or . . . dH. . . . If we set aside those kin types in this class which take the complex forms of W . . . W, W . . . H, or H . . . H, a general rule may be formulated that takes account of the remaining kin types. Let wife's kinsman be regarded as equivalent to wife's parent (corollary: Let kinsman's husband be regarded as equivalent to child's husband):

5. $WP^mc^n \longrightarrow WP \qquad (P^mc^nH \longrightarrow cH)$

The evidence also indicates that restrictions must be placed on rule 5, because one's wife's lineal junior generation kinsmen, and the husbands of one's lineal senior generation kinsmen, are excluded from this in-law class. These may be excluded by restricting the (m) and (n) values in the rule as follows:

$$WP^{\geq 1}c^n \longrightarrow WP \qquad (P^mc^{\geq 1}H \longrightarrow cH)$$

Rule 5 bears a strong formal resemblance to consanguineal rule 2, which specifies that $MFc \longrightarrow MP$ ($Fdc \longrightarrow dc$). In rule 5, the initial female element takes the value of wife (W) rather than mother (M), and the reduction that occurs is to a $/G^1/$ level rather than $/G^2/$. This places the in-law category in a position generationally intermediate to the mother's parent/daughter's child category. Rule 5 is also more generalized, in that it is not restricted to agnatically linked kinsmen; however, it is clear that Onitsha people regard wife's agnates and wife's mother's parents as primary in-laws, while wife's daughter's children and wife's mother's children are called in-laws by courtesy and not by prescription. This, with the patterns associated with rule 4, suggests that rules 4 and 5 may be viewed as transformations of rules 1 and 2 into the context of affinal relations, where they take on more generalized forms.

There are yet other kin types to be considered in connection with the in-law class, for certain spouses of kinsmen's spouses are also members of the class. The term in-law applies to all wives of those wife's kinsmen reduced by rule 5 to "wife's parent," and it applies to all of husband's kinsmen's husbands reduced to "child's husband" by the same rule (i.e. $HP^{m}c^{\geq 1}H$). It also refers to husbands of both senior and junior generation lineal kinsmen of wife. Since we have previously encountered some distinctive demarcations of lineally linked kin, it may prove revealing to examine such categories more closely in this context.

Classification of Spouse's Lineal Kinsman's Spouse

Senior generation

HFW	— nwunye-di	WFW	— ɔgɔ (ɔgɔ-anyi)
HFFW	— nwunye-di	WFFW	
HFMH	— di nne nna di	WFMH	
HMH	— di nne di	WMH	
HMMH	— di nne di	WMMH	
HMFW	— nwunye nnaochie di	WMFW	

Junior generation

HsW	— nwunye di	WsW	— nwunye nwa nwunye
HdH	— ɔgɔ-anyi	WdH	— ɔgɔ-anyi
HdsW	— nwunye-anyi	WdsW	— nwunye nwadiani nwunye
HddH	— ɔgɔ-anyi	WddH	— ɔgɔ-ani.

This distribution suggests the following additional in-law equivalence rule, assuming that senior generation lineal kinsmen of wife are treated as equivalent to wife's parent. Let wife's parent's spouse be regarded as equivalent to wife's parent (corollary: Let spouse's child's husband be regarded as equivalent to child's husband):

6. $WP^{\geq 1}\not{S} \longrightarrow WP \qquad (\not{S}c^{\geq 1}H \longrightarrow cH)$

For the kin types listed here, this works without exception. In addition, certain of spouse's collateral kinsmen's spouses are also reduced to in-law: WFsW, WFdsW, WMFsW, WMsW, HFdH, HFddH, etc. Rule 5 reduces each of these to either WPW or HdH, so that rule 6 may then apply as it stands.

One set of collaterally linked spouses does not reduce to in-law, at least not to the term ɔgɔ alone; $WP^{\geq 1}c^{\geq 1}H$ are called ɔgɔ ngɔkɔ. The form ngɔ- is a nominal related to ɔgɔ; the suffix -kɔ means "together." Thus ɔgɔ-ngɔkɔ may be translated roughly as "co-in-law," for it applies to those persons who stand as cH to the same set of WP as does ego. This set involves the interpenetration of rules 5 and 6 with their respective corollaries; the first half of the two rules would reduce the kin types to WP, while their corollaries would reduce them to cH. The categorical outcome appears to be a combination of the two, a reduction to WPcH, co-in-law.

This category ɔgɔ ngɔkɔ may be regarded as a subclass of ɔgɔ, but it is clear from discussion with informants that these self-reciprocal relations are viewed as "like ego" rather than "like in-laws." This is of course what the kin type WPcH would lead one to expect; it specifies a shared identity in the same sense as does the kin type Fc.

THE ANALYSIS OF STEP-KIN

Each of the rules formulated here has properties which suggest that lineally linked kinsmen have distinctive characteristics in this affinal system. These properties may be clarified through an examination of those kin types which may be classed etically as step-kin.[3] In Onitsha society, as in many others, step-kin tend to be assimilated within the consanguineal framework if it is socially suitable to do so. The following terms for step-kin types were elicited with the specified assumption that the kin types were not socially assimilable to membership in a consanguineal category or group. Maximum differentiation of terminological categories was thereby obtained, and the resulting patterns suggest hypotheses about the significance of the various affinal categories distinguished.

It is evident from this list that Onitsha categories cut across the etic domain of step-kin types as set by the eliciting procedure. Some step-kin are called "our wife," others "our husband," others "in-law," while still others are referred to descriptively. Analysis of these step-kin can be ordered through their focal types. The two reciprocal pairs FW/Hc and MH/Wc are the focal step-kin, all other combinations being genealogically more remote. The first pair, FW/Hc, falls within the application range of rule 4, and both lineally and collaterally linked step-kin derived from this pair are reduced to "our wife" (focal type FW) and "our husband" (focal type Hc). The second focal pair is not susceptible to rule 4; both it and its derived forms are treated in more diverse ways. Both MH and Wc are invariant to reduction rules, are treated descriptively (di nne,

3. See Lounsbury (1965:163) for a definition of step relationships.

Some Types of Step-Kin

Senior generation, ego's kinsman's spouse

Kin type	Term	Group term
FW		nwunye-anyi
FFW		nwunye-anyi
FFsW		nwunye-anyi
MFW	nwunye-nnaochie	"nwunye-anyi"
MFsW	nwunye nnaochie	"nwunye-anyi"
FMsW	nwunye nwanne	"nwunye-anyi"
MMsW	nwunye nwanne	"nwunye-anyi"

Kin type	Term	Group term
MH	di nne	
MMH	di nneochie	
FMH	di nne nna	
FFMH	di nne nna nna	
FFdH		ɔgɔ-anyi
MFdH		ɔgɔ-anyi
FMdH		ɔgɔ-anyi
MMdH		ɔgɔ-anyi

Same generation, ego's kinsman's spouse's kinsman

Kin type	Term
FWc	nwa nwunye nna
FFsWc	nwa nwunye nwanne nna
FMsWc	nwa nwunye nwanne nna
MFsWc	nwa nwa nwunye nnaochie
MMsWc	nwa nwunye nwanne nne
FWFdc	ɔgɔ-anyi
FWMdc	ɔgɔ-anyi
FWFsc	ɔgɔ-anyi
FWMsc	ɔgɔ-anyi

Kin type	Term
MHc	nwa di nne
MFdHc	ɔgɔ-anyi
MMdHc	ɔgɔ-anyi
FFdHC	ɔgɔ-anyi
FMdHc	ɔgɔ-anyi
MHFsc	nwanne di nne
MHMsc	nwanne di nne
MHFdc	nwadiani di nne
MHMdc	nwanne di nne

Junior generation, ego's spouse's kinsman

Kin type	Term
Wc	nwa nwunye
Wsc	nwa nwa nwunye
Wdc	nwadiani nwunye
WFsc	ɔgɔ-anyi
WFdc	ɔgɔ-anyi
WMsc	ɔgɔ-anyi
WMdc	ɔgɔ-anyi

Kin type	Term	Group term
Hc		di-anyi
Hsc		di-anyi
Hdc		di-anyi
HFsc		di-anyi
HFdc	nwadiani di	"di-anyi"
HM	nwanne di	"di-anyi"
HMdc	nwanne di	"di-anyi"

"husband of mother," and nwa nwunye, "child of wife"), and the same is true of husbands of ego's senior generation lineal kinsmen $(P^{\geq 1}H)$ and wife's junior generation lineal kinsmen $(Wc^{\geq 1})$. The husbands of senior generation collateral kinsmen $(P^{\geq 2}c^{\geq 1}H)$ and their reciprocals, the descending generation collateral kinsmen of wives $(WP^{\geq 1}c^{\geq 2})$, are classed as in-laws.

If the collaterally linked step-kin types reduce in this manner, why are the lineally linked ones treated differently? It may be hypothesized that husbands of ascending generation lineal female kinsmen are treated as "potential parents," the descendants of wives as "potential children," and that these positions of "potential kinsman" are demarcated by descriptive terms of the sort shown on this list of step-kin. These possibilities are indeed held in the minds of most informants, and Wc may be referred to as nwa ("child"), MH as nna ("father") under certain social circumstances. The same inference may be drawn for same generation step-kin (step-siblings) as well as for the cross generation ones; children of wives of both lineal and collateral kinsmen (primarily, however, agnates) are ordinarily referred to descriptively, even though their mothers are reduced to "wife" by rule 4. However, the collateral kinsmen of these wives are reduced to in-law by rules 4 and 5. Similarly, both lineal and collateral kinsmen of lineal kinsmen's husbands ($P^{\geqq 1}c^{0}HP^{m}c^{n}$) are treated descriptively, while lineal and collateral kinsmen (the latter not shown on the list) of collateral kinsmen's husbands ($P^{\geqq 1}c^{\geqq 1}HP^{m}c^{n}$) are reduced to in-law by rules 4 and 5.

This patterning suggests three basic ways of classifying what are etically "step-kin" as set by our eliciting requirements: spouse—or "potential spouse," in the case of the collective terms nwunye-anyi or di-anyi; "potential kinsman" (descriptive terms); and in-law (ɔgɔ). This tripartite scheme may be readily applied to the affinal terminology as a whole. Within this framework, the "potential kinsman" category may be viewed as a subclass of the spouse class; it consists of, first, kin types defined through linkage to a husband's senior generation lineal kinsmen, or to senior generation lineal kinsmen's husbands, or to a combination of these types of relations; and second, those defined through linkage to wife's junior generation lineal kinsmen or to the wives of such kinsmen. These are precisely the kinds of linkages most likely to be assimilatable to consanguineal relations in the Onitsha system.

APPENDIX C: ONITSHA CHIEFTAINCY TITLES

The following lists the major titles current or remembered in recent times, according to rank order insofar as this was possible to estimate. For the most senior titles, there was general agreement about ranking, but for the lower levels there was some inconsistency among informants. Cf. Orakwue (1953) and Ifeka (1962).

I. NDICHIE UME

1. Ónôwú (Íyàséle; Ɔ́nuiyi; Ǹgadaba Órumili)
2. Àjíè (Ísàgbá; Úkàdíùgwu; Ìdéjiogù)
3. Ódù (Ósòdi; Ǹkataúkwu)
4. Ɔ̀nyá (Ɔ̀zɔ́ma; Úkanagbaɔjì; Ásakàlakpobi)
5. Ɔgené (Onírà; Ùkpáka)
6. Òwélè (Osowa; Ánya)

II. NDICHIE OKWA

A. Ndichie Ukpo
   1. Ósùmá (Afa; Ákankposi)
   2. Ádazie (Ógulâni; Alɩbɔ́)
   3. Ɔ̀mɔ́dì (Dàíke; Alumaga)
   4. Òzí (Odamagwe; Ògwuya)
   5. Ɔ̀dúà (Ńgu; Álamuzɔ̀)

B. Others
   6. Àkpé (Ɔlɔdi; Jebogwu)
   7. Éde (Ògbʊgbʊgaga)
   8. Òjûdɔ (Enema)
   9. Íke (Ǹkpúmà)
   10. Òzízànɩ (Òbí)
   11. Òjíba (Inwagwe)
   12. Òbolí (Bɔ̀ja)
   13. Gbŏsà (Òbí)
   14. Ójiabʊ̀ (Úgàla)
   15. Ógbuɔba (Anyalagbom)
   16. Òzízànɩ (Déi)

17. Òjôgwú (Ézè)
18. Ɔmɔ́dì Òbele (Ézè)
19. Ɔ̀dúà (Bàlala)
20. Ósùmá Òbele (Ɔ̀gwá)
21. Ójiede (Ézè)
22. Ódù (Oke)
23. Òbíɔba
24. Òkwúagwe

III. NDICHIE OKWARAEZE

1. Ónoli (Ógwudà nà ìyelé)
2. Àkwé (Ísàmá)
3. Èseágbà (Ágbàla Ùdóbi)
4. Ágba (Oriogu)
5. Ìgwúɔba (Ákàlám)
6. Ásagwàli (Ómeikpo)
7. Òjîbá (Ògbúagada)
8. Ìjágwò (Òbí)
9. Ajako (Òbí)
10. Uboh (Negbasele)
11. Àsagba (Òbí)
12. Ágba (Òbele)
13. Ísàmá (Òsuji)
14. Onika
15. Íke (Òbele)
16. Òkwúagwo
17. Àjákɔ
18. Unwolu
19. Ɔza
20. Ojugani
21. Ogbaiko
22. Igedu
23. Abi

IV. SPECIAL CATEGORY

Òkwûgba (Úkedei)

The following lists the tripartite ritual organization, and putative war organization, of the Onitsha chiefs, so far as could be determined from recent informants.

I. ONOWU AND ƆGENE

A. Ndichie Okwa

1. Ɔmɔdi
2. Ozi
3. Akpe
4. Ojiabʊ
5. Ozizanɩ
6. Ojiede

B. Ndichie Okwaraeze

1. Akwe
2. Asagwali

II. AJIE AND ƆNYA

A. Ndichie Okwa

1. Osuma
2. Ike
3. Gbosa
4. Ede
5. Ogbuɔba
6. Ojudɔ

B. Ndichie Okwaraeze

1. Eseagba
2. Igwuɔba

III. ODU AND OWELLE

A. Ndichie Okwa

1. Adazi
2. Ɔdua
3. Ojiba

B. Ndichie Okwaraeze

1. Agba
2. Oboli
3. Ojiba
4. Onoli
5. Ijagwo

APPENDIX D: NINETEENTH-CENTURY ROYAL INSTALLATION SACRIFICES

The following is an exact copy of a list compiled in 1931 that recorded the sacrificial objects traditionally given to the hidden king of Ɔbiɔ clan for his duties in installing a new Onitsha king. The initial remarks refer to the nontraditional nature of the 1900 installation of King Okosi.

LIST OF CEREMONIES AND SACRIFICES BY EKEMBU OBIO IN CONNECTION WITH THE INSTALLATION OF THE OBI OF ONITSHA

(Remarks: The two items of Ogbonuke and Nze were only [*sic*] performed by the late Mr. Samuel Okolo Okosi who refused to perform others stating that Government made him the Obi)

Due: from the intended successor to the throne, to head representative ekembu orbio	OGBONUKE (1) Black sheep, good size, to be killed in respect of the death of predecessor and for the nomination of the new obi. (3) bottles gin, (1) pot palm wine
do	NZE (1) He-goat to be killed for sacrifice to Nze for notifying successor to the throne. (4) bottles gin, (1) pot palm wine
do	ANI ORBIO (1) She-goat to be killed for sacrifice to Ani Orbio for notifying successor to the throne, (1) fowl hen. (5) bottles gin, (2) pots palm wine and fried corn powder (Omumu)
do	KPANNENE (1) She-goat to be killed for sacrifice to Kpannene for notifying successor to the throne. 3 bottles gin, 1 pot palm wine.

ON THE UNDERSTANDING THAT THE SUCCESSOR TO THE THRONE IS FULLY PREPARED: THEN COMES:

ISU-ONICHA and Ceremony (all Onitsha)

That is juju made up with red mat. (1) human being for sacrifice, 1 bullock to be killed, 1 sheep, 2 fowls (cock and hen) (1) fathom cloth, 7 chickens, 60 fowls, 60 bunches guinea grains, 60 goats, 60 razors (Uchee).

In respect of putting work in hand. On completion, he ceases shaking of hand with anybody from that day.

Due: from the intended successor to the throne, to head representative Ekembu Orbio

OBALOGBI

(1) Dog, male, (1) fowl hen, (3) chickens, (3) bunches guinea grains and (6) bottles gin and cowries equivalent to the value of (6) bags = £2.

do

UDO ORBIO (all young men Onitsha)

(3) Human beings for sacrifice.
(1) Bullock to be killed.
(2½) c/s Gin and (8) pot palm wine
(3) goats. (8) fowls, (10) Ugbugbas
(clay pots), 20 bunches guinea grains,
(3) Fishes Ase, (6) bottles palm oil
(6) pots palm wine and 1C/s gin.
[note: from the (10 Ugbugbas) line downwards may refer to another phase of ceremony]
(60) Needles native.

To be given to Orbio.

(2) Human beings or cowries equivalent to the value of 20 bags = £6-13-4
20 bags = 6-13-4

Feast about 20 dishes agbuke, 20c/s gin, 10 pots palm wine, 10 bottles oil and 10 fishes Ase

NKPUEZE FEAST

(1) Human being for sacrifice
(1) bullock to be killed.
(2) goats (1 she and 1 he) to be killed
(3) Fowls to be killed.
(10) Ugbugbas (clay pots)
(20) bunches guinea grains
(3) Fishes Ase, 6 bottles palm oil,

(6) pots palm wine and 1 c/s gin

EGBO

(2) human beings

UKWUAKE

(1) human being

OBULUEZE OZI JUJU

(1) he goat, 1 ram, 1 cock, 7 bunches guinea grains, 7 kola nuts and chalk.

OGWUCWU OGBOLI

(1) He-goat, 1 Ram, 1 cock, 7 bunches guinea grains, 7 kola nuts and chalk

UMUOSUMA EKWENSU

(1) he-goat, 1 ram, 1 cock, 7 bunches guinea grain, 7 kola nuts and chalk

YEARLY SERVICE

5 goats for sacrifice to 5 jujus [to Ɔbiɔ]

YEARLY TRIBUTE [To Ɔbiɔ]

Cowries equivalent to the value of 12 bags = 4.

Amendment. For "Human being" wherever occur, substitute "bullock."

Signed at Waterside Onitsha this 24th day of August, 1931.

Ezeocha His x mark, commoner Igwe

Signature of Informant

BIBLIOGRAPHY

Aberle, D. F., et al.

1950 The Functional Requisites of a Society, *Ethics* 60:100–11.

Alagoa, E. J.

1966 Oral traditions among the Ijo of the Niger Delta, *Journal of African History* 7:405–19.

Allen, William, and T. R. H. Thomson

1848 *A Narrative of the Expedition Sent by Her Majesty's Government to the River Niger, in 1841.* 2 vols. London: Richard Bentley.

Alutu, J. C.

1963 *A Groundwork of Nnewi History.* Enugu: The E.N.I.S. Press.

Apter, D. E.

1965 *The Politics of Modernization.* Chicago: University of Chicago Press.

Arensberg, C. M.

1957 Anthropology as History, in *Trade and Market in the Early Empires,* eds. Karl Polanyi, C. M. Arensberg, and H. W. Pearson. Glencoe, Ill.: Free Press, pp. 97–113.

Armstrong, Robert

1955 The Igala and The Idoma-speaking Peoples, in *Ethnographic Survey of Africa, Western Africa, Part X: Peoples of the Niger-Benue Confluence,* ed. C. D. Forde. London: International African Institute, pp. 77–155.

1962 Glottochronology and African Linguistics, *Journal of African History* 3:283–90.

1964 The Use of Linguistic and Ethnographic Data in the Study of Idoma and Yoruba History, in *The Historian in Tropical Africa,* ed. Jan Vansina, R. Mauny, and L. V. Thomas. London: Oxford University Press, pp. 127–39.

Baikie, W. B.

1856 *Narrative of an Exploring Voyage up the Rivers Kwo'ra and Bi'nue (Commonly Known as the Niger and the Tsadda) in 1854.* London: John Murray, Albemarle Street.

1857 Baikie's Expedition. Great Britain F. O. 2-23: September 28, 1857.

Barnes, J. A.

1961 Physical and Social Kinship, *Philosophy of Science* 28:296–99.

Bascom, W. R.

1944 The Sociological Role of the Yoruba Cult-group, *Memoirs of the American Anthropological Association*, 63:1–75.

Basden, G. T.

1938 *Niger Ibos*. London: Seeley, Service, and Co., Ltd.

Beattie, J. H. M.

1964 Kinship and Social Anthropology, *Man* 64:101–03.

1965a Correspondence. *Man* 65:123.

1965b The Content of Kinship, *Man* 65:51–52.

Bellah, Robert

1964 Religious Evolution, *American Sociological Review* 29:358–74.

Bennett, J. W., and L. A. Despres

1960 Kinship and Instrumental Activities: A Theoretical Inquiry, *American Anthropologist* 62:254–67.

Biobaku, Saburi

1958 An Historical Sketch of the Peoples of Western Nigeria, *Odù* 6:24–28.

Bohannan, Laura, and Paul Bohannan

1953 The Tiv of Central Nigeria, in *Ethnographic Survey of Africa, Western Africa, Part VIII*. London: International African Institute.

Boston, J. S.

1960a Notes on Contact Between the Igala and the Ibo, *Journal of the Historical Society of Nigeria* 2:52–58.

1960b Some Northern Ibo Masquerades, *Journal of the Royal Anthropological Institute* 90:54–65.

1962 Notes on the Origin of Igala Kingship, *Journal of the Historical Society of Nigeria* 2:373–83.

1968 *The Igala Kingdom*. London: Oxford University Press.

Bradbury, R. E.

1957 The Benin Kingdom and the Edo-speaking Peoples of Southwestern Nigeria, in *Ethnographic Survey of Africa, Western Africa, Part XIII*, ed. C. D. Forde. London: International African Institute, pp. 13–171.

1959 Chronological Problems in the Study of Benin History, *Journal of the Historical Society of Nigeria* 1:263–87.

1960 Ehi: Three Stories from Benin, *Odù* 8:40–48.

1964 The Historical Uses of Comparative Ethnography with Special Reference to Benin and the Yoruba, in *The Historian in Tropical Africa*, ed. Jan Vansina, R. Mauny, and L. V. Thomas. London: Oxford University Press, pp. 145–64.

1967 The Kingdom of Benin, in *West African Kingdoms in the Nineteenth Century*, ed. C. D. Forde and P. M. Kaberry. London: Oxford University Press, pp. 1–35

Brown, Paula

1951 Patterns of Authority in West Africa, *Africa* 21:261–77.

1955 The Igbira, in *Ethnographic Survey of Africa, Western Africa, Part X: Peoples of the Niger-Benue Confluence*, ed. C. F. Forde. London: International African Institute, pp. 55–74.

Buck, John

n.d. Journals of the Reverend John Buck, Native Pastor, Onitsha 1871–1880. Church Missionary Society Archives CA/025/4. London.

Burdo, Adolphe

1880 *The Niger and the Benueh*, trans. Mrs. George Sturge. London: Richard Bentley and Son.

Carneiro, R. L., ed.

1967 *The Evolution of Society: Selections from Herbert Spencer's Principles of Sociology*, ed. and intro. Robert Carneiro. Chicago: University of Chicago Press.

Church Missionary Record

1866 Letters. n.s. 11:7.

1871–72 Report. Third series 1–2.

Clifford, Miles

1936 A Nigerian Chiefdom, *Journal of the Royal Anthropological Institute* 66:393–435.

Coser, Lewis

1956 *The Functions of Social Conflict*. Glencoe, Ill.: The Free Press.

Crowther, D. C.

1879 Report on Onitsha, Iyawo (outstation) and Asaba, Lower Niger, 1879. Church Missionary Society Archives CA 013/46. London.

Crowther, S. A.

1855 *Journal of an Expedition up the Niger and Tshadda Rivers Undertaken by Macgregor Laird, Esq., in Connection with the British Government, in 1854*. London: Seeley, Jackson, and Halliday.

1868 Letters. *Church Missionary Record* 39 (n.s. 13):81–82.

1871 Report on a Visit to the Stations on the Niger in the year 1870, *Church Missionary Intelligencer* (n.s. 7):124–28.

1873 Niger Mission Report, *Church Missionary Record* 44 (2nd n.s. 3):217–18.

1874 Report of Bishop Crowther's Annual Visit to the Niger Station in 1873, *Church Missionary Intelligencer* (n.s. 10):152–60.

1875 Bishop Crowther's Charge, *Church Missionary Intelligencer* (n.s. 11):88–91, 121–22.

n.d. Letter to Reverend R. Lang, 31 December 1881. Church Missionary Society Archives G3/A3/01. London.

Crowther, S. A., and J. C. Taylor

1859 *The Gospel on the Banks of the Niger. Journals and Notices of the Native Missionaries Accompanying the Niger Expedition of 1857–59.* London: Church Missionary House.

1864 *The Gospel on the Banks of the Niger.* No. 3 (1863), London.

Curtin, P. D.

1968 Field Techniques for Collecting and Processing Oral Data, *Journal of African History* 9:367–85.

Dike, K. O.

1956 *Trade and Politics in the Niger Delta, 1830–1885.* Oxford: Clarendon Press.

Dobinson, Rev. H. H.

n.d. Notes of Conversations and Pieces of Miscellaneous Information Gathered at Onitsha. Nigerian National Archives, Church Missionary Society N5/1:1890–91. Ibadan.

Durkheim, Emile

1915 *The Elementary Forms of the Religious Life.* Trans. Joseph Ward Swain. London: George Allen and Unwin Ltd.

1964 *The Division of Labor in Society.* Trans. G. Simpson. London: Macmillan.

Egharevba, J.

1960 *A Short History of Benin* (3rd edn). Ibadan: Ibadan University Press.

Eisenstadt, S. N.

1959 Primitive Political Systems: A Preliminary Comparative Analysis, *American Anthropologist* 61:200–19.

1964a Institutionalization and Change, *American Sociological Review* 29:2:235–47.

1964b Social change, Differentiation, and Evolution, *American Sociological Review* 29:375–85.

Erikson, E. H.

1959 The Problem of Ego Identity, *Psychological Issues: Identity and the Life Cycle* 1:101–66.

Evans-Pritchard, E. E.

1940 *The Nuer*. Oxford: Clarendon Press.

Fagan, B. M.

1966 Radiocarbon Dates for Sub-Saharan Africa, IV, *Journal of African History* 7:495–506.

Fallers, L. A.

1956 *Bantu Bureaucracy*. Cambridge: W. Heffer and Sons.

Field, J. M. O.

1940 Bronze Castings at Igbo, Southern Nigeria, *Man* 40:1–6.

Forde, C. D., and G. I. Jones

1950 The Ibo and Ibibio-speaking Peoples of South-Eastern Nigeria, in *Ethnographic Survey of Africa, Western Africa*, Part III, ed. C. D. Forde. London: International African Institute.

Fortes, Meyer

1945 *The Dynamics of Clanship among the Tallensi*. London: Oxford University Press.

1949 *The Web of Kinship among the Tallensi*. London: Oxford University Press.

Fortes and E. E. Evans-Pritchard, eds.

1940 *African Political Systems*. London: Oxford University Press.

Freedman, Maurice

1964 Kinship and Kinship Terms, in *A Dictionary of the Social Sciences*, New York: Free Press of Glencoe, pp. 366–68.

Fried, M. H.

1957 The Classification of Corporate Unilineal Descent Groups, *Journal of the Royal Anthropological Institute* 87:1–30.

1960 On the Evolution of Social Stratification and the State, in *Culture in History: Essays in Honor of Paul Radin*, pp. 713–31. ed. Stanley Diamond. New York: Columbia University Press.

1967 *The Evolution of Political Society*. New York: Random House.

Gellner, Ernest

1957 Ideal language and kinship structure, *Philosophy of Science* 24: 235–42.

1960 The concept of kinship, *Philosophy of Science* 27:187–204.

1963 Nature and society in social anthropology, *Philosophy of Science* 30:236–51.

George, I. T.

n.d. Journal. Church Missionary Society Archives C A3/018. London.

1869 Letters. *Church Missionary Record* 40 (n.s. 14):85–89.

Gluckman, Max

1956 *Custom and Conflict in Africa.* New York: Barnes and Noble.

1962 Les rites de passage, in *Essays On the Ritual of Social Relations,* ed. Max Gluckman. Manchester, Eng.: Manchester University Press, pp. 1–52.

Goodenough, W. H.

1965 Rethinking 'Status' and 'Role': Toward a General Model of the Cultural Organization of Social Relationship, in *The Relevance of Models for Social Anthropology,* ed. Michael Banton. Association of Social Anthropologists Monographs 1. London: Tavistock, pp. 1–24.

Goody, Jack

1959 The Mother's Brother and the Sister's Son in West Africa, *Journal of the Royal Anthropological Institute* 89:59–88.

1961 The Classification of Double Descent Systems, *Current Anthropology* 2:3–25.

1962 *Death, Property, and the Ancestors.* Stanford, Calif.: Stanford University Press.

Great Britain

1888 Foreign Office. Slave Trade, 1880, no. 2: *Correspondence Relating to the Bombardment of Onitsha.* Parliamentary Papers, 1880, v. 74. London.

Greenberg, Joseph

1955 *Studies in African Linguistic Classification.* The Compass Publishing Company, New Haven.

1963 The Languages of Africa, *International Journal of American Linguistics* 29:1:1–177.

Grove, A. T.

1951 *Land Use and Soil Conservation in Parts of Onitsha and Owerri Provinces.* Geological Survey of Nigeria, Bulletin no. 21. Zaria: Gaskiya Corporation.

Harding, R. W.

1963 *The Dispute over the Obiship of Onitsha.* Report of the Inquiry. Official Document no. 6 of 1963. Enugu: The Government Printer.

Harris, Marvin
1968 *The Rise of Anthropological Theory*. New York: Thomas Y. Crowell.

Henderson, H. K.
n.d. *Ritual Roles of Women in Onitsha Ibo Society*. Ph.D. Dissertation, University of California (Berkeley), 1969.

Henderson, R. N.
1966 Generalized Cultures and Evolutionary Adaptability: A Comparison of Urban Efik and Ibo in Nigeria, *Ethnology* 5:365–91.
1967 Onitsha Ibo Kinship Terminology: A Formal Analysis and its Function Applications, *Southwestern Journal of Anthropology* 23:15–51.

Henderson and H. K. Henderson
1966 *An Outline of Traditional Onitsha Ibo Socialization*. Ibadan: Ibadan University Press.

Horton, Robin
1954 The Ohu System of Slavery in a Northern Ibo Village-group, *Africa* 24:311–36.
1956 God, Man, and the Land in a Northern Ibo Village-group, *Africa* 26:17–28.
1961 Destiny and the Unconscious in West Africa, *Africa* 31:110–17.
1967 African Traditional Thought and Western Science, *Africa* 37:50–71, 155–87.

Hsu, F. L. K.
1965 The Effect of Dominant Kinship Relations in Kin and Non-kin Behavior, *American Anthropologist* 67:638–61.

Ifeka, Sam
1962 Onitsha Social Heritage, *Nigerian Spokesman*, May 19–July 2, Onitsha.

Iweka-nuno, I. E.
1924 *History of Obosi and Ibo Land in General*. Onitsha.

Jeffreys, M. D. W.
n.d. *The Divine Umundri Kings of Igbo Land*. Ms. London: International African Institute Library.
1935 The Divine Umundri King, *Africa* 8:346–53.
1936 Additional steps in the Umundri Coronation Ceremony, *Africa* 9:403–06.
1954 Ikenga: The Ibo Ram-headed God, *African Studies* 13:25–40.
1956 The Umundri Tradition of Origin, *African Studies* 15:3:119–31.

John, T. A.

n.d. Letter to S. A. Crowther Received Feb. 5, 1879. Church Missionary Society Archives CA3/022/2. London.

Johnson, Henry

n.d. A Journey up the Niger. Letter dated 14 December, 1877, Church Missionary Society Archives, CA3/023/1. London.

Jones, G. I.

1949 Ibo Land Tenure, *Africa* 19:309–23.

1961 Ecology and Social Structure among the North-Eastern Ibo, *Africa* 31:117–34.

1962 Ibo Age Organization, with Reference to the Cross River and North-Eastern Ibo, *Journal of the Royal Anthropological Institute* 92: 191–212.

1963 *Trading States of the Oil Rivers.* London: Oxford University Press.

Keay, R. W. J.

1949 *An Outline of Nigerian Vegetation.* Lagos: Government Printer.

Kirchoff, P.

1959 The Principles of Clanship in Human Society, in *Readings in Anthropology,* vol. 2, M. H. Fried, ed. New York: Thomas Y. Crowell, pp. 259–70.

Laird, MacGregor and R. A. K. Oldfield

1837 *Narrative of an Expedition into the Interior of Africa, by the River Niger in the Steam-vessels Quorra and Alburkah, in 1832, 1833, and 1834.* 2 vols. London: Richard Bentley.

Lander, Richard, and John Lander

1841 *Journal of an Expedition to Explore the Course and Termination of the Niger; with a narrative of a Voyage down that river to its termination.* Vol. 2. London: John Murray.

Langley, Francis

n.d. Annual Letter Iwayo station, Oct. 5, 1872. Church Missionary Society Archives CA3/025/4. London.

Leach, E. R.

1951 The Structural Implications of Matrilateral Cross-Cousin Marriage, *Journal of the Royal Anthropological Institute* 81:23–55.

1954 *Political Systems of Highland Burma.* Cambridge, Mass.: Harvard University Press.

1957 Aspects of Bridewealth and Marriage Stability among the Kachin and Lakher, *Man* 57:50–55.

1960 Descent, Filiation and Affinity, *Man* 60:9–10.

1961 *Rethinking Anthropology*. London: Athlone Press.

1962 On Certain Unconsidered Aspects of Double Descent Systems, *Man* 62:130–34.

1967 Virgin Birth, *Proceedings of the Royal Anthropological Institute for 1966*, London, pp. 39–49.

Leacock, E. B.

1963 Introduction to Parts I, II, III, and IV, in L. H. Morgan, *Ancient Society*. Ed., intro., and annot. Eleanor Burke Leacock. New York: Meridian Books.

Leonard, A. G.

1906 *The Lower Niger and Its Tribes*. London: Macmillan.

Levine, D. N.

1965 *Wax and Gold*. Chicago: University of Chicago Press.

LeVine, R. A.

1965 Socialization, Social structure, and Intersocietal Images, in *International Behavior: A Social Psychological Analysis*, ed. Herbert Kelman, New York: Holt, Rinehart and Winston, pp. 45–69.

Lévi-Strauss, Claude

1949 *Les Structures élémentaires de la parenté*. Paris: Presses Universitaires de France.

Levy, M. J.

1952 *The Structure of Society*. Princeton, N.J.: Princeton University Press.

Linton, Ralph

1936 *The Study of Man*. New York: Appleton-Century Company.

Lloyd, P. C.

1960 Sacred Kingship and Government among the Yoruba, *Africa* 30:221–37.

1965 The Political Structure of African Kingdoms: An Exploratory Model, in *Political Systems and the Distribution of Power*. Association of Social Anthropologists Monograph 2, ed. Michael Banton. New York: Praeger, pp. 63–112.

Lounsbury, F. G.

1964a A Formal Account of the Crow- and Omaha-type Kinship Terminologies, in *Explorations in Cultural Anthropology*, ed. W. H. Goodenough, New York, McGraw-Hill, pp. 351–93.

1964b The Structural Analysis of Kinship Semantics, in *Proceedings of the Ninth International Congress of Linguists,* ed. Horace G. Lunt, The Hague, Mouton and Co., pp. 1073–93.

1965 Another View of the Trobriand Kinship Categories, *American Anthropologist* 67:5:2:142–85.

Maine, Sir Henry

1861 *Ancient Law.* London.

Mair, Lucy

1962 *Primitive Government.* Baltimore, Md.: Penguin Books.

Marx, Karl

1904 *The Critique of Political Economy.* Trans. I. N. Stone, Chicago: International Library Co.

Mattei, A.

1890 *Bas-Niger, Benoue, Dahomey.* Grenoble.

Mbanefo, Frank

1962 The Iba House in Onitsha, *Nigeria* 72:18–25.

Meek, C. K.

1937 *Law and Authority in a Nigerian Tribe.* London: Oxford University Press.

Middleton, John, and David Tait, eds.

1958 *Tribes without Rulers.* London: Routledge and Kegan Paul.

Middleton and E. H. Winter, eds.

1963 *Witchcraft and Sorcery in East Africa.* London: Routledge and Kegan Paul.

Mockler-Ferryman, A. F.

1892 *Up the Niger.* London: George Philip and Son.

Morgan, Lewis Henry

1871 *Systems of Consanguinity and Affinity of the Human Family.* Smithsonian Contributions to Knowledge, 17.

1877 *Ancient Society.* New York: The World Publishing Company.

Murdock, G. P.

1949 *Social Structure.* New York: Macmillan.

1959 *Africa.* New York: McGraw-Hill.

Nadel, S. F.

1942 *A Black Byzantium.* London: Oxford University Press.

1957 *The Theory of Social Structure.* Glencoe, Ill.: The Free Press.

Needham, R.

1960 "Descent Systems and Ideal Language," *Philosophy of Science* 27:96–101.

1962 *Structure and Sentiment.* Chicago: University of Chicago Press.

Netting, R. M.

1965 Household Organization and Intensive Agriculture: The Kofyar Case, *Africa* 35:422–29.

Noon, J. A.

1944 A Preliminary Examination of the Death Concepts of the Ibo, *American Anthropologist* 44:638–54.

Nzekwu, J. O.

1959 Ofala Festival, *Nigeria* 61:104–22.

Obi, S. N. C.

1963 *The Ibo Law of Property*. London: Butterworths.

O'Connor, D. P.

1936 The Obiship of Onitsha, *The African Advertiser*, Dec. 24, 1936.

Okolo, P. H.

1947 *Onitsha Ebo-Itenani*. Onitsha: Enenia Press.

Onitsha Native Court

1921 Civil Judgment Book, Case no. 180.

1948 Civil Judgment Book, Case no. 142.

Orakwue, J. I.

1953 *Onitsha Custom of Title-taking*. Onitsha: Renascent Africa Press, Ltd.

Ottenberg, Simon

1958 Ibo Oracles and Intergroup Relations, *Southwestern Journal of Anthropology* 14:295–317.

Parsons, Talcott

1951 *The Social System*. Glencoe, Ill.: The Free Press.

1959 An Approach to Psychological Theory in Terms of the Theory of Action, in *Psychology: A Study of a Science*, ed. Sigmund Koch. New York: McGraw-Hill, pp. 612–711.

1960 *Structure and Process in Modern Societies*. Glencoe, Ill.: The Free Press.

1961a An Outline of the Social System, in *Theories of Society*, ed. Parsons, Shils, Naegele, and Pitts, 1:30–79. New York: The Free Press of Glencoe.

1961b The Point of View of the Author, in *The Social Theories of Talcott Parsons*, ed. Max Black. Englewood Cliffs, N.J.: Prentice-Hall, pp. 311–63.

1964 Evolutionary Universals in Society, *American Sociological Review* 29:339–57.

1966 *Societies*. Englewood Cliffs, N.J.: Prentice-Hall.

1968 The Position of Identity in the General Theory of Action, in *The Self in Social Interaction*, ed., C. Gordon and K. Gergen. New York: John Wiley and Sons, 1:11–23.

Parsons, E. Shils, K. Naegele, and J. Pitts, eds.

1961 *Theories of Society*. New York: The Free Press of Glencoe.

Radcliffe-Brown, A. R.

1957 *A Natural Science of Society*. New York: Free Press of Glencoe.

Ryder, A. F. C.

1965 A Reconsideration of the Ife-Benin Relationship, *Journal of African History* 6:25–37.

Sahlins, Marshall

1961 The Segmentary Lineage: An Organization of Predatory Expansion, *American Anthropologist* 63:322–45.

1965a On the Ideology and Composition of Descent Groups, *Man* 65:104–07.

1965b On the Sociology of Primitive Exchange, in *The Relevance of Models for Social Anthropology*, ed. Michael Banton. Association of Social Anthropologists Monographs 1. London: Tavistock, pp. 139–236.

Sahlins and Elman Service, eds.

1960 *Evolution and Culture*. Ann Arbor: University of Michigan Press.

Scheffler, H. W.

1966 Ancestor Worship in Anthropology: Or, Observations on Descent and Descent Groups, *Current Anthropology* 7:541–51.

Schneider, D. M.

1964 The Nature of Kinship, *Man* 64:180–81.

1965 Some Muddles in the Models: Or, How the System Really Works, in *The Relevance of Models for Social Anthropology*, ed. Michael Banton. Association of Social Anthropologists Monograph 1. London: Tavistock, pp. 25–85.

1968 *American Kinship: A Cultural Account*. Englewood Cliffs, New Jersey: Prentice-Hall.

Schneider and George Homans

1955 Kinship Terminology and the American Kinship System, *American Anthropologist* 57:1194–208.

Schneider and J. M. Roberts

1956 *Zuni Kin Terms*. Laboratory of Anthropology, Notebook 3, monograph 1. Lincoln, Neb.: University of Nebraska.

Service, Elman

1962 *Primitive Social Organization*. New York: Random House.

1968 The Prime-mover of Cultural Evolution, *Southwestern Journal of Anthropology* 24:396–409.

Seton, R. S.

1928 Installation of an Attah of Idah, *Journal of the Royal Anthropological Institute* 58:255–78.

Shaw, Thurston

1960 Excavations at Igbo-Ukwu, Eastern Nigeria: An Interim Report, *Man* 60:161–64.

1965 Further Excavations at Igbo-ukwu, Eastern Nigeria: An Interim Report, *Man* 65:181–84.

1967 The Mystery of the Buried Bronzes: Discoveries at Igbo-ukwu, Eastern Nigeria, *Nigeria* 92:55–74.

Shelton, A. J.

1965 The Meaning and Method of Afa Divination among the Northern Nsukka Ibo, *American Anthropologist* 67:1441–55.

Southall, A. W.

1956 *Alur Society*. Cambridge: W. Heffer and Sons.

1965 A Critique of the Typology of States and Political Systems, in *Political Systems and the Distribution of Power*, ed. Michael Banton. Association of Social Anthropologists Monograph 2. New York: Praeger, pp. 113–40.

Spencer, Julius

1901 The History of Asaba and its Kings, *Niger and Yoruba Notes* 85:20–21.

Stevenson, R. F.

1968 *Population and Political Systems in Tropical Africa*. New York: Columbia University Press.

Steward, J. H.

1955 *Theory of Culture Change*. Urbana, Ill.: University of Illinois Press.

Strong, A. C.

n.d. Onitsha Station Log Book 1884–1893. Ibadan: Nigerian National Archives, Church Missionary Society N5/1:1.

Talbot, P. A.

1926 *The Peoples of Southern Nigeria*, vols. 2, 3. London: Oxford University Press.

Taylor, J. C.

n.d. Map of Onitsha Town. Church Missionary Society Archives CA3/037/10. London.

1864 Letters for Year Ending November 1863. *Church Missionary Record* n.s. 9:137–47.

1865 Journals of Taylor from July 1863–September 1864. *Church Missionary Record* 36 (n.s. 10):133–49.

1866 Journals. *Church Missionary Record* 7 (n.s. 11):201–06.

Thomas, N. W.

1913 *Anthropological Report on the Ibo-speaking Peoples of Nigeria. Part I. Law and custom of the Ibo of the Akwa neighborhood, S. Nigeria.* London: Harrison and Sons.

1914 *Anthropological Report on the Ibo-speaking Peoples of Nigeria. Part IV. Law and custom of Ibo of the Asaba District, S. Nigeria.* London: Harrison and Sons.

Tönnies, Ferdinand

1957 *Community and Society (Gemeinschaft und Gesellschaft).* Trans. and intro. C. P. Loomis. East Lansing: Michigan State University Press.

Turner, Victor

1966 "Color Classification in Ndembu Ritual: A Problem in Primitive Classification," in *Anthropological Approaches to the Study of Religion,* ed. Michael Banton. American Association of Social Anthropologists Monograph 3. New York: Praeger, pp. 47–84.

Uchendu, V. C.

1965 *The Igbo of Southeast Nigeria.* New York: Holt, Rinehart, and Winston.

Vansina, Jan

1965 *Oral Tradition.* Trans. H. M. Wright. Chicago: Aldine Publishing Company.

Weber, Max

1947 *The Theory of Social and Economic Organization.* Trans. H. M. Henderson and Talcott Parsons. Glencoe, Ill.: The Free Press.

1958 *The City.* Trans. and ed. Don Martindale and Gertrud Neuwirth. Glencoe, Ill.: The Free Press.

White, Leslie

1949 *The Science of Culture.* New York: Grove Press.

1959 *The Evolution of Culture.* New York: McGraw-Hill.

Williams, John

n.d. Some of Onitsha laws. Church Missionary Society Archives CA3/041/4. London.

Witford, John
1877 *Trading Life in Western and Central Africa.* Liverpool.
Worsley, Peter
1956 The Kinship System of the Tallensi: A Revaluation, *Journal of the Royal Anthropological Institute* 86:37–75.

INDEX

CPSIA information can be obtained
at www.ICGtesting.com
Printed in the USA
BVOW06*0811111116
467471BV00012B/15/P

9 780974 044002